# Organizational Psychology
## a book of readings

*SECOND EDITION*

David A. Kolb
Massachusetts Institute of Technology

Irwin M. Rubin
Massachusetts Institute of Technology

James M. McIntyre
Development Research Associates

Prentice-Hall, Inc., Englewood Cliffs, New Jersey

BEHAVIORAL SCIENCES IN BUSINESS SERIES

Herbert A. Simon, Editor

Printed in the United States of America

10   9   8   7   6   5   4   3

0-13-641167-3

Prentice-Hall International, Inc., *London*
Prentice-Hall of Australia, Pty. Ltd., *Sydney*
Prentice-Hall of Canada, Ltd., *Toronto*
Prentice-Hall of India Private Limited, *New Delhi*
Prentice-Hall of Japan, Inc., *Tokyo*

# Preface

This book is intended as a source of primary material in organizational psychology for the student of management at all three levels—undergraduate, graduate, and in-service. There are represented here the works of numerous authors who have contributed to our understanding of human behavior in groups and organizations. We have tried in this revised edition to choose selections that represent the frontiers of thinking and research about the human side of organizational life. We have particularly sought articles that place a new way of looking at critical organizational problems such as socialization or planned change in the context of other major approaches to the same problem. Articles of this type give the reader an overview of a field of inquiry and at the same time provide an in-depth look at a major new perspective. Several articles in this edition (see the Kolb article on learning, the Boyatzis article on affiliation motivation, and the Berlew article on leadership) were prepared specifically for this volume in order to more fully cover the latest work in the field and to more closely relate the readings book to the exercises and theory in its companion volume *Organizational Psychology: An Experiential Approach*. We have tried throughout the volume to provide a balance of research reports and theoretical essays that were readable enough to be understood by the beginning student and at the same time sufficiently weighty to be of help to the active manager who wants an overview of the field. Through feedback from our students at the Sloan School of Management, M.I.T., and colleagues who have used the book elsewhere, this book is considerably different from the list of readings prepared first in 1967. They have been articulate with their satisfactions and dissatisfactions and have forced us to the realization that our choices cannot always be based on personal preference.

The organization of the book is somewhat unusual for this field. Instead of following the usual logical sequence of individual to group to organization, the subject areas have been divided into fifteen sections with a seemingly random pattern. The sequence as it stands reflects our feeling after teaching the introductory human behavior course several times, that a "logical" sequence does not reflect the real tempo of the classroom experience. To follow the section on "Learning and Problem Solving" with another unit on individual psychology does not necessarily make learning more complete. In our experience it has had just the opposite effect by causing the student to question prematurely the relevance of the course to organizational behavior. We have therefore followed this unit with "Organizational Decision Making" which makes use of the previous section's emphasis on personal style in problem solving in an organizational context. The sequence in which these articles are found is based primarily on pedagogical logic rather than our view of the structure of the discipline.

This book is designed to be used with the text, *Organizational Psychology: An Experiential Approach,* by the same authors. The articles herein form a complete package with the exercises and summaries contained in that volume thus allowing the student to go through all phases of the experiential learning process on which the course is based:

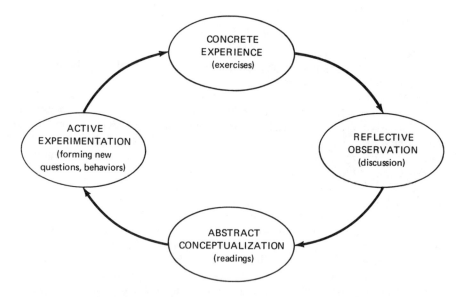

Although designed as a companion volume, this collection of readings stands on its own and should be useful to teachers, managers, and consultants for the breadth of viewpoints and the wealth of data it provides about the field of organizational behavior.

David A. Kolb
Irwin M. Rubin
James M. McIntyre
Cambridge, Mass.

# Contents

# Organizational Decision Making

# Motivation and Organizational Climate

# Achievement Motivation

# The Dynamics of Power and Affiliation Motivation

## Decision Making in Groups

## Interpersonal Perception

## Interpersonal Communication

# Leadership

# Intergroup Relations

# Organizational Structure and Communication

# Personal Growth and Career Development

## Helping and Consulting

## Planned Change and Organization Development

# Organizational Socialization

## ORGANIZATIONAL SOCIALIZATION
## AND THE PROFESSION OF MANAGEMENT

EDGAR H. SCHEIN

. . . I can define my topic of concern best by reviewing very briefly the kinds of issues upon which I have focused my research over the last several years. In one way or another I have been trying to understand what happens to an individual when he enters and accepts membership in an organization. My interest was originally kindled by studies of the civilian and military prisoners of the Communists during the Korean War. I thought I could discern parallels between the kind of indoctrination to which these prisoners were subjected, and some of the indoctrination which goes on in American corporations when college and business school graduates first go to work for them. My research efforts came to be devoted to learning what sorts of attitudes and values students had when they left school, and what happened to these attitudes and values in the first few years of work. To this end I followed several panels of graduates of the Sloan School into their early career.

When these studies were well under way, it suddenly became quite apparent to me that if I wanted to study the impact of an organization on the attitudes and values of its members, I might as well start closer to home. We have a school through which we put some 200 men per year—undergraduates, regular Master's students, Sloan Fellows, and Senior Executives. Studies of our own students and faculty revealed that not only did the student groups differ from each other in various attitude areas, but that they also differed from the faculty. For example, if one takes a scale built up of items which deal with the rela-

The third Douglas Murray McGregor Memorial Lecture of the Alfred P. Sloan School of Management, Massachusetts Institute of Technology. Reprinted by permission of Edgar H. Schein.

tions of government and business, one finds that the Senior Executives in our program are consistently against any form of government intervention, the Sloans are not as extreme, the Master's students are roughly in the middle, and the faculty are in favor of such intervention. A similar line-up of attitudes can be found with respect to labor-management relations, and with respect to cynicism about how one gets ahead in industry. In case you did not guess, Senior Executives are least cynical and faculty are most cynical.

We also found that student attitudes *change* in many areas during school, and that they change away from business attitudes toward the faculty position. However, a recent study of Sloan Fellows, conducted after their graduation, indicated that most of the changes toward the faculty had reversed themselves to a considerable degree within one year, a finding which is not unfamiliar in studies of training programs of all sorts.

The different positions of different groups at different stages of their managerial career and the observed changes during school clearly indicate that attitudes and values change several times during the managerial career. It is the process which brings about these changes which I would like to focus on today—a process which the sociologists would call *occupational socialization*, but which I would prefer to call *organizational socialization* in order to keep our focus clearly on the setting in which the process occurs.

Organizational socialization is the process of "learning the ropes," the process of being indoctrinated and trained, the process of being taught what is important in an organization or some subunit thereof. This process occurs in school. It occurs again, and perhaps most dramatically, when the graduate enters an organization on his first job. It occurs again when he switches within the organization from one department to another, or from one rank level to another. It occurs all over again if he leaves one organization and enters another. And it occurs again when he goes back to school, and again when he returns to the organization after school.

Indeed, the process is so ubiquitous and we go through it so often during our total career, that it is all too easy to overlook it. Yet it is a process which can make or break a career, and which can make or break organizational systems of manpower planning. The speed and effectiveness of socialization determine employee loyalty, commitment, productivity, and turnover. The basic stability and effectiveness of organizations therefore depends upon their ability to socialize new members.

Let us see whether we can bring the process of socialization to life by describing how it occurs. I hope to show you the power of this process, particularly as it occurs within industrial organizations. Having done this, I would like to explore a major dilemma which I see at the interface between organizations and graduate management schools. Schools socialize their students toward a concept of a profession, organizations socialize their new members to be effective members. Do the two processes of socialization supplement each other or conflict? If they conflict, what can we do about it in organizations and in the schools?

## Some Basic Elements of Organizational Socialization

The term socialization has a fairly clear meaning in sociology, but it has been a difficult one to assimilate in the behavioral sciences and in management. To many of my colleagues it implies unnecessary jargon, and to many of my business acquaintances it implies the teaching of socialism—a kiss of death for the concept right there. Yet the concept is most useful because it focuses clearly on the interaction between a stable social system and the new members who enter it. The concept refers to the process by which a new member learns the value system, the norms, and the required behavior patterns of the society, organization, or group which he is entering. It does not include all learning. It includes only the learning of those values, norms, and behavior patterns which, from the organization's point of view or group's point of view, it is necessary for any new member to learn. This learning is defined as the price of membership.

What are such values, norms, and behavior patterns all about? Usually they involve:

1. The basic *goals* of the organization.
2. The preferred *means* by which those goals should be attained.
3. The basic *responsibilities* of the member in the role which is being granted to him by the organization.
4. The *behavior patterns* which are required for effective performance in the role.
5. A set of rules or principles which pertain to the *maintenance of the identity and integrity* of the organization.

The new member must learn not to drive Chevrolets if he is working for Ford, not to criticize the organization in public, not to wear the wrong kind of clothes or be seen in the wrong kinds of places. If the organization is a school, beyond learning the content of what is taught, the student must accept the value of education, he must try to learn without cheating, he must accept the authority of the faculty and behave appropriately to the student role. He must not be rude in the classroom or openly disrespectful to the professor.

By what processes does the novice learn the required values and norms? The answer to this question depends in part upon the degree of prior socialization. If the novice has correctly anticipated the norms of the organization he is joining, the socialization process merely involves a reaffirmation of these norms through various communication channels, the personal example of key people in the organization, and direct instructions from supervisors, trainers, and informal coaches.

If, however, the novice comes to the organization with values and behavior patterns which are in varying degrees out of line with those expected by the organization, then the socialization process first involves a destructive or unfreezing phase. This phase serves the function of detaching the person from his former values, of proving to him that his present self is worthless from the point of view of the organization and that he must redefine himself in terms of the new roles which he is to be granted.

The extremes of this process can be seen in initiation rites or novitiates for religious orders. When the novice enters his training period his old self is symbolically destroyed by loss of clothing, name, often his hair, titles and other self-defining equipment. These are replaced with uniforms, new names and titles, and other self-defining equipment consonant with the new role he is being trained for.

It may be comforting to think of activities like this as being characteristic only of primitive tribes or total institutions like military basic training camps, academies, and religious orders. But even a little examination of areas closer to home will reveal the same processes both in our graduate schools and in the business organizations to which our graduates go.

Perhaps the commonest version of the process in school is the imposition of a tight schedule, of an impossibly heavy reading program, and of the assignment of problems which are likely to be too difficult for the student to solve. Whether these techniques are deliberate or not, they serve effectively to remind the student that he is not as smart or capable as he may have thought he was, and therefore, that there are still things to be learned. As our Sloan Fellows tell us every year, the first summer in the program pretty well destroys many aspects of their self-image. Homework in statistics appears to enjoy a unique status comparable to having one's head shaved and one's clothes burned.

Studies of medical schools and our own observations of the Sloan program suggest that the work overload on students leads to the development of a peer culture, a kind of banding together of the students as a defense against the threatening faculty and as a problem-solving device to develop norms of what and how to study. If the group solutions which are developed support the organizational norms, the peer group becomes an effective instrument of socialization. However, from the school's point of view, there is the risk that peer group norms will set up counter-socializing forces and sow the seeds of sabotage, rebellion, or revolution. The positive gains of a supportive peer group generally make it worthwhile to run the risks of rebellion, however, which usually motivates the organization to encourage or actually to facilitate peer group formation.

Many of our Sloan Fellow alumni tell us that one of the most powerful features of the Sloan program is the fact that a group of some 40 men share the same fate of being put through a very tough educational regimen. The peer group ties formed during the year have proven to be one of the most durable end-results of the educational program and, of course, are one of the key supports to the maintaining of some of the values and attitudes learned in school. The power of this kind of socializing force can be appreciated best by pondering a further statement which many alumni have made. They stated that prior to the program they identified themselves primarily with their company. Following the program they identified themselves primarily with the other Sloan Fellows, and such identification has lasted, as far as we can tell, for the rest of their career.

Let me next illustrate the industrial counterpart of these processes. Many of my panel members, when interviewed about the first six months in their new jobs, told stories of what we finally labelled as "upending experiences." Upending experiences are deliberately planned or accidentally created circumstances which dramatically and unequivocally upset or disconfirm some of the major assumptions which the new man holds about himself, his company, or his job.

One class of such experiences is to receive assignments which are so easy or so trivial that they carry the clear message that the new man is not worthy of being given anything important to do. Another class of such experiences is at the other extreme—assignments which are so difficult that failure is a certainty, thus proving unequivocally to the new man that he may not be as smart as he thought he was. Giving work which is clearly for practice only, asking for reports which are then unread or not acted upon, protracted periods of training during which the person observes others work, all have the same upending effect.

The most vivid example came from an engineering company where a supervisor had a conscious and deliberate strategy for dealing with what he considered to be unwarranted arrogance on the part of engineers whom they hired. He asked each new man to examine and diagnose a particular complex circuit, which happened to violate a number of textbook principles but actually worked very well. The new man would usually announce with confidence, even after an invitation to doublecheck, that the circuit could not possibly work. At this point the manager would demonstrate the circuit, tell the new man that they had been selling it for several years without customer complaint, and demand that the new man figure out why it did work. None of the men so far tested were able to do it, but all of them were thoroughly chastened and came to the manager anxious to learn where their knowledge was inadequate and needed supplementing. According to this manager, it was much easier from this point on to establish a good give-and-take relationship with his new man.

It should be noted that the success of such socializing techniques depends upon two factors which are not always under the control of the organization. The first factor is the initial motivation of the entrant to join the organization. If his motivation is high, as in the case of a fraternity pledge, he will tolerate all kinds of uncomfortable socialization experiences, even to extremes of hell week. If his motivation for membership is low, he may well decide to leave the organization rather than tolerate uncomfortable initiation rites. If he leaves, the socialization process has obviously failed.

The second factor is the degree to which the organization can hold the new member captive during the period of socialization. His motivation is obviously one element here, but one finds organizations using other forces as well. In the case of basic training there are legal forces to remain. In the case of many schools one must pay one's tuition in advance, in other words, invest one's self materially so that leaving the system becomes expensive. In the case of religious orders one must make strong initial psychological commitments in the form of vows and the severing of relationships outside the religious order. The situation is defined as one in which one will lose face or be humiliated if one leaves the organization.

In the case of business organizations the pressures are more subtle but nevertheless identifiable. New members are encouraged to get financially committed by joining pension plans, stock option plans, and/or house purchasing plans which would mean material loss if the person decided to leave. Even more subtle is the reminder by the boss that it takes a year or so to learn any new business; therefore, if you leave, you will have to start all over again. Why not suffer it out with the hope that things will look more rosy once the initiation period is over.

Several of my panel members told me at the end of one year at work that they were quite dissatisfied, but were not sure they should leave because they had invested a year of learning in that company. Usually their boss encouraged them to think about staying. Whether or not such pressures will work depends, of course, on the labor market and other factors not under the control of the organization.

Let me summarize thus far. Organizations socialize their new members by creating a series of events which serve the function of undoing old values so that the person will be prepared to learn the new values. This process of undoing or unfreezing is often unpleasant and therefore requires either strong motivation to endure it or strong organizational forces to make the person endure it. The formation of a peer group of novices is often a solution to the problem of defense against the powerful organization, and, at the same time can strongly enhance the socialization process if peer group norms support organizational norms.

Let us look next at the positive side of the socialization process. Given some readiness to learn, how does the novice acquire his new learning? The answer is that he acquires it from multiple sources—the official literature of the organization; the example set by key models in the organization; the instructions given to him directly by his trainer, coach, or boss; the example of peers who have been in the organization longer and thus serve as big brothers; the rewards and punishments which result from his own efforts at problem solving and experimenting with new values and new behavior.

The instructions and guidelines given by senior members of the organization are probably one of the most potent sources. I can illustrate this point best by recalling several incidents from my own socialization into the Sloan School back in 1956. I came here at the invitation of Doug McGregor from a research job. I had no prior teaching experience or knowledge of organizational or managerial matters. Contrary to my expectations, I was told by Doug that knowledge of organizational psychology and management was not important, but that some interest in learning about these matters was.

The first socializing incident occurred in an initial interview with Elting Morison, who was then on our faculty. He said in a completely blunt manner that if I knew what I wanted to do and could go ahead on my own, the Sloan School would be a great place to be. If I wasn't sure and would look to others for guidance, not to bother to come.

The second incident occurred in a conversation with our then Dean, Penn Brooks, a few weeks before the opening of the semester. We were discussing what and how I might teach. Penn said to me that he basically wanted each of his faculty members to find his own approach to management education. I could do whatever I wanted—so long as I did not imitate our sister school up the river. Case discussion leaders need not apply, was the clear message.

The third incident (you see I was a slow learner) occurred a few days later when I was planning my subject in social psychology for our Master's students. I was quite nervous about it and unsure of how to decide what to include in the subject. I went to Doug and innocently asked him to lend me outlines of previous versions of the subject, which had been taught by Alex Bavelas, or at least to give me some advice on what to include and exclude. Doug was very nice and very patient, but also quite firm in his refusal to give me either outlines or advice. He thought there was really no need to rely on history, and expressed confidence that I could probably make up my own mind. I suffered that term but learned a good deal about the value system of the Sloan School, as well as how to organize a subject. I was, in fact, so well socialized by these early experiences that nowadays no one can get me to coordinate anything with anybody else.

Similar kinds of lessons can be learned during the course of training programs, in orientation sessions, and through company literature. But the more subtle kinds of values which the organization holds, which indeed may not even be well understood by the senior people, are often communicated through peers operating as helpful big brothers. They can communicate the subtleties of how the boss wants things done, how higher management feels about things, the kinds of things which are considered heroic in the organization, the kinds of things which are taboo.

Of course, sometimes the values of the immediate group into which a new person is hired are partially out of line with the value system of the organization as a whole. If this is the case, the new person will learn the immediate group's values much more quickly than those of the total organization, often to the chagrin of the higher levels of management. This is best exemplified at the level of hourly workers where fellow employees will have much more socializing power than the boss.

An interesting managerial example of this conflict was provided by one recent graduate who was hired into a group whose purpose was to develop cost reduction systems for a large manufacturing operation. His colleagues on the job, however, showed him how to pad his expense account whenever they traveled together. The end result of this kind of conflict was to accept neither the cost reduction values of the company nor the cost inflation values of the peer group. The man left the company in disgust to start up some businesses of his own.

One of the important functions of organizational socialization is to build commitment and loyalty to the organization. How is this accomplished? One mechanism is to invest much effort and time in the new member and thereby build up expectations of being repaid by loyalty, hard work, and rapid learning. Another mechanism is to get the new member to make a series of small behavioral commitments which can only be justified by him through the acceptance and incorporation of company values. He then becomes his own agent of socialization. Both mechanisms involve the subtle manipulation of guilt.

To illustrate the first mechanism, one of our graduates went to a public relations firm which made it clear to him that he had sufficient knowledge and skill to advance, but that his values and attitudes would have to be evaluated for a couple of years before he would be fully accepted. During the first several months he was frequently invited to join high ranking members of the organization at their luncheon meetings in order to learn more about how they thought about things. He was so flattered by the amount of time they spent on him, that he worked extra hard to learn their values and became highly committed to the organization. He said that he would have felt guilty at the thought of not learning or of leaving the company. Sending people to expensive training programs, giving them extra perquisites, indeed the whole philosophy of paternalism, is built on the assumption that if you invest in the employee he will repay the company with loyalty and hard work. He would feel guilty if he did not.

The second mechanism, that of getting behavioral commitments, was most beautifully illustrated in Communist techniques of coercive persuasion. The Communists made tremendous efforts to elicit a public confession from a prisoner. One of the key functions of such a public confession, even if the prisoner knew he was making a false confession, was that it committed him publicly. Once he made this commitment, he found himself under strong internal and external pressure to justify why he had confessed. For many people it proved easier to justify the confession by coming to believe in their own crimes than to have to face the fact that they were too weak to withstand the captor's pressure.

In organizations, a similar effect can be achieved by promoting a rebellious person into a position of responsibility. The same values which the new member may have criticized and jeered at from his position at the bottom of the hierarchy suddenly look different when he has subordinates of his own whose commitment he must obtain.

Many of my panel members had very strong moral and ethical standards when they first went to work, and these stood up quite well during their first year at work even in the face of less ethical practices by their peers and superiors. But they reported with considerable shock that some of the practices they had condemned in their bosses were quickly adopted by them once they had themselves been promoted and faced the pressures of the new position. As one man put it very poignantly—"my ethical standards changed so gradually over the first five years of work that I hardly noticed it, but it was a great shock to suddenly realize what my feelings had been five years ago and how much they had changed."

Another version of obtaining commitment is to gain the new member's acceptance of very general ideals like "one must work for the good of the company," or "one must meet the competition." Whenever any counter-organizational behavior occurs one can then point out that the ideal is being violated. The engineer who does not come to work on time is reminded that his behavior indicates lack of concern for the good of the company. The employee who wears the wrong kind of clothes, lives in the wrong neighborhood, or associates with the wrong people can be reminded that he is hurting the company image.

One of my panel members on a product research assignment discovered that an additive which was approved by the Food and Drug Administration might in fact be harmful to consumers. He was strongly encouraged to forget about it. His boss told him that it was the F.D.A.'s problem. If the company worried about things like that it might force prices up and thus make it tough to meet the competition.

Many of the upending experiences which new members of organizations endure are justified to them by the unarguable ideal that they should learn how the company really works before expecting a position of real responsibility. Once the new man accepts this ideal it serves to justify all kinds of training and quantities of menial work which others who have been around longer are unwilling to do themselves. This practice is known as "learning the business from the ground up," or "I had to do it when I first joined the company, now it's someone else's turn." There are clear elements of hazing involved not too different from those associated with fraternity initiations and other rites of passage.

The final mechanism to be noted in a socialization process is the transition to full fledged member. The purpose of such transitional events is to help the new member incorporate his new values, attitudes, and norms into his identity so that they become part of him, not merely something to which he pays lip-service. Initiation rites which involve severe tests of the novice serve to prove to him that he is capable of fulfilling the new role—that he now is a man, no longer merely a boy.

Organizations usually signal this transition by giving the new man some important responsibility or a position of power which, if mishandled or misused, could genuinely hurt the organization. With this transition often come titles, symbols of status, extra rights or prerogatives, sharing of confidential information or other things which in one way or another indicate that the new member has earned the trust of the organization. Although such events may not always be visible to the outside observer, they are felt strongly by the new member. He knows when he has finally "been accepted," and feels it when he becomes "identified with the company."

So much for examples of the process of socialization. Let us now look at some of the dilemmas and conflicts which arise within it.

## Failures of Socialization—Non-conformity and Over-conformity

Most organizations attach differing amounts of importance to different norms and values. Some are *pivotal*. Any member of a business organization who does not believe in the value of getting a job done will not survive long. Other pivotal values in most business organizations might be belief in a reasonable profit, belief in the free enterprise system and competition, belief in a hierarchy of authority as a good way to get things done, and so on.

Other values or norms are what may be called *relevant*. These are norms which it is not absolutely necessary to accept as the price of membership, but which are considered desirable and good to accept. Many of these norms pertain to standards of dress and decorum, not being publicly disloyal to the company, living in the right neighborhood and belonging to the right political party and clubs. In some organizations some of these norms may be pivotal. Organizations vary in this regard. You all know the stereotypes of IBM as a company that requires the wearing of white shirts and hats. In some parts of IBM such values are indeed pivotal; in other parts they are only relevant, and in some parts they are quite peripheral. The point is that not all norms to which the new member is exposed are equally important for the organization.

The socialization process operates across the whole range of norms, but the amount of reward and punishment for compliance or non-compliance will vary with the importance of the norm. This variation allows the new member some degrees of freedom in terms of how far to conform and allows the organization some degrees of freedom in how much conformity to demand. The new man can accept none of the values, he can accept only the pivotal values, but carefully remain independent in all those areas not seen as pivotal, or he can accept the whole range of values and norms. He can tune in so completely on what he sees to be the way others are handling themselves that he becomes a carbon-copy and sometimes a caricature of them.

These basic responses to socialization can be labeled as follows:

| | |
|---|---|
| Type 1 *Rebellion* | Rejection of all values and norms |
| Type 2 *Creative individualism* | Acceptance only of pivotal values and norms; rejection of all others |
| Type 3 *Conformity* | Acceptance of all values and norms |

Most analyses of conformity deal only with the Type 1 and 3 cases, failing to note that both can be viewed as socialization failures. The rebellious individual either is expelled from the organization or turns his energies toward defeating its goals. The conforming individual curbs his creativity and thereby moves the organization toward a sterile form of bureaucracy. The trick for most organizations is to create the Type 2 response—acceptance of pivotal values and norms, but rejection of all others, a response which I would like to call *creative individualism.*

To remain creatively individualistic in an organization is particularly difficult because of the constant resocialization pressures which come with promotion or lateral transfer. Every time the employee learns part of the value system of the particular group to which he is assigned, he may be laying the groundwork for conflict when he is transferred. The engineer has difficulty accepting the values of the sales department, the staff man has difficulty accepting the high pressure ways of the production department, and the line manager has difficulties accepting the service and helping ethic of a staff group. With each transfer, the forces are great toward either conforming or rebelling. It is difficult to keep focused on what is pivotal and retain one's basic individualism.

### Professional Socialization and Organizational Socialization

The issue of how to maintain individualism in the face of organizational socialization pressures brings us to the final and most problematical area of concern. In the traditional professions like medicine, law, and teaching, individualism is supported by a set of professional attitudes which serve to immunize the person against some of the forces of the organization. The questions now to be considered are (1) Is management a profession? (2) If so, do professional attitudes develop in managers? and (3) If so, do these support or conflict with organizational norms and values?

Professionalism can be defined by a number of characteristics:

1. Professional decisions are made by means of general principles, theories, or propositions which are independent of the particular case under consideration. For management this would mean that there are certain principles of how to handle people, money, information, etc. independent of any particular company. The fact that we can and do teach general subjects in these areas would support management's claim as a profession.

2. Professional decisions imply knowledge in a specific area in which the person is expert, not a generalized body of wisdom. The professional is an expert only in his profession, not an expert at everything. He has no license to be a "wise man." Does management fit by this criterion? I will let you decide.

3. The professional's relations with his clients are objective and independent of particular sentiments about them. The doctor or lawyer makes his decisions independent of his liking or disliking of his patients or clients. On this criterion we have a real difficulty since, in the first place, it is very difficult to specify an appropriate single client for a manager, and, in the second place, it is not at all clear that decisions can or should be made independent of sentiments. What is objectively best for the stockholder may conflict with what is best for the enterprise, which, in turn may conflict with what is best for the customer.

4. A professional achieves his status by accomplishment, not by inherent qualities such as birth order, his relationship to people in power, his race, religion, or color. Industry is increasingly moving toward an acceptance of this principle for managerial selection, but in practice the process of organizational socialization may undermine it by rewarding the conformist and rejecting the individualist whose professional orientation may make him look disloyal to the organization.

5. A professional's decisions are assumed to be on behalf of the client and to be independent of self-interest. Clearly this principle is at best equivocal in manager-customer relations, though again one senses that industry is moving closer to an acceptance of the idea.

6. The professional typically relates to a voluntary association of fellow professionals, and accepts only the authority of these colleagues as a sanction on his own behavior. The manager is least like the professional in this regard, in that he is expected to accept a principle of hierarchical authority. The dilemma is best illustrated by the previous example which I gave of our Sloan Fellow alumni who, after the program, related themselves more to other Sloans than to their company hierarchy. By this criterion they had become truly professionalized.

7. A professional has sometimes been called someone who knows better what is good for his client than the client. The professional's expertness puts the client into a very vulnerable position. This vulnerability has necessitated the development of strong professional codes and ethics which serve to protect the client. Such codes are enforced through the colleague peer group. One sees relatively few attempts to develop codes of ethics for managers or systems of enforcement.

On several bases, then, management is a profession, but on several others it is clearly not yet a profession.

This long description of what is a profession was motivated by the need to make a very crucial point. I believe that management education, particularly in a graduate school like the Sloan School, is increasingly attempting to train professionals, and in this process is socializing the students to a set of professional values which are, in fact, in severe and direct conflict with typical organizational values.

For example, I see us teaching general principles in the behavioral sciences, economics, and quantitative methods. Our applied subjects like marketing, operations management, and finance are also taught as bodies of knowledge governed by general principles which are applicable to a wide variety of situations. Our students are given very broad concepts which apply to the corporation as a whole, and are taught to see the relationship between the corporation, the community, and the society. They are taught to value the long-range health and survival of economic institutions, not the short-range profit of a particular company. They come to appreciate the necessary inter-relationships between government, labor, and management rather than to define these as mutually warring camps. They are taught to look at organizations from the perspective of high-ranking management, to solve the basic problems of the enterprise rather than the day-to-day practical problems of staff or line management. Finally, they are taught an ethic of pure rationality and emotional neutrality— analyze the problem and make the decisions independent of feelings about people, the product, the company, or the community. All of these are essentially professional values.

Organizations value many of the same things, in principle. But what is valued in principle by the higher ranking and senior people in the organization often is neither supported by their own behavior, nor even valued lower down in the organization. In fact, the value system which the graduates encounter on their first job is in many respects diametrically opposed to the professional values taught in school. The graduate is immediately expected to develop loyalty and concern for a particular company with all of its particular idiosyncrasies. He is expected to recognize the limitation of his general knowledge and to develop the sort of *ad hoc* wisdom which the school has taught him to avoid. He is expected to look to his boss for evaluation rather than to some group of colleagues outside the company.

Whereas the professional training tells him that knowledge is power, the graduate now must learn that knowledge by itself is nothing. It is the ability to sell knowledge to other people which is power. Only by being able to sell an application of knowledge to a highly specific, local situation, can the graduate obtain respect for what he knows. Where his education has taught the graduate principles of how to manage others and to take the corporate point of view, his organizational socialization tries to teach him how to be a good subordinate, how to be influenced, and how to sell ideas from a position of low power.

On the one hand, the organization via its recruiters and senior people tells the graduate that it is counting on him to bring fresh points of view and new techniques to bear on its problems. On the other hand, the man's first boss and peers try to socialize him into their traditional mold.

A man is hired to introduce linear programming into a production department, but once he is there he is told to lay off because if he succeeds he will make the old supervisors and engineers look bad. Another man is hired for his financial analysis skills but is not permitted access to data worth analyzing because the company does not trust him to keep them confidential. A third man is hired into a large group responsible for developing cost reduction programs in a large defense industry, and is told to ignore the fact that the group is overstaffed, inefficient, and willing to pad its expense accounts. A fourth man, hired for his energy and capability, put it this way as an explanation of why he quit to go into private consulting: "They were quite pleased with work that required only two hours per day; I wasn't."

In my panel of 1962 graduates, 73 per cent have already left their first job and many are on their third or fourth. In the class of 1963, the percentage is 67, and in the class of 1964, the percentage is 50. Apparently, most of our graduates are unwilling to be socialized into organizations whose values are incompatible with the ones we teach. Yet these organizations are precisely the ones who may need creative individualists most.

What seems to happen in the early stages of the managerial career is either a kind of postponement of professional socialization while organizational socialization takes precedence, or a rebelling by the graduate against organizational socialization. The young man who submits must first learn to be a good apprentice, a good staff man, a good junior analyst, and perhaps a good low level administrator. He must prove his loyalty to the company by accepting this career path with good graces, before he is trusted enough to be given a position of power. If he has not lost his education by then, he can begin to apply some general principles when he achieves such a position of power.

The businessman wants the school to provide both the professional education and the humility which would make organizational socialization smoother. He is not aware that teaching management concepts of the future precludes justifying the practices of today. Some professional schools clearly do set out to train for the needs of the profession as it is designed today. The Sloan School appears to me to reject this concept. Instead we have a faculty which is looking at the professional manager of five, ten, or 20 years from now, and is training its graduates in management techniques which we believe are coming in the future.

Symptomatic of this approach is the fact that in many of our subjects we are highly critical of the management practices of today, and highly committed to re-educating those managers like Sloan Fellows and Senior Executives who come back to study at M.I.T. We get across in a dozen different ways the belief that most organizations of today are obsolete, conservative, constipated, and ignorant of their own problems. Furthermore, I believe that this point of view is what society and the business community demands of a good professional school.

It would be no solution to abandon our own vision of the manager of the future, and I doubt that those of you in the audience from business and industry would really want us to do this. What you probably want is to have your cake and eat it too—you want us to teach our students the management concepts of tomorrow, and you want us to teach them how to put these concepts into deep freeze while they learn the business of today. Then when they have proved themselves worthy of advancement and have achieved a position of some influence, they should magically resurrect their education and put it to work.

Unfortunately, socialization processes are usually too powerful to permit that solution. If you succeed in socializing your young graduates to your organizations, you will probably also succeed in proving to them that their education was pretty worthless and might as well be put on a permanent rather than temporary shelf. We have research evidence that many well educated graduates do learn to be complacent and to play the organizational game. It is not at all clear whether they later ever resurrect their educational arsenal.

### What Is to Be Done about This Situation?

I think we need to accept, at the outset, the reality of organizational socialization phenomena. As my colleague, Leo Moore, so aptly put it, organizations like to put their fingerprints on people, and they have every right to do so. By the same token, graduate schools of business have a right and an obligation to pursue professional socialization to the best of their ability. We must find a way to ameliorate the conflicts at the interface, without, however, concluding that either schools or organizations are to blame and should stop what they are doing.

### What the Schools Can Do

The schools, our school in particular, can do several concrete things which would help the situation. First, we can insert into our total curriculum more apprenticeship experience which would bring the realities of organizational life home to the student earlier. But such apprenticeship experiences will not become educational unless we combine them with a second idea, that of providing a practicum on how to change organizations. Such a practicum should draw on each of the course specialties and should be specifically designed to teach a student how to translate his professional knowledge into viable action programs at whatever level of the organization he is working.

Ten years ago we would not have known how to do this. Today there is no excuse for not doing it. Whether the field is operations research, sophisticated quantitative marketing, industrial dynamics, organizational psychology or whatever, we must give our students experience in trying to implement their new ideas, and we must teach them how to make the implementation effective. In effect, we must teach our students to become change-agents, whatever their disciplinary specialty turns out to be. We must teach them how to influence their organizations from low positions of power without sacrificing their professional values in the process. We must teach them how to remain creative individualists in the face of strong organizational socialization pressures.

Combined with these two things, we need to do a third thing. We need to become more involved in the student's efforts at career planning and we need to coordinate our activities more closely with the company recruiters and the university placement officers. At the present I suspect that most of our faculty is quite indifferent to the student's struggles to find the right kind of a job. I suspect that this indifference leaves the door wide open to faulty selection on the part of the student, which can only lead, in the end, to an undermining of the education into which we pour so much effort. We need to work harder to insure that our graduates get jobs in which they can further the values and methods we inculcate.

### What the Companies Can Do

Companies can do at least two things. First, they can make a genuine effort to become aware of and understand their own organizational socialization practices. I fear very few higher level executives know what is going on at the bottom of their organization where all the high priced talent they call for is actually employed. At the same time, I suspect that it is their own value system which ultimately determines the socialization activities which occur throughout all segments of the organization. Greater awareness and understanding of these practices should make possible more rational choices as to which practices to encourage and which to de-emphasize. The focus should be on pivotal values only, not on peripheral or irrelevant ones.

Second, companies must come to appreciate the delicate problems which exist both for the graduate and for his first boss in the early years of the career when socialization pressures are at the maximum. If more companies appreciated the nature of this dilemma they would recognize the necessity of giving some training to the men who will be the first bosses of the graduates.

I have argued for such training for many years, but still find that most company effort goes into training the graduate rather than his boss. Yet it is the boss who really has the power to create the climate which will lead to rebellion, conformity, or creative individualism. If the companies care whether their new hires use one or the other of these adaptation strategies, they had better start looking at the behavior of the first boss and training him for what the company wants and hopes for. Too many bosses concentrate on teaching too many peripheral values and thus undermine the possibilities for creative individualism and organization improvement.

### Conclusion

The essence of management is to understand the forces acting in a situation and to gain control over them. It is high time that some of our managerial knowledge and skill be focused on those forces in the organizational environment which derive from the fact that organizations are social systems who do socialize their new members. If we do not learn to analyze and control the forces of organizational socialization, we are abdicating one of our primary managerial responsibilities. Let us not shrink away from a little bit of social engineering and management in this most important area of the human side of the enterprise.

. . . Much of the material used in this talk is based upon the following publications.

Blau, P. M. & Scott, R. W. *Formal Organizations*. San Francisco: Chandler, 1962.

Goffman, E. *Asylums*. Garden City, N.Y.: Doubleday Anchor, 1961.

Schein, E. H., Schneier, Inge, and Barker, C. H. *Coercive Persuasion*. New York: W. W. Norton, 1961.

Schein, E. H. "Management Development as a Process of Influence," *Industrial Management Review* (M.I.T.), 1961, 2, 59–77.

Schein, E. H. "Forces Which Undermine Management Development," *California Management Review, V*, Summer, 1963.

Schein, E. H. "How to Break in the College Graduate," *Harvard Business Review*, 42, 1964.

Schein, E. H. "Training in Industry: Education or Indoctrination," *Industrial Medicine and Surgery*, 1964, 33.

Schein, E. H. *Organizational Psychology*. Englewood Cliffs, N.J.: Prentice-Hall, 1965.

Schein, E. H. "The Problem of Moral Education for the Business Manager," *Industrial Management Review* (M.I.T.), 1966, 8, 3–14.

Schein, E. H. "Attitude Change During Management Education," *Administrative Science Quarterly*, 1967, 11, 601–628.

Schein, E. H. "The Wall of Misunderstanding on the First Job," *Journal of College Placement*, February/March, 1967.

# THE SOCIALIZATION OF MANAGERS:
# EFFECTS OF EXPECTATIONS ON PERFORMANCE

DAVID E. BERLEW
DOUGLAS T. HALL

This paper is concerned with the socialization of new managers by the companies they join. The focus will be on the effect of the company's initial expectations of the young managers upon their subsequent performance and success. To place the topic in perspective, a simple conceptual model of organizational socialization is proposed, followed by a report on the results of an empirical investigation designed to test the central thesis of the model.

Reprinted from *Administrative Science Quarterly*, 11, No. 2 (September 1966), 207–223. Used by permission of *Administrative Science Quarterly* and the authors.

## Model

### Expectations and Performance

One of the strongest determinants of behavior is the expectations of other people. In the language of role theory, the behavior of a focal person is strongly influenced by the expectations of significant others, sometimes referred to as role senders. For the young manager, the expectations of the company constitute an important class of role forces impinging on him, so that his behavior will be strongly affected by the expectations of his associates.[1,2]

Of particular interest are expectations about his contributions or performance. Role theory would predict that new managers assigned to relatively demanding jobs will perform better than those assigned to less demanding tasks. Direct evidence for this relationship between expectations and performance is provided by Stedry and Kay, who found improvements in the performance of managers assigned difficult goals which they perceived as challenging.[3] Improved performance was not associated with goals perceived either as easy or impossible.[4] Further support for the expectations-performance relationship is provided by Berlew and Hall's finding that a manager tends to improve his performance when his contribution falls short of company expectations.[5]

### Meeting Performance Expectations

When an individual successfully meets performance expectations set for him, he is usually rewarded; e.g., with approval, a good grade, an increase in salary, or a promotion. If the performance expectations are reasonably high, i.e., close to the person's own level of aspiration, he will also feel personal satisfaction at having achieved his goal. These positive outcomes will generally lead to a higher level of aspiration, or the internalization of higher personal standards of performance[6] and a more positive attitude toward the job or task.[7] Moreover, these higher performance standards and positive job attitudes will generalize to task activities that have some psychological relation to the initial activity.[8]

Failure to meet performance expectations has effects quite opposite to those of success. Failure is not rewarded and is frequently punished. If the performance expectations are high, i.e., close to his level of aspiration, the individual will

[1]Edgar H. Schein, "Management Development as a Process of Influence," *Industrial Management Review*, 1 (May 1961), 55–97.

[2]Edgar H. Schein, "How to Break in the College Graduate," *Harvard Business Review*, 42 (November-December 1964), 68–76.

[3]Andrew Stedry and Emanuel Kay, *The Effects of Goal Difficulty on Performance* (Lynn, Mass.: General Electric Company, 1962, mimeo.).

[4]There is considerable evidence that expectations set so high that they are impossible or even perceived as impossible to reach can be as deleterious to both short-run and long-run performance as expectations set so low they can be reached without effort. Overly high company expectations have not been included in the proposed model as a separate situation; however, the description of what happens when an individual fails to meet high initial expectations is directly relevant.

[5]David E. Berlew and Douglas T. Hall, "The Management of Tension in Organizations: Some Preliminary Findings," *Industrial Management Review*, 6 (Fall 1964), 31–40.

[6]Kurt Lewin, "Psychology of Success and Failure," *Occupations*, 14 (June 1936), 926–930.

[7]M. E. Gebhard, "Effects of Success and Failure upon the Attractiveness of Activities as a Function of Experience, Expectations, and Need," *Journal of Experimental Psychology*, 38 (1948), 371–388.

[8]Kurt Lewin, *op. cit.*

generally lower his personal performance goals or standards,[9] his level of performance will tend to drop off,[10] and he will develop negative attitudes toward the task activity or job.

Routine performance, even when no more than that is expected, is not generally rewarded. More important still, successfully meeting company expectations will not bring about internalization of high performance standards or increase in perceived job attractiveness unless the task requirements lie near the person's upper limit of achievement; the feeling of success occurs only if there is a chance for failure.[11] Whatever positive effects result from meeting low performance expectations will be in response to external rewards, which will probably be modest.

When an individual fails to meet low performance expectations, the worst of all possible situations, there will probably be a strong tendency to project blame outward in an attempt to preserve some measure of self-esteem.[12]

### Primacy and Company Expectations

Personality psychologists generally have assumed that attitudes or expectations formed early in life have important implications for later behavior and are more resistant to change than those which develop later in life. It may be instructive to draw an analogy between the socialization of a child and a young adult's entry into a business or industrial organization. The analogy suggests that very early in his organizational career an individual will develop enduring attitudes and aspirations which will have important effects on his future behavior. Of particular interest is the early development of performance standards and job attitudes. From the moment he enters the organization, a new manager is given cues about the quality of performance that is expected and rewarded. The probability that these expectations or standards will be internalized is probably higher when the individual has just joined the organization and is searching for some definition of the reality of his new environment.

In terms of field theory, when the new manager first enters an organization, that portion of his life-space corresponding to the organization is blank. He will feel a strong need to define this area and develop constructs relating himself to it. As a new member, he is standing at the boundary of the organization, a very stressful location,[13] and he is motivated to reduce this stress by becoming incorporated into the "interior" of the company. Being thus motivated to be accepted by this new social system and to make sense of the ambiguity surrounding him, he is more receptive to cues from his environment than he will ever be again, and what he learns at the beginning will become the core of his organizational identity. In terms of Lewin's model of attitude change, the new manager is *unfrozen* and is searching for information and identification models on the basis of which he can change in the direction he feels the organization expects him to change.

The hypothesis submitted to empirical test is derived directly from the pro-

[9]*Ibid.*

[10]K. V. Rao and R. W. Russell, "Effects of Stress on Goal-setting Behavior," *Journal of Abnormal and Social Psychology*, 61 (1960), 380–388.

[11]Kurt Lewin, *op. cit.*

[12]*Ibid.*

[13]Robert L. Kahn, Donald M. Wolfe, J. Dietrick Snoek, and Robert A. Rosenthal, *Organizational Stress: Studies in Role Conflict and Ambiguity* (New York: Wiley, 1964).

posed model: New managers given initial jobs that are demanding (and therefore challenging) will in the next several years perform better and be more successful than new managers given less demanding initial assignments.

## Method

### Subjects

All 62 subjects were college graduates hired originally as management trainees by two operating companies of the American Telephone and Telegraph Company (often referred to simply as the Bell System). At the time of the study, 44 subjects, hired in 1956, were management level employees of an operating company here called Company B. An additional 18 subjects were young managers hired in 1957 by Company D.[14] Most of the subjects joined their company directly from college; a few, however, were employed after completing a tour in the armed forces or a short period of employment in another company.

### Independent Variable

The independent variable was *company expectations*, defined as the type and quality of contribution expected of the employee by the company. This variable was intended to reflect the demands upon an employee which result mainly from the specific job that he held, but which might be modified by salient physical and social characteristics of his work environment. Thus, for example, the company may have certain expectations of an employee because he is functioning as an installation foreman, but these expectations are increased if the company assigns him to work under a difficult supervisor, or as senior telephone company manager in a small town, or makes him foreman of a crew that has proven difficult to handle.

Company expectations were coded in 18 categories which were empirically formulated to reflect the variety of expectations the companies had for managerial employees.[15]

Data on company expectations were derived from in-company and follow-up interview protocols. The in-company interviews were conducted annually

[14]The sample size was determined by the number of subjects employed as college graduates by Company B in 1956 and Company D in 1957 that were still with their respective companies in 1962, and for whom complete assessment and annual interview data were available.

The materials which form the basis of this research were collected by the American Telephone and Telegraph Company as part of the Bell System's Management Progress Study. We are indebted to Dr. Douglas Bray, director of the Management Progress Study, and to W. D. Bachelis, H. W. Clarke, Jr., K. Connors, A. Derks, W. S. Felton, W. H. James, J. P. McKinney, D. B. Muirhead, W. Katkovsky, and J. F. Rychlak. The planning and execution of the research are the sole responsibility of the authors, and the conclusions reached do not necessarily reflect the views of the Management Progress Study.

This research was supported in part by grants from the Russell Sage Foundation, the Foundation for Research on Human Behavior, and the National Aeronautics and Space Administration.

[15]A coding manual with more complete definitions, scoring conventions, and scoring examples is available from the junior author. The categories are: technical competence, learning capacity, imagination, persuasiveness, group membership skills, communication skills, supervisory skills, decision-making, organizing ability, time-energy commitment, sacrifice of autonomy, sociability, acceptance of company norms, self-development, maintenance of public image, loyalty, productivity, and initiative.

with some member of the company's management (usually a middle-management personnel man) able to describe the job held by the subject during the preceding year, the personalities and management styles of his superiors, and the organizational and physical context in which he worked.

The follow-up interview was an annual interview with the subject, of two to three hours. This was conducted by a consulting psychologist, who explored such topics as job responsibilities, major sources of satisfaction or dissatisfaction, relationships with peers, subordinates, and superiors, career aspirations, salary, major occurrences in the past year, significant aspects of personal life, and health. Frequently, the subject's description of his job expanded upon that provided by the personnel manager and the coder's knowledge of positions in the Bell System; however, these data were used for scoring company expectations only when the coders were reasonably sure that the subject's comments were objective descriptions of the job environment.

The company's expectations of a subject in a given year were rated from 1 (low) to 3 (high) on each of the 18 categories and a company expectations score was computed for each year through 1960 for all subjects (yielding four scores for each Company D manager and five for each Company B manager). Using data for a single year drawn from the records of 15 subjects, two coders working independently obtained a reliability index (Spearman rank order correlation) of .97 for company expectations scores.

### Dependent Variables

The dependent variables can be divided into success criteria and performance criteria. The three success criteria were:

1. *1962 Adjusted salary.* Each subject was assigned a score equal to his monthly salary in 1962, corrected (within each company) for differences in starting salary. 1962 was the sixth year of employment for Company D managers and the seventh year for those in Company B.

2. *Global appraisal.* This variable reflects the company's estimate of a subject's overall performance and potential at the end of 1960,[16] his fourth year (Company D) or fifth year (Company B) with the company. On the basis of data included in the in-company interviews after the fourth and fifth year, each subject was rated on a scale ranging from 1 (completely unsatisfactory performance) to 10 (outstanding performance). on a sample of 23 randomly selected subjects, two coders working independently obtained a reliability index (Spearman rank correlation) of .91.

3. *Success index.* This variable was the sum of standardized 1962 adjusted salary and 1960 global appraisal scores, with each given equal weight.

The four performance criteria were:

1. *Average effectiveness.* These scores reflect the company's overall appraisal of a man's performance for each year averaged across five years for Company B subjects and four years for Company D subjects. Annual

[16]The time difference in the salary and global appraisal ratings is due to the fact that salary figures were available through 1962, and global appraisal data were available only through 1960. The authors chose to employ the latest possible success data to demonstrate the continuing impact of initial employment experience, even at the risk of complicating the research design. The correlations between 1960 and 1962 salary were .86 for Company B and .74 for Company D.

in-company interview data were used to rate each subject on a scale ranging from 1 (completely unsatisfactory performance) to 10 (outstanding performance). These yearly ratings were then averaged to obtain an average effectiveness score.

2. *Over contribution.* Each subject's contributions in a given year were rated using the same 18 categories that were used to rate company expectations and the same 1 to 3 rating scale. These 18 category scores were then summed to obtain a single individual contribution score.[17] Each subject's individual contribution score was then subtracted from his company expectations score for the same year to obtain an index of whether he exceeded, met, or fell short of his company's expectations of him in that year. Finally, these yearly indices were summed algebraically across four years for Company D subjects and five years for Company B subjects to obtain an over contribution score for each subject. Annual in-company interview data were used as the primary data source for these ratings.

3. *Cumulative contribution.* A cumulative contribution score was computed by summing the individual contribution scores (see above) across the first four years for Company D subjects and across the first five years for Company B subjects. Each subject's score reflected his overall contribution to his company in his first four or five years' employment.

4. *Performance index.* These scores were computed by summing each subject's standardized scores for average effectiveness, over contribution, and cumulative contribution.

### Intercorrelations of Dependent Variables

From the description of the various performance and success criteria, it should be apparent that each is different in terms either of what it measures or of the method of measurement. Relatively high intercorrelations were found to exist among these variables. Thus, while each may reflect something unique, they all share a marked common variance. Results obtained using each criterion variable separately follow.

## Results

Data bearing on the relationship between company expectations and performance over several years are presented in Table 1; those bearing on the relationship between company expectations and later success are included in Table 2.

The results tend to support the hypothesis. The correlations indicate that Company B managers whose initial jobs were more demanding performed better over a four or five year period than those whose initial jobs were less demanding. Similarly, Company B's college graduates given demanding jobs in their first year with the company were more successful after several years than those given less demanding jobs. The same relationships appear to hold for Company D, although not all of the key correlations between first-year company expectations and the performance and success criteria reach statistical significance. However, the magnitude of the Company D correlations is of the same order

[17]Using data for a single year drawn from the records of 15 subjects, two coders working independently obtained a reliability index (Spearman rank correlation) of .97 for individual contribution scores. (A detailed coding manual is available from the junior author.)

TABLE 1.
Correlations of Company Expectations for First Four and
Five Years with Total Performance Measures

| Year | Average Effectiveness | Over Contribution | Cumulative Contribution | Performance Index |
|------|----------------------|-------------------|------------------------|-------------------|
| Company B (N = 44) | | | | |
| First | .29* | .29* | .69† | .54† |
| Second | .16 | .16 | .61† | .42† |
| Third | .26* | .29* | .78† | .58† |
| Fourth | .14 | .26* | .78† | .56† |
| Fifth | .16 | .11 | .55† | .36† |
| Company D (N = 18) | | | | |
| First | .24 | .12 | .46* | .29 |
| Second | .18 | .00 | .39 | .21 |
| Third | .42* | .09 | .46* | .35 |
| Fourth | .58† | .45* | .53* | .56† |

*p is less than .05 (one-tailed test).
†p is less than .01 (one-tailed test).

TABLE 2.
Correlations of Company Expectations for First Four and
Five Years with Success Measures

| Year | 1962 Adjusted Salary | 1962 Global Appraisal | Success Index |
|------|---------------------|----------------------|---------------|
| Company B (N = 44) | | | |
| First | .33* | .26* | .32* |
| Second | .20 | .32* | .28* |
| Third | .23 | .44† | .37† |
| Fourth | .14 | .31* | .25* |
| Fifth | .32* | .28* | .33* |
| Company D (N = 18) | | | |
| First | .51* | .14 | .37 |
| Second | .02 | −.14 | −.07 |
| Third | .36 | .22 | .33 |
| Fourth | .59† | .59† | .68† |

*p is less than .05 (one-tailed test).
†p is less than .01 (one-tailed test).

as that for Company B, suggesting that with a larger sample more of the correlation coefficients would have been statistically significant.

The correlations between the performance and success criteria and company expectations for years other than the first year are also presented in Tables 1 and 2. What is notable is not that there is a relationship between company expectations and the criteria in years two through five, but that the correlations for the first year are on the average as high as those for later years. Something is happening in the first year which has a strong impact on the trainees' careers.

At least two factors may be contributing to the significant correlations between first-year company expectations and subsequent performance and success: (1) The company somehow managed to assign the best men to the most demanding jobs in the first year; or (2) a demanding job in the first year *leads* to better performance and thus greater success in subsequent years.

After the first year, an additional factor is operating which appears to maintain or increase the correlations between company expectations and both performance and success; performance feedback allows the company to assign men to jobs on the basis of past job performance. Thus, those who perform well will eventually be assigned to the more demanding jobs, whereas those whose performance is poor will be left where they are or reassigned to less demanding positions. As a result, company expectations and performance should gradually draw closer together. If we can assume that those who perform best will also receive the highest rewards (i.e., salary raises and promotions), then the correlations between company expectations and success should also increase. These increases are more pronounced in Company D than in Company B.

To summarize, the significant correlations between later company expectations (i.e., after the first year) and the performance and success criteria are no surprise, because the selection process whereby the best men get channelled into the most responsible jobs has had time to function. However, the relationship between what the company *initially* expects of a new employee and his subsequent performance and success, a relationship that obtains before the selection process has had time to function, has far greater implications.

### Discussion

The results obtained appear to confirm the hypothesis and to provide at least very general support for the socialization model proposed. However, there are several alternative explanations of the results which must be considered. Among these are the following: (1) Are new college employees with the most potential immediately identified by the company and assigned to the most challenging jobs? If so, then their subsequent high-level performance and success can be explained without recourse to any socialization model. (2) Does early assignment to a highly challenging job lead to success only because it increases the candidates' visibility to company executives and not because it leads to better performance? (3) Is a man's performance in his first job a more important determinant of his subsequent performance and success than the initial challenge he encounters?

These issues are not the only ones that can be raised about the socialization model proposed, but they are particularly relevant to the interpretation of the results presented in this paper, and therefore are discussed at some length.

#### Personal Potential and Initial Company Expectations

There can be little doubt that college employees with high potential will generally outperform and be more successful than those with low potential. Granting this, if subjects assigned to the most challenging jobs are also those with highest potential, the results say nothing about the importance of early challenge (except perhaps that if the best men are put in the best jobs they will do better than the weaker men in the more routine jobs). However, it is the stated policy of the Bell System that all new employees are considered equal until their performance proves otherwise. If this policy were in effect for the subjects, such that the most challenging jobs were randomly assigned to both gifted and less gifted candidates in the first year, then the results cannot be so easily dismissed.

To explore the possibility that the best men were initially assigned to the most challenging jobs, correlations were run between 45 personality variables and subjects' first-year company expectations scores. Among the 45 variables were biographical indices, scores on standard personality inventories and intelligence tests, and ratings by psychologists on 25 variables representing qualities or skills considered relevant to managerial performance.[18]

None of the 45 product moment correlations were significant at the .01 level. Only four variables (inner work standards, tolerance of uncertainty, range of interests, and one of five intelligence test scores included) were positively correlated with first-year company expectations at the .05 level of significance.[19] The conclusion is that, in accordance with Bell System policy, the challenging jobs were randomly assigned to trainees. It is worth noting that the operating companies did not have the personality data available to the authors when assigning new employees to jobs, so that even if there had been a conscious attempt to match top candidates with the most challenging jobs, it would have been difficult to accomplish.

### Visibility and Success

The second issue questions the assumption that the relationship between high first-year company expectations and later success is mediated by the development of attitudes, i.e., the internalization of positive job attitudes and high performance standards, which lead to better performance. An alternative possibility is that high visibility is the effective intervening variable; i.e., that young managers who start out in the more responsible jobs are more visible to company executives, and thus have a higher probability of being successful regardless of their job performance.

It would be naive to argue that visibility is unrelated to success in most organizations. However, there is ample evidence to indicate that the visibility stemming from an unusually demanding first assignment was not sufficient to account for the results obtained. The most obvious refutation lies in the fact that first-year company expectations correlate as highly with performance during the first several years of a man's career as with his success at the end of that period. Even stronger evidence is obtained by correlating first-year company expectations and the success index with the performance index held constant by means of partial correlation analysis. This yields insignificant partial correlation coefficients of $-.05$ for Company B and $+.24$ for Company D,

[18]These data were collected in connection with the Management Progress Study at or about the time the subjects joined the Bell System.

[19]Using these same data, as well as more refined indices of managerial aptitude and potential, the Management Progress Study staff was able to predict subsequent performance and success with a relatively high degree of accuracy. These results do not conflict with our findings, nor our argument. We are arguing that performance and success are the result of a variety of qualities and skills *plus* attitudes and performance standards learned on the job. Taken separately, both undoubtedly account for a part of the variance in performance and success. However, when we fully understand the interaction between individual potential and the organizational environment optimal for utilizing and developing that potential, our ability to predict and improve managerial performance and success will increase substantially.

indicating that the relationship between company expectations in the first year and success after six or seven years is not independent of performance during those years.

### First-Year Expectations and Performance

This leads directly to the third issue; i.e., the possibility that a man's performance in his first year is a better predictor of his subsequent performance and success than how much the company expects of him. Relevant correlations of first-year company expectations and first-year performance measures with performance and success indices are presented in Table 3. Both expectations and performance in the first year correlate consistently with later performance and success. The question of whether one is more important than the other is more difficult to answer and must inevitably include the elusive question of causality. The following points are relevant, however: (a) Measures of company expectations and individual performance in a given year are highly correlated. For example, first-year company expectations and the performance index for the first year correlate .56 for Company B and .46 for Company D.[20] (b) If company expectations exceed a man's contributions in a given year, he tends to contribute more the following year.[21] This strongly implies a causal relationship between expectations and contributions. (c) Partial correlation analyses yield mixed results. In the case of Company B, they indicate that first-year performance is not related (r = .09) to success when first-year company expectations are held constant. When the effects of initial performance are removed, however, the relationship between first-year company expectations and success remains strong (r = .22). This suggests that, for this organization, company expectations in the first year are more strongly related to success than is performance in that year.

**TABLE 3.**

Correlations of First-year Company Expectations and Performance
Measures with Total Performance and Success Indices

| First Year | Performance Index | | Success Index | |
|---|---|---|---|---|
| | B | D | B | D |
| Company expectations | .54† | .29 | .32* | .37 |
| Performance measures | | | | |
| Effectiveness | .39† | .74† | .27* | .62† |
| Contribution | .60† | .63† | .29* | .46* |
| Over contribution | .37† | .67† | .07 | .34 |
| Performance index | .55† | .76† | .25* | .53* |

*p is less than .05 (one-tailed test).
†p is less than .01 (one-tailed test).

[20] These correlations would be higher but for the inclusion of over contributions in the performance index. As might be expected, the correlation between how much the company expects of a manager and the degree to which his contribution exceeds those expectations is not high (.20 for Company B; .12 for Company D).

[21] David E. Berlew and Douglas T. Hall, op. cit.

Both first-year variables seem equally important in predicting performance in Company B. The correlation between the (seven-year) performance index and the first-year performance index, with effects of first-year expectations suppressed, is .36. When first-year performance is held constant, the partial correlation between first-year expectations and the performance index is .34.

Performance is very definitely the more important of the two first-year variables in Company D. When first-year performance is held constant, the relationships between first-year company expectations and both the performance index ($r = -.10$) and the success index ($r = .17$) decrease greatly. With initial company expectations held constant, however, first-year performance still correlates .44 with the success index and .74 with the performance index.

Thus, the only safe conclusion that can be drawn from these results is that something important is happening in the first year. In both companies first-year job challenge and individual performance are strongly related to later success and performance.

In terms of company strategy, however, it is unimportant which variable *causes* success and strong performance, since the organization can manipulate both. Its control over job challenge obviously lies in management's function of job assignment. Its control over first-year performance is achieved through the high correlation between first-year performance and first-year company expectations. Thus, although we do not yet understand the relative impact of initial performance and challenge in the *process* of success, we can deduce logically the primary importance of company expectations in the *strategy* of success.

## Conclusions

### Toward a Model of Organizational Socialization

What conclusions can we draw about the process of becoming a successful, high-performing manager? We would speculate that meeting high company expectations in the critical first year leads to the internalization of positive job attitudes and high standards; these attitudes and standards, in turn, would first lead to and be reinforced by strong performance and success in later years. It should also follow that a new manager who meets the challenge of one highly demanding job will be given subsequently a more demanding job, and his level of contribution will rise as he responds to the company's growing expectations of him.

On the other hand, either being assigned to an undemanding job or failing to meet the challenge of a demanding job in the first year may seriously jeopardize a new manager's subsequent performance and success. If he fails to meet high expectations, he will not experience the internal and external rewards that can lead to the internalization of high performance standards and positive job attitudes. If he is given a job which demands little of him, whether he meets expectations or not, he is not likely to win the recognition that can lead to positive job attitudes or the personal satisfaction that will facilitate the internalization of high performance standards. In either case, his failure to develop positive job attitudes means that he will respond primarily to *external* work incentives, and his lack of high personal standards of performance will lead him to do only as much as is expected of him.

It should be emphasized that the results reported in this paper support only the relationship between initial company expectations and later performance; they do *not* bear directly on the intervening variables, i.e., perceived success and failure, rewards, attitudes, and job standards. The data are now available for exploring some of the postulated intervening relationships. Preliminary work has already suggested areas wherein the proposed model is oversimplified. For example, company expectations can be measured objectively, but the same job may be highly challenging for one man and routine for another, thus leading to achievement satisfaction for one and not the other. In order to test the relationships suggested by the model adequately, individual differences such as these must be taken into account.

### The Critical First Year

The key feature of this organizational socialization model is the concept of the first year as a *critical period for learning*, a time when the trainee is uniquely ready to develop or change in the direction of the company's expectations. This year would be analogous to the critical period, probably between six and 18 months, when human infants must either experience a close emotional relationship with another human being or suffer ill effects ranging from psychosis to an inability ever to establish such a relationship.[22] Another example is the puppyhood of dogs; if they do not have extensive contact with human beings during a few crucial weeks, it is difficult and sometimes even impossible ever to domesticate them.[23]

The situation of the new manager just entering upon a career in an organization is not as extreme as either of the examples cited. It is doubtful that his work orientation is "fixed" in his first year, any more than a child's personality is permanently set in his first few years of life. Corrective experiences are certainly possible. However, probably never again will he be so "unfrozen" and ready to learn as he is in his first year. For the benefit of the individual, and of the investment in him, no organization can afford to treat this critical period lightly.

[22]John Bowlby, *Maternal Care and Mental Health* (Geneva: World Health Organization, 1951).

[23]J. Scotts, "The Effects of Selection and Domestication on the Behavior of the Dog," *Journal of the National Cancer Institute*, 15 (May 1954), 739–758.

# Learning and Problem Solving

## ON MANAGEMENT AND THE LEARNING PROCESS

David A. Kolb

Today's highly successful manager or administrator is distinguished not so much by any single set of knowledge or skills but by his ability to adapt to and master the changing demands of his job and career, i.e., by his ability to *learn*. The same is true for successful organizations. Continuing success in a changing world requires an ability to explore new opportunities and learn from past successes and failures. So stated, these ideas are neither new nor particularly controversial. Yet it is surprising that this ability to learn, which is so widely regarded as important, receives little explicit attention by managers and their organizations. There is a kind of fatalism about learning: one either learns or he doesn't. The ability to consciously control and manage the learning process is usually limited to such schoolboy maxims as "Study hard" and "Do your homework."

Part of the reason for this fatalism lies, I believe, in a lack of understanding about the learning process itself. If managers and administrators had a model about how individuals and organizations learn, they would better be able to enhance their own and their organization's ability to learn. This essay describes such a model and attempts to show some of the ways in which the learning process and individual learning styles affect management education, managerial decision making and problem solving, and organizational learning.

### The Experiential Learning Model

Let us begin with a model of how people learn—a model which I call the experiential learning model. The model is labelled experiential for two reasons. The first is historical, tying it to its intellectual origins in the social psychology of Kurt Lewin in the forties and the sensitivity training and laboratory education work of the fifties and sixties. The second reason is to emphasize the important role that experience plays in the learning process, an emphasis that

---

Prepared specifically for this volume.

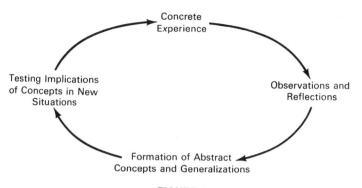

**FIGURE 1**

The Experiential Learning Model

differentiates this approach from other cognitive theories of the learning process. The core of the model is a simple description of the learning cycle, of how experience is translated into concepts which in turn are used as guides in the choice of new experiences (see Figure 1).

Learning is conceived of as a four-stage cycle. Immediate, concrete experience is the basis for observation and reflection. These observations are assimilated into a "theory" from which new implications for action can be deduced. These implications or hypotheses then serve as guides in acting to create new experiences. The learner, if he is to be effective, needs four different kinds of abilities—*concrete experience* abilities (CE), *reflective observation* abilities (RO), *abstract conceptualization* abilities (AC), and *active experimentation* abilities (AE). That is, he must be able to involve himself fully, openly, and without bias in new experiences (CE), he must be able to reflect on and observe these experiences from many perspectives (RO), he must be able to create concepts that integrate his observations into logically sound theories (AC), and he must be able to use these theories to make decisions and solve problems (AE). Yet how difficult this ideal is to achieve! Can anyone become highly skilled in all of these abilities or are they necessarily in conflict? How can one act and reflect at the same time? How can one be concrete and immediate and still be theoretical? Indeed a closer examination of the four-stage learning model reveals that learning requires abilities that are polar opposites and that the learner, as a result, must continually choose which set of learning abilities he will bring to bear in any specific learning situation. More specifically, there are two primary dimensions to the learning process. The first dimension represents the concrete experiencing of events at one end and abstract conceptualization at the other. The other dimension has active experimentation at one extreme and reflective observation at the other. Thus, in the process of learning one moves in varying degrees from actor to observer, from specific involvement to general analytic detachment.

Most cognitive psychologists (e.g., Flavell, 1963; Bruner, 1960, 1966; Harvey, Hunt, and Shroeder, 1961) see the concrete/abstract dimension as a primary dimension on which cognitive growth and learning occur. Goldstein and Scheerer suggest that greater abstractness results in the development of the following abilities:

1. To detach our ego from the outer world or from inner experience
2. To assume a mental set
3. To account for acts to oneself; to verbalize the account
4. To shift reflectively from one aspect of the situation to another
5. To hold in mind simultaneously various aspects
6. To grasp the essential of a given whole: to break up a given into parts to isolate and to synthesize them
7. To abstract common properties reflectively; to form hierarchic concepts
8. To plan ahead ideationally, to assume an attitude toward the more possible and to think or perform symbolically (1941, p. 4)

Concreteness, on the other hand, represents the absence of these abilities, the immersion in and domination by one's immediate experiences. Yet as the circular model of the learning process would imply, abstractness is not exclusively good and concreteness exclusively bad. To be creative requires that one be able to experience anew, freed somewhat from the constraints of previous abstract concepts. In psychoanalytic theory this need for a concrete childlike perspective in the creative process is referred to as regression in service of the ego (Kris, 1952). Bruner (1966), in his essay on the conditions for creativity, further emphasizes the dialectic tension between abstract detachment and concrete involvement. For him, the creative act is a product of detachment and commitment, of passion and decorum, and of a freedom to be dominated by the object of one's inquiry.

The active/reflective dimension is the other major dimension of cognitive growth and learning. As growth occurs, thought becomes more reflective and internalized, based more on the manipulation of symbols and images than overt actions. The modes of active experimentation and reflection, like abstractness/concreteness, stand in opposition to one another. Reflection tends to inhibit action and vice versa. For example, Singer (1968) has found that children who have active internal fantasy lives are more capable of inhibiting action for long periods of time than are children with little internal fantasy life. Kagan (1964) has found on the other hand that very active orientations toward learning situations inhibit reflection and thereby preclude the development of analytic concepts. Herein lies the second major dialectic in the learning process—the tension between actively testing the implications of one's hypotheses and reflectively interpreting data already collected.

**Individual Learning Styles**

As a result of our hereditary equipment, our particular past life experience, and the demands of our present environment, most people develop learning styles that emphasize some learning abilities over others. We come to resolve the conflicts between being active and reflective and between being immediate and analytical in characteristic ways. Some people develop minds that excel at assimilating disparate facts into coherent theories, yet these same people are incapable or uninterested in deducing hypotheses from their theory; others are logical geniuses, but find it impossible to involve and surrender themselves to an experience, and so on. A mathematician may come to place great emphasis on abstract concepts while a poet may value concrete experience more highly.

A manager may be primarily concerned with the active application of ideas while a naturalist may develop highly his observational skills. Each of us in a unique way develops a learning style that has some weak and strong points.

For some time now I have been involved in a program of research studies aimed at identifying different kinds of learning styles and their consequences. The purpose of this research is to better understand the different ways that people learn and solve problems so that we can both make individuals aware of the consequences of their own learning style and of the alternative learning modes available to them, and improve the design of learning experiences to take these learning style differences into account. In this work we have developed a simple self-description inventory, the Learning-Style Inventory (LSI), that is designed to measure an individual's strengths and weaknesses as a learner. The LSI measures an individual's relative emphasis on the four learning abilities described earlier, concrete experience (CE), reflective observation (RO), abstract conceptualization (AC), and active experimentation (AE), by asking him, several different times, to rank order four words that describe these different abilities. For example, one set of four words is "Feeling" (CE), "Watching" (RO), "Thinking" (AC), "Doing" (AE). The inventory yields six scores, CE, RO, AC, and AE, plus two combination scores that indicate the extent to which the individual emphasizes abstractness over concreteness (AC-CE) and the extent to which an individual emphasizes active experimentation over reflection (AE-RO).

The LSI was administered to 800 practicing managers and graduate students in management to obtain a norm for the management population. In general, these managers tended to emphasize active experimentation over reflective observation. In addition, managers with graduate degrees tended to rate their abstract (AC) learning skills higher.[1] While the managers we tested showed many different patterns of scores on the LSI, we have identified four dominant types of learning styles that occur most frequently.[2] We have called these four styles the *converger*, the *diverger*, the *assimilator*, and the *accommodator*.

The *converger's* dominant learning abilities are abstract conceptualization (AC) and active experimentation (AE). His greatest strength lies in the practical application of ideas. We have called this learning style the converger because a person with this style seems to do best in those situations like conventional intelligence tests where there is a single correct answer or solution to a question or problem (*cf.* Torrealba, 1972). His knowledge is organized in such a way that, through hypothetical-deductive reasoning, he can focus it on specific problems. Liam Hudson's (1966) research on this style of learning shows that convergers are relatively unemotional, preferring to deal with things rather than people. They tend to have narrow technical interests, and choose to specialize in the physical sciences. Our research shows that this learning style is characteristic of many engineers.

[1]The details of the inventory construction are described in Kolb (1971). The inventory itself along with management norms appears in Kolb, Rubin, and McIntyre, *Organizational Psychology: An Experiential Approach*, Prentice-Hall, Inc., 1971.

[2]The reason that there are four dominant styles is that AC and CE are highly negatively correlated as are RO and AE. Thus individuals who score high on both AC and CE or on both AE and RO occur with less frequency than do the other four combinations of LSI scores.

The *diverger* has the opposite learning strengths of the converger. He is best at concrete experience (CE) and reflective observation (RO). His greatest strength lies in his imaginative ability. He excels at viewing concrete situations from many perspectives. We have labelled this style "diverger" because a person with this style performs better in situations that call for a generation of ideas such as a "brainstorming" session. Hudson's (1966) work on this learning style shows that divergers are interested in people, and tend to be imaginative and emotional. They have broad cultural interests and tend to specialize in the arts. Our research shows that this style is characteristic of managers from humanities and liberal arts backgrounds. Personnel managers tend to be characterized by this learning style.

The *assimilator's* dominant learning abilities are abstract conceptualization (AC) and reflective observation (RO). His greatest strength lies in his ability to create theoretical models. He excels in inductive reasoning; in assimilating disparate observations into an integrated explanation. He, like the converger, is less interested in people and more concerned about abstract concepts, but he is less concerned with the practical use of theories since it is more important that the theory be logically sound and precise. As a result, this learning style is more characteristic of the basic sciences than the applied sciences. In organizations, this learning style is found most often in the research and planning departments.

The *accommodator* has the opposite learning strengths of the assimilator. He is best at concrete experience (CE) and active experimentation (AE). His greatest strength lies in doing things, in carrying out plans and experiments, and in involving himself in new experiences. He tends to be more of a risk taker than people with the other three learning styles. We have labelled this style "accommodator" because he tends to excel in those situations where he must adapt himself to specific immediate circumstances. In situations where the theory or plan do not fit the "facts," he will most likely discard the plan or theory. (His opposite style type, the assimilator, would be more likely to disregard or reexamine the facts.) The accommodator is at ease with people, but is sometimes seen as impatient and "pushy." His educational background is often in technical or practical fields such as business. In organizations, people with this learning style are found in "action-oriented" jobs often in marketing or sales.

These different learning styles can be illustrated graphically (see Figure 2) by plotting the average LSI scores for managers in our sample who reported their undergraduate college major (only those majors with more than ten people responding are included). Before interpreting this data some cautions are in order. First, it should be remembered that all of the individuals in the sample are managers or managers-to-be. In addition most of these men have completed or are in graduate school. These two facts should produce learning styles that are somewhat more active and abstract than the population at large (as indicated by total sample mean scores on AC-CE and AE-RO, of $+4.5$ and $+2.9$ respectively). The interaction between career, high level of education, and undergraduate major may produce distinctive learning styles. For example, physicists who are not in industry may be somewhat more reflective than those in this sample. Secondly, undergraduate majors are described only in the most gross terms. There are many forms of engineering or psychology. A business major at one school can be quite different than that at another. However, even

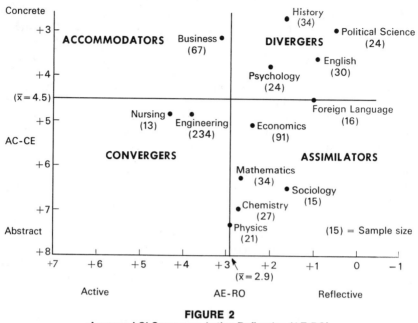

**FIGURE 2**
Average LSI Scores on Active Reflective (AE-RO)
and Abstract/Concrete (AC-CE) by Undergraduate College Major

if we take these cautions into consideration, the distribution of undergraduate majors on the learning-style grid is strikingly consistent with theory.[3] Undergraduate business majors tend to have accommodative learning styles while engineers on the average fall in the convergent quadrant. History, English, political science, and psychology majors all have divergent learning styles. Mathematics and chemistry majors have assimilative learning styles along with economics and sociology. Physics majors are very abstract falling between the convergent and assimilative quadrants. What these data show is that one's undergraduate education is a major factor in the development of his learning style. Whether this is because individuals' learning styles are shaped by the fields they enter or because of selection processes that put people into and out of disciplines is an open question at this point. Most probably both factors are operating—people choose fields which are consistent with their learning styles and are further shaped to fit the learning norms of their field once they are in it. When there is a mismatch between the field's learning norms and the individual's learning style, one will either change or leave the field. Plovnick's (1971) research indicated that the latter alternative is more likely the case. He studied a major university physics department and concluded that the major emphasis in physics education was on convergent learning. He predicted that physics students who had convergent learning styles would be content with their majors whereas physics majors who were divergent in their learning style would be uncertain of physics as a career and would take more courses outside of the physics department than their convergent colleagues. His predictions were con

[3]Many of these differences in LSI scores among disciplines are highly statisticall significant especially when they are grouped into physical sciences, social science and the arts (see Kolb, 1971 for details).

firmed. Those students who are not "fitted" for the convergent learning style required in physics tend to turn away from physics as a profession.

These results pose something of an educational dilemma for the physics department. To contribute in physics today one must know many facts—so learning content is important; and that takes time—time that might be spent developing the convergent skills of divergers. Isn't it simpler to select (implicitly or explicitly) people who already possess these convergent experimental and theoretical skills? Perhaps, but in the process, the creative tension between convergence and divergence is lost. The result of this process may be a program that produces fine technicians but few innovators. Kuhn (1962) put the issue this way, "Because the old must be revalued and reordered when assimilating the new, discovery and invention in the sciences are usually intrinsically revolutionary. Therefore they do demand just that flexibility and open-mindedness that characterize and indeed define the divergent." It may be that one of the reasons why creative contributions in the sciences are made primarily by younger men (Lehman, 1953) is that the learning styles of older men have been shaped by their professional training and experience so that they adapt well to the inquiry norms of their profession but the creative tension is lost.

### Learning Styles and Management Education

Differences in learning styles create similar problems for management education. The manager who comes to the university for midcareer education experiences something of a "culture shock." Fresh from a world of time deadlines and concrete specific problems that he must solve, he is suddenly immersed in a strange slow-paced world of generalities where the elegant solution to problems is sought even when workable solutions have been found. One gets rewarded here for reflection and analysis rather than concrete goal-directed action. The manager who "acts before he thinks—if he ever thinks" meets the scientist who "thinks before he acts—if he ever acts." Our research on learning styles has shown that managers on the whole are distinguished by very strong active experimentation skills and are very weak on reflective observation skills. Business school faculty members usually have the reverse profile. To bridge this gap in learning styles, the management educator must somehow respond to pragmatic demands for relevance and the application of knowledge while encouraging the reflective examination of experience that is necessary to refine old theories and to build new ones. In encouraging reflective observation, the teacher often is seen as an interrupter of action—as a passive "ivory tower" thinker. Indeed this is a critical role to be played in the learning process. Yet if the reflective observer role is not internalized by the students themselves, the learning process can degenerate into a value conflict between teacher and student, each maintaining that theirs is the right perspective for learning.

Neither the faculty nor student perspective alone is valid in my view. Managerial education will not be improved by eliminating theoretical analysis *or* relevant case problems. Improvement will come through the *integration* of the scholarly and practical learning styles. My approach to achieving this integration has been to directly apply the experiential learning model in the classroom (Kolb, Rubin, and McIntyre, 1971). To do this, we created a workbook providing games, role plays, and exercises (concrete experiences) that focus on fifteen central concepts in organizational psychology. These simulations provide a common experiential starting point for managers and faculty to explore the relevance of psychological concepts for their work. In traditional management education methods, the conflict between scholar and practitioner learning styles is exaggerated because the material to be taught is filtered through the learning style of the faculty member in his lectures or his presentation and analysis of cases. The student is "one down" in his own analysis because his data is secondhand and already biased. In the experiential learning approach, this filtering process does not take place because both teacher and student are observers of immediate experiences which they both interpret according to their own learning style. In this approach to learning, the teacher's role is that of a facilitator of a learning process that is basically self-directed. He helps students to experience in a personal and immediate way the phenomena in his field of specialization. He provides observational schemes and perspectives from which to observe these experiences. He stands ready with alternative theories and concepts as the student attempts to assimilate his observations into his own conception of reality. He assists in deducing the implications of the student's concepts and in designing new "experiments" to test these implications through practical "real world" experience.

There are two goals in the experiential learning process. One is a goal to learn the specifics of a particular subject matter. The other goal is to learn about one's own strengths and weaknesses as a learner—i.e., learning how to learn from experience. When the process works well, managers finish their educational experience not only with new intellectual insights, but also with an understanding of their own learning style. This understanding of learning strengths and weaknesses helps in the  back home application of what has been learned and provides a framework for continuing learning on the job. Day-to-day experience becomes a focus for testing and exploring new ideas. Learning is no longer a special activity reserved for the classroom, but becomes an integral and explicit part of work itself.

### Learning Styles and Managerial Problem Solving

We have been able to identify relationships between a manager's learning style and his educational experiences, but how about his current behavior on the job? Do managers with different learning styles approach problem solving and decision making differently? Theoretically, the answer to this question should be "yes" since learning and problem solving are not different processes but the same basic process of adaptation viewed from different perspectives. To illustrate this point I have overlaid in Figure 3 a typical model of the problem-solving process (after Pounds, 1965) on the experiential learning model. In this figure we can see that the stages in a problem-solving sequence generally correspond with the learning-style strengths of the four major learning styles described earlier. The accommodator's problem-solving strengths lie in executing solutions and in initiating problem finding based on some goal or model about how things should be. The diverger's problem-solving strengths lie in identifying the multitude of possible problems and opportunities that exist in reality ("compare model with reality" and "identify differences"). The assimilator excels in the abstract model building that is necessary to choose a

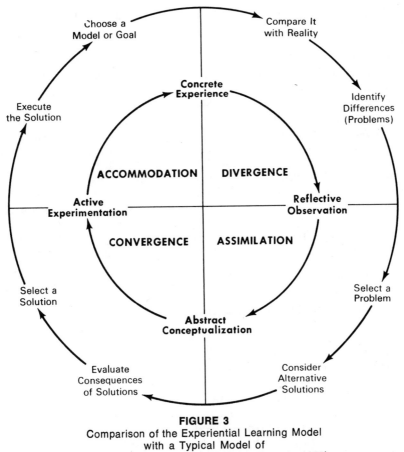

**FIGURE 3**
Comparison of the Experiential Learning Model
with a Typical Model of
the Problem-Solving Process (after Pounds, 1965)

priority problem and alternative solutions. The converger's strengths lie in the evaluation of solution consequences and solution selection.

To date, two studies have been conducted to discover whether there is anything to this theoretical model. The first study was conducted by Charles Stabell (Stabell, 1973) in the Trust Department of a large U.S. midwestern bank. One aim of his study was to discover how the learning styles of investment portfolio managers affected their problem solving and decision making in the management of the assets in their portfolios. While his study involved only thirty-one managers, he found a strong correspondence between the type of decisions these managers faced and their learning styles. More specifically he found that nearly all of the managers in the Investment Advisory section of the department, a high-risk, high-pressure job (as indicated by a large percentage of holdings in common stock, a large percentage of discretionary accounts, and a high performance and risk orientation on the part of clients), had accommodative learning styles (scoring very high on the AE and CE LSI scales). On the other hand, the men in the Personal Trust section, where risk and performance orientation were low and where there were few discretionary accounts and fewer holdings in common stock, scored highest on reflective observation. This finding supports our earlier analysis that high-pressure management jobs develop and select for active experimentation learning skills and inhibit reflective observation learning skills.

Stabell was interested in whether he could identify differences, on the basis of their LSI scores, in the way managers went about making investment decisions. He focused his research on differences between managers with concrete experience (CE) learning skills and abstract conceptualization (AC) learning skills. He asked these managers to evaluate the importance of the information sources that they used in making decisions and found several interesting differences. First, CE managers cited more people as important sources (e.g., colleagues, brokers, and traders) while the AC managers listed more analytically oriented printed material as sources (e.g., economic analyses, industry and company reviews). In addition, it seemed that CE managers sought services that would give them a specific recommendation that they could accept or reject (e.g., a potential list) while the AC managers sought information that they could analyze themselves in order to choose an investment. This analytic orientation of the AC managers is further illustrated by the fact that they tended to use more information sources in their decisions than the CE managers. These data fit well with the learning/problem solving model in Figure 3. The concrete managers prefer go/no go implementation decisions based on personal recommendations while the abstract managers prefer to consider and evaluate alternative solutions themselves.

The second study of the relationship between learning styles and managerial problem solving was a laboratory computer simulation of a production "troubleshooting" problem where the problem solver had to determine which specific type of "widget" was failure prone. This experiment, which is a modification of an earlier problem-solving experiment by Bruner et al. (1956), was conducted by Jerry Grochow as part of his doctoral dissertation (1973). His subjects for the experiment were twenty-two middle-level managers at Massachusetts Institute of Technology's Sloan Fellows program. Grochow was particularly interested in the different types of problem-solving strategies that assimilators and accommodators would use to solve this problem. He predicted that the accommodators would use a strategy that called for little complexity in use and interpretation, little inference from the data, and little cognitive strain in assimilating information, while assimilators would prefer a strategy that had the opposite characteristics—i.e., more complex use and interpretation, and more assimilation strain and required inference. The former strategy, called successive scanning, was simply a process whereby the problem solver scans the data base of widgets for a direct test of his current hypothesis. It requires little conceptual analysis since the current hypothesis is either validated or not in each trial. The latter strategy, called simultaneous scanning, is in a sense an "optimal" strategy in that each data point is used to eliminate the maximum number of data points still possible. This strategy requires considerable conceptual analysis since the problem solver must keep several hypotheses in his head at the same time and deduce the optimal widget to examine in order to test these hypotheses. The results of Grochow's experiment confirmed his hypothesis that accommodators would use successive scanning while assimilators would use the more analytical simultaneous scanning strategy. He further found that managers with accommodative learning styles tended to show more inconsistency in their use of strategies while the assimilative managers were quite consistent in their use of the simultaneous scanning strategy. The accommodative managers seemed to be taking a more intuitive approach, switching strategies as they gathered more data during the experiment. Interestingly enough, Grochow found no differences between accommodative and assimilative managers in the amount of time it took them to solve the problem. Though the two groups used very different styles in this problem, they performed equally well.

The results of both of these studies are consistent with the learning/problem-solving model. Managers' learning styles are measurably related to the way in which they solve problems and make decisions on the job and in the laboratory. Let us now turn to how these different managerial learning/problem-solving styles affect organizational functioning.

### The Organization as a Learning System

Like individuals, organizations learn and develop distinctive learning styles. They, like individuals, do so through their transactions with the environment and through their choice of how to relate to that environment. This has come to be known as the open systems view of organizations. Since many organizations are large and complex, the environment they relate to becomes highly differentiated and diverse. The way the organization adapts to this external environment is to differentiate itself into units each of which deals with just one part of the firm's external conditions. Marketing and sales face problems associated with the market, customers, and competitors; research deals with the academic and technological worlds; production deals with production equipment and raw materials sources; personnel and labor relations deal with the labor market, and so on.

Because of this need to relate to different aspects of the environment the different units of the firm develop characteristic ways of thinking and working together; different styles of decision making and problem solving. These units select and shape managers to solve problems and make decisions in the way their environment demands. In fact, Lawrence and Lorsch define organizational differentiation as *"the difference in cognitive and emotional orientation among managers in different functional departments"* (1967, p. 11).

If the organization is thought of as a learning system then each of the differentiated units that is charged with adapting to the challenges of one segment of the environment can be thought of as having a characteristic learning style that is best suited to meet those environmental demands. The Learning-Style Inventory (LSI) should be a useful tool for measuring this organizational differentiation among the functional units of a firm. To test this we studied about twenty managers from each of five functional groups in a midwestern division of a large American industrial corporation.[4] The five functional groups are described below followed by my hypothesis about the learning style that should characterize each group given the environments to which they relate.

> 1. Marketing (n = 20). This group is made up primarily of former salesmen. They have a non-quantitative "intuitive" approach to their work. Because of their practical sales orientation in meeting

[4]This data was collected by Frank Weisner as part of his Sloan MS thesis (Weisner, 1971). I have reanalysed his data for presentation here.

customer demands, they should have accommodative learning styles —i.e., concrete and active.

2. Research (n = 22). The work of this group is split about 50/50 between pioneer research and applied research projects. The emphasis is on basic research. Researchers should be the most assimilative group—i.e., abstract and reflective, a style fitted to the world of knowledge and ideas.

3. Personnel/Labor Relations (n = 20). In this company, men from this department serve two primary functions, interpreting personnel policy and promoting interaction among groups to reduce conflict and disagreement. Because of their "people orientation," these men should be predominantly divergers, concrete and reflective.

4. Engineering (n = 18). This group is made up primarily of design engineers who are quite production oriented. They should be the most convergent subgroup—i.e., abstract and active, although they should be less abstract than the research group. They represent a bridge between thought and action.

5. Finance (n = 20). This group has a strong computer information systems bias. Finance men given their orientation toward the mathematical task of information system design should be highly abstract. Their crucial role in organizational survival should produce an active orientation. Thus finance group members should have convergent learning styles.

Figure 4 shows the average scores on the active/reflective (AE-RO) and abstract/concrete (AC-CE) learning dimensions for the five functional groups. These results are consistent with the above predictions with the exception of the finance group whose scores are less active than predicted and thus they fall between the assimilative and the convergent quadrant.[5] The LSI clearly differentiates the learning styles that characterize the functional units of at least this one company. Managers in each of these units apparently use very different styles in doing their jobs.

But differentiation is only part of the story of organizational adaptation and effectiveness. The result of the differentiation necessary to adapt to the external environment is the creation of a corresponding internal need to integrate and coordinate the different units. This necessitates resolving in some way the conflicts inherent in these different learning styles. In actual practice this conflict gets resolved in many ways. Sometimes it is resolved through confrontation and integration of the different learning styles. More often, however, it is resolved through dominance by one unit over the other units resulting in an unbalanced organizational learning style. We all know of organizations that are controlled by the marketing department or are heavily engineering oriented, etc. This imbalance can be effective if it matches environmental demands in a stable environment; but it can be costly if the organization is called upon to learn to respond to changing environmental demands and opportunities.

[5] "T" tests for significance of difference between groups on the abstract/concrete dimension yield the following one-tail probabilities that are less than .10. Marketing is more concrete than personnel (p < .10), engineering (p < .05), research (p < .005), and finance (p < .005). Finance and research are more abstract than personnel (on both comparisons p < .005). On the active/reflective dimension, research is more reflective than marketing (p < .05), engineering (p < .05), and to a lesser extent, finance (p < .10).

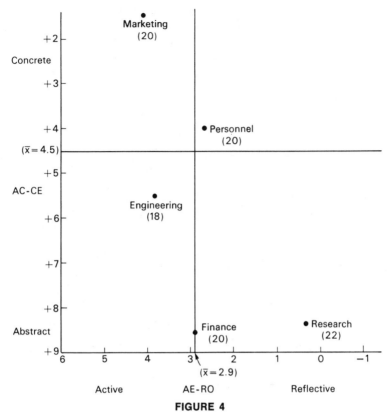

**FIGURE 4**
Average LSI Scores on Active Reflective (AE-RO)
and Abstract/Concrete (AC-CE) by Organizational Function

One important question concerns the extent to which the integrative conflict between units is a function of managers' learning styles rather than merely a matter of conflicting job and role demands. To get at this question we asked the managers in each of the five functional units in the above study to rate how difficult they found it to communicate with each of the other four units. If integrative communication is a function of learning style there should be a correspondence between how similar two units are in their learning style and how easy they find it to communicate. When the average communication difficulty ratings among the five units are compared with differences in unit learning styles, we find that in most cases this hypothesis is confirmed—i.e., those units that are most different in learning style have most difficulty communicating with one another (see Weisner, 1971, pp. 56–59). To test this notion more rigorously we did a more intensive study of communication between the two units who were most different in learning styles, marketing and research. To ascertain whether it was the managers' learning style itself that accounted for communication difficulty, we divided managers in the marketing unit into two groups. One group had learning styles that were similar to those managers in research (i.e., assimilators) while the other group had accommodative learning styles typical of the marketing function. The research group was divided similarly. The results of this analysis are shown in Figure 5. When managers have learning styles similar to another group they have little trouble communicating with that group. When style differences are great, communication difficulty rises. These results suggest that managers' learning styles are an important factor to consider in achieving integration among functional units.

## Managing the Learning Process

To conclude let us return to the problem we began with—how managers and organizations can explicitly manage their learning process. We have seen that the experiential learning model is useful not only for examining the educational process but also for understanding managerial problem solving and organizational adaptation. But how can an awareness of the experiential learning model and our own individual learning style help improve individual and organizational learning? Two recommendations seem important.

First, learning should be an explicit objective that is pursued as consciously and deliberately as profit or productivity. Managers and organizations should budget time to specifically learn from their experiences. When important meetings are held or important decisions are made, time should be set aside to critique and learn from these events. In my experience, all too few organizations

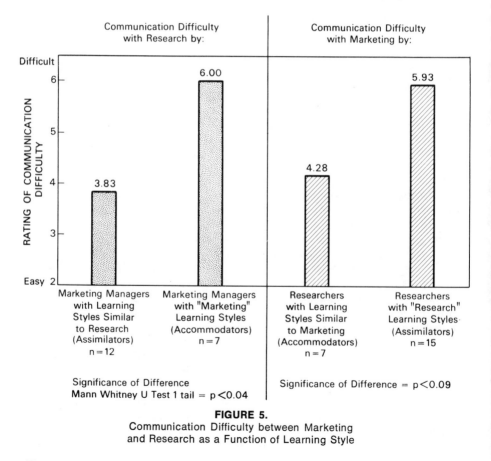

**FIGURE 5.**
Communication Difficulty between Marketing
and Research as a Function of Learning Style

have a climate which allows for free exploration of questions like "What have we learned from this venture?" Usually active experimentation norms dictate "We don't have time, let's move on."

This leads to the second recommendation. The nature of the learning process is such that opposing perspectives, action and reflection, concrete involvement and analytical detachment, are all essential for optimal learning. When one perspective comes to dominate others, learning effectiveness is reduced. From this we can conclude that the most effective learning systems are those that can tolerate differences in perspective. This point can be illustrated by the case of an electronics firm that I have worked with over the years. The firm was started by a group of engineers with a unique product. For several years they had no competitors and when some competition entered the market they continued to dominate and do well because of their superior engineering quality. Today it is a different story. They are now faced with stiff competition in their original product area, and, in addition, their very success has caused new problems. They are no longer a small intimate company but a large organization with several plants in the U.S. and Europe. The company has had great difficulty in responding to these changes because it still responds to problems primarily from an engineering point of view. Most of the top executives in the company are former engineers with no formal management training. Many of the specialists in marketing, finance, and personnel who have been brought in to help the organization solve its new problems feel like "second-class citizens." Their ideas just don't seem to carry much weight. What was once the organization's strength, its engineering expertise, has become to some extent its weakness. Because engineering has flourished at the expense of the development of other organizational functions like marketing and the management of human resources, the firm is today struggling with, rather than mastering, its environment.

**References**

Jerome S. Bruner, *Essays for the Left Hand* (New York: Atheneum, 1966).

Jerome S. Bruner, *The Process of Education* (New York: Vintage Books, 1960).

J. S. Bruner, J. J. Goodnow, and G. A. Austin, *A Study of Thinking* (New York: Wiley and Sons, 1956).

John Flavell, *The Developmental Psychology of Jean Piaget* (New York: Van Nostrand Reinhold Co., 1963).

K. Goldstein and M. Scheerer, "Abstract and Concrete Behavior: An Experimental Study with Special Tests," *Psychological Monographs* 1941, *53, No. 239.*

Jerrold Grochow, "Cognitive Style as a Factor in the Design of Interactive Decision-Support Systems" (Ph.D. Thesis, Massachusetts Institute of Technology Sloan School of Management, 1973).

O. J. Harvey, David Hunt, and Harold Schroder, *Conceptual Systems and Personality Organization* (New York: John Wiley, 1961).

Liam Hudson, *Contrary Imaginations* (Middlesex, England: Penguin Books Ltd., 1966).

Jerome Kagan, Bernice L. Rosman, Deborah Day, Joseph Alpert, and William Phillips, "Information Processing in the Child: Significance of Analytic and Reflective Attitudes," *Psychological Monographs*, 78, No. 1, 1964.

David A. Kolb, "Individual Learning Styles and the Learning Process," (Working paper #535–71, M.I.T. Sloan School, 1971).

David Kolb, Irwin Rubin, and James McIntyre, *Organizational Psychology: An Experiential Approach* (Englewood Cliffs, N.J.: Prentice-Hall, Inc., 1971).

Ernst Kris, *Psychoanalytic Explorations in Art* (New York: International Universities Press, 1952).

Thomas Kuhn, *The Structure of Scientific Revolutions* (Chicago: University of Chicago Press, 1962).

Paul Lawrence and Jay Lorsch, *Organization and Environment* (Boston: Division of Research, Graduate School of Business Administration, 1967).

H. C. Lehman, *Age and Achievement* (Princeton, N.J.: Princeton University Press, 1953).

Mark S. Plovnick, "A Cognitive Ability Theory of Occupational Roles" (Working paper #524–71, Massachusetts Institute of Technology Sloan School of Management, Spring, 1971).

William Pounds, "On Problem Finding" (Working paper #145–65, Massachusetts Institute of Technology Sloan School of Management, 1965).

Jerome Singer, "The Importance of Daydreaming," *Psychology Today*, 1968, *1*, No. 11, pp. 18–26.

Charles Stabell, "The Impact of a Conversational Computer System on Human Problem Solving Behavior," (unpublished working paper, Massachusetts Institute of Technology Sloan School of Management, 1973).

David Torrealba, "Convergent and Divergent Learning Styles" (Master's thesis, Massachusetts Institute of Technology Sloan School of Management 1972).

Frank Weisner, "Learning Profiles and Managerial Styles of Managers" (S.M. thesis, Massachusetts Institute of Technology Sloan School of Management, 1971).

# THE DESIGN OF CROSS-CULTURAL TRAINING: AN ALTERNATIVE TO THE UNIVERSITY MODEL

Roger Harrison
Richard L. Hopkins

### The Problem of Education for Overseas Work

With few exceptions, formal systems of higher education in the United States provide training in the manipulation of symbols rather than of things; reliance on thinking rather than on feeling and intuition; and commitment to understanding rather than to action. These systems were designed originally for the training of scholars, researchers, and professionals, for whom rationality, abstract knowledge, emotional detachment, and verbal skills are primary values. These systems, however, are applied across the board to almost all students, regardless of individual occupational goals. The criteria of performance used to evaluate the effectiveness of the traditional educational experience are familiar to all of us. They consist of tests, papers, reports, and the evaluation of performance on laboratory problems. With few exceptions, these methods of evaluation are verbal and intellectual.

There are attempts to provide action-oriented and experience-based learning models in many institutions of higher learning, but these less intellectual and more emotionally involving learning settings tend to be peripheral and ancillary to the main work of the college or university. Student governments and student organizations, for example, have an ambiguous, unintegrated relationship to the faculty and the classroom. The status of Deans of Students and Directors of Student Activities is cloudy when it is not second-class. The classroom remains a stronghold of rationality.

Reprinted by permission of the authors and the *Journal of Applied Behavioral Science*, Vol. 3, No. 4 (1967), pp. 431–60. ©1967 by NTL Institute for Applied Behavioral Science.

## How the Traditional University Model Fails

When colleges or universities are approached to design or conduct training for work overseas, the resources made available to work on the problem are often those of the traditional part of the organization. Training design is usually based upon the university model.

Until quite recently, for example, the typical Peace Corps university training program was chopped up into components which conformed, by and large, to university departmental lines, and time was assigned to each component on an hourly-block basis: so much to language, so much to technical studies, so much to area studies, and so on. Such a program was more than likely conducted in an environment that differed little from the one the trainee had just escaped, with all or most of its *in loco parentis* rules and regulations, its classrooms and blackboards, its textbooks and reading lists, its blue-book examinations, its air-conditioned dormitories and student-union atmosphere.

In many of these programs the environment was restrictive and authoritarian, a kind of exhausting endurance contest, which the trainee survived by a sort of game-playing designed to get him through the Peace Corps' selection process as painlessly as possible. Recognizing that *something* ought to be different in a Peace Corps program, university project directors typically designed programs that ran from dawn to dark—and beyond—up to as much as 65 or 70 hours a week of intensive instruction for 11 to 15 weeks. Thus, although one of the prime objectives of training was to convince the prospective Volunteer that he was no longer a college student, he was placed in a training environment where he was treated as one.

In any case, the goals and methods of this model focus upon the development of the student's intellectual capacity and on a certain kind of gamesmanship that enables him to *cope* with the training program. There is no manifest concern with his feelings, with an ideal behavior model, or with the interpersonal aspects of the work he may be doing. Students in a typical university setting spend most of their time reading and writing, more time talking about ideas than acting on them; and their professors are much more interested in students' ideas than in their feelings. To be emotional as opposed to being rational and objective, at least in the classroom, is to transgress the bounds of appropriate student or professorial behavior.

Universities and colleges do succeed in influencing students to move toward the traditional goals. Students do become more rational, more critical, more detached, and more adept at the manipulation of words, symbols, and abstractions. In terms of the desired outcome of training for cross-cultural work, the university model can provide an *intellectual* understanding of cultural diversity, of values and assumptions that differ from their own.

### The Missing Interpersonal Links

Nothing in this paper should be construed as suggesting that this kind of understanding is of *no* value or that it is totally irrelevant to overseas work. It does not, however, provide a trainee with all he needs overseas. Its weakness is that in those aspects of overseas performance having to do with interpersonal effectiveness the traditional model offers little help. This is a serious weakness.

The experiences of all our overseas agencies—private, governmental, religious—have demonstrated that the human elements of overseas work are at least as important as the technical ones in the success of a job or mission, and that overseas personnel are much more likely to be deficient in these human aspects of work performance than in technical skills.[1] The gravest problems of Peace Corps Volunteers, said David Riesman in a recent seminar on the Peace Corps as an educative experience, are "emotional and interpersonal."

By interpersonal effectiveness we mean such functions as establishing and maintaining trust and communication, motivating and influencing, consulting and advising—all that complex of activities designed to inculcate change. In overseas jobs, the performance of these relationship activities must take place across differences in values, in ways of perceiving and thinking, and in cultural norms and expectations.

### Divergent Goals Detailed

These requirements suggest a very different set of goals from those of the university model. To sharpen the contrast, here are some important and divergent goals of the two educational enterprises.

| Some Major Goals of University Education | Some Divergent Goals of Overseas Education |
|---|---|
| *Communication:* To communicate fluently via the written word and, to a lesser extent, to speak well. To master the languages of abstraction and generalization, e.g., mathematics and science. To understand readily the reasoning, the ideas, and the knowledge of other persons through verbal exchange. | *Communication:* To understand and communicate directly and often nonverbally through movement, facial expression, person-to-person actions. To listen with sensitivity to the hidden concerns, values, motives of the other. To be at home in the exchange of feelings, attitudes, desires, fears. To have a sympathetic, *empathic* understanding of the feelings of the other. |
| *Decision Making:* To develop critical judgment: the ability to test assertions, assumptions, and opinions against the hard facts and the criteria of logic. To reduce susceptibility to specious argument and to be skeptical of intuition and emotion. To search for the best, most rational, most economical, and elegant solution. | *Decision Making:* To develop ability to come to conclusions and take action on inadequate, unreliable, and conflicting information. To be able to trust feelings, attitudes, and beliefs as well as facts. To search for the *possible* course, the viable alternative, the durable though inelegant solution. |
| *Commitment:* Commitment is to the truth. It requires an ability to stand back from on-going events in order to understand and analyze them and to maintain objectivity in the face of emotionally involving situations. Difficult situations are handled by explanations, theories, reports. | *Commitment:* Commitment is to people and to relationships. It requires an ability to become involved: to be able to give and inspire trust and confidence, to care and to take action in accordance with one's concern. Difficult situations are dealt with by staying in emotional contact with them and by trying to take constructive action. |
| *Ideals:* To value the great principles and ideals of Western society: social justice, economic progress, scientific truth. To value the sacrifice of present rewards and satisfactions for future advancement of these ideals and to find self- | *Ideals:* To value causes and objectives embedded in the here-and-now and embodied in the groups and persons in the immediate social environment. To find satisfaction, enjoyment, and self-esteem from the impact one has |

[1]For an excellent review and statement of these human problems, see Foster, R., *Examples of Cross-cultural Problems Encountered by Americans Overseas—Instructor's Handbook* (Alexandria, Va.: Human Resources Research Office, May 1965).

esteem and satisfaction from one's contribution toward distant social goals.

directly on the lives of others. To be able to empathize with others who live mostly in the present and to work with them toward the limited, concrete goals which are important to them.

*Problem Solving:* A problem is solved when the true, correct, reasonable answer has been discovered and verified. Problem solving is a search for knowledge and truth. It is a largely rational process, involving intelligence, creativity, insight, and a respect for facts.

*Problem Solving:* A problem is solved when decisions are made and carried out which effectively apply people's energies to overcoming some barrier to a common goal. Problem solving is a social process involving communication, interpersonal influence, consensus, and commitment.

Even though the goals on the left are not universally honored in American colleges and universities, they do represent a spirit or ideal of academic excellence. They have a pervasive influence on the values and behavior of educators. They are important goals that have contributed much to our civilization. The transfer of these goals from generation to generation is not the least important function of higher education. The trouble is that they are often not relevant in an action situation.

The goals on the right above are typical of the aims of Americans working closely with counterparts in overseas situations. They are not universal, but they represent the reach and thrust of many persons who are concerned and active in the improvement of overseas effectiveness. These goals are also operative in a number of domestic programs, especially in community development activities.

**Contrasting Learning Styles or Meta-Goals**

University education and cross-cultural training are sharply different, too, in what Schein and Bennis (1965) have called the "meta-goals" of training. Meta-goals are approaches to learning and personal development which the learner acquires in the *process* of being educated in a particular system. In other words, meta-goals represent what the learner learns, in addition to the *content* of instruction, about how to approach and solve subsequent problems outside the classroom.

They represent the problem-solving processes, the learning styles, which the trainee or student becomes committed to in the course of his educational experience. Meta-goals have to do with "learning how to learn." In some learning settings, for example, an authoritative person acts as the source of solutions to problems, while in others the learner must look to peers or to himself for information and suggestions. Such differences can be critical in overseas work.

Below are listed some meta-goals of university education, contrasted with meta-goals which seem appropriate for the cross-cultural situation.

*Meta-Goals of Traditional College and University Classrooms*

*Appropriate Meta-Goals for Cross-Cultural Training*

*Source of Information:* Information comes from experts and authoritative sources through the media of books, lectures, audio-visual presentations. "If you have a question, look it up."

*Source of Information:* Information sources must be developed by the learner from the social environment. Information-gathering methods include observation and questioning of associates, other learners, and chance acquaintances.

*Learning Settings:* Learning takes place in settings designated for the purpose, e.g, classrooms and libraries.

*Problem-Solving Approaches:* Problems are defined and posed to the learner by experts and authorities. The correct problem-solving methods are specified, and the student's work is checked for application of the proper method and for accuracy, or at least for reasonableness of results. The emphasis is on solutions to known problems.

*Role of Emotions and Values:* Problems are largely dealt with at an ideational level. Questions of reason and of fact are paramount. Feelings and values may be discussed but are rarely acted upon.

*Criteria of Successful Learning:* Favorable evaluation by experts and authorities of the quality of the individual's intellectual productions, primarily written work.

*Learning Settings:* The entire social environment is the setting for learning. Every human encounter provides relevant information.

*Problem-Solving Approaches:* The learner is on his own to define problems, generate hypotheses, and collect information from the social environment. The emphasis is on discovering problems and developing problem-solving approaches on the spot.

*Role of Emotions and Values:* Problems are usually value- and emotion-laden. Facts are often less relevant than the perceptions and attitudes which people hold. Values and feelings have action consequences, and action must be taken.

*Criteria of Successful Learning:* The establishment and maintenance of effective and satisfying relationships with others in the work setting. This includes the ability to communicate with and influence others. Often there are no criteria available other than the attitudes of the parties involved in the relationship.

At the level of meta-goals, university education and cross-cultural training diverge significantly. The sources, settings, and approaches of the former tend to be formal, bookish, rational, dependent on authority, and lacking in opportunities to gain competence in learning through interpersonal contact.

*Need for freedom to learn independently.* They differ profoundly along the dimension of freedom. It is here that the inappropriateness of traditional educational systems for overseas work is most evident. The high degree of control and dependence upon authority common in the college classroom does not lead to the development of a learning style facilitative of success in an overseas environment. This is not just because freedom is a good thing and everyone ought to have a lot of it. It is because so much external control implies a dependency on experts and authorities for direction, information, and validation. When the learner is deprived of these sources of support, as he is almost certain to be in the overseas environment, he is in an uncomfortable and sometimes emotionally crippling situation. He not only must solve new problems in a new setting, but he must develop a new learning style, quite on his own. This experience—not knowing how to learn without traditional supports—may be productive of a good deal of the anxiety and depression grouped under the rubric, "culture shock." It is certainly responsible for much individual failure, even when it does not lead to chronic depression and anomie.

Education for cross-cultural applications should train the individual in a system of learning operations that is independent of settings, persons, and other information sources not found in the overseas environment. If the trainee can be educated to be an effective and independent learner, he need not be filled with all the information he can contain before going into his new job. He will have the capacity to generate his own learning as needed. Indeed, he will have to generate his own learning in any case, whether he is trained to do this or not, for the simple reason that no training agency can train for every exotic contingency, for every aspect of life and work in another culture.

*Risks of emotional encounter.* The other dimension on which the two learning models described above differ is that of encounter—the extent to which the emotions, values, and deeper aspects of the self are actively involved, touched, and changed in the learning process. The intellectuality and the formality, the emphasis on ideas and on the written word, the appeals to logic and reason implicit in university education, all combine to encourage an emotional distance from the learning material and a relativism about values.

But it is not possible to maintain such emotional distance from the sights, the smells, the sounds, and the customs of an alien culture. (And for one who is attempting to effect change or to act as an advisor in another culture, it is certainly not desirable, either.) Those aspects of life which in one's own culture are familiar and which would be supportive if they were present overseas (eating habits, standards of hygiene and cleanliness, language, social systems, subliminally perceived signals of all kinds) are *not* present; and their absence is emotionally disruptive. One's assumptions and values are called into question again and again by the most trivial kinds of events. The interpersonal competencies that work well in one's own culture suddenly do not work any more. The cues are different. One can avoid the encounter only by retreating into some kind of physical or emotional enclave, into the kinds of American compounds that wall off "Yankees" from "natives" all over the world.

Education in the classroom teaches one to deal with emotionally loaded questions of value and attitude by analyzing and talking about them in an atmosphere of emotional detachment. Such a scholarly, scientific attitude is appropriate to the task of *understanding*; but by sidestepping direct, feeling-level involvement with issues and persons, one fails to develop the "emotional muscle" needed to handle effectively a high degree of emotional impact and stress. Lacking "emotional muscle," the individual under stress tends to withdraw as much as possible from exposure of his self-esteem or, at the other extreme, he impulsively risks too much in an effort to get the anxiety and suspense over with. Either of these reactions to stress can, and often does, lead to failure overseas. Thus an important objective in training for overseas work should be the development in the trainee of the ability and willingness to take moderate emotional risks in situations where his sense of self-esteem is involved.

The concept of moderate risk taking can be illustrated by examining the alternatives one faces when a friend or colleague has become noticeably unapproachable, cold, and unresponsive. The alternative actions one may take may be classified as low-, moderate-, or high-risk, according to which emotional impact is likely to result to one's self-esteem. Low-risk alternatives might include withdrawal from the relationship or resort to written rather than oral communication. High-risk alternatives might include retaliation with some kind of personal attack on the colleague, reproaches for his unfriendliness, or demands to his face that he change his behavior. The low- and high-risk approaches allow the causes of the situation to remain unknown and not dealt with. They are designed more to ease the tension and uncertainty than to solve the problem.

In contrast, the moderate-risk approach is characterized by a willingness to increase tension somewhat in order to obtain information about the difficulty. Such an approach might take the form of asking the other person if there were anything the matter; indicating that one was puzzled about the behavior of the other; trying to arrange increased interaction in nonwork settings to see whether a relationship could be built on some more personal foundation; and so on. The important thing is not that these attempts be successful in resolving the problem but that they develop more information about it with low risk of further damage to the relationship. They also all involve some increase in tension for the subject, since failure might be painful. Moderate-risk approaches require more ability to stand emotional tension over a period of time than do the others.

The ability to deal directly with a high degree of emotional impact is not likely to be developed in the university classroom. The kinds of problems dealt with in the classroom neither require nor reward attempts to turn the learning situation into an opportunity for interpersonal encounter.

In summary, then, the classroom approach is poorly adapted to training persons to operate in settings, overseas or anywhere else, where they must define and attack problems without the aid of authoritative or expert assistance (freedom), and where the degree of emotional, attitudinal, and value involvement is so high as to require dealing directly and continually with emotionally laden issues (encounter).

### An Alternative Model for Cross-cultural Training

Design principles for cross-cultural training differ from those of the university classroom. The purposes of the former are to: (1) develop in the student more independence of external sources of decision, information, problem definition, and motivation; (2) develop in the student the "emotional muscle" he needs to deal constructively with the strong feelings which are created by conflict and confrontation of values and attitudes; (3) enable him to make choices and commitments to action in situations of stress and uncertainty; and (4) encourage him to use his own and others' feelings, attitudes, and values as *information* in defining and solving human problems.

#### Design Principles

There are a number of design principles which follow directly from these aims and goals.

*Problem solving.* The individual should be continually exposed to situations that require him to diagnose what is going on, define a problem to solve, devise a solution, and take action upon it. Because information and theory which are not used in the problem-solving process will not be readily available to the learner when he must solve problems under stress, *information is not presented which is irrelevant to the solution of real problems which the learner is asked to solve in the here-and-now.*

*Immediate data orientation.* Immediate data are data gathered by observation of the physical environment and experience with persons involved in some problem, as distinguished from second-hand and abstract information obtained from experts and authorities. Learning to use immediate data, particularly from the social environment, frees the learner from dependence on authoritative sources of information. In cross-cultural training designs, problems should be constructed so that their definition and solution require the problem solver to develop information from the persons who are present with him in the problem situation.

*Value orientation.* Almost any action a person takes in a culture other than his own involves a confrontation between his values and those of the host country. In the marketplace, in work situations, in businesses, in social relations of all kinds, the visitor abroad must confront and cope with unfamiliar values and customs. Thus the problems which the learner deals with in training should also require a confrontation with opposing values. Furthermore, it is not enough that the learner examine these value conflicts with interest and detachment. In the cross-cultural application situation he will not be able to escape choices among conflicting values. The choices he makes will have important consequences. Therefore, in the training situation the learner should be confronted with problem-solving situations forcing him to *make choices among competing values which have consequences for his relationships with others in the training situation.*

*Experience-action orientation.* A basic problem in cross-cultural training design may be stated inelegantly as "connecting head and guts." This means that training designs which lead only to understanding are never good enough. Training problems must require that the person *experience* the emotional impact of the phenomena with which he is dealing, as well as understand them. He must be able to translate ideas and values into direct action, with all the attendant risks and difficulties. This requires that the learner influence others to action.

The principle, then, is that training situations should require that discussion and analysis lead to decision and action on the part of the trainee. This would imply, for example, that even the best led "discussion group" is only half a training situation, because it does not lead to action.

*Use of authority.* The authority of the educator or trainer should not be used to diagnose situations, define problems, provide information, or select alternative courses of action for the learner. If these functions are performed for the learner, he learns through dependency on expert or authoritative help.

On the other hand, plunges into anarchy and laissez faire may so traumatize the learner that he must spend most of his energy in defending himself emotionally from the learning situation. If he is allowed to, he may defend himself by sidestepping confrontation with problems and the hard work on their definition and solution which is the heart of the learning process as we have prescribed it. A delicate and unusual use of authority is thus called for.

It is clear that authority must not be used to deprive the learner of the opportunity to have his own experience. In general, he is not provided with information, but encouraged to seek it; he is not given solutions, but asked to come to conclusions on his own; he is not told what action to take or how to take it, only that action is expected of him.

Authority is used to support the learner in his first steps in an unfamiliar learning environment. At the same time, he is not left completely without sources of help. He is encouraged to experiment, to try and fail and try again, to take risks, to express himself and his values in words and action. He is rewarded by those in authority, not for succeeding or getting the right answer or expressing the right opinion, but for engaging actively and wholeheartedly in the learning process.

The restrictive side of this use of authority is that the learner *is* to some extent "fenced in" to keep him in contact with the problems he is expected to solve. Sanctions or punishments are applied, not for "goofing up" but for "goofing off"; not for making mistakes but for failing to act; not for taking an illogical or unreasonable position but for failure to take a stand.

*Use of expertise.* A premise of this model is that a person does not learn to exist effectively in another culture simply by being provided with information about that culture. Although we can predict to some extent the general types of difficulties the learner will have to face in the cross-cultural situation, we cannot predict with any certainty the exact information which he will need to solve the particular difficulties challenging him.

We can, however, specify the conceptual framework which the learner needs to make sense of an alien and ambiguous social situation, and to take action in that situation. The learner's need for expert help is less to provide information about the *content* of the other culture than to teach the problem-solving *processes* and to develop the feeling-thinking linkages which are primary goals of our proposed training designs.

The expert interacts with the learner first through designing situations constructed so that as the learner follows his own natural adaptive styles he will be confronted with the processes and problems which it is desired that he assimilate. These are "free movement" situations in that the learner's specific actions and activities are only loosely prescribed: he is free to solve the problem in almost any way he chooses.

Further, the educator should help the learner reflect about his experience. The process of linking thought and feeling is as difficult when one begins with a concrete problem and moves toward conceptualization of the experience as it is when one starts with ideas and facts and tries to move toward action based upon an intellectual analysis. The educator does not simply construct problems and then sit back while the learner runs through a maze like a rat. At the very least, the educator should ask the learner what meaning the experience had for him and what, if any, connections and generalizations he can make between this particular experience and what he knows about himself, his goals in the cross-cultural situation, his own culture, and the alien culture. His role is that of any teacher working intuitively—to ask the right questions at the right time. Without this kind of guidance, it is just as possible for a person to have an experience-packed and emotionally laden but conceptually meaningless learning experience as it is for him to have an intellectualized and detached but emotionally bland one.

It is not unusual, for example, for returned Peace Corps Volunteers working as staff in a Peace Corps training program to see their overseas career as a kind of kaleidoscope of impactful, difficult, rewarding, but essentially unconnected, experiences. The returned Volunteer often does not have a clear conception of the processes which he used to adapt himself to the culture, to develop sources of information, or to formulate and test hypotheses about problems. When he communicates to trainees he often communicates at the level of "war stories." These anecdotes usually have as their implied message, "It's no use to prepare for much of anything, because whatever you expect, it is not going to come out as you anticipated."

Many of these veterans of the real world seem not to have been able to turn their own experience into real learning or to make it available as training for others. They have been through an experience-based learning situation in their overseas assignment without learning anything which they see as clearly transferable to other social situations. They have not been able to conceptualize their experiences, partly because they were not taught how to do so during their training period. But of course learning has occurred; it is latent, waiting for some structured conceptual framework into which it may be fitted in a coherent way.

The purpose of experience-based cross-cultural training is to inculcate somehow in the learner the ability to see and know what he is learning and has learned, so that he can articulate it afterward and act on his learning consciously. The role prescribed for the teacher, the educator, in such a learning system is one of aiding in an inductive rather than the traditional deductive learning process. He helps the learner to verbalize his feelings, perceptions, and experiences and to draw conclusions and generalizations from them. If the teacher succeeds, the trainee will not only be more successful in the field situation; the entire experience will become a richer and more rewarding one for him. He will, in one degree or another, have learned something about how to learn.

## SOLVING PROBLEMS

RAY HYMAN
BARRY ANDERSON

Psychologists have been experimenting on thinking for more than sixty years. They have observed the problem solving behavior of chickens, rats, chimpanzees, children, adults, mental defectives, psychotics, and so on. They have gathered data on how rats release themselves from puzzle boxes, how chimps employ tools to win bananas, how children combine colorless liquids to find the combination which produces yellow, and so on.

Is there anything that can be said, on the basis of this research, to help people solve practical and technical problems? When we—both of us experimental psychologists—first asked ourselves this question we agreed the answer was "No." It seemed to us that such studies were too far from naturalistic settings to have relevance for problem solving in "real life." But then we looked again at the outcomes of a number of experiments—and we were pleasantly surprised. It seems to us now that there may be a common thread between many of the laboratory experiments and many kinds of problem difficulties that crop up in our daily activities.

Reprinted by permission of the authors and *Science and Technology* (September 1965), pp. 36–41. ©1965 by International Communications, Inc.

When we stand back and survey this heterogeneous body of data, we see one theme that appears again and again. In attempting to solve a given problem, the most typical difficulty is that humans fail to make use of the information *which they have.* Since most of this article will deal with laboratory experiments which are concerned with this difficulty, it may help at this point if we give two examples from "real life."

The first must be as old as the inner tube: It's the homely story of the truck which was stuck in an underpass. Various onlookers tried to be helpful by suggesting ways for extricating the truck, but all these suggestions involved reasonably major deformations—either of the truck or the underpass. Then a little boy suggested letting air out of the tires. Many such stories exist in science and invention. All serve to show the same point: A solution, once stated, can be seen as "obvious."

A classic example involves the invention of the ophthalmoscope. The physiologist Brücke, interested in how the retina of the eye reflects light, devised an instrument to illuminate it. The famous physiologist Helmholtz, while preparing a lecture on Brücke's device, suddenly realized that the rays reflected from the illuminated retina could be used to view the retina itself. Helmholtz used a series of mirrors to reflect light into and out of the eye, and then used a lens to form an image with the light reflected from the retina. This was, as the mathematician Jacques Hadamard points out, "an almost obvious idea, which as it seems, Brücke could hardly have overlooked." But overlook it he did. Why? Here is Helmholtz' explanation: "In this, Brücke was within a hairsbreadth of the invention of the ophthalmoscope. He did not ask himself what optical images are produced by the rays that emerge from an eye into which a light is thrown. For his particular purposes it was not necessary to ask this question, but had it been posed, he would have been able to reply to it as quickly as I have."

Nobody should be surprised when people fail to solve problems for which they lack the necessary information. But it is curious indeed that they fail so frequently when they have all the necessary information.

How is it possible for a person to have the necessary information and not be able to use it? The answer seems to lie in the fact that the brain, like the computer, is divided into a storage unit and a processing unit. While the storage unit can hold a vast amount of information, the capacity of the processing unit is strictly limited. The average person is able to retain and repeat back immediately only about seven unrelated digits. This fact, along with other research, suggests that the processing unit can handle no more than about seven independent items of information at a time. Now any problem of any consequence probably involves more elements than can be handled by the immediate memory span. Unless the processing unit is guided by a systematic search plan, and unless it possesses perfect memory of where it has already looked, it can easily overlook elements or combinations for consideration. Furthermore, not only must the processing unit sift the relevant from the irrelevant—it must also organize the elements into larger units in order to deal with more items in its attempt to construct a workable solution pattern.

The limited attention span and the necessity of "chunking" items of information into larger organization units may contribute to an individual's failure to use available information. He may start his search by looking at the wrong elements. This will not necessarily lead him into trouble. But as he looks at any set of elements he is simultaneously placing them within a tentative organization. And this initial organization—no matter how tentative—serves as a guide to his search process. If it is not an appropriate construction, this organization may prevent him from looking in more appropriate directions. For example, think again of the truck: An inappropriate construction directs one's attention to the top of the truck, since this is where the problem is. And, if your thoughts are channeled by the inappropriate construction, this is where you look for the solution.

How can the problem solver be helped to look in the right direction? In one sense, we cannot answer the question, for we do not know in advance what the right direction is. But in another sense we can answer, by pointing out that the problem solver is more likely to hit upon the correct approach if he tries several approaches. What so frequently produces failure in problem solving is getting stuck on one approach and being unable to abandon it.

The Working Rules

Let us look now at several precepts—or working rules—which may help in the problem-solving process. These precepts fall into two categories: Those intended to keep the problem solver from getting stuck on an incorrect line of attack and those which may be expected to help him get free when he is stuck. In other words, preventive rules and remedial rules.

Four considerations guided our choice of precepts. One, we agreed they must be relevant to overcoming the difficulty people have in making use of information. Two, they must be operational; that is, they should specify concrete actions that the individual can take. Three, they must be applicable at the time the individual finds himself confronted with a problem. (This forced us to exclude many precepts which might be classed as "preparation for problem solving" or "education for problem solving.") And four, they must have some support in psychological research.

Precept I: Run over the elements of the problem in rapid succession several times, until a pattern emerges which encompasses all these elements simultaneously

This precept helps keep you from prematurely fixating upon a subset of the elements required for the solution. It also helps you get the "total picture" before you become lost in the details.

Descartes includes this precept in his *Rules for the Direction of the Mind*.

He describes its application as follows: "If I have first found out by separate mental operations what the relation is between magnitudes A and B, then that between B and C, between C and D, and finally between D and E, that does not entail my seeing what the relation is between A and E, nor can the truths previously learned give a precise knowledge of it unless I recall them all. To remedy this, I would run them over from time to time, keeping the imagination moving continuously in such a way that while it is intuitively perceiving each fact it simultaneously passes on to the next; and this I would do until I had learned to pass from the first to the last so quickly that no stage in the process was left to the care of memory, but I seemed to have the whole in intuition before me at the same time. This method will relieve the memory, diminish the sluggishness of our thinking and definitely enlarge our mental capacity."

Compare this quotation with that of Helmholtz, some 200 years later: "It is always necessary, first of all, that I should have turned my problem over on all sides to such an extent that I had all its angles and complexities 'in my head' and could run through them freely without writing."

This precept serves to keep you from getting stuck on the first one or two interpretations that come to mind. When we jump too quickly from the problem statement to an attempted solution, we frequently get trapped into clinging to an inappropriate direction.

Precept II: Suspend judgment. Don't jump to conclusions

Two examples: In teaching sixth-graders how to ask the right kinds of questions in order to discover the scientific principle underlying a physical event, Suchman found it important to train the children from prematurely guessing at the explanation, for once they had offered an explanation, these children had difficulty revising it or dropping it in the face of contradictory evidence. Bruner and Potter show this in another context: Their experiments show the fixating power of premature judgments. Color slides of familiar objects, such as a fire hydrant, are projected upon a screen and people try to identify the objects while they are still out of focus. Gradually, the focus is improved, through several stages. The striking finding is this: If an individual wrongly identifies an object while it is far out of focus, he frequently still cannot identify it correctly when it is brought sufficiently into focus so that another person—who has not seen the blurred vision—can easily identify it. What this seems to say is this: More evidence is required to overcome an incorrect hypothesis than to establish a correct one. He who jumps to conclusions is less sensitive to new information.

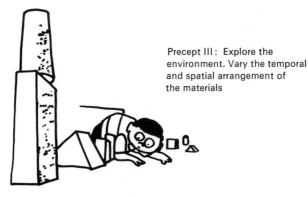

Precept III: Explore the environment. Vary the temporal and spatial arrangement of the materials

This precept serves to keep the mind "loose" by activating a variety of possibilities. It may also help uncover familiar patterns which were masked by an originally unfamiliar arrangement.

The difficulty in many problems frequently resides in the way the elements happen to be ordered. A rearrangement of the elements sometimes reduces the problem to a task that can be handled by standard procedures. The Scotch psychologist Hunter, for example, found his subjects had difficulty specifying the relation of George to Willie when he gave them these two terms: Harry is shorter than George; Harry is taller than Willie. Many eleven-year-old children cannot handle this task, and the adult subjects took considerably more time to give their answers than when the problem was put in its logically equivalent (but more familiar) form: George is taller than Harry; Harry is taller than Willie. In fact, the evidence indicates that subjects actually solve this problem by rearranging the elements until they correspond with the familiar form: A is greater than B; B is greater than C.

Quite frequently, the solution to a difficult problem is suggested to the solver by a slight change in his physical relation to the elements in the problem. In Köhler's famous experiments on chimpanzees, one chimp was faced with the task of obtaining a banana which was beyond arm's reach through the bars of his cage. A stick was available to him, but the stick was behind him and out of his field of vision when he looked at the banana. Later, when he was idly playing with the stick, the banana and the stick accidently became part of the same visual field. When this happened, the chimp instantly made the connection between the stick as a tool for extending his reach and the obtaining of the banana.

**Regaining Flexibility**

Now we shall turn from "preventive" precepts to others which can be looked upon as special operations for accomplishing the following more general precept: If you are getting nowhere on a problem, abandon your approach and try to find a new difficulty as a basis for solving the problem.

Let us begin with the word "direction"—a word employed by Maier to refer to the way in which an individual will attempt to solve a problem. The direction he takes, Maier tells us, depends on what he sees the problem to be. An example: In one of his experiments, Maier gives his subject the task of tying together the ends of two strings which are suspended from the ceiling; the strings are located in such a way that the subject cannot reach one string with his outstretched hand while holding the second string in his other hand. The typical person will see the difficulty as a shortness of reach. Consequently, his "direction" will be toward ways of lengthening his reach—by searching for a stick or hook, for instance. Another person will see the difficulty as a shortness of one of the strings. And consequently, this person will try somehow to make one of the strings longer. Now Maier arranged things so that these obvious solutions could not be used; he wanted to discover some things about "good" reasoners and "poor" reasoners, so he devised his test in a way that required a more imaginative solution: The solution he was looking for required that the subject see the difficulty in terms of getting the second string to come to him. Quite simply, if the subject tied something to the end of that string and then caused it to swing as a pendulum, so as to be grabbed as it swung toward the subject while he held the first string, then the subject would have solved the problem correctly.

The insight Maier gained from this test is this: He found that good reasoners do not persist in one direction if they are getting nowhere. Rather, the good reasoner will jump from one direction to another until he finds a solution. Poor reasoners, on the other hand, persist doggedly in the same direction, even when the difficulty does not yield to their efforts. But he wanted to know more than this. For instance, as he watched people fumble along in the wrong direction he wondered whether this simply indicated that such people were incapable of better reasoning, or whether they were being blocked from considering new directions by some stubborn commitment to the old. To provide himself with an answer to this question, Maier performed another experiment. If people were being blocked as he suspected he reasoned that such people could reach solutions sooner if they were warned against continuing with an unsuccessful experiment. On the other hand, if such people simply were incapable of better reasoning, then such warnings would make little difference, since they would not be able to devise better alternatives anyway. Maier's experiment consisted of giving several hundred college students a one-hour test. Each was asked to solve three problems—one being the two-string problem of a moment ago. The students could do the problems in any order, and they could divide their time among the problems in any way they wished. With half the students, Maier provided the problems with no preliminary comments. With the other group, he prefaced the test with a brief introductory lecture which concluded with the following hints:

1. Locate a difficulty and try to overcome it. If you fail, get it completely out of your mind and seek an entirely different difficulty.
2. Don't be a creature of habit. Don't stay in a rut. Keep your mind open for new meanings.
3. The solution pattern appears suddenly. You cannot force it. Keep your mind open for new combinations and do not waste time on unsuccessful attempts.

As one might expect, this brief lecture produced a significant improvement in performance. The male students who heard the lecture, for example, solved an average of 62% of their problems, while those men who heard no preliminary comments solved only 51% of theirs. Among the young women, the same pattern appeared: 36% for those who heard the lecture, compared with 25% for those who did not.

From these tests and others, Maier concluded that the persistent and initially wrong directions that accompany problem solving actually prevent correct solutions from appearing. "Reasoning," he said. "at least in part, is the overcoming or inhibiting of habitual responses."

Precept IV:
Produce a second
solution after
the first

This precept serves to shift the problem solver's orientation from solution-mindedness to problem-mindedness. In their studies of problem solving, Maier and Hoffman found that when an individual was seeking his first solution to a problem he was dominated by strong pressures to achieve that solution—in other words, he was solution-minded. When he was encouraged—after the first solution had been achieved—to go on to seek a second solution, the second solution was usually a more creative one. This was so, they concluded, because the individual was problem-oriented—he was no longer driven to find *a* solution, for he had already accomplished that; now he was, as Helmholtz would have said, "turning the problem over on all sides." Maier and Hoffman found this precept to increase "creative" solutions from 16% to 52%.

I want to insert a personal observation here—this is Hyman talking now: I have found that unless subjects are told in advance that they will have to produce a second solution, that second solution may be inferior to the first. But I do want to underline the importance of the Maier-Hoffman discovery by stating it again, in a somewhat different form: We can make much better use of the information we have at hand when we are *pushed to the limit*. An example from my own research: I asked a group of people to produce three solutions to the same problem. The problem related to the declining teacher-student ratio in higher education. I gave them statistics and information relevant to the problem and asked each person to write his first solution to the problem of maintaining high-quality education in the face of this declining ratio. Then I asked them to perform some other tasks, and after this interval they were asked again to reconsider the educational problem and write their second solutions. And after another interval I asked them again to produce their third solutions—but on this third go-round I deliberately blocked them from using ideas they were familiar with. I did this by giving each person a copy of his first two solutions, as well as a list of some of the most commonly offered solutions. And I said that these solutions, being already known, should not be considered for solution number three. What we wanted now were solutions that did not make use of any of these ideas. At this point, about one-quarter of the participants threw up their hands in despair. They could think of nothing to do or say. But the others! All were able to come up with at least adequate solutions—involving completely new ideas, in some cases to their own surprise. And as many as 25% of these people came up with truly creative and outstanding answers. They had been blocked from using obvious answers—they had been pushed to the limit.

Precept V: Critically evaluate your own ideas. Constructively evaluate those of others

This precept provides a heuristic for discovering new directions. Its purpose is to guard you against complacency in accepting your own ideas for solving a problem—and also, to help you get new ideas and insights from the attempts others have made at solving the same problem. Torrance, working with students, found that he could increase the creativity of term papers—in which students devised an original research project—by inducing attitudes of constructive evaluation of others' ideas.

I (Hyman) tested this precept with a group of 36 engineers. I asked them, individually, to devise a solution to an automatic warehousing problem. With half the group, I provided some solutions that other engineers had proposed— then I asked these people to list reasons why those solutions could *not* work. (This is the kind of critical task engineers seem well-suited for. They willingly accepted it.) Following this task of critical evaluation, I asked each of these 18 engineers to write out his own solution to the problem. With the second group, I showed the same set of previous solutions, but I asked these men to list as many *strong* points as they could find within those previous solutions. Then, following this constructive evaluation task, these engineers wrote down their own solutions. My next step was to have these 36 solutions evaluated. I mixed them up, thus to prevent anyone's knowing the origin of any particular solution, and gave all 36 solutions to a committee of experts, who rated them for creativity. When the evaluations had been made, it turned out that the solutions of those engineers who had been asked to find strong points were significantly better—more creative—than those who had been asked to look critically at the solutions of others.

Before we can really pin down the extent of, and reasons for, these effects, we must have more information. But one thing that is suggested here is that a positive attitude—or a negative attitude—toward one's own ideas and toward the ideas of others can markedly affect the quality of the solution to a problem. More important, a constructive attitude can easily be induced by the simple expedient of causing the individual to look for weak points in his own first ideas and for strong points in the ideas of others.

Precept VI : When stuck, change your representational system. If a concrete representation isn't
working, try an abstract one, and vice versa

This precept takes advantage of the fact that relationships which are not easy to see in one representational system are often obvious in another. If you have been dealing with a problem in verbal terms, and if you are stuck, then try to switch to a picture, a model, a graph, numbers, or even to other words. If you have been dealing with the problem in non-verbal terms, try mapping the elements into words. A study, by Mawardi, of a group of professional creative thinkers bears this out. She taped sessions in which the group worked on a single problem. Then she classified these sessions into idea units—some were classified as abstract, others as instrumental, metaphor, orientation. She found a very strong tendency within the group to alternate between abstract and concrete modes of thinking.

This precept takes advantage of the fact that a dominant direction will usually weaken with time. Now, surely, to take a break when stuck is the most frequently given advice to problem solvers. But does it really do any good? In two experiments at Stanford, the evidence seemed contradictory: Irvine and Taylor found no advantage in taking a break, while Taylor and LaBerge—in the second experiment—found a definite advantage. The difference was this: There was an advantage when the subjects were allowed to determine their own times for taking breaks. But what is the proper time? And with this question, we must face up to still another question: What is the meaning of "being stuck"? Let us look at the situation in this way: You are getting nowhere with a problem. Why? It may be that your plan of attack is inappropriate. Or it may be that your plan of attack is OK but your perception of the materials is such that they cannot be adapted to your plan. In either case, it is doubtful that a break will help you, for it may only cause you to return to an inappropriate plan or perception. On the other hand, if you have explored the possibilities of your present approach rather thoroughly—and if you cannot think of another approach to try—then you are "stuck" and this would seem a good time to take a break. Put it this way: If you are really stuck, then take a break. But if you simply have not given an approach sufficient thought, then the break won't help.

In talking with someone, you are forced to consider aspects of your problem which you might not otherwise have considered. You cannot take "short cuts" here; you cannot jump across gaps that you might otherwise take for granted. You must return to fundamentals in order to communicate with your listener. And the presence of the listener provides a powerful feedback mechanism which quickly detects obscure or inconsistent points in your story. Where you have to communicate to another person, you have to put yourself in his shoes; this in itself is a powerful precept.

Further, the act of communicating any problem transforms that problem

from a private to a public form. The Swiss psychologist Jean Piaget places great emphasis on this role of communication in the development of the thought process. Piaget has made monumental investigations of how thinking develops in children and he has concluded that thinking—as we recognize it in our society—would never develop in children if they were not forced by society to justify with reasons their behavior to adults and peers. (Quite independently, Russian psychologists have come to the same conclusion.) By being forced repeatedly to communicate his ideas to others, the child gradually masters public forms of representing the world. As he grows older, the child internalizes this public system of representation and thus can check his ideas by recasting them in this public form. For many kinds of thinking, he can now operate independently of the actual presence of others.

But for especially difficult problems, it still helps to communicate with someone. The importance of this precept is illustrated by an incident from contemporary medical research. Dr. Lewis Thomas, in a study involving the enzyme papain, noted a striking phenomenon when he injected the enzyme into the blood stream of a rabbit: The rabbit's ears wilted dramatically. Thomas immediately interrupted his original investigation to try to discover why. He sliced and stained the rabbit's ears. He saw nothing unusual in the connective tissue— where he expected to find changes. He also looked at the cartilage, but he saw nothing obvious there. Like all physicians a few years ago, Thomas had looked upon the cartilage as inactive—he certainly expected to find no changes there. After searching in vain to solve the case of the floppy-eared rabbits, he gave up and returned to his regular work.

About seven years later, Dr. Thomas was teaching second-year medical students how to perform laboratory studies. He decided to demonstrate the floppy-ears phenomenon, feeling it would capture the students' interests. He went through the standard tests again, searching for the cause of the phenomenon. And this time he found it—in the cartilage. What made the difference? Here he was communicating to students; he did not skip or overlook incidental steps and precautions. In his own words: "Well, this time I did what I hadn't done before. I simultaneously cut sections of the ears of rabbits after I'd given them papain *and* sections of normal ears. This is the part of the story that I'm most ashamed of—the only way you could make sense of this change was simultaneously to compare sections taken from the ears of rabbits that had been injected with papain with comparable sections from the ears of rabbits of the same age and size which had not received papain."

Here we see, in striking fashion, how the necessity to rearrange his thinking led the investigator to take precautions he would normally overlook. The result was a discovery which he could have made years earlier.

By phrasing them in a very general form, our eight precepts can be reduced to two:

- Look before you leap.
- After you have leaped, if you find yourself bogged down, find out what you are doing and then do something else.

The usefulness of these precepts depends upon the manner in which they will be applied. And it also depends upon future research—psychological research. But let us add this much for psychological research: As a result of writing this paper, we have discovered that psychological research has more to tell about problem solving than even we had realized. And further—and this may testify to the fruitfulness of the precepts—in trying to communicate what we know to people of the "hard" sciences, we have come up with a number of ideas for doing experiments on problem solving.

# Organizational
# Decision Making

## A NEW LOOK AT MANAGERIAL DECISION-MAKING

VICTOR H. VROOM

### Introduction

While there are many differences in the roles that managers are called upon to play in organizations, all managers are decision-makers. Furthermore, there is little doubt that their effectiveness as managers is largely reflected in their "track record" in making the "right decisions."

Several scholarly disciplines share an interest in the decision-making process. On one hand, we have the fields of operations research and management science, both concerned with how to improve the decisions which are made. Their models of decision-making, which are aimed at providing a rational basis for selecting among alternative courses of action, are termed normative or prescriptive models. On the other hand, we have, in the efforts of psychologists, sociologists, and political scientists, attempts to understand the decisions and choices that people do make. March and Simon were among the first to suggest that an understanding of the decision-making process could be central to an understanding of the behavior of organizations—a point of view that was later amplified by Cyert and March in their behavioral theory of the firm. In this tradition, the goal is understanding rather than improvement, and the models descriptive rather than normative.

Whether the models are normative or descriptive, the common ingredient is a conception of decision-making as an information-processing activity, frequently one which takes place within a single manager. Both sets of models focus on the set of alternative decisions or problem solutions from which the choice is, or should be, made. The normative models are based on the consequences of choices among these alternatives; the descriptive models on the determinants of these choices. Alternatively, one could view the decision-making

Reprinted by permission of the publisher from *Organizational Dynamics* Spring 1973 by AMACOM, a division of American Management Association, Inc.

which occurs in organizations as a social or interpersonal process rather than a cognitive one. A major aspect of the manager's role in the decision-making process is to determine which person or persons should take part in the solution of the problem—or to put it more broadly—which social process should be engaged in the solution of the problem or the making of the decision.

An example may be helpful in illustrating the difference. Let us assume that you are a manager who has five subordinates reporting to you. Each of these subordinates has a clearly defined and distinct set of responsibilities. One of these subordinates resigns to take a position with another organization. Due to a cost-cutting program recently initiated within the firm which makes it impossible to hire new employees, you cannot replace him with someone else. It will be necessary for you to find some way of reallocating the departing subordinate's responsibilities among the remaining four subordinates in such a way as to maintain the present workload and effectiveness of the unit.

The situation described is representative of many with which people in managerial positions are faced. There is some need for action—a problem exists and a solution or decision must be forthcoming. You, as manager, have some area of freedom or discretion (there are a number of possible ways in which the work can be reallocated), but there are also some constraints on your actions. For example, you cannot solve the problem by hiring someone from outside the organization. Furthermore, the solution adopted is going to have effects on people other than yourself (your subordinates are going to have to carry out whatever decision is reached).

Traditionally, efforts to understand or improve the process of decision making in situations such as this one would focus on the events which do (or should) take place within the "head" of the manager. If one's objectives were normative—i.e., to improve decision-making, one might seek to develop an algorithm which would assure selection of the optimal set of work assignments from the total set of possibilities or to develop a set of heuristics (or rules of thumb) for reaching a satisfactory solution to the problem. If one's interests were descriptive—one could obtain from you a protocol of your thoughts as you generated and evaluated alternative solutions and, from such observations, attempt to formulate a model of your decision-making processes which could subsequently be tested against your behavior in other similar situations.

Underlying both approaches is the conviction that the manager is *the* problem-solver or decision-maker—that the task of translating problems into solutions is inevitably his task. In the alternative view of decision-making as a social process, we see the manager's task as determining how the problem is to be solved not the solution to be adopted. In the situation described, one can envision a number of possible decision-making processes that you could employ. You could make the decision by yourself and announce it to your subordinates; you could obtain additional information from your subordinates and then make the decision; you could consult with them either individually or collectively before making the decision, or you could convene them as a group and attempt to reach agreement on the solution to the problem. These alternatives vary in the amount of opportunity afforded your subordinates to participate with you in the solution of the problem.

As with what we have termed the traditional way of looking at the decision-making process, one can distinguish normat've and descriptive questions. The normative questions concern the processes which should be used while the descriptive questions concern the decision-making process which is used.

About four years ago, Philip Yetton, then a graduate student at Carnegie-Mellon University, and I began a major research program in an attempt to answer these questions. A detailed presentation of this work may be found in our forthcoming book, *Leadership and Decision-making*. The purpose of this paper is to present an overview of our approach, methods and major conclusions.

### Toward a Normative Model

We began with the normative question. What would be a rational way of deciding on the form and amount of participation in decision-making that should be used in different situations? We were tired of debates over the relative merits of theory X and theory Y and of the truism that leadership depends upon the situation. We felt that it was time for the behavioral sciences to move beyond such generalities and to attempt to come to grips with the complexities of the phenomena with which they intended to deal.

**TABLE I**

Types of Management Decision Styles

AI   You solve the problem or make the decision yourself, using information available to you at that time.

AII   You obtain the necessary information from your subordinate(s), then decide on the solution to the problem yourself. You may or may not tell your subordinates what the problem is in getting the information from them. The role played by your subordinates in making the decision is clearly one of providing the necessary information to you, rather than generating or evaluating alternative solutions.

CI   You share the problem with relevant subordinates individually, getting their ideas and suggestions without bringing them together as a group. Then *you* make the decision which may or may not reflect your subordinates' influence.

CII   You share the problem with your subordinates as a group, collectively obtaining their ideas and suggestions. Then *you* make the decision which may or may not reflect your subordinates' influence.

GII   You share a problem with your subordinates as a group. Together you generate and evaluate alternatives and attempt to reach agreement (concensus) on a solution. Your role is much like that of chairman. You do not try to influence the group to adopt "your" solution and you are willing to accept and implement any solution which has the support of the entire group.

Table I shows a set of alternative decision processes which we have employed in our research. Each process is represented by a symbol (e.g., AI, CI, GII) which will be used as a convenient method of referring to each process. The first letter in this symbol signifies the basic properties of the process (A stands for autocratic, C for consultative, and G for group). The roman numerals which follow the first letter constitute variants on that process. Thus, AI represents the first variant on an autocratic process, and AII the second variant, etc.[1]

### Conceptual and Empirical Basis of the Model

A model designed to regulate, in some rational way, choices among the decision processes shown in Table I should be based on sound empirical evidence concerning the likely consequences of the styles. The more complete

---

[1]The absence of GI from the code is attributable to the fact that the list of decision processes used in this paper is a part of a larger set of such processes used in broader and more comprehensive models. A complete explication of the entire set of processes and of the models which use them may be found in Vroom and Yetton.

the empirical base of knowledge, the greater the certainty with which one can develop the model and the greater will be its usefulness. To aid in understanding the conceptual basis of the model, it is important to distinguish three classes of outcomes which bear on the ultimate effectiveness of decisions. These are:

1. The quality or rationality of the decision.
2. The acceptance or commitment on the part of subordinates to execute the decision effectively.
3. The amount of time required to make the decision.

The evidence regarding the effects of participation on each of these outcomes or consequences has been reviewed in a chapter written by the author for *The Handbook of Social Psychology*. It was concluded that:

> The results suggest that allocating problem solving and decision-making tasks to entire groups, requires a greater investment of man hours but produce higher acceptance of decisions and a higher probability that the decision will be executed efficiently. Differences between these two methods in quality of decisions and in elapsed time are inconclusive and probably highly variable . . . It would be naïve to think that group decision-making is always more "effective" than autocratic decision-making, or vice versa; the relative effectiveness of these two extreme methods depends both on the weights attached to quality, acceptance, and time variables, and on differences in amounts of these outcomes resulting from these methods, neither of which is invariant from one situation to another. The critics and proponents of participative management would do well to direct their efforts toward identifying the properties of situations in which different decision-making approaches are effective rather than wholesale condemnation or deification of one approach. (Vroom, 1970, pp. 239–240)

Stemming from this review, an attempt has been made to identify these properties of the situation or problem which will be the basic elements in the model. These problem attributes are of two types: 1) those which specify the importance for a particular problem of quality and acceptance, and 2) those which, on the basis of available evidence have a high probability of moderating the effects of participation on each of these outcomes. Table II shows the problem attributes used in the present form of the model. For each attribute a question is provided which might be used by a leader in diagnosing a particular problem prior to choosing his leadership style.

In phrasing the questions, technical language has been held to a minimum. Furthermore, the questions have been phrased in Yes-No form, translating the continuous variables defined above into dichotomous variables. For example, instead of attempting to determine how important the decision quality is to the effectiveness of the decision (attribute A), the leader is asked in the first question to judge whether there is any quality component to the problem. Similarly, the difficult task of specifying exactly how much information the leader possesses that is relevant to the decision (attribute B) is reduced to a simple judgment by the leader concerning whether he has sufficient information to make a high-quality decision.

It has been found that managers can diagnose a situation quite quickly and accurately by answering this set of seven questions concerning it. But how can such responses generate a prescription concerning the most effective leadership style or decision process? What kind of normative model of participation in decision-making can be built from this set of problem attributes?

**TABLE II**
Problem Attributes Used in the Model

| *Problem Attributes* | *Diagnostic Questions* |
|---|---|
| A. The importance of the quality of the decision. | Is there a quality requirement such that one solution is likely to be more rational than another? |
| B. The extent to which the leader possesses sufficient information/expertise to make a high-quality decision by himself. | Do I have sufficient information to make a high quality decision? |
| C. The extent to which the problem is structured. | Is the problem structured? |
| D. The extent to which acceptance or commitment on the part of subordinates is critical to the effective implementation of the decision. | Is acceptance of decision by subordinates critical to effective implementation? |
| E. The prior probability that the leader's autocratic decision will receive acceptance by subordinates. | If you were to make the decision by yourself, is it reasonably certain that it would be accepted by your subordinates? |
| F. The extent to which subordinates are motivated to attain the organizational goals as represented in the objectives explicit in the statement of the problem. | Do subordinates share the organizational goals to be obtained in solving this problem? |
| G. The extent to which subordinates are likely to be in conflict over preferred solutions. | Is conflict among subordinates likely in preferred solutions? |

Figure 1 shows one such model expressed in the form of a decision tree. It is the seventh version of such a model which we have developed over the last three years. The problem attributes, expressed in question form are arranged along the top of the figure. To use the model for a particular decision-making situation, one starts at the left-hand side and works toward the right asking oneself the question immediately above any box that is encountered. When a terminal node is reached, a number will be found designating the problem type[2] and one of the decision-making processes appearing in Table I. AI is prescribed for four problem types (1, 2, 4, and 5): AII is prescribed for two problem types (9 and 10); CI is prescribed for only one problem type (8); CII is prescribed for four problem types (7, 11, 13, and 14); and GII is prescribed for three problem types (3, 6, and 12). The relative frequency with which each of the five decision processes would be prescribed for any manager would, of course, be dependent on the distribution of problem types in his role.

### Rationale Underlying the Model

The decision processes specified for each problem type are not arbitrary. The model's behavior is governed by a set of principles which are intended to be

---

[2]Problem type is a nominal variable designating classes of problems generated by the paths which lead to the terminal nodes.

**FIGURE 1**
Decision Process Flow Chart

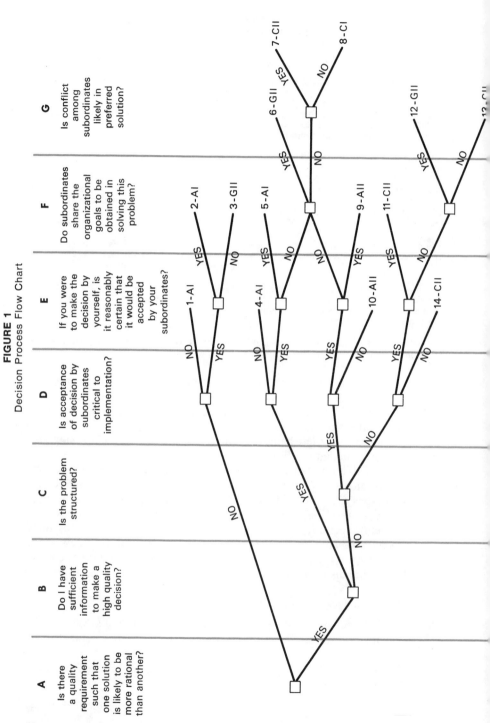

**A**

Is there a quality requirement such that one solution is likely to be more rational than another?

**B**

Do I have sufficient information to make a high quality decision?

**C**

Is the problem structured?

**D**

Is acceptance of decision by subordinates critical to implementation?

**E**

If you were to make the decision by yourself, is it reasonably certain that it would be accepted by your subordinates?

**F**

Do subordinates share the organizational goals to be obtained in solving this problem?

**G**

Is conflict among subordinates likely in preferred solution?

constant with existing evidence concerning the consequences of participation in decision-making on organizational effectiveness.

There are two mechanisms underlying the behavior of the model. The first is a set of seven rules which serve to protect the quality and the acceptance of the decision by eliminating alternatives which risk one or the other of these decision outcomes. Once the rules have been applied, a feasible set of decision processes is generated. The second is a principle for choosing among alternatives in the feasible set where more than one exists.

Let us examine the rules first because they do much of the work of the model. As previously indicated, the rules are intended to protect both the quality and acceptance of the decision. In the form of the model shown, there are three rules which protect decision quality and four which protect acceptance. The seven rules are presented here both as verbal statements and in the more formal language of set theory. In the set theoretic formulation, the letters refer to the problem attributes as stated in question form in Table II. $\bar{A}$ signifies that the answer to question A for a particular problem is *yes*; $\bar{A}$ signifies that the answer to that question is no; $\cap$ signifies intersection; $\Longrightarrow$ signifies "implies"; and $\overline{AI}$ signifies not AI. Thus, A $\cap$ $\bar{B}$ $\Longrightarrow$ $\overline{AI}$ may be read as follows: when both the answer to question A is yes and the answer to question B is no, AI is eliminated from the feasible set.

1. *The Information Rule.* If the quality of the decision is important and if the leader does not possess enough information or expertise to solve the problem by himself, AI is eliminated from the feasible set. (Its use risks a low-quality decision.) (A $\cap$ $\bar{B}$ $\Longrightarrow$ $\overline{AI}$)

2. *The Goal Congruence Rule.* If the quality of the decision is important and if the subordinates do not share the organizational goals to be obtained in solving the problem, GII is eliminated from the feasible set. (Alternatives which eliminate the leader's final control over the decision reached may jeopardize the quality of the decision.) (A $\cap$ $\bar{F}$ $\Longrightarrow$ $\overline{GII}$)

3. *The Unstructured Problem Rule.* In decisions in which the quality of the decision is important, if the leader lacks the necessary information or expertise to solve the problem by himself, and if the problem is unstructured, i.e., he does not know exactly what information is needed and where it is located, the method used must provide not only for him to collect the information but to do so in an efficient and effective manner. Methods which involve interaction among all subordinates with full knowledge of the problem are likely to be both more efficient and more likely to generate a high-quality solution to the problem. Under these conditions, AI, AII, and CI are eliminated from the feasible set. (AI does not provide for him to collect the necessary information, and AII and CI represent more cumbersome, less effective, and less efficient means of bringing the necessary information to bear on the solution of the problem than methods which do permit those with the necessary information to interact.) (A $\cap$ $\bar{B}$ $\cap$ $\bar{C}$ $\Longrightarrow$ $\overline{AI}$, $\overline{AII}$, $\overline{CI}$)

4. *The Acceptance Rule.* If the acceptance of the decision by subordinates is critical to effective implementation, and if it is not certain that an autocratic

decision made by the leader would receive that acceptance, AI and AII are eliminated from the feasible set. (Neither provides an opportunity for subordinates to participate in the decision and both risk the necessary acceptance.) $(D \cap \bar{E} \Longrightarrow \overline{AI}, \overline{AII})$

5. *The Conflict Rule.* If the acceptance of the decision is critical, and an autocratic decision is not certain to be accepted, and subordinates are likely to be in conflict or disagreement over the appropriate solution, AI, AII, and CI are eliminated from the feasible set. (The method used in solving the problem should enable those in disagreement to resolve their differences with full knowledge of the problem. Accordingly, under these conditions, AI, AII, and CI, which involve no interaction or only "one-on-one" relationships and therefore provide no opportunity for those in conflict to resolve their differences, are eliminated from the feasible set. Their use runs the risk of leaving some of the subordinates with less than the necessary commitment to the final decision.) $(D \cap \bar{E} \cap F \Longrightarrow \overline{AI}, \overline{AII}, \overline{CI})$

6. *The Fairness Rule.* If the quality of decision is unimportant, and if acceptance is critical and not certain to result from an autocratic decision, AI, AII, CI, and CII are eliminated from the feasible set. (The method used should maximize the probability of acceptance as this is the only relevant consideration in determining the effectiveness of the decision. Under these circumstances, AI, AII, CI, and CII, which create less acceptance or commitment than GII, are eliminated from the feasible set. To use them is to run the risk of getting less than the needed acceptance of the decision.) $(\bar{A} \cap D \cap \bar{E} \Longrightarrow \overline{AI}, \overline{AII}, \overline{CI}, \overline{CII})$

7. *The Acceptance Priority Rule.* If acceptance is critical, not assured by an autocratic decision, and if subordinates can be trusted, AI, AII, CI, and CII are eliminated from the feasible set. (Methods which provide equal partnership in the decision-making process can provide greater acceptance without risking decision quality. Use of any method other than GII results in an unnecessary risk that the decision will not be fully accepted or receive the necessary commitment on the part of subordinates.) $(A \cap D \cap \bar{E} \cap F \Longrightarrow \overline{AI}, \overline{AII}, \overline{CI}, \overline{CII})$

Once all seven rules have been applied to a given problem, a feasible set of decision processes is given. The feasible set for each of the fourteen problem types is shown in Table 3. It can be seen that there are some problem types for which only one method remains in the feasible set, others for which two methods remain feasible, and still others for which five methods remain feasible.

When more than one method remains in the feasible set, there are a number of alternative decision rules which might dictate the choice among them. The one, which underlies the prescriptions of the model shown in Figure 1, utilizes the number of manhours used in solving the problem as the basis for choice. Given a set of methods with equal likelihood of meeting both quality and acceptance requirements for the decision, it chooses that method which requires the least investment in manhours. On the basis of the empirical evidence summarized earlier, this is deemed to be the method furthest to the left within the feasible set. For example, since AI, AII, CI, CII, and GII are all feasible as in Problem Types 1 and 2, AI would be the method chosen. This decision rule acts to minimize manhours subject to quality and acceptance constraints.

## TABLE III

### Problem Types and the Feasible Set of Decision Processes

| Problem Type | Acceptable Methods |
|---|---|
| 1. | AI, AII, CI, CII, GII |
| 2. | AI, AII, CI, CII, GII |
| 3. | GII |
| 4. | AI, AII, CI, CII, GII* |
| 5. | AI, AII, CI, CII, GII* |
| 6. | GII |
| 7. | CII |
| 8. | CI, CII |
| 9. | AII, CI, CII, GII* |
| 10. | AII, CI, CII, GII* |
| 11. | CII, GII* |
| 12. | GII |
| 13. | CII |
| 14. | CII, GII* |

*Within the feasible set only when the answer to question F is Yes

### Application of the Model

To illustrate how the model might be applied in actual administrative situations, a set of five cases will be presented and analyzed with the use of the model. Following the description of the case, the author's analysis will be given including a specification of problem type, feasible set, and solution indicated by the model. While an attempt has been made to describe these cases as completely as is necessary to permit the reader to make the judgments required by the model, there may remain some room for subjectivity. The reader may wish after reading the case to analyze it himself using the model and then to compare his analysis with that of the authors.

*Case I.* You are manufacturing manager in a large electronics plant. The company's management has always been searching for ways of increasing efficiency. They have recently installed new machines and put in a new simplified work system, but to the surprise of everyone, including yourself, the expected increase in productivity was not realized. In fact, production has begun to drop, quality has fallen off, and the number of employee separations has risen.

You do not believe that there is anything wrong with the machines. You have had reports from other companies who are using them and they confirm this opinion. You have also had representatives from the firm that built the machines go over them and they report that they are operating at peak efficiency.

You suspect that some parts of the new work system may be responsible for the change but this view is not widely shared among your immediate subordinates who are four first-line supervisors, each in charge of a section, and your supply manager. The drop in production has been variously attributed to poor training of the operators, lack of an adequate system of financial incentives, and poor morale. Clearly, this is an issue about which there is considerable depth of feeling within individuals and potential disagreement between your subordinates.

This morning you received a phone call from your division manager. He had just received your production figures for the last six months and was calling to express his concern. He indicated that the problem was yours to solve in any way that you think best, but that he would like to know within a week what steps you plan to take.

You share your division manager's concern with the falling productivity and know that your men are also concerned. The problem is to decide what steps to take to rectify the situation.

*Analysis*

Questions  A (Quality?) = Yes
           B (Manager's Information?) = No
           C (Structured?) = No
           D (Acceptance?) = Yes
           E (Prior Probability of Acceptance?) = No
           F (Goal Congruence?) = Yes
      [G (Conflict?) = Yes]

Problem Type: 12
Feasible Set: GII
Minimum Man-Hours Solution (from Figure 1): GII
Rule Violations: AI violates Rules 1, 3, 4, 5, 7
                 AII violates Rules 3, 4, 5, 7
                 CI violates Rules 3, 5, 7
                 CII violates Rule 7

*Case II.* You are general foreman in charge of a large gang laying an oil pipeline. It is now necessary to estimate your expected rate of progress in order to schedule material deliveries to the next field site.

You know the nature of the terrain you will be traveling and have the historical data needed to compute the mean and variance in the rate of speed over that type of terrain. Given these two variables it is a simple matter to calculate the earliest and latest times at which materials and support facilities will be needed at the next site. It is important that your estimate be reasonably accurate. Underestimates result in idle foremen and workers, and an overestimate results in tying up materials for a period of time before they are to be used.

Progress has been good and your five foremen and other members of the gang stand to receive substantial bonuses if the project is completed ahead of schedule.

*Analysis*

Questions  A (Quality?) = Yes
           B (Manager's Information?) = Yes
           D (Acceptance?) = No

Problem Type: 4
Feasible Set: AI, AII, CI, CII, GII
Minimum Man-Hours Solution (from Figure 1): AI
Rule Violations: None

*Case III.* You are supervising the work of twelve engineers. Their formal training and work experience are very similar, permitting you to use them interchangeably on projects. Yesterday your manager informed you that a request had been received from an overseas affiliate for four engineers to go abroad on extended loan for a period of six to eight months. For a number of reasons, he argued and you agreed that this request should be met from your group.

All your engineers are capable of handling this assignment, and from the standpoint of present and future projects there is no particular reason why any one should be retained over any other. The problem is somewhat complicated by the fact that the overseas assignment is in what is generally regarded in the company as an undesirable location.

Questions A (Quality?) = No
      D (Acceptance?) = Yes
      E (Prior Probability of Acceptance?) = No
      [G (Conflict?) = Yes]

Problem Type: 3
Feasible Set: GII
Minimum Man-Hours Solution (from Figure 1): GII
Rule Violations: AI and AII violate Rules 4, 5, 6
      CI violates Rules 5 and 6
      CII violates Rule 6

*Case IV.* You are the head of a staff unit reporting to the vice-president of finance. He has asked you to provide a report on the firm's current portfolio to include recommendations for changes in the selection criteria currently employed. Doubts have been raised about the efficiency of the existing system in the current market conditions, and there is considerable dissatisfaction with prevailing rates of return.

You plan to write the report, but at the moment you are quite perplexed about the approach to take. Your own specialty is the bond market and it is clear to you that a detailed knowledge of the equity market, which you lack, would greatly enhance the value of the report. Fortunately, four members of your staff are specialists in different segments of the equity market. Together, they possess a vast amount of knowledge about the intricacies of investment. However, they seldom agree on the best way to achieve anything when it comes to the stock market. While they are obviously conscientious as well as knowledgeable, they have major differences when it comes to investment philosophy and strategy.

You have six weeks before the report is due. You have already begun to familiarize yourself with the firm's current portfolio and have been provided by management with a specific set of constraints that any portfolio must satisfy. Your immediate problem is to come up with some alternatives to the firm's present practices and select the most promising for detailed analysis in your report.

*Analysis*

Questions A (Quality?) = Yes
      B (Manager's Information?) = No
      C (Structured?) = No
      D (Acceptance?) = No
      [F (Goal Congruence?) = Yes]
      [G (Conflict?) = Yes]

Problem Type: 14
Feasible Set: CII, GII
Minimum Man-Hours Solution (from Figure 1): CII
Rule Violations: AI violates Rules 1, 3, 5
      AII violates Rules 3 and 5
      CI violates Rules 3 and 5

*Case V.* You are on the division manager's staff and work on a wide variety of problems of both an administrative and technical nature. You have been given the assignment of developing a universal method to be used in each of the five plants in the division for manually reading equipment registers, recording the readings, and transmitting the scorings to a centralized information system. All plants are located in a relatively small geographical region.

Until now there has been a high error rate in the reading and/or transmittal of the data. Some locations have considerably higher error rates than others, and the methods used to record and transmit the data vary between plants. It is probable, therefore, that part of the error variance is a function of specific local conditions rather than anything else, and this will complicate the establishment of any system common to all plants. You have the information on error rates but no information on the local practices which generate these errors or on the local conditions which necessitate the different practices.

Everyone would benefit from an improvement in the quality of the data as it is used in a number of important decisions. Your contacts with the plants are through the quality-control supervisors who are responsible for collecting the data. They are a conscientious group committed to doing their jobs well, but are highly sensitive to interference on the part of higher management in their own operations. Any solution which does not receive the active support of the various plant supervisors is unlikely to reduce the error rate significantly.

*Analysis*

Questions  A (Quality?) = Yes
             B (Manager's Information?) = No
             C (Structured?) = No
             D (Acceptance?) = Yes
             E (Prior Probability of Acceptance?) = No
             F (Goal Congruence?) = Yes

Problem Type: 12
Feasible Set: GII
Minimum Man-Hours Solution (from Figure 1): GII
Rule Violations: AI violates Rules 1, 3, 4, 7
                  AII violates Rules 3, 4, 7
                  CI violates Rules 3 and 7
                  CII violates Rule 7

### Short-Versus Long-Term Models

The model described above seeks to protect, if relevant, the quality of the decision, to create any necessary acceptance of the decision, and to expend the least number of manhours in the process. In view of its attention to conditions surrounding the making and implementation of a particular decision rather than any long-term considerations, it could be termed a short-term model.

It seems likely, however, that the leadership methods which may be optimal for short-term results may be different from those which would be optimal when executed over a longer period of time. Consider a leader who has been uniformly pursuing an autocratic style (AI or AII) and, perhaps as a consequence, has subordinates who cannot be trusted to pursue organization goals (attribute F) and who might be termed "yes men" (attribute E). An examination of the structure of the time-minimizing model reveals that with few exceptions, the leader would be instructed by the model to continue his present autocratic style.

It appears likely, however, that the use of more participative methods would, in time, change the status of these problem attributes so as to develop ultimately a more effective problem-solving system. In the example given above, an autocratic approach would be indicated to maximize short-run benefits, but a higher degree of participation might maximize performance aggregated over a longer period.

A promising approach to the development of a long-term model is one which places less weight on manhours as the basis for choice of method within the feasible set. Given a long-term orientation, one would be interested in the trade-off between manhours in problem-solving and team development, both of which increase with participation. Viewed in these terms, the time-minimizing model places maximum relative weight on manhours and no weight on development and hence chooses the style furthest to the left within the feasible set. A model which places less weight on manhours and more weight on development would, if these assumptions are correct, choose a style further to the right within the feasible set.

### Toward a Descriptive Model of Leader Behavior

So far we have been concerned with the normative questions defined at the outset. But how do managers really behave? What considerations affect these decisions about how much to share their decision-making power with their subordinates? In what respects is their behavior different from or similar to that of the model? These questions are but a few of those that we attempted to answer in a large-scale research program[3] aimed at gaining a greater understanding of the factors that do influence managers in their choice of decision processes to fit the demands of the situation. Two rather different research methods have been utilized in studying these factors.

The first investigation utilized a method which we have come to term "recalled problems." Over 500 managers from eleven different countries and representing a variety of firms were asked to provide a written description of a problem which they had recently had to solve in their managerial capacity. These varied in length from one paragraph to several pages and covered virtually every facet of managerial decision-making. For each case, the manager was asked to indicate which of the decision processes shown in Table I they used to solve the problem. Finally, each manager was asked to answer the questions shown in Table II corresponding to the problem attributes used in the normative model.

The wealth of data, both qualitative and quantitative, served two purposes. Since each manager had diagnosed a situation which he had encountered in terms that are used in the normative model and had indicated the methods that he had used in dealing with it, it is possible to determine what differences if any there were between the model's behavior and his own behavior. Secondly, the written cases provided the basis for the construction of a standard set of cases used in later research to determine the factors which influence managers to share or retain their decision-making power. Each case depicted a manager faced with a problem to solve or decision to make. The cases span a wide range of managerial problems including production scheduling, quality control, portfolio management, personnel allocation, and research and development. In each case

[3]This research program has been financially supported by the McKinsey Foundation, General Electric Foundation, Smith Richardson Foundation, and by the Office of Naval Research.

a person could readily assume the role of the manager described, and could be asked to indicate which of the decision processes he would use if actually faced with that situation.

In most of our research, a set of thirty cases has been used and the subjects have been several thousand managers who were participants in management development programs in the United States and abroad. The cases for use in the set were selected not randomly but systematically. We desired cases which could not only be coded unambiguously in the terms used in the normative model, but which would also permit the assessment of the effects of each of the problem attributes used in the model on the person's behavior. The solution was to select cases in accordance with an experimental design such that they varied in terms of the seven attributes used in the model and variation in each attribute was independent of each other attribute. Several such standardized sets of cases have been developed, and over a thousand managers have now been studied using this approach.

To summarize all of the things that we have learned in the course of this research is well beyond the scope of this paper, but it is possible to discuss some of the highlights. Since the results obtained from the two research methods— recalled and standardized problems—are quite consistent, the major results can be presented independent of the method used.

Perhaps the most striking finding is the weakening of the widespread view that participativeness is a general trait which managers exhibit in different amounts. To be sure, there were differences among managers in their general tendencies to utilize participative methods as opposed to autocratic ones. On the standardized problems, these differences accounted for about 10 percent of the total variance in decision process observed. These differences in behavior between managers, however, were small in comparison with differences within managers. On the standardized problems, no manager has indicated that he would use the same decision process on all problems or decisions, and most use all five methods under some circumstances.

Some of this variance in behavior within managers can be attributed to widely shared tendencies to respond to some situations by sharing power and others by retaining it. It makes at least as much sense to talk about participative and autocratic situations as it does to talk about participative and autocratic managers. In fact, on the standardized problems, the variance in behavior across problems or cases is about three times as large as the variance across managers!

What are the characteristics of an autocratic as opposed to a participative situation? An answer to this question would constitute a partial descriptive model of this aspect of the decision-making process and has been our goal in much of the research that we have conducted. From our observations of behavior on both recalled problems and on standardized problems, it is clear that the decision-making process employed by a typical manager is influenced by a large number of factors, many of which are also utilized in the normative model. Following are several conclusions which are substantiated by the results on both recalled and standardized problems: Managers use decision processes providing less opportunity for participation 1) when they possess all the necessary information than when they lack some of the needed information, 2) when the problem which they face is well structured rather than unstructured, 3) when their subordinates' acceptance of the decision is not critical for the effective implementation of the decision or when the prior probability of acceptance of an autocratic decision is high, and 4) when the personal goals of their subordinates are *not* congruent with the goals of the organization as manifested in that problem.

So far we have been talking about relatively common or widely shared ways of dealing with organizational problems. Our results strongly suggest that there are some ways of "tailoring" one's approach to the situation which distinguish managers from one another. Theoretically, these can be thought of as differences among managers in decision rules about when to encourage participation. Statistically, they are represented as interactions between situational variables and personal characteristics.

Consider, for example, two managers who have identical distributions of use of the five decision processes shown in Table I on a set of thirty cases. In a sense, they are equally participative (or autocratic). However, the situations in which they permit or encourage participation in decision-making on the part of their subordinates may be very different. One may restrict the participation of his subordinates to decisions without a quality requirement whereas the other may restrict their participation to problems with a quality requirement. The former would be more inclined to use participative decision processes (like GII) on such decisions as what color the walls would be painted or when the company picnic would be held. The latter would be more likely to encourage participation in decision-making on decisions which have a clear and demonstrable impact on the organization's success in achieving its external goals.

Use of the standardized problem set permits the assessment of such differences in decision rules which govern choices among decision-making processes. Since the cases are selected in accordance with an experimental design, it can indicate differences in the behavior of managers attributable not only to the existence of a quality requirement in the problem but also in the effects of acceptance requirements, conflict, information requirements, and the like.

The research using both recalled and standardized problems has also enabled us to examine similarities and differences between the behavior of the normative model and the behavior of a typical manager. Such an analysis reveals, at the very least, what behavioral changes would be expected if managers began using the normative model as the basis for choosing their decision-making processes.

A typical manager says he would (or did) use exactly the same decision process as that shown in Figure 1 in about forty percent of the situations. In two-thirds of the situations, his behavior is consistent with the feasible set of methods proposed in the model. Thus, in about one-third of the situations, his behavior violates at least one of the seven rules underlying the model.

The four rules designed to protect the acceptance or commitment of the decision have substantially higher probabilities of being violated than do the three rules designed to protect the quality or rationality of the decision. One of the acceptance rules, the Fairness Rule (Rule 6) is violated about three-quarters of the time that it could have been applicable. On the other hand, one of the quality rules, the Information Rule, (Rule 1) is violated in only about three percent of occasions in which it is applicable. If we assume for the moment that these two sets of rules have equal validity, these findings strongly suggest that the decisions made by the typical manager are more likely to prove ineffective due to deficiencies of acceptance by subordinates than due to deficiencies in decision quality. Another striking difference between the behavior of the model and of the typical manager lies in the fact that the former shows far greater variance with the situation. If a typical manager voluntarily used the model as the basis for choosing his methods of making decisions, he would become both more autocratic and more participative. He would employ autocratic methods more frequently in situations in which his subordinates were unaffected by the decision and participative methods more frequently when his subordinates' cooperation and support were critical and/or their information and expertise required.

It should be noted that the typical manager to which we have been referring is merely a statistical average of the several thousand that have been studied over the last three or four years. There is a great deal of variance around that average. As evidenced by their behavior on standardized problems, some managers are already behaving in a manner which is highly consistent with the model while others' behavior is clearly at variance with it.

### A New Technology for Leadership Development

The investigations that have been summarized here were conducted for research purposes to shed some light on the determinants and consequences of participation in decision-making. In the course of the research, we realized that those managers who were contributing their time as subjects in the research were perceiving this investment as valuable in its own right and as contributing to their own learning and development. The fortunate coincidence of interest between the personal goals of the managers and our own research objectives both made the research task easier and began to suggest that the data collection procedures, with appropriate additions and modifications, might also serve as a valuable approach to leadership development. From this realization evolved an important by-product of the research activities—a new approach to leadership development based on the concepts in the normative model and the empirical methods of the descriptive research.

This approach is based on the assumption that one of the critical skills required of all leaders is the ability to adapt their behavior to the demands of the situation and that one component of this skill involves the ability to select the appropriate decision-making process for each problem or decision he confronts.

In Chapter 8 of Vroom and Yetton a leadership development program is described which is aimed at providing intensive training in that skill. It is not intended to "train" participants in the use of the model but rather to encourage them to examine their own leadership style and to ask themselves whether the methods they are using are most effective for their own organization. A critical part of the program involves the use of a set of standardized cases, each depicting a leader faced with an administrative problem to solve. Each person is asked to specify the decision-making process that he would use if faced with each situation. His responses are processed by computer which generates a highly detailed analysis of his leadership style which is provided to him in the course of the program. The responses for all participants in the course are typically processed simultaneously, permitting the economical representation of differences between the person and other participants in the same program.

In its present form, a single computer printout for a person consists of three 15″ x 11″ pages, each filled with graphs and tables highlighting different features of his behavior. Understanding the results requires a detailed knowledge of the concepts underlying the model which has already been developed in one of the previous phases of the training program. The printout is accompanied by a manual which aids in the explanation of results and provides a suggested set of steps to be followed in extracting full meaning from the printout.

Following are a few of the questions which the printout answers:

1. How autocratic or participative am I in my dealings with subordinates in relationship to other participants in the program?
2. What decision processes do I use more or less frequently than the average?
3. How close does my behavior come to that of the model? How frequently does my behavior agree with the feasible set? What evidence is there that my leadership style reflects the pressure of time as opposed to a concern with the development of my subordinates? How do I compare in these respects with other participants in the class?
4. What rules do I violate most frequently and least frequently? How does this compare with other participants? On what cases did I violate these rules? Does my leadership style reflect more concern with getting decisions that are high in quality or decisions that are accepted?
5. What circumstances cause me to behave in an autocratic fashion; what circumstances cause me to behave participatively? In what respects is the way in which I attempt to vary my behavior with the demands of the situation similar to that of the model?

When a typical manager receives his printout, he immediately goes to work trying to understand what it tells him about himself. After most of the major results have been understood, he goes back to the set of cases to reread those on which he has violated rules. Typically, managers show an interest in discussing and comparing their results with others in the program. Gatherings of four to six people comparing their results and their interpretations of them, often for several evening hours, were such a common feature that they have recently been institutionalized as part of the procedure.

It should be emphasized that the method of providing feedback to managers on their leadership style is just one part of the total training experience but it is an important part. The program is sufficiently new so that, to date, no long-term evaluative studies have been undertaken. The short-term results, reported in detail in Vroom and Yetton, look quite promising and can be summarized by the following comment written by one of the participants in an experimental version of the program.

The (computer) output was perhaps the most informative personalized and comprehensive piece of relatively immediate feedback which I have ever received. I would venture to say that not many managers ever get a chance to confront their leadership style and scrutinize it . . . It will indeed be unfortunate if we never consider the implications of how we treat our subordinates in the business world for the remainder of our careers.

**Conclusion**

As with participation in decision-making, there are many concepts and applications developed within the social sciences, the utility of which is likely to vary with the situation. Decentralization, management by objectives, job enrich-ment, and sensitivity training are among the "treatments" frequently recom-mended as valuable but which are likely to have differential effects and to be of differential value under different conditions. In such instances, there are multiple consequences of each treatment and estimates of their ability in a particular situation inevitably involve judgments concerning the value of each consequence and the probability of its occurrence in that situation.

The efforts reported in this paper rest on the conviction that social scientists can be of greater value in solving problems of organizational behavior if their prescriptive statements deal with the complexities involved in the phenomena with which they study.

The normative model described in this paper is but one small step in that direction. Some might argue that it is premature for social scientists to be prescriptive. Our knowledge is too limited and the issues too complex to war-rant prescriptions for action—even those which are based on a diagnosis of situational demands. It is also true, however, that organizational problems per-sist and that their leaders cannot await the time for the behavioral sciences to perfect their disciplines before attempting to cope with them. Is it likely that models which encourage them to deal analytically with the forces impinging upon them would produce less rational choices than those which they now make? The criterion for social utility is not perfection but improvement over present practice.

Perhaps the most convincing argument for the development of normative models is the fact that in developing and using them their weaknesses can be identified. Insofar as their weaknesses stem from a lack of basic knowledge, this deficiency can be remedied through further research. A strong case can be made for the value of continued interplay between the worlds of practice and social science based on their potential contributions to one another.

# THE PROCESS OF
# PROBLEM FINDING

WILLIAM F. POUNDS

## Introduction

As a result of research efforts over the past twenty years, a number of extremely effective analytical techniques are currently available for the solution of management problems. Linear programming is used routinely in the specification of optimum cattle feeds and fertilizers. Decision rules based on inventory models form the basis for production and inventory control systems in a wide variety of manufacturing companies. Simulation is evolving from a means for doing research on complex managerial problems to a process which can provide useful information to managers on a real-time basis.

Like other technological changes, these methods raise a number of social and organizational issues within the organizations which use them, but their net contribution is no longer seriously in doubt. As a result, in most large organizations and in many smaller ones, operating managers either are themselves aware of these methods or have ready access to help and advise in their application if it is required.

But the manager's job is not only to solve well-defined problems. He must somehow identify the problems to be solved. He must somehow assess the cost

Reprinted by permission of the author. Sloan School Working Paper No. 145–65, Massachusetts Institute of Technology (November 1965).

The research underlying this paper was supported in part by a grant from the National Aeronautics and Space Administration.

The author gratefully acknowledges the many contributions of Professor E.H. Bowman to all phases of this study and particularly those he made to the planning and execution of the company study.

of analysis and its potential return. He must allocate resources to questions before he knows their answers. To many managers and students of management the availability of formal problem solving procedures serves only to highlight those parts of the manager's job with which these procedures do *not* deal— problem identification, the assignment of problem priority, and the allocation of scarce resources to problems. These tasks which must be performed without the benefit of a well-defined body of theory may be among the most critical of the manager's decision-making responsibilities.

This paper is concerned primarily with the first of these tasks—problem identification. It reviews some research which is relevant to understanding decisions of this type, presents a theoretical structure, and reports some results of an empirical study of the process by which managers in a successful industrial organization define their problems.

Because this research was stimulated in part by an interest in the relationship between the so-called new techniques of management and what might be called normal managerial behavior, similarities between these two modes of management which are suggested both by the theory and the empirical evidence are briefly noted.

## Background

Prior to 1945 our understanding of most cognitive tasks within industrial organizations was not much better than our understanding of the process of problem finding is today. Inventory levels were maintained, production schedules were determined, and distribution systems were designed by individuals who, through years of experience, had learned ways to get these jobs done. With few exceptions these individuals could not be explicit about how they performed these tasks and, as a result, training for these jobs was a slow process and the development and testing of new procedures was difficult indeed.

So it is with the process of problem finding today. All managers have discovered ways to maintain a list of problems which can occupy their working hours—and other hours as well. They frequently find it difficult, however, to be explicit about the process by which their problems are selected—and, as a result, training for managerial positions is slow and the development and testing of new and possibly better problem finding procedures is difficult.

Since 1945, however, some progress has been made in understanding certain cognitive tasks in the areas of production and inventory control. Decision rules have been derived from mathematical models of particular tasks and in a number of cases these rules have performed as well or better than the complex intuitive process they have replaced. The significant fact about these developments for this discussion is, not the economic impact of such rules (although it has been significant), but rather the implication that the essential processes by which important decisions are made may be carried out satisfactorily by simple explicit decision rules which are easy to teach and execute and easy to improve through analysis, simulation or experimentation.

Of course it is possible to discount these accomplishments by saying that inventory decisions were always rather simple ones to make. The validity of such arguments, however, seems suspiciously dependent on knowledge of what has been accomplished and on a lack of knowledge of inventory systems.

It is true, however, that mathematical analysis has not been able to suggest decision rules for a wide variety of managerial tasks. Jobs like product design, personnel selection, and others including the definition of problems seem to require symbols and analytical procedures not readily represented by standard mathematical forms. Some other means for discovering the (hopefully simple, explicit) decision rules by which such tasks are performed is clearly required.

Some progress in this direction has already been made. Encouraged both by the success of the analytical approach to decision problems, and by the availability of large digital computers, Newell, Simon and others have been studying human decision behavior since the early 1950s. They have focussed their attention primarily on tasks which would facilitate the development of a methodology for approaching decision situations not readily describable in mathematical terms. They have considered the decision processes involved in proving theorems in symbolic logic[1] and plane geometry.[2] They have considered decision processes involved in playing games like chess[3] and checkers.[4] They have worked on the assembly line balancing problem[5] and on trust investment.[6] The relevance of this research to the problem of problem finding can perhaps best be illustrated by considering the work on chess.

### Research on Chess

Chess is a game with rules simple enough for almost anyone to learn and yet it is complex enough that even the largest computer cannot play it by working out the consequences of all possible moves. Chess is a game of strategy in which individual moves are not always possible to evaluate without considering future moves. Chess moves are inconvenient to describe in mathematical terms and few people can be explicit about how they play chess. For these reasons and several others, chess was an attractive medium in which to attempt to unravel human decision processes which could not be modeled mathematically.

Three aspects of the work on chess playing behavior are relevant to this discussion. First, simple explicit decision rules were discovered which play very good chess. This result has been tested by programming computers with such rules and observing the quality of play which resulted in response to the play of human experts. Second, the decision rules for chess playing were derived from observations, interviews, and the writing of chess masters. Thus it is not necessary that simple explicit decision rules be derived from mathematical or theoretical considerations. They can be abstracted from humans who have themselves never systematically considered the process of their own decision

[1]Newell, A., J, C. Shaw, and H. A. Simon, "Empirical Explorations of the Logic Theory Machine," *Proceedings of the Western Joint Computer Conference* (February, 1957), pp. 218–230.

[2]Gelernter, H. L., "Realization of a Geometry Theorem Proving Machine," *UNESCO Conference on Information Processing Proceedings* (1959).

[3]Newell, A., J. C. Shaw, and H. A. Simon, "Chess-Playing Programs and the Problem of Complexity," *IBM Journal of Research and Development* (October, 1958), pp. 320–335.

[4]Samuel, A. L., "Some Studies in Machine Learning, Using the Game of Checkers," *IBM Journal of Research and Development*, Vol. 3, No. 3 (July, 1959), pp. 210–230.

[5]Tonge, F. M., *A Heuristic Program for Assembly-Line Balancing.* Englewood Cliffs, N. J.: Prentice-Hall, 1961.

[6]Clarkson, G. P. E., *Portfolio Selection: A Simulation of Trust Investment.* Englewood Cliffs, N.J.: Prentice-Hall, 1962.

making. And, third, the decision rules by which humans play chess appear to be separable into three rather distinct classes: rules for defining alternative moves, rules for evaluating alternative moves, and rules for choosing a move from among evaluated alternatives. H. A. Simon has called these three classes of behavior respectively intelligence, design, and choice,[7] and on the basis of his work both on chess and other decision-making situations has concluded that the process of intelligence or alternative definition is the key to effective behavior.

The work on chess and other complex tasks does not directly suggest how managers go about finding and defining the problems to which they devote their time. It does suggest, however, that tasks of this same order of complexity may be understood through careful observation of and abstraction from the behavior of human experts. It further suggests that, if useful insights into managerial problem finding can be gained, they may contribute significantly to managerial effectiveness.

## An Empirical Study of Managerial Problem Finding

Since it was possible to gain useful insights into the process by which humans play chess by observing experts, it seemed likely that insights into the process of managerial problem finding might be derived from careful observation of successful managers. Arrangements were made therefore to interview, observe, and interrogate about 50 executives in a decentralized operating division of a large technically based corporation which will be referred to as the Southern Company.

The work of the study consisted of four relatively distinct activities. First, interviews were conducted during which executives were asked to describe the problems they faced and the processes by which they had become aware of these problems. Second, observations were made of meetings during which problems were identified, discussed, and sometimes solved. Third, investigations were made of the source and disposition of several specific problems. And, fourth, a questionnaire was devised and administered to each executive who participated in the study.

As data began to accumulate from each of these activities it became clear that a major objective of the study would be to discover some level of abstraction which would preserve what seemed to be essential details of the managerial situations being observed and at the same time provide a structure which would convert isolated anecdotes into data from which some generalizations might be drawn. This structure will be described in the following pages together with some of the observations it explains. Observations made outside this particular study will also be reported.

## A Theoretical Structure

The process of management, like any number of other industrial tasks, can be viewed as the sequential execution of elementary activities. In describing their own work, executives find it easy to think and talk in terms of elementary

[7]Simon, H. A., *The New Science of Management Decision.* New York: Harper and Brothers, 1960, pp. 1–4.

activities like making out the production schedule, reading the quality control report, visiting a customer, etc. The attractive feature of this view of managerial work is that elementary tasks can be defined at almost any level of detail.

Clearly the task of preparing a production schedule is itself made up of more elementary tasks like collecting data on orders and labor availability, which are themselves made up of even more elementary activities. On the other hand, one can aggregate elements like production scheduling into larger units of analysis like managing production.

A choice of some level of abstraction cannot be avoided. For purposes of this study the level chosen was that which the managers themselves used. Thus even at the theoretical level, advantage was taken of the fact that the managers' language had evolved as a useful means for processing information about their jobs.

Elements of managerial activity will be referred to as *operators*. An operator transforms a set of input variables into a set of output variables according to some predetermined plan. For example, the operator "lay out a production schedule," takes machine capacities, labor productivities, product requirements, and other input variables and yields man, product, machine, and time associations covering some appropriate period of time.

Since the action of an operator produces an effect which is more or less predictable, operators are frequently named for their effect on the environment. For example, the operator "lay out production schedule" changes the production organization from one with no schedule to one with a schedule. The operator "hire qualified lathe operator" changes the size of the work force.[8]

The word "problem" is associated with the difference between some existing situation and some desired situation. The problem of reducing material cost for example indicates a difference between the existing material cost and some desired level of material cost. The problems of hiring qualified engineers and of reducing finished goods inventories similarly define differences to be reduced.

Because problems are defined by differences and operators can be executed to reduce differences, strong associations are formed between problems and operators. The "problem" of devising a production schedule can ordinarily be "solved" by applying the operator "lay out production schedule." The problem of "increasing sales volume" can sometimes be "solved" by applying the operator "revise advertising budget."

Since operator selection is triggered by the difference to be reduced, the process of problem finding is the process of defining differences. Problem solving on the other hand is the process of selecting operators which will reduce differences.

The manager defines differences by comparing what he perceives, to the output of a *model* which predicts the same variables. For example, a difference might be defined by comparing an idle machine to a production schedule which implies high machine utilization. In this case the production schedule is the model used to define a difference. A difference might be defined by comparing a $10\%$ reject rate in a department to a budgeted rate of $2\%$. In this case the budget is the model. A difference might be defined by comparing available data to that required for a special report. The problem of understanding problem

---

[8]Because this paper is concerned primarily with problem finding, the process of operator selection and execution will not be discussed. The definitions are included here only to complete the description of the theoretical structure.

finding therefore is eventually reduced to the problem of understanding the models which managers use to define differences. The next section of this paper will discuss the models which are used by successful operating managers.

Before that discussion it should be noted that the theoretical framework proposed here has drawn on ideas discussed by Miller, Galanter, and Pribram,[9] who in turn refer to some basic work by Newell, Shaw, and Simon.[10] Figure 1 presents a flow chart of the process described in this section and indicates the relationship of these ideas to those which have been proposed by others.

### Managerial Models for Problem Finding

Because the models to be described here were not on hand at the beginning of the study, it is not possible to supply good data on the relative frequency or other statistics on their use.

### Historical Models

On the assumption that recent past experience is the best estimate of the short term future, managers maintain a wide variety of models based on the continuity of historical relationships: April sales exceed March sales by ten percent; Department X runs 5% defective product; the cost of making item Y is $10.50 per thousand; the lead time on that raw material is three weeks, etc. Because the manager's world is complex and these models tend to be simple, discrepancies frequently arise between these models' predictions and what actually takes place. Such discrepancies are a major source of problems to which managers devote their time.

Why is our inventory account drifting out of line? Why is our reject rate so high this week? What has happened to make so many deliveries late? What can be done to reverse this trend in absenteeism? Why is our safety record suddenly so good? All of these problems and a host of others like them can keep a manager and his organization busy all day every day. All these problems are triggered by discrepancies from historical models.

For the most part these models are non-explicit. The manager "carries them in his head" or "just knows." In a number of cases, however, these models are strongly supported by routine reports. Pieces of paper on which are printed: monthly P & L statements, weekly reports of sales totals, daily reports of orders behind schedule, semi-annual inventories, and many other items of interest flow across the manager's desk in a steady stream and, except in its historical context, each one has little meaning to the manager or anyone else.[11]

Recognizing this fact, most management reports in the Southern Company were prepared in such a way that current figures and recent reports of the same variables appeared side by side. Trends or sharp variations in any variable could be easily noted.

The confidence placed in such analysis was clearly indicated by the fact that a large number of variables were added to routine reports following an unan-

[9]G. A. Miller, E. Galanter, and K. H. Pribram, *Plans and the Structure of Behavior,* New York: Henry Holt and Company, 1960.

[10]Newell, A., J. C. Shaw, and H. A. Simon, "Report on a General Problem-Solving Program," *Proceedings of the ICIP,* Paris (June, 1960). (Reprinted in *Computers and Automation,* 8: 10–7, July, 1960, as "A General Problem-Solving Program for a Computer.")

[11]Budgets which can also provide context for such data will be discussed in the next section.

Figure 1

A Flow Chart of Managerial Behavior

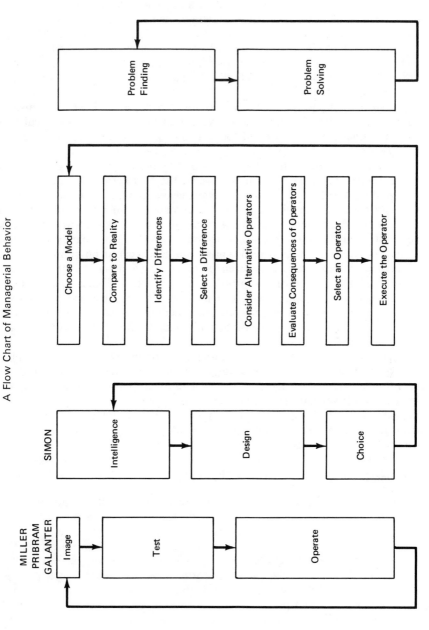

ticipated fluctuation in corporate profits. After several months managers could review their history of "Return on Sales," "Return on Investment," and many other variables in addition to those previously reported.

The importance of routine reports as well as the use of an historical model to identify a problem were both illustrated when the rejection rate of one department moved past an historic high and thereby attracted attention to the Quality Assurance organization. A number of other examples could be cited. Forty-two out of 52 managers agreed with the statement that "most improvements come from correcting unsatisfactory situations" and for the most part unsatisfactory situations were defined by departures from historically established models of performance.

Departures of performance in a favorable direction, i.e., lower than historical cost or higher than historical sales, were used to modify the historical model not to define a problem *per se*. Several managers reported that better-than-average performance was frequently used as evidence of what could be accomplished when reduced cost allowances or increased profit expectations were being discussed. At the time of this study, the Southern Company was doing very well relative to its own past performance and a number of managers shared the sentiments of one who reported, "This year is going too well." They were clearly concerned about their ability to continue to meet what would become a new historical standard. Several were already working on that problem-to-be.

In another company, wage incentive standards based on running averages of past production rates have been observed to yield significant innovations. In one case a 400% increase in productivity was accomplished on an inspection operation over a period of eighteen months with no decrease in quality. By basing production requirements on past accomplishments, workers were encouraged to find their own methods and pace and they did so with completely satisfactory results.

Besides serving as triggers for corrective and innovative problem solving, historical models are used extensively in the process of devising plans for future operations. These plans are in turn converted into budget objectives and these budget objectives can sometimes serve as models which trigger managerial problem solving. Because of the complex process by which they are devised, managerial planning models will be discussed separately from the more straightforward historical ones.

## Planning Models

Managers in the Southern Company devoted substantial amounts of time to planning future operations. Detailed projections of operating variables for the coming year and less detailed projections for the coming five years were presented annually to corporate officers by each Product Department Manager. When approved—perhaps after some modification—these projections were used periodically to evaluate managerial performance (as well as for other purposes).

In view of the importance attributed to planning by the Southern Company, it might be expected that planning models would constitute an important part of the problem finding process. In fact they did not. Historical models were more influential on managerial behavior than planning models. To understand why, it is necessary to examine both the function of planning models and the process by which they were devised.

Among other things, plans are organizationally defined limits of managerial independence. So long as the manager is able to perform at least as well as his plan requires, he expects, and is normally granted, the right to define his problems as he sees fit. That is to say, as long as meeting his plan does not itself constitute a problem, the manager can use other criteria for defining his problems. If, however, he is unable to perform as well as he planned, he can expect to attract the attention of higher levels of management and to receive substantial assistance in problem identification. In other words, he will lose, perhaps only temporarily, the right to manage.

One product department manager put the matter this way, "The best way to remain in charge is to be successful." Other managers strongly supported this position. Success was defined relative to the predictions of the planning model.

In view of the fact that unfavorable deviations in performance were far more undesirable to managers than favorable deviations, it is not surprising that planning models were not simple descriptions of what the managers expected would happen. On the contrary, planning models represented the minimum performance the manager could reasonably expect if several of his plans failed or were based on the minimum organizational expectations of managerial performance, whichever was higher. Planning models were in general very conservatively biased historical models.

For the most part these biases in plans were not injected surreptitiously. After approving a manager's plan, upper level managers always inquired about how he would deal with various contingencies. At this point the manager would reveal some but usually not all of his "hedges" against uncertainty. If he could report a number of conservative estimates and contingent plans to back up the plan being proposed, this was viewed as highly desirable.

In aggregating departmental plans further "adjustments" were made which led the plan to depart from expectations. In some cases these adjustments shifted expected profits from one department to another to "make the package look OK." In other cases already conservative departmental estimates were "rounded down" to further cover contingencies. Some of these adjustments were made explicit at higher levels.

Even with all its conservative biases, the division's plan still exceeded the corporation's minimum profit and volume expectations. It is not surprising, therefore, that the planning model was a far less important source of management problems than historical models. Extrapolations of past performance simply implied much higher levels of performance than the planning model called for. Only in those cases (not observed) where the corporate expectations required improvements over historical trends would one expect planning models to be important in the process of problem finding.

## Other People's Models

Some models which define problems for the manager are maintained by other people. A customer whose model of product quality is violated by the product he receives may notify the manager of the producing organization of this fact and thereby define a problem for him. A higher level manager may lack information to complete an analysis and this discrepancy can define a problem for a lower level manager. An employee may need a decision on vacation policy and his request will define a problem for his supervisor. A basic function of an organization structure is to channel problems which are identified by its various members to individuals especially qualified to solve them. Managers as well as other members of the organization do not always work on problems defined by their own models.

In the Southern Company invitations to attend meetings, requests to prepare reports, and requests for projects of various kinds whether made by superiors, subordinates, or peers were rarely questioned by managers as appropriate ways to spend their time. While it was easy to get sometimes vehement testimony as to the uselessness of many of these activities, the behavior of managers clearly indicated the strong influence of other people's models.

One reason for the influence of these models may be the cost to the manager of doubting them. Any attempt to validate each request made on him could easily imply a heavier workload on the manager than the simple execution of the work requested. In addition, by providing "good service" the manager builds (or at least many believe they build) a store of goodwill among other managers toward his own requests.

Confidence in other people's models is sufficient in many cases to provide the manager with an insurmountable workload. A survey of highly successful middle managers who were participating in an executive program at Massachusetts Institute of Technology indicated that such models provided the vast bulk of their workload. In those rare cases where these models left some free time, several of these managers indicated they "walked around the shop" or "talked with people"—indicating perhaps a reluctance on their part to undertake problems which were not defined by someone else.

During the course of the company study, several clear examples of the influence of these models were observed. In a series of interviews, managers were asked to specify the problems currently faced by them and their organizations. Most of them mentioned from five to eight problems. Later in the same interview, each manager was asked to describe in broad terms his own activities for the previous week. In reviewing the data from these interviews as they were collected, it was noted that no manager had reported any activity which could be directly associated with the problems he had described.

In order to be sure that this result was not due to some semantic problem, this point was discussed with several managers—in some cases during the first interview with them and in some cases as a follow-up question.

One manager found the point both accurate and amusing. He smiled as he replied. "That's right. I don't have time to work on *my* problems—I'm too busy." Another manager took a different tack in agreeing with the general conclusion. He replied rather confidentially, "I don't really make decisions. I just work here." In further discussion with a number of managers, the power of other people's models was repeatedly indicated. The influence of these models was also noted in the case of a rather involved project which was observed in some detail.

The Plant Engineering Department (using a quite different model)[12] decided to look at the desirability of revising the management of the company's 21 fork trucks. Besides scheduling and other operating questions which were investigated by people within the Engineering Department, studies of the contract under which the trucks were leased and an economic evaluation of leasing versus buying trucks were also felt to be required.

The Manager of Plant Engineering called representatives of the Comptroller's

[12]Discussed on pages 92–95.

organization and the Legal Department to a meeting where the project was discussed in some detail. This discussion clearly indicated that the project was risky both from the point of view of economic payoff and political considerations. The representatives accepted their tasks, however, and in due course their studies were completed. In neither case did the studies take much time, but the assumption that it was the job of the Accounting Department and the Legal Department to serve the Plant Engineering Department was clear. A problem found by someone in the organization carries with it substantial influence over the problems on which other parts of the organization will work.

Even clearer evidence of the power of other people's models was the time devoted by all the managers in the Southern Company to the preparation of reports "required" by higher management. These reports ranged in their demands on managerial time from a few minutes in the case of a request for routine information to several man months of work on the preparation of a plan for the coming year's operations. In reply to the question "If you were responsible for the whole company's operations would you require more, the same or less planning?" 52 managers responded as follows:

| | | |
|---|---|---|
| More | — | 4 |
| Same | — | 32 |
| Less | — | 16 |

For many managers the expectations of the organization were consistent with their own ideas of the time required for effective planning. For a number of others, however, the influence of other people was clear.

It is difficult in discussing these models as a source of problems to avoid a negative connotation due to the widely held ethic which values individual problem definition. Two points are worth emphasizing therefore. First, the study was conducted to find out how managers do define their problems—not how they should do so—although that, of course, may be a long term objective of this work. Second, both the organization and the individuals described here would, by almost any standards, be judged to be highly successful and this fact should be included in any attempt to evaluate their behavior.

Because historical, planning, and other people's models require almost no generalization to make them relevant to particular events of interest to the manager, and because these three types of models can easily generate more problems than the manager can reasonably hope to deal with, it is not surprising, perhaps, that models requiring somewhat more generalization are less important elements of the process of problem finding. It is true, however, that on occasion managers draw on experiences other than their own to define problems for themselves and their organizations.

### Extra-Organizational Models

Trade journals which report new practices and their effects in other organizations can sometimes define useful areas for managerial analysis. Customers frequently serve the same function by reporting the accomplishments of competitors in the area of price, service, and/or product quality. General Motors is known for its practice of ranking the performance measures of a number of plants producing the same or similar products and making this information available to the managers of these facilities. The implication is strong in these comparisons that problems exist in plants where performance is poor relative to other plants.

In using all such extra-organizational models to define intra-organizational problems, the manager must resolve the difficult question of model validity. "Is the fact that our West Coast plant has lower maintenance costs relevant to our operations? After all, they have newer equipment." "Is the fact that our competitor is lowering his price relevant to our pricing policy? After all, our quality is better." Etc. There are enough attributes in any industrial situation to make it unlikely indeed that any extra-organizational model will fit the manager's situation perfectly. Judgments on the question of model validity must frequently be made by operating managers.

In the Southern Company one clear case was observed where two extra-organizational models were employed in an attempt to define a problem.

A member of the Plant Engineering Department attended a meeting of an engineering society at which a technique called "work sampling" was discussed in the context of several successful applications in other plants. This model of a current engineering practice, which had not been employed by his department, led this man to consider the problem of finding an application for work sampling in the Southern Company. Clearly if this technique could be successfully applied, it would reduce the difference between his department and his extra-organizational model.

A few days later this engineer noticed an idle, unattended fork truck in one of the manufacturing shops and he immediately thought that an analysis of fork truck operations might be the application he was looking for. He discussed this idea with his supervisors and they agreed that the project should be undertaken.

In a sense, a study of fork trucks was a strange problem for Plant Engineering personnel to undertake because fork trucks were not their responsibility. Each product department paid rental charges on the trucks it used to a leasing company which provided maintenance service as a part of their contract. The product departments were also responsible for the operation of the trucks. Production workers operated the trucks on an *ad hoc* basis as a part of their regular duties. No full-time drivers were assigned. Because of the lack of direct responsibility for fork trucks, Plant Engineering was aware from the beginning of the project that its primary task would be to convince the product departments that their fork trucks indeed constituted a problem.

To provide the department managers with evidence on this point, in addition to the internal work sampling study, a survey of fork truck operations was made in six nearby plants engaged in similar manufacturing operations. The explicit purpose of the survey was to define a basis (an extra-organizational model) on which internal fork truck operations could be evaluated.

The work sampling study indicated the following activity levels for the set of 21 trucks rented by the product departments:

| | |
|---|---|
| 1. Travel Loaded | 22.2% |
| 2. Travel Unloaded | 11.9% |
| 3. Travel Empty | 10.4% |
| 4. Idle Empty | 43.1% |
| 5. Idle with Driver | 2.5% |
| 6. Loaded no Driver | 9.9% |

Combining categories 1, 2, and 3 as "usage" categories, a 44.5% "utilization factor" resulted.

The six-company survey yielded in part the following results:

1. The number of trucks operated by the surveyed companies ranged from 6 to 50 with an average of 21 (same as Southern Company).
2. Utilizations ranged from 50% to 71% with an average of 63% (18.5% higher than Southern Company).
3. Responsibility for trucks was centralized in all six companies (contrary to Southern Company).
4. Trucks were controlled through dispatching or scheduling on five of the six companies (some companies used radio control) (contrary to Southern Company).
5. All companies owned rather than leased their trucks (contrary to Southern Company).
6. All reporting companies performed their own maintenance of their trucks (contrary to Southern Company).
7. Three companies licensed their drivers, and assigned them full time to driving (contrary to Southern Company).

The fact that the surveyed companies on the average operated the same number of trucks as the Southern Company was clearly cited as evidence supporting the validity of this extra-organizational model.

A comparison of company practice to these survey results led Plant Engineering to draw the following conclusions which are quoted from their report:

1. Utilization of trucks is 20% lower than average.
2. Dispatching or scheduling of trucks from central group should be considered.
3. Radio control of some units shall be investigated.
4. Central responsibility for trucks should be established.
5. Trucks should be purchased not leased.
6. Operator training and licensing should be instituted.

In the opinion of Plant Engineering, therefore, the survey and work sampling study had established the existence of not one but a number of related problems.

Because the six-company survey and the work sampling study had defined the problem in aggregate terms, the analysis and recommendations proceeded at this level. The Plant Engineering Department decided to make their recommendation on the basis of an overall utilization of 60% (the average utilization found in the six-company survey) which implied a reduction of five trucks. They then looked at their work sampling data and re-allocated trucks among departments to bring individual truck utilization figures as close to 60% as possible. The recommended re-allocation in fact implied a saving of five trucks. The recommendation went on to suggest that Product Departments "compensate [for this reduction in trucks] by establishing sharing arrangements between departments."

The recommendation also proposed "permanent [full time] licensed drivers." "The drivers will report administratively to the Vehicles and Grounds Foreman [Plant Engineering]. Drivers will be assigned from presently available men doing driving. Men not selected as drivers will work at jobs vacated by permanent drivers in addition to their other duties. No men will be dropped." As a result of a study which had indicated that leasing was preferable to buying the fork trucks, no change in ownership or maintenance was proposed. The annual savings anticipated from the recommended changes amounted to $7,250/year.

It is interesting to note that the recommendations themselves constituted problems for the Product Department Managers. The task of "establishing sharing arrangements among departments" had not been resolved by the study and remained a thorny problem. The task of transferring qualified production workers to full-time truck driving duties [and the Plant Engineering Department] involved not only complex problems of morale and labor relations but also involved economic trade-offs not evaluated by the study. The task of redefining departmental work procedures to relate to centrally controlled truck services was similarly unresolved. In return for these problems the seven product department managers could expect to share in an annual saving of $7,250.

Their response to the recommendation was less than enthusiastic. They agreed, after some bargaining, to return one truck to the leasing company, but were not willing to pursue the matter any further than this.

Despite this rather negative conclusion it is interesting to note that most managers considered the fork truck study a success. The validity of using the extra-organizational model derived from the survey as a means to define the problem was never questioned and an evaluation of the existing policy on this basis was considered well-justified.

It was clear, however, that extra-organizational models did not carry with them the same direct implications as models based on intra-organizational experience. The observation that the company's central office used time clocks to control tardiness of clerical personnel was not viewed as relevant to discussion of this same problem at the divisional level. The comment, "We have never done that," was sufficient to discredit this evidence.

A more complicated use of extra-organizational models occurred in the case of several managers who had had personal experience in other organizations. In several situations they used this experience to define intra-organizational problems by emphasizing the personal element of this experience as evidence of its validity and by de-emphasizing (or not mentioning) where this experience was gained.

Extra-organizational models have a natural disadvantage as sources of problems because of the question of model validity which can always be raised against them. When extra-organizational experience agrees with local experience (historical model) it is seen as valid but since it agrees with the local experience it defines no problem. When extra-organizational experience disagrees with local experience and might therefore define a problem, the discrepancy itself raises the question of model validity. This attribute of extra-organizational models may serve to explain the fact that they were a relatively weak source of management problems in the Southern Company. Forty-seven out of 52 managers agreed with the statement "Most of our new ideas are generated within the Company."

In the case of new organizations, of course, historical models are not available and extra-organizational models become more influential. One such situation was observed in the Southern Company.

A promising new product was moving from the later stages of development into the early stages of production and sales. A new product department was formed on an informal basis and the standard procedures of accounting data collection and reporting were instituted. No one expected the new department to be profitable immediately but after some months an executive at the product group level used a model not based on the history of the new department but one based on the performance of other departments to define a problem. He described the process this way:

> "The numbers [on the monthly reports] were horrifying. I asked for a report and I got fuzzy answers that I didn't believe so I said 'Fellows, I'm taking over the right to ask questions.'"
>
> "In asking questions I found I could pick holes in their analysis of the situation. Everything was loose."
>
> "I analyzed their orders and found with their overhead they couldn't make money."
>
> "The department was reorganized."

In new organizations extra-organizational models can be quite powerful sources of management problems.

### Some Normative Questions

The principal objective of this study was to find a relatively simple theoretical structure to explain the process of problem finding used by the managers at the Southern Company, and the set of four models just described represents that structure. These models, which range from ones maintained by other members of the organization, through simple historical and planning models, to those which apply the experience of other organizations to local situations, have been tested against the rather massive sample of data collected at the Southern Company and have been found sufficient to explain all these observations. That is to say, it is possible to trace all the observed behavior back to differences defined by one of these four classes of models. To this extent the study was successful.

But observations like these, even after abstraction into a theoretical structure, are only observations. They do not suggest the consequences of using other kinds of models or using these same models with different frequencies. They do not suggest how managers might behave more effectively than they do.

Isolated observations cannot define differences. Observations must be compared to a model before normative questions can be answered.

One way to generate such comparisons would be to conduct comparative studies within and among a number of organizations. As a result of this work one could answer questions like: "Are these same models used by unsuccessful managers? If so, how can the difference in performance be explained? If not, what models are used? Do managers in other organizations use these models with different frequencies or under different circumstances? Are there systematic differences in the use of these models at different levels of the organization?" All such questions could be answered by careful study of several organizations or several levels of the same organization and these extra-organizational models might serve to suggest management improvements. Until such studies are completed, however, the only models which can be used to evaluate the behavior observed in the Southern Company are some which were not used there.

## Scientific Models

When compared to models used in the physical and social sciences for quite similar purposes, the models used by the managers in the Southern Company (and elsewhere) are almost startling in their naivete. In the same company, electrical engineers explicitly used quite complex theoretical models to help them define problems associated with the design of a relatively simple electronic control system. Mechanical engineers similarly employed a variety of quite general theories in the design of new high-speed production equipment. In neither- of these cases did the engineers base their predictions on their own experience except in a very general sense. They quite confidently applied theories derived from the observations of others and the equipment which resulted from their work required relatively little redesign after construction.

Managers on the other hand based their expectations on relatively small samples of their own experience. Their rather simple theories, as has already been noted, yielded rather poor predictions and managers therefore spent a substantial amount of time problem solving either on their own problems or on those defined by others.

The behavior of scientists (an extra-organizational model) suggests that there is an alternative to this rather frantic approach to a complex world. When discrepancies arise between a model and the environment, one can undertake to improve the model rather than to change the environment. In fact, a scientist might even go so far as to suggest that, until one has a fairly reliable model of the environment, it is not only foolish but perhaps even dangerous to take action when its effect cannot be predicted.

If carried to an extreme, of course, the scientist's tendency to search for better models of the world as it is, would leave no time for taking action to change it, and it seems unlikely that this allocation of time and talent would be an appropriate one for the operating manager. In the Southern Company, it must be remembered, those managers who based their actions on very simple models which took very little of their time to construct were judged to be quite successful by their organization.

On the other hand, the increasing use by managers of more sophisticated modeling techniques like those mentioned earlier in this paper may suggest that the balance between model building and action taking is shifting. A number of companies now base changes in distribution systems, production and inventory control systems, quality control systems, advertising allocation systems, etc. on the predictions of relatively complex models which are based on substantial bodies of theory and empirical evidence.

To the extent that these models fail to describe events which take place they, just like the simpler models they replace, can serve to define problems. To the extent that these more complete models take into account events which the manager cannot, or prefers not to, control, these models can serve to protect the manager from problems on which he might otherwise waste his energy.

While it may be true that these more explicit scientific models will gradually replace simple intuitive models, several reasons suggest that the change will take some time. First, as has been frequently noted, many operating managers today find the language of the new techniques foreign despite increasing attempts to change this situation through training. Second, the new techniques often involve even more generalization than extra-organizational models and honest questions of model validity will tend to delay their widespread use. And third, the process of problem finding currently used will perpetuate itself simply by keeping managers so busy that they will find little time to learn about and to try these new methods of problem finding.

More important than any of these reasons, however, may be one which, curiously, has been created by the advocates of management science.

In most, if not all, of the literature describing them, model-building techniques are described as means for solving management problems. In their now classical book on operations research, Churchman, Ackoff and Arnoff, for example, suggest model building as a step which should follow "formulating the problem."[13] The process by which the problem should be formulated, however, is left totally unspecified—and this is where managers as well as students of management frequently report their greatest difficulty. They can see the process by which these techniques can solve problems but they cannot see how to define the problems.

The theory which has been proposed here suggests that problem definition cannot precede model construction. It is impossible to know, for example, that a cost is too high unless one has some basis (a model) which suggests it might be lower. This basis might be one's own experience, the experience of a competitor, or the output of a scientific model. Similarly, one cannot be sure that his distribution costs will be reduced by linear programming until a model is constructed and solved which suggests that rescheduling will lower costs. The imperfections of an inventory system are revealed only by comparing it to some theoretical model—therefore, they cannot be defined until after the model has been built. The logical inconsistency which suggests that problems must be clearly defined in order to justify model construction is very likely an important reason that scientific models will only slowly be recognized by operating managers as important aids in the definition of their problems.

Despite their current disadvantages, the so-called new techniques of model building are, as has already been noted, making significant contributions to management effectiveness. They represent, therefore, not only a means for evaluating current managerial behavior, but also are becoming a new class of models which can be used by managers to define their problems.

### The Problem of Model Selection

The study of managers in the Southern Company indicates that concepts like image and intelligence, which have been proposed to explain the process of problem finding, can be made somewhat more operational. A rather small set of model classes have been defined which constitute sufficient stimuli to trigger a fairly large sample of managerial behavior. This is not to say that further observations may not indicate the need for additional model classes or that further work is not required to make the process of managerial model building even more operational and testable. The study of the Southern Com-

---

[13]Churchman, C. W., R. L. Ackoff, and E. L. Arnoff, *Introduction to Operations Research.* New York: John Wiley and Sons, Inc., 1957, pp. 12–13.

pany represents perhaps only an encouraging start at understanding an important and little understood area of management.

Even with these initial insights, however, it is possible to see where major theoretical gaps still exist. Chief among these is the problem of model selection.

As has already been noted, the requests of other people are sufficient to define a full time job for many managers. The problem of investigating and taking corrective action on discrepancies from historical trends can keep any manager busy all the time. The construction of extra-organizational and/or scientific models and the actions which they trigger are similarly time-consuming. Even after the manager has constructed the models he will use to define his problems, he must somehow select from among the differences which are simultaneously defined by these models. Personal requests, historical discrepancies, extra-organizational ideas, and the stimuli of scientific models do not in general define differences one at a time. The choice of the discrepancy to attend to next may be as important a process as the construction of the models which define them. It seems clear, however, that we must understand the process by which differences are defined before we can worry seriously about understanding the process of selecting from among them. The study in the Southern Company, therefore, largely ignored the priority problem and concentrated on difference definitions only.

It is impossible, however, to observe managers at work without getting some rough ideas about how they deal with the priority problem. Telephone calls for example are very high priority stimuli. A ringing telephone will interrupt work of virtually every kind. This priority rule is complicated sometimes by an intervening secretary, but many managers pride themselves on always answering their own phone.

One manager reported that he always worked on problems which would "get worse" before he worked on static problems. Thus, he dealt with a problem involving a conflict between a foreman and a troublesome employee before pressing forward on a cost reduction program.

Perhaps the most explicit priorities in the Southern Company were established by means of deadlines. Most problems defined by other members of the organization carried with them a time at which, or by which, the request should be satisfied. Certain reports were due monthly, a fixed number of working days after the end of the preceding month. Meetings were scheduled at stated times. Annual plans were required on a specified date. While a number of such requests might face a manager simultaneously, they almost never would have the same deadline and by this means the manager could decide which to do when. The fact that most problems triggered by other people's models carried deadlines may explain why these problems seemed to be given so much attention. When asked to indicate "Which problems do you usually get to first, time deadline, big payoff or personal interest?" 43 out of 52 managers indicated time deadline.

From a theoretical point of view one could view the flow of problems through an organization as analogous to the flow of jobs through a job shop and perhaps apply some of the theories which have been developed there to understand and perhaps prescribe the process of priority assignment. Managers, for example, must trade off relative lateness of their tasks with the duration of the tasks just as a foreman loading machines in a machine shop. Once the problem of problem definition is well understood it would appear that some theory is already available to structure the process assigning problem priorities.

**Summary and Conclusions**

Applying the same reasoning which had proved useful in understanding the process by which chess is played, a study which involved interviews and observations of managers in a successful industrial organization was conducted in order to gain some insight into the process by which managers find and define their problems. A theoretical structure was devised which organized managerial problems by means of the models used to define them.

Four classes of models proved sufficient to explain the sample of data collected during the study. These models—largely inexplicit and intuitive in nature —were compared to more formal models used by engineers and scientists. No value judgments could be made on the basis of this comparison, but the recent trend in model sophistication may indicate that managers will spend more time building models to guide their attention and proportionately less in problem solving.

The array of models used by and available to managers suggests that an understanding of the process by which problems are defined will not constitute a complete theory of problem finding. A process which assigns priorities to a set of simultaneously defined problems remains to be specified.

# STRATEGIES, STRUCTURES, AND PROCESSES OF ORGANIZATIONAL DECISION

James D. Thompson
Arthur Tuden

Despite the apparent importance of decision-making for theories of administration and the considerable attention recently devoted to the topic, present models and knowledge of decision-making have generated few hypotheses about administration, and they have not been adequately linked with organizational models.

A major deficiency of most decision models has been that they are economically logical models seeking to describe maximization processes. These *econo-logical* models have utility as criteria against which to reflect behavior, but they have contributed little toward the explanation or prediction of behavior.

Simon has achieved a major break-through with his "satisficing" model.[1] This is much more than the mere substitution of one word or one concept for another, for Simon's model is a *psycho-logical* model designed to describe and predict behavior. Its full significance seems not yet to be widely recognized.

---

Reprinted from James D. Thompson and Arthur Tuden, *Comparative Studies in Administration* (Pittsburgh: University of Pittsburgh Press, 1959) by permission from the author and publisher.

[1]Herbert A. Simon, "A Behavioral Model of Rational Choice," *Quarterly Journal of Economics,* February, 1955; reprinted in Simon, *Models of Man,* New York: John Wiley & Sons, 1957.

This psychological model of decision-making is essentially one dealing with individual human beings. It applies equally to purposive choices of a personal or an organizational nature. Its generalizability is, however, both a source of power and of limitation, for it does not deal explicitly with the particular phenomena which surround the making of decisions in organizational contexts.

As a companion to the psychological model, therefore, we wish to develop *sociological* models. We believe they will point to important decision-making behavior which has been observed in organizations but which is neither described nor predicted by econological or psychological models.

We will attempt to show (1) that there are several types of decisions to be made in and on behalf of collective enterprises, (2) that each type of decision calls for a different strategy or approach, (3) that there are several varieties of organizational structures which facilitate these several strategies, and (4) that the resulting behavior defines variations in decision processes. It has been our purpose to construct models which are neither culture-bound nor discipline-bound, containing no evaluative or normative elements.

**Working Definitions**

"Choice" from among alternatives seems to be the end-point of decision-making, but the term "decision" will not be confined simply to ultimate choice. Rather, "decision" will refer to those activities which contribute to choice, including recognizing or delimiting and evaluating alternatives as well as the final selection. Thus an individual may have responsibility for making a final choice on behalf of an organization, but if others help him delimit or evaluate alternatives we will not describe that individual as *the* decider.[2]

The term "decision" in this paper should also be understood to refer to organizational decisions. Personal decisions, i.e., choices presumed by an individual to have consequences only for himself, are excluded.[3] Likewise, unconscious choices or habits are not within the scope of this paper.

The term "decision unit" will be used to refer to that individual or group within an organization which has power, responsibility, or authority to choose, on a particular issue, for the organization. To illustrate, in American jurisprudence, "the court" may be the appropriate organization, but the power to decide certain issues is assigned to a single presiding judge as the decision unit; other issues are assigned to a jury as the decision unit; still others are assigned to a panel of justices as the decision unit.

**Types of Decision Issues**

The notion of differing types of issues calling for decisions is not new. More than a decade ago Simon distinguished ethical from factual decisions[4] but no one seems to have extended his analysis. More recently there has been considerable discussion of decision-making under the differential conditions of certainty,

---

[2]For the notion of "composite decisions" see Herbert A. Simon, *Administrative Behavior*, New York: Macmillan, 1957. See also R. Tannenbaum and F. Massarik, "Participation by Subordinates in the Managerial Decision Making Process," *Canadian Journal of Economics and Political Science*, August, 1950.

[3]This distinction is made by Chester I. Barnard, *Functions of the Executive*, Cambridge, Mass.: Harvard University Press, 1936.

[4]Simon, *Administrative Behavior* (first edition), 1945.

risk, and uncertainty.[5] Dorwin Cartwright has suggested distinguishing among judgment, preference-ranking, and "actual decision-making" (which he defines as commitment to action).[6] There have, however, been few attempts to build typologies of issues or decisions.

A typology of issues will enable the sorting out of (a) those aspects of decision situations which *confront* decision units from (b) those actions which decision units may take in such situations.

The main elements of decision—found both in the econological and psychological models available—seem to be three: (1) alternative courses of action, (2) differential consequences of the several alternatives (means), and (3) evaluation of the potential outcomes on some scale of desirability (ends).[7]

We will work with two of those three variables, dropping "alternative courses of action," since by definition a unit called upon to decide is aware of at least one pair of alternatives. Before working with the remaining two variables, however, we wish to redefine them slightly in order to achieve greater generalizability.

The notion of "consequences of alternative courses of action" assumes only a concern with present and future, not with past actions. Yet it seems reasonable, for example, to conceive of the trial jury as a decision unit which works backward from one present fact, e.g., a corpus delecti, to choose one of several possible past actions which may account for the present fact. This sequence may also characterize certain decisions in scientific research and in audits or inspections. The notion of *causation*, as applied to several alternatives, seems to us to subsume both questions of present and future states and questions of past actions which may explain present states.

We would also like to avoid some of the possible implications of such terms as desirability scale, which is inanimate, and to substitute for them some term with more explicit behavioral overtones. For this purpose we will speak of *preferences about outcomes*. In conceiving of our major variables as *causation* and *preferences*, we have gained a certain flexibility without losing the value of previous work on economic models. The means-ends approach falls within our scheme, but we have the added advantage of being able to include other approaches too.

Since we are dealing with organizations—social systems—it cannot be taken for granted that causation will be "known" as soon as a decision issue appears, nor can it be assumed that the organization is certain of its preferences regarding the several alternatives apparent. Often the organization's decision unit cannot simply choose, but must act to determine what its knowledge or beliefs are regarding cause-and-effect relationships, and what its preferences are about the postulated effects.

[5]For examples, see the collection of papers edited by M. J. Bowman, *Expectations, Uncertainty and Business Behavior*, New York: Social Science Research Council, 1958; and R. D. Luce and H. Raiffa, *Games and Decisions*, New York: John Wiley & Sons, 1957.

[6]In Bowman, *op. cit.*

[7]We believe this is not inconsistent with the statements of such diverse writers as Simon, *Models of Man* (*op. cit.*); Irwin D. J. Bross, *Design for Decision*, New York: The Macmillan Co., 1953; Richard C. Snyder in Roland Young (ed.) *Approaches to the Study of Politics*, Evanston: Northwestern University Press, 1958; Jacob Marschak in Paul Lazarsfeld (ed.) *Mathematical Thinking in the Social Sciences*, Glencoe, Illinois: The Free Press, 1954; and Bernard Berelson in Berelson, Paul Lazarsfeld and William McPhee, *Voting*, Chicago: University of Chicago Press, 1954.

Now, if the two variables *causation* and *preferences* are reflected against the additional question of whether there is *agreement or consensus within the decision unit* about those two matters, it is possible to construct a four-fold typology of decision issues.

|  | PREFERENCES ABOUT POSSIBLE OUTCOMES | |
|---|---|---|
|  | AGREEMENT | DISAGREEMENT |
| BELIEFS ABOUT CAUSATION — AGREEMENT | COMPUTATION | COMPROMISE |
| DISAGREEMENT | JUDGMENT | INSPIRATION |

The labels in the four cells—computation, judgment, compromise, and inspiration—are descriptive of four *strategies* which we believe are appropriate for the four types of decision issues. In the following section we will elaborate on those strategies, and connect them with certain types of social structures. For the time being we will deal only with "pure" cases.

### Pure Strategies and Structures

*Decision by Computation.* Where there is agreement regarding both causation and preference, i.e., where a preference hierarchy is understood and where knowledge is available or believed to be available, decision-making is a technical or mechanical matter. In its extreme form, this situation requires no genuine choice, since the problem-solution appears as common sense.[8]

But in many instances, the appropriate techniques for equating cause-effect knowledge with known preferences are quite complicated. The data may be so voluminous for example, that only an electronic calculator can make sense of them. Likewise, the particular sequences of action involved in the techniques may be hard to master and difficult to carry out, so that only the highly trained specialist can arrive at an appropriate choice. In either event, the strategy for decision is straight-forward analysis, and we term this decision by computation.

*A Structure for Computation.* Assuming for the moment complete freedom to build an organization which will face *only* computation issues, and that our guiding norms are economy of effort and efficiency of performance, what kind of organization shall we build?

This will be an organization of specialists, one for each kind of computation problem we can anticipate, and we want to introduce four constraints or rules to: (1) prohibit our specialists from making decisions in issues lying outside their spheres of expert competence, (2) bind each specialist to the organization's preference scale, (3) route all pertinent information to each specialist, and (4) route every issue to the appropriate specialist.

---

[8]Simon notes that what he terms "programmed" choice situations sometimes elicit behavior which suggests that the choice has been made in advance. In these cases, he says, there is a well-established procedure that leads through a series of steps to a determinate decision. He also stresses that programmed decisions may involve a very great amount of computation before choice is actually made. See his paper in Bowman, *op. cit.*

The organization which we have just built contains the heart of what Max Weber described as the "pure type" of bureaucracy. This bureaucratic model is clearly expressed in the "formal" or "official" structure of the great majority of business firms, governmental agencies, and military units. For each of these, presumably, preferences can be stated with some clarity. Members are appointed to positions only so long as they embrace those preferences. Moreover, bureaucracy is formulated on the assumption that rules or procedures can be established for classes of cases or problems, and that the events which will call for organizational decisions are repetitive or serial events for which expert competence can be developed.[9] Candidates for these positions are expected to hold licenses or degrees indicating successful completion of training for the specialized positions, or to pass tests.

It is in these organizations that the concept and practice of "delegation" seems most widespread, and that decision units officially are comprised of single individuals. Expert specialization means that the organization can enjoy the economy of assigning problems to individuals or their electronic counterparts.

*Decision by Majority Judgment.* Where causation is uncertain or disputed, although preferences are clearly known and shared, decision-making takes on new difficulties. Lacking in acceptable "proof" of the merits of alternatives, the organization must rely on judgment.[10] Triangulation illustrates this simply and clearly. Each member of the three-man team is presumed competent by virtue of his training and his equipment to make a judgment, but because none has indisputable and complete evidence, none is permitted to make the decision alone, and no member may outvote or override the judgment made by other members. But triangulation is a special case of the more general problem— special because each judge focuses on the same empirical phenomenon from his own special vantage point. More frequent, perhaps, is the case where there is not only differential perception but also differential interpretation, and this is most clearly illustrated by the voting situation in which the collective judgment determines the decision. We will refer to this strategy of organizational decision as one of majority judgment.

*A Structure for Majority Judgment.* What kind of organization shall we build as an ideal one to handle only judgmental problems? This is to be an organization of wise and knowing men, operating according to constraints or rules which: (1) require fidelity to the group's preference hierarchy, (2) require all members to participate in each decision, (3) route pertinent information about causation to each member, (4) give each member equal influence over

---

[9] Bowman, in *Expectations, Uncertainty, and Business Behavior, op. cit.*, commenting on the papers read at the conferences, notes that only two authors focus on cases involving nonseriability. She comments that "Neglect of the higher degrees of uncertainty (or nonseriability) was undoubtedly deliberate in some instances, reflecting the hypothesis that businessmen ignore parameters about which they cannot at least make reasonably informed guesses, and that they commonly avoid taking actions the outcomes of which are characterized by extreme uncertainty . . . . However, problems involving the more extreme degrees of uncertainty were probably by-passed for another reason, the obvious difficulty of dealing with them systematically." p. 5.

[10] See Leon Festinger's important distinction between "social reality" and "external reality" as bases for the validation of opinions of group members. Festinger, "Informal Social Communication," *Psychological Review*, 1950, pp. 271–292.

the final choice, and (5) designate as ultimate choice that alternative favored by the largest group of judges—the majority.

What we have just described may be labelled, for lack of a better term, a *collegium.* This concept has been used in ecclesiastical literature to refer to a self-governing voluntary group, with authority vested in the members.[11] Whatever this type of organization is labelled, the social science literature does not seem to contain formal models of it, as it does for bureaucracy.

Nevertheless, this type of organization is described in case studies of "voluntary associations" and in the constitutions and by-laws of many organizations, including many American universities and trade unions. All of these not only take steps to "get out the vote," but incorporate into their by-laws provisions requiring a quorum for the transaction of official business. Direct elections of governmental officials approximate the collegial situation, with each literate citizen-of-age presumed to have equal competence and influence at the polls.

Governing boards of directors or trustees are also established on the collegial principle, with the requirement of a quorum in order for judgments to be binding.[12]

*Decision by Compromise.* On occasion there may be agreement by all parties as to the expected consequences or causes of available alternatives, but lack of consensus over preferences toward such "facts." Neither computation nor collective judgment is "appropriate" for this type of issue, for the blunt fact is that if one preference is satisfied, another is denied. An organization facing this situation may fall apart through schism, civil war, or disinterest, unless some common item or point can be found on the several extant preference scales. It can be illustrated by imagining an organization composed of two factions. For faction A, the preference scale runs 1, 2, and 3, while for faction B, the scale is 4, 5, and 6. In this case, in order for either faction to obtain at least an acceptable solution the other must be denied all satisfaction, and this presages the end of the organization. If the preference scales run 1, 2, and 3, in that order, and 3, 4, and 5, both factions can attain a modicum of satisfaction by choosing 3. The appropriate strategy where causation is conceded but preferences are in dispute thus appears to be one which will arrive at the common preference. We will refer to this strategy as decision by compromise.

*A Structure for Compromise.* Now the task is to construct an ideal organization to handle compromise types of issues economically and efficiently.

Whereas computation problems call for the smallest possible decision unit, and collective judgment for the widest possible participation, compromise seems to require a decision unit of intermediate size. What we want is a structure to facilitate bargaining, and since this involves detailed and subtle exploration of the several factional preference scales, the decision unit must be small enough to permit sustained and often delicate interchange. On the other hand, there is the requirement that all factions—or certainly all important factions—be

[11] Max Weber discussed the "colleagiality" or collegial system, but used the term more loosely than we propose to do here. See Hans Gerth and C. Wright Mills, *From Max Weber: Essays in Sociology*, New York: Oxford University Press, 1946, pp. 236–244.

[12] The typical conception of the corporation as pyramidal in form, with ultimate authority peaking in the office of the president, is thus misleading. It would be more descriptive to think of the corporation as a wigwam, with a group at the top.

involved in the decision. This leads, we think, to the *representative body* as the appropriate structure.

For this purpose, we will build rules or constraints into our organization to: (1) require that each faction hold as its *top* priority preference the desire to reach agreement, i.e., to continue the association, (2) ensure that each faction be represented in the decision unit, (3) give each faction veto power, and (4) give each faction all pertinent, available information about causation.

The United Nations Security Council approximates this type of decision unit, if we assume that the member nations represent all important blocs. Federations often provide the representative structure for boards of directors. The American Congress appears to fit this pattern, with the "veto" requirement relaxed because of the size of the body. It is possible to conceive of the Congress as an arena for bargaining and compromise, rather than judgment, with the vote considered merely a mechanical device for measuring at any point in time the current state of negotiations.[13]

The representative decision unit, operating toward compromise, is also seen, though less formally, in many loosely organized societies in the form of "consensus decision-making" by councils of tribal chiefs or elders.[14] In these instances power is relatively diffused, so that a "veto" of an alternative by any one member of the decision unit prevents the choice of that alternative. While not necessarily elected, members of the decision unit have to maintain followings and thus may be considered representatives. This is clearly brought out in the studies cited.

The American trial jury for capital cases can also be seen as an attempt to ensure bargaining or weighing of the evidence against the conflicting preferences of freeing the innocent and punishing the guilty. The jury situation differs from many other compromise situations in that each member of the unit is presumed to be an advocate of *both* of the competing values (rather than an advocate of one factional position) who "bargains with himself." The requirement of unanimity for the jury seeks to remove the decision from the area of majority judgment to one of arriving at a choice endorsable by all members of the decision unit.

*Decision by Inspiration.* The fourth and in our typology the final type of issue is one in which there is disagreement both as to causation and as to preferences. This is, of course, a most dangerous situation for any group to be in; certainly by definition and probably in fact the group in this situation is nearing disintegration. While this situation seems to be far removed from the usual discussions of decision-making, we believe it has empirical as well as theoretical relevance.

The most likely action in this situation, we suspect, is the decision not to face the issue. Organizations which appear to be slow to seize opportunities or to respond to environmental events may, on close inspection, be organizations which contain disagreement as to both preferences and causation. To the extent

[13]This view seems consistent with the findings of Stephen A. Bailey, *Congress Makes a Law*, New York: Columbia University Press, 1950; and E. Latham, *The Group Basis of Politics*, Ithaca, N.Y.: Cornell University Press, 1952. See also Latham in Heinz Eulau, S. Eldersveld, and M. Janowitz (eds.) *Political Behavior*, Glencoe, Illinois: The Free Press, 1956.

[14]For example, see F. M. and M. M. Keesing, *Elite Communication in Samoa*, Stanford, Conn.: Stanford University Press, 1956; W. B. Miller. "Two Concepts of Authority," *American Anthropologist*, April, 1955 (Chapter 7 in the present volume); and M. Nash, "Machine Age Maya: The Industrialization of a Guatemalan Community," *American Anthropologist*, Part 2, April, 1958.

that the organization in this predicament can avoid an issue, it may at least maintain itself as an organization. If it is forced to choose, however, the organization is likely to dissolve—unless some innovation can be introduced.

Anthropologists have recorded on numerous occasions institutionalized means of gaining inspiration by referring "insoluable" problems to supernatural forces, and it is no secret that responsible public officials in "less superstitious" nations call on Divine Guidance when they must make momentous decisions for which there is no precedent and the consequences are highly uncertain. A related device is for the group to rely on a *charismatic* leader.

As Weber pointed out,[15] the charismatic leader is thought by his followers to have solutions or at least the wisdom to find them. Frequently he offers a new set of ideals or preferences which rally unity out of diversity, by shifting attention. Pointing to a real or fancied threat from outside is one ancient device for this.

The 1958 election of deGaulle and adoption of the new French communante seems to reflect the charismatic or inspirational type of situation.[16] But it also seems possible for individuals in nominal positions of leadership to attain and articulate enough imagination to create a new vision or image and thereby pull together a disintegrating organization. This seems consistent with the conclusion of Karl Deutsch and his colleagues as to the importance of innovation and invention in bringing about political integration.[17] Whatever the particular form of leadership exercised, we believe that decisions of this type—where there has been dissensus about both causation and preferences—are *decisions by inspiration*.

*A Structure for Inspiration.* It is difficult to conceive of an ideal structure for decision by inspiration, for the thinking of the social scientist is oriented toward pattern and organization, while the situation we face here is one of randomness and disorganization. If these situations occur it probably is seldom by design. Nevertheless, an attempt to deliberately construct such a situation might be instructive for the student of organization.

What we are trying to build now has been labelled by Durkheim as a state of *anomie*, normlessness, or deregulation.[18] As a rough approximation, anomie occurs when former goals or values have lost their meaning or significance or

[15]Gerth and Mills, *op. cit.*

[16]Although nominally a choice by vote, the majority approached unanimity, and it seems that voters were not asked to judge his ability to solve such specific problems as the war in Africa, but rather were asked to impute to him and endorse qualities of omnipotence.

[17]Deutsch, et al. *Political Community and the North Atlantic Area*, Princeton, N.J.: Princeton University Press, 1957. They say: "... our studies of the more promising strategies of integration have left us strongly impressed with the importance of political innovation and invention. Many of the decisive advances in bringing about political integration involved the making of political decisions in a manner such that improbable or original measures were adopted rather than their more obvious or probable alternatives. Many of the central institutions of amalgamated security communities thus were original and highly improbable at the time they were adopted. The American Articles of Confederation, the Federal constitution—... none of these has any close counterpart in the 18th century politics or law .... It seems worth adding that a number of amalgamated political communities were wrecked precisely as a consequence of decisions which were highly probable at the time and place at which they were made." p. 114.

[18]Emile Durkheim, *Suicide*, transl. by J. A. Spaulding and George Simpson, Glencoe, Ill.: The Free Press, 1951. See also Robert K. Merton, *Social Theory and Social Structure*, Glencoe, Ill.: The Free Press, 1957, Chapters 4 and 5.

when such goals appear unobtainable with the means available. Thus, our problem is to create a situation of chaos, but to do so with an aggregation of persons who in some sense can be considered to constitute a group or collectivity. We will therefore call for the following constraints: (1) the individuals or groups must be interdependent and thus have some incentive for collective problem-solving,[19] (2) there must be a multiplicity of preference scales and therefore of factions, with each faction of approximately equal strength, (3) more information must be introduced than can be processed, and it must be routed through multiple communication channels,[20] and (4) each member must have access to the major communication networks, in case inspiration strikes.

While it is doubtful if empirical cases of organizational anomie are deliberately created, there seems to be evidence that the more carefully structured organizations do sometimes find themselves in a state of anomie. The routed military organization, for example, is characterized by de-emphasis of military values and an abundance of rumors, contradictory information, and loss of contact or faith in nominal leaders.

Anomie and inspiration probably appear in less stark form in formal organizations, for the most part. Befuddled administrators of organizations caught up in forces which are not understood may and sometimes do rely on decision by inspiration in one of two forms: (a) imitation of more prestigeful and successful organizations, or (b) importation of prestigeful and authoritative management consultants to tell them what they should want and how to go after it.

In each of these illustrations the effect is to convert the *anomic* situation into something resembling a computational situation, and to rely upon a decision unit composed of one individual, as in the case of bureaucracy. The basis for designating the "expert" differs, of course. But the production of a new vision, image, or belief, is basically a creative kind of activity and it is doubtful if either voting or bargaining structures are likely to produce it.

*Designation of Decision Units.* Our argument to this point, regarding types of pure issues, pure strategies, and pure structures, can be diagrammed thus:

|  |  | PREFERENCES ABOUT POSSIBLE OUTCOMES | |
|---|---|---|---|
|  |  | AGREEMENT | NON-AGREEMENT |
| BELIEFS ABOUT CAUSATION | AGREEMENT | COMPUTATION IN BUREAUCRATIC STRUCTURE | BARGAINING IN REPRESENTATIVE STRUCTURE |
|  | NON-AGREEMENT | MAJORITY JUDGMENT IN COLLEGIAL STRUCTURE | INSPIRATION IN "ANOMIC STRUCTURE" |

[19]This does not guarantee, of course, that the various factions will remain members of the organization, for we have not ruled out the possibility that they will exploit other resources as substitutes for those provided by the organizations.

[20]Dissensus over causation might be achieved by *withholding* pertinent information about cause and effect, but this is not foolproof because organization members can invent *fictions* to fill in the missing gaps. Dubin describes organization fictions as ways of dealing with the unknown, and suggests that fictions can provide the ideological goals and purposes necessary to an organization, as well as beliefs regarding the efficacy of available means. See "Organization Fictions" in Robert Dubin (ed.), *Human Relations in Administration*, Englewood Cliffs, N.J.: Prentice-Hall, 1951.

Note what this suggests about differences in composition of decision units. For a computation issue, the "ideal" decision unit consists of an individual, acting on behalf of the entire organization. For the voting type of issue, the decision unit is made up of the entire membership. In the compromise situation, a group of representatives or delegates constitute the ideal decision unit. In the inspiration situation, the individual again becomes the most appropriate decision unit.

This typology has some distinct parallels to the work of March, Simon and Guetzkow who discuss four major processes: (1) problem-solving, (2) persuasion, (3) bargaining, and (4) "politics." These four processes are treated, however, simply as processes whereby organizations resolve conflict, which seems to us to be only one aspect of organizational decision phenomena. Moreover, they quickly collapse the four process categories into two: analytic and bargaining.[21]

It seems ironic that the only discipline whose focus has traditionally spanned all four types of situations has been the least productive of decision models.[22] Political science typically has dealt with three branches of government—executive (or bureaucratic); legislative (or bargaining); and judiciary (or collegial). Its interest in statesmen, great men, and leaders seems to cover the fourth (anomic or inspirational) situation.

**Mixed Situations**

There are a variety of reasons why the purity of our illustrations may be relatively infrequent.[23] A major proposition of this essay is that usually an organization adopts one of the four strategies—computation, collective judgment, compromise, or inspiration—as its dominant strategy, and bases its structure on that strategy.

To the extent that this is true, we can expect or predict several kinds of organizational difficulties which will be presented to administrators when the organization faces issues or problems which do not fit the formal neatness of our pure types.[24] We can also expect difficulties if the appropriate constraints are not present within the particular decision unit. Finally, we can predict that problems will arise if an issue calling for one strategy is presented to a decision unit built to exercise a different kind of strategy.

### Confusion of Issues

The difficulties of means-ends distinctions are as real for operating organizations as for scientific observers. Psychological time perspectives have much

[21] See James G. March and Herbert A. Simon, with the collaboration of Harold Guetzkow, *Organizations*, New York: John Wiley, 1958.
[22] Recent exceptions to this generalization include Snyder, *op. cit.*, and Morton Kaplan, *System and Process in International Relations*, New York: John Wiley, 1957. Kaplan identified chain-of-command decision-making units; persuasive decision-making units; and veto decision-making units.
[23] On the other hand we have no proof that the pure examples are rare. Millions of organizational decisions of a computational nature, for example, probably are made every day in bureaucracies. The mixed situations may be more noticeable and memorable because of the difficulties they pose rather than because they are more frequent.
[24] It also has implications for personnel recruitment processes, but we will not deal with that matter in this paper.

to do with whether a particular issue is seen as one of means or ends. Despite the fact that social systems of various kinds generally are expected by members to persist through time, their members may attach different valences to varying periods of the future. The holder of the short-run viewpoint may see an issue as one of preferences, while the long-run adherent sees the issue as one of causation.

In a dynamic and complex organization, moreover, the range of possible outcomes widens rapidly as the time-span is extended.[25] If this is true, then members of an organization probably are less inclined to grant the competence of experts for long-run decisions, even when they would grant the ability of the same experts for short-run matters.

Thus different members of an organization or of its decision unit may respond to the same stimulus in varying ways, some seeing it as a matter for computation, others as a judgment matter, and still others as requiring bargaining.

### Absence of Structural Constraints

One constraint common to all of the pure structures described earlier, except for the case where the decision unit is an individual, was that each judge, each bargainer, each faction, had equal power to influence the choice. While this usually is a formal specification for such units as trial juries, legislatures, or boards, we know that such units in fact exhibit inequality of membership. Strodtbeck, for example, reports that sex and social status affect the amount of participation of jury members in the decision process, the perceptions that fellow jurors have of their competence as jurors, and the degree to which they influence the outcome.[26] Such factors as party loyalty and party discipline, seniority, political skills, and the endorsement of pressure groups may affect the legislator's ability to make his voice heard as loudly as the next one. Within bureaucracies there are well-known inequalities between offices and divisions which formally are equal, and such scholars as Dalton have documented some of the reasons why computational experts may temper their computations with other considerations.[27]

Another constraint common to all but the anomic structure was that each participant in the decision unit have access to all available, pertinent information about causation. In fact, despite all of the attention given to communication in modern organizations, the condition called for by this constraint is at best approximated but seldom achieved. Colleagues of the expert in a bureaucracy, then, may grant the competence and good intentions of an official, but refuse to honor his decision on grounds that he did not know the local or "real" situation. Well informed minorities may control the collegial body whose other members are ill-informed, and "private information" obtained by one faction may make a mockery of the compromise situation.

This listing is intended to be illustrative rather than exhaustive. Relaxation of other constraints, peculiar to particular structures, will be discussed below.

[25]This is suggested by the decision trees of decision theorists. See Luce and Raiffa, *Games and Decisions, op. cit.*

[26]F. L. Strodtbeck, Rita M. James and C. Hawkins, "Social Status in Jury Deliberations," *American Sociological Review*, December, 1957. Similar observations have been made in the hospital setting by A. H. Stanton and M. S. Schwartz, *The Mental Hospital*, New York: Basic Books, 1954.

[27]Melville Dalton, "Conflicts Between Staff and Line Managerial Officers," in *American Sociological Review*, June, 1950.

If organizations were completely pliable, it would be a relatively simple thing to assign each problem to a decision unit designed especially for it. But, of course, organizations would cease to be organizations if they were completely pliable. Regularity, pattern and structure are inescapable.

Presumably the basic structures which prescribe the standing or regular decision units of organizations are established because they are expected to be appropriate for the *typical* problems those organizations will face. In some organizations, at least, precedent and tradition lead members to expect that *all* decisions will be made by the decision units and processes established for typical decisions. This undoubtedly will vary with the history of the organization and with the social and cultural attitudes surrounding it. In our own society and decade, it is not unusual to hear officials of bureaucracies complain that committee participation (on judgment problems) interferes with their work—by which they seem to mean expert computation in their own offices. On the other hand, we frequently hear university faculty members, conditioned to expect collegial decisions, complain when department heads or deans make purely computational decisions.[28] There are also situations, particularly in certain types of military units, when members are dismayed if leaders so much as ask their opinions. For some in the military organization, the commander must be an expert and every issue must be a computational one.

Thus the attitudes and expectations of members may make it difficult for organizations to create *ad hoc* or alternative decision units to deal with problems for which basic, traditional structures are ill-suited.

Another important source of structural rigidity is the shifting nature of human knowledge. Types of problems which at one time are identified by members of a group as appropriate for judgment may at another time be defined as computational problems, as the group changes its beliefs about cause-and-effect relations. We will have more to say about an opposite trend below, but the dominant "scientific" trend on the American scene in recent years has been to remove more and more items from the sphere of opinion to demonstrable "certainty."

Thus problems which once called for voting or inspirational strategies have become problems for computation or bargaining, and traditional structures are threatened. The city manager movement threatens both the party organization and the council by redefining certain types of problems as no longer subject to bargaining or voting but as appropriate for expert computation. The increasing scope of required expertise forces the American Congress to establish bureaucratic agencies to make decisions which once were prerogatives of the legislature—and Congress then becomes jealous of its own creations.

### Expansion Tendencies in Decision Issues

Decision issues appear to be broader, more complex, and more time-consuming as we move from computation issues to voting to bargaining issues. There is reason to believe that, left to their own devices, members of social

---

[28]This often is *expressed* by questioning their competence.

systems tend to expand decision issues. In a revealing summary of community issues and the course of their disposition, Coleman[29] notes a tendency for transformation of issues from specific to general, and from disagreement to antagonism. Bales also notes in small problem-solving groups that interpersonal tensions mount as the decision process moves from orientation to evaluation to control.[30]

As knowledge becomes increasingly pluralistic, in the sense that new specialized logics are developed, the bureaucracy encompasses not one but several sets of beliefs about appropriate means to organizational ends. Thus the competence of the single expert becomes doubted and members define issues as calling for judgment rather than computation. If, for example, the expert can be forced to admit that his is but a professional opinion—a tactic in jury trials—the way is cleared to insist that others be consulted and a balance of judgments obtained. This has also been a common practice in communities where public health experts have decided to introduce fluoride into the public water supply.[31]

It is clear that in the past several decades, American corporations have shown a proliferation of specialized staff agencies, each with its own logic for maximizing a particular function or procedure. As the beliefs about causation have thus become increasingly pluralistic, there has been a plea for the development of "generalists," but also there seems to have been a corresponding increase in the use of decision units appropriate to judgmental issues.[32] Committees, conferences, staff meetings, and "clearance" procedures have not only proliferated but have been dignified on wall charts—at least to the extent of dotted lines.

With problems which appear to call for judgment, the heat of debate can lead proponents of the several alternatives to overstate their cases and discount missing information; often it also leads them to refer to more general but extraneous organization preferences as a means of finding moral justification for the selection of the alternative they endorse. When this occurs, the issue is no longer one of judgment regarding causation, but becomes one of dispute over (relevant) ends and thus subject to compromise.

The issue which seems a natural for bargaining may verge on the anomic, since it frequently generates difficulties in the identification and exploration of causation. Inherently emphasizing preference conflict, the bargaining structure leads its members to discount causation theories endorsed by opponents and to overemphasize their own. This hampers the effort to get the "facts" and where preferences already are at issue, disputes over facts create anomic situations. Moreover, if one faction is adamant or unwilling to "bargain fairly," there is a tendency for the other faction or factions to seek to expand the issue into a larger, more general category, and to threaten the adamant faction with trouble on unrelated matters. This, too, tends toward anomie.

[29]James S. Coleman, *Community Conflict*, Glencoe, Ill.: The Free Press, 1957.

[30]Robert F. Bales, "The Equilibrium Problem in Small Groups," in Talcott Parsons, Robert F. Bales, and Edward A. Shils, *Working Papers in the Theory of Action,* Glencoe, Ill.: The Free Press, 1953.

[31]See Coleman, *op. cit.*

[32]For a report on the increasing use of committees for key decisions on new products, on personnel policy, production volume, and long-range planning, see "Committees: Their Role in Management Today," *Management Review*, October, 1957.

We can now offer the general proposition that an important role for administration is to *manage* the decision *process*, as distinct from *making the decision*. We are not suggesting that administrators do one to the exclusion of the other, but if issues are not automatically crystallized, the ideal structural constraints are not automatically present, or appropriate decision units are not automatically selected, it may fall to administrators to take action which will facilitate decisions.

The following discussion is not offered as exhaustive, but as illustrative of the potential utility of considering administrative roles with respect to the decision process.[33]

Where a time dimension is not clearly implied by the nature of the issue, one role of administration is to delineate, by fiction or otherwise, such a time dimension. This facilitates the sorting out of means from ends, by the decision unit, and thus tends to contain the issue from expanding into a more complex one.

When there are many alternatives available, a role of administration is to provide machinery for elimination of all but a few. This can be particularly important when an issue is assigned to a voting unit, which seems to be able to operate effectively only on binary problems. At one level of generality this is an important role for Congressional committees.[34] At a more general level of analysis this is the function of political parties in the two party system; the necessary compromises of platform and candidates are achieved before the issue is put to the electorate. By way of contrast, in multi-party France the function of compromising a plurality of interests devolved on the legislature more than on intraparty processes, and was an important factor in the lack of effectiveness of the Fourth Republic.[35]

In the bargaining situation the important role of administration may be to obtain initial mutual commitment to reaching agreement, and to maintain this commitment as taking priority over factional preferences. This approach may guard the issue from expanding into one of anomie, for as Dubin points out, mutual commitment to the necessity for reaching agreement in effect moves the issue in the direction of judgment and voting.[36] One method of handling the bargaining issue, and seemingly an indispensable one when the preference

[33]For a similar conclusion, though approached differently, see Philip Selznick, *Leadership in Administration*, Evanston, Ill.: Row Peterson and Co., 1957.

N.W. Chamberlain, in a study of the corporate decision-making process as applied to the transfer of employees, notes the distinction between deciding and managing the decision process, and offers a number of stimulating hypotheses. See Chamberlain, *Management in Motion*, New Haven, Conn.: Labor and Management Center, Yale University, 1950.

[34]See Latham, *Group Basis of Politics, op. cit.*

[35]For an analysis of this see Duncan MacRae, "Factors in the French Vote," *American Journal of Sociology*, November, 1958.

[36]Suggested by his analysis of union-management relations. See "Power and Union-Management Relations," *Administrative Science Quarterly*, June, 1957.

Bernard Berelson makes a related point. Surveying political voting research he writes, "... it would seem to be at least likely that the *same* avowed principles underlie political positions at every point on the continuum from left to right. ... Democratic theorists have pointed out what is so often overlooked because too visible, namely, that an effective democracy must rest upon a body of political and moral consensus. ... In this circumstance, a seeming consensus

scales do not contain common items, is to place the particular issue in a larger context. This can be done by "horse-trading," thus assuring the losing faction on the present issue of priority treatment on a future issue.[37]

Another role of administration which seems to be important under certain conditions is that of crystallizing consensus about preferences. Ambiguity in a decision situation may result in lack of knowledge, on the part of members of a decision unit, of the similarities of their preferences. When this is the case, an administrator who can sense the agreement and articulate it may play a vital part in organizational decision. In this connection it appears that timing may be as important as sensitivity to cues. Keesing and Keesing, observing formal group deliberation in Samoa, note that a senior elite person may choose to speak early if he wants to give guidance to the discussion *or knows that prior informal consultations have made clear a unanimous stand*, but that usually he will let others carry the active roles, making his pronouncements after the debate has pretty well run its course.[38]

A final suggestion regarding possible roles of administrators in facilitating organizational decision-making concerns the extremely complicated kinds of issues that frequently face administrators of "loose" organizations. We have in mind such social systems as the community (as viewed by a mayor, council, or manager); the school district (as viewed by the superintendent or board), or the bloc of nations (as viewed by their diplomats and officials). We refer to these as "loose" organizations because only a portion of the relevant "members" are directly subject to the hierarchy of authority. In the legal sense, that is, some of the groups are not "members," although in the behavioral sense they are.[39]

When such organizations face important and complicated issues, we believe, it may become necessary for administrators to redefine the issue into a series of issues, each assigned to an appropriate decision unit. It may also be that there are patterns in the sequence in which the series is handled. For example, in order to achieve a "community decision" on a fluoridation or school bond issue, it may be necessary to *first* get agreement and commitment of the powerful elements on preferences. This might be done "informally" in the smokefilled room, by compromise, and it might include the important choice as to whether to tackle the issue at all. After that decision is made, the *second* step might be to frame a judgmental issue for presentation to an electorate. Finally, within the limits of the majority decision, specialists can be presented with such issues as the proper equipment for fluoridation or the most appropriate timing for bond issues.

---

which is accepted at its face value is far better than no consensus—and a seeming consensus is sometimes reflected in loyalty to the same symbols even though they carry different meanings. A sense of homogeneity is often an efficient substitute for the fact of homogeneity. . . . What this means, then, is that the selection of means to reach agreed-upon ends is more likely to divide the electorate than the selection of the ends themselves." See Berelson in Heinz Eulau, S. J. Eldersveld, and M. Janowitz (eds.) *Political Behavior*, Glencoe, Ill.: The Free Press, 1956, p. 110.

[37] The important role of the larger context in facilitating decisions was suggested to us by Professor Bela Gold, School of Business Administration, University of Pittsburgh.

[38] *Elite Communication in Samoa, op. cit.*

[39] Such "loose" organizations are found in industry, too. For an instructive analysis of this, see Valentine F. Ridgway, "Administration of Manufacturer-Dealer Systems," *Administrative Science Quarterly*, March, 1957.

We feel rather safe in predicting that there is a cumulative effect in this sequence. Weakness in the first step probably forecasts trouble in succeeding steps, and so on.

### Administrative Tendencies to Narrow Issues

It seems apparent that in terms of time and effort, issues increase in "cost" in the same order in which they increase in breadth; computation is the quickest and simplest and involves the fewest members; judgment by voting membership is slower and diverts the energies of many; and bargaining usually is a drawn out energy-consuming process.

Organizations operate in environmental contexts and hence cannot always take a leisurely approach in making decisions. The actions of competitors or of potential collaborators and clientele frequently place time deadlines on issues. Moreover, the interrelatedness of the parts of large organizations may mean that delay at one point suspends activities at others, and when costs must be reckoned closely this fact exerts serious pressures to have issues settled promptly.[40]

Thus if an issue can be defined in more than one way, responsible officials may be tempted to define it in an easier, faster and less frustrating way, i.e., as calling for computation rather than judgment, or as appropriate for voting rather than bargaining.[41] In some cases the pressures of time, or habit, may lead administrators to force issues into molds which are patently inappropriate.

### Timing of Choice and Consensus

Except in situations where force can be brought to bear on members, it appears that consensus or acceptance of both means and ends is necessary for effective organizational action.

The four types of issues posited above are successively "broader" in the sense that they incorporate into the issue itself the necessity of finding or building consensus. It is only in the simplest type—computation—that consensus on means and ends exists prior to the decision. The judgment issue involves finding a cause and effect hypothesis about which a majority can agree. The bargain-

---

[40] Rose Laub Coser, comparing medical and surgical wards in a hospital, finds that the emergency nature of the surgical setting results in decision-making by fiat, whereas the more tentative, diagnostic atmosphere in the medical ward results in decision-making by deliberation and consensus. See Coser, "Authority and Decision-Making in a Hospital: A Comparative Analysis," *American Sociological Review*, February, 1958, (Chapter 8 in the present volume).

[41] March, Simon, and Guetzkow see this tendency. They write: "Because of these consequences of bargaining, we predict that the organizational hierarchy will perceive (and react to) all conflict as though it were in fact individual rather than intergroup conflict. More specifically, we predict that almost all disputes in the organization will be defined as problems in analysis, that the initial reaction to conflict will be problem-solving and persuasion, that such reactions will persist even when they appear to be inappropriate, that there will be a greater explicit emphasis on common goals where they do not exist than where they do, and that bargaining (when it occurs) will frequently be concealed within an analytic framework." (In *Organizations, op. cit.*, p. 131.)

Lipset, surveying political sociology, writes: "Inherent in bureaucratic structures is a tendency to reduce conflicts to administrative decisions by experts; and thus over time bureaucratization facilitates the removing of issues from the political arena." In Robert K. Merton, Leonard Broom, and Leonard S. Cottrell, Jr. (eds.) *Sociology Today*, New York: Basic Books, 1958, p. 102.

ing issue involves finding a preference on which consensus can be established. The anomic situation requires the creation of both preferences and causation-beliefs acceptable to a majority.

If the fact or the fiction of consensus is not present at the time a choice is made—and this may frequently be the case when rapid decisions are necessary—the required consensus must be achieved following choice. The hypothesis here is that for organizational decisions to be implemented effectively both consensus and choice are necessary. If, for reasons of expediency, choice is made *before* consensus is achieved, the burden of achieving consensus *following* choice remains.

This hypothesis, if accurate, has important implications not only for decision-making but for the larger administrative process of which decision is a part.

**Conclusion**

We have attempted to develop a format for studying decision processes in organizations, by identifying four major types of decision issues and pairing them with four major strategies for arriving at decisions. For each strategy we have suggested, there is an appropriate structure. Obviously there are many combinations and permutations of issues, strategies, and structures, but we believe that the format suggested points to a limited number of such arrangements, and that patterns can be found in them. We hope we have shown that this approach to organizational decision processes has important implications for theory and application.

What has been presented here can be considered no more than a first approximation. The empirical evidence along these lines has not been collected systematically, and further conceptual development undoubtedly will be necessary. It is possible, for example, that added leverage can be gained by distinguishing between "lack of agreement" and "disagreement," and thus developing a nine-fold typology of issues.[42] This format could also be extended into an analysis of how decisions are blocked or prevented. Such an extension should tell us something about the important area of belligerent behavior in or between organizations, and it should also provide a useful test of the models presented here.

Whatever the eventual results, we hope we have made the case for development of sociological models of decision processes, which can be joined with the psychological "satisficing" model to their mutual advantage.

[42]Suggested by Professor Frederick L. Bates, Department of Sociology, Louisiana State University, in private communication.

# Motivation and
# Organizational Climate

## MOTIVATION IN WORK GROUPS:
## A TENTATIVE VIEW

James V. Clark

This paper represents an attempt to examine a number of different researches in the field of organizational behavior and to see if their similarities can be highlighted and tentatively explained by the use of Maslow's need-hierarchy concept.[1]

A recent research experience of mine (so far published only in case form)[2] suggested for me that this process might be a useful way of generating new hypotheses and methods of measurement. The present paper is presented in the hope that others can be stimulated in the same way.

More specifically, this paper makes no claim that the answers concerning employee motivation and its determinants are all in. Neither does it claim that the questions generated by the examination of several researches from the point of view of the need-hierarchy concept are all presently researchable in a strict operational sense. Rather, the paper puts up what, for me, appears to be a potentially operational scheme for analyzing motivation and its organizational determinants. With such a scheme, it appears possible to study a number of different organizations comparatively, an effort which the field of organizational behavior needs.

I do believe, therefore, that the use of this theory puts us in a somewhat

Reprinted from *Human Organization*, 19 (1960–1961), 199–208 by permission from the author and the Society for Applied Anthropology.

[1]A. H. Maslow, *Motivation and Personality*, Harper and Bros., New York, 1954.
[2]"Century Co., (A)—(I)," Harvard Business School, EA-A 321–329.

better position than that outlined in a recent research on worker motivation by Herzberg *et al.*:

> This concept [Maslow's need hierarchy] has led many people to feel that the worker can never be satisfied with his job. How are you going to solve the dilemma of trying to motivate workers who have a continuously revolving set of needs? Since each individual may present at any one time a different scramble of his psychological need list, a systematic personnel practice hoping to cater to the most prepotent needs of its entire working force is defeated by the nature of the probabilities. Forgetting for a moment the individual "need hierarchies," it can be argued that there is sufficient homogeneity within various groups of employees to make for a relative similarity of "need hierarchies" within each group. Even so, the changes in prepotency for the group will occur, and personnel administration will have to keep up with them. For some who hold to this point of view personnel administration is reduced to the essential of labor-management bargaining. For others it means that personnel programs must be geared to be sensitive to the changes that are continually taking place in the needs of the employees. And since this can be done only by the supervisors, the training of supervisors in understanding human motivation, the factors underlying it, and the therapeutic or manipulative skills with which to cope with it is the most essential ingredient to any industrial-relations program.[3]

As this paper will show, I am not opposed to sensitive firstline administrators. However, other variables relating to satisfaction and productivity will be highlighted and in such a way as to suggest that the development of worker motivation is not a random scramble but is perhaps predictable, with only a modicum of sensitivity to employee needs.

### The Need-Hierarchy Model

Let us start with McGregor's summary of Maslow's concepts, which is concise and simply put.

As most readers are probably aware, Maslow views an individual's motivations not in terms of a series of drives, but rather in terms of a hierarchy, certain "higher" needs becoming activated to the extent certain "lower" ones become satisfied. McGregor summarized these as follows:[4]

#### Physiological Needs

> Man is a wanting animal—as soon as one of his needs is satisfied, another appears in its place. This process is unending. It continues from birth to death.

> Man's needs are organized in a series of levels—a hierarchy of importance. At the lowest level, but preeminent in importance when they are thwarted, are his *physiological needs*. Man lives for bread alone, when there is no bread. Unless the circumstances are unusual, his needs for love, for status, for recognition are inoperative when his stomach has been empty for awhile. But when he eats regularly and adequately, hunger ceases to be

---

[3]Frederick Herzberg, Bernard Mausner, and Barbara Bloch Synderman, *The Motivation to Work*, John Wiley & Sons, New York, 1959.
[4]Douglas M. McGregor, 5th Anniversary Convocation, School of Industrial Management, Massachusetts Institute of Technology, Cambridge, Massachusetts.

an important motivation. The same is true of the other physiological needs of man—for rest, exercise, shelter, protection from the elements.

*A satisfied need is not a motivator of behavior*! This is a fact of profound significance that is regularly ignored in the conventional approach to the management of ["normal"] people. Consider your own need for air; except as you are deprived of it, it has no appreciable motivating effect upon your behavior.

## Safety Needs

When the physiological needs are reasonably satisfied, needs at the next higher level begin to dominate man's behavior, to motivate him. These are called *safety needs*. They are needs for protection against danger, threat, deprivation. Some people mistakenly refer to these as needs for security. However, unless man is in a dependent relationship where he fears arbitrary deprivation, he does not demand security. The need is for the "fairest possible break." When he is confident of this he is more willing to take risks. But when he feels threatened or dependent, his greatest need is for guarantees, for protection, for security.

The fact needs little emphasis that, since every industrial employee is in a dependent relationship, safety needs may assume considerable importance. Arbitrary management actions, behavior which arouses uncertainty with respect to continued employment or which reflects favoritism or discrimination, unpredictable administration of policy—these can be powerful motivators of the safety needs in the employment relationship at *every level*, from worker to vice president.

## Social Needs

When man's physiological needs are satisfied and he is no longer fearful about his physical welfare, his *social needs* become important motivators of his behavior—needs for belonging, for association, for acceptance by his fellows, for giving and receiving friendship and love.

Management knows today of the existence of these needs, but it often assumes quite wrongly that they represent a threat to the organization. Many studies have demonstrated that the tightly knit, cohesive work group may, under proper conditions, be far more effective than an equal number of separate individuals in achieving organizational goals.

Yet management, fearing group hostility to its own objectives, often goes to considerable lengths to control and direct human efforts in ways that are inimical to the natural "groupiness" of human beings. When man's social needs—and perhaps his safety needs, too—are thus thwarted, he behaves in ways which tend to defeat organizational objectives. He becomes resistant, antagonistic, uncooperative. But this behavior is a consequence, not a cause.

## Ego Needs

Above the social needs—in the sense that they do not become motivators until lower needs are reasonably satisfied—are the needs of greater significance to management and to man himself. They are the *egoistic* needs, and they are of two kinds:

1. Those needs that relate to one's self-esteem—needs for self-confidence, for independence, for achievement, for competence, for knowledge.

2. Those needs that relate to one's reputation—needs for status, for recognition, for appreciation, for the deserved respect of one's fellows.

Unlike the lower needs, these are rarely satisfied; man seeks indefinitely for more satisfaction of these needs once they have become important to him. But they do not appear in any significant way until physiological, safety, and social needs are all reasonably satisfied.

The typical industrial organization offers few opportunities for the satisfaction of these egoistic needs to people at lower levels in the hierarchy. The conventional methods of organizing work, particularly in mass-production industries, give little heed to these aspects of human motivation. If the practices of scientific management were deliberately calculated to thwart these needs, they could hardly accomplish this purpose better than they do.

### Self-Fulfillment Needs

Finally—a capstone, as it were, on the hierarchy of man's needs—there are what we may call the needs for *self-fulfillment*. These are the needs for realizing one's own potentialities, for continued self-development, for being creative in the broadest sense of that term.

It is clear that the conditions of modern life give only limited opportunity for these relatively weak needs to obtain expression. The deprivation most people experience with respect to other lower-level needs diverts their energies into the struggle to satisfy those needs, and the needs for self-fulfillment remain dormant.

For purposes of initial explanation and simplicity, McGregor spoke in terms of separate steps or levels. Actually, Maslow suggests that these levels are interdependent and overlapping, each higher-need level emerging before the lower needs have been satisfied completely. In our society, most people tend to be partially satisfied in each need area and partially unsatisfied. However, most individuals tend to have higher satisfaction at the lower-need level than at higher-need levels. Maslow helps to explain this by picturing the average citizen as (for illustrative purposes) 85 percent satisfied in his physiological needs, 70 percent satisfied in his safety needs, 50 percent in his belonging needs, 40 percent in his egoistic needs, and 10 percent in his self-fulfillment needs.

### Some Suggested Uniformities Among Different Researches

Exhibit 1 shows how the need-hierarchy concept might be utilized to relate and explain the findings of a number of different studies. In other words, it takes McGregor's generalization of Maslow's theory, attempts to relate it to some existing studies, and concludes that workers under this or that combination of environmental conditions behave *as if* they were motivated in such-and-such a fashion.

Before we turn to this exhibit, however, a word of caution is in order. This way of relating and thinking about different organizational behavior researches is by no means perfect. First of all, the propositions which follow from the need-hierarchy theory are extremely difficult to test in a research sense. Secondly, the variety of environmental and internal-system factors affecting work-group behavior cannot be categorized so as to make all known descriptions of work situations directly comparable from some one point of view. Finally, almost all

EXHIBIT 1

## Some Relations Between Conditions in the Work Group's Environment, Motivation, Satisfaction, Productivity, and Turnover-Absenteeism

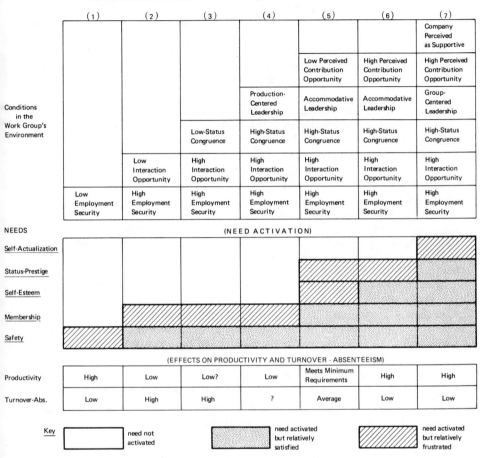

| | (1) | (2) | (3) | (4) | (5) | (6) | (7) |
|---|---|---|---|---|---|---|---|
| **Conditions in the Work Group's Environment** | | | | | | | Company Perceived as Supportive |
| | | | | | Low Perceived Contribution Opportunity | High Perceived Contribution Opportunity | High Perceived Contribution Opportunity |
| | | | | Production-Centered Leadership | Accommodative Leadership | Accommodative Leadership | Group-Centered Leadership |
| | | | Low-Status Congruence | High-Status Congruence | High-Status Congruence | High-Status Congruence | High-Status Congruence |
| | | Low Interaction Opportunity | High Interaction Opportunity | High Interaction Opportunity | High Interaction Opportunity | High Interaction Opportunity | High Interaction Opportunity |
| | Low Employment Security | High Employment Security | High Employment Security | High Employment Security | High Employment Security | High Employment Security | High Employment Security |

**NEEDS** — (NEED ACTIVATION)

Self-Actualization
Status-Prestige
Self-Esteem
Membership
Safety

(EFFECTS ON PRODUCTIVITY AND TURNOVER - ABSENTEEISM)

| | | | | | | | |
|---|---|---|---|---|---|---|---|
| Productivity | High | Low | Low? | Low | Meets Minimum Requirements | High | High |
| Turnover-Abs. | Low | High | High | ? | Average | Low | Low |

Key:
need not activated
need activated but relatively satisfied
need activated but relatively frustrated

researches leave out, or find uncontrollable, some variables that are necessary for complete comparability. Nevertheless, some available researches suggest uniformities consistent with the need-hierarchy concept.

Exhibit 1 shows how a number of different "givens" in a work-group's environment can prevent or frustrate an individual's opportunity for need satisfaction at different levels of the need hierarchy. The exhibit is based on the assumption that all individuals have a potential for activating all the needs on the need hierarchy. Likewise, the exhibit assumes that an individual does not necessarily suspend or forget his unrealized needs during his hours on the job. Actually, in industrial situations, there are few data to support the first assumption, many data to support the second. Therefore, the exhibit can usefully be regarded as a tentative explanation of how and why most people, or an "average worker," would most typically react under different conditions at work.

The extreme left-hand scale of the middle block of graphs in Exhibit 1 represents the various levels of the need hierarchy (exclusive of the physiological needs). (In Maslow's description of his need hierarchy, the status-prestige need and the self-esteem need are placed side by side about the membership need. They are placed one on top of the other here for graphic simplicity.)

The remaining columns of the middle block depict the pattern of an individual's need activation and satisfaction under a number of different external conditions. These patterns will be discussed in this paper in relation to certain researches. (It is not possible to show all possible combinations of external conditions: researches have not been conducted under such a wide variety of conditions.)

Across the bottom of the exhibit are two rows which show "productivity" and "turnover and absenteeism" for each column. These are by no means definitely established results but the researches examined in this paper often suggested certain tendencies in regard to these variables which are shown. Consequently, by beginning with human needs, we can move to the relationship between the satisfaction of these needs, external conditions, and productivity and turnover-absenteeism.

*Column 1* illustrates a situation in which employment security is extremely low. Such conditions might exist whenever alternative employment is unavailable (as in a depression) or is deemed by the workers to be not as desirable as present employment and where workers feel unprotected from a management which is perceived as arbitrary in its layoff and firing procedures.

Research by Goode and Fowler[5] in an automobile feeder plant illustrates this condition. In their study of a low morale, nonunion plant a small group of high service employees, for whom the job had become an absolute economic necessity, consistently produced according to management expectations. Turnover among other workers, for whom the job was less important, was high. They quit or were fired for not producing enough.

Interestingly enough, related situations were described some time ago, and were alluded to by Mitchell,[6] when he noted that the pace or work was slower in the flush times of 1900-1902 than it had been in the dull times of 1894-1896. He quoted a sample bit of testimony from the period. The superintendent of a company manufacturing electrical machinery said:

> ... Five years ago men did not restrict their output, union or non-union men, because they wanted to hold their jobs, and a man would do anything and all he was told to do. Now a man knows that all he has to do is to walk across the street and get another job at the same rate of pay. ...

Obviously, a group's productivity does not always increase in depression times: it fell off in the bank-wiring room[7] shortly before the final layoffs. The suggestion being made here is that under employment conditions which an individual perceives as economically threatening *and* arbitrary (and such conditions probably exist most often in a depression), his higher needs cannot motivate. He is "stuck" on the safety level and his behavior can only work

[5]W. F. Goode and Irving Fowler, "Incentive Factor in a Low Morale Plant," *American Sociological Review*, XIV, No. 5 (1949).

[6]W. C. Mitchell, *Business Cycles and Their Causes*, University of California Press, Berkeley, Cal., 1941.

[7]F. J. Roethlisberger and W. J. Dickson, *Management and the Worker*, Harvard University Press, Cambridge, Mass., 1952.

toward the immediate goal of economic survival. Under conditions of this kind, financial rewards tend to be the primary incentives which motivate workers toward higher productivity.

### Frustrated Membership Needs

Columns 2 through 4 all show situations in which membership needs are active, but frustrated. They are shown separately, because apparently they occur under different environmental conditions.

*Column 2* shows a situation where workers are less concerned with employment security, because they have it, but where the job technology imposes physical or spatial requirements where interaction is impossible or severely restricted. This condition reflects and is labelled "low interaction opportunity." Such conditions and their effects on satisfaction were described in two automobile assembly plant studies.

Walker and Guest[8] rated jobs according to their "mass production characteristics" (noise, repetitiveness, restricted opportunity for movement, etc.). Workers holding such jobs often reported social isolation to be an important reason for job dissatisfaction. Moreover, absenteeism and turnover (extremely high throughout the automotive industry) were nearly twice as high for persons whose jobs exhibited "extreme mass production characteristics."

Another study of automobile assembly workers by Jasinski[9] showed that the men resented not being able to follow conventional conversation patterns; looking at the listener, being able to pause for conversation, and to complete the "talk." A correlation was found between an individual's desire to talk on the job and his attitude toward his job: the higher the desire to talk, the less interesting the job.

It is possible that Van Zelst's study[10] of sociometrically restructured construction work groups may be illustrative of what happens when opportunities to interact are increased.

When men were allowed to work alongside others whom they themselves had chosen, turnover, labor cost and materials cost all dropped.

The inference can be drawn that these results occurred because membership level motivation was satisfied and higher needs became activated.

Another research, "The Case of the Changing Cage,"[11] suggests what happens to a work group's productivity and satisfaction when interaction opportunities are suddenly lowered. (In this case, however, interaction opportunity was decreased by a combination of physical changes and another variable we will discuss later, leadership behavior.)

Workers in a voucher-check filing unit in an insurance company worked together well, kept up with the work load and expressed feelings of satisfaction. Their work area was inside a wire cage surrounded by filing cabinets and boxes

[8]Charles R. Walker and Robert H. Guest, *The Man on the Assembly Line*, Harvard University Press, Cambridge, Mass., 1952.

[9]Frank J. Jasinski, "Technological Delimitation of Reciprocal Relationships: A Study of Interaction Patterns in Industry," *Human Organization*, XV, No. 2 (1956).

[10]R. J. Van Zelst, "Sociometrically Selected Work Teams Increase Productivity," *Personnel Psychology*, V, No. 3 (1953).

[11]Cara B. Richards and Henry F. Dobyns, "Topography and Culture: The Case of the Changing Cage," *Human Organization*, XVI, No. 1 (1957).

through which the group's supervisors could not see. For efficiency purposes, the cage was moved to a new area in which the filing cabinets were arranged so that supervisors could see into the cage and restrict worker interaction. The workers could no longer engage in social activities which had been important to them (games, chatting, eating, etc.). Their output declined drastically, the amount of time spent in nonwork activities increased substantially, and the workers expressed considerable dissatisfaction with the new setup.

In short, it appears that if there are any major physical or spatial technological factors which restrict opportunities for interaction (under conditions where safety-level needs are not primary) membership needs will be frustrated and, consequently, any higher-need levels will not be activated.

*Column 3* illustrates a situation in which safety-level considerations are relatively unimportant because they are satisfied, interaction opportunities are high, but where workers are placed in low-status congruence work groups.

The need-hierarchy explanation of this situation would be as follows: safety needs are not active and membership needs are active but frustrated because social-status differences among persons in the work group are too large for the group to deal with effectively. Therefore no indications of higher-level needs are present. As a consequence, people would not see their work as something to which they could or should contribute. But why should low- or high-status congruence affect membership motivation?

In Zaleznik, Christensen, and Roethlisberger's recent study, a "theory of social certitude" was advanced to explain this on an individual level:

> In the condition of social certitude, the individual may be high, middle, or low in total status. But at whatever level, his status factors are well established. As a social entity, therefore, he can place himself and be placed readily in the structure of a group. People relate to him in terms of common expectations of behavior toward a person well established at this particular level of status. In turn, the individual knows what to expect from others. These expectations may or may not be functional for the group or the individual—there may be a more productive role for an individual than his status, well established as it is, allows him to play. Nevertheless, in a condition of social certitude the individual becomes "structured" into a group. Whether he is structured into the group at a high rank or low rank will depend on the level of the individual's total status.
>
> The condition of ambiguity, where the individual's status factors are out of line, provides no readily apparent social position for him. As an ambiguous social entity, the group has no clear expectations regarding behavior from or toward such an individual. On the one hand, being high in one or more dimensions of status seems to require the form of behavior associated with a high status person. On the other hand, being simultaneously low in one or more dimensions of status seems to require behavior associated with a low status person. These mixed expectations create ambiguities and consequently anxiety in social relationships.[12]

This theory was advanced to explain why group members are attracted to or repelled by an *individual* whose status factors are out of line: some very high, some very low. Such an individual is ambiguous in relation to the group majority. The term "group-status congruence" refers to a collection of people who

[12]A. Zaleznik, C. R. Christensen, and F. J. Roethlisberger, *The Motivation, Productivity and Satisfaction of Workers, A Prediction Study*, Harvard University Division of Research, Graduate School of Business Administration, Boston, Mass., 1958.

share similar status factors, even if the factors themselves may be out of line with one another for a given individual. In this kind of a situation, an individual who exhibits status factors different from the majority tends to be avoided by the majority even if his status factors are in line with one another. He is likely to be described by others as "not our class" or "not our kind of person."[13] The four combinations between an individual and his group (high group-status congruence, high individual-status congruence; high group-status congruence, low individual-status congruence, etc.) have not been studied as such. At the present time, loosely stated, it appears that if, under most conditions, an individual has status factors to some extent different from the majority of people in the small-group social structure to which he belongs, he will tend to be regarded as ambiguous by that majority, and hence will be regarded with anxiety.

Clark's supermarket research[14] was concerned with differences in group-status congruence between stores.

He found that groups with high group-status congruence (which he called "high status factors in common" groups) exhibited low turnover and low absenteeism, both indications of membership-need level satisfaction. Moreover, he further found that stores which had high-status congruent groups in them also tended to have higher labor efficiency ratings. In addition, he found that members of these groups tended to speak of their work as more satisfying.

Adams' bomber crew study[15] was somewhat similar.

He showed that crews with high group-status congruence tended to report feelings of satisfaction with group membership. However, Adams also showed that while crews with high-status congruence showed high technical performance up to a point, beyond that point, as group-status congruence increased, technical performance decreased.

Therefore, while Clark's and Adams' studies showed similar results in the relation between group-status congruence and membership satisfaction, their findings on group-status congruence and performance were less clear.[16] It is difficult to explain with confidence why Adams' highest technical performance groups were low-status congruent. Comparable data on social structure, motivation, satisfaction, and formal leadership might have provided clearer explanations.

Not only the possible difference between these two studies, but the findings of other researches in the general area of status and how people react to it, all indicate that not enough is known yet about this subject to offer inclusive explanations for work-group behavior. For example, Zaleznik's machine shop workers[17] had developed a social structure which offered its members at least a minimal level of satisfaction. In comparison to other studies, his workers

[13]James V. Clark, *Some Unconscious Assumptions Affecting Labor Efficiency in Eight Supermarkets* (unpublished D.B.A. thesis), Harvard Graduate School of Business Administration, 1958.

[14]*Ibid.*

[15]Stuart Adams, "Status Congruency as a Variable in Small Group Performance," *Social Forces*, XXXII, 16–22.

[16]However, the two studies do not necessarily contradict each other on this point, since Clark studied no stores with status-congruence measures as high as some of the bomber crews studied by Adams. Also, the two studies used different status factors, and different ways to measure group-status congruence. Clark's research is continuing in an attempt to test for lower labor efficiency under conditions of higher group-status congruence.

[17]A. Zaleznik, *Worker Satisfaction and Development,* Harvard University Division of Research, Graduate School of Business Administration, Boston, Mass., 1956.

could be said to have exhibited low individual and group-status congruence, although the congruence apparently was high enough for the group to form: it contained no Bolsheviks or Andaman Islanders. In short, the existing findings in this area suggest, but not conclusively, that under most industrial conditions, a group will be more cohesive to the extent to which its members exhibit individual and/or group-status congruence. (An important exception will be discussed under Column 7 of Exhibit 1).

The remaining columns, 4 through 7, show those situations where neither technological restrictions on interaction, nor the given sentiments of workers (e.g., notions of member attraction stemming from status factors in common) are such as to prevent the formation of a satisfying social structure. Rather the constrictions on group development portrayed here stem largely from the behavior of the formal leader of the work group.

### Leadership Behavior

Since leadership is important here, it will be useful, before turning to the columns themselves, to describe roughly the leadership behavior under three different types.[18] The labels "accommodative," "production-centered," and "group-centered" will be briefly described, in that order.

The first, "accommodative," refers to situations where the leader's behavior neither challenges a group, nor seriously violates its norms of how a leader should behave. The group's determination of its own work procedures is left alone. As a result, the formal leader does not seriously threaten the group's survival as a group.

This condition is a common one and was described in the following reports:

In the Whirlwind Corporation[19] a group of workers developed an improved tool capable of increasing their productivity on a certain item fifty percent. Actually, they increased productivity ten percent and used the remaining time to improve quality on some other products. A methods engineer was assigned to study the problem but the group withheld information about the tool from him. For some time, the foreman was aware of this but was "satisfied to let the men handle it their own way." He reasoned that at little expense he was able to get out production of high quality.

In Roy's research in a piecework machine shop[20] workers had an elaborate set of restriction-of-output activities. The foreman instructed new men in parts of this system. To one man he said:

> Say, when you punch off day work onto piecework, you ought to have your piecework already started. Run a few, then punch off day work, and you'll have a good start. You've got to chisel a little around here to make money.

In the Century Company,[21] workers in one area (B) reported that their foreman left them completely alone and had for several years. Prior to that time, he had supervised the men closely but they had taught him not to, by telling him that they would refuse to work if he didn't let them alone.

[18]It is beyond the scope of this article to evaluate these labels or to offer a different classification scheme.

[19]Paul Pigors and Charles H. Myers, *Personnel Administration, A Point of View and a Method*, McGraw-Hill Book Co., New York, 1956.

[20]Donald Roy, "Efficiency and the Fix: Informal Intergroup Relations in a Piecework Machine Shop," *American Journal of Sociology*, LX, No. 3 (1954).

[21]"Century Co. (A)—(I)," *op. cit.*

Although the three situations above point to different degrees of foreman involvement in the group, the uniformity among them is that the leader has abdicated any influence in the setting of work procedures. The group determines its procedures. A variety of labels other than "accommodative" have been devised to describe such a foreman: "laissez-faire," "abdicratic," etc.

Other researches have pointed to the "production-centered" pattern of leadership behavior (and, moreover, suggested certain relations between such leadership and productivity).

In a study of productivity and leadership in an insurance company,[22] certain leaders were characterized as seeing their job primarily in terms of methods, procedures, and standards of production. Called production-centered leaders, by the researchers, it was noted that such leaders headed seven out of ten low-producing sections.

In the Century Company (I) case,[23] one foreman said this about his idea of a good worker:

> A good man is a man who is reasonable. . . . He does what the company tells him he should do. He does not try to do what he thinks he should do, but he does what he is told.

The people working for this foreman had these kinds of things to say about him:

> Whenever my foreman sees a man sitting down, he comes up to him and gives him something to do. . . . I don't think he'll be happy until he sees everybody running around all the time. [Our] foreman shouldn't yell at a man in front of everybody or nail him down. . . . This makes friction and breaks down the group.

Borrowing the phrase from the above-mentioned insurance company research, the Century Company researchers labelled this foreman "production-centered."

This kind of leader is the direct opposite of the accommodative type, in that he allows the employees little or no influence in the setting-up of work procedures. Influence is supposed to move downward only according to such a supervisor. Although we are calling such a leader production-centered, others have described him as "authoritarian," "autocratic," and "task-centered."

"Group-centered" leadership was indicated in the same two studies.

In the insurance company,[24] "employee-centered leadership" referred to supervisors who saw their job primarily in terms of the organization, training, and motivation of subordinates. Such supervisors headed six of seven high-producing sections. The researchers said that:

> The supervisors of the high-producing sections . . . regard supervision as the most important part of their work. . . . Their method of supervision appears to be one of setting up certain general conditions for their employees and thus permitting their employees to work out the details of when and how the work will be handled.

In the Century Company case (I),[25] one foreman said this about his idea of a good worker:

[22]Daniel Katz, N. Maccoby, and Nancy Morse, *Productivity, Supervision and Morale in an Office Situation*, Part I, Institute for Social Research, Ann Arbor, Mich., 1950.
[23]"Century Co. (A)—(I)," *op. cit.*
[24]Daniel Katz, N. Maccoby, and Nancy Morse, *op. cit.*
[25]"Century Co. (A)—(I)," *op. cit.*

In my estimation, a good furnace worker is a man who has confidence in himself. . . . A foreman should show confidence in his men, and this should be real confidence. I'm always ready to show confidence in a man, even though at first sight I might think he doesn't deserve it. What I do is give some directions to a man and then let him do his work without always being on his back. I want him to be free to do his work. . . . I realize that this requires a lot of talking on the part of the foreman. The men have to learn to trust their foreman. A foreman has to talk to his men to let himself be known by them. . . . Another thing, I like to tease the men, because it's one way for me to talk to them. It shows them I'm not dangerous.

The workers spoke about this foreman as follows:

Last week when———was our foreman we did not have any trouble. There were no complaints, no grievances, no beefs. It was hot and he understood that we were having more difficulty working at this temperature than at other times. After all, a man needs encouragement.

He knows how to run the men. I wish we could keep him for a long time. . . . We're not the only ones that have noticed he is good. Everywhere he has been in the company, people have been glad to work for him.

The researchers classified this foreman as "group-centered."

This kind of leader has been described as "democratic," "group-centered," "employee-centered," etc. In this paper, the group-centered label will be used. Regardless of the label, however, it can be seen that such a leader allows and encourages a *mutual* influence relationship with his men. Both the leader and his subordinates play a role in the setting-up of work procedures and the mutuality is made legitimate and encouraged by this kind of leader.

Returning to the Exhibit 1 diagram, *Column 4* shows the effects of the production-centered leadership condition in a situation where group formation potential is present. The behavior of a leader allowing low-influence opportunity, as described above, would tend to prevent a group from forming a satisfying relationship with each other and to its environment. Because workers are more consciously forced to attend to their work, their membership needs are frustrated.

The Century Company[26] cases showed two groups of furnace workers, both with equal numbers of high and low individually status-congruent people. Workers in furnace area "A" had a production-centered foreman and exhibited less social development, while workers in furnace area "B" had an accommodative foreman and showed more social development. The researchers made an attempt to assess motivation, also, and there was considerably lower indication of membership need activation in area A than in area B. Moreover, of those judged active at this need level in area A, the majority appeared frustrated.

This study shows an instance in which membership needs were frustrated by a production-centered foreman: by holding workers rigidly to their required activities, he never permitted the social group to form, even though it was potentially capable of so forming. Incidentally, while accurate productivity data were not available for the two particular shift crews studied, area A as a whole (all four shift crews together) was producing much less than area B.

If production-centered leadership is introduced into a group that has already

[26] *Ibid.*

formed, however, there is some evidence to suggest that the group continues to function as a group: they unite around their hostility to management.

The "Case of the Changing Cage"[27] alluded to before illustrates this (although it contains no information about status congruence). The supervisor believed that he could better control output by looking into this cage and thereby reducing nonwork behavior. In the old cage, he could not see in, but in the new cage he could. The result, however, was the nonwork activities actually increased (although they were less visible: the group went underground).

Whether or not such a situation is indicative of frustrated membership needs is difficult to say. Perhaps it can be said, though, that this group was simply elaborating its membership needs: under this condition, the nonwork behavior offered the only *possibility* for need satisfaction.

Columns 1 through 4 have all illustrated how environmental conditions can restrict the development of social structure in work groups. In addition, they also illustrated motivational consequences at lower-need levels only. The remaining columns show situations in which there is indication that higher-need levels can become activated. Since, in a formal organization, people activated at these higher-need levels show a tendency to contribute their judgment and productiveness to the organization's task, the term "contributive motivation" may sometimes be a useful shorthand for all the need levels above the membership level. We shall use it occasionally in the rest of this paper.

*Column 5* shows two changes in comparison to Column 4. One, the satisfaction of membership needs, comes from the accommodative leader who, by not threatening the group too much, allows it to form and perpetuate itself. The second change is the frustration of the esteem needs, due to the introduction of a condition which might be labelled "low-perceived contribution opportunity." This refers to a worker's perception of a technological process as being predetermined for the most part. Here, except for the opportunity for an occasional change in setup, technology, etc., a member of a social group at work sees no continuing opportunity to contribute anything, to make a difference, to initiate, along with other members of this group, something useful on his environment. The Column 5 situation has often been described in organizational behavior research at the worker level because it is undoubtedly the most common. The self-esteem and status-prestige needs are released, because membership needs are relatively satisfied, but, since the workers' jobs prevent any satisfying feelings of group competence or mastery to emerge, and because the accomodative foreman has no concept of getting his group involved in setting up any of its own procedures, the esteem needs are frustrated. Typical comments of workers in such situations are:

> A job is a job.
> You have to work so it might as well be here as anywhere.
> This job isn't bad: it's a nice bunch of guys but any moron could do the work [etc.].

It appears as if the "regulars" in the Zaleznik, Christensen, Roethlisberger prediction study[28] and the famous bank-wiring room workers[29] illustrate this

[27]Cara Richards and Henry Dobyns, *op. cit.*

[28]A. Zaleznik, C. R. Christensen, and F. J. Roethlisberger, *op. cit.*

[29]Where there is a suggestion (untested) that social structure was determined by individual status congruence. *Cf.* F. J. Roethlisberger and W. J. Dickson, *op. cit.*

column. Under such conditions, workers' productivity and satisfaction are determined mainly by their position in the social structure, since they are "stuck" on the membership level. Little, if any, opportunity for the satisfaction of contributive motivation exists.

*Column 6* differs from Column 5 in that it shows the satisfied self-esteem need under conditions of a high perceived contribution opportunity, but a frustrated status-prestige need (frustrated by the lack of recognition on the part of an accommodative foreman) which the worker would feel was justified by his competence. The accommodative leader allows a group to develop simply by not being around or bothering to impede it. His *not* being around or *not* understanding the forces which motivate productiveness (i.e., self-esteem around job competence) make him less likely to reward the work with verbal or economic recognition of these perceived skills.

This motivational pattern and these environmental conditions were seen in the previously referred to Century Company case.[30] Workers in one furnace area (B) were glad their foreman was not around to interfere with their nonwork activities and their exercising of skill and judgment in their work. However, they resented the fact that he did not *understand* the extent of their technical competence and hence could not reward them adequately when it came time for him to evaluate them.

Before leaving Columns 1 through 6, which all illustrate one or another form of what Roethlisberger has called "frozen groups,"[31] another condition should be mentioned: "perception of company supportiveness." It has not been studied in enough situations to allow us to place it somewhere in Columns 1 through 6; however two studies suggest its importance.

Seashore[32] found that high cohesive groups tended to produce significantly higher than average when they reported a high perception of company supportiveness and to produce significantly lower than average when they reported a low perception of company supportiveness.

In a piecework machine shop studied by Collins, *et al.*,[33] a work group had an elaborate system of output restriction. The accommodative foreman knew about and actively supported the system. The general superintendent, however, exerted much effort in an attempt to break it up. He told workers they should not accept group pressure to conform and that they were foolish and dishonest if they did. The men saw the overall company as being hostile toward them and went to considerable lengths to restrict output: they often finished their day's work in three or four hours, they had jigs and fixtures which increased their hourly productivity but which were unknown to management, etc.

*Column 7* shows a condition that has only recently been analytically studied on a continuing basis in industry. However, studies concerning group participation in the process of instituting technological change (e.g., the well-known relay assembly test room[34] and Coch and French[35] studies) might illustrate this

[30]"Century Co. (A)—(I)," *op. cit.*

[31]A. Zaleznik, *op. cit.*

[32]S. F. Seashore, *Group Cohesiveness in the Industrial Work Group*, Survey Research Center, University of Michigan, Ann Arbor, Mich., 1954.

[33]Orville Collins, Melville Dalton, and Donald Roy, "Restriction of Output and Social Cleavage in Industry," *Applied Anthropology*, V, No. 3 (1946).

[34]F.J. Roethlisberger and W. J. Dickson, *op cit.*

[35]L. Coch and J. R. P. French, "Overcoming Resistance to Change," *Human Relations*, I, 512–532.

situation for temporary periods where workers were involved in, and given recognition for, their ability to contribute to important organizational problems. Perhaps, too, the Lamson Company case[36] points to such a condition.

Skilled, experienced oil refinery workers were taken off their old job, given an extensive training course, and placed in a new tower. For several months they worked alongside the engineers who were installing and "de-bugging" the new and complicated equipment. Their suggestions were encouraged and accepted by the engineers and the men's behavior indicated they were highly satisfied with the experience.

Workers in such situations appear to be motivated at the higher need levels and to exist under maximal environmental conditions: they have a high opportunity to interact, a task to which they see a high opportunity to contribute and a leader who sets up a high opportunity for mutual influence between himself and his subordinates. Moreover, we can infer, too, that such workers would exist in an organizational environment which they saw as supportive. In addition, one study in an electronics factory (not yet published) suggests that the remaining environmental condition, high-status congruence, is a prerequisite for the motivation pattern seen in Column 7.

However, in a recently published research by Barnes,[37] members of an engineering group exhibited low individual and group-status congruence, yet had high opportunity to interact, high opportunity for mutual influence and a high contribution opportunity. A few individuals, considered as a collection, had high group-status congruence, yet the social structure was not determined by this fact. Moreover, much of the group looked as if they might be exhibiting the need pattern seen in Column 7.

Barnes' research suggests, therefore, that, when all other conditions are met, a group's social behavior is not "frozen" by the status factors its members brought with them. If one is interested in the growth and development of individuals in an organization, Barnes' study points to a helpful situation.

### Summary and Conclusion

By carefully examining Exhibit 1 we have attempted to describe factors which both release and constrain different motivations in members of industrial work groups. In addition, we have shown how, according to Maslow's theory, relative satisfaction of certain needs may release other needs which alter the picture. Roughly, the following diagram illustrates this process, and is nothing more than a simplified restatement of Exhibit 1.

Incidentally, the similarity between Exhibit 2 and the small group conceptual scheme of Homans'[38] is obvious. "Contribution opportunity" refers to the extent to which an individual's "required activities" are not so highly programmed that no room is left for the individual's contribution to them. "Interaction opportunity" refers to the extent to which an individual's "required interactions" do not limit him from getting together, on a social as well as task basis, with others. "Influence opportunity," a function of leadership behavior, has an effect

[36]"Lamson Co.," Harvard Business School, HP 318.

[37]Louis B. Barnes, *Organizational Systems and Engineering Groups*, Harvard University Division of Research, Graduate School of Business Administration, Boston, Mass., 1960.

[38]George C. Homans, *The Human Group*, Harcourt, Brace & Co., New York, 1950.

EXHIBIT 2

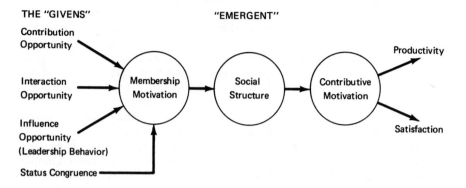

on an individual's motivation because of the kinds of "given sentiments" most of us appear to have about leadership: when we are closely controlled or highly programmed, this violates our expectations of a satisfying superior-subordinate behavior. "Status congruence" refers to another large body of "given sentiments" most people seem to have: ideas about status and class which are widespread in our culture.

Any emergent small group behavior feeds back on the givens, however, as Homans and others have observed. And Exhibit 2 is oversimplified insofar as this feedback is not shown. Nevertheless, its importance is obvious, particularly if one must understand and/or deal with a group through time. For example, a foreman of a work group which, for various reasons, was producing too little might change his leadership behavior from accommodative to production-centered, thus, perhaps, frustrating membership and self-esteem needs. Another example of such feedback might exist in a group under a group-centered leader who allowed mutual influence opportunities and whose members were active at the membership and contributive levels. Conceivably, these members would see continuous contribution opportunities in their jobs, thereby releasing further contributive motivation. Another example, and one which a number of my colleagues at the Harvard Business School and myself hope to test specifically in a current project, is the possibility that the structure of a group operating on higher need levels will be less determined by the status congruence of its members than it was at an earlier time, when it was operating more at the membership level.

In conclusion, the obvious fact remains to be emphasized that better techniques for the measurement of need activation in workers must be developed before this broad-stroke explanatory theory can be refined, altered, or rejected in the organizational behavior area. Only one of the studies cited—and that not yet published except in case form[39]—made an explicit attempt to assess motivation in Maslow's terms.

Research takes time, though, and those of us concerned directly with the immediate here-and-now problems of executives cannot always wait for our own and others' patient and time-consuming testing of intriguing notions of potential utility to practicing administrators. And, it seems to me, an adminis-

[39] "Century Co. (A)—(I)," *op. cit.*

trator *can* use this general way of thinking to predict, at least on a gross basis, that certain consequences are quite likely to follow from the "givens" in any situation. Such a prediction might be economically valuable to him. He might, for example, behave differently during a technological or organizational change than he would have if he were not aware of the suggested effects of low interaction opportunity and contribution potential on motivation, social structure and productivity, and satisfaction. Conversely, if he were experiencing severe problems of dissatisfaction in his work force he might seek to understand them in terms of this theory, and thereby highlight some "givens" which might be changed: interaction opportunity, for example. Such a change might cut down grievances, or even avert a strike.

Hopefully, this paper may serve to stimulate some better ways of testing the utility of Maslow's concepts for the study of organizational behavior. Certainly we are in need of integrative and operational concepts that both form the basis for replicable and comparative research and offer some utility to the practicing administrator.

## CLIMATE AND MOTIVATION: AN EXPERIMENTAL STUDY

GEORGE H. LITWIN

AUTHOR'S NOTE: The concepts and research presented in this paper are developed more fully in *Motivation and Organizational Climate* by George H. Litwin and Robert A. Stringer, Jr. (Boston: Harvard University, Graduate School of Business Administration, Division of Research, 1968).

The experimental study described here was designed to test certain hypotheses regarding the influence of leadership style and organizational climate on the motivation and behavior of organization members. The study involved the creation of several simulated business organizations. Three research objectives were established: first, to study the relationship of leadership style and organizational climate; second, to study the effects of organizational climate on individual motivation, measured through content analysis of imaginative thought; third, to identify the effects of organizational climate on such traditional variables as personal satisfaction and organizational performance.

An important methodological objective was the development of an experimental design consistent with a molar conception of organizational climate. The experimental design allowed only one variable input, leadership style, and measured the climate and motivation that were produced. Rather than focusing on the series of organizational and psychological occurrences following from

Reprinted, with permission of author, from *Organizational Climate: Explorations of a Concept,* Renato Tagiuri and George H. Litwin, eds. (Boston: Harvard University, Graduate School of Business Administration, Division of Research, 1968), pp. 169–90.

various "natural" leadership styles, an attempt was made to create three distinct styles, and to measure their effects. Less emphasis was placed on the mechanism through which leadership style influences climate than on the specific nature of the climates produced and their effects on motivation.

### Background and Theory

This study draws on recent systematic research and theory-building in the field of human motivation carried on by McClelland (1961), Atkinson (1958, 1964), and others. Atkinson (1964, pp. 240–314) has developed a formal model of motivational behavior which puts considerable emphasis on environmental determinants of motivation. The assumptions underlying the Atkinson model can be roughly restated as follows:

1. All individuals have certain basic motives or needs. These motives represent behavior potentials and influence behavior only when aroused.
2. Whether or not these motives are aroused depends upon the situation or environment perceived by the individual.
3. Particular environmental properties serve to stimulate or arouse various motives. In other words, a specific motive will not influence behavior until the motive is aroused by an appropriate environmental influence.
4. Changes in the perceived environment result in changes in the pattern of aroused motivation.
5. Each kind of motivation is directed to the satisfaction of a different kind of need. The pattern of aroused motivation determines behavior, and a change in the pattern of aroused motivation will result in a change of behavior.

Several motives have been identified and studied (see Atkinson, 1958). Among the most significant of these are: the *need for achievement* (*n* Achievement), defined as the need for success in relation to an internalized standard of excellence; the *need for affiliation* (*n* Affiliation), defined as the need for close interpersonal relationships and friendships with other people; and the *need for power* (*n* Power), defined as the need to control or influence others and to control the means of influencing others. Systematic methods for measuring the strength of these motives through content analysis of thematic apperceptive stories have been developed and validated (Atkinson, 1958).

It is useful to think that each kind of motivation (achievement, affiliation, power) has a "characteristic" kind of behavior associated with it. Achievement-motivated individuals set high but realistic goals, are likely to plan ahead, enjoy taking personal responsibility, and are desirous of prompt and concrete feedback on the results of their actions. Affiliation-motivated individuals seek warm relationships and friendship. They are not concerned with getting ahead but enjoy jobs where they can be with people and help people. Power-motivated individuals tend to seek positions of power or influence; they are politicians, executives, military officers, and teachers.

In the Atkinson model, two situational or environmental determinants of motivation are described, expectancy and incentive value. Expectancy refers to the subjective probability or likelihood of need satisfaction (or frustration). Incentive value is the amount of satisfaction or frustration the person attaches to the outcome of a behavior sequence. These variables are rather particularistic and molecular—in any real life situation, many hundreds of expectancies and incentive values might be generated. The assessment of expectancies and incentive values has proven feasible in the controlled laboratory studies that have been conducted by Atkinson and his associates (see Atkinson and Feather, 1966), but such assessment is extremely difficult, if not impossible, in complex social situations. . . .

The concept of organizational climate fits the need for a broader, more molar framework for describing the environmental influence on motivation. As defined earlier in this volume, organizational climate is the quality or property of the organizational environment that (a) is perceived or experienced by organization members and (b) influences their behavior. In this study, the term organizational climate refers specifically to the motivational properties of the organizational environment; that is, to those aspects of climate that lead to the arousal of different kinds of motivation. In Atkinson's terms, organizational climate is the summary of the *total pattern of expectancies and incentive values that exist in a given organizational setting.*

Through a series of theoretical analyses and empirical studies, a climate measurement instrument with reasonable reliability and validity was developed (see Litwin and Stringer, 1968). The instrument is a 31-item questionnaire which provides scores on the following six dimensions:[1]

1. *Structure:* the feeling the workers have about the constraints in their work situation; how many rules, regulations, and procedures there are.
2. *Responsibility:* the feeling of being your own boss; not having to double-check all your decisions.
3. *Risk:* the sense of riskiness and challenge in the job and in the work situation.
4. *Reward:* the feeling of being rewarded for a job well done; the emphasis on reward versus criticism and punishment.
5. *Warmth and Support:* the feeling of general "good fellowship" and helpfulness that prevails in the organization.
6. *Conflict:* the feeling that management isn't afraid of different opinions or conflict; the emphasis placed on settling differences here and now.

**Methodology**

Experimental Design

Three simulated business organizations were created, each with 15 members plus a president, who was a member of the research staff. The presidents were instructed regarding the leadership style they were to maintain. The particular leadership styles, and hypotheses regarding their effects, are described below.

Leadership style was the major variable input. All other factors were controlled as carefully as possible. The physical locations were identical, the technology and essential tasks were the same, and the members of the organizations were matched with respect to age, sex, background, motive patterns, and per-

[1]Dr. Herbert H. Meyer of the General Electric Company collaborated in the development of this questionnaire. The development of two later forms of this questionnaire and their respective scoring dimensions are described in more detail in Dr. Meyer's paper, "Achievement Motivation and Industrial Climates," in *Organizational Climate: Explorations of a Concept,* Renato Tagiuri and George H. Litwin, eds. (Boston: Harvard University, Graduate School of Business Administration, Division of Research, 1968).

sonality characteristics. The design represents a refinement of a classic study conducted by Lewin, Lippitt, and White (1939).

Each simulated business operated in a 100-seat classroom. The work involved the production of miniature construction models of radar towers and radar-controlled guns of various kinds from "Erector Set" parts. A typical product was comprised of from 30 to 50 parts. The businesses had three major tasks and three corresponding functional departments—production, product development, and control (or accounting). The president appointed people to each department, selected department managers, and was responsible for establishing job specifications and operating procedures.

The businesses were responsible to a simulated government agency, which released specifications for new products and product changes and requested bids on product orders of various sizes. Although each business started with the same product line, additions to and shifts in the product line were required. The simulated agency utilized a cost-plus control procedure, and the presidents were responsible for the preparation of detailed accounting statements showing material usage, labor efficiency, productivity, and contract by contract performance.

The 15 subjects assigned to each business included 13 men and 2 women. The subjects ranged in age from 18 to 29 years. All were hired (at an average hourly wage of $1.40) to participate in a study of "competitive business organizations." The 45 subjects were selected from an initial subject pool of 78 because they composed the "best" matched groups. The dimensions along which the groups were matched were: age, college major, business or other work experience, $n$ Achievement, $n$ Affiliation, and $n$ Power scores, and California Psychological Inventory personality profiles (particularly overall elevation, and elevation in the major areas). Attention was given to careful matching with respect to initial motive scores, since aroused motivation was a major output measure.

The experiment was conducted over a two-week period, comprising eight actual days of organizational life. The work day averaged about six hours. During the course of the experiment, daily observations were made and periodic readings were taken using questionnaires and psychological tests. These data were used to provide feedback to the presidents indicating to what extent they were achieving the intended leadership styles.

### Organization A: British Radar

The president placed strong emphasis on the maintenance of a formal structure. Members of the organization were assigned roles, their spheres of operation were tightly defined, and they were held responsible for the strict performance of their duties. Seriousness, order, and relative status were heavily stressed. All levels of management were encouraged to exercise position-based authority, and deviation from explicit organizational rules was punished. Communication was allowed only through strict vertical channels, was formal in nature, and was only permitted to cover matters directly related to the task. A conservative policy was maintained toward the task, the managerial credo being that reliable and consistent quality was more important than product innovation.

It was expected that in the climate thus produced the workers or participants would react against the formal structure and that boredom and aggression against the symbols of authority would be high. General job satisfaction was expected to be low.

### Organization B : Balance Radar

A loose, informal structure was endorsed by the president of Organization B. He stressed friendly, cooperative behavior, group loyalty, and teamwork, and he tried to reflect these values in his own behavior. Group decision making was encouraged at every level. Punishment was dispensed with and was replaced with a relaxed atmosphere of encouragement and assistance. To insure the absence of conflict and frustration, managers were encouraged to pay special attention to the self-development and personal well-being of the workers. Group meetings were established in which the workers could get to know one another better.

It was expected that the climate of Organization B would lead to a feeling of group unity among the members. It was assumed that this unity, being born out of affiliative norms, would be more focused on interpersonal relationships than on task excellence. Thus, it was felt that, while job satisfaction would be high, efficiency would be only moderate.

### Organization C : Blazer Radar

High productivity was valued by the president of Organization C. Each participant was encouraged to set his own goals and to take personal responsibility for results. Efforts to be innovative and creative were supported and reinforced by management. Competitive feedback was given frequently so that progress toward goals could be easily evaluated. Rewards for excellent performance were given in the form of recognition and approval, as well as in promotions and pay raises. An attempt was made to create a feeling of pride and team-work in the organization through emphasis on competition against an external standard. Members were encouraged to seek each other's help around task issues, and no formal system of communications was instituted.

The researchers expected that worker enthusiasm would be high, along with personal commitment and involvement. While productivity would therefore be high, it was felt that the emphasis on improved performance would induce the workers to report that even better performance could be achieved.

### Summary and Hypotheses

Exhibit 1 is a summary representation of the leadership style inputs for the three simulated business organizations. It represents, in generic terms, the directives given by the researchers to the presidents. The vertical divisions are a rough attempt to correlate the leadership style inputs with the dimensions of climate to which they seem most clearly related.

The researchers formulated a series of hypotheses regarding the experimental effects of climate on aroused motivation. The hypotheses, as originally stated for each organization, are set forth below:

1. The climate created in Organization A will stimulate or arouse *need for power* relative to the other two climates, and the strength of the aroused *need for achievement* and *need for affiliation* will be correspondingly reduced.

2. Relative to the other two climates, the climate of Organization B will arouse the *need for affiliation*. The *need for power* will be correspondingly reduced, and the *need for achievement* will be relatively unaffected.
3. The climate of Organization C will arouse the *need for achievement* relative to the other two climates, and the *need for affiliation* and *need for power* will not be affected.

Exhibit 2 summarizes the hypotheses concerning the motive arousal effects of the three experimentally induced climates. It should be noted that each leadership style was intended to create a climate that would make one motive more salient. Thus, the climates, and the leadership styles designed to create them, can be characterized as power-related (Organization A), affiliative (Organization B), and achieving (Organization C).

The connection between leadership style and motivation can be analyzed through a comparison of Exhibits 1 and 2. The leadership style inputs for the

**EXHIBIT 1**

Summary of Leadership Style Inputs

| Climate Dimension | Organization A (*British*) | Organization B (*Balance*) | Organization C (*Blazer*) |
|---|---|---|---|
| 1. Structure | maintain order<br><br>exercise authority and control | maintain informality | maintain informality |
| 2. Standards, Responsibility | | | set high standards for individuals and organization<br><br>encourage innovation |
| 3. Reward and Punishment | criticize poor performance<br><br>criticize deviation from rules | avoid individual punishment<br><br>give general, positive rewards (unconditional positive regard) | give individual and organizational rewards, praise, promotion<br><br>reward excellent performance |
| 4. Warmth and Support | | create warm, friendly relationships<br><br>create relaxed, easygoing atmosphere | give individual and organizational support |
| 5. Cooperation and Conflict | | stress cooperation<br><br>avoid conflicts<br><br>create warm, personal relationships with subordinates | stress cooperation in work<br><br>tolerate personal and task-related conflict |
| 6. Risk and Involvement | stress conservatism<br><br>avoid deep involvement | | stress moderate risks, create pride in organization, stress challenge, fun and excitement of work |

**EXHIBIT 2**

Summary of Hypotheses Concerning
the Motivational Effects* of Climate

| Motive | Organization A (British) | Organization B (Balance) | Organization C (Blazer) |
|---|---|---|---|
| n Achievement | reduction effect | no effect | arousal effect |
| n Affiliation | reduction effect | arousal effect | no effect |
| n Power | arousal effect | reduction effect | no effect |

*Effects are statements of change relative to other business groups, as measured by thematic apperceptive measures of motivation.

president of Organization A, for example, are meant to discourage behavior which would lead to the fulfillment of either the *need for achievement* or the *need for affiliation*. Each directive reduces either the incentive value or expectancy (or both) of satisfaction associated with these needs. Similarly, the leadership directives of Organization B generally increase the expectancy and incentive value of feelings associated with the members' *need for affiliation*. Applying the Atkinson model, one would expect a need to be aroused when the incentive and expectancy of success are high and to be reduced when they are low.

The climate model affords a level of generalization and collectivity which greatly simplifies the task of identifying motivational determinants. Rather than dealing with individual incentives and expectancies, it tries to measure the total situational influence. As previously stated, climate represents some sort of sum of the expectancies and incentive values generated in a situation. The present experiment was intended to demonstrate the relationship between climate and three specific kinds of aroused motivation. The design was an attempt to study the arousal effects of climate on one motive at a time, in order to provide clear demonstration of these relationships.

**Results and Discussion**

Effects of Leadership Style on Climate

Observation, interview, and questionnaire data revealed three distinct social and work environments emerging during the course of the experiment. Exhibit 3 summarizes the climate questionnaire data collected for each week. Statistically significant differences among the three organizations are demonstrated for all the climate dimensions.

Observation data indicate that Organization A was characterized by isolation, organizational formality, and an avoidance of conflict. The climate data indicate high scores on the Structure dimension, and low scores on Responsibility, Reward, and Warmth and Support. These data seem to reflect the feelings of the members about the climate, as indicated in responses to open-ended questions and in post-study interviews. They reported that the climate was highly constraining, conservative, cold, and formal. Conflicts (between managers and workers) were reported to be widespread but suppressed. High scores on the Conflict dimension, intended to measure the capacity to confront conflict openly, were apparently generated by the presence of considerable unresolved conflict.

## EXHIBIT 3
### Mean Climate Dimension Scores in the Three Simulated Organizations (Measured in Week I and Week II).

| Climate Dimension | Organization A (British) | | Organization B (Balance) | | Organization C (Blazer) | | F-Ratios | |
|---|---|---|---|---|---|---|---|---|
| | week I | week II | week I | week II | week I | week II | week I | week II |
| Structure | 19.8 | 21.4 | 13.4 | 15.1 | 14.3 | 16.0 | 16.1** | 20.4** |
| Responsibility | 12.6 | 11.6 | 13.9 | 15.3 | 15.6 | 16.3 | 3.0* | 15.0** |
| Risk | 9.7 | 8.5 | 10.3 | 10.3 | 11.8 | 12.4 | 4.7* | 17.8** |
| Reward | 18.0 | 15.7 | 29.4 | 27.2 | 27.7 | 22.5 | 39.7** | 58.4** |
| Warmth and Support | 15.8 | 14.6 | 26.8 | 24.8 | 22.7 | 24.2 | 62.1** | 82.2** |
| Conflict | 9.2 | 9.6 | 5.0 | 5.8 | 7.1 | 6.6 | 23.6** | 23.3** |

*p < .05.
**p < .01.

Organization B developed norms of friendliness and equality. These characteristics are demonstrated in the consistently high scores on the dimensions of Warmth and Support and Reward. The data are supported by statements of the members that the climate was relaxed, friendly, very loosely structured, and personally satisfying.

Organization C was characterized by activity, teamwork, competitiveness, and an enjoyment of work. The climate data in Exhibit 3 indicate high scores on Responsibility, Risk, Reward, and Warmth and Support. The members described the climate as loosely structured and high in rewards for individual initiative.

### Effects of Climate on Motivation

*Immediate Effects.* On the second, fifth, and seventh days of the eight-day simulation, the participants were asked to complete an individual report describing in several paragraphs their thoughts, feelings, concerns, and actions during the past several days. These descriptions were scored for $n$ Achievement, $n$ Affiliation, and $n$ Power, using standardized content analysis procedures (see Atkinson, 1958). The scores thus derived represent measures of aroused motivation, and differences among the three organizations in these motivation scores can be assumed to describe the arousal effects of the induced climates.

Exhibit 4 graphically depicts the levels of aroused motivation in the three climates. Exhibit 5 shows the results of a series of One-way Analyses of Variance of the data presented in Exhibit 4. Almost all the differences in aroused motivation among the three climates are statistically significant (as can be seen from the F-Ratios). *All the hypotheses regarding the arousal effects of the experimental climates are confirmed.* Organization A created a high level of power motivation; Organization B created a high level of affiliation motivation; and Organization C created a high level of achievement motivation.

*The hypotheses regarding the reduction effects of the experimental climates are not generally confirmed.* While Organization A did create the lowest average level of achievement motivation, as was hypothesized, there was no difference between the level of aroused affiliation motivation in Organizations A and C.

## EXHIBIT 4
### The Effects of Climate on Situationally Aroused Motivation

n Achievement          n Power          n Affiliation

High
Low
Week 1   Week 2   Week 1   Week 2   Week 1   Week 2

———— Organization A (British)
— — — Organization B (Balance)
- - - - Organization C (Blazer)

## EXHIBIT 5
### Results of One-Way Analyses of Variance
### for Aroused Motivation Scores Derived from the
### Individual Reports for Three Simulated Organizations

| Data Collected[a] | Motivation Content | F-Ratio[b] | Significance Level |
|---|---|---|---|
| First Testing | n Achievement | 3.87 | .05 |
| (Day 2) | n Affiliation | 3.49 | .05 |
| | n Power | .89 | — |
| Second Testing | n Achievement | 6.39 | .01 |
| (Day 5) | n Affiliation | 13.86 | .01 |
| | n Power | 3.74 | .05 |
| Third Testing | n Achievement | 9.98 | .01 |
| (Day 7) | n Affiliation | 11.11 | .01 |
| | n Power | 3.27 | .05 |

aThe simulated business organizations were run for 8 days, and individual reports were collected on three occasions, on Day 2, Day 5, and Day 7. The aroused motivation scores were derived from several open-ended questions requiring description of the person's thoughts, feelings, concerns, and actions.
bBased on One-Way Analyses of Variance of differences between the three organizations (N = 15 in each).

Furthermore, Organization B created, by the seventh day, a moderate but significant arousal of power motivation.

*Long-Term Effects.* A standardized thematic apperception instrument* was

*The Test of Imagination, developed by McClelland and used extensively in his studies (McClelland, 1961).

## EXHIBIT 6
### The Effects of Climate on Changes in Need for Achievement

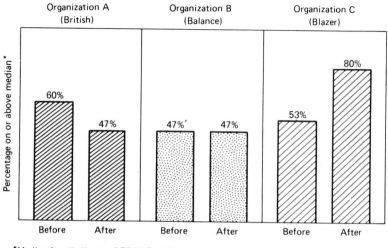

Organization A (British)    Organization B (Balance)    Organization C (Blazer)

Percentage on or above median*

Organization A: Before 60%, After 47%
Organization B: Before 47%', After 47%
Organization C: Before 53%, After 80%

*Median for all climates BEFORE = 10
Median for all climates AFTER = 7

## EXHIBIT 7
### The Effects of Climate on Changes in Need for Affiliation

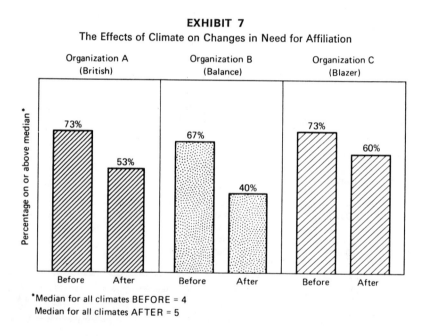

Organization A (British)    Organization B (Balance)    Organization C (Blazer)

Percentage on or above median*

Organization A: Before 73%, After 53%
Organization B: Before 67%, After 40%
Organization C: Before 73%, After 60%

*Median for all climates BEFORE = 4
Median for all climates AFTER = 5

used to measure the overall change in $n$ Achievement, $n$ Affiliation, and $n$ Power. These tests were administered several days "before" and "after" the simulation experience. The bar graphs in Exhibits 6, 7, and 8 outline the results. A One-way Analysis of Variance of the *change scores* for each of the climates showed that none of the changes was significant. All $n$ Achievement scores declined, while $n$ Affiliation and $n$ Power showed some increase.

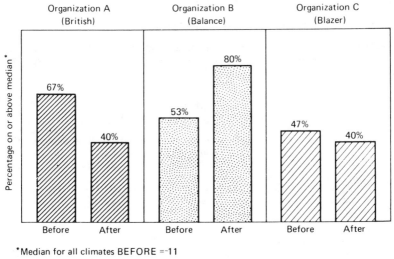

**EXHIBIT 8**

The Effects of Climate on Changes in Need for Power

| Organization A (British) | Organization B (Balance) | Organization C (Blazer) |

*Median for all climates BEFORE = -11
Median for all climates AFTER = 13

The general decline in *n* Achievement was anticipated. In hiring the subjects, the researchers introduced an array of "arousal" cues. For example, subjects were told that the simulation would be competitive, and that there were a limited number of positions available. In other words, when the subjects took the initial tests, they were excited and tended to score high in *n* Achievement.

The fact that none of the motive changes was statistically significant suggests that the climate conditions did not affect the more generalized (and stable) patterns of expectancy and thematic response elicited by the standardized instrument. The situationally specific cues in the individual report questionnaire did elicit the varying patterns of thematic response that were hypothesized. The more general cues in the standardized instrument did not elicit such patterns of varying thematic response. The length of time the participants lived and worked in the experimentally generated climates may have been the critical factor in determining the extent to which more general and stable behavior tendencies were affected. The eight-day climate experience in this study does not appear to have created lasting changes in motive strength.

Though the motive scores did not change significantly, the trend, for *n* Achievement, was in the direction that was hypothesized. Relative to the other businesses, *n* Achievement scores in Organization C showed some gain. For *n* Affiliation, there were no differences among the three businesses. For *n* Power, Organization B showed some gain.

Although the hypotheses concerning the effects of climate on before-after measures of motivation were not confirmed, other measures of personality did reveal significant before-after changes. Three scales on the California Psychological Inventory (CPI) showed significant before-after changes. These scales were: Self-Acceptance, Responsibility, and Communality. Without going into the detailed definitions of these scales, the results indicate that the members of Organization A became less content with themselves, less accepting of others, and more anxious and impatient. Members of Organization B changed little on these dimensions, and members of Organization C tended to grow in responsibility, patience, and resourcefulness.

### Effects of Climate on Satisfaction and Performance

The researchers were interested in measuring the effects of climate on job satisfaction and performance. Exhibit 9 summarizes the immediate effect of climate on these two measures.

**EXHIBIT 9**

Effects of Climate on Performance and Satisfaction

| | Organization A (British) | Organization B (Balance) | Organization C (Blazer) |
|---|---|---|---|
| Performance | | | |
| Profit; ( ) = Loss | $7.70 | $(5.30) | $72.30 |
| % Profit; ( ) = Loss | .81% | (.80%) | 11.7% |
| No. of new products developed | 4 | 6 | 8 |
| Materials-Saving Innovations (estimates) | $0.00a | $25.10 | $43.80 |
| Units Rejected by Government | 0 | 1 | 4 |
| Satisfactionb | low (3.2)* | high (6.4) | high (5.8) |

aBritish never deviated from government specifications, and their material charges were used as a base figure.

bSatisfaction as described here was measured in response to the question, "How satisfying has your job and your participation been?" on a 9-point rating scale, after 7 days of work in the organization. The numbers shown are the mean scores for the 15 people in each organization.

*An Analysis of Variance shows that the means are significantly different from each other (p < .05), and further analysis shows that the Balance mean is significantly different from the other two.

*Satisfaction.* Measures of satisfaction were collected at three points during the two-week simulation.* Satisfaction was reported to be high in Organizations B and C, and consistently low in Organization A. The sources of satisfaction in Organizations B and C may be quite different. Organization B aroused affiliation motivation, and the suggestion is that members are reporting satisfaction with the warm, friendly, relaxed atmosphere. Organization C aroused achievement motivation, and the suggestion is that members are reporting satisfaction with the challenging goals and the rewards for excellent performance.

*Performance.* Organization C significantly outperformed its two competitors. This company was able to introduce more new products, enjoyed the highest profits, and cut material costs substantially. This last factor probably contributed to the relatively high number of rejects.

Organization A enjoyed the best "quality" reputation. This is because it never attempted to "cut corners," and was very conservative in its bidding. It was not able to innovate and generally showed a marked degree of inflexibility in the changing marketplace.

*Responses to the question, "How satisfying has your job and your participation been?"

Organization B, with the poorest profit showing, did enjoy a good "quality" image. It also was able to encourage innovation. Its bids were generally competitive with those of Organization A, but Organization B was unprofitable because it supported an extremely high (unfavorable) labor variance.

It should be noted that the members of Organization A repeatedly stated that if they had been "allowed" to maintain a stable one or two product line, their efficiency and productivity would have been much improved. The structured climate prohibited organizational adaptability in this simulated marketplace.

A summary of the data on satisfaction and performance in relation to motive arousal follows:

| Organization | Motive Aroused | Satisfaction | Performance |
|---|---|---|---|
| A | n Power | Low | Low |
| B | n Affiliation | High | Low |
| C | n Achievement | High | High |

## Conclusions

1. A major conclusion of this experimental study is that distinct organizational climates can be created by varying leadership style. Such climates can be created in a short period of time, and their characteristics are quite stable.

2. Once created, these climates seem to have significant, often dramatic, effects on motivation, and correspondingly on performance and job satisfaction. Each of the three experimentally induced climates aroused a different motivational pattern.

3. Organizational climates may effect changes in seemingly stable personality traits. This conclusion is somewhat tentative. Motive strength, as measured by a standardized thematic apperceptive instrument, was not significantly affected, but certain personality dispositions, measured through a standardized empirically validated personality test, were affected by the climate.

4. These findings suggest that organizational climate is an important variable in the study of human organizations. The climate concept should aid, first, in understanding the impact of organizations on the person and the personality. If significant changes in relatively stable personality factors can be created in *less than two weeks,* then we can imagine how living in a given climate for a *period of years* could dramatically affect many aspects of personal functioning, capacity for productive effort, commitment to long-term relationships (such as friendships and marriage), etc. An understanding of climate will aid in the study of the management process, particularly with regard to the effects different styles of management have on people, on organizational performance, and on organizational health.

## References

Atkinson, J. W., ed. (1958) *Motives in Fantasy, Action, and Society.* Princeton: Van Nostrand.

Atkinson, J. W. (1964) *An Introduction to Motivation.* Princeton: Van Nostrand.

Atkinson, J. W., and N. T. Feather, eds. (1966) A *Theory of Achievement Motivation*. New York: Wiley.

Lewin, K., R. Lippitt, and R. K. White (1939) "Patterns of Aggressive Behavior in Experimentally Created 'Social Climates,' " *Journal of Social Psychology,* 10: 271–299.

Litwin, G. H. and R. A. Stringer, Jr. (1968) *Motivation and Organizational Climate.* Boston: Division of Research, Harvard Business School.

McClelland, D. C. (1961) *The Achieving Society.* Princeton: Van Nostrand.

# Achievement
# Motivation

## THAT URGE TO ACHIEVE

David C. McClelland

Most people in this world, psychologically, can be divided into two broad groups. There is that minority which is challenged by opportunity and willing to work hard to achieve something, and the majority which really does not care all that much.

For nearly twenty years now, psychologists have tried to penetrate the mystery of this curious dichotomy. Is the need to achieve (or the absence of it) an accident, is it hereditary, or is it the result of environment? Is it a single, isolatable human motive, or a combination of motives—the desire to accumulate wealth, power, fame? Most important of all, is there some technique that could give this will to achieve to people, even whole societies, who do not now have it?

While we do not yet have complete answers for any of these questions, years of work have given us partial answers to most of them and insights into all of them. There is a distinct human motive, distinguishable from others. It can be found, in fact tested for, in any group.

Let me give you one example. Several years ago, a careful study was made of 450 workers who had been thrown out of work by a plant shutdown in Erie, Pennsylvania. Most of the unemployed workers stayed home for a while and then checked back with the United States Employment Service to see if their old jobs or similar ones were available. But a small minority among them behaved differently: the day they were laid off, they started job-hunting.

They checked both the United States and the Pennsylvania Employment

Reprinted by permission from *THINK Magazine*, published by IBM, © 1966 by International Business Machines Corporation, and from the author.

Office; they studied the "Help Wanted" sections of the papers; they checked through their union, their church, and various fraternal organizations; they looked into training courses to learn a new skill; they even left town to look for work, while the majority when questioned said they would not under any circumstances move away from Erie to obtain a job. Obviously the members of that active minority were differently motivated. All the men were more or less in the same situation objectively: they needed work, money, food, shelter, job security. Yet only a minority showed initiative and enterprise in finding what they needed. Why? Psychologists, after years of research, now believe they can answer that question. They have demonstrated that these men possessed in greater degree a specific type of human motivation. For the moment let us refer to this personality characteristic as "Motive A" and review some of the other characteristics of the men who have more of the motive than other men.

Suppose they are confronted by a work situation in which they can set their own goals as to how difficult a task they will undertake. In the psychological laboratory, such a situation is very simply created by asking them to throw rings over a peg from any distance they may choose. Most men throw more or less randomly, standing now close, now far away, but those with Motive A seem to calculate carefully where they are most likely to get a sense of mastery. They stand nearly always at moderate distances, not so close as to make the task ridiculously easy, nor so far away as to make it impossible. They set moderately difficult, but potentially achievable goals for themselves, where they objectively have only about a 1-in-3 chance of succeeding. In other words, they are always setting challenges for themselves, tasks to make them stretch themselves a little.

But they behave like this only if *they* can influence the outcome by performing the work themselves. They prefer not to gamble at all. Say they are given a choice between rolling dice with one in three chances of winning and working on a problem with a one-in-three chance of solving in the time allotted, they choose to work on the problem even though rolling the dice is obviously less work and the odds of winning are the same. They prefer to work at a problem rather than leave the outcome to chance or to others.

Obviously they are concerned with personal achievement rather than with the rewards of success *per se*, since they stand just as much chance of getting those rewards by throwing the dice. This leads to another characteristic the Motive A men show—namely, a strong preference for work situations in which they get concrete feedback on how well they are doing, as one does, say in playing golf, or in being a salesman, but as one does not in teaching, or in personnel counseling. A golfer always knows his score and can compare how well he is doing with par or with his own performance yesterday or last week. A teacher has no such concrete feedback on how well he is doing in "getting across" to his students.

### The *n* Ach Men

But why do certain men behave like this? At one level the reply is simple: because they habitually spend their time thinking about doing things better. In fact, psychologists typically measure the strength of Motive A by taking samples of a man's spontaneous thoughts (such as making up a story about a picture they have been shown) and counting the frequency with which he mentions doing things better. The count is objective and can even be made these days with the help of a computer program for content analysis. It yields what is referred to technically as an individual's $n$ Ach score (for "need for Achievement"). It is not difficult to understand why people who think constantly about "doing better" are more apt to do better at job-hunting, to set moderate, achievable goals for themselves, to dislike gambling (because they get no achievement satisfaction from success), and to prefer work situations where they can tell easily whether they are improving or not. But why some people and not others come to think this way is another question. The evidence suggests it is not because they are born that way, but because of special training they get in the home from parents who set moderately high achievement goals but who are warm, encouraging and nonauthoritarian in helping their children reach these goals.

Such detailed knowledge about one motive helps correct a lot of common sense ideas about human motivation. For example, much public policy (and much business policy) is based on the simpleminded notion that people will work harder "if they have to." As a first approximation, the idea isn't totally wrong, but it is only a half-truth. The majority of unemployed workers in Erie "had to" find work as much as those with higher $n$ Ach, but they certainly didn't work as hard at it. Or again, it is frequently assumed that *any* strong motive will lead to doing things better. Wouldn't it be fair to say that most of the Erie workers were just "unmotivated"? But our detailed knowledge of various human motives shows that each one leads a person to behave in *different* ways. The contrast is not between being "motivated" or "unmotivated" but between being motivated toward A or toward B or C, etc.

A simple experiment makes the point nicely: subjects were told that they could choose as a working partner either a close friend or a stranger who was known to be an expert on the problem to be solved. Those with higher $n$ Ach (more "need to achieve") chose the experts over their friends, whereas those with more $n$ Aff (the "need to affiliate with others") chose friends over experts. The latter were not "unmotivated"; their desire to be with someone they liked was simply a stronger motive than their desire to excel at the task. Other such needs have been studied by psychologists. For instance, the need for Power is often confused with the need for Achievement because both may lead to "outstanding" activities. There is a distinct difference. People with a strong need for Power want to command attention, get recognition, and control others. They are more active in political life and tend to busy themselves primarily with controlling the channels of communication both up to the top and down to the people so that they are more "in charge." Those with high $n$ Power are not as concerned with improving their work performance daily as those with high $n$ Ach.

It follows, from what we have been able to learn, that not all "great achievers" score high in $n$ Ach. Many generals, outstanding politicians, great research scientists do not, for instance, because their work requires other personality characteristics, other motives. A general or a politician must be more concerned with power relationships, a research scientist must be able to go for long periods without the immediate feedback the person with high $n$ Ach requires, etc. On the other hand, business executives, particularly if they are in positions of real responsibility or if they are salesmen, tend to score high in $n$ Ach. This is true even in a Communist country like Poland: apparently there, as well as in a private enterprise economy, a manager succeeds if he is concerned about improving all the time, setting moderate goals, keeping track of his or the company's performance, etc.

**Motivation and Half-Truths**

Since careful study has shown that common sense notions about motivation are at best half-truths, it also follows that you cannot trust what people tell you about their motives. After all, they often get their ideas about their own motives from common sense. Thus a general may say he is interested in achievement (because he has obviously achieved), or a businessman that he is interested only in making money (because he has made money), or one of the majority of unemployed in Erie that he desperately wants a job (because he knows he needs one); but a careful check of what each one thinks about and how he spends his time may show that each is concerned about quite different things. It requires special measurement techniques to identify the presense of $n$ Ach and other such motives. Thus what people say and believe is not very closely related to these "hidden" motives which seem to affect a person's "style of life" more than his political, religious or social attitudes. Thus $n$ Ach produces enterprising men among labor leaders or managers, Republicans or Democrats, Catholics or Protestants, capitalists or Communists.

Wherever people begin to think often in $n$ Ach terms, things begin to move. Men with higher $n$ Ach get more raises and are promoted more rapidly, because they keep actively seeking ways to do a better job. Companies with many such men grow faster. In one comparison of two firms in Mexico, it was discovered that all but one of the top executives of a fast growing firm had higher $n$ Ach scores than the highest scoring executive in an equally large but slow-growing firm. Countries with many such rapidly growing firms tend to show above-average rates of economic growth. This appears to be the reason why correlations have regularly been found between the $n$ Ach content in popular literature (such as popular songs or stories in children's textbooks) and subsequent rates of national economic growth. A nation which is thinking about doing better all the time (as shown in its popular literature) actually does do better economically speaking. Careful quantitative studies have shown this to be true in Ancient Greece, in Spain in the Middle Ages, in England from 1400–1800, as well as among contemporary nations, whether capitalist or Communist, developed or underdeveloped.

Contrast these two stories for example. Which one contains more $n$ Ach? Which one reflects a state of mind which ought to lead to harder striving to improve the way things are?

*Excerpt from story A* (4th grade reader): "Don't Ever Owe a Man—The world is an illusion. Wife, children, horses and cows are all just ties of fate. They are ephemeral. Each after fulfilling his part in life disappears. So we should not clamour after riches which are not permanent. As long as we live it is wise not to have any attachments and just think of God. We have to spend our lives without trouble, for is it not time that there is an end to grievances?

So it is better to live knowing the real state of affairs. Don't get entangled in the meshes of family life."

*Excerpt from story B* (4th grade reader): "How I Do Like to Learn—I was sent to an accelerated technical high school. I was so happy I cried. Learning is not very easy. In the beginning I couldn't understand what the teacher taught us. I always got a red cross mark on my papers. The boy sitting next to me was very enthusiastic and also an outstanding student. When he found I couldn't do the problems he offered to show me how he had done them. I could not copy his work. I must learn through my own reasoning. I gave his paper back and explained I had to do it myself. Sometimes I worked on a problem until midnight. If I couldn't finish, I started early in the morning. The red cross marks on my work were getting less common. I conquered my difficulties. My marks rose. I graduated and went on to college."

Most readers would agree, without any special knowledge of the *n* Ach coding system, that the second story shows more concern with improvement than the first, which comes from a contemporary reader used in Indian public schools. In fact the latter has a certain Horatio Alger quality that is reminiscent of our own McGuffey readers of several generations ago. It appears today in the textbooks of Communist China. It should not, therefore, come as a surprise if a nation like Communist China, obsessed as it is with improvement, tended in the long run to outproduce a nation like India, which appears to be more fatalistic.

The *n* Ach level is obviously important for statesmen to watch and in many instances to try to do something about, particularly if a nation's economy is lagging. Take Britain, for example. A generation ago (around 1925) it ranked fifth among 25 countries where children's readers were scored for *n* Ach—and its economy was doing well. By 1950 the *n* Ach level had dropped to 27th out of 39 countries—well below the world average—and today, its leaders are feeling the severe economic effects of this loss in the spirit of enterprise.

### Economics and *n* Ach

If psychologists can detect *n* Ach levels in individuals or nations, particularly before their effects are widespread, can't the knowledge somehow be put to use to foster economic development? Obviously detection or diagnosis is not enough. What good is it to tell Britain (or India for that matter) that it needs more *n* Ach, a greater spirit of enterprise? In most such cases, informed observers of the local scene know very well that such a need exists, though they may be slower to discover it than the psychologist hovering over *n* Ach scores. What is needed is some method of developing *n* Ach in individuals or nations.

Since about 1960, psychologists in my research group at Harvard have been experimenting with techniques designed to accomplish this goal, chiefly among business executives whose work requires the action characteristics of people with high *n* Ach. Initially, we had real doubts as to whether we could succeed, partly because like most American psychologists we had been strongly influenced by the psychoanalytic view that basic motives are laid down in childhood and cannot really be changed later, and partly because many studies of intensive psychotherapy and counseling have shown minor if any long-term personality effects. On the other hand we were encouraged by the nonprofessionals: those enthusiasts like Dale Carnegie, the Communist ideologue or the Church missionary, who felt they could change adults and in fact seemed to be doing so. At any rate we ran some brief (7 to 10 days) "total push" training courses for businessmen, designed to increase their $n$ Ach.

**Four Main Goals**

In broad outline the courses had four main goals: (1) They were designed to teach the participants how to think, talk and act like a person with high $n$ Ach, based on our knowledge of such people gained through 17 years of research. For instance, men learned how to make up stories that would code high in $n$ Ach (i.e., how to think in $n$ Ach terms), how to set moderate goals for themselves in the ring toss game (and in life). (2) The courses stimulated the participants to set higher but carefully planned and realistic work goals for themselves over the next two years. Then we checked back with them every six months to see how well they were doing in terms of their own objectives. (3) The courses also utilized techniques for giving the participants knowledge about themselves. For instance, in playing the ring toss game, they could observe that they behaved differently from others—perhaps in refusing to adjust a goal downward after failure. This would then become a matter for group discussion and the man would have to explain what he had in mind in setting such unrealistic goals. Discussion could then lead on to what a man's ultimate goals in life were, how much he cared about actually improving performance v. making a good impression or having many friends. In this way the participants would be freer to realize their achievement goals without being blocked by old habits and attitudes. (4) The courses also usually created a group *esprit de corps* from learning about each other's hopes and fears, successes and failures, and from going through an emotional experience together, away from everyday life, in a retreat setting. This membership in a new group helps a man achieve his goals, partly because he knows he has their sympathy and support and partly because he knows they will be watching to see how well he does. The same effect has been noted in other therapy groups like Alcoholics Anonymous. We are not sure which of these course "inputs" is really absolutely essential—that remains a research question—but we were taking no chances at the outset in view of the general pessimism about such efforts, and we wanted to include any and all techniques that were thought to change people.

The courses have been given: to executives in a large American firm, and in several Mexican firms; to underachieving high school boys; and to businessmen in India from Bombay and from a small city—Kakinada in the state of Andhra Pradesh. In every instance save one (the Mexican case), it was possible to demonstrate statistically, some two years later, that the men who took the course had done better (made more money, got promoted faster, expanded their businesses faster) than comparable men who did not take the course or who took some other management course.

Consider the Kakinada results, for example. In the two years preceding the course 9 men, 18 percent of the 52 participants, had shown "unusual" enterprise in their businesses. In the 18 months following the course 25 of the men, in other words nearly 50 percent, were unusually active. And this was not due to a general upturn of business in India. Data from a control city, some forty-five miles away, show the same base rate of "unusually active" men as in Kakinada before the course—namely, about 20 percent. Something clearly happened in Kakinada: the owner of a small radio shop started a chemical plant; a banker was so successful in making commercial loans in an enterprising way that he was promoted to a much larger branch of his bank in Calcutta; the local political leader accomplished his goal (it was set in the course) to get the federal government to deepen the harbor and make it into an all-weather port; plans are far along for establishing a steel rolling mill, etc. All this took place without any substantial capital input from the outside. In fact, the only costs were for four 10-day courses plus some brief follow-up visits every six months. The men are raising their own capital and using their own resources for getting business and industry moving in a city that had been considered stagnant and unenterprising.

The promise of such a method of developing achievement motivation seems very great. It has obvious applications in helping underdeveloped countries, or "pockets of poverty" in the United States, to move faster economically. It has great potential for businesses that need to "turn around" and take a more enterprising approach toward their growth and development. It may even be helpful in developing more $n$ Ach among low-income groups. For instance, data show that lower-class Negro Americans have a very low level of $n$ Ach. This is not surprising. Society has systematically discouraged and blocked their achievement striving. But as the barriers to upward mobility are broken down, it will be necessary to help stimulate the motivation that will lead them to take advantage of new opportunities opening up.

### Extreme Reactions

But a word of caution: Whenever I speak of this research and its great potential, audience reaction tends to go to opposite extremes. Either people remain skeptical and argue that motives can't really be changed, that all we are doing is dressing Dale Carnegie up in fancy "psychologese," or they become converts and want instant course descriptions by return mail to solve their local motivational problems. Either response is unjustified. What I have described here in a few pages has taken 20 years of patient research effort, and hundreds of thousands of dollars in basic research costs. What remains to be done will involve even larger sums and more time for development to turn a promising idea into something of wide practical utility.

### Encouragement Needed

To take only one example, we have not yet learned how to develop $n$ Ach really well among low-income groups. In our first effort—a summer course for bright underachieving 14-year-olds—we found that boys from the middle class improved steadily in grades in school over a two-year period, but boys from the lower class showed an improvement after the first year followed by a drop back to their beginning low grade average [see the chart on the following page]. Why? We speculated that it was because they moved back into an environment in which neither parents nor friends encouraged achievement or upward mobility. In other words, it isn't enough to change a man's motivation if the environment in which he lives doesn't support at least to some degree his new efforts. Negroes striving to rise out of the ghetto frequently confront this

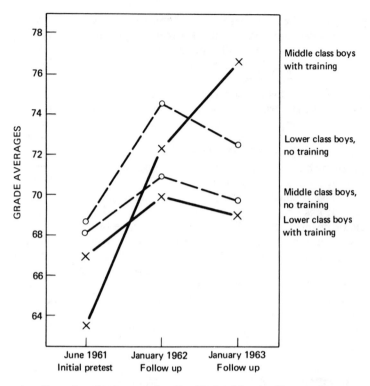

In a Harvard study, a group of underachieving 14-year-olds was given a six-week course designed to help them do better in school.

Some of the boys were also given training in achievement motivation, or *n* Ach (solid lines). As graph reveals, the only boys who continued to improve after a two-year period were the middle-class boys with the special *n* Ach training.

Psychologists suspect the lower-class boys dropped back, even with *n* Ach training, because they returned to an environment in which neither parents nor friends encouraged achievement.

problem: they are often faced by skepticism at home and suspicion on the job, so that even if their *n* Ach is raised, it can be lowered again by the heavy odds against their success. We must learn not only to raise *n* Ach but also to find methods of instructing people in how to manage it, to create a favorable environment in which it can flourish.

Many of these training techniques are now only in the pilot testing stage. It will take time and money to perfect them, but society should be willing to invest heavily in them in view of their tremendous potential for contributing to human betterment.

# MOTIVATION OF RESEARCH AND DEVELOPMENT ENTREPRENEURS: DETERMINANTS OF COMPANY SUCCESS[1]

HERBERT A. WAINER
IRWIN M. RUBIN

In an attempt to associate need for achievement ($n$ Ach) and economic development, McClelland (1961) looks to the entrepreneur as the one who translates $n$ Ach into economic development. The entrepreneur in McClelland's scheme is "the man who organizes the firm (the business unit) and/or increases its productive capacity [p. 205]."

The present authors' aim was to test McClelland's macro theory of economic growth at the micro level of organizational performance. The principal interest in considering McClelland's work stems from his discussions of who entrepreneurs are and of their different behavioral styles predicted from differences in need patterns. McClelland's underlying assumption is that entrepreneurs have a high $n$ Ach and that in business situations this high $n$ Ach will lead them to behave in certain ways and have certain tendencies.

Based on McClelland's discussion, the present authors raised the proposition that the degree to which an entrepreneur is motivated by $n$ Ach directly influences his skill as an entrepreneur and consequently his enterprise's performance. The major hypothesis to be tested concerns the relationship between an entrepreneur's level of $n$ Ach and his company's performance.

Schrage (1965), in testing the relationship between the entrepreneur's $n$ Ach and company performance, reported that companies run by entrepreneurs who have a high $n$ Ach tend to have either high profits or losses ($\pm 3\%$ of sales), while those run by low $n$ Ach entrepreneurs tend to have low profits or losses ($\leq 3\%$ of sales). Reanalysis of his data by the present authors sheds considerable doubt on the validity of his findings. The primary source of doubt was a

Abridged from the *Journal of Applied Psychology*, Vol. 53, No. 3 (1969) by permission of the publisher and author.

[1]The research presented in this paper was supported in part by grants from the Massachusetts Institute of Technology Center for Space Research and by the National Aeronautics and Space Administration (NsG-235 and NsG-496). However the findings and views reported are those of the authors and do not necessarily reflect those of the supporting agencies. This work was done in part at the Massachusetts Institute of Technology Computation Center.

The authors wish to acknowledge the work done by Charles W. McLaughlin, a master's degree candidate in the Massachusetts Institute of Technology, Sloan School of Management, in the collection of data for this paper.

discrepancy between the scores Schrage used for $n$ Ach and those subsequently derived when the same protocols were rescored by the Motivation Research Group at Harvard. The fact that his results departed markedly from established theory further substantiates this concern.

In addition to the relationship between $n$ Ach and company performance, the authors were interested in the interrelationships among three needs, $n$ Ach, need for power ($n$ Pow), and the need for affiliation ($n$ Aff), with respect to company performance. $n$ Pow is defined by Atkinson (1958) as "that disposition, directing behavior toward satisfactions contingent upon the control of the means of influencing another person [p. 105]."

$n$ Aff is concerned with the establishment, maintenance, or restoration of positive affective relationships with other people, that is, friendships. Statements of liking or desire to be liked, accepted, or forgiven are manifestations of this motive (Atkinson, 1958). McClelland's (1961) discussion of the joint product of $n$ Pow and $n$ Aff in relation to dictatorship stimulated this aspect of the inquiry. He found that $n$ Pow was not related to economic growth but was related to style of leadership. More specifically, the combination of a high $n$ Pow and a low $n$ Aff was associated with the tendency of a country to resort to totalitarian methods as a style of leadership.

The present authors propose that $n$ Ach has behavioral manifestations different than either $n$ Pow or $n$ Aff in terms of the individual's relationships with people. $n$ Pow and $n$ Aff are interpersonally oriented needs. Implicit in their definitions is the existence of other human beings whom the $n$ Pow or $n$ Aff motivated individual can influence and control, or with whom he can be friends. $n$ Ach, on the other hand, seems to be a more internalized need. The $n$ Ach motivated individual may need other people to help him satisfy his $n$ Ach, but the nature of his relationship with them, or more appropriately his effectiveness with them, will be determined by other needs. The authors suggest that $n$ Ach is a primary consideration determining noninterpersonally related behavior that leads to high company performance. $n$ Pow and $n$ Aff are primary considerations determining interpersonal behavior that affects company performance. $n$ Pow and $n$ Aff, then, can be looked upon as having strong implications as determinants of management style.

Numerous other attempts have been made to identify those personality traits which differentiate leaders from nonleaders or effective leaders from ineffective leaders. These studies have, in general, failed to find any consistent pattern of differentiating traits. In a broad sense, the present research is analogous to these prior efforts in that it seeks to explain company performance on the basis of certain personality characteristics of the president. Steps were taken, however, in anticipation of two potential problem areas: (*a*) that personality description and measurement themselves are not yet adequate; (*b*) that the groups studied have usually been markedly different from one another and this may have concealed a relation between personality and the exercise of leadership that would have appeared within a more homogeneous set of groups or situations.

The major personality variable of interest in the present study is the need for achievement. On the basis of the existing body of research, McClelland's version of the Thematic Apperception Test (TAT) was deemed a reliable means of measuring $n$ Ach (Atkinson, 1958; McClelland, 1961). With respect to the second problem area, a very homogeneous set of groups has been examined, thus mitigating the potential influence of the "situation."

For these reasons, the focus in this study was upon the new, small, technically based enterprise. The entrepreneur president of such a company has placed himself in a situation where his $n$ Ach, to the extent that it exists, can readily be translated into concrete behavior. He starts the company, hires the people, and motivates them, sells, plans, takes risks, and so on. It is his personality and motivation that mold the company in its every aspect. Furthermore, in such situations, the entrepreneur's efforts and decisions are likely to be very important in determining the initial success of the venture.

## Method

Fifty-one small technically based companies in the Boston area comprised the sample. All were at least 4 but less than 10 years old at the time of the study and all were "spin-offs" from one of the Massachusetts Institute of Technology research laboratories or industrial laboratories around the Boston area. They ranged in business activities from service, such as computer software development, to manufacturing, such as special purpose computers and welded modules. Company and entrepreneurial personality information were gathered from the entrepreneur president. The typical entrepreneur, based on the central tendencies for the total sample of entrepreneurs, was approximately 36 years of age when he started his new enterprise, was educated to the master's degree level, and had considerable experience at a technically advanced research laboratory prior to starting his new enterprise. Among the information gathered were company

**TABLE 1**
Means, Medians, and Ranges of Variables Measured

| Variable | M | Mdn | Range |
|---|---|---|---|
| $n$ Ach | 5.9 | 5.0 | −5 to 18 |
| $n$ Pow | 9.7 | 9.5 | 0 to 19 |
| $n$ Aff | 3.5 | 3.0 | 0 to 16 |
| Growth rate | .40 | .375 | 0.0 to 2.10 |

yearly sales figures and scores on McClelland's version of the TAT for each entrepreneur. The yearly sales figures were used as the basis for determining the growth rate, defined in detail below. The index of performance was derived from the growth rate. The TATs were scored for $n$ Ach, $n$ Pow, and $n$ Aff by the Motivation Research Group at Harvard University. The resulting scores were the basis for analysis of the strength of various needs in relation to performance.[2]

Growth rate is defined as follows: *annual increase in the logarithm of sales volume between the second and most recent year reported.* For example, Company A is 7 yr. old. Its second-year sales were $100,000 and its last year (seventh) sales were $950,000. These two sales values are plotted on

[2]Average intercoder reliabilities of scores from the Motivation Research Group are in the high .80 range.

semilog paper. The growth rate is indicated by the percent rate of change from year to year. This is, of course, constant over the 7 years. The growth rate in this case would be approximately .56. Table 1 summarizes the general characteristics of the four variables with which this paper is concerned. The method of analysis in all cases was a comparison of high, moderate, and low groups.

## Results

### Need Strength versus Company Performance

The major hypothesis in this study predicts a direct and positive relationship between an entrepreneur's $n$ Ach and the performance of his company. No directional hypotheses were specified concerning the relationships between $n$ Pow, $n$ Aff, and company performance.[3]

Referring to Table 2, it can be seen that, within the range of moderate to high $n$ Ach, a very marked positive relationship exists between $n$ Ach and company performance. The growth rate of those companies led by entrepreneurs with a high $n$ Ach was almost 250% higher (.73 versus .21) than those companies led by entrepreneurs with a moderate $n$ Ach. Here again, however, the relationship is not purely linear since the low $n$ Ach group has a mean performance score slightly *higher* than the moderate $n$ Ach group but still significantly lower than the high $n$ Ach group.

$n$ Pow, as can be seen from Table 2, is completely unrelated to company performance. $n$ Aff, on the other hand, exhibits a mildly negative, nonlinear, relationship to company performance. The data were then examined to see if the observed relationship between $n$ Ach and $n$ Aff influenced the relationship found between $n$ Ach and performance.[4] No such contamination was found. Of those who were classified in the low $n$ Aff group ($n = 13$), only six fell into the high $n$ Ach group. $n$ Ach, in other words, directly affects company performance, independent of its relationship to $n$ Aff.

The results of this section are summarized graphically in Figure 1. The percentage of companies within each subgroup (high, moderate, low), whose performance is above that of the median for the total sample of entrepreneurs, is plotted for each of the needs. Seventy-nine percent of those companies led by entrepreneurs whose $n$ Ach was high had a growth rate which was above the median for the total sample of entrepreneurs.

### Joint Products of Needs versus Performance

The previous section focused on variations in company performance resulting from each of the three needs ($n$ Ach, $n$ Pow, and $n$ Aff) taken singularly. The aim in this section is to explore the question of whether or not any *pattern* of need strengths appears to be associated with high company performance. In examining the data, it was noticed that, in addition to the very wide differences

[3]The following are the Kendall Tau correlations between the three needs and company performance (growth rate). $n$ Ach versus performance: $T = .15$, $p < .08$, $N = 51$ (one-tailed). $n$ Pow versus performance: $T = .05$, $p < .64$, $N = 51$. $n$ Aff versus performance: $T = -.11$, $p < .28$, $N = 51$.

[4]The three needs were found to be related: $n$ Ach was positively related to $n$ Pow and negatively related to $n$ Aff; $n$ Pow was negatively related to $n$ Aff.

**TABLE 2**

Relationship between *n* Ach, *n* Pow, and *n* Aff
and Growth Rate

| Need | Code for Mann-Whitney U results[a] | Strength | Mean growth rate |
|---|---|---|---|
| | A | High ($\geq$ 9) $N = 14$ | .73 |
| *n* Ach | B | Moderate ($4 \geq X \leq 8$) $N = 19$ | .21 |
| | C | Low ($\leq$ 3) $N = 18$ | .36 |
| | A | High ($\geq$ 13) $N = 15$ | .38 |
| *n* Pow | B | Moderate ($8 \geq X \leq 12$) $N = 19$ | .47 |
| | C | Low ($\leq$ 7) $N = 17$ | .36 |
| | A | High ($\geq$ 4) $N = 20$ | .33 |
| *n* Aff | B | Moderate ($2 \geq X \leq 3$) $N = 18$ | .30 |
| | C | Low ($\leq$ 1) $N = 13$ | .67 |

[a]Results of Mann-Whitney *U* tests: *n* Ach versus growth rate: A versus B. $p < .0001$; A versus C, $p < .006$; B versus C, $p < .08$, one tailed. *n* Pow versus growth rate: A versus B, $p < .80$; A versus C, $p < .90$; B versus C, $p < .80$, two-tailed. *n* Aff versus growth rate: A versus B, $p < .81$; A versus C. $p < 16$; B versus C, $p < .10$, two-tailed.

in company performance noted *between* high, moderate, and low *n* Ach groups, there existed substantial variations in company performance *within* each of these three groups. In other words, although the high *n* Ach group exhibited very high performance in comparison with the moderate and low *n* Ach groups, the range of performance scores *within* the high *n* Ach group was from .14 to 2.10. Similar within-group ranges were observed in the other two *n* Ach groupings.

An attempt was made, therefore, to determine whether these within-group variations could be attributed to variations in the strengths of the other two needs being investigated, *n* Pow and *n* Aff. The authors have further split the samples into high versus low performers (at the median performance score *within* each *n* Ach group) and compared levels of *n* Pow and *n* Aff within each of these new subgroups.

The following patterns emerge from the data. . . . Within the low *n* Ach group, variations in performance are unaffected by variations in *n* Pow or *n* Aff. Within the moderate *n* Ach group, *n* Pow is identical for high versus low performers, while high performers within this group have a significantly higher *n* Aff. Finally, within the high *n* Ach group, *n* Aff is identical for high versus low performers, while high performers within this group have a significantly lower *n* Pow.

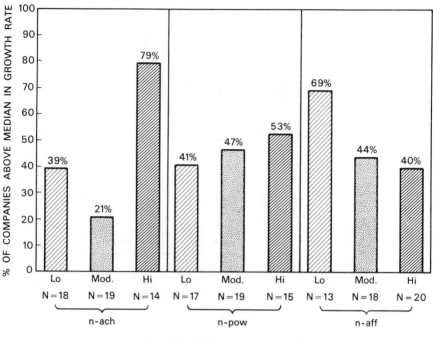

**FIGURE 1**

Percentage of Companies Above Median Growth Rate as a Function of the President's Achievement, Power, and Affiliation Motivation

COMPANY PRESIDENTS MOTIVATION

In summary, the *highest performing companies* in this sample were led by entrepreneurs who exhibited a high *n* Ach and a moderate *n* Pow. Those entrepreneurs who had a high *n* Ach coupled with a high *n* Pow performed less well than their high *n* Ach counterparts who exhibited only a moderate level of *n* Pow.[5] Within the moderate *n* Ach group, higher performing companies were led by entrepreneurs who had a high *n* Aff.

## Discussion

The major hypothesis tested in this study predicted a positive relationship between an entrepreneur's level of *n* Ach and his company's performance. The authors' findings strongly support the conclusion that high *n* Ach is associated with high company performance, but the relationship between *n* Ach and performance is not linear across the entire range of *n* Ach scores. The relationship is markedly linear for the entrepreneurs whose *n* Ach is moderate to high. However, these entrepreneurs who scored low in *n* Ach were not significantly lower performers than those whose *n* Ach was moderate.

[5]When the authors use the phrases "moderate *n* Pow" or "high *n* Pow," they are using as their reference point the distribution of scores observed in this study sample. Their specification, for example, of *high n* Pow as being $\geq$ 13.0 was made *prior* to the analyses under discussion in this section. Consequently, classification of a mean *n* Pow of 13.1 as high and a mean *n* Pow of 9.4 as moderate is consistent with their a priori definitions.

In an attempt to explain this nonlinearity it seems reasonable to assume that other needs or factors are influencing the entrepreneurial behavior of individuals who are not moderate to high in their level of $n$ Ach. It is extremely likely that some threshold level of $n$ Ach is necessary before one could assume that the strength of the need is significantly affecting the individual's behavior. In addition, it is obvious that the authors do not see $n$ Ach as being the only (or for that matter the most important) factor that influences company performance. They are arguing, however, that where the need exists in sufficient strength to influence entrepreneurial behavior significantly, company performance in general will improve.

A secondary aim in this study was to explore the question of whether a certain pattern or combination of needs was most often associated with high performance. In the introduction to this paper, it was suggested than $n$ Pow and $n$ Aff were needs whose behavioral manifestations were interpersonal in character. Satisfaction of these two needs, by definition, involves relationships with other people. $n$ Ach, on the other hand, is much more individualistic in character. Satisfaction of one's $n$ Ach, although often involving contact with other people, has behavioral manifestations which are qualitatively different in nature than either $n$ Pow or $n$ Aff.

The results of this study suggest that the combination of a high $n$ Ach and a moderate $n$ Pow characterizes the highest performing companies in the sample. In other words, a high (as opposed to moderate) level of $n$ Pow appeared to counterbalance to some extent the positive benefits of a high level of $n$ Ach.

One possible explanation for this finding lies in the relationship between $n$ Pow and various styles of leadership. The lower an individual's $n$ Pow, the more permissive or laissez-faire his style of leadership, the higher his $n$ Pow, the more autocratic or authoritarian his style of leadership. The middle of the $n$ Pow spectrum represents a mixed influence of the two extreme styles which is best described as democratic.[6] Prior research (Lippitt & White, 1958) has suggested that in certain situations the most effective leadership style is democratic and that performance of groups controlled in this manner is better than that of groups controlled by either of the other two styles.

Somewhat more difficult to explain is the finding concerning the positive differential effect on company performance, within the moderate $n$ Ach group, of a high versus low $n$ Aff level. It may be that for those individuals who have only a moderate level of $n$ Ach, a high level of $n$ Aff enables them to form close interpersonal relationships with their colleagues. In this way, the moderate $n$ Ach individual may be able to acquire the assistance he needs from his colleagues, some of whom may well have a higher level of $n$ Ach than he himself has.

Interpretations in this area of need combinations must be viewed, at this point, as speculative and suggestive of further research. Analysis of the results of this study indicates that more complex relationships do have to be examined if a realistic view of performance determined by personality is to be gained. Future research should include replications of this study and the use of larger samples for the investigation of these hypotheses.

---

[6]The authors have assumed, of course, that high $n$ Pow leaders are more likely to exercise an autocratic style of leadership and low $n$ Pow leaders a laissez-faire style.

## References

Atkinson, J. W. *Motives in Fantasy, Action, and Society.* Princeton, N.J.: Van Nostrand, 1958.

Lippitt, R. and R. K. White. "An Experimental Study of Leadership and Group Life." In *Readings in Social Psychology.* New York: Holt, Rinehart & Winston, 1958.

McClelland, D. C. *The Achieving Society.* Princeton, N.J.: Van Nostrand, 1961.

Schrage, H. "The R & D Entrepreneur: Profile of Success." *Harvard Business Review,* 1965.

# The Dynamics of Power
# and Affiliation Motivation

## THE TWO FACES OF POWER

David C. McClelland

For over twenty years now I have been studying a particular human motive—the need to Achieve, the need to do something better than it has been done before. As the investigation advanced, it became clear that the need to Achieve (technically $n$ Achievement) was one of the keys to economic growth because men who are concerned about doing things better have become active entrepreneurs and created the growing business firms which are the foundation stones of a developing economy (see McClelland, 1961). Some of these heroic entrepreneurs could be regarded as leaders in the sense that their activities established the economic base for the rise of a civilization, but they seldom were leaders of men. The reason is simple: $n$ Achievement is a one man game which need not involve other people at all. Boys who are high in $n$ Achievement like to build things or make things with their hands, presumably because they can tell easily whether they have done a good job of work. A boy who is trying to build as tall a tower as possible out of blocks can measure very precisely and easily how well he has done. He is in no way dependent on someone else to tell him how good it is. So in the pure case the man with high $n$ Achievement is not dependent on the approval of others; he is concerned with improving his own performance, and as an ideal type, he is most easily conceived as a sales-

---

Reprinted by permission of the author and publisher. Copyright by the Board of Editors of the *Journal of International Affairs*, reprinted from Vol. 24, No. 1.

This paper has been prepared as a commentary on the lack of leadership in contemporary America as noted by John Gardner in his paper, "The anti-leadership vaccine."

man or an owner-manager of a small business, where he is in a position to watch carefully whether his performance is improving.

But in studying such men and their role in economic development, I ran head on into problems of leadership, power and social influence which n Ach clearly did not prepare a man to cope with. For as a one-man firm grows larger, it obviously requires some division of function, some organizational structure. Organizational structure involves relationships among people, and sooner or later someone in the organization has to pay attention to getting people to work together, or to dividing up the tasks to be performed, or to supervising the work of others, and so on. Yet it is fairly clear that a high need to Achieve does not equip a man to deal effectively with managing human relationships. For instance, a salesman with high n Achievement does not necessarily make a good sales manager. For as a manager, his task is not to sell, but to inspire others to sell which involves a different set of personal goals and different strategies for reaching them. I shall never forget the moment when I learned that the president of one of the most successful achievement-oriented firms we had been studying scored exactly zero in n Achievement! Up to this point I had fallen into the easy assumption that a man with a high need to Achieve does a better job, gets promoted faster, and ultimately ends up as president of a company. How then was it possible for a man to be head of an obviously achieving company and yet score so low in n Achievement? At the time I was tempted to dismiss the finding as measurement error, but now I see it as a dramatic way of calling attention to the fact that stimulating achievement motivation in others requires a different motive and a different set of skills than wanting achievement satisfaction for oneself. For some time now our research on achievement motivation has shifted its focus from the individual with high n Achievement to the climate which encourages him and rewards him for doing well (see Litwin & Stringer, 1968). For no matter how high a person's need to Achieve may be, he cannot succeed if he has no opportunities, if the organization keeps him from taking initiative or does not reward him if he does. As a simple illustration of this point, we have found in our recent research in India that it did no good to raise achievement motivation through training if the man was not in charge of his business. That is to say, even though he might now be "all fired up" and prepared to be more active and entrepreneurial, he could not in fact do much so long as he was working for someone else who had the final say as to whether any of the things he wanted to do would in fact be done. In short, the man with high n Achievement seldom can act alone, even though he might like to. He is caught up in an organizational context in which he is being managed, controlled or directed by others. Thus to understand better what happens to him, we must shift our attention to those who are managing him, to those who are concerned about organizational relationships, to the leaders of men.

Since managers are primarily concerned with influencing others, it seems obvious that they should be characterized by a high need for Power and that by studying the power motive we could learn something about the way effective managerial leaders work. That is to say, if A gets B to do something, A is at one and the same time a leader (i.e., he is leading B), and exercising some kind of influence or power over B. Thus leadership and power are two closely related concepts and if we want to understand effective leadership better, we may begin by studying the power motive in thought and action. What arouses thoughts of being powerful? What kinds of strategies does the man employ who thinks constantly about gaining power? Are some strategies more effective than others in influencing people? In pursuing such a line of inquiry, we are adopting an approach which worked well in another area. Studying the achievement motive led to a better understanding of business entrepreneurship. Analogously, studying the power motive complex may help us understand managerial leadership better.

But there is one striking difference between the two motive systems which is apparent from the outset. In general, individuals are proud of having a high need to Achieve, but dislike being told they have a high need for Power. What is it about the concern for power which distinguishes it from most other motives which are socially approved? It is a fine thing to be concerned about doing things well (*n* Achievement) or making friends (n Affiliation), but why is it reprehensible to be concerned about having influence over others (*n* Power)? The vocabulary behavioral scientists use to describe power relations is strongly negative in tone. Consider one of the major works that deals with people concerned with power, *The Authoritarian Personality*. In it they are pictured as harsh, sadistic, fascist, Machiavellian, prejudiced, and neurotic. Ultimately, concern for power leads to Nazi-type dictatorships, to the slaughter of innocent Jews, to political terror, police states, brainwashing and exploitation of helpless masses who have lost their freedom. Even less political terms for power have a distinctively negative flavor: dominance-submission, competition, zero sum game (if I win, you lose). It is small wonder that people don't particularly like being told they have a high need for Power.

The negative reactions to the exercise of power became vividly apparent to me in the course of our recent research efforts to develop achievement motivation (McClelland and Winter, 1969). Out of our extensive research on the achievement motive, we conceived of ways in which it might be increased through short intensive courses. At first people were interested and curious. It seemed like an excellent idea to develop a fine motive like *n* Achievement, particularly among under-achievers in school or relatively inactive businessmen in underdeveloped countries. But most people were also skeptical. Could we really do it? It turned out that many remained interested only so long as they were really skeptical about our ability to change motivation. As soon as it became apparent that we could indeed change people, and in a relatively short period of time, then many observers started to worry. Was it really ethical to change people's personalities? Weren't we brainwashing them? What magical power were we employing to change an underlying personality disposition which had presumably been laid down in childhood and laboriously stabilized over the years? We then became aware of the fundamental dilemma confronting anyone who gets involved in the "influence game." He may think that he is exercising leadership, i.e., influencing people for their own good, but if he succeeds, he is likely to be accused of manipulating people. We thought our influence attempts were benign. In fact we were a little proud of ourselves. After all, weren't we giving people a chance to be more successful at business and in school? Yet we soon found ourselves attacked as potentially dangerous "brainwashers." To some extent ordinary psychotherapy avoids these accusations because the power the therapist has seems to be relatively weak. Therapy doesn't work very well or very quickly, and when it does the therapist can say that the patient did most of the work himself.

But consider the following anecdote. Johnny was a bright but lazy sixth grade student in math. His parents were quite concerned that he was not motivated to work harder and were delighted when the psychologists explained that they had some new techniques for development motivation that they would like to expose Johnny to. After all, he spent practically all of his evenings watching TV and the parents felt that he could surely be employing his time better. Soon after the motivation training regime started in school, they noticed a dramatic change in his behavior. Now he spent all his time studying math. He never watched television but stayed up late working long hours and soon got way ahead of his class in advanced mathematics. Then the parents began to worry. What in the world had the psychologists done to their Johnny to produce such a dramatic change in his behavior? They wanted him changed, but not *that* much. They reacted very negatively to the power that the psychologists seemed to have had over him.

An experience like this was enough to make us yearn for the detached scientist, consulting expert role so vividly described by John Gardner (1965) as the preferred role for more and more young people today. For the scientist ordinarily does not intervene (i.e., exercise power) directly in human or social affairs. He observes the interventions of others, reports, analyses, and advises, but never takes responsibility himself. In this case our research had led us to intervene actively and even that small, relatively benign exercise of influence led to some pretty negative responses from the public. My own view is that young people avoid leadership roles not so much because their professors brainwash them into believing it is better to be a professional, but because in our society in our time and perhaps in all societies at all times, the exercise of power is often viewed very negatively. People are suspicious of a man who wants power. He is suspicious of himself. He doesn't want to be in a position where he might be thought to be seeking power and influence in order to exploit others.

Yet clearly this negative face of power is only part of the story. Power must have a positive face too. For after all, people cannot help influencing each other. Organizations cannot function without some kind of authority relationships. Surely it is necessary and desirable for some people to concern themselves with management, with working out influence relationships that make it possible to achieve the goals of the group. A man who is consciously concerned about working out the proper channels of influence is surely better able to contribute to group goals than a man who neglects or represses power problems and lets working relationships grow up higgledy-piggledy. So our problem is to try to understand these two faces of power. When is it bad and when is it good? Why is it often perceived as dangerous? What aspects are viewed favorably? When is it proper and when improper, to exercise influence? Are there different kinds of power?

It will not be possible to answer all of these questions definitively, but recent research on the power motive as it functions in human beings will help us understand the two faces of power a little better. Let us begin with the curious fact that turned up in the course of what are technically "arousal" studies. When an experimenter gets interested in a new motive, he ordinarily begins to study it by trying to arouse it in a variety of ways to see how it influences what a person thinks about. Then these alterations in thought content are worked into a code or a scoring system which will capture the extent to which he is concerned about achievement or power or whatever motive state has been aroused. Thus, Veroff (1957), when he began the study of the power motive, asked student candidates for office to write imaginative stories while they were waiting for the election returns to be counted. He contrasted these stories with those written by other students who were not candidates for office. That is, he assumed that the students waiting to hear if they had been elected were in a state of aroused power motivation and that their stories would reflect this fact as contrasted with stories of students not in such a state. From the differences in story content he derived a coding system for $n$ Power (need for Power) which centered on the greater concern for having influence over others present in the stories of student candidates for election. Later arousal studies by Uleman (1965) and Winter (1967) further defined the essence of $n$ Power as a concern for having a *strong impact on others*. That is, when power motivation was aroused in a variety of ways, students thought more often about people having strong impact on others. This is true not only for student candidates for office awaiting election returns, but also for student experimenters who are about to demonstrate their power over subjects by employing a winning strategy in a competitive game that they had been taught beforehand (Uleman, 1965).

What surprised us greatly was to discover that drinking alcohol also increased such power thoughts in men. This discovery was one of those happy accidents that sometimes occurs in scientific laboratories when two studies thought to be unrelated are proceeding side by side. Certainly when we began studying the effects of social drinking on fantasy, we had no idea that alcohol would increase power fantasies. Yet we early found that it increased sex and aggression fantasies and one day it occurred to us that certain types of exploitative sex and certainly aggression were instances of "having impact" on others and therefore could be considered part of an $n$ Power scoring definition. We later found that drinking in small amounts increases the frequency of power thoughts even outside the field of sex and aggression altogether. This finding by itself did not at first mean very much to us, but it served to focus attention on two further questions. What was the relationship between $n$ Power and drinking! And is it worthwhile to distinguish between a more primitive sex and aggression power imagery, as aroused by heavy drinking, and a more socialized type of interpersonal influence aroused in other ways? Winter (1967) conducted an extensive study of power fantasies and related activities among college students that shed some light on both of these questions. He found that some students with high $n$ Power scores did in fact tend to drink more heavily, and that some of them held more offices in student organizations. The interesting fact was that these were not the same people. That is, a student with high $n$ Power either drank more heavily or he was a club officer, though he was usually not both, possibly because heavy drinking would prevent him from being elected to a responsible office. In other words, Winter identified alternative manifestations of the power drive—either heavy drinking or holding office. Clearly these activities appear to lie along some dimension of inhibition of socialization, with drinking representing a less socialized, more primitive expression of power whereas holding public office represents a more socialized form of having impact.

Other studies have added to this picture, and while it is still not altogether clear, its main outlines can be readily sketched. There are two faces of power. One might be described as a kind of unsocialized concern for personal dominance. It is aroused in men by drinking alcohol and probably by other techniques like threat of physical violence that have not yet been tested experimentally. At the fantasy level, it expresses itself in terms of thoughts of exploitative sex and physical aggression. At the level of action, it leads to heavier drinking, more trouble from drinking, more casual sexual contacts (in which the goal seems to be sexual exploitation rather than love), and a tendency to watch TV shows dealing with crime and violence.

The other face of the power motive is more socialized. It is aroused by the possibility of winning an election, or the expectancy that one will be able to win over another in a competitive game. At the fantasy level it expresses itself in terms of more conventional thoughts of persuasion and interpersonal influence. So far as activities are concerned, people concerned with the more socialized aspect of power participate more often in competitive sports, even as adults, and end up more often as officers in the organizations which they join. It is useful to think of the two aspects of the power motive as having developed at different points in the life of a child. The more direct and less socialized form of expressing .power, as in direct physical aggression, appears to occur earlier as the child tries to get what he wants simply by pushing another child out of the way. Later on he must learn more acceptable and more inhibited means of influencing other people.

Certain characteristics of the power syndrome cannot readily be classified as belonging to either aspect of it exclusively. Consider for example the control of resources. If someone wants to have impact on others, he should accumulate resources like physical strength, wealth or information which can be used to impress other people or control what they do. If he is stronger, he can threaten to beat up someone if he doesn't do what he says. If he is richer, he can reward the other person for compliance or punish him by withdrawal of funds for noncompliance. Or if he knows something that the other person does not know, he can use this information to influence what happens to the other person. In his study of university students Winter employed a measure of what he called *prestige possessions* which included such things as a refrigerator, a well-equipped bar, certain types of collegiate "artifacts" (like pins, beer mugs, etc.), owning a motorcycle, and so on. He found that ownership of prestige supplies was significantly correlated with the *n* Power score, but more significantly it belonged to the cluster of activities which we have described as expressing unsocialized personal power desires. At least at the college level, control of these resources goes with exploitative sex and heavy drinking. Yet a moment's reflection will show that prestige symbols may be an important part of more socialized influence attempts. Thus when we were trying to convince Indian businessmen that they should come to our motivation training courses because their achievement motivation could be developed, we relied heavily on the prestige of scientific findings and our association with a major American university. A political leader must employ the prestige of his office and his distinguished record of public service as means of persuading people to accept his leadership in public affairs. In such cases it seems safer to conclude that the characteristic does not belong exclusively to either the negative or positive aspect of the power syndrome. Rather it can be employed either in the service of a primitive or a more socialized power attempt.

We have made some progress in distinguishing two aspects of the power motive, but what exactly is the difference between the way the two are exercised? Again a clue came from a very unexpected source. It is traditional in the literature of social psychology and political science to describe a leader as someone who can evoke feelings of obedience or loyal submission in his followers. A leader is sometimes said to have charisma if, when he makes a speech, for example, the members of his audience are swept off their feet and feel they must submit to his overwhelming authority and power. In the extreme case they are like iron filings that have been polarized by a powerful magnet. He is recognized as supernatural or superhuman; they feel submissive, loyal, devoted, obedient to his will. Certainly this is one common description of what was happening in mass meetings addressed by Hitler or Lenin. As great demagogues they established their power over the masses which followed loyally, obediently.

Winter wished to find out just exactly what kinds of thoughts the members of an audience had when exposed to a charismatic leader. In other words he wanted to find out if this common picture of what was going on in the minds of the audience was in fact accurate. So he exposed a group of business school students to a film of John F. Kennedy's Inaugural Address as President of the United States sometime after he had been assassinated. There was no doubt that this film was a highly moving and effective presentation of a charismatic leader for such an audience at this time. After the film was over he asked them to write imaginative stories as usual and contrasted the themes of their stories with those written by a comparable group of students after they had seen a film explaining some aspects of modern architecture. Contrary to expectation, he did not find that the students exposed to the Kennedy film thought more afterward about submission, following, obedience, or loyalty. Instead the frequency of power themes in their stories increased. It is certainly not too far fetched to interpret this as meaning that they felt strengthened and uplifted by the experience. They felt more powerful, rather then less powerful and submissive. This is an extremely interesting finding because it suggests that the traditional way of explaining the influence a leader has on his followers has not always been entirely correct. He does not force them to submit and follow him by the sheer overwhelming magic of his personality and persuasive powers. This in fact is to interpret leadership in terms of the kind of primitive aspect of the power syndrome we described above, and leadership has been discredited in this country because social scientists have often used this primitive power image to explain how the leader gets his effects. Rather he is influential in quite a different way by strengthening and inspiriting his audience. Max Weber, who is the source of much of the sociological treatment of charisma, recognized that such leaders obtained their effects through "begeisterung," a word which means "inspiritation" rather more than its usual translation, "enthusiasm."[1] The leader arouses confidence in his followers. They feel better able to accomplish whatever goals he and they share. Much has been made of whether his ideas as to what will inspire his followers came from God, from himself, or from some intuitive sense of what the people need and want. But whatever the source he cannot inspire them unless he expresses vivid goals and aims which in some sense they want. And of course the more he is meeting their needs, the less "persuasive" he has to be. But in no case does it make much sense to speak as if his role is to force submission. Rather it is to strengthen and uplift, to make people feel like origins, not pawns (deCharms, 1968). His message is not so

[1]For a fuller discussion of what Weber and other social scientists have meant by charisma, see Eisenstadt, 1968, and Tucker, 1968.

much: "Do as I say because I am strong and know best. You are children with no wills of your own and must follow me because I know better," but "Here are the goals which are true and right and which we share. Here is how we can reach them. You are strong and capable. You can accomplish these goals." His role is to clarify what goals the group should achieve and then create confidence in its members that they can achieve them. John Gardner has described these two aspects of the leadership role very well when he said that leaders "can conceive and articulate goals that lift people out of their petty preoccupations, carry them above the conflicts that tear a society apart, and unite them in the pursuit of objectives worthy of their best efforts" (1965).

So the more socialized type of power motivation cannot and does not express itself in a leadership pattern which is characterized by more primitive methods of trying to have personal impact. Social scientists have been too much impressed by the dominance hierarchies established by brute force among lower animals in their thinking about the power motive. Such methods may be effective in very small groups, but if a human leader wants to be effective in influencing large groups, he must come to rely on much more subtle, and socialized forms of influence. He necessarily gets more interested in formulating the goals toward which groups of people can move. And if he is to move the group toward achieving them, he must help define the goals clearly and persuasively and then he must be able to strengthen the will of the individual members of the group to work for those goals. To be sure, if he is a gang leader, he may display power characteristics like exploitative sex and physical aggression which we have been characterizing as typical of less socialized forms of power, but even here to the extent that he is a leader of a large group he is effective because he knows how to encourage them to pursue such goals, perhaps in this case by the technique of his own example in displaying more primitive, less socialized forms of power.

Some further light on the two faces of power was shed by our experience in trying to exert social leadership by offering achievement motivation development courses for business leaders in small cities in India. As noted above, when we began to succeed in these efforts, some observers began to wonder whether we were coarsely interfering in people's lives, perhaps spreading some new brand of American imperialism by foisting achievement values on a people that had gotten along very well without them. Their reaction is not unlike the one just described in which an outsider seeing a leader sway an audience concludes that he must have some mysterious magical power over the audience. Did we have a similar kind of "power over" the Indian businessmen who came for motivation training? Were we a new type of psychological Machiavelli?

Certainly we never thought we were. Nor, we are certain, did the businessmen perceive us as very powerful agents. How then did we manage to influence them? What happened was very much like the process of social leadership as described by John Gardner. First, we set before the participants certain goals which we felt would be desired by them—namely, to be better businessmen, to improve economic welfare in their community, to make a contribution in this way to the development of their country as a whole, to provide a pilot project that the rest of the underdeveloped might copy, and to advance the cause of science. These goals ranged all the way from the specific and personal—improving one's business—to improving the community, the nation and the world. In our experience neither a personal selfish appeal nor an altruistic social appeal is as effective by itself as the combination of the two. At any rate, these certainly were objectives that interested the businessmen we contacted. Second, we provided them with the means of achieving these goals, namely, the courses in achievement motivation development which we explained were designed to make them personally better able to move quickly and efficiently toward these objectives. What we had to offer were some new types of training in goal setting, planning, and risk taking which research had shown would help a man become a more effective entrepreneur. All of this was explained as a simple matter of fact which it was. No one was pressured to undergo this training or pursue these goals. If there was any pressure perceived, it is clearly in the eyes of the outside observer noting the effects of our intervention; it was not in the minds of the participants at the time. Third, the major goal of all of our educational exercises was to make the participants feel strong, like origins rather than pawns. Thus we insisted that the initial decision to come must be their own. They should not come out of a sense of obligation or desire to conform. In fact we pictured the training as so difficult that a high degree of personal involvement would be necessary to complete it. During the training we never set goals for them. They set their own goals for what they would try to do either in the course or for the next few months after the course. We never made psychological analyses of their test behavior which we either kept for our private diagnosis or presented to them as evidence of our superior psychological knowledge. Rather we taught them to analyze their own test records and to make their own decisions as to what a test score meant. After the course they set up their own association to work together for common community goals. We did not provide them with technical information about various types of new businesses they might enter. If they wanted such information, they had to go search for it themselves. We did not have a fixed order of presenting course materials, but constantly asked the participants to criticize the material as it was presented and to direct the staff as to what new types of presentation were desirable. Thus it turned out that we had behaved all along like effective leaders in our ceaseless efforts to make the participants feel strong, competent and effective on their own. We expressed in many ways our faith in their ability to act as origins and solve their own problems. In the end many of them justified our faith. They became more active, as we expected them to, and once again validated the ubiquitous psychological finding that what you expect other people to do they will in fact tend to do (see Rosenthal, 1968). Furthermore we have good evidence that we succeeded only with those businessmen whose sense of personal efficacy was increased. This expresses the ultimate paradox of social leadership and social power: to be an effective leader, you have to turn all your so-called followers into leaders. No wonder the situation is a little confusing not only to the would-be leader, but also to the social scientist observing the process!

Now let us put together the various bits and pieces of evidence about the nature of power and see what kind of a picture they make. The negative face of power is characterized by the dominance-submission mode. If I win, you lose. It is more primitive in the sense that the strategies employed are adopted earlier in life before the child is sufficiently socialized to learn more subtle techniques of influence. In fantasy it expresses itself in thoughts of exploitative sex and direct physical aggression. In real life it leads to fairly simple direct means of feeling powerful—like drinking heavily, chasing women, acquiring some kinds of "prestige supplies," or watching "the fights" on television. It does not lead to effective social leadership for the simple reason that a person whose power drive is fixated at this level tends to treat other people as pawns rather than as origins. And people who feel they are pawns tend to be passive and useless to the leader who is getting his childish satisfaction from dominating them. As Galbraith points out, slaves are the poorest, most inefficient form of labor ever devised by man. If a leader wants to have real far reaching influence, he must make his followers feel powerful and able to accomplish things on their own.

The positive face of power is characterized by a concern for group goals, for finding what goals will move them, for helping the group to formulate them, for taking some initiative in providing members of the group with the means of achieving such goals, and for giving group members the feeling of strength and competence they need to work hard for such goals. In fantasy it leads to a concern with persuading, forming new organizations, expressing the viewpoint of a given organization and so on. In real life, it leads to an interest in sports, politics, and holding office. It treats members of a group more as origins than as pawns. Even the most dictatorial leaders have not succeeded without instilling in at least some of their followers a sense of power and strength to pursue the goals he has set. This is often hard for outside observers to believe, but that is because they do not experience the situation as it is experienced by inside group members. One of the characteristics of being an outsider who notices only the success of an influence attempt is that he tends to convert what is a positive face of power into its negative version. He believes the leader must have "dominated" because he was so effective whereas in fact direct domination could never have produced so large an effect.

Why? Why is a successful influence attempt so often perceived as an instance of personal domination by a leader? One answer lies in the simplifying nature of social perception. The observer notices that a big change in the behavior of a group of people has occurred. He also can single out one or two people as having been leaders in some way involved in the change. He does not know how the leaders operated to bring about the change since he was not that intimately involved in the process. So he tends to perceive it as an instance of application of primitive power, or simple dominance and submission. The more effective a leader is, the more personal power tends to be attributed to him, no matter how he goes about getting his effects.

There is also a realistic basis for the frequent misperception of the nature of leadership. In real life the actual leader is balancing on a knife edge between expressing personal dominance and the more socialized type of leadership. He may present first one face of power, then the other. The reason lies in the simple fact that even if he is a socialized leader, he must take initiative in helping the group form its goals. How much initiative? How persuasive should he attempt to be? At what point does his clear enthusiasm for certain goals verge over into personal, authoritarian insistence that those goals are the right ones whatever the members of the group may think? If he takes no initiative, he is no leader. If he takes too much, he becomes a dictator, particularly if he tries to shut off the process by which members of the group can participate in shaping the group goals. Furthermore, there is a particular danger for the man who has demonstrated his competence in shaping group goals and in inspiriting group members to pursue them, for in time both he and they may assume that he knows best and he may almost imperceptibly shift from being a democratic to an authoritarian leader. There are safeguards against slipping from the more socialized to the less socialized expressions of power. One is psychological: the leader must thoroughly learn the lesson that his role is not to dominate and treat people like pawns, but to give strength to others and make them feel like origins. If they are to be truly strong, he must continually consult them and be aware of their wishes and desires. A firm faith in people as origins prevents the development of the kind of cynicism that so often characterizes authoritarian leaders. The other safeguard is social: democracy provides a system whereby the group can throw out the leader if they feel he is no longer properly representing them or formulating goals with them that the group wants to achieve.

Despite these safeguards, Americans remain unusually suspicious of the leadership role for fear that it will become the vehicle of personal abuse of power. Students do not aspire to leadership roles because they are sensitive to the negative face of power and suspicious of their own motives. Furthermore, they know if they are in a position of leadership, they will be under constant surveillance by all sorts of groups which are ready to accuse them of personal abuse of power. Americans have probably less respect for authority than almost any people in the world. The reasons are not hard to find. Many Americans immigrated here in the first place to avoid tyranny in other countries. We have come to hate and fear authority in many of its forms because of its excesses elsewhere. As a nation, we are strongly committed to an ideology of personal freedom and noninterference by government. We cherish our free press as a guardian of our freedom because it can ferret out tendencies toward the misuse or abuse of personal power before they become dangerous to the public. In government and also in many other types of organizations, we have developed elaborate systems of checks and balances or divisions of power which make it hard for any one person or group to abuse power. In government power is divided three ways—among the executive, the legislative and the judicial branches. In business it is divided among management, labor, and the owners. In the universities the trustees, the administration and students share power. In many of these organizations there is also a system for rotating leadership to make sure that no one gains enough power over time to misuse it. A Martian observer might conclude that as a nation we are excessively, almost obsessively, worried about the abuse of power.

But the wonder of it is that any leadership can be exercised under such conditions. For look at the situation from the point of view of a would-be leader. He knows that if he takes too much initiative, or even if he doesn't, he is very likely to be severely attacked by some sub-group as a malicious, power hungry status seeker. If he is in any way a public figure, he may be viciously attacked by the press for any mis-step or chancy episode in his past life. Even though the majority of the people are happy with his leadership, a small vociferous minority can make his life unpleasant. Furthermore, he knows that he will not be the only leader trying to formulate group goals. If he is a Congressman, he has to work not only with his fellow Congressmen, but with representatives of independent sources of power in the Presidency and the bureaucracy. If he is a college president, he has to cope with the relatively independent sources of power in his trustees, the faculty and the student body. If he is a business manager, he must share power with labor leaders. Furthermore, he knows that his tenure of office is very likely to be temporary. It is chancy whether he will get in a position to exert leadership. So there is no use preparing for it. If he does get in he won't stay long. So he should spend his time now preparing for what he will do before and after his short tenure in office. Under these conditions why would any promising young man aspire to be a leader? He begins by doubting his motives and ends by concluding that even if he believes his motives to be altruistic, the game is scarcely worth the candle. In other words, the anti-leadership vaccine, which John Gardner speaks of, is partly supplied by the negative face that power wears in our society and the extraordinary lengths we have gone to protect ourselves against it.

It is much safer to pursue a career as a professional advisor where one is assured some continuity of service, freedom from public attack (because after all one is not responsible for decisions), certainty that one's motives are good, and the peace of mind that comes from knowing that power conflicts have to be settled by someone else.

Is there any remedy for the situation? How can immunity against the anti-leadership vaccine be strengthened? For some immunity surely needs to be built up if our society is not to go floundering about for lack of leadership. I would personally concoct a remedy which is one part changes in the system, one part rehabilitation of the positive face of power, and one part adult education. Let me explain each ingredient in turn. I feel least confident in speaking about the first one because I am neither a political scientist, a management expert, nor a revolutionary, yet as a psychologist I do feel that America's concern about the possible misuse of power verges at times on a neurotic obsession. To control the abuses of power, is it really necessary to divide authority so extensively and to give such free license to anyone to attack a leader in any way he likes? Doesn't this make the leadership role unnecessarily difficult? John Gardner, I am sure, is aware of how difficult it is to get qualified people to want to be college presidents in present-day America. But who in his right mind would want the job under most operating conditions today? A president has great responsibility—for raising money, for setting goals for the institution that faculty, students and trustees can share, for student discipline, for appointment of a distinguished faculty and so forth—yet he often has only a very shaky authority with which to carry out these responsibilities. What authority he has, he must share with the faculty (many of whom he cannot remove no matter how violently they disagree with the goals set for the university), with the trustees and with the students who speak with one voice one year and quite a different one two years later. I am not now trying to defend ineffective college presidents no matter what they do. I am simply trying to point out that our social system makes his role an extraordinarily difficult one. Furthermore, other democratic nations, like Britain, have not found it necessary to go to such extremes to protect their liberty against possible encroachment by power hungry leaders. Some structural reform definitely seems called for. It is beyond the scope of this paper to say what it might be. The possibilities range all the way from a less structured system in which all organizations are conceived as temporary with task force leaders (see Bennis and Slater, 1968) to a system in which leaders are given more authority or offered greater protection from irresponsible attack. But surely the problem deserves serious attention. If we want better leaders, we will have to find ways of making the conditions under which they work less frustrating.

The second ingredient in my remedy for the antileadership vaccine is rehabilitation of the positive face of power. This paper is an effort in that direction.

Its major thesis is that many people, including both social scientists and potential leaders, have consistently misunderstood or misperceived the way in which effective social leadership takes place. They have confused it regularly, as we have pointed out, with the more primitive exercise of personal power. The error is perpetuated by people who speak of leaders as "making decisions." Such a statement only serves to obscure the process by which the decision is arrived at. It suggests that the leader is making a decision arbitrarily without consulting anyone, exercising his power or authority for his own ends. It is really more proper to think of an effective leader as an educator. In fact the word "educate" comes from the Latin *educāre* meaning "to lead out." The relationship between leading and educating is much more obvious in Latin than it is in English, although the Latin word *dux* (leader) does appear in several English words like conductor, as in the sense of a leader of an orchestra. Effective leaders are educators: they lead people out by helping set goals for a group, communicating them widely throughout the group, taking initiative in formulating means of achieving the goals, and finally, inspiriting the members of the group to feel strong enough to work hard for those goals. Such an image of the exercise of power and influence in a leadership role should not frighten anybody and should convince more people that power exercised this way is not only not dangerous but of the greatest possible use to society.

Our experience in developing businessmen in India has led me to propose the third ingredient in my formula for producing better leaders—namely, psychological education for adults. What impressed me greatly about the results we obtained in India was the apparent ease with which adults can be changed, by the methods we used. The dominant view in American psychology today is still that basic personality structure is laid down very early in life and is very hard to change later on. Whether the psychologist is a Freudian or a learning theorist, he believes that early experiences are critical and shape everything a person can learn, feel and want throughout his entire life span. As a consequence many educators have come to be rather pessimistic about what can be done for the poor, the black or the dispossessed who have had damaging experiences early in life. Such traumatized individuals have developed non-adaptive personality structures that are difficult, if not impossible, to change later in life, or so the reasoning goes. Yet our experience with the effectiveness of short-term training courses in achievement motivation for adult businessmen in India and elsewhere does not support this view. I have seen men change, many of them quite dramatically, after only a 10-day exposure to our specialized techniques of psychological instruction. They have changed the way they thought, the way they talked, and what they spent their time doing; their businesses improved. The message is clear: adults can be changed, often with a relatively short exposure to specialized techniques of psychological education. The implication for the present discussion is obvious: if it is true, as John Gardner argues, that many young men have learned from their professors in the colleges and universities that the professional role is preferable to the leadership role, then psychological education offers society a method of changing their views and self conceptions when they are faced with leadership opportunities. The type of psychological education needed will of course differ somewhat from the simple emphasis on achievement motivation in the courses offered for entrepreneurs. More emphasis would have to be given to managing motivation in others. More explanations would have to be given of the positive face of leadership as an educational enterprise to give participants a better idea of how to be effective leaders. But such alterations in the nature of the courses are quite feasible. In fact they have been tried out and repeatedly we have discovered that leaders are not so much born as made. And we have been working in places where most people would feel there was not much leadership potential—namely, among the poor and dispossessed. Yet we have found over and over again that even among people who have never thought of themselves as leaders or attempted to have influence in any way in poverty areas, real leadership performance can be elicited by our specialized techniques of psychological education. We need not be so pessimistic about possibilities for change in adults. Real leaders have been developed in such disadvantaged locations as the Delmarva Peninsula in the United States, the black business community in Washington, D.C., or the relatively stagnant small cities of India. So I can end on an optimistic note. Even if the leadership role today is becoming more and more difficult and people tend to avoid it for a variety of reasons, science has again come at least partly to the rescue by providing society with new techniques for developing the leaders that are needed for the world of tomorrow.

**References**

Bennis, W. G. and P. E. Slater. *The Temporary Society*. New York: Harper & Row, 1968.

Eisenstadt, S. N. *Charisma, Institution Building, and Social Transformation: Max Weber and Modern Sociology*. Chicago, Illinois: The University of Chicago Press, 1968.

Litwin, G. H. and R. A. Stringer. *Motivation and Organizational Climate*. Harvard University, Graduate School of Business Administration, Division of Research, 1966.

McClelland, D. C. *The Achieving Society*. Princeton, N.J.: Van Nostrand, 1961.

McClelland, D. C. *et al., Alcohol and Human Motivation*. New York: The Free Press (in press).

McClelland, D. C. and D. G. Winter. *Motivating Economic Achievement*. New York: The Free Press, 1969.

Tucker, R. C. "The Theory of Charismatic Leadership." *Daedalus*, 1968, *97*, 731–756.

Uleman, J. "A New TAT Measure of the Need for Power." Unpublished doctoral dissertation, Harvard University, 1965.

Veroff, J. "Development and Validation of a Projective Measure of Power Motivation." *Journal of Abnormal and Social Psychology*, 1957, *54*, 1–8.

Weber, M. *Theory of Social and Economic Organization*. New York: The Free Press, 1957.

Winter, D. G. "The Need for Power in College Men: Action Correlates and Relationship to Drinking." Chapter 5 in D. C. McClelland *et al., Alcohol Power and Inhibition*. Princeton, N.J.: Van Nostrand (in press).

Winter, D. G. "Power Motivation in Thought and Action." Unpublished doctoral dissertation, Harvard University, 1967.

# POWER TACTICS

Norman H. Martin
John Howard Sims


Executives—whether in business, government, education, or the church—have power and use it. They maneuver and manipulate in order to get a job done and, in many cases, to strengthen and enhance their own position. Although they would hate the thought and deny the allegation, the fact is that they are politicians. "Politics," according to one of the leading authorities in this complex and fascinating field, "is . . . concerned with relationships of control or of influence. To phrase the idea differently, politics deals with human relationships of superordination and subordination, of dominance and submission, of the governors and the governed."[1] In this sense, everyone who exercises power must be a politician.

It is true, as many others have pointed out in different connections, that we in this country have an instinctive revulsion against the term "power." It carries immoral connotations for us, despite the definitions of men like R.H. Tawney, the economic historian, who divorces it from any ethical attributes by calling it simply "the capacity of an individual or group of individuals to modify the conduct of other individuals or groups in the manner which he desires, and to prevent his own conduct from being modified in the manner which he does not."[2]

Furthermore, though we glorify ambition in the abstract, we frown on its practice and are distressed at the steps which must be taken if ambition is to be translated into actual advancement. Thus when power is coupled with ambition, we shy away and try to pretend that neither really exists.

But the fact is that we use power and exercise our ambitions just the same—troubled though we may be by the proverbial New England conscience which "doesn't prevent you from doing anything—it just keeps you from enjoying it!"

The complexity of the problem is increased when we recall that the real source of power is not the superior but the subordinate. Men can only exercise that power which they are allowed by other men—albeit their positions are buttressed by economic, legal, and other props. The ultimate source of power is the group; and a group, in turn, is made up of people with consciousness and will, with emotion and irrationality, with intense personal interests and tenaciously held values.

---

Reprinted from *Harvard Business Review* (November-December 1956), pp. 25–29, by permission of the authors and publisher. © 1956 by the President and Fellows of Harvard College; all rights reserved.

[1] V. O. Key, Jr., *Politics, Parties and Pressure Groups* (2d ed.; New York: Thomas Y. Crowell Co., 1948), p. 3.

[2] R. H. Tawney, *Equality* (4th ed.; London: George Allen & Unwin, Ltd., 1952), p. 175.

The human being resists being treated as a constant. Knowledge, reason, and technical know-how will not suffice as means of control but give way to the arts of persuasion and inducement, of tactics and maneuver, of all that is involved in interpersonal relationships. Power cannot be given; it must be won. And the techniques and skills of winning it are at the same time the methods of employing it as a medium of control. This represents the political function of the power-holder.

In such a light, we see why the successful functioning and advancement of the executive is dependent, not only on those aspects of an enterprise which are physical and logical, but on morale, teamwork, authority, and obedience—in a word, on the vast intricacy of human relationships which make up the political universe of the executive.

The real question then becomes: How can power be used most effectively? What are some of the political stratagems which the administrator must employ if he is to carry out his responsibilities and further his career? This is an area that has carefully been avoided by both students and practitioners of business— as if there were something shady about it. But facts are facts, and closing our eyes to them will not change them. Besides, if they are important facts, they should be brought into the open for examination.

Accordingly, we present here some of the findings of the first stage of a fairly extensive investigation of just how the executive functions in his political-power environment. We have searched the biographies of well-known leaders of history, from Alexander to Roosevelt; we have explored the lives of successful industrialists like Rockefeller and Ford; and we have interviewed a number of contemporary executives.

There follows an account of certain tactics which we have found to be practiced by most men whose success rests on ability to control and direct the actions of others—no doubt, raw and oversimplified when reduced to a few black-and-white words, but for this very reason more likely to be provocative. With further refinement, these generalizations will serve as hypotheses in the succeeding stages of our research, but in the meantime we present them to businessmen to look at openly and objectively—to ask, "Do we not use just such techniques frequently?" and, if so, to ponder, "How can we best operate in this particular area, for our own interest as managers and for the good of people under us?"

*Taking counsel.* The able executive is cautious about how he seeks and receives advice. He takes counsel only when he himself desires it. His decisions must be made in terms of his own grasp of the situation, taking into account the views of others when he thinks it necessary. To act otherwise is to be subject, not to advice, but to pressure; to act otherwise too often produces vacillation and inconsistency.

Throwing a question to a. group of subordinates is all too often interpreted as a delegation of power, and the executive may find himself answered with a decision instead of counsel. He must remember that he, not the group under him, is the responsible party. If an executive allows his subordinates to provide advice when he does not specifically call for it, he may find himself subject, not only to pressure, but to conflicting alignments of forces within his own ranks. A vague sort of policy which states, "I am always ready to hear your advice and ideas on anything," will waste time, confuse issues, dilute leadership, and erode power.

*Alliances.* In many respects, the executive system in a firm is composed of complexes of sponsor-protégé relationships.[3] For the protégé, these relationships provide channels for advancement; for the sponsor, they build a loyal group of followers. A wise administrator will make it a point to establish such associations with those above and below him. In the struggles for power and influence that go on in many organizations, every executive needs a devoted following and close alliances with other executives, both on his own level and above him, if he is to protect and to enhance his status and sphere of influence.

Alliances should not be looked upon, however, merely as a protective device. In addition, they provide ready-made systems of communication, through which the executive can learn firsthand how his decisions are being carried out, what unforeseen obstacles are being encountered, and what the level of morale in the organization is at any moment.

*Maneuverability.* The wise executive maintains his flexibility, and he never completely commits himself to any one position or program. If forces beyond his control compel a major change in company policy, he can gracefully bend with the wind and co-operate with the inevitable, thus maintaining his status.

An executive should preserve maneuverability in career planning as well. He ought never to get in a situation that does not have plenty of escape hatches. He must be careful, for instance, that his career is not directly dependent on the superior position of a sponsor. He should provide himself with transferable talents, and interfirm alliances, so that he will be able to move elsewhere if the conditions in his current organization become untenable.

*Communication.* During recent years emphasis has been placed on the necessity for well-dredged channels of communication which run upward, downward, and sideways. Top management should supply its subordinates with maximum information, according to this theory; subordinates, in turn, must report fully to their chiefs.

It is possible, however, that executives have been oversold on maximizing the flow of information. It simply is not good strategy to communicate everything one knows. Instead, it may often be advantageous to withhold information or to time its release. This is especially true with reference to future plans—plans which may or may not materialize; it is also valid in the case of information that may create schism or conflict within the organization; and it is prudent when another executive is a threat to one's own position. Furthermore, information is an important tactical weapon, and should be considered as such.

It would appear, then, that executives should be concerned with determining "who gets to know what and when" rather than with simply increasing the flow. Completely open communication deprives the executive of the exclusive power of directing information which should be his.

*Compromising.* The executive should accept compromise as a means of settling differences with his tongue in his cheek. While appearing to alter his view, he should continue to press forward toward a clear-cut set of goals. It is

[3]See Norman H. Martin and Anselm S. Strauss, "Patterns of Mobility within Industrial Organizations," *Journal of Business,* April 1956, p. 101.

frequently necessary to give ground on small matters, to delay, to move off on tangents, even to suffer reverses in order to retain power for future forward movement. Concessions, then, should be more apparent than real.

*Negative timing.* The executive is often urged to take action with which he is not in agreement. Sometimes pressure for such action arises from the expectations of subordinates, the influence of his associates with his superiors, the demands of custom and tradition, or other sources he would be unwise to ignore.

To give in to such demands would be to deny the executive's prerogative; to refuse might precipitate a dangerous crisis, and threaten his power. In such situations the executive may find it wise to use what might be called the technique of "negative timing." He initiates action, but the process of expedition is retarded. He is considering, studying, and planning for the problem; there are difficulties to be overcome and possible ramifications which must be considered. He is always *in the process* of doing something but never quite does it, or finally he takes action when it is actually too late. In this way the executive escapes the charge of dereliction, and at the same time the inadvisable program "dies on the vine."

*Self-dramatization.* Most vocal communication in which an executive engages—whether with his superiors, his colleagues, or his subordinates—is unpremeditated, sincere, spontaneous. His nonvocal communication—the impression projected by his posture, gestures, dress, or facial expressions—is commonly just as natural.

But executives would do well to re-examine this instinctive behavior, for many of them are overlooking an important political stratagem. The skill of the actor—whose communication is "artistic" as opposed to "natural"—represents a potential asset to an administrator. Dramatic art is a process by which selections from reality are chosen and arranged by the artists for the particular purpose of arousing the emotions, of convincing, of persuading, of altering the behavior of the audience in a *planned direction.*

The actor's purpose is no different from that of the manager who wants to activate his subordinates in certain specific directions—to secure a certain response from those with whom he communicates. The actor's peculiar gift is in deliberately shaping his own speech and behavior to accomplish his purpose. The element of chance, the variable of the unknown, is diminished, if not removed; and rehearsal with some foreknowledge of what is to occur takes place. The *how* of communicating is considered as well as the *what.*

Of course, this is no easy task. The effectiveness of the actor's performance depends on his ability to estimate what will stimulate the audience to respond. And once he makes his choices, he must be able to use them skilfully. His voice and body must be so well disciplined, so well trained, that the images he chooses may be given life. The question is, How can an executive acquire the skill of artistic communication?—How can he learn to dramatize himself?

The development of sharper powers of observation is the first step. Having witnessed effective communication—whether a TV drama or an actual meeting of the board of directors—the executive should try to determine what made it effective. He should pay attention to *how* a successful man handled himself, not what he said or did. Formal classes can provide the executive with control over his voice—its pitch, tone, color, speed, diction; training can do the same for his body—gesture, posture, and mime. Most important, the executive should seize any opportunity to gain actual experience in putting such skills to work, in amateur theatricals or "role-playing" sessions.

It would be foolish to deny that such skills cannot be entirely learned; to some extent they depend on the unknowns of flair, talent, and genius. But such an acknowledgment does not excuse the executive from making an effort, for the range of possible improvement is very great.

*Confidence.* Related to, but not identical with, self-dramatization is the outward appearance of confidence. Once an executive has made a decision, he must look and act decided. In some instances genuine inner conviction may be lacking, or the manager may find it difficult to generate the needed dynamics. The skilful executive who finds himself in such a situation will either produce the effect of certainty or postpone any contact with his associates in order to avoid appearing in an unfavorable light.

Thus, the man who constantly gives the impression of knowing what he is doing—even if he does not—is using his power and increasing it at the same time.

*Always the boss.* Warm personal relations with subordinates have sometimes been considered the mark of a good executive. But in practice an atmosphere of social friendship interferes with the efficiency of an operation and acts to limit the power of the manager. Personal feelings should not be a basis for action—either negative or positive. The executive should never permit himself to be so committed to a subordinate as a friend that he is unable to withdraw from this personal involvement and regard the man objectively as an element in a given situation.

Thus, a thin line of separation between executive and subordinate must always be maintained. The situation should be one of isolation and contact—of the near and far—of marginality. No matter how cordial he may be, the executive must sustain a line of privacy which cannot be transgressed; in the final analysis, he must always be the boss. If we assume, then, that the traditional "open-door" policy of the modern executive is good strategy, we must always ask the question: "How far open?"

The foregoing discussion will undoubtedly raise questions, and even indignation, in the minds of some readers. In the last two decades, the finger of censure has often been pointed at the interpersonal relations in the management of industrial organizations, questioning whether they are harmonious with a democratic society and ideology.[4] Executives have been urged to adopt practices and programs aimed at "democratizing" their businesses. Perhaps they have even developed a sense of guilt from the realization of their own position of authority and that they cannot be completely frank, sincere, honest, and aboveboard in their interpersonal relations. We live in an era of "groupiness"; we are bombarded with admonitions which insist that everyone who is participating in an enterprise should have a part in the management of it.

In the light of such a trend even the terminology used in this article—"power," "maneuver," "tactics," "techniques"—appears disturbing when set down in

[4] See Thomas C. Cochran, "Business and the Democratic Tradition," *Business Review*, March-April, 1956, p. 39.

black and white. But in fact it is neither immoral nor cynical to recognize and describe the actual daily practices of power. After all, sweeping them under the rug—making believe that they are not actually part of the executive's activity— does not cause them to vanish. Open and honest discussion of the political aspects in the administrator's job exposes these stratagems to the constructive spotlight of knowledge. They exist; therefore, we had better take a look at them and see what they are really like.

As we delve deeper into the study of political tactics in business management, the contrast with modern human relations theory and practice will stand out in ever-sharper relief. Mutual confidence, open communication, continuing consultation and participation by subordinates, friendship, and an atmosphere of democracy seem hard to reconcile with much of the maneuvering and power plays that go on in the nation's offices and factories every day.

Yet businessmen must develop some rationale of executive behavior which can encompass the idealism of democracy and the practicality of politics—and, at the same time, be justified in terms of ultimate values. If they do not, they will feel like hypocrites as the day-to-day operation of their offices clashes with their speeches before women's clubs. The old cliché that "business is business" is no longer satisfying to the general public nor to the executive himself.

One way to try to fit human relations theory and political tactics together is to state that the means or ways of exercising power are neutral. In and of themselves, they have no moral value. They take on moral qualities only in connection with the ends for which they are used. Power can be used for good or ill according to this theory, and we should have the courage and knowledge to use it wisely. Conscious, deliberate, and skilled use of executive power means responsible use of power. If men in the past have employed power for evil ends, that is unfortunate; it is just as true that other men, if they had made use of business politics in an effective fashion, might have been a greater force for good.

The difficulty with this line of thought lies in the well-known pitfalls inherent in the timeless means-ends controversy. In real life, what are means and what are ends? Can you achieve good ends by bad means? If the way one man conducts his relationship with another has no moral implications, what human activity does have moral significance?

Others may take the position that "so long as my general philosophy is sound and moral, the specific actions I have to take in the course of my job don't matter." But one may question the validity of a philosophy of life that breaks down every time it comes into contact with reality.

Still another formula could be found in the statement, "The good of the company comes before that of an individual. If I have to violate moral codes and democratic principles in dealing with one man, that is too bad for him. But I cannot allow any single person to overshadow the interests of all our other employees, stockholders, and customers." The skeptical listener might then raise the issue of collectivism versus individualism, and ask whether the general welfare really overrides the worth and dignity of the individual. Can we build a society on the idea of the individual's importance if we violate the principle whenever it interferes with what we consider to be the good of the group?

There are, of course, other approaches, but they too are fraught with internal contradictions. The riddle, then, remains unsolved; the conflict between the use of power and the principles of democracy and enlightened management is unrelieved. Businessmen, who face this paradox every day in countless situations, cannot avoid the responsibility of explaining or resolving it. If a viable philosophy of management is to be developed, they must contribute their ideas—for the sake of their own peace of mind, if nothing else.

If this article succeeds in getting more businessmen to do some thinking along this line, then it will have served its purpose.

## THE NEED FOR CLOSE RELATIONSHIPS AND THE MANAGER'S JOB

Richard E. Boyatzis

The results of research on the affiliative motive are somewhat contradictory although they tend to relate high levels of this motive with poor performance as a manager. Boyatzis (1972) proposed a new theory of affiliation motivation in which he claimed there are two forms of the motive: one is called *affiliative assurance* and the other *affiliative interest*. With these types of affiliation motivation in mind, prior findings are reconciled into clear patterns of behavior: one would lead to effective performance of a manager's job, and the other would not.

The results of research on the affiliative motive are somewhat contradictory and relate high levels of this motive with poor performance as a manager. Boyatzis (1972) proposed a new theory of affiliation motivation in which he claimed there are two forms of the motive: one is called *affiliative assurance* and the other *affiliative interest*. With these types of affiliation motivation in mind, prior findings are reconciled into clear patterns of behavior: one would lead to effective performance of a manager's job, and the other would not.

### The Manager and His Subordinate

Past research on the affiliation motive has shown that a person with a high level of that motive would act in some ways which are necessary to a manager's job, such as communicating with others and understanding their feelings. Such a person may also exhibit behavior which inhibits the manager in effectively performing his job, such as seeking the approval of subordinates.

A corporate unit or "spin-off" (research and development organizations, in particular) headed by a manager with a high need for affiliation does not do as well as do other similar organizations (Harris, 1969; Wainer and Rubin, 1969). Such a manager prefers to work in collaboratively structured groups and in a relaxed atmosphere (deCharms, 1957; French, 1955). Both of these situational factors are often difficult to establish because of economic pressures and requirements of the marketplace.

---

Prepared specifically for this volume.

A manager with a high need for affiliation would strive for approval from his subordinates and superiors (Byrne, 1961), he would be sensitive to others' facial expressions and their feelings (Atkinson and Walker, 1956), and if the manager and his subordinate were to disagree, the manager would change his attitude to one which was more acceptable to the subordinate's, especially if the manager likes the subordinate (Burdick and Burnes, 1958; Byrne, 1961).

If this manager with a high need for affiliation were given a choice as to which of his subordinates he would like to work with on a task, he would choose the subordinate with whom he has a close, friendly relationship—even if this person were less competent to perform the task than another subordinate (French, 1956). He would also choose a subordinate less likely to reject his offer, rather than choose a more qualified subordinate (Rosenfeld, 1964).

The manager with a high need for affiliation is so concerned about his relationships that performance objectives of his job become confused. The goal of building and maintaining friendly relations supersedes a concern over the effectiveness of his organizational unit's performance toward corporate objectives. But, he sincerely believes that friendly relations are *necessary* to healthy corporate performance.

In contrast to these findings, several studies have shown that a person with affiliation motivation demonstrates behavior which contributes to the effectiveness of corporate performance. Lawrence and Lorsch (1967) report that effective "integrators" (managers whose function is to integrate the work of various people or units) rank higher in the need for affiliation than their less effective peers.

Kolb and Boyatzis (1970) showed that people who were effective at helping others change their behavior were higher in the need for affiliation than their less effective counterparts. This is relevant because one of the manager's functions is to "help" his subordinates develop their behavioral skills to more effectively perform their present job, as well as to aid the subordinate in planning his career development.

After several days with this effective affiliation motivated manager, you would notice that he spent more time communicating with subordinates (Noujaim, 1968) and writing, calling, and visiting friends (Lansing and Heyns, 1959) than would other managers you know. The disposition to communicate with others is a critical aspect of the manager's job. Without that communication, it is very difficult to integrate people's efforts in a manner which builds their commitment to their work.

The evidence is somewhat contradictory. On the one hand, managers with high affiliation motivation exhibit behavior which interferes with their job and the poor performance of their organizational units show it. On the other hand, aspects of a manager's job require some of the behavior demonstrated by a person with affiliation motivation. Is it a matter of degree—i.e., do managers who show ineffective behavior stemming from affiliative concerns have levels of affiliation motivation which are too high? Or is it a function of the way in which they experience and express their affiliation motive?

### Grasping or Concern?

A manager may have a low, moderate, or high concern about close relationships relative to his other concerns, such as concerns about having impact on others, prestige or reputation, attempting to do better against a standard of excellence, or doing something unique, to mention a few.

Affiliative concerns which are moderate or high with respect to other concerns may lead a manager to increase the performance of his unit and develop commitment in his subordinates, or it may cause him to act in a way which interferes with his job. The difference in the effects of a person's affiliative motive is determined by the *type* of affiliation motive.

As a result of methodological and conceptual difficulties, I contend that the research on the need for affiliation taps primarily the *affiliative assurance* form of the motive. The early experiments performed in an attempt to develop a method of measuring the need for affiliation based their research on a definition of affiliation motive as a striving for close relationships in the sense of security needs (Shipley and Veroff, 1952; Atkinson, Heyns, and Veroff, 1954). The arousal of the motive in these studies consisted of having individual members of fraternities stand, while others in his group described them on an adjective checklist (used in two studies), or using people adversely affected by being rejected from a fraternity during a rush period (used in one study). Both techniques bias the measuring system in a way which causes the measure of affiliation motivation to tap the person's concerns about being evaluated, being accepted or rejected more than his unanxious concerns about being a part of close relations. The component of anxiety about being rejected or negatively evaluated by friends was probably present in people who participated in the studies.

A preliminary attempt to separate the affiliative assurance motive from the affiliative interest motive demonstrated support for the theory, but lacked enough substantial results to consider it a definitive theoretical and methodological solution to the problem of measuring affiliation motives (Boyatzis, 1972). The support found did confirm the basic notion that the two forms exist, and they do determine different forms of interpersonal behavior.

A manager with a high affiliative assurance motive will basically be concerned about obtaining assurance as to the security and strength of his close relations. He will be anxious about not being rejected. This concern leads him to look for "proof" of others' commitments to him and to avoid issues or conflict which may threaten the stability of the relationship. He would tend to be jealous or possessive of his subordinates (and possibly of his superior), search for communications which support the closeness of the relationship, and look for signs of approval from the others around him. He would avoid conflict situations by smoothing things over, or abdicating his role in intervening to resolve the conflict. *It is this assurance form of affiliation motivation which would interfere with a person's work as a manager.* It would be his "grasping" onto close relationships which would drain his energy and absorb his time. He would spend time seeking approval and security, rather than doing his job.

The manager with an assurance motive would be concerned about the subordinate's feelings toward him and the job. He would be looking for acceptance and approval from the subordinate. This manager would equate the subordinate's happiness in the job with acceptance of the manager as a person, and would not feel comfortable confronting the subordinate with negative feedback on job performance. He might even ignore this type of information to avoid the interpersonal situation of telling the subordinate. The rules of behavior in his relationship to his subordinates would include much concern but little openness —for example, the subordinate would not be allowed to disagree with the manager or give him negative feedback because it would threaten the relationship. The manager would not look forward to a transfer or promotion of him or his subordinates, but, instead would like to keep them all in the family. The objectives of this manager's organizational unit would be ambiguous to his subordinates. Although corporate objectives would be evident, the manager would actually be spending time working on the relationships, and at times, at the expense of performance objectives.

The manager with predominantly an affiliative interest motive would want the subordinate to feel a part of a human organization. The rules of behavior in his relationships would include interpersonal concern and openness, and because the relationship was in the context of the whole organization, there would be a sense of closeness evolved from working together toward performance objectives. This would not threaten, or diminish, the manager's feelings of closeness to his subordinates.

This type of manager could evaluate a subordinate's piece of work, give him negative or positive feedback, and not communicate a positive or negative overall evaluation of the subordinate as a person. As a result of the openness and concern over the subordinate's welfare, a climate of trust would be established which would encourage the subordinate to make his motives or concerns clear to the manager. This would enable the manager to direct the subordinate's work more effectively, designing his subordinate's job in a manner which responded to his motives or concerns.

Such a manager would be enthusiastic about the transfer or promotion of one of his subordinates, not feeling the separation as a loss and would look forward to establishing a close relationship with a new subordinate.

*It is the affiliative interest form of the motive which would lead to increased managerial effectiveness.* Such a person's show of "concern" would not occur at the expense of goal-oriented behavior.

Most organizational theorists emphasize the importance of personnel feeling as a part of an organization. The manager with an affiliative interest motive can stimulate those feelings on a human level by making it clear that the subordinate's thoughts and feelings are important to him. The manager with an assurance motive has a tendency to confuse his subordinates. They are not sure whether the quality of interpersonal relationships is the most important factor on the job, or if it is performance toward organizational objectives. The objectives of this manager's performance are often toward building and maintaining a set of close relationships.

In his relationship to his superior, the manager with an assurance motive would be looking for approval and acceptance. He would exaggerate in his mind the relevance of positive feedback and would tend to ignore negative feedback. With some negative feedback, he might assume that the superior did not like him as a person and he would not utilize the information to improve performance, but begin to withdraw from the job.

He would do things which would please the superior and make him notice. Constantly seeking more personal contact, such a manager would not take moderate risks in job assignments and would prefer to stay away from challenging tasks which might result in failure. He might also do the opposite, which is to accept task assignments which are high-risk (challenging, but hardly attainable) in the hope that if he succeeds, his superior would appreciate him greatly.

The manager with an affiliative interest motive would be able to separate interpersonal relationships and job performance issues. Feedback to him, or from him to his superior, could be related to a task and not have implications for the future quality of their relationship. Informal meetings with the interest-type manager and his superior would be more relaxed than such encounters with an assurance-type manager.

The reader should remember that the affiliation motive is but one of many motives of the individual. The character of the person's affiliative motive will interact with his other motives in a variety of ways. Providing a person who has either type of affiliative motive with a warm, interpersonal environment in which to work will stimulate him. In particular, a person with an assurance motive will not be able to devote energy to objectives other than maintaining relationships if he does not feel like an accepted part of the organizational unit. A manager with such a motive may find it difficult to stimulate goal-oriented thinking and behavior in his subordinates because of his needs.

**Toward a Genuine Concern**

Managers with relatively low concerns about close relationships compared to other concerns will find the performance of their organizational unit increasing and turnover decreasing if they develop the ability to demonstrate genuine concern toward others around them.

Managers with high affiliative assurance motives would find the performance of their units increasing if they could realize that people around them do not necessarily want to reject them. Their relationships are a part of a work organization whose main objectives are performance toward corporate objectives. The concerns for assurance are this manager's needs, not his subordinates' or superior's needs.

A healthy and productive organization is a humane effort toward corporate performance objectives. By increasing the behavior which would appear to emanate from an affiliative interest motive, a manager will create a climate of interpersonal concern and trust which builds the capability of the organization to reach its objectives and grow.

J. W. Atkinson, R. W. Heyns, and J. Veroff, "The Effect of Experimental Arousal of the Affiliation Motive on Thematic Apperception," *Journal of Abnormal and Social Psychology*, 1954, *49*, 405–410.

J. W. Atkinson, and Walker, "The Affiliation Motive and Perceptual Sensitivity to Faces," *Journal of Abnormal and Social Psychology*, 1956, *53*, 38–41.

R. E. Boyatzis, "A Two-Factor Theory of Affiliation Motivation" (unpublished doctoral dissertation, Harvard University, 1972).

H. A. Burdick, and A. J. Burnes, "A Test of 'Strain Toward Symmetry' Theories," *Journal of Abnormal and Social Psychology*, 1958, *57*, 367–370.

D. Byrne, "Anxiety and the Experimental Arousal of the Affiliation Need," *Journal of Abnormal and Social Psychology*, 1961, *63*, 660–662.

D. Byrne, "Interpersonal Attraction as a Function of Affiliation Need and Attitude Similarity," *Human Relations*, 1961, *14*, 283–289.

R. deCharms, "Affiliation Motivation and Productivity in Small Groups," *Journal of Abnormal and Social Psychology*, 1957, *55*, 222–226.

E. G. French, "Some Characteristics of Achievement Motivation," *Journal of Experimental Psychology*, 1955, *50*, 232–236.

E. G. French, "Motivation as a Variable in Work Partner Selection," *Journal of Abnormal and Social Psychology*, 1956, *53*, 96–99.

H. Harris, "An Experimental Model of the Effectiveness of Project Management Offices" (unpublished Master's dissertation, Massachusetts Institute of Technology, 1969).

D. A. Kolb, and R. E. Boyatzis, "On the Dynamics of the Helping Relationship," *Journal of Applied Behavioral Sciences*, 1970.

J. B. Lansing, and R. W. Heyns, "Need for Affiliation and Four Types of Communication," *Journal of Abnormal and Social Psychology*, 1959, *58*, 365–372.

P. R. Lawrence, and J. W. Lorsch, "New Management Job: The Integrator," *Harvard Business Review*, 1967, *45*, 142–151.

K. Noujaim, "Some Motivational Determinants of Effort Allocation and Performance" (unpublished doctoral dissertation, Massachusetts Institute of Technology, 1968).

H. Rosenfeld, "Social Choice Conceived as a Level of Aspiration," *Journal of Abnormal and Social Psychology*, 1964, *3*, 491–499.

T. E. Snipley, and J. Veroff, "A Projective Measure of Need for Affiliation," *Journal of Experimental Psychology*, 1952, *43*, 349–356.

H. A. Wainer, and I. M. Rubin, "Motivation of Research and Development Entrepreneurs," *Journal of Applied Psychology*, 1969, *53*, 178–184.

# Decision Making
# in Groups

## THE NATURE OF
## HIGHLY EFFECTIVE GROUPS

RENSIS LIKERT

We concluded in Chapter 8 that the form of organization which will make the greatest use of human capacity consists of highly effective work groups linked together in an overlapping pattern by other similarly effective groups. The highly effective work group is, consequently, an important component of the newer theory of management. It will be important to understand both its nature and its performance characteristics. We shall examine these in this chapter, but first a few words about groups in general.

Although we have stressed the great potential power of the group for building effective organizations, it is important to emphasize that this does *not* say that all groups and all committees are highly effective or are committed to desirable goals. Groups as groups can vary from poor to excellent. They can have desirable values and goals, or their objectives can be most destructive. They can accomplish much that is good, or they can do great harm. There is nothing *implicitly* good or bad, weak or strong, about a group.

The nature of the group determines the character of its impact upon the development of its members. The values of the group, the stability of these values, the group atmosphere, and the nature of the conformity demanded by the group determine whether a group is likely to have a positive or negative impact upon the growth and behavior of its members. If the values of the group are seen by the society as having merit, if the group is stable in its adherence to these values, and if the atmosphere of the group is warm, supportive, and full of understanding, the group's influence on the development of its members will be positive. A hostile atmosphere and socially undesirable or unstable values produce a negative impact upon the members' growth and behavior.

Loyalty to a group produces pressures toward conformity. A group may demand conformity to the idea of supporting, encouraging, and giving recognition for individual creativity, or it may value rigidity of behavior, with seriously narrowing and dwarfing consequences. This latter kind of pressure for conformity keeps the members from growing and robs the group of original ideas. Many writers have pointed to these deleterious effects of conformity. They often overlook the capacity of groups to stimulate individual creativeness by placing a high value on imaginative and original contributions by their members. As Pelz's findings, reported in Chapter 2, demonstrate, groups can contribute significantly to creativity by providing the stimulation of diverse points of view within a supportive atmosphere which encourages each individual member to pursue new and unorthodox concepts.

Some business executives are highly critical of groups—or committees—and the inability of committees to accomplish a great deal. Their criticisms are often well warranted. In many instances, committees are wasteful of time and unable to reach decisions. Sometimes the decisions, when reached, are mediocre. Moreover, some members of management at various hierarchical levels use committees as escape mechanisms—as a way to avoid the responsibility for a decision.

The surprising thing about committees is not that many or most are ineffective, but that they accomplish as much as they do when, relatively speaking, we know so little about how to use them. There has been a lack of systematic study of ways to make committees effective. Far more is known about time-and-motion study, cost accounting and similar aspects of management than is known about groups and group processes. Moreover, in spite of the demonstrated potentiality of groups, far less research is being devoted to learning the role of groups and group processes and how to make the most effective use of them in an organization than to most management practices. We know appreciably less about how to make groups and committees effective than we know about most matters of managing.

We do know that groups can be powerful. The newer theory takes this into account and tries to make constructive use of the group's potential strength for developing and mobilizing human resources.

In this and other chapters the use of the term "group" may give the impression that groups have the capacity to behave in ways other than through the behavior of their members. Thus, such expressions appear as the "group's goals," "the group decides," or the "group motivates." In many instances, these expressions are used to avoid endless repetition of the words, "the members of the group." In other instances, something more is meant. Thus, in speaking of "group values," the intent is to refer to those values which have been established by the group through a group-decision process involving consensus. Once a decision has been reached by consensus, there are strong motivational forces, developed within each individual as a result of his membership in the group and his relationship to the other members, to be guided by that decision. In this sense, the group has goals and values and makes decisions. It has properties which may not be present, as such, in any one individual. A group may be divided in opinion, for example, although this may not be true of any one member. Dorwin Cartwright puts it this way: "The relation between the individual members and the group is analogous to the distinction made in mathematics between the properties of a set of elements and the properties of the elements within a set. Every set is composed of elements, but sets have properties which are not identical with the properties of the elements of the set."

## The Highly Effective Work Group

Much of the discussion of groups in this chapter will be in terms of an ideal organizational model which the work groups in an organization can approach as they develop skill in group processes. This model group, of course, is always part of a large organization. The description of its nature and performance characteristics is based on evidence from a variety of sources. Particularly important are the observational and experimental studies of small groups such as those conducted by the Research Center for Group Dynamics (Cartwright & Zander, 1960; Hare et al., 1955; Institute for Social Research, 1956; Institute for Social Research, 1960; Thibaut & Kelly, 1959). Extensive use is made of data from studies of large-scale organizations (see Chapters 2 to 4). Another important source is the material from the National Training Laboratories (Foundation for Research on Human Behavior, 1960d; National Training Laboratories, 1953; National Training Laboratories, 1960; Stock & Thelen, 1958). The NTL has focused on training in sensitivity to the reactions of others and in skills to perform the leadership and membership roles in groups.

In addition to drawing upon the above sources, the description of the ideal model is derived from theory. Some of the statements about the model for which there is little or limited experimental or observational data have been derived directly from the basic drive to achieve and maintain a sense of importance and personal worth. At several points in this chapter and Chapter 12 the author has gone appreciably beyond available specific research findings. The author feels, however, that the generalizations which are emerging based on research in organizations and on small groups, youth, and family life, personality development, consumer behavior, human motivation, and related fields lend strong support to the general theory and the derivations contained in this book.

It has been necessary to go beyond the data in order to spell out at this time in some detail the general pattern of the more complex but more effective form of organization being created by the higher-producing managers. The author hopes that the theory and model proposed will stimulate a substantial increase in basic and developmental research and that they will be tested and sharpened by that research.

The body of knowledge about small groups, while sufficiently large to make possible this description of the ideal model, is still relatively limited. Without question, as the importance of the work group as the basic building block of organizations becomes recognized, there will be a great increase in the research on groups and our knowledge about them. The over-all pattern of the model described here will be improved and clarified by such research. Our understanding of how to develop and use groups effectively will also be greatly advanced.

The following description of the ideal model defines what we mean by *a highly effective group*. The definition involves reference to several different variables. Each of them can be thought of as a continuum, i.e., as a characteristic which can vary from low to high, from unfavorable to favorable. For example, a group can vary from one in which there is hostility among the members to one in which the attitudes are warm and friendly. The ideal model is at the favorable end of each variable.

## The Nature of Highly Effective Work Groups

The highly effective group, as we shall define it, is always conceived as being a part of a larger organization. A substantial proportion of persons in a company are members of more than one work group, especially when both line and staff are considered. As a consequence, in such groups there are always linking functions to be performed and relationships to other groups to be maintained. Our highly effective group is not an isolated entity.

All the persons in a company also belong to groups and organizations outside of the company. For most persons, membership in several groups both within and outside the company is the rule rather than the exception. This means, of course, that no single group, even the highly effective work group, dominates the life of any member. Each member of the organization feels pressures from membership in several different groups and is not influenced solely by loyalty to any one group.

Since the different groups to which a person belongs are apt to have somewhat different and often inconsistent goals and values, corresponding conflicts and pressures are created within him. To minimize these conflicts and tensions, the individual seeks to influence the values and goals of each of the different groups to which he belongs and which are important to him so as to minimize the inconsistencies and conflicts in values and goals. In striving for this reconciliation, he is likely to press for the acceptance of those values most important to him.

The properties and performance characteristics of the ideal highly effective group are as follows:

1. The members are skilled in all the various leadership and membership roles and functions required for interaction between leaders and members and between members and other members.

2. The group has been in existence sufficiently long to have developed a well-established, relaxed working relationship among all its members.

3. The members of the group are attracted to it and are loyal to its members, including the leader.

4. The members and leaders have a high degree of confidence and trust in each other.

5. The values and goals of the group are a satisfactory integration and expression of the relevant values and needs of its members. They have helped shape these values and goals and are satisfied with them.

6. In so far as members of the group are performing linking functions, they endeavor to have the values and goals of the groups which they link in harmony, one with the other.

7. The more important a value seems to the group, the greater the likelihood that the individual member will accept it.

8. The members of the group are highly motivated to abide by the major values and to achieve the important goals of the group. Each member will do all that he reasonably can—and at times all in his power—to help the group

achieve its central objectives. He expects every other member to do the same. This high motivation springs, in part, from the basic motive to achieve and maintain a sense of personal worth and importance. Being valued by a group whose values he shares, and deriving a sense of significance and importance from this relationship, leads each member to do his best. He is eager not to let the other members down. He strives hard to do what he believes is expected of him.

9. All the interaction, problem-solving, decision-making activities of the group occur in a supportive atmosphere. Suggestions, comments, ideas, information, criticisms are all offered with a helpful orientation. Similarly, these contributions are received in the same spirit. Respect is shown for the point of view of others both in the way contributions are made and in the way they are received.

There are real and important differences of opinion, but the focus is on arriving at sound solutions and not on exacerbating and aggravating the conflict. Ego forces deriving from the desire to achieve and maintain a sense of personal worth and importance are channeled into constructive efforts. Care is taken not to let these ego forces disrupt important group tasks, such as problem-solving. Thus, for example, a statement of the problem, a condition which any solution must meet, a suggested solution, or an item of relevant fact are all treated as from the group as a whole. Care is taken so that one statement of the problem is not John's and another Bill's. A suggested solution is not referred to as Tom's and another as Dick's. All the material contributed is treated as *ours*: "One of our proposed solutions is *A*, another is *B*." In all situations involving actual or potential differences or conflict among the members of the group, procedures are used to separate the ego of each member from his contribution. In this way, ego forces do not stimulate conflict between members. Instead, they are channeled into supporting the activities and efforts of the group.

The group atmosphere is sufficiently supportive for the members to be able to accept readily any criticism which is offered and to make the most constructive use of it. The criticisms may deal with any relevant topic such as operational problems, decisions, supervisory problems, interpersonal relationships, or group processes, but whatever their content, the member feels sufficiently secure in the supportive atmosphere of the group to be able to accept, test, examine, and benefit from the criticism offered. Also, he is able to be frank and candid, irrespective of the content of the discussion: technical, managerial, factual, cognitive, or emotional. The supportive atmosphere of the group, with the feeling of security it provides, contributes to a cooperative relationship between the members. And this cooperation itself contributes to and reinforces the supportive atmosphere.

10. The superior of each work group exerts a major influence in establishing the tone and atmosphere of that work group by his leadership principles and practices. In the highly effective group, consequently, the leader adheres to those principles of leadership which create a supportive atmosphere in the group and a cooperative rather than a competitive relationship among the members. For example, he shares information fully with the group and creates an atmosphere where the members are stimulated to behave similarly.

11. The group is eager to help each member develop to his full potential. It sees, for example, that relevant technical knowledge and training in interpersonal and group skills are made available to each member.

12. Each member accepts willingly and without resentment the goals and

expectations that he and his group establish for themselves. The anxieties, fears, and emotional stresses produced by direct pressure for high performance from a boss in a hierarchical situation is not present. Groups seem capable of setting high performance goals for the group as a whole and for each member. These goals are high enough to stimulate each member to do his best, but not so high as to create anxieties or fear of failure. In an effective group, each person can exert sufficient influence on the decisions of the group to prevent the group from setting unattainable goals for any member while setting high goals for all. The goals are adapted to the member's capacity to perform.

13. The leader and the members believe that each group member can accomplish "the impossible." These expectations stretch each member to the maximum and accelerate his growth. When necessary, the group tempers the expectation level so that the member is not broken by a feeling of failure or rejection.

14. When necessary or advisable, other members of the group will give a member the help he needs to accomplish successfully the goals set for him. Mutual help is a characteristic of highly effective groups.

15. The supportive atmosphere of the highly effective group stimulates creativity. The group does not demand narrow conformity as do the work groups under authoritarian leaders. No one has to "yes the boss," nor is he rewarded for such an attempt. The group attaches high value to new, creative approaches and solutions to its problems and to the problems of the organization of which it is a part. The motivation to be creative is high when one's work group prizes creativity.

16. The group knows the value of "constructive" conformity and knows when to use it and for what purposes. Although it does not permit conformity to affect adversely the creative efforts of its members, it does expect conformity on mechanical and administrative matters to save the time of members and to facilitate the group's activities. The group agrees, for example, on administrative forms and procedures, and once they have been established, it expects its members to abide by them until there is good reason to change them.

17. There is strong motivation on the part of each member to communicate fully and frankly to the group all the information which is relevant and of value to the group's activity. This stems directly from the member's desire to be valued by the group and to get the job done. The more important to the group a member feels an item of information to be, the greater is his motivation to communicate it.

18. There is high motivation in the group to use the communication process so that it best serves the interests and goals of the group. Every item which a member feels is important, but which for some reason is being ignored, will be repeated until it receives the attention that it deserves. Members strive also to avoid communicating unimportant information so as not to waste the group's time.

19. Just as there is high motivation to communicate, there is correspondingly strong motivation to receive communications. Each member is genuinely interested in any information on any relevant matter that any member of the group can provide. This information is welcomed and trusted as being honestly and sincerely given. Members do not look "behind" the information item and attempt to interpret it in ways opposite to its purported intent. This interest of group members in information items and the treatment of such items as valid reinforces the motivation to communicate.

20. In the highly effective group, there are strong motivations to try to influence other members as well as to be receptive to influence by them. This applies to all the group's activities: technical matters, methods, organizational problems, interpersonal relationships, and group processes.

21. The group processes of the highly effective group enable the members to exert more influence on the leader and to communicate far more information to him, including suggestions as to what needs to be done and how he could do his job better, than is possible in a man-to-man relationship. By "tossing the ball" back and forth among its members, a group can communicate information to the leader which no single person on a man-to-man basis dare do. As a consequence, the boss receives all the information that the group possesses to help him perform his job effectively.

22. The ability of the members of a group to influence each other contributes to the flexibility and adaptability of the group. Ideas, goals, and attitudes do not become frozen if members are able to influence each other continuously.

Although the group is eager to examine any new ideas and methods which will help it do its job better and is willing to be influenced by its members, it is not easily shifted or swayed. Any change is undertaken only after rigorous examination of the evidence. This stability in the group's activities is due to the steadying influence of the common goals and values held by the group members.

23. In the highly effective group, individual members feel secure in making decisions which seem appropriate to them because the goals and philosophy of operation are clearly understood by each member and provide him with a solid base for his decisions. This unleashes initiative and pushes decisions down while still maintaining a coordinated and directed effort.

24. The leader of a highly effective group is selected carefully. His leadership ability is so evident that he would probably emerge as a leader in any unstructured situation. To increase the likelihood that persons of high leadership competence are selected, the organization is likely to use peer nominations and related methods in selecting group leaders.

An important aspect of the highly effective group is its extensive use of the principle of supportive relationships. An examination of the above material reveals that virtually every statement involves an application of this principle.

## Leadership Functions

Several different characteristics of highly effective groups have been briefly examined. The role of the leader in these groups is, as we have suggested, particularly important. Certain leadership functions can be shared with group members; others can be performed only by the designated leader. In an organization, for example, the leader of a unit is the person who has primary responsibility for linking his work group to the rest of the organization. Other members of the group may help perform the linking function by serving as linking pins in overlapping groups other than that provided by the line organization, but the major linking is necessarily through the line organization. The leader has full responsibility for the group's performance and for seeing that his group meets the demands and expectations placed upon it by the rest of the organization of which it is a part. Other members of the group may share this responsibility at times, but the leader can never avoid full responsibility for the adequate performance of his group.

Although the leader has full responsibility, he does not try to make all the decisions. He develops his group into a unit which, with his participation, makes better decisions than he can make alone. He helps the group develop efficient communication and influence processes which provide it with better information, more technical knowledge, more facts, and more experience for decision-making purposes than the leader alone can marshal.

Through group decision-making each member feels fully identified with each decision and highly motivated to execute it fully. The over-all performance of the group, as a consequence, is even better than the excellent quality of the decisions.

The leader knows that at times decisions must be made rapidly and cannot wait for group processes. He anticipates these emergencies and establishes procedures with his group for handling them so that action can be taken rapidly with group support.

The leader feels primarily responsible for establishing and maintaining at all times a thoroughly supportive atmosphere in the group. He encourages other members to share this responsibility, but never loses sight of the fact that as the leader of a work group which is part of a larger organization his behavior is likely to set the tone.

Although the leader accepts the responsibility associated with his role of leader of a group which is part of a larger organization, he seeks to minimize the influence of his hierarchical position. He is aware that trying to get results by "pulling rank" affects adversely the effectiveness of his group and his relationship to it. Thus, he endeavors to deemphasize status. He does this in a variety of ways that fit his personality and methods of leading, as for example by:

- Listening well and patiently
- Not being impatient with the progress being made by the group, particularly on difficult problems
- Accepting more blame than may be warranted for any failure or mistake
- Giving the group members ample opportunity to express their thoughts without being constrained by the leader pressing his own views
- Being careful never to impose a decision upon the group
- Putting his contributions often in the form of questions or stating them speculatively
- Arranging for others to help perform leadership functions which enhance their status

The leader strengthens the group and group processes by seeing that all problems *which involve the group* are dealt with by the group. He never handles such problems outside of the group nor with individual members of the group. While the leader is careful to see that all matters which involve and affect the whole group are handled by the whole group, he is equally alert not to undertake in a group-meeting agenda items or tasks which do not concern the group. Matters concerning one individual member and only that member are, of course, handled individually. Matters involving only a subgroup are handled by that subgroup. The total group is kept informed, however, of any subgroup action.

The leader fully reflects and effectively represents the views, goals, values, and decisions of his group in those other groups where he is performing the function of linking his group to the rest of the organization. He brings to the group of which he is the leader the views, goals, and decisions of those other groups.

In this way, he provides a linkage whereby communication and the exercise of influence can be performed in both directions.

The leader has adequate competence to handle the technical problems faced by his group, or he sees that access to this technical knowledge is fully provided. This may involve bringing in, as needed, technical or resource persons. Or he may arrange to have technical training given to one or more members of his group so that the group can have available the necessary technical know-how when the group discusses a problem and arrives at a decision.

The leader is what might be called "group-centered," in a sense comparable with the "employee-centered" supervisor described in Chapter 2. He endeavors to build and maintain in his group a keen sense of responsibility for achieving its own goals and meeting its obligations to the larger organization.

The leader helps to provide the group with the stimulation arising from a restless dissatisfaction. He discourages complacency and passive acceptance of the present. He helps the members to become aware of new possibilities, more important values, and more significant goals.

The leader is an important source of enthusiasm for the significance of the mission and goals of the group. He sees that the tasks of the group are important and significant and difficult enough to be challenging.

As an over-all guide to his leadership behavior, the leader understands and uses with sensitivity and skill the principle of supportive relationships.

Many of these leadership functions, such as the linking function, can be performed only by the designated leader. This makes clear the great importance of selecting competent persons for leadership positions.

## Roles of Membership and Leadership

In the highly effective group, many functions are performed either by the leader or by the members, depending upon the situation or the requirements of the moment. The leader and members, as part of their roles in the group, establish and maintain an atmosphere and relationships which enable the communication, influence, decision-making, and similar processes of the group to be performed effectively. This means not only creating positive conditions, such as a supportive atmosphere, but also eliminating any negative or blocking factors. Thus, for example, groups sometimes have to deal with members who are insensitive, who are hostile, who talk too much, or who otherwise behave in ways adversely affecting the capacity of the group to function. In handling such a problem, the group makes the member aware of his deficiency, but does this in a sensitive and considerate manner and in a way to assist the member to function more effectively in the group. The members of most ordinary groups stop listening to a member who expresses himself in a fuzzy or confused manner. In a highly effective group, the members feed back their reaction to the person involved with suggestions and assistance on how to make his contributions clear, important, and of the kind to which all will want to listen. Friendly assistance and coaching can help a member overcome excessive talking or help him to learn to think and express himself more clearly.

Benne and Sheats (1948) have prepared a description of the different roles played in well-functioning groups. These roles may at times be performed by one or more group members, at other times by the leader. The list, while prepared on the basis of roles in discussion and problem-solving groups, is useful in considering the functions to be performed in any work group which is part of a larger organization.

The following material is taken from the Benne and Sheats article (pp. 42–45) with slight modifications. Group roles are classified into two broad categories:

1. *Group task roles.* These roles are related to the task which the group is deciding to undertake or has undertaken. They are directly concerned with the group effort in the selection and definition of a common problem and in the solution of that problem.

2. *Group building and maintenance roles.* These roles concern the functioning of the group as a group. They deal with the group's efforts to strengthen, regulate, and perpetuate the group as a group.

### Group Task Roles

The following analysis assumes that the task of the group is to select, define, and solve common problems. The roles are identified in relation to functions of facilitation and coordination of group problem-solving activities. Each member may, of course, enact more than one role in any given unit of participation and a wide range of roles in successive participations. Any or all of these roles may be performed, at times, by the group "leader" as well as by various members.

*A. Initiating-contributing:* suggesting or proposing to the group new ideas or a changed way of regarding the group problem or goal. The novelty proposed may take the form of suggestions of a new group goal or a new definition of the problem. It may take the form of a suggested solution or some way of handling a difficulty that the group has encountered. Or it may take the form of a proposed new procedure for the group, a new way of organizing the group for the task ahead.

*B. Information seeking:* asking for clarification of suggestions made in terms of their factual adequacy, for authoritative information and facts pertinent to the problems being discussed.

*C. Opinion seeking:* seeking information not primarily on the facts of the case, but for a clarification of the values pertinent to what the group is undertaking or of values involved in a suggestion made or in alternative suggestions.

*D. Information giving:* offering facts or generalizations which are "authoritative" or involve presenting an experience pertinent to the group problem.

*E. Opinion giving:* stating beliefs or opinions pertinent to a suggestion made or to alternative suggestions. The emphasis is on the proposal of what should become the group's view of pertinent values, not primarily upon relevant facts or information.

*F. Elaborating:* spelling out suggestions in terms of examples or developed meanings, offering a rationale for suggestions previously made, and trying to deduce how an idea or suggestion would work out if adopted by the group.

*G. Coordinating:* showing or clarifying the relationships among various ideas and suggestions, trying to pull ideas and suggestions together or trying to coordinate the activities of various members or sub-groups.

*H. Orienting:* defining the position of the group with respect to its goals by summarizing what has occurred, departures from agreed upon directions or goals are pointed to, or questions are raised about the direction the group discussion is taking.

*I. Evaluating:* subjecting the accomplishment of the group to some standard or set of standards of group functioning in the context of the group task. Thus, it may involve evaluating or questioning the "practicality," the "logic," or the "procedure" of a suggestion or of some unit of group discussion.

*J. Energizing:* prodding the group to action or decision, attempting to stimulate or arouse the group to "greater" activity or to activity of a "higher quality."

*K. Assisting on procedure:* expediting group movement by doing things for the group—performing routine tasks, e.g., distributing materials, or manipulating objects for the group, e.g., rearranging the seating or running the recording machine, etc.

*L. Recording:* writing down suggestions, making a record of group decisions, or writing down the product of discussion. The recorder role is the "group memory."

## Group Building and Maintenance Roles

Here the analysis of member-functions is oriented to those activities which build group loyalty and increase the motivation and capacity of the group for candid and effective interaction and problem-solving. One or more members or the leader may perform each of these roles.

*A. Encouraging:* praising, showing interest in, agreeing with, and accepting the contributions of others; indicating warmth and solidarity in one's attitudes toward other group members, listening attentively and seriously to the contributions of group members, giving these contributions full and adequate consideration even though one may not fully agree with them; conveying to the others a feeling that—"that which you are about to say is of importance to me."

*B. Harmonizing:* mediating the differences between other members, attempting to reconcile disagreements, relieving tension in conflict situations through jesting or pouring oil on troubled waters, etc.

*C. Compromising:* operating from within a conflict in which one's ideas or position is involved. In this role one may offer a compromise by yielding status, admitting error, by disciplining oneself to maintain group harmony, or by "coming half-way" in moving along with the group.

*D. Gate-keeping and expediting:* attempting to keep communication channels open by encouraging or facilitating the participation of others or by proposing regulation of the flow of communication.

*E. Setting standards or ideals:* expressing standards for the group or applying standards in evaluating the quality of group processes.

*F. Observing:* keeping records of various aspects of group process and feeding such data with proposed interpretations into the group's evaluation of its own procedures. The contribution of the person performing this role is usually best received or most fittingly received by the group when this particular role has been performed by this person at the request of the group and when the report to the group avoids expressing value judgments, approval, or disapproval.

*G. Following:* going along with the group, more or less passively accepting the ideas of others, serving as an audience in group discussion and decision.

The *group task roles* all deal with the intellectual aspects of the group's work. These roles are performed by members of the group during the problem-solving process, which usually involves such steps as:

1. Defining the problem
2. Listing the conditions or criteria which any satisfactory solution to the problem should meet
3. Listing possible alternative solutions
4. Obtaining the facts which bear on each possible solution
5. Evaluating the suggested solutions in terms of the conditions which a satisfactory solution should meet
6. Eliminating undesirable solutions and selecting the most desirable solution

The *group building and maintenance roles* are, as the label suggests, concerned with the emotional life of the group. These roles deal with the group's attractiveness to its members, its warmth and supportiveness, its motivation and capacity to handle intellectual problems without bias and emotion, and its capacity to function as a "mature" group.

The membership roles proposed by Benne and Sheats, while they are not definitive or complete, nevertheless point to the many complex functions performed in groups and dealt with by leader and members. The members of a highly effective group handle these roles with sensitivity and skill, and they see that the emotional life of the group contributes to the performance of the group's tasks rather than interfering with them.[1]

The highly effective group does not hesitate, for example, to look at and deal with friction between its members. By openly putting such problems on the table and sincerely examining them, they can be dealt with constructively. An effective group does not have values which frown upon criticism or which prevent bringing friction between members into the open. As a consequence, it does not put the lid on these emotional pressures, causing them to simmer below the surface and be a constant source of disruption to the performance of group tasks. The intellectual functions of any group can be performed without bias and disruption only when the internal emotional tensions and conflicts have been removed from the life of the group. Differences in ideas are stimulating and contribute to creativity, but emotional conflict immobilizes a group.

Group building and maintenance functions and group task functions are interdependent processes. In order to tackle difficult problems, to solve them creatively, and to achieve high performance, a group must be at a high level of group maintenance. Success in task processes, fortunately, also contributes to the maintenance of the group and to its emotional life, including its attraction to members and its supportive atmosphere.

In the midst of struggling with a very difficult task, a group occasionally may be faced with group maintenance problems. At such times, it may be necessary for the group to stop its intellectual activity and in one way or another to look at and deal with the disruptive emotional stresses. After this has been done, the group can then go forward with greater unity and will be more likely to solve its group task constructively.

[1]Although the Benne and Sheats list does not define each category unambiguously, it is useful in helping a group analyze and improve its processes. Another list has been prepared by Bales (1950) which has relatively precise definitions. The Bales list will be of interest to those who wish to do research on group processes or who wish to observe and analyze them systematically.

The leader and the members in the highly effective group know that the building and maintenance of the group as well as the carrying out of tasks need to be done well. They are highly skilled in performing each of the different membership and leadership roles required. Each member feels responsible for assuming whatever role is necessary to keep the group operating in an efficient manner. In performing these required roles, the member may carry them out by himself or in cooperation with other group members. Each exercises initiative as called for by the situation. The group has a high capacity to mobilize fully all the skills and abilities of its members and focus these resources efficiently on the jobs to be done.

The larger the work group, the greater the difficulty in building it into a highly effective group. Seashore (1954) found that group cohesiveness, i.e., attraction of the members to the group, decreased steadily as work groups increased in size. This finding is supported also by other data (Indik, 1961; Revans, 1957).

To facilitate building work groups to high levels of effectiveness it will be desirable, consequently, to keep the groups as small as possible. This requirement, however, must be balanced against other demands on the organization, such as keeping the number of organizational levels to a minimum. This suggests the desirability of running tests and computing the relative efficiencies and costs of different-sized work groups. It is probable also that the optimum size for a group will vary with the kind of work the group is doing.

The highly effective group as described in this chapter, it will be recalled, is an "ideal model." It may sound completely unattainable. This does not appear to be the case. There is impressive evidence supporting the view that this ideal can be approximated, if not fully reached, in actual operations in any organization. This evidence is provided by the highest-producing managers and supervisors in American industry and government. If the measurements of their work groups and the reports of their work-group members are at all accurate, some of these managers have built and are operating work groups strikingly similar to our ideal model.

This chapter started by observing that groups can have constructive or destructive goals and can achieve these goals fully or partially, that there is nothing inherently good or bad about groups. If we reflect on the nature and functional characteristics of the highly effective group, however, some qualification of our initial comments may be warranted. In the highly effective group, the members can and do exercise substantial amounts of influence on the group's values and goals. As a consequence, these goals reflect the long-range as well as the short-range needs, desires, and values of its members. If we assume that the long-range desires and values will reflect, on the average, some of the more important long-range values and goals of the total society, we can draw some inferences about the highly effective group. These groups will, in terms of probability, reflect the constructive values and goals of their society. They are likely to be strong groups seeking "good" goals.

# FACTORS INFLUENCING THE EFFECTIVENESS OF HEALTH TEAMS

IRWIN RUBIN

RICHARD BECKHARD

## Introduction

In the first part of the article, several key variables known to be of importance in any group situation are discussed. These variables are drawn from behavioral science knowledge and their dynamics. The particular relevance of these general variables to a specific situation is discussed next. The situation chosen is an interdisciplinary health team[1] working to deliver comprehensive family-centered care[2] to the residents of a low-income urban area. The success or failure of such a highly interdependent diverse group is, in large measure, a function of how well they work together—their group process.[3] Finally, in the last section, we discuss one alternative response to the question: What can you do about it? A model is described for intervening directly into the life of a team to help them improve the way they work together. An actual case study of the application of this model is then discussed.

While many readers will not themselves be members of an interdisciplinary health team, the concepts discussed and issues raised should nonetheless be easily generalizable. By combining both theory and practice, this article will enable the reader to more easily see the "real world" relevance of group process.

## The Dynamics of Groups

In this section, we will present and briefly define seven selected characteristics or variables known to be of importance in any group situation. Each character-

---

Abridged and reprinted from I. M. Rubin and R. Beckhard, "Factors Influencing the Effectiveness of Health Teams." *Milbank Quarterly*, July, 1972, p. 317–335.

[1]The "average" team in this center consisted of a full-time internist, a full-time pediatrician, two full-time nurses, and four to six full-time family health workers drawn from the community. Available on a part-time basis were a dentist, a psychiatrist, in addition to the back-up support of X-rays, labs, and the like. A team was responsible for 1,500 families in a particular geographical area.

[2]We pay little attention in this paper to the very important question of the organization of which the health team is a part. For an intensive discussion of the organizational issues involved in the delivery of health care see R. Beckhard, "The Organizational Issues in Team Delivery of Health Care," *Milbank Quarterly*, 1971.

[3]For an excellent and readable description of group process, see E. H. Schein, *Process Consultation*. Reading, Mass.: Addison-Wesley Publishing Co., 1969.

istic can be viewed as a scale or yardstick against which one can ask the question: Is this particular group (made up of certain kinds of people, trying to do a given task in this situation) located where it needs to be on each of these scales to function most effectively?

### Goals or Mission

A team or group has a *purpose*. There exists a reason (or reasons) for the formation of the group in the first place. In any group, therefore, there will be issues like:

(a) How clearly defined are the goals? Who sets the goals?
(b) How much agreement is there among members concerning the goals? How much commitment?
(c) How clearly measurable is goal achievement?
(d) How do group goals relate to broader organizational goals? To personal goals?

Since a group's very existence is to achieve some goal or mission, these issues are of central importance.

### Role Expectations—Internal

In working to achieve their goals, group members will play a variety of *roles*. There exists among the members of a group a set of multiple expectations concerning role behavior. Each person, in effect, has a set of expectations of how each of the other members[4] *should* behave as the group works to achieve its goals. In any group, therefore, there exists questions about:

a) the extent to which such expectations are clearly defined and communicated (role ambiguity);

b) the extent to which such expectations are compatible or in conflict (role conflict); and

c) the extent to which any individual is capable of meeting these multiple expectations (role overload).

These role expectations are messages "sent" between the members of a group. Generally, the more uncertain and complex the task, the more salient are issues of role expectations.

### Role Expectations—External

Any individual is a member of several groups. Each group of which he is a member has expectations which can influence his behavior. The Director of Pediatrics in a hospital, for example, is "simultaneously" the manager of his group, a subordinate, a member in a group of peers (directors of the functional areas), a member of a hospital staff, a father, husband, etc.

[4]For an excellent study of this concept of role sets see R. N. Kahn, *et al., Organizational Stress: Studies in Role Conflict and Ambiguity* (New York: Wiley, 1964).

Each of these "reference" groups, as they are called, holds expectations of a person's behavior. Together they can be ambiguous, in conflict, or create overload. These multiple *reference group* loyalties can create significant problems for an individual in terms of his behavior as a *member* of a particular group. While the source of the conflicts involved in the question of reference group loyalties is external to a particular group, they can have significant *internal* effects.

### Decision-making

A group is a problem-solving, decision-making mechanism. This is not to imply that an entire group must always make all decisions as a group. The issue is one of relevance and appropriateness; *who* has the relevant information and *who* will have to implement the decision. A group can choose from a range of decision-making mechanisms including decision by default (lack of group response), unilateral decision (authority rule), majority vote, consensus, or unanimity.

Each form is appropriate under certain conditions. Each will have different consequences both in terms of the amount of information available for use in making the decision, and the subsequent commitment of members to implement the decision.

Similarly, when a group faces a conflict it can choose to (a) ignore it, (b) smooth over it, (c) allow one person to force a decision, (d) create a compromise, or (e) confront all the realities of the conflict (facts and feelings), and attempt to develop an innovative solution. The choices it makes in both of these areas will significantly influence group functioning.

### Communication Patterns

If, indeed, a group is a problem-solving, decision-making mechanism, then the effective flow of information is central to its functioning. Anything which acts to inhibit the flow of information will detract from the group effectiveness.

There are a range of factors which affect information flow. At a very simple level there are architectural and geographical issues. Meeting space can be designed to facilitate or hinder the flow of communication. Geographically separated facilities may be a barrier to rapid information exchange. There are also numerous more subtle factors. Participation—frequency, order, and content—may follow formal lines of authority or status. High-status members may speak first, most, and most convincingly on all issues. The best sources of information needed to solve a problem will, however, vary with the problem. Patterns of communication based exclusively on formal lines of status will not meet many of the group's information needs. People's feelings of freedom to participate, to challenge, to express opinions also significantly affect information flow.

### Leadership

Very much related to the processes of decision-making and communication is the area of leadership. To function effectively, a group needs many *acts of leadership*—not necessarily one "leader" but many leaders. People often misinterpret such a statement as saying "good groups are leaderless." This is not the intent. Depending on the situation and the problem to be solved, different people *can* and *should* assume leadership. The formal leader of a group may be in the best position to reflect the "organization's" position on a particular problem. Someone else may be a resource in helping the formal leader and another member clarify a point of disagreement. All are examples of *necessary acts of leadership*. It is highly unlikely that in any group there will be one person capable of meeting all of a group's leadership needs.

### Norms

Norms are unwritten (often untested explicitly) rules governing the behavior of people in groups. They define what behavior is "good or bad," "acceptable or unacceptable" if one is to be a functioning member of this group. As such, they become very powerful *determinants* of group behavior and take on the quality of laws—"It's the way we do things around here!" Their existence is most clear when they are violated—quiet uneasiness, shifting in one's seat, joking reminders, are observable. Repeated violation of norms often leads to expulsion—psychological or physical.

Norms take on particular potency because they influence all of the other areas previously discussed. Groups develop norms governing leadership, influence, communication patterns, decision-making, conflict resolution, and the like. Inherently, norms are not good or bad. The issue is one of appropriateness—does a particular norm help or hinder a group's ability to work.

These seven factors, then, are characteristics of any group situation. Where a particular group needs to be on each of these "yardsticks" is a function of the situation. We turn now to look at these factors within the setting of health teams.

### The Dynamics of a Health Team

Our intention in this section is to look at these factors affecting group functioning and to relate them to a group[5] setting (community-based, total health care). The center in which we have worked[6] is the particular situation from which we will draw examples and observations. However, the issues raised are, in our view, very broadly relevant.

### Goals or Mission

A health team striving to provide "comprehensive family-centered health care" faces uncertainties substantially different from those one might find in a

[5]By group practice we mean situations wherein people are together over long periods of time working on a common task. More temporary groups like the group formed to do a particular operation in a hospital are not included in our discussion. Even in many temporary groups, such as short duration task forces or committees, many of the process factors discussed can be observed to be in operation.

[6]For a more detailed preliminary report of our activities in this setting see: Fry, R. E. and Lech, B. A., "An Organizational Development Approach to Improving the Effectiveness of Neighborhood Health Care Teams: A Pilot Program," Unpublished Master's thesis, Sloan School of Management, Massachusetts Institute of Technology, June, 1971. (Copies available from Dr. Martin Luther King, Jr. Health Center, 3674 Third Avenue, Bronx, New York 10456.)

hospital setting. The goals[7] in a hospital are relatively clear: remove the gall stone, deliver the baby. Success is measurable and clear. Seldom are social factors of prime importance. The thrust is curative and the emphasis is medical.

The community-oriented health teams we have studied experience considerable uncertainty over their mission. "Comprehensive" means the team cannot ignore *social* problems and emphasize the "relative security and certainty" of medical problems. There is considerable anxiety generated because the team does not really know when and if it is succeeding. The questions of *priorities* and time allocations become complicated; how does one decide between competing activities in the absence of clearly defined goals? A team member wonders if she should spend half a day trying to arrange for a school transfer for a child or should she see the other patients scheduled for visits.

No one member of the team has been trained to be knowledgeable in all the areas required. Yet, the complexity of the task demands that doctors become involved in social problems; nurses become the supervisors of paraprofessional family health workers who are an integral part of the team; and these community-based family health workers become knowledgeable in diagnosing and treating psychiatric problems. This is not to say everyone should become an expert at solving all problems. The requirements are for considerable information collection, sharing, and group planning so that the *team* has all the available information to deploy its total resources to the task.

The anxieties and frustrations created by the complexity of the task are *inevitable*—an inherent part of providing "comprehensive" care.[8] A major team dilemma is one of managing short- versus long-run considerations—to give itself short-run security and direction while not losing sight of its long-run vague and global goal.

### Role Expectations—Internal and External

The nature of the task—comprehensive family-centered health care—demands a highly diverse set of skills, knowledge, backgrounds. In creating a team, many "cultures" are of *necessity* being mixed and asked to work together.

As a result of educational background and training, the doctors are accustomed to being primary (if not sole) authority and most expert in medical issues. The specialist role for which they have been so well trained and which is so appropriate in a hospital setting comes under pressure. As a team member, in addition to his specialist skills, the doctor is asked to become more of a generalist. He needs to teach other health workers some of his medical knowledge. He also needs to *learn* from them more about the social problems facing the community and the character, mores, and values of the particular patient population.

[7] If one takes a *total* hospital as a group, many similar issues appear. Revens, for example, argues that the central task in a hospital is the management of anxiety. This is very analogous to the position we take *vis-à-vis* a health team. The only difference is that the problems are more visible in the smaller social system of an ongoing group. See R. W. Revens, *Standards for Morale: Cause and Effect in Hospitals.* (London: Oxford University Press, 1964).

[8] A very useful tool for diagnosing the forces impinging upon a team is called life space or force field analysis. For more detail, see Fry and Lech, *op. cit.*, and an article by Kurt Lewin, in W. Bennis, K. Benne, and R. Chin, *The Planning of Change*, 2nd ed. (New York: Holt, Rinehart, and Winston, 1969).

Doctors tend to maintain strong psychological ties with their professional specialty groups. The stronger these ties for a physician, the more difficult it will be for him to develop needed team loyalty. His sense of professionalism stems from these external reference groups. The careful hospital-type workup he has been so well trained to do may not be feasible or appropriate in the face of the hectic schedule generated by large numbers of patients. The conflict may become one around "professional standards." Comprehensive group practice may require a redefinition of these standards and perhaps even the redefinition of a professional.

Both the nurses and family health workers tend to bring a history of submissiveness. The nurses have been trained to be submissive to doctors. In this setting, nurses find themselves as *coordinators* of the work of a team *including doctors*—a complete role reversal.

Family health workers in this case are local community residents who, after six months of clinical training, suddenly find themselves defined as "colleagues" with middle-class physicians. They bring a deep concern for social problems coupled with the best understanding of what will or will not work with patients (their friends and relatives!). The team needs their knowledge of the cultural norms of the community and their commitment to social issues. Their background and passive posture is often a barrier to the realization of these expectations.

Whereas the nurses and doctors have a professional reference group, the family health workers as yet have none. The resulting feelings of "homelessness" are heightened by their liaison role at the interface between the team and the community.[9] Their membership and acceptance in the community is crucial to the team's ability to be of service. They alone can serve to bridge the cultural gaps which exist.[10]

This set of conditions differs markedly from the hospital setting where strong reference group loyalties and clearly defined role expectations are common. Behaviors learned during one's individual preparation are appropriately applicable in the vast majority of situations. Although professionals and paraprofessionals work in the same organization, seldom, if ever, are they asked to work in highly interdependent on-going stable groups.

A part of being a member of a highly interdependent team is the need to develop new loyalties and learn how to do some new things—not anticipated or covered during individual training. In fact, it is very unlikely that, in the face of the mission of providing "comprehensive family-centered health care," clearly defined, complete job descriptions will ever be feasible.[11] This reality puts great stress on a team's ability to learn and adapt by itself. In response to a particular problem, the question cannot be "Whose job is it?" but may instead have to be "Who on the team is capable?" or "Who needs to learn how to handle this situation?"

[9]Such people have been called marginal men. A foreman in a factory is another example since he is caught between the management culture and the worker culture.
[10]The very notion of a team approach to the delivery of health care may, for example, force a redefinition of the norm of privacy between doctor and patient. The norm may need to be adapted to encompass team and patient.
[11]Many organizations are realizing the needs for such fluid role relationships. A job is now viewed as "a man in action in a particular situation at a particular moment." Such "job descriptions" must be constantly renegotiated and updated to account for *both* changes in the man and the situation.

The inherent uncertainties in its mission and the diverse mix of skills represented on a health team suggest that decisions can seldom be appropriately made in a routine, programmable, or unilateral manner. This is in sharp contrast to the majority of cases in the hospital setting where there is the relative clarity and certainty of the goals and clearly defined roles and lines of authority.

One difficulty in any on-going team is the need to differentiate a variety of decision-making situations. In an attempt to be "democratic and participative" a team might try to make all decisions by consensus as a team. This represents a failure to distinguish, for example, (a) who has the information necessary to make a decision, (b) who needs to be *consulted before* certain decisions get made, and (c) who needs to be informed of a decision, after it has been made. Under certain circumstances, the team may need to strive for unanimity or consensus; in other cases, majority vote may be appropriate.

Perhaps the greatest barrier to effective decision-making in highly interdependent health teams stems again from the "cultural" backgrounds of team members. Doctors are used to making decisions by themselves or in collaboration with peers of equal status—other doctors or highly educated professionals. At the other extreme, the community residents who work on the team are used to being passive dependent recipients of others' decisions. Yet many times, on a health team, the doctor and the community workers *are and must behave as peers*—neither one possessing all the information needed to solve a particular problem or make a particular decision. Furthermore, there are many times when the doctor is the one who needs information held by another health worker. When a conflict develops, the required discussion which will lead to consensus is difficult to achieve; forcing, compromise, or decision by default may result. Commitment to decisions is low with the result being that many decisions have to be remade several times—"I thought we decided that last week!" or "Didn't we decide that you would do such and such?"

The team approach to delivery of health care puts great stress on the need for numerous and various inputs to many decisions. When the decision-making process is inappropriate, less information is shared, commitment is lowered, and anxiety and frustration are increased.

### Communication Patterns/Leadership

Issues of communication patterns and leadership can be handled together for, as was true in the case of decision making as well, the central theme is one of "influence." The leadership or influence structure—to which we have all become so accustomed via our family, educational, and organizational experiences and which is appropriate for a hospital operating room, for example—will be incapable of responding to the diversity of issues with which a health team must deal. In this setting, *each member* is a resource. He must have open channels to all the other members. Because of the complexities in this type of group, a number of communication norms are required: openness (leveling) and a *person-to-person* relationship which has enough mutual trust to enable each person to "tell it like it is."

Team practice cannot work if *roles* talk to *roles*—a much more personal mutual dependency is required. Influence, communication frequency, and leadership should be determined by the nature of the problem to be solved not by hierarchical position, by seating position, educational background, or social status.

With respect to leadership, in particular, the teams we have studied relied on the model they knew best—in this case, *"follow the doctor."* Continued reliance on that model will result in an overemphasis on medical versus social issues, a lack of shared commitment to decisions (which doctors sometimes interpret as "lack of professional attitude"), and less than complete sharing of information, all of which affect the task performance directly.

### Norms

Much of what we have described is reflected in a group's *norms*. The teams we have studied have exhibited several powerful norms:

(a) "In making a decision, silence means consent."

(b) "Doctors are more important than other team members," "We don't disagree with them"; "We wait for them to lead."

(c) Conflict is dangerous, *both* task conflicts and interpersonal disagreements—"It's best to leave sleeping dogs lie."

(d) Positive feelings, praise, support are not to be shared—"We're all 'professionals' here to do a job."

(e) The precision and exactness demanded by our task negate the opportunity to be *flexible* with respect to our own internal group processes. (This may be a carryover from the hospital operating room environment where the last thing you need is an innovative idea as to how to do things better!)

The effects of these norms, and others like them, is to guarantee that a team gets caught in a negative spiral.[12] While the norms are those of rigidity, the complexity of the environment and the task to be done demand flexibility. The frustrating, anxiety-provoking quality of the task places great demands for some place to recharge one's emotional battery. The team is potentially such a place.

In addition to these specific norms of flexibility, support, and openness of communication, there are a set of higher order norms which are essential. Task uncertainty and environmental changes require that a team develop a capacity to become self-renewing—to become a *learning* organism. Learning requires a climate which legitimizes controlled experimentation, risk taking, failure, and evaluation of outcomes. In the absence of norms which support and reinforce these kinds of behaviors, a team will end up fighting two enemies—*its task and itself.*

There exists, in other words, a unique connection between what a team does (its *task*) and how it goes about doing it (its *internal group processes*). At a very simple level, the health care analogy would be: If a team is to treat a family as an integrated unit (its task), the team itself must, in many ways, operate as a highly integrated "family unit" (its internal group processes). Without this ability

---

[12]It is in this regard that our thinking is very similar to Revens'. The ineffective management of inherent anxiety results in more anxiety creating a negative feedback loop and a self-reinforcing downward spiral. See Fry and Lech, *op. cit.*

to maintain itself a health team will, like many other "pieces of equipment," eventually burn itself out. In the interim, work continues to get done but more and more energy is demanded to "move the machine forward."

To summarize, the "internal process" issues we have discussed will occur in any group. They cannot be wished away or ignored for long without some cost. Nor are they the result—as is frequently assumed—of basic personality problems. More often team members have difficulty functioning together because of ambiguous goal orientations, unclear role expectations, dysfunctional decision-making procedures, and other such process issues.

If a health team is first to survive and second to grow, it must, as we have said, develop an attitude and a capability for building and renewing itself as a team. It can do this first by becoming aware of how its internal group processes influence its ability to function and second by learning how to manage these process or maintenance needs in a more productive manner.

We turn now to a brief case illustration of an effort aimed at helping health teams move closer to this ideal of becoming self-renewing or learning organisms.

### A Case Study of a Health Team Improvement Effort[13]

Our efforts at helping teams improve their functioning relied heavily upon a very simple but powerful model—the action research approach.[14] The basic flow of activities can be depicted in the following manner:

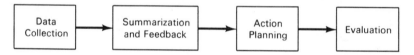

In this setting, the initial activity with a health team involved interviewing each member individually—using both openended questions and checklist ratings. Questions asked related directly to the seven process factors discussed earlier such as team goals, level of participation, decision-making styles, etc. These data were then summarized and fed back *anonymously* to the entire team.

Team members' reactions to the data presented during this feedback session were varied. For some, the result was one of surprise—"I didn't realize people felt that way about this team!" Others were surprised to find many of their own concerns widely shared. Before the feedback session, many people believed they were the only ones experiencing certain difficulties. The most frequent reaction could be characterized as follows: "These problems have been around—*under the surface*—for a long time. Now they have been collected, summarized, and are out on the table for all of us to see."

The teams, in other words, were provided with an *image* or *picture* of their present state based on information (feelings as well as facts) collected from the

[13]Our initial efforts at dividing into two health teams are reported in detail in Fry and Lech, *op. cit.* We have to date completed initial interventions with six health teams. Similar activities are planned for other teams in the future as well as follow-up activities to reinforce our initial efforts. Four of our students—Ron Fry, Bern Lech, Marc Gerstein, and Mark Plovnick—have worked closely with us in these efforts.

[14]For an excellent description of this model and its applicability in a wide variety of situations see R. Beckhard, *Organization Development: Strategies and Models.* Reading, Mass.: Addison-Wesley Publishing Co., 1969.

most valid sources available—the team members themselves. As a result of the interview feedback process, teams *owned* the information (verbatim quotes were used to exemplify a particular issue) and *shared* the image of their present state —"It's out on the table for all of us to see." These two elements of *shared ownership* helped to create a heightened desire and commitment on the part of team members to solve their problems.

In order to cope with the large number of complex problems reflected in the information and to move most effectively into action planning, the health teams had to:

a) prioritize the multiple issues reflected in their data;

b) decide upon the most appropriate format to use (total group, homogeneous versus heterogeneous subgroups, etc.) to generate solution alternatives;

c) develop a clear and shared set of *change objectives* or goals—an image of what a more ideal or improved state would be;

d) allocate individual and subgroup responsibilities to implement chosen actions; and

e) specify mechanisms and procedures for checking progress (follow-up).

The problem-solving skills, attitudes, norms, etc., needed to accomplish the above "process work" were *very similar* to behaviors needed to successfully accomplish "task work." This unique connection between task and process can be clarified with the following example.

A salient problem in each health team concerned their regularly scheduled 1½ hour weekly team conference meetings. These meetings represented the one time each week when the entire team met together. The intent was to discuss patient family cases, learn from each other's experiences, work on common problems and the like. The pervasive feeling with regard to these meetings was one of frustration and dissatisfaction. They were dull, a waste of time, and a time for some people to "lecture" about their pet topics.

The way the team managed itself (its process) during these meetings in fact made the situation more difficult. The negative spiral to which we referred earlier was operating to drain energy and commitment required to solve patient problems.

The specific action plans developed and subsequent team improvement interventions were, in each case, a product of the particular issues reflected in the data collected initially from a team. Regardless of the problem, the same action research model, with minor variations was applied. For example, action plans aimed at improving the team conference meeting included:

(a) the formation of agenda planning committees:

(b) systems of rotating chairmen to help all team members enhance their skills at running a meeting;

(c) designation of observers, on a rotating basis, to help the team evaluate— *at the end of each meeting*—the impact of its own group dynamics.[15]

[15]In several cases, these observers were part of the next agenda planning committee. The data collected by the observers, in other words, was quickly used as an input into the next action planning phase.

While many consultant interventions were aimed at helping a team to solve problems it *presently* felt, longer run considerations also guided consultant behavior. Whenever feasible, a team was helped to see the connection between *what* they were doing (their task) and *how* they were going about it (their internal group process). This expanded awareness helped to develop an attitude (norm) toward change which legitimized *managed experimentation and learning.* In other words, if a team is to become self-renewing, it must be willing to experiment in a *controlled way*—to try new ways of working, evaluate and learn from the consequences of these efforts, and use this new learning in the planning and implementation of future efforts. On the assumption that the action research approach we used represented a generalizable problem-solving model, we continuously worked to help the teams to internalize this model so that they could apply it when confronted with future problems.

# Interpersonal
# Perception

## EMPATHY REVISITED:[1] THE PROCESS OF
## UNDERSTANDING PEOPLE

FRED MASSARIK
IRVING R. WECHSLER

Mike Corey walked into his office, fifteen minutes behind schedule. Through the glass partition Mike caught a glimpse of his boss. Arthur Blick looked up briefly as Mike slid into his chair. A number of signs obscured the full view: "Tomorrow We Finally Have to Get Organized," "THINK," "Wait Till Next Time—You Have Done Enough Damage for Now." Mike tried to look inconspicuous, though his mind was working rapidly. He was late for the third straight day. Oh, there were good reasons all right . . . one day his wife needed to be driven downtown and *she* wasn't ready—one day he had a terrible headache . . . and then . . . today. . . . His thoughts shifted abruptly—it really didn't matter as long as Blick was in a good mood. . . . Mike had some very definite ideas about what kind of guy his boss was. Usually he wasn't a bad sort; businesslike, but human too. If you had a big problem, he probably would listen. Still he was so darn changeable, and you had to hit him "just right" if you wanted to get along. This morning Blick seemed preoccupied . . . he looked up as if he hardly saw you, yet the way he spun back to his desk telegraphed "bad news."

This was Jean Krugmeier's first day on her job. She liked being an employment interviewer. People were interesting, and it would be a novel experience to sit behind a desk all day. The initial two interviews proceeded uneventfully. The third applicant wanted to be foreman of the shipping gang. He was a young, burly 250 pounder who said that he used to work in the steel mills near Gary. He spoke loudly, with much self-assurance. "Some sort of a bully—a leering Casanova of the hot-rod set," Jean thought. Jean always did dislike guys like this, especially this sort of massive redhead. Just like her kid brother used to be—

©1959 by the Regents of the University of California. Reprinted from *California Management Review*, Vol. I, No. 2, 36–46, by permission of the Regents.

[1]The area covered by this article has been subject to systematic study only in very recent years. It is still much in flux, and few findings of certainty are as yet available. As we seek to lay out some of the problems, methods, and results with which this research is concerned, we are much aware of the tentative nature of our comments. The technically-inclined reader is urged to examine R. Tagiuri and L. Petrullo, *Person Perception and Interpersonal Behavior* (Stanford, Conn.: Stanford University Press, 1958); F. Heider, *Psychology of Interpersonal Relations* (New York: John Wiley and Sons, 1958); and U. Bronfenbrenner, J. Harding, and M. Gallwey, "The Measurement of Skill in Social Perception" in D. C. McClelland, *et al., Talent and Society* (Princeton, N.J.: Van Nostrand Co., 1958).

"a real pest!" The more he bragged about his qualifications, the more Jean became annoyed. It wouldn't do to let her feelings show; interviewers are supposed to be friendly and objective. She smiled sweetly, even if she did have a mild suspicion that her antagonism might be coming through. "I am sorry, we cannot use you just now," she said. "You don't seem to have the kind of experience we are looking for. But we'll be sure to keep your application in the active file and call you as soon as something comes up. Thank you for thinking of applying with us."

### Looking at Social Perception

These anecdotes serve to illustrate the all-pervasive role that *social perception* plays in our lives. Forming impressions of people is a part of our daily experience, yet we rarely single out the process for explicit consideration.

Mike Corey was very much concerned with making the correct perceptual assessment of Arthur Blick's mood for the morning. Of course, he reacted without specifically worrying about his *empathy*.[2] He did what came naturally. The physical obstructions in the glass partition between the two offices were not the only barriers between these men. Mike's own views, attitudes, and feelings contributed to the difficulties, and so in turn did Blick's behavior, which provided Mike with only a limited amount of information (or *cues*). The fact that the entire relationship was set in the context of a given office situation both aided and impeded the extent to which Mike Corey could accurately perceive the relevant aspects of his boss's personality.

Jean Krugmeier probably does not think of herself as a prejudiced person. She may associate the term "prejudice" primarily with racial intolerance. She argues vociferously that people must have an "open mind." Still, like all of us, she too has "blind spots" and uses "shortcut thinking" which gives her a distorted picture of reality. Her feelings about burly redheaded men are very much like any other prejudice. They are supported by a *stereotype* that, in essence, says: "All of them are alike!" Thus, Jean's feelings may be irrational, her mind may be closed, and her social perception less than accurate because she subconsciously prevents relevant information about people "of this sort" from reaching her.

#### The Illusion of Objectivity

Most of us pride ourselves on our ability to look at people in a dispassionate, objective manner. Yet the psychological realities are that every time we have a personal contact we *do* form favorable or unfavorable impressions that influence our social behavior. We all have some positive or negative feeling in our interpersonal experiences. We *do* like or dislike in varying degrees, even if we are not always willing or able to recognize our true feelings.

*Social perception* is the means by which people form impressions of and, hopefully, understand one another. *Empathy*, or *social sensitivity*, is the extent to which they succeed in developing *accurate impressions*, or actual understanding, of others.[3] Social perception is not always rational or conscious; thus it

[2] In this context, we shall treat as synonymous the concepts *empathy*, *understanding of people*, *social sensitivity*, and *accuracy in social perception*.

[3] Many complexities are involved in the actual measurement of social sensitivity. The definition given here is a kind of practical shortcut, useful for most everyday applications. For a consideration of the conceptual issues, see, for example, N. L. Gage and L. J. Cronbach, "Conceptual and Methodological Problems in Interpersonal Perception," *Psychological Review*, LXII (1955), 411–422; and L. J. Cronbach, "Processes Affecting Scores on 'Understanding of Others' and 'Assumed Similarity,'" *Psychological Bulletin*, LII (1955), 177–193.

follows that empathy is not necessarily the result of conscious, rational effort. For some, it may just seem to "happen," while others may develop it only after much training and living experience.

Three basic aspects of social perception must be considered: (1) *the perceiver*, the person who is "looking" and attempting to understand; (2) *the perceived*, the person who is being "looked at" or understood; and (3) *the situation*, the total setting of social and nonsocial forces within which the act of social perception is lodged.[4] We have already encountered "perceivers" Mike Corey and Jean Krugmeier, and their respective "perceived" counterparts, Arthur Blick and the burly job applicant.

### The Perceivers and the Perceived

Perceivers and perceived need not be single individuals. Entire *social groupings* may do the "looking" or may be "looked at." We can, for example, conceive of the social perceptions existing between two rival departments of a corporation, with each department viewing the other with possible hostility or competitive jealousy. Similarly, we may distinguish social perceptions among small work groups, among large companies, and even among nations. Indeed any group of people, as well as any given person, can be a principal participant in the process of social perception.

The perceiver and perceived are not billiard balls on a flat table top. Their interactions do not usually produce obvious one-to-one cause-and-effect relations, for the perceived and the perceiver both possess personalities of great complexity. Social perception develops in the give-and-take among these *personalities-in-action*.

What is termed "personality" for the individual may be viewed as a unique pattern of "group characteristics" for the social grouping, be it work group, department, company, or nation. This pattern does not result from a simple addition of the personalities of individual members, although these individual personalities do have an impact. Rather, the social grouping's "personality" results from its formal and informal traditions, and from its accepted ways of "doing things." For example, some groups operate rigidly "according to the book;" others are more flexible and freewheeling. Some groups are highly integrated, with close and supportive relationships existing among their members; others are torn by antagonistic cliques and by intense rivalries. Some groups set high and constant standards for the admission of new members; others are more open and lax in their membership requirements.[5]

### Patterns of Perceiving

The process of social perception can be graphically portrayed in a variety of ways. If $I$ stands for "individual," and $G$ for any grouping of individuals (and if the arrow stands for the act of perceiving), we may consider such relations as the following:

[4]This approach is in harmony with Robert Tannenbaum and Fred Massarik, "Leadership: A Frame of Reference," *Management Science*, IV, 1 (October, 1957), 1–19.

[5]Among the better-known approaches to the analysis of a group's personality is that of J. K. Hemphill and C. M. Westie, "The Measurement of Group Dimensions," *Journal of Psychology*, XXIX (1950), 325–342. Many sociologists have also made important contributions in this area; see, for example, Robert Dubin, *The World of Work* (Englewood Cliffs, N.J.: Prentice-Hall, 1958); and Melville Dalton, *Men That Manage* (New York: John Wiley and Sons, in press).

Type-A *I* → *I* (Individual to Individual)
Type-B *I* → *G* (Individual to Grouping)
Type-C *G* → *I* (Grouping to Individual)
Type-D *G* → *G* (Grouping to Grouping)

Our anecdotes were of the Type-A variety—one individual perceiving another individual. Jean Krugmeier's perception of the job applicant, however, was influenced by a Type-B perception, her view of all burly, red-headed men—a view that she as an individual held for a broader (though tenuous) grouping of persons. Under conditions beyond those already described, Mike Corey may be perceived in a Type-C relationship by his fellow employees, a grouping that may view him with envy and anger because of his ability to get away with lateness without apparent untoward consequences.

Type-D perceptions become important particularly in attempts to analyze the nature of complex organizations, such as large sections or departments, entire firms, or other entities composed of various subgroups. For instance, a management consultant may wish to assess the way in which the Sales Department views the Credit Department—how the Research Section sees the Development Branch—or how Employee Relations relates to Wage and Salary Administration—and vice versa.

The four types of perceptual processes noted so far are relatively straightforward: Type-A, interindividual perception; Type-B, an individual's perception of a grouping; Type-C, a grouping's perception of an individual; and Type-D, intergroup perception. Yet in each type countless obvious as well as hidden distortions can and do occur which prevent the perceiver from obtaining a faithful image. These breakdowns in communications, which we shall need to explore further at a later point, magnify their effects when we consider what might be termed *higher-order perception.*

As Mike Corey, for instance, forms his perceptions of Arthur Blick, he also considers the way in which Blick reciprocates. In other words, Corey is very much concerned to know how Blick feels about him. Corey makes assumptions about Blick's view of him which may or may not be correct. He may "think" that Blick hardly saw him, when—if he were to probe Blick's true reaction—he might learn that Blick saw Corey very well indeed and was actively annoyed with his repeated tardiness. The extent to which one accurately recognizes someone else's reactions to oneself defines a special kind of social sensitivity— the ability to assess correctly what another person "thinks" about you.

Above, we are dealing with a "perception of a perception." We may conceive of a theoretically infinite series of social perceptions that begin as follows:

1. First-order perceptions: how the perceiver views the perceived (as illustrated by Types A, B, C, and D).
2. Second-order perceptions: how the perceiver "thinks" the perceived views the perceiver.
3. Third-order perceptions: how the perceiver "thinks" the perceived views "the perceiver's perception of the perceived," *etc.*

By the time we reach third-order perceptions, the pattern has become immensely problematical. Any further higher order adds to the complexity. Fortunately, most of our actual perceptions governing interactions with others probably do not get more involved than those defined by the first or second order.

### One Empathy—or Many?

There may be several different "empathies." Some perceivers seem more skillful in seeing beneath the surface and in ferreting out correct perceptions from vast networks of superficial psychological defenses. Others are more capable in hurdling the abyss that separates their actual observations of cues from the more remote recesses of behavior that they are seeking to understand. Some excel in painstakingly accumulating fragments of perceptual evidence and piecing them together. Others have a unique capacity for the elegant sweep that pulls together quickly and accurately a broad complexity of social phenomena.

Understanding social groupings rather than individuals involves unique problems and may require different skills of perception from those needed in understanding individuals. The talent for sizing up group opinion is probably different from the "diagnostic skills" needed for understanding a specific employee. An executive of a large corporation, for instance, may excel in accurately assessing opinions and attitudes of union and work force, but he may need to sharpen his skills in empathizing with his fellow corporate officers.

The probable existence of several "empathies" is not surprising if we consider the diversity of the factors at work. We have available a tremendous variety of cues that we may draw on in order to understand how another person thinks or feels, and these make differential demands upon our skills to draw inferences that will yield accurate perceptions.

### Cues: Raw Material of Perceiving

Cues are often direct: through words, gestures, facial expressions, and specific behavioral acts, they are transmitted to the perceiver (interpreter) directly by the perceived (communicator), sometimes consciously, sometimes subconsciously. At other times, the perceiver gets his insights second hand—as by gossip, through reference letters, or by comments overheard during a coffee-break.

Some cues are more obvious in their apparent meaning. A broad smile and a friendly hello usually reflect a clear expression of personal warmth, while a vague wave of the hand is considerably more ambiguous and thus more difficult to interpret.

Some cues are more clear-cut than others. A girl's approximate age—the beautician's art notwithstanding—is likely to be more easily assessable than the meaning of a Mona Lisa-like smile; and despite best intentions, it may be virtually impossible to base an analysis of a person's basic psychological motivations on a casual martini-clouded social contact.

The psychological leap to be made from the cues available to what we seek to understand presents another consideration. As Mike Corey viewed his boss Blick, he had knowledge of Blick's customary office behavior. He had observed Blick before and under roughly similar conditions. Past cues provided a good base of present generalizations. On the other hand, Mike Corey might want to join Blick's country-club set. There he would need some insights into the latter's social behavior. Corey would search for some implicit theory, derived from Blick's on-the-job reactions, the only reactions with which he is actually familiar. He would try to extrapolate from Blick's available pattern of cues into a relatively distant and different situation, and risk empathic failure in the process.

The perceiver brings to the task of understanding others two sets of interrelated characteristics: (1) his general background, *demographic characteristics;* and (2) his unique self, *personality characteristics.*

*Demographic characteristics* are those broad sociological aspects of the individual which, for the most part, are easily definable, specific, and outside the more subtle ebb-and-flow of personality as such. Age, sex, nationality, religion, number of siblings, occupation, and economic level are illustrative.

When the psychologist Ronald Taft[6] reviewed studies on the relation of certain demographic attributes to social perceptual skill (especially empathy for individuals rather than for social groupings), he formed conclusions such as the following: (a) ability to judge emotional expression in others increases with age in children, but does not seem to increase further with age in adulthood; (b) sex differences in empathy are negligible, but there may be a very slight edge in favor of women.

Thus it seems that when dealing with adults, such as those encountered in business, age alone provides no free ticket to social perceptual wisdom. Although —hopefully—age may bring increases in some areas of technical knowledge, the process of getting older in and of itself does not lead to heightened empathy. Further, there does not seem to be much substance to the widely held assumption that women are "better judges" of people than men; the controversy on this point is not fully resolved.

More significant relationships emerge from an analysis of dynamic *personality characteristics.* Taft's attempt to find common threads in the web of available research leads him to postulate rather substantial association between emotional adjustment and empathy. A person's emotional adjustment hinges primarily on how he sees himself and how he feels about himself—it is closely linked to his *self-concept.*

One's self-concept provides a kind of psychological "base of operations" that inevitably affects relations with family, friends, business associates, and strangers. Some aspects of the self-concept are at the surface of personality; these are the *publicly held attitudes*—the things we don't mind telling other people about ourselves and our views of the world. And there are some feelings about the self of which we are aware, but which we do not want to share with others—these are the *privately held attitudes* to the self. And buried still deeper are the *subconscious and unconscious aspects*—feelings about "who" we are and "what" we are that somehow we cannot face up to, even to ourselves. The theories of psychoanalysis and depth psychology deal at length with these "disassociated" parts of the self, which as subtly disturbing, often powerful sources of internal turmoil may affect and hinder a person's effective functioning.

**Barriers and Aids to Empathy**

The individual who has resolved most of his internal conflicts appears in a better position to direct his energies to the understanding of others. He is likely not to meet "booby traps" of his own unconscious devising that prevent accurate perception. The *healthy personality* is based upon a fundamental self-

[6]See R. Taft, "The Ability to Judge People," *Psychological Bulletin,* LII (1955), 1–23.

acceptance at all levels—public to unconscious. It relies on an openness to experience, a willingness to respond realistically to relevant cues; it exhibits a lack of dogmatism and a capacity for responding to the world flexibly and dynamically. When we are under pressure, or in a state of anxiety, we are less likely to perceive accurately the motives and actions of those about us. It is only when we have reached a fair give-and-take balance between ourselves and the world that we are in a secure position to venture important human relations judgments.

In light of this, is it likely that in a Nirvana of perfect psychological equilibrium all social perceptions would be accurate? On the basis of what we know, the answer is no. In order to understand others, there must be some driving force, some motivation, some problem. Such cause or problem implies the èxistence of some tensions within the perceiver. In a fully tensionless state—in a hypothetical state of perfect adjustment—there could be no reason to care about understanding anything or anybody. As a result there would be little meaningful social perception or social interaction. As too many cooks are said to spoil the broth, too many tranquilizers seem to spoil the well-springs of human understanding. While excess tension reduces empathy, its complete absence induces a state of apathy.

### The Special Case of Self-Insight

Empathy and self-insight tend to go hand in hand, although the evidence is by no means all in.[7] Fortunate, they say, is the individual who knows how much or how little he truly knows about himself—who is aware of his own capacities, limitations, motivations, and attitudes.

The sole tool that we bring to the task of understanding others is our own personality. The cues we receive from the outside must be processed through the perceptual equipment that is "us"—through lenses of our own background and expectations. If we are to be successful in assessing the meaning of cues that impinge on us, we must become aware of the distortions that may be introduced by our "built-in" perceptual equipment.

A realistic view of our perceptual limitations, and of the kinds of aberrations we tend to introduce in what we see and hear, should help us to make allowances in interpreting the world around us. If, for instance, we are aware that people who seem to be weak and submissive make us irrationally angry, we may be able to develop safeguards against our own unreasonable anger and ultimately gain a more realistic understanding of the motivations of the other person.

Self-insight does not come easy. Many factors militate against it. Central among these is our system of *psychological defenses*—the ways in which we systematically and unconsciously protect ourselves from facing what might be real or imagined threats to our personal security.

These protective distortions—which frequently concern our perceptions of others—help us make reality more palatable. There is no human being alive who is without some pattern of psychological defenses. Unfortunately, the cost of excessive utilization of defenses is the progressive removal from reality. Without some controlled and mild forms of self-delusion, adjustment of the

[7]See, for example, J. S. Bruner and R. Tagiuri, "The Perception of People" in G. Lindzey (editor), *Handbook of Social Psychology*, II (Cambridge, Mass.: Addison-Wesley Publishing Co., 1954), 645–646.

ordinary everyday sort may be difficult. Yet the defenses that we bring into play as we seek to understand ourselves and others seduce us into various states of unreality; they make us see that which is *not* there, and hide that which might be apparent.

In our illustrations of Mike Corey and Jean Krugmeier, not much may have been at stake. However, similar processes, affected by the distortions of psychological defenses, influence decisions of major importance: for example, the selection and promotion of top management personnel, the establishment of budgetary commitments, the theme of advertising campaigns, or the assessment of company performance.

### The Force of Attitude

One particularly pervasive pattern of personal defenses found in industry, which interferes with the process of understanding others, is characterized by a high degree of *authoritarianism*, with concurrent *rigidity in perception* and *intolerance for ambiguity*. The authoritarian person seems to need to view the world in clearly defined segments, some strictly black, others strictly white. He does not make much room for gradations—things are clearly good or abominably bad, people friendly or hostile, nations with us or against us. Thus, the authoritarian unconsciously fails to recognize subtle but significant interpersonal phenomena, because he is unable to evaluate shades of gray for what they are.[8] Extreme nonauthoritarian personalities—"nothing is definite—all is a matter of shading"—also encounter difficulties in understanding others since they too have a singularly single-minded view of what the world and its inhabitants are like.

The attitudes with which we approach the task of understanding others, then, do a great deal to determine just what we will be able to see. Attitudes basically serve as organizing forces that order in some preliminary manner the potential chaos and complexity confronting us. They give meaning to what we are prepared to see and hear. As such, they serve a necessary and useful function.

### "Playing the Odds"

The question of whether the holding of stereotypes is necessarily detrimental to accurate social perception deserves consideration. If we define a "stereotype" as an *inaccurate* perception of a given grouping, it follows logically that stereotypes are hindrances. But, more generally, we *do* need to be able to type people by means of broad and flexible generalizations. In that sense, a realistic view of a group of individuals (a kind of "accurate stereotype") may increase the odds for accuracy in our perception of others. Thus we may make assumptions about the characteristics of a specific company's board of directors, about the honor graduates of a college, or about women secretaries. We frame enlightened guesses concerning the manner in which a directive will be interpreted by first-line supervision, the way in which a sales campaign on bottled beer will be received by the housewives in Suburbia, or how the new profit-sharing plan suggested by the union's bargaining committee will strike the company attorney.

[8]See T. W. Adorno, E. Frenkel-Brunswik, D. J. Levinson, and R. N. Sanford, *The Authoritarian Personality* (New York: Harper & Bros., 1950).

This kind of "typing," while based upon prior perceptions of individuals and groups, necessarily is a kind of oversimplification; still its use in a consciously wary manner is a constant necessity if we are to relate to people.

Since understanding people involves relative probabilities of being right, caution is always in order. We must ever attempt to remain open to a constant flow of new information which may help us alter our perceptions in the light of changing circumstances. It is the danger of fossilization—the pitfall of "hardening" perceptions irrationally—that needs to be avoided.

### Link Between Perceiver and Perceived

The personality of the perceived also determines the success of social perception. Ultimately it is the relationship that emerges between perceiver and perceived which becomes crucial. *Communication* linking the two—the sending and receiving of messages (involving feelings as well as content)—becomes raw material underlying the process of understanding others. Cues are messages from the perceived to the perceiver. In each instance, the perceiver "samples" certain small units of behavior that come from the perceived. While these samples in a statistical sense are neither random nor necessarily representative, they form the basis for generalizations that constitute predictions about the behavior of others. As communications develop, a person becomes both perceiver and perceived—sending and receiving cues of great variety and with high speed.

In the relationship between perceiver and perceived it becomes important for the perceiver to elicit cues from the perceived which will do the most to reveal, on a sample basis, the relevant aspects of the perceived's feelings, thoughts, and potential behavior. This ability to break through a person's outer veneer, to penetrate false fronts, has two facets: (1) the perceiver's *skill in facilitating the "sending" of cues* by the perceived, and (2) the perceiver's *skill in picking up and interpreting properly* the cues that have been sent.

Jean Krugmeier, for example, by eliciting fully the attitudes and aspirations of her job applicant might have succeeded in bringing to the surface relevant cues that might have made possible a more sensible evaluation of his potential. She might have reduced the applicant's defensiveness by proving herself receptive to his comments and accepting of him as a person, by listening for his feelings as well as meaning, and by communicating to him her understanding of his point of view.

As we engage in the process of understanding people, our hope for ever increasing accuracy rests partially with our ability to get *feedback* on how others view the accuracy of our perceptions. We must remain in tune with the reactions of others—not in order to become blind automata, but rather to doublecheck and review the validity of our own perceptions.

### The Danger of "Expertise"

Usually we receive feedback from members of our own *reference groups*—our families, friends, and business associates. These are the people whose opinions about us usually matter to us. Especially parents and close relatives who have provided us with experiences which make us what we are often continue to give us, as Robert Burns so aptly put it, "the giftie . . . to see oorsels as ithers see us."

At times, the validity of our insights and understanding of people is assessed by experts, by psychiatrists or psychologists who have been trained in personality diagnosis and behavior prediction. Unfortunately, research has shown that some of these experts, in spite of their intellectual grasp of interpersonal relations, are rather inept judges of people. This startling paradox has some rather persuasive explanations to account for it. First, intellect alone—though a slight help—does not guarantee empathy. More importantly, for some people too much knowledge is a dangerous thing! For them, there exists the danger of *overreaching*. They are confronted with the ever present temptation to read into cues complex "deeper" meanings which in reality may not be there at all. This is the pitfall of imagining psychological ghosts behind each casual remark, simply because of some intellectual predisposition to make interpretations at more esoteric levels.

For experienced clinicians, the process of feedback here again proves to be a partial safeguard. If all too often our views of others, though psychologically "sophisticated," find no confirmation, either by the subject of our perception or through the perceptions of other observers, we may suspect that we are overreaching in our search for perceptual accuracy.

### The Situation: Arena for Feelings

Regardless of the specific situation in which social perception takes place, some positive feelings of varying intensity will be exchanged between perceiver and perceived. These feelings condition the process of social perception. They set up *halos* which reduce the accuracy of empathic judgments. If we believe that some persons "can do no wrong," if we are enamored of their righteousness and virtue, if we blindly approve of everything they do—we will be unable accurately to assess their less desirable characteristics or behaviors. The inverse is equally true; pervasive hostility and prejudice also obliterate any chance for a realistic appraisal of people's positive characteristics.

A more subtle manifestation of the impact of feelings on perceptual accuracy can be found in the process of *naive projection* (assuming similarity), the attributing by the perceiver of his own characteristics to the perceived. If few cues are available to the perceiver, if he is unable to utilize those that are available, or if his feelings toward the other person are in fact similar to those he has about himself, projection may become his significant *modus operandi*. The vacuum that might be filled by meaningful cues is taken up by assumptions implying that the perceived resembles the perceiver.

Assuming similarity to another person is neither intrinsically a barrier nor a block to accurate social perception. If the perceived really *is* much like the perceiver with respect to the characteristics involved in the judgment, assuming similarity is clearly warranted. Although some unique psychological perceptual skill may or may not have been at work, accurate social perception will result.

One can visualize an extreme situation in which the major prerequisite for social perceptual accuracy is the knack for picking out associates who resemble us with regard to relevant personality dimensions. If we succeed in this selection, be our choice conscious or unconscious, all we may need in order to understand them is to assume that they are, more or less, replicas of ourselves. Obviously, reality rarely permits this uncritical, though convenient, approach. More likely we may find that we assume similarity where none exists, thus hindering social sensitivity by the unwarranted assumption.

A blind assumption, on the other hand, that we do *not* resemble others (or a particular "other") can also lead to misperception. In most cases, the perceiver and the perceived do share in common some attitudes, feelings, and similar personality characteristics. The challenge confronting us is to recognize those elements that we have in common with other individuals, while at the same time noting the differences that make us unique. Likewise, when dealing with many people, we need to learn to discriminate the relevant differences among them, while remaining aware of the similarities which they, as a group, share. Thus, as a particular boss considers a group of subordinates, he must ask—and answer—these four questions:

1. In what respects is each of these persons like me?
2. In what respects does each of these persons differ from me?
3. In what ways do all these people resemble one another?
4. In what ways is each of these people unique from every other?

Clearly, this is a large order.

The *relative stress* with which people relate to one another also influences their ultimate empathy toward each other. As superiors, for instance, we may find it relatively easy to size up properly the feelings and attitudes of our subordinates; as subordinates our anxieties may becloud our perceptions of our superiors' intent and attitudes. The well-known phenomenon of "seeing red" when angered and the notion that "love is blind" represent classic illustrations of the befogging effect of strong emotions on social perception. Most accurate social perception, it seems, occurs under conditions which do not involve extremely charged feelings.

Because each individual approaches the task of social perception in his own particular situation, his personal receptivity will be influenced by the nature of this situation. An executive who operates in an environment of "yes-men" may come to be attuned to hearing "yes," even if the real sound is more like "maybe." An amusing cartoon series of medical specialists on vacation shows a plastic surgeon fascinated by the Sphinx in Egypt, a urologist intrigued by the shapes of swimming pools, and a gynecologist marveling at the fertile life in the farm's pigsty.

The *broader culture*, too, provides certain expectations and highlights specific types of cues. The "Man in the Gray Flannel Suit," the "Rate Buster," the "Organization Man," the "Huckster," the "Tycoon"—all of these are cultural types which are readily found on the American business scene, and whose existence is typically recognized by those of us who share a common cultural heritage.

### Pay-Off for Empathy

Whatever its correlates and roots, empathy provides a "road map" defining properly the social world confronting the perceiver. There is no guarantee, however, that even the most understanding perceiver will be able to behave appropriately, even if his road map is clear and accurate. He further requires an adequate repertoire of behaviors—*behavioral flexibility*—to provoke the kinds of action that will most effectively attain the goals he seeks.

Social sensitivity and social effectiveness do not necessarily go hand in hand. In *The Outsider*, Colin Wilson[9] draws the portrait of the cultural hero who sees too much, whose perceptions penetrate all too well, but who tragically lacks

[9]Colin Wilson, *The Outsider* (Boston: Houghton Mifflin Co., 1956).

the customary social skills for functioning within the reality that he perceives.

"Seeing too much," if not buttressed by an appropriate range of available behaviors, can indeed prove a threat to self and others and thereby reduce ultimate social effectiveness. In terms of actual pay-off, having too much empathy may well be as detrimental as having too little. Seeing the surrounding social world in proper perspective is useful only if knowledge can be successfully implemented by action.

As an executive faces the myriad decisions he needs to make, it becomes quite clear that he must master two tasks: he must learn to see accurately the human, as well as the inanimate, factors of the total scene; and he must acquire the skills of action which, while based upon accurate perception, tap well-springs of behavior that ultimately lead to the successful attainment of personal and organizational goals.

Social effectiveness can be developed. For some people, dealing with feelings is as easy as recognizing and manipulating facts. For others, the world of emotions is mysterious indeed. The improvement of social skills is a many-sided challenge. Neither intellectual learning nor emotional experience alone suffice. Nor is the heightening of social sensitivity the sole sacrosanct cure-all. Experiences are needed that reach the full personality. Increased social effectiveness depends on a "tool-kit" of appropriate behaviors, in addition to enhanced understanding of social situations. Special clinically-oriented training experiences[10] hold promise to bring about integrated intellectual, emotional and behavioral learnings that can make for greater effectiveness in dealing with others.

[10]Sensitivity Training is one approach designed to improve a person's social sensitivity and behavioral flexibility. For a description see, for example, Irving R. Weschler, Robert Tannenbaum, and John H. Zenger, *Yardsticks for Human Relations Training*, Adult Education Association Monograph No. 2 (Chicago: Adult Education Association, 1957). Similar programs sponsored by the National Training Laboratories in Group Development are described in numerous publications, especially those authored by Leland P. Bradford.


# PERCEPTION: IMPLICATIONS FOR ADMINISTRATION

SHELDON S. ZALKIND
TIMOTHY W. COSTELLO

Management practice is being increasingly influenced by behavioral science research in the areas of group dynamics, problem solving and decision making, and motivation. One aspect of behavior which has not been fully or consistently emphasized is the process of perception, particularly the recent work on person perception.

Reprinted from *Administrative Science Quarterly*, VII (September, 1962), 218–35, by permission of the authors and the publisher. Portions of this article were originally presented at the Eighth Annual International Meeting of The Institute of Management Sciences in Brussels, August 1961.

In this paper we shall summarize some of the findings on perception as developed through both laboratory and organizational research and point out some of the administrative and managerial implications. We discuss first some basic factors in the nature of the perceptual process including need and set; second, some research on forming impressions; third, the characteristics of the perceiver and the perceived; fourth, situational and organizational influences on perception; and finally, perceptual influences on interpersonal adjustment.

### Nature of the Perceptual Process

What are some of the factors influencing perception? In answering the question it is well to begin by putting aside the attitude of naïve realism, which suggests that our perceptions simply register accurately what is "out there." It is necessary rather to consider what influences distort one's perceptions and judgments of the outside world. Some of the considerations identified in the literature up to the time of Johnson's 1944 review of the research on object perception (where distortion may be even less extreme than in person perception) led him to suggest the following about the perceiver:[1]

1. He may be influenced by considerations that he may not be able to identify, responding to cues that are below the threshold of his awareness. For example, a judgment as to the size of an object may be influenced by its color even though the perceiver may not be attending to color.
2. When required to form difficult perceptual judgments, he may respond to irrelevant cues to arrive at a judgment. For example, in trying to assess honesty, it has been shown that the other person's smiling or not smiling is used as a cue to judge his honesty.
3. In making abstract or intellectual judgments, he may be influenced by emotional factors—what is liked is perceived as correct.
4. He will weigh perceptual evidence coming from respected (or favored) sources more heavily than that coming from other sources.
5. He may not be able to identify all the factors on which his judgments are based. Even if he is aware of these factors he is not likely to realize how much weight he gives to them.

These considerations do not imply that we respond only to the subtle or irrelevant cues or to emotional factors. We often perceive on the basis of the obvious, but we are quite likely to be responding as well to the less obvious or less objective.

In 1958, Bruner, citing a series of researches, described what he called the "New Look" in perception as one in which personal determinants of the perceptual process were being stressed.[2] Bruner summarized earlier work and showed the importance of such subjective influences as needs, values, cultural background, and interests on the perceptual process. In his concept of "perceptual readiness" he described the importance of the framework or category system that the perceiver himself brings to the perceiving process.

[1]D. M. Johnson, "A Systematic Treatment of Judgment," *Psychological Bulletin*, XLII (1945), 193–224.
[2]J. S. Bruner, "Social Psychology and Perception," in *Readings in Social Psychology*, ed. E. Maccoby, T. Newcomb, and E. Hartley (3d ed.; New York, 1958), pp. 85–94.

Tapping a different vein of research, Cantril described perceiving as a "transaction" between the perceiver and the perceived, a process of negotiation in which the perceptual end product is a result both of influences within the perceiver and of characteristics of the perceived.[3]

One of the most important of the subjective factors that influence the way we perceive, identified by Bruner and others, is *set*. A study by Kelley illustrated the point.[4] He found that those who were previously led to expect to meet a "warm" person, not only made different judgments about him, but also behaved differently toward him, than those who were expecting a "cold" one. The fact was that they simultaneously were observing the same person in the same situation. Similarly, Strickland indicated the influence of set in determining how closely supervisors feel they must supervise their subordinates.[5] Because of prior expectation one person was trusted more than another and was thought to require less supervision than another, even though performance records were identical.

### Forming Impressions of Others

The data on forming impressions is of particular importance in administration. An administrator is confronted many times with the task of forming an impression of another person—a new employee at his desk, a visiting member from the home office, a staff member he has not personally met before. His own values, needs, and expectations will play a part in the impression he forms. Are there other factors that typically operate in this area of administrative life? One of the more obvious influences is the physical appearance of the person being perceived. In a study of this point Mason was able to demonstrate that people agree on what a leader should look like and that there is no relationship between the facial characteristics agreed upon and those possessed by actual leaders.[6] In effect, we have ideas about what leaders look like and we can give examples, but we ignore the many exceptions that statistically cancel out the examples.

In the sometimes casual, always transitory situations in which one must form impressions of others it is a most natural tendency to jump to conclusions and form impressions without adequate evidence. Unfortunately, as Dailey showed, unless such impressions are based on important and relevant data, they are not likely to be accurate.[7] Too often in forming impressions the perceiver does not know what is relevant, important, or predictive of later behavior. Dailey's research furthermore supports the cliché that, accurate or not, first impressions are lasting.

Generalizing from other research in the field, Soskin described four limitations on the ability to form accurate impressions of others.[8] First, the impres-

[3]H. Cantril, "Perception and Interpersonal Relations," *American Journal of Psychiatry*, CXIV (1957), 119–26.

[4]H. H. Kelley, "The Warm–Cold Variable in First Impressions of Persons," *Journal of Personality*, XVIII (1950), 431–39.

[5]L. H. Strickland, "Surveillance and Trust," *Journal of Personality*, XXVI (1958), 200–215.

[6]D. J. Mason, "Judgments of Leadership Based upon Physiognomic Cues," *Journal of Abnormal and Social Psychology*, LIV (1957), 273–74.

[7]C. A. Dailey, "The Effects of Premature Conclusion upon the Acquisition of Understanding of a Person," *Journal of Psychology*, XXIII (1952), 133–52.

[8]W. E. Soskin, "Influence of Information on Bias in Social Perception," *Journal of Personality*, XXII (1953), 118–27.

sion is likely to be disproportionately affected by the type of situation or surroundings in which the impression is made and influenced too little by the person perceived. Thus the plush luncheon club in which one first meets a man will dominate the impression of the man himself. Second, although impressions are frequently based on a limited sample of the perceived person's behavior, the generalization that the perceiver makes will be sweeping. A third limitation is that the situation may not provide an opportunity for the person perceived to show behavior relevant to the traits about which impressions are formed. Casual conversation or questions, for example, provide few opportunities to demonstrate intelligence or work characteristics, yet the perceiver often draws conclusions about these from an interview. Finally, Soskin agrees with Bruner and Cantril that the impression of the person perceived may be distorted by some highly individualized reaction of the perceiver.

But the pitfalls are not yet all spelled out; it is possible to identify some other distorting influences on the process of forming impressions. Research has brought into sharp focus some typical errors, the more important being stereotyping, halo effect, projection, and perceptual defense.

### Stereotyping

The word "stereotyping" was first used by Walter Lippmann in 1922 to describe bias in perceiving peoples. He wrote of "pictures in people's heads," called stereotypes, which guided (distorted) their perception of others. The term has long been used to describe judgments made about people on the basis of their ethnic group membership. For example, some say, "Herman Schmidt [being German] is industrious." Stereotyping also predisposes judgments in many other areas of interpersonal relations. Stereotypes have developed about many types of groups, and they help to prejudice many of our perceptions about their members. Examples of stereotypes of groups other than those based on ethnic identification are bankers, supervisors, union members, poor people, rich people, and administrators. Many unverified qualities are assigned to people principally because of such group memberships.

In a research demonstration of stereotyping, Haire found that labeling a photograph as that of a management representative caused an impression to be formed of the person, different from that formed when it was labeled as that of a union leader.[9] Management and labor formed different impressions, each seeing his opposite as less dependable than his own group. In addition, each side saw his own group as being better able than the opposite group to understand a point of view different from its own. For example, managers felt that other managers were better able to appreciate labor's point of view than labor was able to appreciate management's point of view. Each had similar stereotypes of his opposite and considered the thinking, emotional characteristics, and interpersonal relations of his opposite as inferior to his own. As Stagner pointed out, "It is plain that unionists perceiving company officials in a stereotyped way are less efficient than would be desirable. Similarly, company executives who see all labor unions as identical are not showing good judgment or discrimination."[10]

[9]M. Haire, "Role Perceptions in Labor–Management Relations: An Experimental Approach," *Industrial Labor Relations Review*, VIII (1955), 204–16.
[10]R. Stagner, *Psychology of Industrial Conflict* (New York, 1956), p. 35.

One of the troublesome aspects of stereotypes is that they are so widespread. Finding the same stereotypes to be widely held should not tempt one to accept their accuracy. It may only mean that many people are making the same mistake. Allport has demonstrated that there need not be a "kernel of truth" in a widely held stereotype.[11] He has shown that while a prevalent stereotype of Armenians labeled them as dishonest, a credit reporting association gave them credit ratings as good as those given other ethnic groups.

Bruner and Perlmutter found that there is an international stereotype for "businessmen" and "teachers."[12] They indicated that the more widespread one's experience with diverse members of a group, the less their group membership will affect the impression formed.

An additional illustration of stereotyping is provided by Luft.[13] His research suggests that perception of personality adjustment may be influenced by stereotypes, associating adjustment with high income and maladjustment with low income.

### Halo Effect

The term "halo effect" was first used in 1920 to describe a process in which a general impression which is favorable or unfavorable is used by judges to evaluate several specific traits. The "halo" in such case serves as a screen keeping the perceiver from actually seeing the trait he is judging. It has received the most attention because of its effect on rating employee performance. In the rating situation, a supervisor may single out one trait, either good or bad, and use this as the basis for his judgment of all other traits. For example, an excellent attendance record causes judgments of productivity, high quality of work, and so forth. One study in the U.S. Army showed that officers who were liked were judged more intelligent than those who were disliked, even though they had the same scores on intelligence tests.

We examine halo effect here because of its general effect on forming impressions. Bruner and Taguiri suggest that it is likely to be most extreme when we are forming impressions of traits that provide minimal cues in the individual's behavior, when the traits have moral overtones, or when the perceiver must judge traits with which he has had little experience.[14] A rather disturbing conclusion is suggested by Symonds that halo effect is more marked the more we know the acquaintance.[15]

A somewhat different aspect of the halo effect is suggested by the research of Grove and Kerr.[16] They found that knowledge that the company was in receivership caused employees to devalue the higher pay and otherwise superior working conditions of their company as compared to those in a financially secure firm.

[11]G. Allport, *Nature of Prejudice* (Cambridge, Mass., 1954).

[12]J. S. Bruner and H. V. Perlmutter, "Compatriot and Foreigner: A Study of Impression Formation in Three Countries," *Journal of Abnormal and Social Psychology*, LV (1957), 253–60.

[13]J. Luft, "Monetary Value and the Perception of Persons," *Journal of Social Psychology*, XLVI (1957), 245–51.

[14]J. S. Bruner and A. Taguiri, "The Perception of People," in *Handbook of Social Psychology*, ed. G. Lindzey (Cambridge, Mass., 1954), chap. xvii.

[15]P. M. Symonds, "Notes on Rating," *Journal of Applied Psychology*, VII (1925), 188–95.

[16]A. Grove and W. A. Kerr, "Specific Evidence on Origin of Halo Effect in Measurement of Morale," *Journal of Social Psychology*, XXXIV (1951) 165–70.

Psychologists have noted a tendency in perceivers to link certain traits. They assume, for example, that when a person is aggressive he will also have high energy or that when a person is "warm" he will also be generous and have a good sense of humor. This logical error, as it has been called, is a special form of the halo effect and is best illustrated in the research of Asch.[17] In his study the addition of one trait to a list of traits produced a major change in the impression formed. Knowing that a person was intelligent, skillful, industrious, determined, practical, cautious, and warm led a group to judge him to be also wise, humorous, popular, and imaginative. When warm was replaced by cold, a radically different impression (beyond the difference between warm and cold) was formed. Kelley's research illustrated the same type of error.[18] This tendency is not indiscriminate; with the pair "polite—blunt," less change was found than with the more central traits of "warm—cold."

In evaluating the effect of halo on perceptual distortion, we may take comfort from the work of Wishner, which showed that those traits that correlate more highly with each other are more likely to lead to a halo effect than those that are unrelated.[19]

### Projection

A defense mechanism available to everyone is projection, in which one relieves one's feelings of guilt or failure by projecting blame onto someone else. Over the years the projection mechanism has been assigned various meanings. The original use of the term was concerned with the mechanism to defend oneself from unacceptable feelings. There has since been a tendency for the term to be used more broadly, meaning to ascribe or attribute any of one's own characteristics to other people. The projection mechanism concerns us here because it influences the perceptual process. An early study by Murray illustrates its effect.[20] After playing a dramatic game, "Murder," his subjects attributed much more maliciousness to people whose photographs were judged than did a control group which had not played the game. The current emotional state of the perceiver tended to influence his perceptions of others; i.e., frightened perceivers judged people to be frightening. More recently, Feshback and Singer revealed further dynamics of the process.[21] In their study, subjects who had been made fearful judged a stimulus person (presented in a moving picture) as both more fearful and more aggressive than did non-fearful perceivers. These authors were able to demonstrate further that the projection mechanism at work here was reduced when their subjects were encouraged to admit and talk about their fears.

Sears provides an illustration of a somewhat different type of projection and its effects on perception.[22] In his study projection is seeing our own undesirable

[17]S. Asch, "Forming Impressions of Persons," *Journal of Abnormal and Social Psychology*, LX (1946), 258–90.

[18]Kelley, *op. cit.*

[19]J. Wishner, "Reanalysis of 'Impressions of Personality,'" *Psychological Review*, LXVII (1960), 96–112.

[20]H. A. Murray, "The Effect of Fear upon Estimates of the Maliciousness of Other Personalities," *Journal of Social Psychology*, IV (1933), 310–29.

[21]S. Feshback and S. D. Singer, "The Effects of Fear Arousal upon Social Perception," *Journal of Abnormal and Social Psychology*, LV (1957), 283–88.

[22]R. R. Sears, "Experimental Studies of Perception. I. Attribution of Traits," *Journal of Social Psychology*, VII (1936), 151–63.

personality characteristics in other people. He demonstrated that people high in such traits as stinginess, obstinacy, and disorderliness, tended to rate others much higher on these traits than did those who were low in these undesirable characteristics. The tendency to project was particularly marked among subjects who had the least insight into their own personalities.

Research thus suggests that our perceptions may characteristically be distorted by emotions we are experiencing or traits that we possess. Placed in the administrative settings, the research would suggest, for example, that a manager frightened by rumored organizational changes might not only judge others to be more frightened than they were, but also assess various policy decisions as more frightening than they were. Or a general foreman lacking insight into his own incapacity to delegate might be oversensitive to this trait in his superiors.

### Perceptual Defense

Another distorting influence, which has been called perceptual defense, has also been demonstrated by Haire and Grunes to be a source of error.[23] In their research they ask, in effect, "Do we put blinders on to defend ourselves from seeing those events which might disturb us?" The concept of perceptual defense offers an excellent description of perceptual distortion at work and demonstrates that when confronted with a fact inconsistent with a stereotype already held by a person, the perceiver is able to distort the data in such a way as to eliminate the inconsistency. Thus, by perceiving inaccurately, he defends himself from having to change his stereotypes.

## Characteristics of Perceiver and Perceived

We have thus far been talking largely about influences on the perceptual process without specific regard to the perceiver and his characteristics. Much recent research has tried to identify some characteristics of the perceiver and their influence on the perception of other people.

### The Perceiver

A thread that would seem to tie together many current findings is the tendency to use oneself as the norm or standard by which one perceives or judges others. If we examine current research, certain conclusions are suggested:

1. *Knowing oneself makes it easier to see others accurately.* Norman showed that when one is aware of what his own personal characteristics are, he makes fewer errors in perceiving others.[24] Weingarten has shown that people with insight are less likely to view the world in black-and-white terms and to give extreme judgments about others.[25]

2. *One's own characteristics affect the characteristics he is likely to see in others.* Secure people (compared to insecure) tend to see others as warm rather

[23] M. Haire and W. F. Grunes, "Perceptual Defenses: Processes Protecting an Original Perception of Another Personality," *Human Relations*, III (1958), 403–12.

[24] R. D. Norman, "The Interrelationships among Acceptance-Rejection, Self-Other, Insight into Self, and Realistic Perception of Others," *Journal of Social Psychology*, XXXVII (1953), 205–35.

[25] E. Weingarten, "A Study of Selective Perception in Clinical Judgment," *Journal of Personality*, XVII (1949), 369–400.

than cold, as was shown by Bossom and Maslow.[26] The extent of one's own sociability influences the degree of importance one gives to the sociability of other people when one forms impressions of them.[27] The person with "authoritarian" tendencies is more likely to view others in terms of power and is less sensitive to the psychological or personality characteristics of other people than is a non-authoritarian.[28] The relatively few categories one uses in describing other people tend to be those one uses in describing oneself.[29] Thus traits which are important to the perceiver will be used more when he forms impressions of others. He has certain constant tendencies, both with regard to using certain categories in judging others and to the amount of weight given to these categories.[30]

3. *The person who accepts himself is more likely to be able to see favorable aspects of other people.*[31] This relates in part to the accuracy of his perceptions. If the perceiver accepts himself as he is, he widens his range of vision in seeing others; he can look at them and be less likely to be very negative or critical. In those areas in which he is more insecure, he sees more problems in other people.[32] We are more likely to like others who have traits we accept in ourselves and reject those who have the traits which we do not like in ourselves.[33]

4. *Accuracy in perceiving others is not a single skill.* While there have been some variations in the findings, as Gage has shown, some consistent results do occur.[34] The perceiver tends to interpret the feelings others have about him in terms of his feeling toward them.[35] One's ability to perceive others accurately may depend on how sensitive one is to differences between people and also to the norms (outside of oneself) for judging them.[36] Thus, as Taft has shown, the ability to judge others does not seem to be a single skill.[37]

Possibly the results in these four aspects of person perception can be viewed most constructively in connection with earlier points on the process of perception. The administrator (or any other individual) who wishes to perceive someone else accurately must look at the other person, not at himself. The things

[26]J. Bossom and A. H. Maslow, "Security of Judges as a Factor in Impressions of Warmth in Others," *Journal of Abnormal and Social Psychology*, LV (1957), 147–48.

[27]D. T. Benedetti and J. G. Hill, "A Determiner of the Centrality of a Trait in Impression Formation," *Journal of Abnormal and Social Psychology*, LX (1960), 278–79.

[28]E. E. Jones, "Authoritarianism as a Determinant of First-Impressions Formation," *Journal of Personality*, XXIII (1954), 107–27.

[29]A. H. Hastorf, S. A. Richardson, and S. M. Dombusch, "The Problem of Relevance in the Study of Person Perception," in *Person Perception and Interpersonal Behavior*, ed. R. Taguiri and L. Petrullo (Stanford, Calif., 1958).

[30]L. J. Cronbach, "Processes Affecting Scores on 'Understanding of Others' and 'Assumed Similarity,'" *Psychology Bulletin*, LII (1955), 173–93.

[31]K. T. Omwake, "The Relation between Acceptance of Self and Acceptance of Others Shown by Three Personality Inventories," *Journal of Consulting Psychology*, XVIII (1954), 443–46.

[32]Weingarten, *op. cit.*

[33]R. M. Lundy et al., "Self Acceptability and Descriptions of Sociometric Choices," *Journal of Abnormal and Social Psychology*, LI (1955), 260–62.

[34]N. L. Gage, "Accuracy of Social Perception and Effectiveness in Interpersonal Relationships," *Journal of Personality*, XXII (1953), 128–41.

[35]R. Taguiri, J. S. Bruner, and R. Blake, "On the Relation between Feelings and Perceptions of Feelings among Members of Small Groups," in *Readings in Social Psychology*.

[36]U. Bronfenbrenner, J. Harding, and M. Gallway, "The Measurement of Skill in Social Perception," in *Talent and Society*, ed. McClelland et al. (Princeton, N.J., 1958), pp. 29–111.

[37]R. Taft, "The Ability To Judge People," *Psychological Bulletin*, LII (1955), 1–21.

that he looks at in someone else are influenced by his own traits. But if he knows his own traits, he can be aware that they provide a frame of reference for him. His own traits help to furnish the categories that he will use in perceiving others. His characteristics, needs, and values can partly limit his vision and his awareness of the differences between others. The question one could ask when viewing another is: "Am I looking at him, and forming my impression of his behavior in the situation, or am I just comparing him with myself?"

There is the added problem of being set to observe the personality traits in another which the perceiver does not accept in himself, e.g., being somewhat autocratic. At the same time he may make undue allowances in others for those of his own deficiencies which do not disturb him but might concern some people, e.g., not following prescribed procedures.

### The Perceived

Lest we leave the impression that it is only the characteristics of the perceiver that stand between him and others in his efforts to know them, we turn now to some characteristics of the person being perceived which raise problems in perception. It is possible to demonstrate, for example, that the status of the person perceived is a variable influencing judgments about his behavior. Thibaut and Riecken have shown that even though two people behave in identical fashion, status differences between them cause a perceiver to assign different motivations for the behavior.[38] Concerning co-operativeness, they found that high status persons are judged as wanting to co-operate and low status persons as having to co-operate. In turn, more liking is shown for the person of high status than for the person of low status. Presumably, more credit is given when the boss says, "Good morning," to us than when a subordinate says the same thing.

Bruner indicated that we use categories to simplify our perceptual activities. In the administrative situation, status is one type of category, and the role provides another. Thus the remarks of Mr. Jones in the sales department are perceived differently from those of Smith in the purchasing department, although both may say the same thing. Also, one who knows Jones's role in the organization will perceive his behavior differently from one who does not know Jones's role. The process of categorizing on the basis of roles is similar to, if not identical with, the stereotyping process described earlier.

Visibility of the traits judged is also an important variable influencing the accuracy of perception.[39] Visibility will depend, for example, on how free the other person feels to express the trait. It has been demonstrated that we are more accurate in judging people who like us than people who dislike us. The explanation suggested is that most people in our society feel constraint in showing their dislike, and therefore the cues are less visible.

Some traits are not visible simply because they provide few external cues for their presence. Loyalty, for example, as opposed to level of energy, provides few early signs for observation. Even honesty cannot be seen in the situations in which most impressions are formed. As obvious as these comments might be, in forming impressions many of us nevertheless continue to judge the presence

---

[38]J. W. Thibaut and H. W. Riecken, "Some Determinants and Consequences of the Perception of Social Causality," *Journal of Personality*, XXIV (1955), 113–33.

[39]Bruner and Taguiri, *op. cit.*

of traits which are not really visible. Frequently the practical situation demands judgment, but we should recognize the frail reeds upon which we are leaning and be prepared to observe further and revise our judgments with time and closer acquaintance.

## Situational Influences on Perception

Some recent research clearly points to the conclusion that the whole process of interpersonal perception is, at least in part, a function of the *group* (or interpersonal) context in which the perception occurs. Much of the research has important theoretical implications for a psychology of interpersonal relations. In addition, there are some suggestions of value for administrators. It is possible to identify several characteristics of the interpersonal climate which have direct effect on perceptual accuracy. As will be noted, these are characteristics which can be known, and in some cases controlled, in administrative settings.

Bieri provides data for the suggestion that when people are given an opportunity to interact in a friendly situation, they tend to see others as similar to themselves.[40] Applying his suggestion to the administrative situation, we can rationalize as follows: Some difficulties of administrative practice grow out of beliefs that different interest groups in the organization are made up of different types of people. Obviously once we believe that people in other groups are different, we will be predisposed to see the differences. We can thus find, from Bieri's and from Rosenbaum's work, an administrative approach for attacking the problem.[41] If we can produce an interacting situation which is co-operative rather than competitive, the likelihood of seeing other people as similar to ourselves is increased.

Exline's study adds some other characteristics of the social context which may influence perception.[42] Paraphrasing his conclusions to adapt them to the administrative scene, we can suggest that when a committee group is made up of congenial members who are willing to continue work in the same group, their perceptions of the goal-directed behavior of fellow committee members will be more accurate, although observations of purely personal behavior (as distinguished from goal-directed behavior) may be less accurate.[43] The implications for setting up committees and presumably other interacting work groups seem clear: Do not place together those with a past history of major personal clashes. If they must be on the same committee, each must be helped to see that the other is working toward the same goal.

An interesting variation in this area of research is the suggestion from Ex's work that perceptions will be more influenced or swayed by relatively unfamiliar people in the group than by those who are intimates.[44] The concept needs

---

[40] J. Bieri, "Change in Interpersonal Perception Following Interaction," *Journal of Abnormal and Social Psychology*, XLVIII (1953), 61–66.

[41] M. E. Rosenbaum, "Social Perception and the Motivational Structure of Interpersonal Relations," *Journal of Abnormal and Social Psychology*, LIX (1959), 130–33.

[42] R. V. Exline, "Interrelations among Two Dimensions of Sociometric Status, Group Congeniality and Accuracy of Social Perception," *Sociometry*, XXIII (1960), 85–101.

[43] R. V. Exline, "Group Climate as a Factor in the Relevance and Accuracy of Social Perception," *Journal of Abnormal and Social Psychology*, LV (1957), 382–88.

[44] J. Ex, "The Nature of the Relation between Two Persons and the Degree of Their Influence on Each Other," *Acta Psychologica*, XVII (1960), 39–54.

further research, but it provides the interesting suggestion that we may give more credit to strangers for having knowledge, since we do not really know, than we do to our intimates, whose backgrounds and limitations we feel we do know.

The *organization*, and one's place in it, may also be viewed as the context in which perceptions take place. A study by Dearborn and Simon illustrates this point.[45] Their data support the hypothesis that the administrator's perceptions will often be limited to those aspects of a situation which relate specifically to his own department, despite an attempt to influence him away from such selectivity.

Perception of self among populations at different levels in the hierarchy also offers an opportunity to judge the influence of organizational context on perceptual activity. Porter's study of the self-descriptions of managers and line workers indicated that both groups saw themselves in different terms, which corresponded to their positions in the organization's hierarchy.[46] He stated that managers used leadership-type traits (e.g., inventive) to describe themselves, while line workers used follower-type terms (e.g., co-operative). The question of which comes first must be asked: Does the manager see himself this way because of his current position in the organization? Or is this self-picture an expression of a more enduring personal characteristic that helped bring the manager to his present position? This study does not answer that question, but it does suggest to an administrator the need to be aware of the possibly critical relationship between one's hierarchical role and self-perception.

### Perceptual Influences on Interpersonal Adjustment

Throughout this paper, we have examined a variety of influences on the perceptual process. There has been at least the inference that the operations of such influences on perception would in turn affect behavior that would follow. Common-sense judgment suggests that being able to judge other people accurately facilitates smooth and effective interpersonal adjustments. Nevertheless, the relationship between perception and consequent behavior is itself in need of direct analysis. Two aspects may be identified: (1) the effect of accuracy of perception on subsequent behavior and (2) the effect of the duration of the relationship and the opportunity for experiencing additional cues.

First then, from the applied point of view, we can ask a crucial question: Is there a relationship between accuracy of social perception and adjustment to others? While the question might suggest a quick affirmative answer, research findings are inconsistent. Steiner attempted to resolve some of these inconsistencies by stating that accuracy may have an effect on interaction under the following conditions: when the interacting persons are co-operatively motivated, when the behavior which is accurately perceived is relevant to the activities of these persons, and when members are free to alter their behavior on the basis of their perceptions.[47]

[45]D. C. Dearborn and H. A. Simon, "Selective Perception: A Note on the Departmental Identifications of Executives," *Sociometry*, XXI (1958), 140–44.

[46]L. W. Porter, "Differential Self-Perceptions of Management Personnel and Line Workers," *Journal of Applied Psychology*, XLII (1958), 105–9.

[47]I. Steiner, "Interpersonal Behavior As Influenced by Accuracy of Social Perception," *Psychological Review*, LXII (1955), 268–75.

Where the relationship provides opportunity only to form an impression, a large number of subjective factors, i.e., set, stereotypes, projections, etc., operate to create an early impression, which is frequently erroneous. In more enduring relationships a more balanced appraisal may result, since increased interaction provides additional cues for judgment. In his study of the acquaintance process, Newcomb showed that while early perception of favorable traits caused attraction to the perceived person, over a four-month period the early cues for judging favorable traits became less influential.[48] With time, a much broader basis was used which included comparisons with others with whom one had established relationships. Such findings suggest that the warnings about perceptual inaccuracies implicit in the earlier sections of this paper apply with more force to the short-term process of impression forming than to relatively extended acquaintance-building relationships. One would thus hope that rating an employee after a year of service would be a more objective performance than appraising him in a selection interview—a hope that would be fulfilled only when the rater had provided himself with opportunities for broadening the cues he used in forming his first impressions.

## Summary

Two principal suggestions which increase the probability of more effective administrative action emerge from the research data. One suggestion is that the administrator be continuously aware of the intricacies of the perceptual process and thus be warned to avoid arbitrary and categorical judgments and to seek reliable evidence before judgments are made. A second suggestion grows out of the first: increased accuracy in one's self-perception can make possible the flexibility to seek evidence and to shift position as time provides additional evidence.

Nevertheless, not every effort designed to improve perceptual accuracy will bring about such accuracy. The dangers of too complete reliance on formal training for perceptual accuracy are suggested in a study by Crow.[49] He found that a group of senior medical students were somewhat less accurate in their perceptions of others after a period of training in physician-patient relationships than were an untrained control group. The danger is that a little learning encourages the perceiver to respond with increased sensitivity to individual differences without making it possible for him to gauge the real meaning of the differences he has seen.

Without vigilance to perceive accurately and to minimize as far as possible the subjective approach in perceiving others, effective administration is handicapped. On the other hand research would not support the conclusion that perceptual distortions will not occur simply because the administrator says he will try to be objective. The administrator or manager will have to work hard to avoid seeing only what he wants to see and to guard against fitting everything into what he is set to see.

---

[48]T. M. Newcomb, "The Perception of Interpersonal Attraction," *American Psychologist*, XI (1956), 575–86.

[49]W. J. Crow, "Effect of Training on Interpersonal Perception," *Journal of Abnormal and Social Psychology*, LV (1957), 355–59.

We are not yet sure of the ways in which training for perceptual accuracy can best be accomplished, but such training cannot be ignored. In fact, one can say that one of the important tasks of administrative science is to design research to test various training procedures for increasing perceptual accuracy.

# Interpersonal
# Communication

## DEFENSIVE
## COMMUNICATION

JACK R. GIBB

One way to understand communication is to view it as a people process rather than as a language process. If one is to make fundamental improvement in communication, he must make changes in interpersonal relationships. One possible type of alteration—and the one with which this paper is concerned—is that of reducing the degree of defensiveness.

### Definition and Significance

"Defensive behavior" is behavior which occurs when an individual perceives threat or anticipates threat in the group. The person who behaves defensively, even though he also gives some attention to the common task, devotes an appreciable portion of his energy to defending himself. Besides talking about the topic, he thinks about how he appears to others, how he may be seen more favorably, how he may win, dominate, impress or escape punishment, and/or how he may avoid or mitigate a perceived or an anticipated attack.

Such inner feelings and outward acts tend to create similarly defensive postures in others; and, if unchecked, the ensuing circular response becomes increasingly destructive. Defensive behavior, in short, engenders defensive listening, and this in turn produces postural, facial, and verbal cues which raise the defense level of the original communicator.

Defensive arousal prevents the listener from concentrating upon the message. Not only do defensive communicators send off multiple value, motive, and affect

---

Reprinted from the *Journal of Communication*, XI, No. 3 (September, 1961), 141–48, by permission of the author and the publisher.

cues, but also defensive recipients distort what they receive. As a person becomes more and more defensive, he becomes less and less able to perceive accurately the motives, the values, and the emotions of the sender. The writer's analyses of tape recorded discussions revealed that increases in defensive behavior were correlated positively with losses in efficiency in communication.[1] Specifically, distortions became greater when defensive states existed in the groups.

The converse also is true. The more "supportive" or defense reductive the climate the less the receiver reads into the communication distorted loadings which arise from projections of his own anxieties, motives, and concerns. As defenses are reduced, the receivers become better able to concentrate upon the structure, the content, and the cognitive meanings of the message.

### Categories of Defensive and Supportive Communication

In working over an eight-year period with recordings of discussions occurring in varied settings, the writer developed the six pairs of defensive and supportive categories presented in Table 1. Behavior which a listener perceives as possessing any of the characteristics listed in the left-hand column arouses defensiveness, whereas that which he interprets as having any of the qualities designated as supportive reduces defensive feelings. The degree to which these reactions occur depend upon the personal level of defensiveness and upon the general climate in the group at the time.[2]

TABLE 1

Categories of Behavior Characteristic of Supportive
and Defensive Climates in Small Groups

| Defensive Climates | Supportive Climates |
|---|---|
| 1. Evaluation | 1. Description |
| 2. Control | 2. Problem orientation |
| 3. Strategy | 3. Spontaneity |
| 4. Neutrality | 4. Empathy |
| 5. Superiority | 5. Equality |
| 6. Certainty | 6. Provisionalism |

Evaluation and Description

Speech or other behavior which appears evaluative increases defensiveness. If by expression, manner of speech, tone of voice, or verbal content the sender seems to be evaluating or judging the listener, then the receiver goes on guard. Of course, other factors may inhibit the reaction. If the listener thinks that the speaker regards him as an equal and is being open and spontaneous, for example, the evaluativeness in a message will be neutralized and perhaps not even

[1]J.R. Gibb, "Defense Level and Influence in Small Groups," in *Leadership and Interpersonal Behavior*, ed. L. Petrullo and B. M. Bass (New York: Holt, Rinehart & Winston, 1961), pp. 66–81.

[2]J. R. Gibb, "Sociopsychological Processes of Group Instruction," in *The Dynamics of Instructional Groups*, ed. N. B. Henry (Fifty-ninth Yearbook of the National Society for the Study of Education, Part II, 1960), pp. 115–35.

perceived. This same principle applies equally to the other five categories of potentially defense-producing climates. The six sets are interactive.

Because our attitudes toward other persons are frequently, and often necessarily, evaluative, expressions which the defensive person will regard as non-judgmental are hard to frame. Even the simplest question usually conveys the answer that the sender wishes or implies the response that would fit into his value system. A mother, for example, immediately following an earth tremor that shook the house, sought for her small son with the question: "Bobby, where are you?" The timid and plaintive "Mommy, I didn't do it" indicated how Bobby's chronic mild defensiveness predisposed him to react with a projection of his own guilt and in the context of his chronic assumption that questions are full of accusation.

Anyone who has attempted to train professionals to use information-seeking speech with neutral affect appreciates how difficult it is to teach a person to say even the simple "Who did that?" without being seen as accusing. Speech is so frequently judgmental that there is a reality base for the defensive interpretations which are so common.

When insecure, group members are particularly likely to place blame, to see others as fitting into categories of good or bad, to make moral judgments of their colleagues, and to question the value, motive, and affect loadings of the speech which they hear. Since value loadings imply a judgment of others, a belief that the standards of the speaker differ from his own causes the listener to become defensive.

Descriptive speech, in contrast to that which is evaluative, tends to arouse a minimum of uneasiness. Speech acts which the listener perceives as genuine requests for information or as material with neutral loadings is descriptive. Specifically, presentations of feelings, events, perceptions, or processes which do not ask or imply that the receiver change behavior or attitude are minimally defense-producing. The difficulty in avoiding overtone is illustrated by the problems of news reporters in writing stories about unions, Communists, Negroes, and religious activities without tipping off the "party" line of the newspaper. One can often tell from the opening words in a news article which side the newspaper's editorial policy favors.

### Control and Problem Orientation

Speech which is used to control the listener evokes resistance. In most of our social intercourse someone is trying to do something to someone else—to change an attitude, to influence behavior, or to restrict the field of activity. The degree to which attempts to control produce defensiveness depends upon the openness of the effort, for a suspicion that hidden motives exist heightens resistance. For this reason attempts of non-directive therapists and progressive educators to refrain from imposing a set of values, a point of view, or a problem solution upon the receivers meet with many barriers. Since the norm is control, non-controllers must earn the perceptions that their efforts have no hidden motives. A bombardment of persuasive "messages" in the fields of politics, education, special causes, advertising, religion, medicine, industrial relations, and guidance has bred cynical and paranoidal responses in listeners.

Implicit in all attempts to alter another person is the assumption by the change agent that the person to be altered is inadequate. That the speaker secretly views the listener as ignorant, unable to make his own decisions, uninformed, immature, unwise, or possessed of wrong or inadequate attitudes is a subconscious perception which gives the latter a valid base for defensive reactions.

Methods of control are many and varied. Legalistic insistence on detail, restrictive regulations and policies, conformity norms, and all laws are among the methods. Gestures, facial expressions, other forms of non-verbal communication, and even such simple acts as holding a door open in a particular manner are means of imposing one's will upon another and hence are potential sources of resistance.

Problem orientation, on the other hand, is the antithesis of persuasion. When the sender communicates a desire to collaborate in defining a mutual problem and in seeking its solution, he tends to create the same problem orientation in the listener; and, of greater importance, he implies that he has no predetermined solution, attitude, or method to impose. Such behavior is permissive in that it allows the receiver to set his own goals, make his own decisions, and evaluate his own progress—or to share with the sender in doing so. The exact methods of attaining permissiveness are not known, but they must involve a constellation of cues, and they certainly go beyond mere verbal assurances that the communicator has no hidden desires to exercise control.

### Strategy and Spontaneity

When the sender is perceived as engaged in a stratagem involving ambiguous and multiple motivations, the receiver becomes defensive. No one wishes to be a guinea pig, a role player, or an impressed actor, and no one likes to be the victim of some hidden motivation. That which is concealed, also, may appear larger than it really is, with the degree of defensiveness of the listener determining the perceived size of the suppressed element. The intense reaction of the reading audience to the material in the *Hidden Persuaders* indicates the prevalence of defensive reactions to multiple motivations behind strategy. Group members who are seen as "taking a role," as feigning emotion, as toying with their colleagues, as withholding information, or as having special sources of data are especially resented. One participant once complained that another was "using a listening technique" on him!

A large part of the adverse reaction to much of the so-called human relations training is a feeling against what are perceived as gimmicks and tricks to fool or to "involve" people, to make a person think he is making his own decision, or to make the listener feel that the sender is genuinely interested in him as a person. Particularly violent reactions occur when it appears that someone is trying to make a stratagem appear spontaneous. One person has reported a boss who incurred resentment by habitually using the gimmick of "spontaneously" looking at his watch and saying, "My gosh, look at the time—I must run to an appointment." The belief was that the boss would create less irritation by honestly asking to be excused.

Similarly, the deliberate assumption of guilelessness and natural simplicity is especially resented. Monitoring the tapes of feedback and evaluation sessions in training groups indicates the surprising extent to which members perceive the strategies of their colleagues. This perceptual clarity may be quite shocking to the strategist, who usually feels that he has cleverly hidden the motivational aura around the "gimmick."

This aversion to deceit may account for one's resistance to politicians who are suspected of behind-the-scenes planning to get his vote; to psychologists whose listening apparently is motivated by more than the manifest or content-level interest in his behavior, or to the sophisticated, smooth, or clever person whose "oneupmanship" is marked with guile. In training groups the role-flexible person frequently is resented because his changes in behavior are perceived as strategic maneuvers.

Conversely, behavior which appears to be spontaneous and free of deception is defense reductive. If the communicator is seen as having a clean id, as having uncomplicated motivations, as being straightforward and honest, and as behaving spontaneously in response to the situation, he is likely to arouse minimal defense.

### Neutrality and Empathy

When neutrality in speech appears to the listener to indicate a lack of concern for his welfare, he becomes defensive. Group members usually desire to be perceived as valued persons, as individuals of special worth, and as objects of concern and affection. The clinical, detached, person-is-an-object-of-study attitude on the part of many psychologist-trainers is resented by group members. Speech with low affect that communicates little warmth or caring is in such contrast with the affect-laden speech in social situations that it sometimes communicates rejection.

Communication that conveys empathy for the feelings and respect for the worth of the listener, however, is particularly supportive and defense reductive. Reassurance results when a message indicates that the speaker identifies himself with the listener's problems, shares his feelings, and accepts his emotional reactions at face value. Abortive efforts to deny the legitimacy of the receiver's emotions by assuring the receiver that he need not feel bad, that he should not feel rejected, or that he is overly anxious, though often intended as support giving, may impress the listener as lack of acceptance. The combination of understanding and empathizing with the other person's emotions with no accompanying effort to change him apparently is supportive at a high level.

The importance of gestural behavioral cues in communicating empathy should be mentioned. Apparently spontaneous facial and bodily evidences of concern are often interpreted as especially valid evidence of deep-level acceptance.

### Superiority and Equality

When a person communicates to another that he feels superior in position, power, wealth, intellectual ability, physical characteristics, or other ways, he arouses defensiveness. Here, as with the other sources of disturbance, whatever arouses feelings of inadequacy causes the listener to center upon the affect loading of the statement rather than upon the cognitive elements. The receiver then reacts by not hearing the message, by forgetting it, by competing with the sender, or by becoming jealous of him.

The person who is perceived as feeling superior communicates that he is not willing to enter into a shared problem-solving relationship, that he probably does not desire feedback, that he does not require help, and/or that he will be likely to try to reduce the power, the status, or the worth of the receiver.

Many ways exist for creating the atmosphere that the sender feels himself equal to the listener. Defenses are reduced when one perceives the sender as being willing to enter into participative planning with mutual trust and respect. Differences in talent, ability, worth, appearance, status, and power often exist, but the low defense communicator seems to attach little importance to these distinctions.

### Certainty and Provisionalism

The effects of dogmatism in producing defensiveness are well known. Those who seem to know the answers, to require no additional data, and to regard themselves as teachers rather than as co-workers tend to put others on guard. Moreover, in the writer's experiment, listeners often perceived manifest expressions of certainty as connoting inward feelings of inferiority. They saw the dogmatic individual as needing to be right, as wanting to win an argument rather than solve a problem, and as seeing his ideas as truths to be defended. This kind of behavior often was associated with acts which others regarded as attempts to exercise control. People who were right seemed to have low tolerance for members who were "wrong"—i.e., who did not agree with the sender.

One reduces the defensiveness of the listener when he communicates that he is willing to experiment with his own behavior, attitudes, and ideas. The person who appears to be taking provisional attitudes, to be investigating issues rather than taking sides on them, to be problem solving rather than debating, and to be willing to experiment and explore tends to communicate that the listener may have some control over the shared quest or the investigation of the ideas. If a person is genuinely searching for information and data, he does not resent help or company along the way.

### Conclusion

The implications of the above material for the parent, the teacher, the manager, the administrator, or the therapist are fairly obvious. Arousing defensiveness interferes with communication and thus makes it difficult—and sometimes impossible—for anyone to convey ideas clearly and to move effectively toward the solution of therapeutic, educational, or managerial problems.

# BARRIERS AND GATEWAYS
# TO COMMUNICATION

CARL R. ROGERS
F. J. ROETHLISBERGER

**Part I**

It may seem curious that a person like myself, whose whole professional effort is devoted to psychotherapy, should be interested in problems of communication. What relationship is there between obstacles to communication and providing therapeutic help to individuals with emotional maladjustments?

Actually the relationship is very close indeed. The whole task of psychotherapy is the task of dealing with a failure in communication. The emotionally maladjusted person, the "neurotic," is in difficulty, first, because communication within himself has broken down and, secondly, because as a result of this his communication with others has been damaged. To put it another way, in the "neurotic" individual parts of himself which have been termed unconscious, or repressed, or denied to awareness, become blocked off so that they no longer communicate themselves to the conscious or managing part of himself; as long as this is true, there are distortions in the way he communicates himself to others, and so he suffers both within himself and in his interpersonal relations.

The task of psychotherapy is to help the person achieve, through a special relationship with a therapist, good communication within himself. Once this is achieved, he can communicate more freely and more effectively with others. We may say then that psychotherapy is good communication, within and between men. We may also turn that statement around and it will still be true. Good communication, free communication, within or between men, is always therapeutic.

It is, then, from a background of experience with communication in counseling and psychotherapy that I want to present two ideas: (1) I wish to state what I believe is one of the major factors in blocking or impeding communication, and then (2) I wish to present what in our experience has proved to be a very important way of improving or facilitating communication.

Reprinted from *Harvard Business Review* (July-August 1952), pp. 46–52. ©1952 by the President and Fellows of Harvard College; all rights reserved.

EDITORS' NOTE: Mr. Rogers' and Mr. Roethlisberger's observations are based on their contributions to a panel discussion at the Centennial Conference on Communications, Northwestern University, October 1951. A complete report of this conference may be secured by writing to the Publications Office, Northwestern University, Evanston, Illinois.

I should like to propose, as a hypothesis for consideration, that the major barrier to mutual interpersonal communication is our very natural tendency to judge, to evaluate, to approve (or disapprove) the statement of the other person or the other group. Let me illustrate my meaning with some very simple examples. Suppose someone, commenting on this discussion, makes the statement, "I didn't like what that man said." What will you respond? Almost invariably your reply will be either approval or disapproval of the attitude expressed. Either you respond, "I didn't either; I thought it was terrible," or else you tend to reply "Oh, I thought it was really good." In other words, your primary reaction is to evaluate it from *your* point of view, your own frame of reference.

Or take another example. Suppose I say with some feeling, "I think the Republicans are behaving in ways that show a lot of good sound sense these days." What is the response that arises in your mind? The overwhelming likelihood is that it will be evaluative. In other words, you will find yourself agreeing, or disagreeing, or making some judgment about me such as "He must be a conservative," or "He seems solid in his thinking." Or let us take an illustration from the international scene. Russia says vehemently, "The treaty with Japan is a war plot on the part of the United States." We rise as one person to say, "That's a lie!"

This last illustration brings in another element connected with my hypothesis. Although the tendency to make evaluations is common in almost all interchange of language, it is very much heightened in those situations where feelings and emotions are deeply involved. So the stronger our feelings, the more likely it is that there will be no mutual element in the communication. There will be just two ideas, two feelings, two judgments, missing each other in psychological space.

I am sure you recognize this from your own experience. When you have not been emotionally involved yourself and have listened to a heated discussion, you often go away thinking, "Well, they actually weren't talking about the same thing." And they were not. Each was making a judgment, an evaluation, from his own frame of reference. There was really nothing which could be called communication in any genuine sense. This tendency to react to any emotionally meaningful statement by forming an evaluation of it from our own point of view is, I repeat, the major barrier to interpersonal communication.

### Gateway: Listening with Understanding

Is there any way of solving this problem, of avoiding this barrier? I feel that we are making exciting progress toward this goal, and I should like to present it as simply as I can. Real communication occurs, and this evaluative tendency is avoided, when we listen with understanding. What does that mean? It means to see the expressed idea and attitude from the other person's point of view, to sense how it feels to him, to achieve his frame of reference in regard to the thing he is talking about.

Stated so briefly, this may sound absurdly simple, but it is not. It is an approach which we have found extremely potent in the field of psychotherapy. It is the most effective agent we know for altering the basic personality structure of an individual and for improving his relationships and his communications with others. If I can listen to what he can tell me, if I can understand how it seems to him, if I can see its personal meaning for him, if I can sense the emotional flavor which it has for him, then I will be releasing potent forces of change in him.

Again, if I can really understand how he hates his father, or hates the company, or hates Communists—if I can catch the flavor of his fear of insanity, or his fear of atom bombs, or of Russia—it will be of the greatest help to him in altering those hatreds and fears and in establishing realistic and harmonious relationships with the very people and situations toward which he has felt hatred and fear. We know from our research that such empathic understanding—understanding *with* a person, not *about* him—is such an effective approach that it can bring about major changes in personality.

Some of you may be feeling that you listen well to people and yet you have never seen such results. The chances are great indeed that your listening has not been of the type I have described. Fortunately, I can suggest a little laboratory experiment which you can try to test the quality of your understanding. The next time you get into an argument with your wife, or your friend, or with a small group of friends, just stop the discussion for a moment and, for an experiment, institute this rule: "Each person can speak up for himself only *after* he has first restated the ideas and feelings of the previous speaker accurately and to that speaker's satisfaction."

You see what this would mean. It would simply mean that before presenting your own point of view, it would be necessary for you to achieve the other speaker's frame of reference—to understand his thoughts and feelings so well that you could summarize them for him. Sounds simple, doesn't it? But if you try it, you will discover that it is one of the most difficult things you have ever tried to do. However, once you have been able to see the other's point of view, your own comments will have to be drastically revised. You will also find the emotion going out of the discussion, the differences being reduced, and those differences which remain being of a rational and understandable sort.

Can you imagine what this kind of an approach would mean if it were projected into larger areas? What would happen to a labor-management dispute if it were conducted in such a way that labor, without necessarily agreeing, could accurately state management's point of view in a way that management could accept; and management, without approving labor's stand, could state labor's case in a way that labor agreed was accurate? It would mean that real communication was established, and one could practically guarantee that some reasonable solution would be reached.

If, then, this way of approach is an effective avenue to good communication and good relationships, as I am quite sure you will agree if you try the experiment I have mentioned, why is it not more widely tried and used? I will try to list the difficulties which keep it from being utilized.

*Need for Courage.* In the first place it takes courage, a quality which is not too widespread. I am indebted to Dr. S. I. Hayakawa, the semanticist, for pointing out that to carry on psychotherapy in this fashion is to take a very real risk, and that courage is required. If you really understand another person in this way, if you are willing to enter his private world and see the way life appears to him, without any attempt to make evaluative judgments, you run the risk of being changed yourself. You might see it his way; you might find yourself influenced in your attitudes or your personality.

This risk of being changed is one of the most frightening prospects many of us can face. If I enter, as fully as I am able, into the private world of a neurotic or psychotic individual, isn't there a risk that I might become lost in that world? Most of us are afraid to take that risk. Or if we were listening to a Russian Communist, or Senator Joe McCarthy, how many of us would dare to try to see the world from each of their points of view? The great majority of us could not *listen;* we would find ourselves compelled to *evaluate,* because listening would seem too dangerous. So the *first* requirement is courage, and we do not always have it.

*Heightened Emotions.* But there is a second obstacle. It is just when emotions are strongest that it is most difficult to achieve the frame of reference of the other person or group. Yet it is then that the attitude is most needed if communication is to be established. We have not found this to be an insuperable obstacle in our experience in psychotherapy. A third party, who is able to lay aside his own feelings and evaluations, can assist greatly by listening with understanding to each person or group and clarifying the views and attitudes each holds.

We have found this effective in small groups in which contradictory or antagonistic attitudes exist. When the parties to a dispute realize that they are being understood, that someone sees how the situation seems to them, the statements grow less exaggerated and less defensive, and it is no longer necessary to maintain the attitude, "I am 100% right and you are 100% wrong." The influence of such an understanding catalyst in the group permits the members to come closer and closer to the objective truth involved in the relationship. In this way mutual communication is established, and some type of agreement becomes much more possible.

So we may say that though heightened emotions make it much more difficult to understand *with* an opponent, our experience makes it clear that a neutral, understanding, catalyst type of leader or therapist can overcome this obstacle in a small group.

*Size of Group.* That last phrase, however, suggests another obstacle to utilizing the approach I have described. Thus far all our experience has been with small face-to-face groups—groups exhibiting industrial tensions, religious tensions, racial tensions, and therapy groups in which many personal tensions are present. In these small groups our experience, confirmed by a limited amount of research, shows that this basic approach leads to improved communication, to greater acceptance of others and by others, and to attitudes which are more positive and more problem-solving in nature. There is a decrease in defensiveness, in exaggerated statements, in evaluative and critical behavior.

But these findings are from small groups. What about trying to achieve understanding between larger groups that are geographically remote, or between face-to-face groups that are not speaking for themselves but simply as representatives of others, like the delegates at Kaesong? Frankly we do not know the answers to these questions. I believe the situation might be put this way: As social scientists we have a tentative test-tube solution of the problem of breakdown in communication. But to confirm the validity of this test-tube solution and to adapt it to the enormous problems of communication breakdown between classes, groups, and nations would involve additional funds, much more research, and creative thinking of a high order.

Yet with our present limited knowledge we can see some steps which might be taken even in large groups to increase the amount of listening *with* and decrease the amount of evaluation *about*. To be imaginative for a moment, let us suppose that a therapeutically oriented international group went to the Russian leaders and said, "We want to achieve a genuine understanding of your views and, even more important, of your attitudes and feelings toward the United States. We will summarize and resummarize these views and feelings if necessary, until you agree that our description represents the situation as it seems to you."

Then suppose they did the same thing with the leaders in our own country. If they then gave the widest possible distribution to these two views, with the feelings clearly described but not expressed in name-calling, might not the effect be very great? It would not guarantee the type of understanding I have been describing, but it would make it much more possible. We can understand the feelings of a person who hates us much more readily when his attitudes are accurately described to us by a neutral third party than we can when he is shaking his fist at us.

*Faith in Social Sciences.* But even to describe such a first step is to suggest another obstacle to this approach of understanding. Our civilization does not yet have enough faith in the social sciences to utilize their findings. The opposite is true of the physical sciences. During the war when a test-tube solution was found to the problem of synthetic rubber, millions of dollars and an army of talent were turned loose on the problem of using that finding. If synthetic rubber could be made in milligrams, it could and would be made in the thousands of tons. And it was. But in the social science realm, if a way is found of facilitating communication and mutual understanding in small groups, there is no guarantee that the finding will be utilized. It may be a generation or more before the money and the brains will be turned loose to exploit that finding.

### Summary

In closing, I should like to summarize this small-scale solution to the problem of barriers in communication, and to point out certain of its characteristics.

I have said that our research and experience to date would make it appear that breakdowns in communication, and the evaluative tendency which is the major barrier to communication, can be avoided. The solution is provided by creating a situation in which each of the different parties comes to understand the other from the *other's* point of view. This has been achieved, in practice, even when feelings run high, by the influence of a person who is willing to understand each point of view empathically, and who thus acts as a catalyst to precipitate further understanding.

This procedure has important characteristics. It can be initiated by one party, without waiting for the other to be ready. It can even be initiated by a neutral third person, provided he can gain a minimum of cooperation from one of the parties.

This procedure can deal with the insincerities, the defensive exaggerations, the lies, the "false fronts" which characterize almost every failure in communication. These defensive distortions drop away with astonishing speed as people find that the only intent is to understand, not to judge.

This approach leads steadily and rapidly toward the discovery of the truth, toward a realistic appraisal of the objective barriers to communication. The dropping of some defensiveness by one party leads to further dropping of defensiveness by the other party, and truth is thus approached.

This procedure gradually achieves mutual communication. Mutual communication tends to be pointed toward solving a problem rather than toward attacking a person or group. It leads to a situation in which I see how the problem appears to you as well as to me, and you see how it appears to me as well as to you. Thus accurately and realistically defined, the problem is almost certain to yield to intelligent attack; or if it is in part insoluble, it will be comfortably accepted as such.

This then appears to be a test-tube solution to the breakdown of communication as it occurs in small groups. Can we take this small-scale answer, investigate it further, refine it, develop it, and apply it to the tragic and well-nigh fatal failures of communication which threaten the very existence of our modern world? It seems to me that this is a possibility and a challenge which we should explore.

**Part II**

In thinking about the many barriers to personal communication, particularly those that are due to differences of background, experience, and motivation, it seems to me extraordinary that any two persons can ever understand each other. Such reflections provoke the question of how communication is possible when people do not see and assume the same things and share the same values.

On this question there are two schools of thought. One school assumes that communication between A and B, for example, has failed when B does not accept what A has to say as being fact, true, or valid; and that the goal of communication is to get B to agree with A's opinions, ideas, facts, or information.

The position of the other school of thought is quite different. It assumes that communication has failed when B does not feel free to express his feelings to A because B fears they will not be accepted by A. Communication is facilitated when on the part of A or B or both there is a willingness to express and accept differences.

As these are quite divergent conceptions, let us explore them further with an example. Bill, an employee, is talking with his boss in the boss's office. The boss says, "I think, Bill, that this is the best way to do your job." Bill says, "Oh yeah!" According to the first school of thought, this reply would be a sign of poor communication. Bill does not understand the best way of doing his work. To improve communication, therefore, it is up to the boss to explain to Bill why his way is the best.

From the point of view of the second school of thought, Bill's reply is a sign neither of good nor of bad communication. Bill's response is indeterminate.

Author's Note: For the concepts I use to present my material I am greatly indebted to some very interesting conversations I have had with my friend, Irving Lee.—*F.J.R.*

But the boss has an opportunity to find out what Bill means if he so desires. Let us assume that this is what he chooses to do, i.e., find out what Bill means. So this boss tries to get Bill to talk more about his job while he (the boss) listens.

For purposes of simplification, I shall call the boss representing the first school of thought "*Smith*" and the boss representing the second school of thought "*Jones*." In the presence of the so-called same stimulus each behaves differently. Smith chooses to *explain;* Jones chooses to *listen.* In my experience Jones's response works better than Smith's. It works better because Jones is making a more proper evaluation of what is taking place between him and Bill than Smith is. Let us test this hypothesis by continuing with our example.

### What Smith Assumes, Sees, and Feels

Smith assumes that he understands what Bill means when Bill says, "Oh yeah!" so there is no need to find out. Smith is sure that Bill does not understand why this is the best way to do his job, so Smith has to tell him. In this process let us assume Smith is logical, lucid, and clear. He presents his facts and evidence well. But, alas, Bill remains unconvinced. What does Smith do? Operating under the assumption that what is taking place between him and Bill is something essentially logical, Smith can draw only one of two conclusions: either (1) he has not been clear enough, or (2) Bill is too damned stupid to understand. So he either has to "spell out" his case in words of fewer and fewer syllables or give up. Smith is reluctant to do the latter, so he continues to explain. What happens?

If Bill still does not accept Smith's explanation of why this is the best way for him to do his job, a pattern of interacting feelings is produced of which Smith is often unaware. The more Smith cannot get Bill to understand him, the more frustrated Smith becomes and the more Bill becomes a threat to his logical capacity. Since Smith sees himself as a fairly reasonable and logical chap, this is a difficult feeling to accept. It is much easier for him to perceive Bill as uncooperative or stupid. This perception, however, will affect what Smith says and does. Under these pressures Bill comes to be evaluated more and more in terms of Smith's values. By this process Smith tends to treat Bill's values as unimportant. He tends to deny Bill's uniqueness and difference. He treats Bill as if he had little capacity for self-direction.

Let us be clear. Smith does not see that he is doing these things. When he is feverishly scratching hieroglyphics on the back of an envelope, trying to explain to Bill why this is the best way to do his job, Smith is trying to be helpful. He is a man of goodwill, and he wants to set Bill straight. This is the way Smith sees himself and his behavior. But it is for this very reason that Bill's "Oh yeah!" is getting under Smith's skin.

"How dumb can a guy be?" is Smith's attitude, and unfortunately Bill will hear that more than Smith's good intentions. Bill will feel misunderstood. He will not see Smith as a man of goodwill trying to be helpful. Rather he will perceive him as a threat to his self-esteem and personal integrity. Against this threat Bill will feel the need to defend himself at all cost. Not being so logically articulate as Smith, Bill expresses this need, again, by saying, "Oh yeah!"

### What Jones Assumes, Sees, and Feels

Let us leave this sad scene between Smith and Bill which I fear is going to terminate by Bill's either leaving in a huff or being kicked out of Smith's office.

Let us turn for a moment to Jones and see what he is assuming, seeing, hearing, feeling, doing, and saying when he interacts with Bill.

Jones, it will be remembered, does not assume that he knows what Bill means when he says, "Oh yeah!" so he has to find out. Moreover, he assumes that when Bill said this, he had not exhausted his vocabulary or his feelings. Bill may not necessarily mean one thing; he may mean several different things. So Jones decides to listen.

In this process Jones is not under any illusion that what will take place will be eventually logical. Rather he is assuming that what will take place will be primarily an interaction of feelings. Therefore, he cannot ignore the feelings of Bill, the effect of Bill's feelings on him, or the effect of his feelings on Bill. In other words, he cannot ignore his relationship to Bill; he cannot assume that it will make no difference to what Bill will hear or accept.

Therefore, Jones will be paying strict attention to all of the things Smith has ignored. He will be addressing himself to Bill's feelings, his own, and the interactions between them.

Jones will therefore realize that he has ruffled Bill's feelings with his comment "I think, Bill, this is the best way to do your job." So instead of trying to get Bill to understand him, he decides to try to understand Bill. He does this by encouraging Bill to speak. Instead of telling Bill how he should feel or think, he asks Bill such questions as, "Is this what you feel?" "Is this what you see?" "Is this what you assume?" Instead of ignoring Bill's evaluations as irrelevant, not valid, inconsequential, or false, he tries to understand Bill's reality as he feels it, perceives it, and assumes it to be. As Bill begins to open up, Jones's curiosity is piqued by this process.

"Bill isn't so dumb; he's quite an interesting guy" becomes Jones's attitude. And that is what Bill hears. Therefore Bill feels understood and accepted as a person. He becomes less defensive. He is in a better frame of mind to explore and re-examine his own perceptions, feelings, and assumptions. In this process he perceives Jones as a source of help. Bill feels free to express his differences. He feels that Jones has some respect for his capacity for self-direction. These positive feelings toward Jones make Bill more inclined to say, "Well, Jones, I don't quite agree with you that this is the best way to do my job, but I'll tell you what I'll do. I'll try to do it that way for a few days, and then I'll tell you what I think."

### Conclusion

I grant that my two orientations do not work themselves out in practice in quite so simple or neat a fashion as I have been able to work them out on paper. There are many other ways in which Bill could have responded to Smith in the first place. He might even have said, "O.K., boss, I agree that your way of doing my job is better." But Smith still would not have known how Bill felt when he made this statement or whether Bill was actually going to do his job differently. Likewise, Bill could have responded to Jones in a way different from my example. In spite of Jones's attitude, Bill might still be reluctant to express himself freely to his boss.

The purpose of my examples has not been to demonstrate the right or wrong way of communicating. My purpose has been simply to provide something concrete to point to when I make the following generalizations:

(1) Smith represents to me a very common pattern of misunderstanding. The misunderstanding does not arise because Smith is not clear enough in expressing himself. It arises because of Smith's misevaluation of what is taking place when two people are talking together.

(2) Smith's misevaluation of the process of personal communication consists of certain very common assumptions, e.g., (a) that what is taking place is something essentially logical; (b) that words in themselves apart from the people involved mean something; and (c) that the purpose of the interaction is to get Bill to see things from Smith's point of view.

(3) Because of these assumptions, a chain reaction of perceptions and negative feelings is engendered which blocks communication. By ignoring Bill's feelings and by rationalizing his own, Smith ignores his relationship to Bill as one of the most important determinants of the communication. As a result, Bill hears Smith's attitude more clearly than the logical content of Smith's words. Bill feels that his individual uniqueness is being denied. His personal integrity being at stake, he becomes defensive and belligerent. As a result, Smith feels frustrated. He perceives Bill as stupid. So he says and does things which only provoke more defensiveness on the part of Bill.

(4) In the case of Jones, I have tried to show what might possibly happen if we made a different evaluation of what is taking place when two people are talking together. Jones makes a different set of assumptions. He assumes (a) that what is taking place between him and Bill is an interaction of sentiments; (b) that Bill—not his words in themselves—means something; (c) that the object of the interaction is to give Bill an opportunity to express freely his differences.

(5) Because of these assumptions, a psychological chain reaction of reinforcing feelings and perceptions is set up which facilitates communication between Bill and him. When Jones addresses himself to Bill's feelings and perceptions from Bill's point of view, Bill feels understood and accepted as a person; he feels free to express his differences. Bill sees Jones as a source of help; Jones sees Bill as an interesting person. Bill in turn becomes more cooperative.

(6) If I have identified correctly these very common patterns of personal communication, then some interesting hypotheses can be stated:

(a) Jones's method works better than Smith's, not because of any magic, but because Jones has a better map than Smith of the process of personal communication.

(b) The practice of Jones's method, however, is not merely an intellectual exercise. It depends on Jones's capacity and willingness to see and accept points of view different from his own, and to practice this orientation in a face-to-face relationship. This practice involves an emotional as well as an intellectual achievement. It depends in part on Jones's awareness of himself, in part on the practice of a skill.

(c) Although our colleges and universities try to get students to appreciate intellectually points of view different from their own, very little is done to help them to implement this general intellectual appreciation in a simple face-to-face relationship—at the level of a skill. Most educational institutions train their students to be logical, lucid, and clear. Very little is done to help them to listen more skillfully. As a result, our educated world contains too many Smiths and too few Joneses.

(d) The biggest block to personal communication is man's inability to listen intelligently, understandingly, and skillfully to another person. This deficiency in the modern world is widespread and appalling. In our universities, as well as elsewhere, too little is being done about it.

(7) In conclusion, let me apologize for acting toward you the way Smith did. But who am I to violate a long-standing academic tradition!

# Leadership

## HUMAN RELATIONS
## OR
## HUMAN RESOURCES?

Raymond E. Miles

The proselyting efforts of the advocates of participative management appear to have paid off. The typical modern manager, on paper at least, broadly endorses participation and rejects traditional, autocratic concepts of leadership and control as no longer acceptable or, perhaps, no longer legitimate.

However, while participation has apparently been well merchandised and widely purchased, there seems to be a great deal of confusion about what has been sold and what has been bought. Managers do not appear to have accepted a single, logically consistent concept of participation. In fact, there is reason to believe that managers have adopted two different theories or models of participation—one for themselves and one for their subordinates.

These statements reflect both my analysis of the development of the theory of participative management and my interpretation of managers' attitudes toward these concepts.

My views are based in part on a number of recent surveys of managers' beliefs and opinions. The most recent of these studies, which I conducted, was begun with a group of 215 middle and upper level managers in West Coast companies, and has been continued with a sample of over 300 administrators from public agencies.[1] This study was designed to clarify further certain aspects

---

Reprinted from *Harvard Business Review*, July-August, 1965. ©1965 by the President and Fellows of Harvard College; all rights reserved.

Author's Note: This article has benefited greatly from the comments of Professors Mason Haire and George Strauss of the University of California, Berkeley.
[1]See Raymond E. Miles, "Conflicting Elements in Managerial Ideologies," *Industrial Relations*, October 1964, pp. 77–91. The subsequent research with public administrators is still being conducted, and reports have not yet been published.

of managers' attitudes uncovered by earlier research under the direction of Dale Yoder of Stanford[2] and Profs. Mason Haire, Edwin Ghiselli, and Lyman Porter of the University of California, Berkeley.[3]

This series of studies involved the collection of questionnaire data on managers' opinions about people and on their attitudes toward various leadership policies and practices. Several thousand managers in all, both here and abroad, have participated.

This article is not intended to summarize all of the findings on managers' leadership attitudes available from these studies. Rather, my primary purpose is to construct a theoretical framework that may explain some of the principal dimensions of managers' views and some of the implications of their beliefs and opinions, drawing on the research simply to illustrate my views.

### Participative Theories

While the suggestion that managers have accepted a two-sided approach to participation may be disturbing, it should not be too surprising. Management theorists have frequently failed to deal with participation in a thorough and consistent manner. Indeed, from an examination of their somewhat ambivalent treatment of this concept, it is possible to conclude that they have been selling two significantly different models of participative management.

> One of the scholars' models which we will designate the *human relations* model, closely resembles the concept of participation which managers appear to accept for use with their own subordinates.

> The second, and not yet fully developed, theory, which I have labeled the *human resources* model, prescribes the sort of participative policies that managers would apparently like their superiors to follow.

I shall develop and examine these two models, compare them with managers' expressed beliefs, and consider some of the implications of managers' dual allegiance to them.

Both the *human relations* and the *human resources* models have three basic components:

1. A set of assumptions about people's values and capabilities.
2. Certain prescriptions as to the amount and kind of participative policies and practices that managers should follow, in keeping with their assumptions about people.
3. A set of expectations with respect to the effects of participation on subordinate morale and performance.

This third component contains the model's explanation of how and why participation works—that is, the purpose of participation and how it accomplishes this purpose. In outline form, the models may be summarized as shown in Exhibit 1.

[2]See Dale Yoder, "Management Theories as Managers See Them," *Personnel*, July-August 1962, pp. 25–30; "Management Policies for the Future," *Personnel Administration*, September-October 1962, pp. 11–14 ff.; Dale Yoder et al, "Managers' Theories of Management," *Journal of the Academy of Management*. September 1963, pp. 204–211.

[3]See Mason Haire, Edwin Ghiselli, and Lyman W. Porter, "Cultural Patterns in the Role of the Manager," *Industrial Relations*. February 1963, pp. 95–117, for a report on the Berkeley studies.

This approach is not new. As early as the 1920's, business spokesmen began to challenge the classical autocratic philosophy of management. The employee was no longer pictured as merely an appendage to a machine, seeking only economic rewards from his work. Managers were instructed to consider him as a "whole man" rather than as merely a bundle of skills and aptitudes.[4] They were urged to create a "sense of satisfaction" among their subordinates by showing interest in the employees' personal success and welfare. As Bendix notes, the "failure to treat workers as human beings came to be regarded as the cause of low morale, poor craftsmanship, unresponsiveness, and confusion."[5]

The key element in the *human relations* approach is its basic objective of making organizational members *feel* a useful and important part of the overall effort. This process is viewed as the means of accomplishing the ultimate goal of building a cooperative and compliant work force. Participation, in this model, is a lubricant which oils away resistance to formal authority. By discussing problems with his subordinates and acknowledging their individual needs and desires, the manager hopes to build a cohesive work team that is willing and anxious to tangle with organizational problems.

One further clue to the way in which participation is viewed in this approach is provided in Dubin's concept of "privilege pay."[6] The manager "buys" cooperation by letting his subordinates in on departmental information and allowing them to discuss and state their opinions on various departmental problems. He "pays a price" for allowing his subordinates the privilege of participating in certain decisions and exercising some self-direction. In return he hopes to obtain their cooperation in carrying out these and other decisions for the accomplishment of departmental objectives.

Implicit in this model is the idea that it might actually be easier and more efficient if the manager could merely make departmental decisions without bothering to involve his subordinates. However, as the advocates of this model point out, there are two parts to any decision—(1) the making of the decision and (2) the activities required to carry it out. In many instances, this model suggests, the manager might do better to "waste time" in discussing the problem with his subordinates, and perhaps even to accept suggestions that he believes may be less efficient, in order to get the decision carried out.

In sum, the *human relations* approach does not bring out the fact that participation may be useful for its own sake. The possibility that subordinates will, in fact, bring to light points which the manager may have overlooked, if considered at all, tends to be mentioned only in passing. This is treated as a potential side benefit which, while not normally expected, may occasionally occur. Instead, the manager is urged to adopt participative leadership policies as the least-cost method of obtaining cooperation and getting his decisions accepted.

In many ways the *human relations* model represents only a slight departure

[4]See Reinhard Bendix, *Work and Authority in Industry* (New York, John Wiley and Sons, 1956), pp. 287–340.

[5]*Ibid.*, p. 294.

[6]Robert Dubin, *The World of Work* (Englewood Cliffs, New Jersey, Prentice-Hall, Inc., 1958), pp. 243–244. It should be noted that Dubin treats the concept of privilege pay within a framework which goes beyond the *human relations* approach and, in some respects, is close to the *human resources* model.

from traditional autocratic models of management. The method of achieving results is different, and employees are viewed in more humanistic terms, but the basic roles of the manager and his subordinates remain essentially the same. The ultimate goal sought in both the traditional and the *human relations* model is compliance with managerial authority.

### Human Resources Model

This approach represents a dramatic departure from traditional concepts of management. Though not yet fully developed, it is emerging from the writings of McGregor, Likert, Haire, and others as a new and significant contribution to management thought.[7] The magnitude of its departure from previous models is illustrated first of all in its basic assumptions concerning people's values and abilities, which focus attention on all organization members as reservoirs of untapped resources. These resources include not only physical skills and energy, but also creative ability and the capacity for responsible, self-directed, self-controlled behavior. Given these assumptions about people, the manager's job cannot be viewed merely as one of giving direction and obtaining cooperation. Instead, his primary task becomes that of creating an environment in which the total resources of his department can be utilized.

The second point at which the *human resources* model differs dramatically from previous models is in its views on the purpose and goal of participation. In this model the manager does not share information, discuss departmental decisions, or encourage self-direction and self-control merely to improve subordinate satisfaction and morale. Rather, the purpose of these practices is to improve the decision making and total performance efficiency of the organization. The *human resources* model suggests that many decisions may actually be made more efficiently by those directly involved in and affected by the decisions.

Similarly, this model implies that control is often most efficiently exercised by those directly involved in the work in process, rather than by someone or some group removed from the actual point of operation. Moreover, the *human resources* model does not suggest that the manager allow participation only in routine decisions. Instead, it implies that the more important the decision, the greater is his *obligation* to encourage ideas and suggestions from his subordinates.

In the same vein, this model does not suggest that the manager allow his subordinates to exercise self-direction and self-control only when they are carrying out relatively unimportant assignments. In fact, it suggests that the area over which subordinates exercise self-direction and control should be continually broadened in keeping with their growing experience and ability.

The crucial point at which this model differs dramatically from other models is in its explanation of the causal relationship between satisfaction and performance. In the *human relations* approach improvement in subordinate satisfaction is viewed as an intervening variable which is the ultimate cause of improved

[7]See particularly Douglas McGregor, *The Human Side of Enterprise* (New York, McGraw-Hill Book Company, Inc., 1960); Rensis Likert, *New Patterns of Management* (New York, McGraw-Hill Book Company, Inc., 1961); and Mason Haire, "The Concept of Power and the Concept of Man," in *Social Science Approaches to Business Behavior*, edited by George Strother (Homewood, Illinois: The Dorsey Press, Inc., 1962), pp. 163–183.

# EXHIBIT 1
## Two Models of Participative Leadership

| *Human Relations* | *Human Resources* |
|---|---|

### ATTITUDES TOWARD PEOPLE

1. People in our culture share a common set of needs—to belong, to be liked, to be respected.

2. They desire individual recognition but, more than this, they want to feel a useful part of the company and their own work group or department.

3. They will tend to cooperate willingly and comply with organizational goals if these important needs are fulfilled.

1. In addition to sharing common needs for belonging and respect, most people in our culture desire to contribute effectively and creatively to the accomplishment of worthwhile objectives.

2. The majority of our work force is capable of exercising far more initiative, responsibility, and creativity than their present jobs require or allow.

3. These capabilities represent untapped resources which are presently being wasted.

### KIND AND AMOUNT OF PARTICIPATION

1. The manager's basic task is to make each worker believe that he is a useful and important part of the department "team."

2. The manager should be willing to explain his decisions and to discuss his subordinates' objections to his plans. On routine matters, he should encourage his subordinates to participate in planning and choosing among alternative solutions to problems.

3. Within narrow limits, the work group or individual subordinates should be allowed to exercise self-direction and self-control in carrying out plans.

1. The manager's basic task is to create an environment in which his subordinates can contribute their full range of talents to the accomplishment of organizational goals. He must attempt to uncover and tap the creative resources of his subordinates.

2. The manager should allow, and encourage, his subordinates to participate not only in routine decisions but in important matters as well. In fact, the more important a decision is to the manager's department, the greater should be his effort to tap the department's resources.

3. The manager should attempt to continually expand the areas over which his subordinates exercise self-direction and self-control as they develop and demonstrate greater insight and ability.

### EXPECTATIONS

1. Sharing information with subordinates and involving them in departmental decision making will help satisfy their basic needs for belonging and for individual recognition.

2. Satisfying these needs will improve subordinate morale and reduce resistance to formal authority.

3. High employee morale and reduced resistance to formal authority may lead to improved departmental performance. It should at least reduce intradepartment friction and thus make the manager's job easier.

1. The overall quality of decision making and performance will improve as the manager makes use of the full range of experience, insight, and creative ability in his department.

2. Subordinates will exercise responsible self-direction and self-control in the accomplishment of worthwhile objectives that they understand and have helped establish.

3. Subordinate satisfaction will increase as a byproduct of improved performance and the opportunity to contribute creatively to this improvement.

---

Note : It may fairly be argued that what I call the *human relations* model is actually the product of popularization and misunderstanding of the work of pioneers in this field. Moreover, it is true that some of the early research and writings of the human relationists contain concepts which seem to fall within the framework of what I call the *human resources* model. Nevertheless, it is my opinion that while the early writers did not advocate the *human relations* model as presented here, their failure to emphasize certain of the *human resources* concepts left their work open to the misinterpretations which have occurred.

performance. Diagrammatically, the causal relationship can be illustrated as in Exhibit II.

**EXHIBIT 2**
Human Relations Model

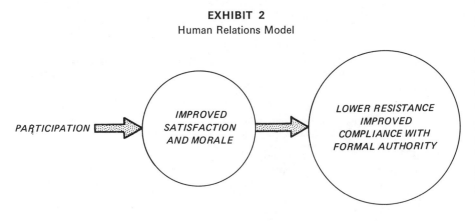

In the *human resouces* model the causal relationship between satisfaction and performance is viewed quite differently. Increased subordinate satisfaction is not pictured as the primary cause of improved performance; improvement results directly from creative contributions which subordinates make to departmental decision making, direction, and control. Subordinates' satisfaction is viewed instead as a by-product of the process—the result of their having made significant contributions to organizational success. In diagram form the *human resources* model can be illustrated as in Exhibit III.

**EXHIBIT 3**
Human Resources Model

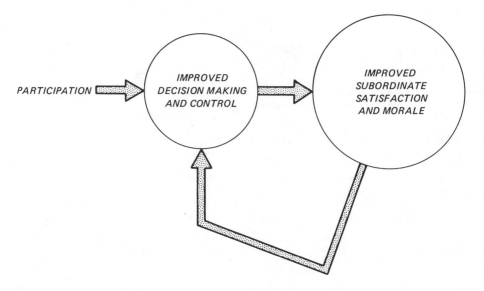

The *human resources* model does not deny a relationship between participation and morale. It suggests that subordinates' satisfaction may well increase as they play more and more meaningful roles in decision making and control. Moreover, the model recognizes that improvements in morale may not only set the stage for expanded participation, but create an atmosphere which supports creative problem solving. Nevertheless, this model rejects as unsupported the concept that the improvement of morale is a necessary or sufficient cause of improved decision making and control. Those improvements come directly from the full utilization of the organization's resources.

### Managers' Own Views

Which approach to participative management do managers actually follow? It was suggested earlier that managers' views appear to reflect both models. When they talk about the kind and amount of participation appropriate for their subordinates, they express concepts that appear to be similar to those in the *human relations* model. On the other hand, when they consider their own relationships with their superiors, their views seem to flow from the *human resources* model. A brief review of the relevant findings suggests some of the bases for this interpretation.

*Participation for subordinates.* When we look at managers' views on the use of participative policies and practices with the subordinates who report to them, two points seem clear:

> Managers generally accept and endorse the use of participative concepts. However, they frequently doubt their subordinates' capacity for self-direction and self-control, and their ability to contribute creatively to departmental decision making.

In the Stanford studies, an overwhelming majority of managers indicated their agreement with statements emphasizing the desirability of subordinate participation in decision making.[8] In the Berkeley studies, a majority of the managers in each of 11 countries, including the United States, indicated their agreement with such concepts as sharing information with subordinates and increasing subordinate influence and self-control.[9] Similarly, in my recent studies, managers overwhelmingly endorsed participative leadership policies.

On the other hand, while managers appear to have great faith in participative policies, they do not indicate such strong belief in their subordinates' capabilities. For example, the Berkeley group in their international study found that managers tended to have a "basic lack of confidence in others" and typically did not believe that capacity for leadership and initiative was widely distributed among subordinates.[10] In my own study, managers in every group to date have rated their subordinates and rank-and-file employees well below themselves, particularly on such important managerial traits as *responsibility*, *judgment*, and *initiative*.

But if managers do not expect creative, meaningful contributions from their subordinates, why do they advocate participative management? A reasonable

[8]Yoder *et al.*, "Managers' Theories of Management," *op. cit.*
[9]Haire, Ghiselli, and Porter, *op. cit.*
[10]Haire, Ghiselli, and Porter, *op. cit.*

answer seems to be that they advocate participative concepts as a means of improving subordinate morale and satisfaction. This interpretation gains support from my recent studies. Here, managers were asked to indicate their agreement or disagreement with statements predicting improved morale and satisfaction and statements predicting improved performance as the result of following various participative leadership policies. In connection with each of these policies, managers indicated consistently greater agreement with the predictions of improved morale than with the predictions of improved performance.

The fact that managers appear to have serious doubts about the values and capabilities of those reporting to them seems to rule out their acceptance of the *human resources* model for use with their subordinates. On the other hand, the fact that they do endorse participation and seem quite certain about its positive impact on morale suggests a close relationship between their views and those expressed in the *human relations* model. Moreover, the types of participative policies which managers most strongly advocate seem to support this interpretation.

In my research, managers indicate strongest agreement with policies that advocate sharing information and discussing objectives with subordinates. However, they tend to be somewhat less enamored with the policies which suggest increasing subordinate self-direction and self-control. This pattern of participation seems much closer to that of the *human relations* approach than to the pattern advocated in the *human resources* model.

*Participation for themselves.* When I examined managers' views toward their relationships with their own superiors, a much different pattern of responses became evident:

1. Managers in my studies tend to see little, if any, difference between their own capabilities and those of their superiors. In fact, they tend to rate themselves equal to, if not higher than, their superiors on such traits as *creativity, ingenuity, flexibility,* and *willingness to change.*
2. When asked to indicate at which levels in their organizations they feel each of the participative policies would be most appropriate, managers invariably feel most strongly that the full range of participative policies should be used by their own superiors.

More importantly, they also tend to be most certain that these participative policies will result in improved organizational performance *at their own level.*

Thus, when managers discuss the type of participative policies which their superiors should follow with managers at their own level, they appear to espouse the *human resources* model. They see themselves as reservoirs of creative resources. Moreover, the fact that they frequently view themselves as more flexible and willing to change than their superiors suggests that they feel their resources are frequently wasted. Correspondingly, they expect improvement in organizational performance to result from greater freedom for self-direction and self-control on their part.

### Reasons Behind Views

If the evidence of the current survey does represent managers' attitudes toward participative leadership, one serious question immediately comes to mind. How can managers desire one type of authority and control relationship with their superiors and at the same time advocate another type with their subordinates? A general answer, of course, is that this pattern of attitudes is just human nature. We tend not only to think more highly of ourselves than we do of others, but also to want more than we are willing to give. There are, however, other logical, more specific explanations for managers' reluctance to accept the *human resources* model for use with their subordinates.

In the first place, the *human relations* model has been around much longer, and an exceptionally good selling job has been done in its behalf. The causal relationship among participation, satisfaction, and performance, despite a lack of empirical validation, has become common wisdom. The *human resources* model, on the other hand, has not been as fully or systematically developed, and has not been the subject of as hard a sell. Managers may "feel" some of the concepts expressed in the *human resources* model and intuitively grasp some of their implications for their relationships with their superiors, but little pressure has been put on them to translate their attitudes into a systematic model for use with their subordinates.

A second explanation for managers' failure to accept the *human resources* model for use with their subordinates is that they are simply reluctant to "buy" a theory that challenges concepts to which they are deeply and emotionally attached. There is no question that the *human resources* model does attack a number of traditional management concepts. Two of the bedrock concepts that are directly challenged deal with: (1) the origins and applicability of management prerogatives, and (2) the source and limits of control.

The *human resources* model recognizes no definable, immutable set of management prerogatives. It does not accept the classical division between those who think and command and those who obey and perform. Instead, it argues that the solution to any given problem may arise from a variety of sources, and that to think of management (or any other group) as sufficient in and of itself to make all decisions is misleading and wasteful.

This approach does not directly challenge the "legal" right of management to command. It suggests, however, that there is a higher "law of the situation" that thoughtful managers will usually observe, deferring to expertise wherever it may be found. In this model the manager's basic obligation is not to the "management team" but to the accomplishment of departmental and organizational objectives. The criterion of success, therefore, is not the extent to which orders are carried out but the results obtained.

Admitting that he may not have all the answers is as difficult for the manager as for any of the rest of us. He has been taught to hide his deficiencies, not to advertise them. Holding on to information, maintaining close control, and reserving the right to make all decisions are ways by which the manager can ensure his importance. Further many organizations have reinforced this type of behavior either (a) by failing to emphasize the manager's obligation to develop and utilize his human resources or (b) by failing to reward him when he does make this effort.

In the area of control the *human resources* model challenges the traditional concept that control is a scarce resource. In traditional theory there is presumed to be a virtually fixed amount of control. This fixed amount can be distributed in a variety of ways, but control given to one group must eventually be taken away from another. Given this concept, the manager is reluctant to allow his subordinates any real degree of self-control—what he gives up to them, he loses himself. In fact, it is frequently this basic fear of losing control which limits the amount of participation that managers are willing to allow.

The *human resources* model does not accept this lump-of-control theory. Instead, it argues that the manager increases his total control over the accomplishment of departmental objectives by encouraging self-control on the part of his subordinates. Control is thus an additive and an expanding phenomenon. Where subordinates are concerned with accomplishing goals and exercising self-direction and self-control, their combined efforts will far outweigh the results of the exercise of any amount of control by the manager.

Moreover, the fact that subordinates desire to exercise greater self-control does not mean that they reject the manager's legitimate concern for goal accomplishment. Rather, there is evidence that they in fact seek a partnership that will allow them to play a larger role, yet also will allow for a corresponding increase in management's control activity.[11]

In all, the fact that managers are reluctant to adopt a model which forces them to rethink, and perhaps restructure, their perceptions of their own roles and functions is not surprising. It is also not surprising that some writers in this field have hesitated to advocate a model which challenges such deeply held concepts. The *human relations* approach is easy to "buy," since it does not challenge the manager's basic role or status. It is correspondingly easy to sell, since it promises much and actually demands little. The *human resources* model, on the other hand, promises much but also demands a great deal from the manager. It requires that he undertake the responsibility of utilizing all the resources available to him—his own and those of his subordinates. It does not suggest that it will make his job easier; it only acknowledges his obligation to do a much better job.

### Logical Implications

The nature of the evidence to date does not warrant any firm or sweeping conclusions. Nevertheless, it does suggest enough support for the interpretations made here to make it worthwhile, and perhaps imperative, to draw some logical implications from the fact that managers seem to have adopted two apparently conflicting attitudes regarding participative management.

The first implication, and the easiest one to draw, is that, given managers' present attitudes, the *human resources* model has little chance of ever gaining real acceptance as a guide to managers' relationships with their subordinates. Managers at every level view themselves as capable of greater self-direction and self-control, but apparently do not attribute such abilities to their subordinates. As long as managers throughout the organizational hierarchy remain unaware that the kind of participation *they* want and believe *they* are capable of handling is also the kind their subordinates want and feel they deserve, there would seem to be little hope for the *human resources* approach being actually put into practice.

A second, and somewhat more complex, implication of managers' current views is that real participation will seldom be found in modern organizations. Participation, in the *human relations* model, is viewed as an "ought" rather

<hr>

[11] See Clagget C. Smith and Arnold Tannenbaum. "Organizational Control Structure: A Comparative Analysis," *Human Relations*, November 1963, pp. 299–316.

than a "must." The manager is under no basic obligation to seek out and develop talent, or to encourage and allow participation; it is something which he "probably should do" but not something for which he is made to feel truly responsible. Viewing participation in this fashion, the manager often junks it when problems arise or pressure builds up from above—the very times when it might be expected to produce the greatest gains.

A third implication, closely related to the second, is that the benefits which the *human resources* approach predicts from participative management will not accrue as long as managers cling to the *human relations* view. From the *human relations* model, a manager may draw a rule for decision making which says that he should allow only as much participation, self-direction, and self-control as is required to obtain cooperation and reduce resistance to formal authority. In the area of job enlargement, for example, the manager following the *human relations* model would be tempted to enlarge his subordinates' jobs just enough to improve morale and satisfaction, with little real concern for making full use of their abilities. This limited approach borders on pseudoparticipation and may be interpreted by subordinates as just another manipulative technique.

The *human resources* model, on the other hand, does not hold the manager to so limited a decision rule. In fact, it affirms that he is obligated to develop and encourage a continually expanding degree of responsible participation, self-direction, and self-control. The only limiting factors legitimate in this approach are the basic requirements of capacity to perform and the need for coordination. The manager following the *human resources* model would therefore continually expand subordinates' responsibility and self-direction up to the limits of their abilities, and/or to the point at which further expansion would produce a wasteful overlap among the responsibilities of members of his department. Even these limits, however, are far from absolute. The *human resources* model suggests that with subordinates' broadened abilities and expanded information, voluntary cooperation can erase much of the need for specific job boundaries.

A fourth and final implication can be drawn from managers' confused and conflicting attitudes toward participative management. Managers' attitudes, as suggested earlier, in part reflect the ambivalent and inconsistent treatment which scholars have given to participative leadership concepts, and are not likely to change until theorists firm up their own thinking.

## Some Final Comments

It must be clear at this point that I feel that management scholars should focus their attention on developing and promoting the application of the *human resources* approach. While I cannot, at this stage, base my preference for the *human resources* model on solid empirical evidence, there is one strong argument for its potential usefulness. It is the fact that managers up and down the organizational hierarchy believe their superiors should follow this model.

Critics of the *human resources* approach have argued that (1) its costs outweigh its benefits because in its final form the *human resources* model prescribes management by committee at every level, which results in wasted effort and the inability to act in crisis situations; and (2) this approach is unsuitable for organizations or organizational groups whose members have neither the desire nor the ability to meet its challenge.

In answer to the first charge, this approach does imply a need for additional information flow to subordinates at all levels, and I admit that collecting and disseminating information increases costs.

However, information collected and *used* at lower levels may be less costly than information collected for use at upper levels that is subsequently ignored or misused. Further, and more important, the application of the *human resources* model does not require—in fact, would make unnecessary—committee-type sharing of routine departmental tasks.

This model would suggest that subordinates are generally willing to go along with their superiors' decisions on more or less routine matters, particularly when they are well informed and feel free to call important points to their bosses' attention. Moreover, this approach implies that many matters are to be delegated directly to one or more subordinates who, in most instances, will coordinate their own activities. At the same time, this model emphasizes that full and extended discussion by the whole department will be utilized where it can do the most good—on complex and important problems that demand the full talent and complete concern of the group. One could argue that under these circumstances crises should arise less often and consensus should be more quickly reached when they do arise.

There is no quick and easy answer to the second charge that the *human resources* model is more adaptable to and more easily applied with some groups than with others. Note, however, that it is the *human relations* approach, and not the *human resources* model, which promises quick and easy application. The latter cannot be put into full-blown practice overnight in any situation, particularly where subordinates have been conditioned by years of traditional or pseudoparticipative techniques of leadership. It involves a step-by-step procedure wherein the manager expands subordinates' responsibilities and participation in keeping with their developing abilities and concerns. High expectations and full support, coupled with an open recognition of the inevitability of occasional shortcomings, are required to achieve successful application.

Finally, there is a familiar ring to the critics' charge that many organization members are either unwilling or unable to contribute creatively, or to accept any real measure of responsibility. In fact, this charge brings us back once again to the heart of the conflict in managers' attitudes toward participation—their own view that subordinates are suited only for the *human relations* type of participation, while they themselves are well suited for the full range of participation suggested in the *human resources* model.

# LEADERSHIP AND ORGANIZATIONAL EXCITEMENT

DAVID E. BERLEW

## Introduction

In the last several years, an increasing number of individuals—often new graduates and professionals—have rejected secure positions in apparently well-managed organizations in favor of working alone or joining up with a few friends in a new organization. Usually they do not leave in protest, but in search of "something more." The nature of this "something more" is the subject of this paper.

Many executives have blamed this disenchantment with established organizations on changes in Western society which have made an increasing number of people unsuited for organizational life. They often express the view that changes in child-rearing practices and the breakdown of discipline in the family and in our schools has produced a generation which cannot or will not exercise the self-discipline and acceptance of legitimate authority required for bureaucratic organizations as we know them to function.

Because it has been so acceptable to fault society, the leadership of most organizations has felt little need to look inward for the source of the problem and to analyze their own and their organization's failure to attract and hold some of the best-trained people our society produces.

Those organizations which have tried to change to keep pace with society have often been frustrated. In analyzing our failure to stem the tide of increasing alienation in the workplace, Walton (1972) describes "a parade of organization development, personnel, and labor relations programs that promised to revitalize organizations," such as job enrichment, participative decision making, management by objectives, sensitivity training or encounter groups, and productivity bargaining. He argues that while each application is often based on a correct diagnosis, it is only a partial remedy, and therefore the organizational system soon returns to an earlier equilibrium. His prescription is a systemic approach leading to comprehensive organization design or redesign.

Whether we are concerned with organizations which have viewed the problem as outside of their control or those which have been frustrated in their attempts to change, one factor which has not been adequately explored and understood is that of effective organization leadership. Only an organization with strong leadership will look within itself for causes of problems which can be blamed easily on outside forces. Exceptional leadership is required to plan

---

Prepared specifically for this volume.

and initiate significant change in organizations, whether it is one of Walton's partial remedies or comprehensive organization redesign. Short-term benefits from change projects often result from leadership behavior which excites members of an organization about the *potential* for change rather than from actual change introduced.

## Current Leadership Models

Almost without exception, theories of managerial leadership currently in vogue postulate two major dimensions of leadership behavior (House, 1971, Korman, 1966). One dimension concerns the manager's or leader's efforts to accomplish organizational tasks. Various writers have given this dimension different names, including task or instrumental leadership behavior, job-centered leadership, initiating structure and concern for production. The second dimension is concerned with the leader's relations with his subordinates; it has been labelled social-emotional leadership behavior, consideration, concern for people, and employee-centered leadership. Measures of the effects of leadership also usually fall into two categories: indices of productivity and of worker satisfaction. A leader or manager who is good at organizing to get work done, and who relates well to his subordinates, should have a highly productive group and satisfied workers.

There is nothing wrong with two-factor models of managerial leadership as far as they go, but they are incomplete. They grew out of a period in history when the goal was to combine the task efficiency associated with scientific management with the respect for human dignity emphasized by the human relations movement. They did not anticipate a point in time when people would not be fulfilled even when they were treated with respect, were productive, and derived achievement satisfaction from their jobs.

As a result, two-factor theories of managerial leadership tell us more about management than about leadership. They deal with relationships between man and his work, and between men and other men, but they do not tell us why some organizations are excited or "turned-on" and others are not. They do not help us understand that quality of leadership which can ". . . lift people out of their petty pre-occupations . . . and unify them in pursuit of objectives worthy of their best efforts" (Gardner, 1965).

## Leadership and Emotion in Organizations

In an effort to help fill that void, the outline of a model relating types of leadership to the emotional tone in organizations is presented in Figure 1. Stages 1 and 2 of the model are derived from familiar theories of work motivation (Herzberg, 1966; Maslow, 1968; McGregor, 1967) and the two-factor models of leadership discussed earlier. Angry or resentful workers (Stage 1) are primarily concerned with satisfying basic needs for food, shelter, security, safety, and respect as human beings. Organizations in Stage 1 try to improve their situations by eliminating "dissatisfiers" through improved working conditions, compensation and fringe benefits, and by providing fair or "decent" supervision. The type of leadership associated with a change from an angry or resentful emotional tone to one of neutrality, or from Stage 1 to Stage 2, has been labelled *custodial*. These leaders are neutral, lacking either strong positive or negative feelings about their work or the organization. In the absence of "dissatisfiers," they tend to become increasingly concerned with group membership or "belonging" and opportunities to do inherently satisfying work and to receive recognition. In order to increase employee satisfaction organizations at Stage 2 introduce improvements such as job enrichment, job enlargement, job rotation, participative management, and effective (as opposed to decent) supervision. Changes are oriented toward providing work that is less routine and more interesting or challenging, building cohesive work teams, and giving employees more say in decisions that directly affect them. The type of leadership associated with this movement from neutral to satisfied workers, or from Stage 2 to Stage 3, has been labelled *managerial*.

Most of the advances in organization theory and management practice in the last few decades have related to Stage 2: defining and controlling the elements of supervision and the organizational environment which result in high productivity with high satisfaction. While these advances have been substantial, and have led, in most cases, to healthier, more effective organizations, they have not prevented the increasing alienation of professional employees.

The addition of Stage 3 to the model to extend the emotional tone continuum to include *organizational excitement* is an attempt to deal with this phenomenon of the 1970's—the increasing number of professionals and new graduates who are rejecting secure positions in established organizations. The model suggests that for this small but growing element of the population, the satisfaction of needs for membership, achievement, and recognition is no longer enough. The meaning they seek has less to do with the specific tasks they perform as individuals than the impact of their individual and collective efforts—channelled through the organization—on their environment. The feelings of potency which accompany "shaping" rather than being shaped or giving up (and dropping out) are a source of excitement. So, too, are the feelings which stem from commitment to an organization which has a value-related mission and thus takes on some of the characteristics of a cause or a movement. At the extreme, this can lead to total involvement or total *identification*—the breaking down of boundaries between the "self" and the organization so that the "individual becomes the organization" and the "organization becomes the individual."

### Stage 3 Leadership

Although Stage 3 leadership must involve elements of both custodial and managerial leadership, the dominant mode is charismatic leadership. The word "charisma" has been used in many ways with many meanings. Here we will define it in terms of three different types or classes of leadership behavior which provide meaning to work and generate organizational excitement. These are:

- the development of a "common vision" for the organization related to values shared by the organization's members,
- the discovery or creation of value-related opportunities and activities within the framework of the mission and goals of the organization, and
- making organization members feel stronger and more in control of their own destinies, both individually and collectively.

**FIGURE 1**

Organizational Emotions and Modes of Leadership

| | Stage 1 | Stage 2 | Stage 3 |
|---|---|---|---|
| EMOTIONAL TONE: | Anger or Resentment | Neutrality | Satisfaction Excitement |
| LEADERSHIP MODE: | CUSTODIAL | MANAGERIAL | CHARISMATIC |
| FOCAL NEEDS OR VALUES: | Food<br>Shelter<br>Security<br>Fair treatment<br>Human dignity | Membership<br>Achievement<br>Recognition | Meaningful work<br>Self-reliance<br>Community<br>Excellence<br>Service<br>Social Responsibility |
| FOCAL CHANGES OR IMPROVEMENTS: | Working conditions<br>Compensation<br>Fringe benefits<br>Equal opportunity<br>Decent supervision<br>Grievance procedures | Job enrichment<br>Job enlargement<br>Job rotation<br>Participative management<br>Management by objectives<br>Effective supervision | Common vision<br>Value-related opportunities<br>and activities<br>Supervision which<br>strengthens subordinates |

The first requirement for Stage 3 or charismatic leadership is a common or shared vision of what the future *could be*. To provide meaning and generate excitement, such a common vision must reflect goals or a future state of affairs that is valued by the organization's members and thus important to them to bring about.

The notion that men do not live by bread alone has been recognized for centuries by religious and political leaders. All inspirational speeches or writings have the common element of some vision or dream of a better existence which will inspire or excite those who share the author's values. This basic wisdom too often has been ignored by managers.

A vision, no matter how well articulated, will not excite or provide meaning for individuals whose values are different from those implied by the vision. Thus, the corporate executive who dreams only of higher return on investment and earnings per share may find his vision of the future rejected and even resented by members of his organization. Indeed, he may even find his vision of a profitable corporate future questioned by stockholders concerned with the social responsibility of corporations. Progressive military leaders may articulate a vision or mission congruent with the needs and values of the young people they are trying to attract to an all volunteer service, only to discover that the same vision conflicts with the values of their senior officers.

An important learning from group theory and research is that informal groups tend to select as leader the individual who is most representative of the group's needs and values. Thus his hopes and aspirations, and the goals toward which he will lead the group, are automatically shared by the group's members.

One problem for heads of complex organizations is that if they are to function as leaders (as opposed to custodians or managers) they must represent and articulate the hopes and goals of many different groups, the young and the old, the unskilled and the professional, the employee and the stockholder, the minority and the majority, union and management. Only the exceptional leader can instinctively identify and articulate the common vision relevant to such diverse groups. But to fail to provide some kind of vision of the future, particularly for employees who demand meaning and excitement in their work, is to make the fatal assumption that man can and will live by bread alone.

There are dangers as well as advantages to a common vision. If top management does not sincerely believe in the desirability of the vision they articulate, they are involved in an attempt to manipulate which will probably backfire. Another danger might be called the "Camelot phenomenon": the articulation of a shared vision that is both meaningful and exciting, but so unrealistic that people must inevitably be disillusioned and disappointed. Whether the responsibility in such cases lies with the seducer or the seduced is difficult to say, but the end result is a step backward into cynicism.

Finally, the effectiveness of the common vision depends upon the leader's ability to "walk the talk": to behave in ways both small and large that are consistent with the values and goals he is articulating. In this regard, my experience in the Peace Corps taught me that the quickest way to destroy or erode the power of a common vision is for the leader to allow himself to be sidetracked into bargaining over details instead of concentrating all of his attention on identifying, tracking, and talking to the value issue involved. For example, at a meeting where Volunteers are reacting negatively to a proposed reduction in their living allowance, the Peace Corps Director or leader cannot afford to get involved in a discussion of whether or not female Volunteers will be able to afford pantyhose with their reduced allowance. The role of the leader is to keep alive the common vision which attracted Volunteers to the Peace Corps in the first place: in this case, the idea of a group of Americans whose help will be more readily accepted if they live at about the same standard as their local coworkers.

### Value-Related Opportunities and Activities

It is a mistake to assume that individuals who desert or reject established organizations are basically loners. In fact, many start or join new organizations, often at considerable personal sacrifice in terms of income, security, and working conditions. It is revealing to analyze these "new" organizations for sources of meaning or excitement which may be lacking in more mature organizations. A list of opportunities present in many of the younger organizations in our society are presented in Figure 2, along with values related to those opportunities.

**FIGURE 2**

Sources of Meaning in Organizations:
Opportunities and Related Values

| Type of Opportunity | Related Need or Value |
| --- | --- |
| 1. A chance to be tested; to make it on one's own | Self-reliance<br>Self-actualization |
| 2. A social experiment, to combine work, family, and play in some new way | Community<br>Integration of life |
| 3. A chance to do something *well*—e.g., return to real craftsmanship; to be really creative | Excellence<br>Unique accomplishment |
| 4. A chance to do something *good*—e.g., run an honest, no rip-off business, or a youth counselling center | Consideration<br>Service |
| 5. A chance to change the way things are—e.g., from Republican to Democrat or Socialist, from war to peace, from unjust to just. | Activism<br>Social responsibility<br>Citizenship |

A Chance To Be Tested

Many of us go through life wondering what we could accomplish if given the opportunity. Our Walter Mitty fantasies place us in situations of extreme challenge and we come through gloriously. Few of us, however, have an opportunity to test the reality of our fantasies, as society increasingly protects us from getting in over our heads where we might fail and thus hurt the organization or ourselves. This is especially true of corporations where managers are moved along slowly, and only after they have had sufficient training and experience to practically insure that they will not have too much difficulty with their next assignment.

As a Peace Corps Country Director in the mid-sixties, I was struck by the necessity of having to place many Volunteers without adequate training or experience in extremely difficult situations, and the readiness—even eagerness—of most Volunteers to be tested in this way. Some Volunteers rose to the challenge in remarkable ways, others held their own, and some could not handle the stress. Volunteers who were severely tested and succeeded were spoiled for the lock-step progression from challenge to slightly more difficult challenge which most established organizations favor to protect both themselves and the individual from failure. The same thing happens in wars and other emergency situations where planned development and promotion systems break down.

The point is that many (not all) people want an opportunity to be tested by an extraordinary challenge, and such opportunities rarely exist in established organizations. As a result, some who are most able and most confident leave the shelter of the established organization to measure themselves against a value of independence and self-reliance.

### Social Experimentation

A great deal has been written about the increasing superficiality of personal relationships in our society and the resulting loneliness and alienation. Organizations have responded with efforts to build cohesive work teams and to provide individuals doing routine, independent work with opportunities to talk with coworkers on the job. These gestures have not begun to meet the needs of persons who have been influenced by the counter-culture's emphasis on authentic relationships as opposed to role-regulated relationships, and the need to reduce social fragmentation by carrying out more of life's functions—working, child-rearing, playing, loving—with the same group of people.

Established organizations do not provide these kinds of opportunities. Many prohibit husbands and wives from working together. Child-care centers, if they exist, are separate from the parents' workplace, and the workplace is geographically and psychologically separated from the home. As a result, individuals who desire more integrated lives often leave established organizations and form new organizations, such as businesses in which wives and children can play a role and professional firms whose members live as well as work together.

### A Chance to Do Something Well

Established organizations fight a continual battle between controlling costs and maintaining standards of excellence, and standards are usually compromised. This is not cynicism: A group of skilled metal workers, machinists and mechanics can nearly always produce a better automobile than General Motors if cost is no object. The opportunity to seek true excellence, to produce the very best of something, is a strong attraction, even though the market may be extremely limited and the economic viability of the venture questionable. Individuals frustrated by the need to cut corners in established organizations find the alternative of a new organization committed to excellence an attractive one, and they will work long hours at low pay to make it financially viable.

### A Chance to Do Good

Still others desert established organizations in the belief that they are compromising standards of honesty and consideration in their struggle to survive in "the capitalistic jungle." They form organizations to do *good*: to provide honest, no rip-off services or products, or services which they believe a "good" community should have such as free schools, legal, medical, and counselling services for the deprived, or low-income housing.

### A Chance to Change the Way Things Are

Finally, many thoughtful individuals leave established organizations because they view them as too interwoven with or dependent upon the system to be an effective force for change. So they form new organizations as vehicles for bringing about change, whether it is to increase our appreciation of art, to eliminate discrimination, or to protect the environment.

The critical difference between these new organizations and established organizations is that the newer ones provide opportunities and activities closely related to the values of their members and also within the framework of the mission and goals of the organization. This is true even when the organization is as intent on making money as any established corporation (as they often are), and when they resemble a modern version of a nineteenth-century sweatshop (as they often do). Members of these organizations are not against profit making *per se* or hard work, or putting the organization before the individual. But there must be a reason for doing these things; they are not ends in themselves. The reason comes from a common vision of what they are trying to create together, as well as opportunities to behave in a value-congruent manner. These factors justify and even make desirable those characteristics of organizations which otherwise would be rejected as unnecessary or exploitative.

Few, if any, progressive executives will find the types of opportunities and values noted above distasteful or undesirable. Many, however, will conclude that it is simply unrealistic to expect to find such opportunities in a large corporation or government agency under pressure from stockholders or the voting public to maximize profits or minimize expenditures.

However, such opportunities *do* exist in large, established organizations, and where they do not, they can often be created. For example, established organizations do not have to be tied to a step-by-careful-step advancement ladder. AT&T, for example, has experimented with a system whereby potential new hires for management positions are offered exceptionally challenging year-long assignments, and are told that depending on their performance, they will either leapfrog ahead or be asked to leave the company. It provides confident individuals with a series of opportunities to test themselves. If implemented successfully, it benefits the organization by attracting and developing self-reliant managers while quickly weeding out security seekers and poor performers.

While it takes managerial leadership to introduce such changes, it takes charismatic leadership to recognize the value relevance of such a program and to integrate it with the organization's mission in such a way that it creates and sustains excitement. Too often such programs go unrecognized or unexploited as sources of increased organizational excitement simply because of a limited conception of leadership.

There are many other things that established organizations are doing or could do which qualify the right type of leadership. Our organizations and institutions have, for the most part, been quite uncreative about countering or controlling the increasing fragmentation of work and family life, and the many problems which result. I know from my own experience the extreme differences in the quality of my relationships with my wife and children now that I work at home a few days a week compared to when I spent fifty to eighty hours at the office or out of town and came home tired and irritable, often with home-work. I doubt if I am much different from most other professionals in this regard. Why not actively recruit husbands and wives, as work teams when possible, and with child-care facilities nearby? Or, where possible, encourage employees to work at home on individual projects when they may have fewer interruptions than at the office?

Many organizations have a manifest commitment to excellence in their products and services, and to carrying out their corporate responsibilities toward the community. Occasionally they are in a position to spearhead social change. Too frequently, however, the value-relevant message seems directed toward customers or stockholders and only secondarily toward organization members. When it is directed toward members, it usually comes from a staff department such as corporate relations or the house organ rather than directly from the senior-line officers. This is public relations, not leadership, and whereas charisma might substitute for public relations, public relations, no matter how good, cannot substitute for charisma.

### Making Others Feel Stronger

The effective Stage 3 leader must lead in such a way as to make members of his organization feel stronger rather than weaker. To achieve the organization's goals as well as to meet the needs of his more confident and able employees, his leadership must encourage or enable employees to be Origins rather than Pawns.

Richard deCharms (1968; 1969) has described Origins and Pawns in the following terms:

> An Origin is a person who feels that he is director of his life. He feels that what he is doing is the result of his own free choice; he is doing it because he wants to do it, and the consequences of his activity will be valuable to him. He thinks carefully about what he wants in this world, now and in the future, and chooses the most important goals ruling out those that are for him too easy or too risky . . . he is genuinely self-confident because he has determined how to reach his goals through his own efforts . . . he is aware of his abilities and limitations. In short, an Origin is master of his own fate.
>
> A Pawn is a person who feels that someone, or something else, is in control of his fate. He feels that what he is doing has been imposed on him by others. He is doing it because he is forced to, and the consequences of his activity will not be a source of pride to him. Since he feels that external factors determine his fate, the Pawn does not consider carefully his goals in life, nor does he concern himself about what he himself can do to further his cause. Rather he hopes for Lady Luck to smile on him.

Clearly, there may only be a few people in the real world of human beings who are *always* guiding their own fate, checking their own skill, and choosing their own goals, but some people act and feel like Origins more of the time than do other people. Similarly, there are only a few people who *always* feel pushed around like Pawns.

Some individuals—parents, teachers, managers—have the ability to relate on a one-on-one basis in ways that make another person feel and behave more like an Origin and less like a Pawn. Certain types of leaders can apparently affect entire groups of people the same way.

In an experiment conducted at Harvard University (Winter, 1967), a group of business-school students were shown a film of John F. Kennedy delivering his inaugural address. After viewing the film, samples of the students' thoughts or fantasies were collected by asking them to write short imaginative stories to a series of somewhat ambiguous pictures. The thoughts of students exposed to the Kennedy film reflected more concern with having an impact on others and being able to influence their future and their environment than the thought samples of students exposed to a neutral control film. J.F.K. made them feel like Origins.

Replicating this experiment in a number of leadership training sessions, I have found the same thing: Exposure to a certain type of leader—such as John F. Kennedy—leaves people feeling stronger, more confident of being able to determine their own destinies and have an impact on the world. It was this type of reaction to J.F.K. that attracted many young people to the Peace Corps to "change the world" during the early and mid-sixties.

It is difficult to assess precisely what it was about Kennedy's leadership that had this strengthening effect. We do know that he articulated a vision of what should be which struck a resonant chord, particularly in young people and citizens of developing nations. He also projected extremely high expectations of what young people could do to remake their country, if not the world, in terms of their own values.

Although most organization leaders cannot count on such dramatic moments as a presidential inauguration, or perhaps on their oratorical powers, they nonetheless do have a powerful effect on whether those around them feel and behave like Origins or Pawns. A number of factors determine the effect they have on others in this critical area.

### Beliefs about Human Nature

One important factor is the manager's beliefs or assumptions about human nature. If he believes that the average human being has an inherent dislike of work and will avoid it if he can, that most people must be coerced or controlled to get them to put forth effort toward the achievement of organizational objectives, and that he wishes to avoid responsibility, has relatively little ambition and wants security above all, then the manager will organize and manage people as if they were Pawns, and they will tend to behave as Pawns. If, on the other hand, the manager believes that the expenditure of physical and mental effort in work is as natural as play or rest, that individuals will exercise self-direction and self-control in the service of objectives to which they are committed, and that commitment to objectives is a function of the rewards associated with their achievement, including psychological rewards, then he will organize and manage people in quite a different way, with the result that they will tend to behave more like Origins than like Pawns (McGregor, 1960).

### High Expectations

Another important factor is the expectations a manager has about the performance of his subordinates. To some extent, all of us are what others expect us to be, particularly if the others in question are people we respect or love. A dramatic demonstration of this phenomenon is the strong positive relationship between a teacher's expectations of how well a student will do and the student's actual performance, a relationship which persists even when the teacher's positive expectations are based on invalid information (Rosenthal and Jacobson, 1968). A second study, done in a corporate setting, demonstrated that new managers who were challenged by their initial assignments were better performers after five years than new managers who were initially assigned to relatively unchallenging tasks, despite the fact that the potential of the two groups was about the same (Berlew and Hall, 1966).

### Reward versus Punishment

Some managers tend to focus their attention on mistakes: to intervene when there are problems, and to remain uninvolved when things are going well. Other managers look for opportunities to reward good performance. An overbalance in the direction of punishing mistakes as opposed to rewarding excellence lowers self-confidence and is relatively ineffective in improving performance. Rewarding examples of effective action, however, both increases self-confidence and improves performance.

### Encouraging Collaboration

Americans have a tendency to compete when the situation does not demand it, and even sometimes when competition is self-defeating (as when individuals or units within the same organization compete). Diagnosing a situation as win-lose, and competing, insures that there are losers; and losing is a weakening process. If a situation is, *in fact*, win-lose in the sense that the more reward one party gets the less the other gets, competition and the use of competitive strategies is appropriate. This is usually the situation that exists between athletic teams or different companies operating in the same market. Diagnosing a situation as win-win and collaborating is a strengthening process because it allows both parties to win. A situation is *in fact*, win-win when both parties may win, or one can win only if the other succeeds, as is usually the case *within* a company or a team.

The leader who is effective in making people feel stronger recognizes collaborative opportunities where they exist and does not allow them to be misdiagnosed as competitive. When he identifies instances of unnecessary competition within his organization, he uses his influence to change the reward system to induce collaborative rather than competitive behavior. If confronted with a competitive situation which he cannot or does not want to alter, however, he does not hesitate to use competitive strategies.

### Helping Only When Asked

It is extremely difficult to help someone without making them feel weaker, since the act of helping makes evident the fact that you are more knowledgeable, powerful, wiser, or richer than the person you are trying to help. Those familiar with this dynamic are not surprised that some of the nations that the U.S. has most "helped" through our foreign aid resent us the greatest, particularly if we have rubbed their nose in their dependence by placing plaques on all the buildings we have helped them build, the vehicles we have provided, and the public works projects we have sponsored.

Yet the fact remains that there are real differences between individuals and groups in an organization, and help-giving is a real requirement. The effective Stage 3 leader gives his subordinates as much control over the type and amount of help they want as he can without taking untenable risks. He makes his help readily available to those who might come looking for it, and he gives it in such a way as to minimize their dependence upon him. Perhaps most important, he is sensitive to situations where he himself can use help and he asks for it, knowing that giving help will strengthen the other person and make him better able to receive help.

### Creating Success Experiences

A leader can make others feel stronger, more like Origins, by attempting to design situations where people can succeed, and where they can feel responsible and receive full credit for their success. People, whether as individuals or organizations, come to believe in their ability to control their destiny only as they accumulate successful experiences in making future events occur—in setting and reaching goals. The leader's role is to help individuals and units within his organization accumulate such experiences.

When an organization, through its leadership, can create an environment which has a strengthening effect on its members, it leads to the belief that, collectively, through the organization, they can determine or change the course of events. This, in turn, generates organizational excitement. It also becomes an *organization* which has all the characteristics of an Origin.

### Some Unanswered Questions

In this paper, I have tried to analyze one aspect of the problem of alienation in the workplace: the increasing attrition of professionals and new graduates from established organizations. I have tried to suggest the nature and source of the meaning and excitement they are seeking in their work, and the type of organizational leadership required to meet their needs. However, a number of questions have been left unasked which must be explored before any conclusions can be drawn.

One such question has to do with the relationship between organizational excitement and productivity. We know there are many productive organizations —some of our major corporations, for example—which cannot be called excited or "turned-on." We have also seen excited organizations expending tremendous amounts of energy accomplishing very little. In the case of excited but unproductive organizations, it is clear that they are overbalanced in the direction of Stage 3 leadership and need effective *custodial* and *managerial leadership* to get organized and production-oriented rather than solely impact-oriented. The case of efficient and productive organizations that are not excited is more complex. Would General Motors or ITT be better off if they could create a higher level of organizational excitement? Would they attract or hold better people, or are they better off without those who would be attracted by the change? Are such corporations headed for problems which can only be dealt with by an emphasis on Stage 3 leadership, or have we overstated the magnitude of the social change that is taking place?

A second question concerns the relevance of the model to different types of organizations. There is little question of the relevance of charismatic leadership and organizational excitement to such as the Peace Corps, the United Nations, religious organizations, political groups, community action organizations, unions, and the military. The same is true of start ups where new industrial or business organizations are competing against heavy odds to carve out a piece of the market. What is not so clear is whether it is any less relevant to large, established corporations and government bureaucracies. Quite possibly, it is precisely the element which is missing from some government agencies, and one of the key elements which give one great corporation the edge over another.

While more questions have been raised than answered, there should be no confusion about one point. Just as man cannot live by bread alone, neither can he live by spirit alone. Organizations must have elements of custodial and managerial leadership to achieve the necessary level of efficiency to survive. It is not proposed that Stage 3 or charismatic leadership increases efficiency; indeed, it may reduce the orderly, professional, totally rational approach to work which managerial leadership tries to foster. However, it does affect motivation and commitment, and organizations will face heavy challenges in these areas in the coming decade.

## References

David E. Berlew, and Douglas T. Hall, "The Socialization of Managers: Effects of Expectations on Performance," *Administrative Science Quarterly*, 11, No. 2 (1966), 207–223.

Richard deCharms, *Personal Causation* (New York: Academic Press, 1968).

Richard deCharms, "Origins, Pawns, and Educational Practice," in G. S. Lessor (ed.) *Psychology and the Educational Process* (Glenview, Ill.: Scott, Foresman and Co., 1969).

John W. Gardner, "The Antileadership Vaccine," *Annual Report of the Carnegie Corporation of New York*, 1965.

Frederick Herzberg, *Work and the Nature of Man* (Cleveland: The World Publishing Company, 1966).

Robert J. House, "A Path Goal Theory of Leader Effectiveness," *Administrative Science Quarterly*, 16, No. 3 (1971), 321–338.

Abraham K. Korman, "Consideration, Initiating Structure, and Organizational Criteria—A Review," *Personnel Psychology*, 1966, Vol. 19, 349–361.

Abraham H. Maslow, *Toward a Psychology of Being*, 2d ed. (New York: D. Van Nostrand Company, Inc., 1968).

Douglas McGregor, *The Human Side of Enterprise* (New York: McGraw-Hill Book Company, 1960).

Douglas McGregor, *The Professional Manager* (New York: McGraw-Hill Book Company, 1967).

Robert Rosenthal, and Lenore Jacobson, *Pygmalion in the Classroom* (New York: Holt, Rinehart and Winston, Inc., 1968).

Richard E. Walton, "How to Counter Alienation in the Plant," *Harvard Business Review*, Nov.-Dec., 1972.

David G. Winter, *Power Motivation in Thought and Action*. (Ph.D. dissertation, Harvard University, Department of Social Relations, January, 1967.)

# Intergroup Relations

## REACTIONS TO
## INTERGROUP COMPETITION
## UNDER WIN-LOSE CONDITIONS

ROBERT R. BLAKE
JANE SRYGLEY MOUTON

Study of key problems of relations *between* groups is central for understanding and dealing constructively with a number of difficulties experienced in contemporary society. The opportunities for enriched decision-making are many if conditions of collaboration between groups which historically have been in conflict can be achieved. Findings from investigations concerning the dynamics of intergroup competition under win-lose conditions are summarized below (3). Results from application of these experimental findings have led to the conclusion that the industrial ethic which causes groups to interact with one another on a competitive win-lose basis can be replaced by one which makes it possible for groups to approach their differences in points of view from a problem-solving orientation based on openness and reinforced by mutual respect and trust. How this revision in basic approach is coming about will be discussed later on.

The investigations reported below are woven around a standard sequence of intergroup conflict so that the research findings are presented along with the natural chronology of the competitive situation itself. These findings will not be encumbered with statistical tests and statements of probabilities since all of the major trends described meet acceptable standards of a significance. Furthermore,

Reprinted from *Management Science*, Vol. 4, No. 4 (July 1961). Used by permission of *Management Science* and the authors.
Received December 1960.
Paper delivered to the 7th International Meeting of the Institute of Management Sciences, New York, October, 1960.

the results to be presented are representative of a much larger body of systematic experimental work which it would be difficult to compress into a few pages.[1]

### Creating Intergroup Conflict

In one company, all managerial people within a given segment of the organization have been through laboratory training programs.[2] The general plan of a laboratory is that dilemmas of various sorts are created. As people work themselves out of these dilemmas, they learn by evaluating the conditions that produced the difficulties and those that led to their resolution. The learning is by experiencing and then generalizing, rather than by studying cases or teaching in the ordinary classroom sense (11).

In these laboratories there usually are two or four groups, each composed of from 9 to 12 people. These groups have an autonomous existence of their own. They continue to meet throughout the laboratory period of 10 days or two weeks. They become very highly involved in their internal affairs, which are characterized initially by power struggles, difficulty in creating a satisfactory agenda, clique formations among members, etc. During this time, as groups are developing, members are stopping to examine why such phenomena are occurring and what their implications are for organization life.

After the group has met maybe twelve or fourteen hours, a problem is provided for members to work on so they can measure their effectiveness as a problem-solving group. Furthermore, the problem is presented in such a way that everyone recognizes that one group will be the winner and one group the loser. Sometimes there are two groups present in the situation and sometimes four. In any event, *pairs* are in competition so that there will be one winner and one loser for every two groups. The same problem is assigned to all groups routinely in the evening around 7 pm, and it can be worked on for any number of hours up to 8 am. Frequently the ingroup work phase goes on until 4 or 5 am. The problem is delivered to the secretary and she types it, without designation as to which group produced it.

### Impact of Competition on Member Behavior

After it is understood by group members that there will be a victor and a vanquished, much of the social poise and gracefulness of senior, middle and junior managers disappear under the pressure of creating a product and meeting the adversary.

#### Changes in Cohesion

The problem-solving period is a time when cohesion builds very rapidly. Ranks close and members are united in their efforts.

Evaluations of the "goodness" of one's own group can be taken as an approximate measure of the attractiveness of the group to each of its members. Members

[1] These studies were supported by Grant M-2447, Behavior of Group Representatives under Pressure, National Institute of Health and by a grant from Esso Division of The Humble Oil and Refining Company.

[2] The incompany laboratory training programs are similar to ones conducted by The Human Relations Training Laboratory of The University of Texas, and The National Training Laboratories at Arden House.

routinely indicated how "good" they thought their groups were to be at the end of each meeting. The question was, "How do you feel about your group?" The answer was on a nine-point scale from "Worst possible" to "Best possible" group. The same scale also was answered at points along the way during the intergroup competition.

Figure 1 shows the feelings of cohesion reported by 12 different groups with each block showing results for experiments where groups were competing with one another two at a time.

Figure 1
Development Group Trends in Cohesion
During Ingroup and Intergroup Phases

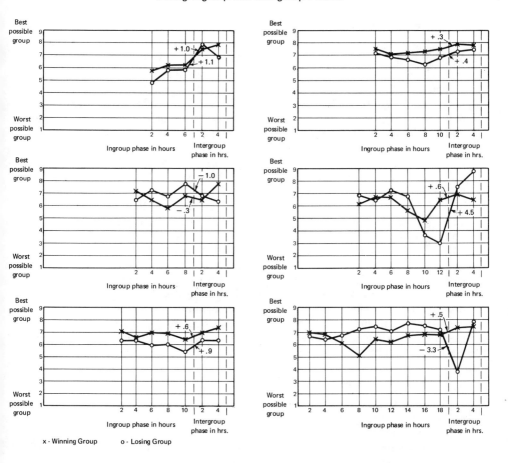

x - Winning Group      o - Losing Group

From Figure 1 it is apparent that group members rarely thought themselves to be as low as "average" even before competition was introduced. All groups rated themselves to be something better than "average." These graphs point to the natural "superiority complex" of groups. A commonly shared feeling, regardless of the group in which one holds membership, is that, "Poor though it may be, my group is at least a little above average!" In almost all of the group ratings in Figure 1, or 60 out of 64 times, cohesion was scored as above "average" even before intergroup competition begins.

Now intergroup competition is introduced. At this point, 9 of the 12 groups showed an even *further* increase in the degree they think their groups to be "good."

Why is it that competition heightens positive identification with one's own group through making members of a group uniformly feel it is even a better group than it was before it entered into competitive relations? Here is an item of the first significance. Under competition, members close ranks. They become more single-minded. Now they have a clear goal—to win. The unity of direction achieved is not deliberate, as members do not focus the issue for discussion on whether "our" group is better. Here is evidence of concordance in feelings linked to membership affiliations under competitive conditions (4).

### Distortions in Judgment

The next morning, groups first examine the quality of competing solutions. The solutions were distributed so that each member got his own solution and solutions of the other groups to examine for similarities and differences. Figure 2 depicts a situation where there were four groups in simultaneous competition rather than two, so each group was analyzing its own solution plus the other three and judging all of the four solutions in terms of adequacy, on a nine-point scale, from totally adequate to totally inadequate.

The graph shows that each group evaluated its own solution as best. The Red Group said it was best. The Black Group said it was best. The Purple Group said it was best. The Green Group said it was best, with the exception of a little bit of similarity, because there was one very statesmanlike gentleman who felt that invidious comparisons ought not to be made, but that members should be objective. He was able to hold the group in line for a short while but later on the collaboration broke down in this group.

Findings such as these indicate that group members have a solid identification with their own group's position. The result is strong pressure toward a more favorable evaluation of own position, with rejections, or at least downgrading, of solutions by other groups. The striking aspect is that these similarities in group members' behavior appear without opportunity of communication among members to influence understanding or to pressure toward agreement (5). This is similar to what occurs when management feels its position is the best, and labor feels that its proposals are better.

### Attack the Adversary: Disregard the Neutrals

The next step is to say to each of the groups, "Now that you have had an opportunity to study all the solutions, formulate questions to ask from each of the other three groups, so as to improve the evaluation of the similarities and differences when intergroup contact is established." There were four groups, and prior to this time none of the groups knew which other group would be its adversary. After each group was told who its adversary was to be, its members were asked to spend another hour or so formulating questions that they might like to ask of each of the other three groups.

The results are shown in Fig. 3. Group 1 sent twelve questions to its adversary, six to one of the neutrals, and four to the other. Group 2 sent 12 to its competitor, 1 to one neutral, and three to the other. Group 3 sent nine to its

Figure 2
Judgmental Tendencies for Own and Other's Solutions
When Adversaries Are Not Identified

Figure 2
Judgmental Tendencies for Own and Other's Solutions
When Adversaries Are Not Identified

| GROUP JUDGING | C | SOLUTIONS PRODUCED BY | | | |
|---|---|---|---|---|---|
| | | Red | Black | Green | Purple |
| Red | Totally Adequate / Totally Inadequate | (7.1) | (5.3) | (5.0) | (6.0) |
| Black | Totally Adequate / Totally Inadequate | (4.4) | (7.2) | (5.8) | (5.4) |
| Green | Totally Adequate / Totally Inadequate | (6.0) | (6.6) | (6.6) | (6.3) |
| Purple | Totally Adequate / Totally Inadequate | (3.1) | (5.0) | (4.1) | (6.7) |

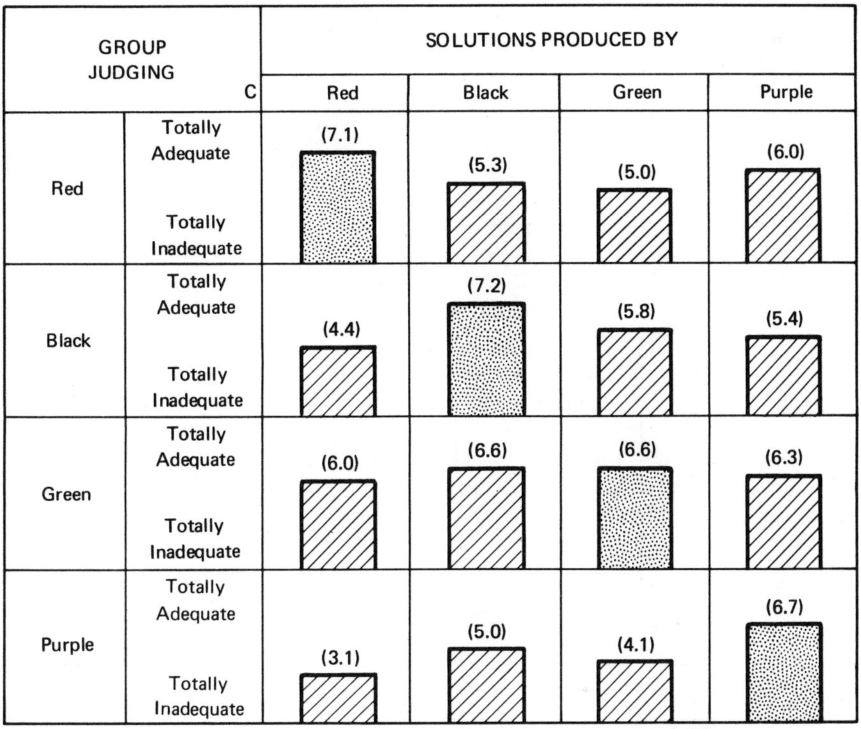

The significant trend is for group members to place a higher assessment on their own group's product than on products by other groups developed under the same circumstances.

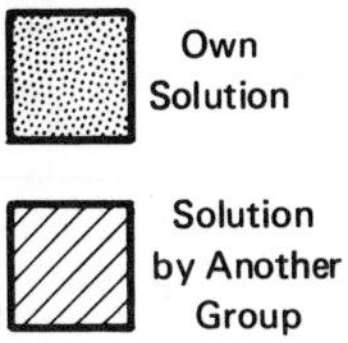

Own Solution

Solution by Another Group

adversary, and Group 4 sent 13 to its adversary and faced only one of the other groups with one question.

After studying the qualitative content of these questions, there is yet to be a question whose answer would ńot embarrass those who respond to it. The questions are always designed to weaken the position of the person to whom they are asked. Individual adjustment, then, is conditioned by membership considerations. The target of a group's attack is the group which is considered its strongest adversary, not the group which seems to have the most unclear position or the most complex one (3).

### Knowledge of Own and Competitor's Positions

During the period while this competition had been going on, a true-false test regarding the contents of the solutions had been developed. At the point in the intergroup competition where members of both groups indicated *full* under-

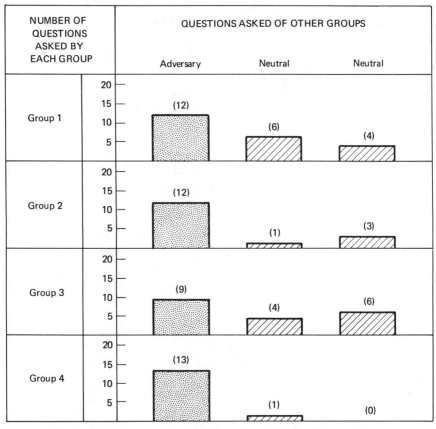

Figure 3
Number of Questions Sent to Adversaries and to Neutrals
During Intergroup Competition

When provided the opportunity to challenge the quality of another group's product,
neutrals are more or less disregarded, but adversaries are targets of attack.

standing of the other group's solution, as well as of their own, an intergroup knowledge test was introduced. No indication, prior to that time, had been given that participants were to be tested. The test was administered before a winner or a loser was determined.

There were forty answers on each of these true-false tests. Ten were true for Group A, but false for Group B. Ten were true for Group B but false for Group A. Ten were true for both A and B, and ten were true for neither group. The question here is whether or not the perception of *content* of competing positions is any way influenced by membership. The data in Figure 4 show that there is yet to be a group that knew more about the other group's solution than it did about its own. This is true in spite of the systematic effort that was made to insure complete understanding through questions, through comparison, through representative negotiation, and everything else (6).

What kind of errors do people make? Figure 5 gives an analysis of the com-

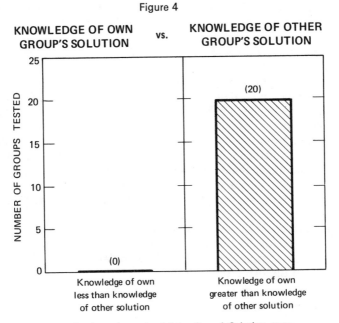

Figure 4

## KNOWLEDGE OF OWN GROUP'S SOLUTION vs. KNOWLEDGE OF OTHER GROUP'S SOLUTION

NUMBER OF GROUPS TESTED

(0) — Knowledge of own less than knowledge of other solution

(20) — Knowledge of own greater than knowledge of other solution

*Even after intensive study of Other Group's Solution, group members of the Opposing Group do not understand it as well as they understand their own.*

Figure 5

## KINDS OF ERRORS ON COMMON ITEMS FROM INTERGROUP KNOWLEDGE TEST

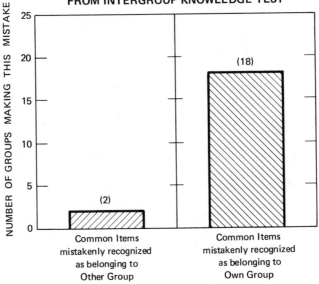

NUMBER OF GROUPS MAKING THIS MISTAKE

(2) — Common Items mistakenly recognized as belonging to Other Group

(18) — Common Items mistakenly recognized as belonging to Own Group

*What two groups actually share in common is difficult for Group Members to recognize.*

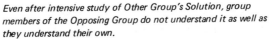

mon items—ones that are found in the positions of both Group A and Group B. In only two cases were common items mistakenly recognized as belonging to the other group. In 18 of the groups the mistake was in assuming that these items belong to one's own position alone and were not shared in common with the other group. These graphs are a little old now and there are about 40 more comparisons to be added, but the trend is the same: 2 to 18.

To state it differently, here are two findings stemming from trends toward uniformities in membership behavior associated with protection of group interests which have unusual significance in determining barriers to the resolution of conflict between groups. They suggest that under competitive conditions members of one group perceive that they understand the other's proposal when in fact they do *not*. Inadequate understanding makes it all the more difficult for competing groups to view each other's proposals realistically. Areas they share in common are likely to go unrecognized and in fact be seen as characteristic of one's own group only. Under conditions of competition, areas of true agreement go undiscovered (7). Membership considerations arise not only in emotion of an ingroup sort, loyalty to own group position, but also in areas of cognition —in an analytical, comprehensive view of the similarities and differences actually existing between the two group solutions (7).

**Resolution of the Conflict**

One procedure for resolving the conflict between the competing groups is for each group to elect a representative to interact in public with a representative of the competing group to determine which is the better of the two solutions.

### Selection of Representatives

The characteristics of the people who are elected as representatives have been evaluated. Representatives are easily characterized as task leaders, not the social leaders. They are the hard driving members of the group; the people who keep the group on its course. Some of their characteristics are shown in Figure 6, where high ranking spokesmen were seen to have quite different characteristics from those not chosen to be spokesmen. They were seen, for example, as offering constructive evaluations, finding ways to be helpful, assuming the leader role, contributing to the problem solutions, expressing themselves clearly and concisely, and so on. On the bottom of Figure 6 personal characteristics that failed to distinguish high from low ranking spokesmen are presented. Many of the personal characteristics often thought to be important to success in becoming a representative turn out to be irrelevant. Examples are: opinionated rather than factual, mannerisms, self-repetition and so on (8).

Summarizing the general picture, it seems as though strong, active, participating, capable people "come to the surface" under elective conditions. People seem to have "good sense" regarding those who can represent them in a satisfactory manner. Yet, as reported below, individuals who are constructive and helpful on an ingroup basis are incompetent to adjudicate differences between their own and contesting groups.

### Negotiation between Representatives

When representatives meet, they are expected to select one solution as the winner. They have the freedom to make the decision. The data shown in Figure 7,

## Figure 6

### HOW MEMBERS DESCRIBE THOSE THEY WANT
### TO REPRESENT THEM

x - HIGH CHOICE FOR REPRESENTATIVE
o - LOW CHOICE FOR REPRESENTATIVE

ITEMS THAT DISCRIMINATE

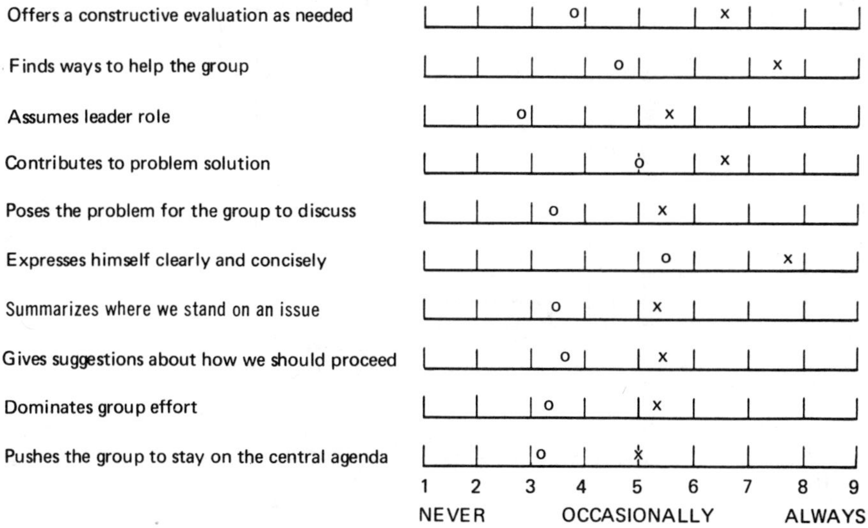

| Item | o position | x position |
|---|---|---|
| Offers a constructive evaluation as needed | ~4 | ~6.5 |
| Finds ways to help the group | ~5 | ~7.5 |
| Assumes leader role | ~3 | ~5 |
| Contributes to problem solution | ~4.5 | ~6 |
| Poses the problem for the group to discuss | ~3.5 | ~5 |
| Expresses himself clearly and concisely | ~6 | ~8 |
| Summarizes where we stand on an issue | ~3.5 | ~5 |
| Gives suggestions about how we should proceed | ~3.5 | ~5 |
| Dominates group effort | ~3 | ~5 |
| Pushes the group to stay on the central agenda | ~3 | ~4.5 |

```
1     2     3     4     5     6     7     8     9
NEVER        OCCASIONALLY              ALWAYS
```

ITEMS THAT DO NOT DISCRIMINATE

| | |
|---|---|
| Expresses personal needs to group | Accurately understands behavior of others |
| Opinionated rather than factual | Senses when to talk and when to listen |
| Mannerisms diminish effectiveness | Interest and involvement fluctuate |
| Views only from own point of view | Sees general problem as well as specifics |
| Repeats himself | Makes others feel at ease |

for 33 such comparisons, show how many representatives have been able to come to agreement. Loyalty of representatives to their group is at a peak during intergroup competition. Thirty-one out of thirty-three representatives held firm to create a deadlock, while 2 gave up so that a decision could be reached (9).

The repetitiveness of the phenomenon across competitions, therefore, tells how strong the motivation to win is, of the person into whose hands is placed his group's fate. Spokesmen are committed people. They elect to *conform* to group expectation rather than to solve the assigned problem.

Now then, in the university under laboratory conditions, competition can be created where representatives, for reasons of experimentation, can be instructed to give up. Under conditions of capitulation by one representative a basis is provided for formulating a definition of a hero and a traitor. A hero is a person whose membership standing is good, who goes out and contacts the enemy and "brings home the bacon." A traitor is a person whose membership is in good standing, who goes out and contacts the group, but who lets himself be influ-

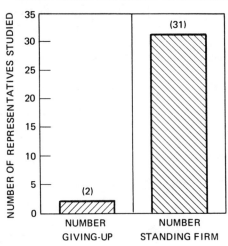

Figure 7

LOYALTY OF REPRESENTATIVES TO THEIR
GROUPS DURING INTERGROUP COMPETITION

enced by the other group's point of view and thereby sells out his own group
(1, 10).

### Reactions to the Arbiter

Eventually a judge is brought in to make the decision. An outsider, or a
neutral person, is used, who can make the decision without partiality. He is a
model of the arbiter under industrial conditions. Unlike the representative, the
arbiter is always able to make a decision (3). The interesting findings, however,
are with respect to the *perception* of the judge. Those whose position he advanced
by his judgment see him as fairminded and impartial, fully competent to handle
intellectual materials and in other ways quite scholarly and analytically skillful.
From the standpoint of those whose position he defeats, he is a weak person to
whom not even the most elementary assignment would be given because he
simply cannot understand.

## Aftermath of Victory and Defeat

Finally, through the action of the arbiter, one group is victorious; the other
group is vanquished. Competition is over, and the groups go back together to
continue their ingroup development on an autonomous basis. Here is the place
that is most interesting to study experimentally. What is the aftermath of victory
and defeat?

### Leadership Replacement in the Defeated Group

What is the impact of victory and defeat on the persons who influenced the
groups during the competitive period? Results in Figures 8 and 9 to a significant
degree parallel the hero and traitor reactions to a winning and losing representative discussed above.

Figure 8

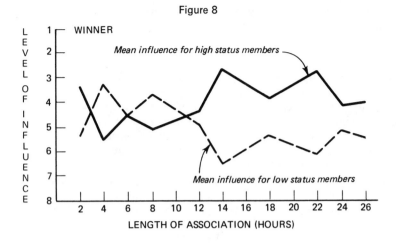

In the losing groups, by comparison with the winning groups, members challenged the old leadership. Soon it became apparent that the former leaders had lost some of their strength, at least for a while. They no longer seemed to be so trustworthy as they were thought to be prior to leading the group into defeat.

The figures show two aspects of leadership. One is that the high status persons increased in influence under periods of stress. The other is what happened to these people after victory and defeat. Intergroup competition was introduced after 12 hours of meeting. In both the winning and losing groups, leaders emerged from among the high status members. Their influence was strong during the 2-hour ingroup problem-solving phase represented in the figures at 14 hours of association. In both the winning and losing groups, the high status members or the "leaders" declined somewhat in influence during the competition, but the dramatic change took place after 18 hours when the verdict of victory or defeat was rendered. In the winning group, Figure 8, those who led the group to victory increased in status. In the defeated group, those who led, led the group into failure. Their influence in the post defeat period, shown in Figure 9, dropped to the lowest level during the life of the group. There seemed to be a compulsion

Figure 9

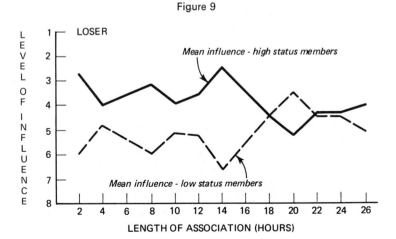

among members of defeated groups to place responsibility for their fate on the individuals who led it to defeat.

### Changes in Atmosphere

During the entire sequence of competition, after each group meeting, members checked words which characterized the atmosphere which prevailed in their group. They checked the same list of nine words before competition was started, during the competition, and after the competition was over. These were used as indications of change. Each group member checked any three of the nine words. These words included work, cooperation, rewarding, fight, flight, tension, sluggish, play and competitive.

Changes in group atmosphere characterized by work and cooperation are shown in Figure 10. On the left side is the amount of work and cooperation during the ingroup problem-solving phase. Both winners and losers were iden-

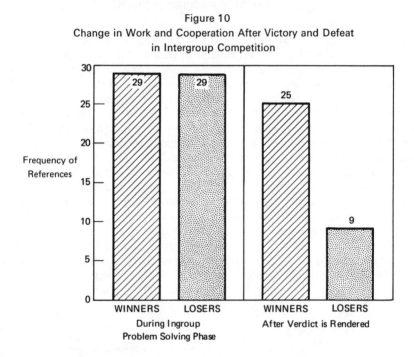

Figure 10
Change in Work and Cooperation After Victory and Defeat
in Intergroup Competition

tical with respect to the amount of work and cooperation present before victory and defeat were awarded. After victory and defeat though, the winners stayed rather work oriented and cooperative.

However, the work orientation has dissipated significantly in the defeated groups. So the question is, "What are they doing if they are not working and cooperating?" Figure 11 shows changes in group atmosphere associated with feelings such as tension, flight (going away from the problem), fighting and competitiveness. Again, the groups were almost identical during the intergroup phase, with no differences evident between the eventual winners and losers. What happens is that after the verdict is rendered, fighting, flighting and com-

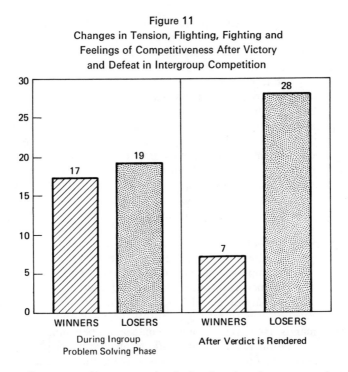

Figure 11
Changes in Tension, Flighting, Fighting and
Feelings of Competitiveness After Victory
and Defeat in Intergroup Competition

petitiveness disappear almost completely in the victorious group but increase to a significant degree in the vanquished group.

What the vanquished were really doing was this. They started out by saying, "It was not we who were defeated, it was the judge that couldn't make a wise decision." That is always the first reaction: the judge, the arbiter, is wrong. The second reaction was, "Well, wait. Maybe we had better examine the two solutions. Since we have been defeated, maybe the judge is right and we need to find out why. So as the defeated group we have to find out why. We have to find out who and what did us in." It becomes a very lean and hungry group. It wants to get its muscles into shape so that if another competition comes along, it doesn't get left behind.

The feeling in the winning group is just the opposite. Another way of characterizing the victorious group is that it becomes "fat and happy." They say, "We did a good job. Let's knock off." They are free to do so, so they do.

### Application of the Win-Lose Dynamics in Labor-Management Relations

Now I would like to describe the applications of experiments concerned with bringing about intergroup collaboration where the history of relationship has been characterized by tension and strife. The example given below is a description of the successful efforts of two companies to replace management-union conflict by cooperation.

The application setting involves union and management relations at the bargaining table. This situation defines a deep and difficult area of relationship between groups, where the atmosphere is too tense, at best, and at worst, saturated with suspicion, distrust, defensiveness, and hostility and open warfare. In two such situations, intensive efforts are underway to convert an intergroup labor-management situation of historical competition, conflict, and warfare to a situation of more statesmanlike intergroup collaboration and problem solving.

The general procedure involved first gaining an understanding of win-lose dynamics as basic to the reduction of competitive intergroup relations. The second step was, through deliberate effort, to avoid falling into the pitfalls that arise when each of the contending groups has its own unique and preferred solution to any given problem. One of the most important of these was to try to avoid creating the conditions under which an opposition group becomes a *defeated* group as described earlier in this paper. Another was in trying to create conditions under which the facts surrounding an area of disagreement could be seen in bold relief rather than leaving them unexplored or accepting them at reputational or argumentative levels. Many of the important considerations involved in taking both of these steps can be gleaned from the systematic generalizations regarding intergroup warfare that have been summarized above.

One of the two examples of application involves a bargaining situation in a 16 man unit; eight men from management and eight from the union. The union approached the bargaining table with sixty-odd fixed demands. Management's initial reaction was to take a defensive, negative and rejecting attitude toward the demands. However, since all management personnel had undergone an intensive orientation regarding the pitfalls of intergroup conflict and also the conditions that foster intergroup problem solving, they were able to examine their own attitudes of resentment and antagonism *before* intergroup contact of a win-lose sort had had the opportunity to arise. Rather than an immediate or impulsive repudiation by management of the sixty-odd demands, they were accepted in good faith as the basis for preliminary interaction. The demands were grouped into topic areas which then became the targets for exploratory discussions.

What kind of attitude did this kind of acceptance of their demands produce in the union? Where it had anticipated rejections and immediate win-lose conflict, it discovered that the attitude of management was one of listening and of constructive interest in wanting to get at the roots of difficulties, to solve them in a mutually acceptable manner. As so often happens, here, too, when the hand of help, understanding, and collaboration was extended, a hand of help, understanding, and collaboration was returned. By this stage, both union and management had adopted an orientation to problem solving which permitted them to explore procedures that could aid in searching out the facts behind these problems under conditions of greater openness and mutual trust and respect.

The basic strategy that evolved involved establishing a number of subgroups, each consisting of two union and two management representatives, to accept a single responsibility. It was their obligation to investigate and to establish the *facts* behind each of the identified problem areas. The subgroups were *not* to work on solutions. The secret in separating fact-finding from the development of solutions was that negotiators were better able to agree on the facts *per se* since they did not have to examine the implications of these facts simultaneously in terms of solutions.

In due course the joint subgroups reported the facts to the total union and management bargaining team. At this point a fascinating result was to be observed. In many cases, the facts developed and agreed on in the subgroups were conspicuously different than the "facts" that either management or the union had thought to lie behind the problem *before* the subgroup investigations took place. Furthermore, the uniform reaction was that the definition of the facts by subgroup investigations produced a higher quality of understanding and analysis of the problem than had been possible based on the "facts" originally perceived to be correct by each group analyzing the problem area separately and from its own point of view.

Given a mutually acceptable statement of facts within each problem area, the situation was ripe to search for solutions which would meet the common needs of both union and management as well as the needs unique to each. The procedure adopted for taking the step toward finding acceptable solutions in each problem area involved breaking the total group of 16 into two subgroups of eight, with each composed of four from management and four from the union. Each group of eight, working independently of the other, used the facts as previously agreed upon as the basis for searching for solutions, though, of course, as new facts became evident they also were included in the basic approach. Rather than a management proposal being presented and countered with an alternate union proposal (the typical approach that leads too commonly to win-lose competition), each eight-man group explored the widest possible spectrum of alternate solutions in a tentative way prior to placing evaluations of utility on any of them. The next step involved evaluating each suggested solution as to its adequacy for satisfying the common needs shared by both groups and the needs unique to each. This step led more or less naturally to a priority ordering of suggested solutions in terms of overall adequacy as well as to further revision and refinement of the better solutions by incorporating desirable elements of inferior solutions into them.

In the final stage, the two eight-men subgroups reunited into a total bargaining group of 16 to compare the quality of the solutions by one group with the solutions by the other. They were able to evaluate, and when necessary to further modify, the most highly agreed on suggested solutions as the basis for formalized agreements. This sequential procedure for problem solving between groups has proved outstandingly successful as a basis for statesmanlike union-management problem solving.

### Conclusion

Now I want to place the behavioral science concepts and methods and their concrete applications such as given above in a broader context than has hitherto been mentioned. It is this. I gain the firm impression that systematic behavioral science methods and generalizations are beginning to provide a sound basis for the emergence of a new industrial ethic. The ethic in another sense, however, is not new, but rather it is ages old. It is the ethic of openness, mutual respect and trust as the basis for trying to understand problems from the other person's or other group's point of view, and from the standpoint of the legitimate needs that must be recognized and met for effective intergroup problem-solving to occur. It replaces an ethic that has come all too frequently to be embraced as the basis for doing business in modern times. The ethic, which must inevitably be replaced, is based on secrecy, mutual suspicion and common distrust. It leads to arguing from the standpoint of selfish, vested interests and to using power as the basis for forcing an adversary to submit rather than to using common sense and decency as an important foundation for collaboration.

Behavioral science generalizations point the way. They say, "With adequate insight and sound problem-solving procedures, problems *can* be approached and solved, not on the basis of win-lose dynamics, but from the standpoint that everyone can win."

**References**

1. Blake, R. R. Psychology and the crisis of statesmanship. *Amer. Psychologist,* 1958, 13, 87–94.
2. Blake, R. R. Gaining acceptance of new ideas in the power structure of an organization. *Proceedings,* 12th Annual Institute of Industrial Engineering, 1960.
3. Blake, R. R. and Mouton, Jane Srygley. *Group Dynamics—Key to Decision Making.* Houston, Texas: Gulf Publishing Co., April, 1961.
4. Blake, R. R. and Mouton, Jane Srygley. Competition, communication and conformity. In I. Berg & B. M. Bass. *Conformity and deviation.* New York: John Wiley & Sons, . . . 1961.
5. Blake, R. R. and Mouton, Jane Srygley. Judgmental tendencies in intergroup competition. *J. abnorm. soc. Psychology,* . . . 1960.
6. Blake, R. R. and Mouton, Jane Srygley. Comprehension of own and outgroup positions under intergroup competition. *Confl. Resol.,* . . . 1961.
7. Blake, R. R. and Mouton, Jane Srygley. Comprehension of points of communality in competitive solutions. *Sociometry,* . . . 1961.
8. Blake, R. R. and Mouton, Jane Srygley. Perceived characteristics of elected representatives. *J. abnorm. soc. Psychol.,* . . . May, 1961.
9. Blake, R. R. and Mouton, Jane Srygley. Loyalty to ingroup positions of representatives during intergroup competition. *Sociometry,* . . . 1961.
10. Blake, R. R. and Mouton, Jane Srygley. Heroes and traitors: two patterns of representing groups in a competitive situation. *Int. J. Sociometry,* . . . 1961.
11. *Proceedings,* Austin, Texas: The Human Relations Training Laboratory, 1960.

## TACTICS OF LATERAL RELATIONSHIP: THE PURCHASING AGENT

GEORGE STRAUSS

This is a study of the tactics used by one functional group in an organization—purchasing—to influence the behavior of other functional departments of relatively equal status. It deals in part with "office politics" and "bureaucratic gamesmanship."

Reprinted from *Administrative Science Quarterly*, 7, No. 2 (1962): 161–186. Used by permission of Administrative Science Quarterly and George Strauss.

Most studies of human relations in management have dealt with *vertical* relations between superiors and subordinates or between line and staff.[1] Yet the purchasing agent's[2] internal relationships (as opposed to his external relationships with salesmen) are almost entirely *lateral*; they are with other functional departments of about the same rank in the organizational hierarchy—departments such as production scheduling, quality control, engineering, and the like. Most agents receive relatively little attention from their superiors; they must act on their own, with support being given by higher management only in exceptional cases. They are given broad freedom to define their own roles and are "controlled" chiefly by the client departments with which they deal.

Although purchasing is technically a staff department, its relations with other departments can best be analyzed in terms of work flow rather than according to the typical staff-line concept. At the beginning of the typical work flow the sales department receives an order; on the basis of this the engineering department prepares a blueprint; next the production scheduling department initiates a work order for manufacturing and a requisition for purchasing; with this requisition the purchasing department buys the needed parts.

But this process does not always work smoothly. Each department has its specialized point of view which it seeks to impose on others, and each department is struggling for greater authority and status. The purpose of this exploratory study is to illustrate the range of tactics available in the interdepartmental conflict which almost always results.

### Research Method

The research methodology included a considerable number of informal contacts with agents, observation of them at work for periods of up to one week, twenty-five formal interviews, a written questionnaire, a review of purchasing journals, and an analysis of how agents, both individually and in groups, handled specially prepared case problems.[3] In the selection of firms to be studied there was a strong bias in favor of those with large engineering staffs, since agents in these firms face the most complex problems.

The discussion which follows will be largely impressionistic and will deal with broad aspects of tactics used by purchasing agents, since their problems vary greatly and various means are used to solve them. It should also be noted that the examples illustrate extreme cases, which, being extreme, illustrate some

[1] There have been many studies of lateral relations within or among primary work groups, but such studies have been concerned primarily with rank-and-file workers, not management. Three notable studies of horizontal relations within management are Melville Dalton, *Men Who Manage* (New York, 1959); Elliot R. Chapple and Leonard Sayles, *The Measure of Management* (New York, 1961); and Henry A. Landsberger, "The Horizontal Dimension in a Bureaucracy," *Administrative Science Quarterly*, 6 (1961), 298–332.

[2] Henceforth, I shall refer to the purchasing agent as the "agent."

[3] I am indebted for assistance to the Buffalo and Northern California Association of Purchasing Agents and to the chairmen of their respective Committees for Professional Development, Messrs. Roger Josslyn and M. J. McMahon. Helpful criticism was provided by Profs. Delbert Duncan, E. T. Malm, and Lyman Porter at the University of California, Berkeley; Prof. John Gullahorn of Michigan State College; Prof. Leonard Sayles at Columbia University; and Dean Arthur Butler and Prof. Perry Bliss at the University of Buffalo. Part of the research was done while the author was a research associate at the Institute of Industrial Relations, University of California, Berkeley.

of the basic dilemmas which most agents face, though often in an attenuated form. This study is primarily concerned with the agent himself, the man who heads the purchasing office. It does not directly concern the buyers and expediters under him or the added complications that occur when divisions or plant agents have a staff relationship with a corporation-wide purchasing office.

## Causes of Friction

The agent originally had two primary functions: (1) to negotiate and place orders at the best possible terms—but only in accordance with specifications set by others—and (2) to expedite orders, that is, to check with suppliers to make sure that deliveries are made on time. This arrangement gave the agent broad power in dealing with salesmen but made him little more than an order clerk in terms of power or status within the company.

The ambitious agent feels that placing orders and expediting deliveries are but the bare bones of his responsibilities. He looks upon his most important function as that of keeping management posted about market developments: new materials, new sources of supply, price trends, and so forth. And to make this information more useful, he seeks to be consulted before the requisition is drawn up, while the product is still in the planning stage. He feels that his technical knowledge of the market should be accorded recognition equal to the technical knowledge of the engineer and accountant.

Specifically, the ambitious agent would like to suggest (1) alternative materials or parts to use, (2) changes in specifications or redesign of components which will save money or result in higher quality or quicker delivery, and (3) more economical lot sizes, and to influence (4) "make or buy" decisions. The agent calls these functions "value analysis."

One way of looking at the agent's desire to expand his influence is in terms of interaction. Normally orders flow in one direction only, from engineering through scheduling to purchasing. But the agent is dissatisfied with being at the end of the line and seeks to reverse the flow. Value analysis permits him to initiate for others. Such behavior may, however, result in ill feeling on the part of other departments, particularly engineering and production scheduling.

### Conflicts with Engineering

Engineers write up the *specifications* for the products which the agents buy. If the specifications are too tight or, what is worse, if they call for one brand only, agents have little or no freedom to choose among suppliers, thus reducing their social status internally and their economic bargaining power externally. Yet engineers find it much easier to write down a well-known brand name than to draw up a lengthy functional specification which lists all the characteristics of the desired item. Disagreements also arise because, by training and job function, engineers look first for quality and reliability and thus, agents charge, are indifferent to low cost and quick delivery, qualities of primary interest to purchasing.

All these problems are aggravated by the "completion barrier." Usually the agent seeks to change specifications only after the engineer has already committed his plans to blueprints and feels he has completed his work—in fact, he may be starting another project; the agent's interference inevitably threatens the engineer's feeling of accomplishment and completion. In any case engineers are jealous of their professional status and often resent the efforts of the agent to suggest new techniques or materials. These are areas in which the engineer feels that he is uniquely competent. Finally, agents are particularly anxious to prevent "backdoor selling" which occurs when a salesman bypasses them and seeks to influence someone else in the organization (usually an engineer) to requisition the salesman's product by name or—more subtly—to list specifications which only this product can meet. Backdoor selling threatens the agent's status in two ways: (1) it encourages specification by brand and (2) it makes both salesmen and engineers less dependent on him.

### Conflicts with Production Scheduling

The size of the order and the date on which it is to be delivered are typically determined by production scheduling. The agent's chief complaint against scheduling is that delivery is often requested on excessively short notice—that schedulers engage in sloppy planning or "cry wolf" by claiming they need orders earlier than they really do—and thus force the agent to choose from a limited number of suppliers, to pay premium prices, and to ask favors of salesmen (thus creating obligations which the agent must later repay). Schedulers, on the other hand, claim that "short lead times" are not their fault, but the fault of departments farther up the line, such as engineering (which delays its blueprints) or sales (which accepts rush orders). In addition agents claim that schedulers order in uneconomic lot sizes and fail to consider inventory costs or the savings from quantity discounts. In some instances, as we shall see, the purchasing agent seeks to solve these problems through combining production scheduling, inventory control, and purchasing into one "materials handling" department, which he hopes he will head.

### Techniques for Dealing with Other Departments

Normally the agent attempts to fill requisitions as instructed. The majority of interdepartmental contacts are handled routinely and without friction in accordance with standard operating procedures. Yet many difficult problems cannot be easily programmed. Other departments are constantly placing pressures on the agent, who must take countermeasures, if only to preserve the *status quo*. And if the purchasing agent wishes to expand his power aggressively, as many do, he will inevitably run into conflict.

Understandably, then, successful agents have developed a variety of techniques for dealing with other departments, particularly when they wish to influence the terms of the requisitions received. These techniques will first be summarized briefly under five general headings and then be discussed in greater detail.

1. *Rule-oriented tactics*
   a. Appeal to some common authority to direct that the requisition be revised or withdrawn.
   b. Refer to some rule (assuming one exists) which provides for longer lead times.

    *c.* Require the scheduling department to state in writing why quick delivery is required.

    *d.* Require the requisitioning department to consent to having its budget charged with the extra cost (such as air freight) required to get quick delivery.

2. *Rule-evading tactics*

    *a.* Go through the motions of complying with the request, but with no expectation of getting delivery on time.

    *b.* Exceed formal authority and ignore the requisitions altogether.

3. *Personal-political tactics*

    *a.* Rely on friendships to induce the scheduling department to modify the requisition.

    *b.* Rely on favors, past and future, to accomplish the same result.

    *c.* Work through political allies in other departments.

4. *Educational tactics*

    *a.* Use direct persuasion, that is, try to persuade scheduling that its requisition is unreasonable.

    *b.* Use what might be called indirect persuasion to help scheduling see the problem from the purchasing department's point of view (in this case it might ask the scheduler to sit in and observe the agent's difficulty in trying to get the vendor to agree to quick delivery).

5. *Organizational-interactional tactics*

    *a.* Seek to change the interaction pattern, for example, have the scheduling department check with the purchasing department as to the possibility of getting quick delivery *before* it makes a requisition.

    *b.* Seek to take over other departments, for example, to subordinate scheduling to purchasing in an integrated materials department.

Note that neither the over-all categories nor the tactics listed under them are all-exclusive and that there is a great deal of over-lapping. They are proposed not as comprehensive tools of analysis, but merely as fairly common examples of bureaucratic gamesmanship.

Each agent interviewed in the study was evaluated in terms of his reported success (in terms of specific accomplishments) in getting other departments to accept a wider role for purchasing. Although this measure was crude and subjective,[4] there seemed to be quite clear differences between the tactics used by those who looked upon their job description as a defensive bastion and those who sought to expand their power beyond it. (Note that success is measured here in terms of expansion of power, rather than money saved for the company.)

**Rule-Oriented Tactics**

The tactics listed below are rule-oriented in the sense that the agent's approach is perfectly legitimate under the formal rules of the organization. Agents who emphasize these tactics seem to fit into Melville Dalton's category of "systematizers."

---

[4] *Reported* success obviously involves a fair amount of wishful thinking—aspiration rather than accomplishment—but for the general character of this study this limitation was not too serious. It should be emphasized, however, that whether an agent was a successful expansionist depended not only on his own personality and his choice of techniques but also on the institutional characteristics of the organization in which he worked.

According to traditional organizational theory, whenever two executives on about the same level cannot agree, they should take the problem to their common superior for solution. Yet, most agents looked upon this as a drastic step, to be taken only when other means failed.

Only five of the agents interviewed mentioned appealing to their superior as a reasonably common means of dealing with interdepartmental problems. In three cases low status seemed to be largely responsible for their inability to handle problems on their own.

Two of these agents were new to the job. For example, one was a man in his early twenties, who had only a few months' experience and who commented that his chief problems were his age and his inability to understand what engineers were talking about. This man met daily to review his problems with his boss and commented that his boss ran interference for him, at least in big problems.

The purchasing agent of a large scientific laboratory was very successful in extending his authority. In dealing with research departments, however, he used the laboratory manager "as a buffer between me and the department heads." But in regard to equipment-maintenance departments, whose heads had much lower status than did the scientists, he commented that "if there were differences, I would discuss them with them. If we didn't agree, the laboratory manager would have to arbitrate. But this has never happened here." Significantly, this agent did not have a college degree, while many of the scientists were Ph.D's.

The other two agents who frequently worked through their superiors came from branch plants of nation-wide firms, which placed strong emphasis on individual responsibility to live within rigid rules.

The more expansionist agents rarely relied on their superiors to help them in interdepartmental disputes (in part because they had little success in doing this). They often explained that they would take problems to a man's superior if necessary but that they rarely found it necessary. Many repeated versions of the following:

> We have a policy against engineers having lunch with salesmen. Since the engineer is on my level I couldn't *tell* him to stop it. But in a nice way I could talk to him. If this didn't work, I'd see the plant manager.
> *Q*: Have you ever done this [appealed to the boss]?
> *A*: No.

The general feeling, particularly among stronger agents, was that too frequent reference to the superior would weaken their relations both with the superior and with their fellow employees. ("After all, you've got to live with them.") To bring in top management too often would, in effect, be an admission that the agent could not handle his own problems. Moreover, there is a myth in many corporations of being "one great big happy family," and, as a consequence, it is difficult to bring conflicts out in the open. Furthermore, since the agent is usually the aggressor, in the sense that he is seeking to expand his power beyond its formal limits, he is unlikely to go to the boss unless his case is unusually good.

On the other hand, the threat of going to the boss loses its effectiveness as a weapon if the threat is *never* carried out. The following quotation summarizes a common position:

> It depends on how much fuss you want to make. If it is really important, you can tell him you will discuss it with his boss. But, I don't want you to get the wrong impression. If you have to resort to this, you are probably falling down on the job. By and large, we have a good relationship with our engineers. However, there are times when you have to take a tough position. You aren't doing your job if you always go along with them in a wishy-washy fashion.

One agent explained how he "educated" engineers to accept substitute products instead of insisting on one brand.

> We prepared our evidence and we were all set to take it to the top—and then, at the last minute, we backed down and told them it was too late in the game. But we indicated that in the future we would take similar issues to the top and they knew we would. So there has been much more understanding. . . . You have to risk making a few enemies once in a while.

### Use of Rules

A second traditional bureaucratic means of dealing with other departments is to cite applicable rules or to rely on a formal statement of authority (such as a job description). For instance, an agent may circumvent pressure to place an order with a given company by referring to company rules requiring competitive bidding on all purchases in excess of $10,000. Most agents agreed, in theory, that rules of this sort are useful weapons, but they varied greatly in the extent to which they relied upon them in practice.

Some agents went very much "by the book," day in and day out. In general, these were men without college training, and they worked for larger, rule-oriented companies that were not changing rapidly. In answer to questions, these men often said, "This matter is governed by corporate policy" or made references to manuals and procedures. They also had a tendency to draw the lines of responsibility quite tightly, so that there were few areas of joint decision making; for example, "Engineering has the final word as far as specs are concerned. But we decide from whom to buy, provided they meet the specs." On the other hand, many agents operated very effectively without any formal written statement of their authority; their authority was understood by everybody in the organization and there was no need to put it in writing.

The evidence suggests that the most successful expansionists preferred to operate informally until there was an open conflict with another department. When this happened, they were very glad to refer to rules to bolster their position. Thus, paradoxically, we found strong agents who worked hard to introduce purchasing manuals and then paid relatively no attention to them in daily practice. In effect these agents take the position of "speak softly and carry a big stick." Indeed, the use of rules involves an implicit threat to appeal to higher management if the rules are not obeyed. ("When everyone in the organization knows what your responsibility is—and that you are backed up—then there is no need to mention it constantly.")

If flexibly used, procedure manuals provide the agent with an added bargaining weapon in dealing with other departments. Even though he may permit rules in the manual to be ignored most of the time, he can always do this as a favor in return for which he may ask favors. And the rules put a legal stamp on his efforts whenever he decides to ensnarl another department in a mass of red tape. But the expansionist agent must be careful not to become too rule-oriented. After all, his goal is to expand his influence beyond the areas over which the rules give him definite authority—not to retreat behind them.

### Requiring Written Acceptance of Responsibility

Another bureaucratic technique used by many agents is to require others to justify their decisions in writing. For example, if a production scheduler orders a part for delivery with very short lead time, the agent can ask him to explain in writing why there is such a rush. He hopes the scheduler will be embarrassed unless he has a good excuse—and in any case, the effort will make him reluctant to make such last-minute requests in the future. Certainly this helps expose the scheduler who constantly cries "wolf."

Agents may ask for written explanations to clear themselves. Just as often, however, this is done to make others hesitate or to have evidence against them later. In insisting that such reports be written, the purchasing agent can refer to company rules or to possible audits. Thus in asking for such a statement, agents often say, "I need it to document my records."

Again, it is the weaker, noncollege agent who makes the most persistent use of such tactics. Many seem to feel that an approach of this sort is cowardly and defeatist. As one put it, "If you are trying to get a man to say 'yes,' I don't see any value in forcing him to put his 'no' in writing. Then he will never move." And another said, "I suppose you do punish an engineer by forcing him to give you a long written explanation, but that's hardly the way to win friends or advance your point of view." Furthermore, "You can always ask an engineer to give you a formal test result, but if he wishes he can always make the test fail."

### Financial Charges

Cost-accounting procedures may also be used as a lever. A number of agents made comments like this:

> Whenever I get a request for a rush delivery, I ask the department which wants it whether they are willing to authorize overtime[5] or air freight. Since this gets charged against their budget, they usually hesitate a bit. If they go along I know they really need it. And if they have too many extra charges the auditor starts asking questions.

This tactic resembles the one previously discussed, particularly when the agent enters a statement into his records that the product would have been cheaper had the requisition been received on time. (Some companies charge inbound freight to the budget of the purchasing or traffic department; in such cases purchasing's leverage is somewhat less effective.)

Some companies have what is often called an efficiency (or profit) improvement plan. According to such a plan each department (and sometimes each executive) receives credit[6] for the cost savings which can be attributed to the department's activities. Agents in two companies reported that engineers showed

---

[5]That is, the vendor is authorized to make an extra charge for having his men work overtime.

[6]Though there is no direct pay-off, performance under the plan is often taken into account in determining bonuses or promotions.

little enthusiasm for value analysis because the purchasing department got all the credit, even though part of the work was done by the engineering department. The situation greatly improved in one of these companies when "primary" credit was transferred to engineering, with purchasing retaining "participating" credit.

## Rule-Evading Tactics

### Literal Compliance

In dealing with pressures from other departments the agent can always adopt a policy of passive resistance—that is, he can go through the motions in hopes of satisfying the demands. This tactic of feigned acceptance[7] is often used with production scheduling. For instance, after completing a lengthy phone call in which he half-heartedly tried to persuade a vendor to make a very quick delivery, an agent commented, "My buyer tried already and I knew that they just weren't going to be able to deliver that soon. Still production scheduling was screaming and they threatened to go to the plant manager. So I tried to handle it in such a way as not to hurt my relations with the vendor. They knew why I had to call."

This game of passive resistance can be skillfully played in such a way as to set a trap for the other department.

*Example.* One agent told how he dealt with an engineer who had placed a requisition for one company's products after having been lavishly entertained by its salesman. The agent wrote a long memo explaining why he felt this to be a poor choice and presented it to the engineer in a fashion which he knew the engineer would reject. The agent then placed the order. As he had predicted, the products arrived late and were totally inappropriate. The subsequent investigation led both to this engineer's transfer and demotion and to other engineers having greater respect for the agent's advice.[8]

It should be noted, however, that these tactics were reported by only a minority of agents. In almost every case the agent was "weak" (in terms of expansionism) or worked in large companies where there was considerable emphasis on following formal rule books. Instead of passively seeming to accept unreasonable requests, the stronger agents actively oppose them.

### Exceeding Authority

Occasionally agents may revise the terms of requisitions on their own initiative, even though they have no formal authority to do so. For instance, an agent may extend a lead time if he knows the production scheduler has set the delivery date much earlier than is really required. Where a requisition calls for a given brand, he may purchase a substitute which he feels sure is an equivalent. Or, he may buy a larger quantity than requested in order to take advantage of quantity discounts.

When an agent revises requisitions in this manner, he may or may not tell the requisitioning department what he is doing. In either case he is exceeding his formal authority. In effect, he is daring the requisitioning department to

[7]Dalton, *op. cit.*, p. 232.
[8]A tactic like this can always backfire. The agent himself may be blamed for the failure.

make an issue of it. This requires considerable courage. No sensible agent will expose himself in this way unless (1) his over-all political position is secure and (2) he feels the terms of the original requisition were clearly so unreasonable that the requisitioning department will hesitate to raise the issue and expose its mistake.

Most agents were reluctant to use this tactic. Even if they could safely change orders in a given case, continual flouting of the requisitioning department's desires would create too much antagonism in the long run.

## Personal-Political Tactics

Friendships and exchange of favors are used in almost every organization to get things done and to oil the wheels of formal bureaucracy. The agent is no exception to this rule; yet the author found to his surprise that informal relations played a less important role than he had expected. Agents, on the whole, seemed oriented to doing things "through channels."

None of the tactics which follow are contemplated by the company's formal scheme; all involve the use of personal relations. It would seem that Dalton's "adapters" would make greatest use of these tactics.

### Friendships

Most agents prefer to deal with friends. Friendships help reduce the kinds of tensions to which agents are commonly subject. Even where friendship is not involved, it is easier to deal with people when you know their idiosyncrasies and special interests. Not surprisingly, comments like this were common: "[In handling problems] friendships count a lot. Many of the people here started when I did twenty-five years ago. We are all at about the same level and most of them are pretty good friends of mine. A lot is a matter of trust and confidence."

Agents seem to rely on friendship contacts as a means of communication and of getting quick acceptances of proposals that could be justified on their merits in any case. Rarely do agents rely on friendship alone. As one put it, "You can accomplish some things on the basis of friendship, but you can't do too much or you will strain your friendship."

### Exchange of Favors

To some extent agents operate on the principle of "reward your friends, punish your enemies," and are involved in a network of exchange of favors—and sometimes even reprisals. Favors of various sorts may be given. Most agents are under pressure to make personal purchases, for example, to help someone in management buy a set of tires at wholesale rates. Since there are usually no formal rules as to such extracurricular purchasing, the agent has a strong incentive to help those who help him most. Similarly an agent is in a position to suggest to a salesman that it might be strategic to take a "co-operative" engineer to lunch. And there are always people in management who would like him to do a favor for a friend or relative who is a salesman or who owns a small business.

Other favors are more work-related. An agent may expedite delivery for a production scheduler who normally gives plenty of lead time for his orders but who now has a real emergency on his hands. Or he may rush parts for an engineer who is building a prototype model. "If a man is reasonable with me," one agent commented, "I'll kill myself to get him what he wants." The agent is less likely to exert himself for the man who has been unco-operative in the past. Yet, in general, agents seem to play down the exchange of favors, perhaps because they have relatively few favors to offer, other than trivial ones such as personal purchases or lunches for salesmen.[9]

The use of reprisals can be seen most clearly in dealing with salesmen. As one agent put it, "I play ball with those who play ball with me. If a salesman operates behind my back, he's going to have a hell of a time getting me to give him an order." Reprisals are more risky in dealing with management.

*Example.* One assistant agent, for example, told how he "delayed" getting catalogues for "uncooperative" engineers and gave "slow service" to engineers who habitually cried wolf. However, both this man's supervisor and his personnel director expressed concern over his poor human relations and his tendency to antagonize others.

The typical agent, however, seemed to feel that if he used such techniques he ran the risk of permanently impairing his relations with others. Furthermore, these techniques might always backfire; for example, if production were delayed because components were delivered late, he would be blamed.

### Interdepartmental Politics

In addition to their personal relations with people, agents inevitably get involved in interdepartmental power struggles. Indeed, as the following quotation suggests, the agent is often a man in the middle, subject to conflicting pressures from all sides:

Production scheduling wants quick delivery, engineering wants quality, manufacturing wants something easy-to-make, accounting wants to save money, quality control has their own interests. And then you've got to deal with the supplier—and present the supplier's position back to your own organization (sometimes you think you are wearing two hats, you represent both the supplier and the company). Everybody has his own point of view and only the agent sees the over-all picture.

Much of the agent's time is spent seeking informal resolution of such problems[10]—and in these meetings he often acts as a mediator. The following is a common situation:

*Example.* Production scheduling has been pushing hard to get early delivery of a particular component (perhaps because the sales department has been pressing for increased production). In response to this pressure the vendor puts new, inexperienced men on the job. But when the components are delivered, quality control declares the work is sloppy, rejects it *in toto*, and wants to disqualify the vendor from doing further work for the company. Production

---

[9]Reciprocity in the broader sense, as suggested by Gouldner and others, is, of course, inherent in the entire framework of relations discussed here. Cf. Alvin W. Gouldner, "The Norm of Reciprocity: A Preliminary Statement," *American Sociological Review*, 25 (1960), 161–177.

[10]Dalton (*op. cit.*, pp. 227–228) points out the function of meetings in short-circuiting formal means of handling problems.

scheduling and the vendor are naturally upset; the vendor insists that the defects are trivial and can be easily remedied; and purchasing is placed in the difficult position of trying to mediate the issue.

If the agent is not careful in situations like this, he may become a scapegoat; everyone may turn on him and blame him for the unhappy turn of events. On the other hand, the successful agent is able to play one pressure off against another and free himself—or he may enlist the support of a powerful department to back him. If he is shrewd, he can get both sides to appeal to him to make the final decision and thus gain prestige as well as bestow favors which he may later ask returned.

Like it or not, agents of necessity engage in power politics. In doing this, they necessarily develop allies and opponents. Each department presents a special problem.

1. *Engineering.* Unless the relationship with engineering is handled with great tact, engineering tends to become an opponent, since value analysis invades an area which engineers feel is exclusively their own. Purchasing is at a disadvantage here. Engineers have the prestige of being college-trained experts, and engineering is much more strongly represented than purchasing in the ranks of higher management.

2. *Manufacturing.* There is often a tug of war between purchasing and manufacturing over who should have the greatest influence with production scheduling. These struggles are particularly sharp where purchasing is trying to absorb either inventory control or all of production scheduling.

3. *Comptroller.* The comptroller is rarely involved in the day-to-day struggles over specifications or delivery dates. But when purchasing seeks to introduce an organizational change which will increase its power—for example, absorbing inventory control—then the comptroller can be a most effective ally. But the agent must present evidence that the proposed innovation will save money.

4. *Sales.* Sales normally has great political power, and purchasing is anxious to maintain good relations with it. Sales is interested above all in being able to make fast delivery and shows less concern with cost, quality, or manufacturing ease. In general, it supports or opposes purchasing in accordance with these criteria. But sales is also interested in reciprocity—in persuading purchasing "to buy from those firms which buy from us."

5. *Production scheduling.* Relations with production scheduling are often complex. Purchasing normally has closer relations with production scheduling than any other department, and conflicts are quite common. Yet these departments are jointly responsible for having parts available when needed and, in several companies at least, they presented a common front to the outside world. Unfortunately, however, production scheduling has little political influence, particularly when it reports relatively low down in the administrative hierarchy.

The shrewd agent knows how to use departmental interests for his own ends. Two quotations illustrate this:

> Engineering says we can't use these parts. But I've asked manufacturing to test a sample under actual operating conditions—they are easy to use.

Even if engineering won't accept manufacturing's data, I can go to the boss with manufacturing backing me. On something like this, manufacturing is tremendously powerful.

[To get acceptance of new products] I may use methods and standards. Or I might go to engineering first and then to methods and standards if engineering shows no interest. If I go to methods and standards I got to emphasize the cost-saving aspect [as contrasted to engineering's interest in quality].

### Educational Tactics

Next we come to a set of tactics designed to persuade others to think in purchasing terms.

#### Direct Persuasion

Direct persuasion—the frank attempt to sell a point of view—is, of course, the agent's typical means of influencing others. Successful persuasion means "knowing your products backwards and forwards. . . building your case so that it can't be answered. . . knowing what you are talking about."

Most agents feel it essential that they have complete command of the facts, particularly if they are to bridge the status gap and meet engineers on equal terms. As one of them said, "The engineer thinks he is the expert; the only way you can impress him is to know more than he does." Thus many agents go to considerable lengths to acquire expertise; they spend a great deal of time learning production processes or reading technical journals.

Yet some of the stronger agents pointed out that too much expertise can be dangerous in that it threatens the other man's status. "Never put a man in a corner. Never prove that he is wrong. This is a fundamental in value analysis. It doesn't pay to be a know-it-all." Thus some agents look upon themselves primarily as catalysts who try to educate others to think in purchasing terms:

> Actually it is an asset not to be an engineer. Not having the [engineering] ability myself, I've had to work backwards. I can't tell them what to do but I can ask questions. They know that I'm not trying to design their instrument . . . . You have to give the engineer recognition. The less formal you are in dealing with them the better. It doesn't get their dander up.

#### Indirect Persuasion

Recognizing the danger of the frontal approach, agents often try forms of indirection—manipulation, if you like—which are designed to induce the other departments to arrive at conclusions similar to those of the agent but seemingly on their own. For example:

> We were paying $45.50 a unit, but I found a vendor who was producing a unit for $30 which I felt would meet our needs just as well. There was a lot of reluctance in engineering to accept it, but I knew the engineer in charge of the test was susceptible to flattery. So I wrote a letter for general distribution telling what a good job of investigating he was doing and how much money we'd save if his investigation was successful. . . . That gave

him the motivation to figure out how it *could* work rather than how it *could not* work.

Indirect persuasion often involves presenting the facts and then letting the other person draw his own conclusions. The agent may ask the engineer to run a test on a product or even simply attach a sample of the product to an inter-office buck slip, asking, "Can we use this?" Similarly, choosing which salesmen may see engineers, he can indirectly influence the specification process. (In fact, once an agent decides that a product should be introduced, he and the salesman will often co-ordinate their strategies closely in order to get it accepted by others in management.)

Most agents feel engineers should have no part in negotiating prices; they feel this would be encroaching on purchasing's jurisdiction. But one successful agent encourages engineers to help out in the bargaining because "that's the best way I know to make these engineers cost conscious." Another arranges to have foremen and production schedulers sit in while he negotiates delivery dates with salesmen. "In that way they will know what I'm up against when they give me lead times which are too short for normal delivery."

### Organizational-Interactional Techniques

Organizational factors play an important part in determining (1) whether the agent's relations with other departments will be formal or informal (for example, whether most contacts will be face-to-face, by phone, or in writing), (2) whether it will be easy or hard for other departments to initiate for purchasing, and (3) whether purchasing can make its point of view felt while decisions are being considered—or can intervene only after other departments have already taken a position. All these involve interaction patterns. We shall consider here only two types of organizational changes: informal measures which make it easier for other departments to initiate change in the usual flow of orders and formal changes involving grants of additional authority.

#### Inducing Others to Initiate Action

In most of the examples discussed here, the agent seeks to initiate change in the behavior of other departments. He is the one who is trying to change the engineer's specifications, the production scheduler's delivery schedules, and so forth. The other departments are always at the receiving (or resisting) end of these initiations. As might be expected, hard feelings are likely to develop if the initiations move only one way.[11]

Recognizing this, many of the stronger agents seem to be trying to rearrange their relations with other departments so that others might initiate changes in the usual work flow more often for them. Specifically they hope to induce the other departments to turn instinctively to purchasing for help whenever they have a problem—and at the earliest possible stage. Thus one agent explained that his chief reason for attending production planning meetings, where new

---

[11] Actually, of course, initiations do occur in both directions. The production schedulers initiate for the agent when they file requisitions and the engineers initiate when they determine specifications. This normal form of programmed, routine initiation is felt to be quite different from the agent's abnormal attempts to introduce innovation. This distinction is quite important.

products were laid out, was to make it easier for others to ask him questions. He hoped to encourage engineers, for example, to inquire about available components before they drew up their blueprints. Another agent commented, "I try to get production scheduling to ask us what the lead times for the various products are. That's a lot easier than our telling them that their lead times are unreasonable after they have made commitments based on these."

Some purchasing departments send out what are, in effect, ambassadors to other departments. They may appoint purchase engineers, men with engineering background (perhaps from the company's own engineering group) who report administratively to purchasing but spend most of their time in the engineering department. Their job is to be instantly available to provide information to engineers whenever they need help in choosing components. They assist in writing specifications (thus making them more realistic and readable) and help expedite delivery of laboratory supplies and material for prototype models. Through making themselves useful, purchase engineers acquire influence and are able to introduce the purchasing point of view before the "completion barrier" makes this difficult. Similar approaches may be used for quality control.

Work assignments with purchasing are normally arranged so that each buyer can become an expert on one group of commodities bought. Under this arrangement the buyer deals with a relatively small number of salesmen, but with a relatively large number of "client" departments within the organization. A few agents have experimented with assigning men on the basis of the departments with which they work rather than on the basis of the products they buy. In one case work assignments in both purchasing and scheduling were so rearranged that each production scheduler had an exact counterpart in purchasing and dealt only with him. In this way closer personal relations developed than would have occurred if the scheduler had no specific individual in purchasing to contact.

Even the physical location of the agent's office makes a difference. It is much easier for the agent to have informal daily contacts with other departments if his office is conveniently located. Some companies place their agents away from the main office, to make it easier for salesmen to see them. Although this facilitates the agents' external communications, it makes their internal communications more difficult. Of course, those companies that have centralized purchasing offices and a widespread network of plants experience this problem in an exaggerated form. Centralized purchasing offers many economic advantages, but the agent must tour the plants if he is not to lose all contact with his client departments.

Value analysis techniques sharply highlight the agent's organizational philosophy. Some agents feel that value analysis should be handled as part of the buyer's everyday activities. If he comes across a new product which might be profitably substituted for one currently used, he should initiate engineering feasibility studies and promote the idea ("nag it" in one agent's words) until it is accepted. Presumably purchasing then gets the credit for the savings, but resistance from other departments may be high. Other agents, particularly those with college training, reject this approach as unnecessarily divisive; they prefer to operate through committees, usually consisting of engineers, purchasing men, and production men. Though committees are time consuming, communications are facilitated, more people are involved, more ideas are forthcoming—and, in addition, the purchasing department no longer has the sole responsibility for value analysis.

To the extent that he allows others to take the initiative, the agent himself must take a passive role. Not all agents are emotionally prepared to do this.[12] Some feel that it smacks too much of the "order clerk." A number commented, in effect, "I don't want to be everyone's door mat." Many asked questions like, "How far do you go in cost estimating, in getting quotes for hypothetical orders? . . . What do you do if a man throws a label at you and says get me some of this? After all, our time is limited."

### Formal Organizational Change

The final approach is for the agent to seek to expand the formal grant of authority given his department (which might mean a larger budget too), as, for example, to place other functions such as traffic, stores, or even inventory control and production scheduling in one combined materials department. Agents who exert their energies in this direction generally reject the "human relations" or "participative" approach to management. They like to resolve problems through memoranda ("it helps keep emotions down") and are not particularly optimistic about the possibilities of converting other departments to think in purchasing terms ("after all every department has its own point of view—that's natural"). They spend considerable time developing statistical means of measuring their own efficiency and that of their subordinates, and they are more likely to be in companies that have similar philosophies. For example, one agent explained why value analysis in his organization was concentrated in the purchasing department, "[Our company] doesn't believe in joint assignments or committees. If a man isn't competent to do the job himself, then we find another man. We don't want weak sisters." And another argued, "The responsibility must be concentrated in one department or another. It can't fall between two stools."[13]

## Choice of Techniques

The foregoing list of tactics is presented not as a formal typology but merely to illustrate the *range* of techniques available to the agent. Most agents use all of these techniques at one time or another, depending on the problem. A different technique might well be used in introducing a major policy change than in handling routine orders. In trying to promote changes, one agent observed:

> You have to choose your weapons. I vary them on purpose. . . . I ask myself, who has the final decision? How does the Chief Engineer operate? What does he delegate? What does he keep for himself? It all involves psychological warfare. Who are the people to be sold? Who will have the final say?

[12]After all, a certain type of active, initiating sort of personality is required if the agent is to bargain successfully with suppliers; it is hard for the same individual to adopt a passive role within the organization.

[13]Yet it could be argued that the committee system does not itself divide responsibility; it merely recognizes the fact that responsibility for value analysis is of necessity divided among departments.

And even in dealing with one problem, a mixture of tactics will generally be used. Nevertheless, the over-all strategies used by various agents seem to vary greatly in terms of which tactics receive the greatest emphasis.

1. Some agents seek formal grants of power (for example, to get inventory placed under purchasing); others merely seek influence (for example, to persuade inventory control to order in more economic lot sizes).

2. Some agents want to influence decisions *before* they are made (for example, through encouraging engineers to turn instinctively to purchasing for help whenever they are even considering the use of a new component); others *after* (for example, through having their decisions upheld often enough for engineering to hesitate to make an issue of a request whenever purchasing questions a specification).

3. Some agents think in terms of their long-run position and thus seek to improve procedures; whereas others are interested chiefly in exerting their influence in each conflict as it comes along.

We have already noted a difference between successful expansionists and those content with their roles as they are. On the whole, expansionists seemed to be more likely to choose informal tactics such as indirect persuasion, inducing others to make changes in the work flow, and interdepartmental politics. They had long-run strategies and sought to influence decisions before they were made. Those who were successful in achieving more formal power were also well aware of the value of informal influence; those who merely *talked* about formal power seemed to be relatively unsuccessful even in informal influence. In fact, one of the most noticeable characteristics of successful expansionists was their flexibility. Most were equally adept at using both formal and informal tactics and were not averse to turning the formal organization against itself.

Differences in success in expansionism seem to be due to a number of factors:

1. *Technology.* Obviously the agent cannot expand very much in a service industry or one where only raw materials are bought. He has his greatest chance for power in companies which make goods to order and in which there is a great deal of subcontracting.

2. *Management philosophy.* Where lines of authority are sharply drawn, the agent has little chance to extend his influence—except through direct seizure of another department's power, which is not easy. Note the comments of one agent in a highly rule-oriented company:

> We are a service department. . . We must see that parts are here at the proper time. . . . I usually let engineering pretty much make its own decisions. I may try to persuade an engineer to accept a new product. But if he says "no" all I can do is wait till he gets transferred and try to persuade his successor.

Of the agents interviewed, the most successful was one in a company which had just introduced a new management and in which all relationships were in flux.

3. *Education.* Purchasing agents who were college graduates seemed to be more expansionist than those who were not. This may be due to their higher level of aspiration. Moreover, any company that appoints a college graduate may well expect to grant him greater influence. The college-trained man may

feel more as an equal of the engineer and therefore more willing to come into conflict with him.

Furthermore, the more educated men (and particularly those with a business school background) seemed more prone to rely on techniques that were informal and not rule-oriented. Specifically, they were less likely to rely on formal statements of authority, to require others to take formal responsibilities for decisions, or to insist that an agent should "yell loudly whenever his rights are violated"; and they were more willing to work through committees.[14]

## Conclusion

Traditional organization theory emphasizes authority and responsibility; it deals largely with two types of relationships: (1) those between superiors and subordinates, which it conceives as being primarily authoritarian (though perhaps modifiable by participation, general supervision, and the like) and (2) those of staff and line, which are nonauthoritarian. Though the purchasing department is traditionally classified as a staff department, my own feeling is that the staff-line dichotomy in this case (as perhaps for most other purposes) tends to obscure more problems than it illuminates. As we have seen, the purchasing department's relations with other departments cannot be explained by any one simple phrase, such as "areas of responsibility," "exchange of favors," "advice," "control," or the like. Instead the skillful agent blends all these approaches and makes use of authoritarian and persuasive tactics as the situation requires. His effectiveness is largely dependent on the political power he is able to develop.

Recent authors have suggested that the study of organization should begin first with "the work to be done and resources and techniques available to do it."[15] The emphasis is on the technology of the job ("technology" being defined broadly to include marketing problems and the like as well as external environment) and the relationships between people which this technology demands. "Organizations should be constructed from the *bottom up*, rather than from the *top down*. In establishing work-group boundaries and supervisory units, management should start with the actual work to be performed, an awareness of who must co-ordinate his job with whom, when, and where."[16]

Some of us who are interested in this area are groping toward a concept of *work flow*, meaning the communications or interactions required by the job and including the flow of raw materials and products on the assembly line, the flow of paper work when a requisition moves through engineering, scheduling, and purchasing, as well as the flow of instruction, which may move down the the chain of command from president to janitor.

[14]These conclusions are consistent with the findings of the questionnaire sample ($N = 142$). The results are in the direction indicated for both degree of education and business school background (each taken separately) although only three out of eight relationships are significant at the .05 level. The questionnaire data are somewhat suspect, however, since the values which agents report are not always consistent with their observed behavior: in answering questionnaires many agents seem to place greater emphasis on formal techniques than they do in practice.

[15]Wilfred Brown, *Explorations in Management* (London, 1960), p. 18. See Chapple and Sayles, *op. cit.;* William F. Whyte, *Men at Work* (Homewood, Ill., 1961).

[16]George Strauss and Leonard R. Sayles, *Personnel: The Human Problems of Management* (Englewood Cliffs, N.J., 1960), p. 392. The sentence is Sayles's.

This has been an exploratory study of the interrelationship between power struggles and lateral work flow. Of particular interest in this study, are: (1) the agent's strong desire for increased status, which upsets the stability of his relationship with other departments, (2) his attempts to raise his status through influencing the terms of the requisitions he receives and thus make interactions flow both ways, (3) the relatively limited interference on the part of higher management, which makes the lateral relationship especially important for the agent, (4) the "completion barrier," which requires the agent to contact an engineer before a blueprint is finished if the agent is to be successful in influencing the terms of the requisition, and (5) the differing vested interests or terms of reference of the various departments, which make agreement more difficult.

Finer mapping and more intensive research into interdepartmental relations is required; interactions should be precisely counted[17] and work should be done with specialties other than purchasing.

[17]Albert H. Rubenstein of Northwestern University has completed an unpublished quantitative study of communications within a purchasing department.

# Organizational Structure and Communications

## ORGANIZATION DESIGN: AN INFORMATION PROCESSING VIEW

Jay R. Galbraith

The empirical research of the last fifteen years on the structure of large organizations seems to confirm the hypothesis of Herbert Simon that human cognitive limits are a basic limiting factor in determining organization structures (Simon, 1957, pp. 196–206). This observation is derived from what is called modern contingency theory. A basic premise of this theory is that the most effective method of organizing is contingent upon some attributes of the organization's environment (Lawrence and Lorsch, 1967). While current research is devoted to discovering what these attributes are, there is a school of thought which suggests that the degree of uncertainty is the primary attribute. This paper takes that point of view and develops an explanation as to why that is the case. In so doing, the organization design strategies for coping with cognitive limits are articulated.

### Information Processing Model

The basic proposition is that the greater the uncertainty of the task, the greater the amount of information that has to be processed between decision-makers during the execution of the task. If the task is well understood prior to performing it, much of the activity can be preplanned. If it is not understood, then during the actual task execution more knowledge is acquired which leads to changes in resource allocations, schedules, and priorities. All these changes require information processing *during* task performance. Therefore, *the greater the task uncertainty, the greater the amount of information that must be processed among decision-makers during task execution in order to achieve a given*

---

A revised version of Sloan School of Management Working Paper No. 425–69, Massachusetts Institute of Technology, 1969. Reprinted by permission of the author.

**313**

*level of performance.* The basic effect of uncertainty is to limit the ability of the organization to preplan or to make decisions about activities in advance of their execution. Therefore, it is hypothesized that the observed variations in organizational forms are variations in the strategies of organizations to 1) increase their ability to preplan, 2) increase their flexibility to adapt to their inability to preplan, or 3) to decrease the level of performance required for continued viability. Which strategy is chosen depends on the relative costs of the strategies. The function of the framework is to identify these strategies and their costs.

### Mechanistic Model

The framework is best developed by keeping in mind a hypothetical organization. Assume it is large and employs a number of specialist groups and resources in providing the output. After the task has been divided into specialist subtasks, the problem is to integrate the subtasks around the completion of the global task. This is the problem of organization design. The behaviors that occur in one subtask cannot be judged as good or bad *per se.* The behaviors are more effective or ineffective depending upon the behaviors of the other subtask performers. There is a design problem because the executors of the behaviors cannot communicate with all the roles with whom they are interdependent. Therefore the design problem is to create mechanisms that permit coordinated action across large numbers of interdependent roles. Each of these mechanisms, however, has a limited range over which it is effective at handling the information requirements necessary to coordinate the interdependent roles. As the amount of uncertainty increases, and, therefore, information processing increases, the organization must adopt integrating mechanisms which increase its information processing capabilities.

#### 1. Coordination by Rules or Programs

For routine predictable tasks, March and Simon have identified the use of rules or programs to coordinate behavior between interdependent subtasks (March and Simon, 1958, Chapter 6). To the extent that job-related situations can be predicted in advance, and behaviors specified for these situations, programs allow an interdependent set of activities to be performed without the need for inter-unit communication. Each role occupant simply executes the behavior which is appropriate for the task-related situation with which he is faced.

#### 2. Hierarchy

As the organization faces greater uncertainty, its participants face situations for which they have no rules. At this point, the hierarchy is employed on an exception basis. The recurring job situations are programmed with rules while infrequent situations are referred to that level in the hierarchy where a global perspective exists for all affected subunits. However, the hierarchy also has a limited range. As uncertainty increases, the number of exceptions increases until the hierarchy becomes overloaded.

314

### 3. Coordination by Targets or Goals

As the uncertainty of the organization's task increases, coordination increasingly takes place by specifying outputs, goals, or targets (March and Simon, 1958, p. 145). Instead of specifying specific behaviors to be enacted, the organization undertakes processes to set goals to be achieved and the employees select the behaviors which lead to goal accomplishment. Planning reduces the amount of discretion exercised at lower levels. Like the use of rules, planning achieves integrated action and also eliminates the need for continuous communication among interdependent subunits as long as task performance stays within the planned task specifications, budget limits, and targeted completion dates. If it does not, the hierarchy is again employed on an exception basis.

The ability of an organization to coordinate interdependent tasks depends on its ability to compute meaningful subgoals to guide subunit action. When uncertainty increases because of introducing new products, entering new markets, or employing new technologies, these subgoals are incorrect. The result is more exceptions, more information processing, and an overloaded hierarchy.

**Design Strategies**

The ability of an organization to successfully utilize coordination by goal setting, hierarchy, and rules depends on the combination of the frequency of exceptions and the capacity of the hierarchy to handle them. As the task uncertainty increases, the organization must again take organization design action. It can proceed in either of two general ways. First, it can act in two ways to reduce the amount of information that is processed. And second, the organization can act in two ways to increase its capacity to handle more information. The two methods for reducing the need for information and the two methods for increasing processing capacity are shown schematically in Figure 1. The effect of all these actions is to reduce the number of exceptional cases referred upward into the organization through hierarchical channels. The assumption is that the critical limiting factor of an organizational form is its ability to handle the nonroutine, consequential events that cannot be anticipated and planned for in advance. The nonprogrammed events place the greatest communication load on the organization.

### Creation of Slack Resources

As the number exceptions begin to overload the hierarchy, one response is to increase the planning targets so that fewer exceptions occur. For example, completion dates can be extended until the number of exceptions that occur are within the existing information-processing capacity of the organization. This has been the practice in solving job shop scheduling problems (Pounds, 1963). Job shops quote delivery times that are long enough to keep the scheduling problem within the computational and information-processing limits of the organization. Since every job shop has the same problem, standard lead times evolve in the industry. Similarly budget targets could be raised, buffer inventories employed, etc. The greater the uncertainty, the greater the magnitude of the inventory lead time or budget needed to reduce an overload.

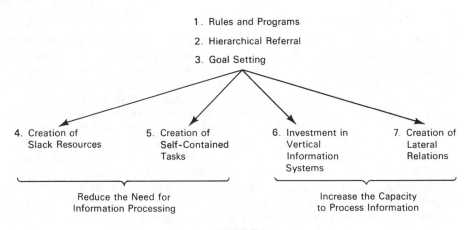

1. Rules and Programs

2. Hierarchical Referral

3. Goal Setting

4. Creation of
Slack Resources

5. Creation of
Self-Contained
Tasks

6. Investment in
Vertical
Information
Systems

7. Creation of
Lateral
Relations

Reduce the Need for
Information Processing

Increase the Capacity
to Process Information

**FIGURE 1**
Organization Design Strategies

All of these examples have a similar effect. They represent the use of slack resources to reduce the amount of interdependence between subunits (March and Simon, 1958, Cyert and March, 1963). This keeps the required amounts of information within the capacity of the organization to process it. Information processing is reduced because an exception is less likely to occur, and reduced interdependence means that fewer factors need to be considered simultaneously when an exception does occur.

The strategy of using slack resources has its costs. Relaxing budget targets has the obvious cost of requiring more budget. Increasing the time to completion date has the effect of delaying the customer. Inventories require the investment of capital funds which could be used elsewhere. Reduction of design optimization reduces the performance of the article being designed. Whether slack resources are used to reduce information or not depends on the relative cost of the other alternatives.

The design choices are among which factors to change (lead time, overtime, machine utilization, etc.) to create the slack and by what amount should the factor be changed. Many operations research models are useful in choosing factors and amounts. The time-cost, trade-off problem in project networks is a good example.

### Creation of Self-Contained Tasks

The second method of reducing the amount of information processed is to change the subtask groupings from resource-(input) based to output-based categories and supply each group with the resources it needs to supply the output. For example, the functional organization could be changed to product groups. Each group would have its own product engineers, process engineers, fabricating and assembly operations, and marketing activities. In other situations, groups can be created around product lines, geographical areas, projects, client groups, markets, etc., each of which would contain the input resources necessary for creation of the output.

The strategy of self-containment shifts the basis of the authority structure from one based on input, resource, skill, or occupational categories, to one based on output or geographical categories. The shift reduces the amount of information processing through several mechanisms. First, it reduces the amount of output diversity faced by a single collection of resources. For example, a professional organization with multiple skill specialties, providing service to three different client groups, must schedule the use of these specialties across three demands for their services and determine priorities when conflicts occur. But, if the organization changed to three groups, one for each client category, each with its own full complement of specialties, the scheduled conflicts across client groups disappears and there is no need to process information to determine priorities.

The second source of information reduction occurs through a reduced division of labor. The functional or resource specialized structure pools the demand for skills across all output categories. In the example above, each client generates approximately one-third of the demand for each skill. Since the division of labor is limited by the extent of the market, the division of labor must decrease as the demand decreases. In the professional organization, each client group may have generated a need for one-third of a computer programmer. The functional organization would have hired one programmer and shared him across the groups. In the self-contained structure, there is insufficient demand in each group for a programmer—so the professionals must do their own programming. Specialization is reduced, but there is no problem of scheduling the programmer's time across the three possible uses for it.

The cost of the self-containment strategy is the loss of resource specialization. In the example, the organization foregoes the benefit of a specialist in computer programming. If there is physical equipment, there is a loss of economies of scale. The professional organization would require three machines in the self-contained form but only one large time-shared machine in the functional form. But those resources which have large economies of scale or for which specialization is necessary may remain centralized. Thus, it is the degree of self-containment that is the variable. The greater the degree of uncertainty, other things equal, the greater the degree of self-containment.

The design choices are the basis for the self-contained structure and the number of resources to be contained in the groups. No groups are completely self-contained or they would not be part of the same organization. But one product divisionalized firm may have eight of fifteen functions in the division while another may have twelve of fifteen in the divisions. Usually accounting, finance, and legal services are centralized and shared. Those functions which have economies of scale, require specialization, or are necessary for control, remain centralized and not part of the self-contained group.

The first two strategies reduced the amount of information by lower performance standards and creating small autonomous groups to provide the output. Information is reduced because an exception is less likely to occur and fewer factors need to be considered when an exception does occur. The next two strategies accept the performance standards and division of labor as given, and adapt the organization so as to process the new information which is created during task performance.

### Investment in Vertical Information Systems

The organization can invest in mechanisms which allow it to process information acquired during task performance without overloading the hierarchical communication channels. The investment occurs according to the following logic. After the organization has created its plan or set of targets for inventories, labor utilization, budgets, and schedules, unanticipated events occur which generate exceptions requiring adjustments to the original plan. At some point, when the number of exceptions becomes substantial, it is preferable to generate a new plan rather than make incremental changes with each exception. The issue then is how frequently should plans be revised—yearly, quarterly, or monthly? The greater the frequency of replanning, the greater the resources—such as clerks, computer time, input-output devices, etc.—required to process information about relevant factors.

The cost of information-processing resources can be minimized if the language is formalized. Formalization of a decision-making language simply means that more information is transmitted with the same number of symbols. It is assumed that information-processing resources are consumed in proportion to the number of symbols transmitted. The accounting system is an example of a formalized language.

Providing more information, more often, may simply overload the decision-maker. Investment may be required to increase the capacity of the decision-maker by employing computers, various man-machine combinations, assistants-to, etc. The cost of this strategy is the cost of the information-processing resources consumed in transmitting and processing the data.

The design variables of this strategy are the decision frequency, the degree of formalization of language, and the type of decision mechanism which will make the choice. This strategy is usually operationalized by creating redundant information channels which transmit data from the point of origination upward in the hierarchy where the point of decision rests. If data is formalized and quantifiable, this strategy is effective. If the relevant data are qualitative and ambiguous, then it may prove easier to bring the decisions down to where the information exists.

### Creation of Lateral Relationships

The last strategy is to selectively employ joint decision processes which cut across lines of authority. This strategy moves the level of decision making down in the organization to where the information exists but does so without reorganizing around self-contained groups. There are several types of lateral decision processes. Some processes are usually referred to as the informal organization. However, these informal processes do not always arise spontaneously out of the needs of the task. This is particularly true in multi-national organizations in which participants are separated by physical barriers, language differences, and cultural differences. Under these circumstances, lateral processes need to be designed. The lateral processes evolve as follows with increases in uncertainty.

1. *Direct Contact.* This contact can be between managers who share a problem. If a problem arises on the shop floor, the foreman can simply call the design engineer and they can jointly agree upon a solution. From an information-processing view, the joint decision prevents an upward referral and unloads the hierarchy.

2. *Liaison Roles.* When the volume of contacts between any two departments grows, it becomes economical to set up a specialized role to handle this

communication. Liaison men are typical examples of specialized roles designed to facilitate communication between two interdependent departments and to bypass the long lines of communication involved in upward referral. Liaison roles arise at lower and middle levels of management.

3. *Task Forces.* Along with direct contact and liaison roles—like the integration mechanisms before them—task forces have a limited range of usefulness. They work when two managers or functions are involved. When problems arise involving seven or eight departments, the decision-making capacity of direct contacts is exceeded. Then these problems must be referred upward. For uncertain, interdependent tasks, such situations arise frequently. Task forces are a form of horizontal contact which is designed for problems of multiple departments.

The task force is made up of representatives from each of the affected departments. Some are full-time members; others may be part-time. The task force is a temporary group. It exists only as long as the problem remains. When a solution is reached each participant returns to his normal tasks.

To the extent that they are successful, task forces remove problems from higher levels of the hierarchy. The decisions are made at lower levels in the organization. In order to guarantee integration, a group problem-solving approach is taken. Each affected subunit contributes a member and, therefore, provides the information necessary to judge the impact on all units.

4. *Teams.* The next extension is to incorporate the group decision process into the permanent decision processes. That is, as certain decisions consistently arise, the task forces become permanent. These groups are labeled teams. There are many design issues concerned in team decision making such as at what level do they operate, who participates, etc. (See Galbraith, 1973, Chapters 6 and 7). One design decision is particularly critical. This is the choice of leadership. Sometimes a problem exists largely in one department so that the department manager is the leader. Sometimes the leadership passes from one manager to another. As a new product moves to the marketplace, the leader of the new product team is first the technical manager followed by the production and then the marketing manager. The result is that if the team cannot reach a consensus decision and the leader decides, the goals of the leader are consistent with the goals of the organization for the decision in question. But quite often obvious leaders cannot be found. Another mechanism must be introduced.

5. *Integrating Roles.* The leadership issue is solved by creating a new role— an integrating role (Lawrence and Lorsch, 1967, Chapter 3). These roles carry the labels of product managers, program managers, project managers, unit managers (hospitals), materials' managers, etc. After the role is created, the design problem is to create enough power in the role to influence the decision process. These roles have power even when no one reports directly to them. They have some power because they report to the general manager. But if they are selected so as to be unbiased with respect to the groups they integrate and to have technical competence, they have expert power. They collect information and equalize power differences due to preferential access to knowledge and information. The power equalization increases trust and the quality of the joint decision process. But power equalization occurs only if the integrating role is

staffed with someone who can exercise expert power in the form of persuasion and informal influences rather than exert the power of rank or authority.

6. *Managerial Linking Roles.* As tasks become more uncertain, it is more difficult to exercise expert power. The role must get more power of the formal authority type in order to be effective at coordinating the joint decisions which occur at lower levels of the organization. This position power changes the nature of the role which for lack of a better name is labeled a managerial-linking role. It is not like the integrating role, because it possesses formal position power but is different from line managerial roles in that participants do not report to the linking manager. The power is added by the following successive changes:

a) The integrator receives approval power of budgets formulated in the departments to be integrated.

b) The planning and budgeting process starts with the integrator making his initiation in budgeting legitimate.

c) The linking manager receives the budget for the area of responsibility and buys resources from the specialist groups.

These mechanisms permit the manager to exercise influence even though no one works directly for him. The role is concerned with integration but exercises power through the formal power of the position. If this power is insufficient to integrate the subtasks and creation of self-contained groups is not feasible, there is one last step.

7. *Matrix Organization.* The last step to is create the dual authority relationship and the matrix organization (Galbraith, 1971). At some point in the organization, some roles have two superiors. The design issue is to select the locus of these roles. The result is a balance of power between the managerial-linking roles and the normal-line organization roles. Figure 2 depicts the pure matrix design.

The work of Lawrence and Lorsch is highly consistent with the assertions concerning lateral relations (Lawrence and Lorsch, 1967, Lorsch and Lawrence,

**TABLE 1**

|  | Plastics | Food | Container |
|---|---|---|---|
| % new products in last ten years | 35% | 20% | 0% |
| Integrating Devices | Rules | Rules | Rules |
|  | Hierarchy | Hierarchy | Hierarchy |
|  | Planning | Planning | Planning |
|  | Direct Contact | Direct Contact | Direct Contact |
|  | Teams at 3 levels | Task forces |  |
|  | Integrating Dept. | Integrators |  |
| % Integrators/Managers | 22% | 17% | 0% |

(Adopted from Lawrence and Lorsch, 1967, pp. 86–138 and Lors :h and Lawrence, 1968.)

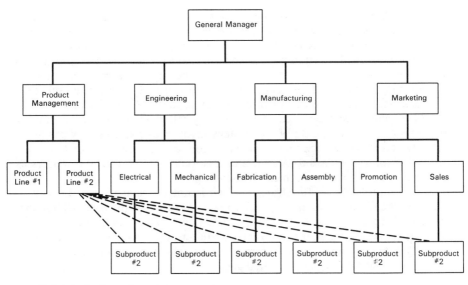

— — — Technical authority over the product

———— Formal authority over the product (in product organization, these relationships may be reversed)

**FIGURE 2**
Pure Matrix Organization

1968). They compared the types of lateral relations undertaken by the most successful firm in three different industries. Their data are summarized in Table 1. The plastics firm has the greatest rate of new product introduction (uncertainty) and the greatest utilization of lateral processes. The container firm was also very successful but utilized only standard practices because its information-processing task is much less formidable. Thus, the greater the uncertainty, the lower the level of decision making and the integration is maintained by lateral relations.

Table 1 points out the cost of using lateral relations. The plastics firm has 22 percent of its managers in integration roles. Thus, the greater the use of lateral relations, the greater the managerial intensity. This cost must be balanced against the cost of slack resources, self-contained groups, and information systems.

**Choice of Strategy**

Each of the four strategies has been briefly presented. The organization can follow one or some combination of several if it chooses. It will choose that strategy which has the least cost in its environmental context. (For an example, see Galbraith, 1970.) However, what may be lost in all of the explanations is that the four strategies are hypothesized to be an exhaustive set of alternatives. That is, if the organization is faced with greater uncertainty due to technological change, higher performance standards due to increased competition, or diversifies its product line to reduce dependence, the amount of information processing is increased. *The organization must adopt at least one of the four strategies when faced with greater uncertainty.* If it does not consciously choose one of the four, then the first, reduced performance standards, will happen automatically. The task information requirements and the capacity of the organization to process information are always matched. If the organization does not consciously match them, reduced performance through budget overruns, schedule overruns will occur in order to bring about equality. Thus, the organization should be planned and designed simultaneously with the planning of the strategy and resource allocations. But if the strategy involves introducing new products, entering new markets, etc., then some provision for increased information must be made. Not to decide is to decide, and it is to decide upon slack resources as the strategy to remove hierarchical overload.

There is probably a fifth strategy which is not articulated here. Instead of changing the organization in response to task uncertainty, the organization can operate on its environment to reduce uncertainty. The organization, through strategic decisions, long-term contracts, coalitions, etc., can control its environment. But these maneuvers have costs also. They should be compared with costs of the four design strategies presented above.

### Summary

The purpose of this paper has been to explain why task uncertainty is related to organizational form. In so doing, the cognitive limits theory of Herbert Simon was the guiding influence. As the consequences of cognitive limits were traced through the framework, various organization design strategies were articulated. The framework provides a basis for integrating organizational interventions, such as information systems and group problem solving, which have been treated separately before.

### Bibliography

Richard Cyert, and James March, *The Behavioral Theory of the Firm* (Englewood Cliffs, N.J.: Prentice-Hall, Inc., 1963).

Jay Galbraith, "Environmental and Technological Determinants of Organization Design: A Case Study" in Lawrence and Lorsch (eds.), *Studies in Organization Design* (Homewood, Ill.: Richard D. Irwin Inc., 1970).

Jay Galbraith, "Designing Matrix Organizations," *Business Horizons*, Feb., 1971, pp. 29–40.

Jay Galbraith, *Organization Design* (Reading, Mass.: Addison-Wesley Publishing Co., 1973).

Paul Lawrence, and Jay Lorsch, *Organization and Environment* (Boston: Division of Research, Harvard Business School, 1967).

Jay Lorsch, and Paul Lawrence, "Environmental Factors and Organization Integration" (paper read at the Annual Meeting of the American Sociological Association, August 27, 1968, Boston, Mass.).

James March, and Herbert Simon, *Organizations* (New York: John Wiley & Sons, 1958).

William Pounds, "The Scheduling Environment," in Muth and Thompson (eds.), *Industrial Scheduling* (Englewood Cliffs, N.J.: Prentice-Hall, Inc., 1963).

Herbert Simon, *Models of Man* (New York: John Wiley & Sons, 1957).

# COMMUNICATIONS IN THE
# RESEARCH AND DEVELOPMENT
# LABORATORY

THOMAS J. ALLEN

Ask any manager of research and development what are the most serious problems affecting the efficiency of his work, and his answer will almost certainly involve some aspect of communication. The communication of ideas is central to the research and development process, and without effective communication among its participants, the quality of the work must necessarily suffer.

Despite its importance, however, little has been known until quite recently about the manner in which scientific or technological information actually passes from one person to another. This article presents results from a series of studies conducted over the past few years in the Sloan School of Management to explore the process of information flow in research and development organizations.

Two rather general conclusions result from earlier studies at the Sloan School: First of all, surprisingly few ideas flow into the laboratory directly from the scientific or technological literature; in the case of some 19 research and development projects studied, for example, only 15 per cent of the "idea generating messages" could be attributed to the literature. And more significant for management, perhaps, is the finding that extra-organizational channels consistently perform more poorly than internal information channels in the provision of technical information; this was first seen in the case of proposal competitions where teams which relied more heavily on information sources outside of their parent organization consistently produced proposals of poor technical quality. Lack of technical capability within the laboratory was largely

Reprinted from Technology Review, 70, No. 1 (October-November, 1967): 31–37. Used with permission of *Technology Review* and Thomas J. Allen. Copyright by the Alumni Association of the Massachusetts Institute of Technology.

responsible for the decision to use outside sources, and inverse relations were found between the use of such sources and the size of the laboratory's technical staff and its ratio to the laboratory's total employment. Laboratories which do not have the necessary technical manpower resources attempted unsuccessfully to substitute through reliance upon outside technical personnel.

On the other hand the use of internal consultants bears a weak but consistently positive relation to performance. It is best, of course, to have the information already available among the proposal team members; but when information must be sought, as indeed it often must, then sources within the information seeker's organization seem much more capable than outside sources of fulfilling the need.

But among academic scientists, W.O. Hagstrom in his book *The Scientific Community* found a strong positive relation between performance and extra-organizational communication. In this instance, the organization (an academic department) occupies a subsidiary position to a more inclusive social system—the "invisible college" or academic discipline. While the communication process (in Hagstrom's case) is external to the academic department, it is *internal to the academic discipline.*

The concept of a shared coding scheme produces a rather simple and straightforward explanation for all of this. In industrial and governmental situations, the laboratory organization assumes an overwhelming importance, demanding loyalty and affiliation far beyond that required by academic departments. The members of such organizations acquire shared coding schemes, or common ways of ordering the world, through their common experience and organization that can be quite different from the schemes held by other members of their particular discipline. This is not true of the academic scientists, whose alignments seem to develop more strongly with others who share their peculiar research interests than with those who share a particular university or department; in other words, an "invisible college" now becomes the mediator of the coding scheme.

It is possible, of course, to hypothesize upon devices to reduce the organizational boundary impedance. One of these possibilities, which may well arise spontaneously, is a two-step process in which certain key individuals able to do so act as bridges linking the organization members to the outside world. Information then enters the organization through these individuals, operating within and transmitting between two coding schemes.

The possibility that such individuals exist, who in effect straddle the closed society of the organization and the wide open one of the outside world, function efficiently in both, and cross easily between them, holds obvious significance for their potential usefulness in information transfer. Recent studies in the Sloan School have sought to identify such people in connection with an examination of the flow of information both into and within the confines of research organizations.

But before turning directly to this particular problem, let us briefly review a body of research on the flow of information in a somewhat different context.

## Public Opinion Research

Twenty years ago, P. F. Lazarsfeld, B. Berelson and H. Gaudet, to explain a phenomenon which they observed in decision-making during the course of the 1940 election campaign, first proposed what has become known as the two-step information flow hypothesis. It appeared that ideas flow from radio and print to opinion leaders and from them to the remainder of the population. Instead of a simple direct connection between mass media and the general public, the process is more complex, involving the individual's social attachments to other people and the character of the opinions and activities which he shares with them. Thus the response of an individual to a communicated message cannot be accounted for without reference to his social environment and to the character of his interpersonal relations. This two-step flow was found to be mediated by "opinion leaders" who in every stratum of society perform a relay function: controlling the flow, for example, of political information from mass media to electorate and thus influencing the vote. The opinion leaders proved to be considerably more exposed than the rest of the population to the formal media of communication. And they were most likely to be exposed to the media appropriate to the sphere of their principal concern, and to have a greater number of interpersonal contacts outside of their own groups.

This hypothesis appears well established in the wide context of public opinion. An obvious next step is to ask whether it is relevant to the far more specific problem of communications in research and development organizations.

Our earliest studies gave some evidence that members of an engineer's immediate work group or colleagues in other parts of the organization are often instrumental in delivering information to him or making him aware of the existence of a particular source. Repeatedly we found that several sources, rather than one single one, had contributed to the discovery or formulation of a particular idea. In one case, for example, an engineer's colleague hears a paper at a conference of the Society of Automotive Engineers, associates the device described with a problem the engineer is tackling, and tells him about it. The engineer follows up the lead by searching the literature, writing the man who delivered the paper, and making arrangements with a vendor who can supply some of the hardware. Another case is quite similar. A vendor visits a particular engineer and tells him about a new piece of equipment that his company has developed. The engineer knows of a colleague to whose problems this equipment might be relevant and suggests that the vendor call on him; the application turns out to be appropriate.

These instances, stated exactly as they were related to the interviewers, are not isolated occurrences. Very frequently an intermediary directly relays information he has obtained from another source, or indirectly assists in the transaction. The early studies certainly suggest the possibility of a two-step flow in technological communication.

## Networks of Communication

The evidence I have cited encouraged us to design a second series of studies, aimed at defining both the nature of the process by which information flows into the organization and the channels through which information proceeds among the scientists within it.

Turning first to information exchange within the organization, we investigated the influence of two factors on the structure of the network through which technical information flows. These were the organization's formal structure—the work groups as they appear officially on the organization chart—and its informal structure—patterns of friendship and social encounters. We examined the impact of these factors on communications in two organizations; the first was a small laboratory in which 34 professionals were actively engaged in work on new materials and devices in the fields of direct energy conversion and solid state electronics, both for military and industrial applications, and the second a department of a large aerospace firm.

We asked the scientists in the two laboratories the following questions:

1. Socialization: Name the three or four persons from the laboratory with whom you meet most frequently on social occasions.
2. Work group: Name the people whom you consider to be members of your present work group.
3. Technical discussion: Name the three or four people with whom you most frequently discuss technical matters.
4. Special information: Please think back to the last technical assignment you completed and try to identify the most difficult technical obstacle or subproblem you had to resolve in the course of this job. Indicate the sources of information which were especially helpful in overcoming this obstacle.
5. Research idea: To whom in the laboratory would you first express an idea for a new research project?

Our questionnaire to the small laboratory employees also included two questions dealing with individuals' methods of gathering information. These asked the number of technical periodicals read regularly and the extent to which personal friends outside their organization and technical specialists inside were used as sources of information.

The figures accompanying this article summarize our results; in compiling them we used three different criteria to measure information flow—technical discussion, information to overcome central research problems, and discussions of research ideas (from questions three, four, and five, above).

Scientists in both the laboratories we studied tended largely to discuss technical matters with the individuals with whom they also met socially. In the small laboratory this results largely, but not entirely, from the rather tight clique found among the Ph. D.'s in the group. As a matter of fact, the relation between socializing and technical discussion is not statistically significant when we consider the Ph. D.'s alone. In the larger research and development department, by contrast, the choice of individuals for technical discussion does not appear to be related to any differentiation of status.

The two other criteria of information flow show less obvious connection with the social network than does technical discussion. Only in the larger laboratory in the case of the upward flow of research ideas, in fact, is there any significant relationship. Nevertheless, since the technical discussions between colleagues are certainly an important mechanism for transferring technical imformation of various sorts, and even though we cannot determine from these data what is the primary impetus (that is, whether socialization brings about transfer of information or technical discussions lead on to social contacts), we conclude that the laboratory's informal structure has an important position in information transfer.

The question of the impact of the formal structure of the organization upon communication remains. Comparison between the work groups and the social

## Figure 1 : Socialization-Choices

These figures illustrate the pattern of relationships among the members of a small research and development laboratory.
In the left pair of charts the arrows indicate the direction of socialization choices; at the right the pattern of technical discussion choices. Since two distinct cliques were evident, those holding and not holding Ph.D. degrees are shown separately in these diagrams.

## Figure 2: Technical Discussion-Choices

The large circle labeled "non-Ph.D." at the left, representing the Ph.D. to non-Ph.D. choices, shows practically no social intercourse between the two groups. The circle labeled "Ph.D." above gives an indication of which non-Ph.D.'s choose into the Ph.D. group. Nine non-Ph.D.'s do so but in only two cases, subjects 24 and 28, is the choice reciprocated. Reciprocal choices are indicated by the double-headed arrows. Non-respondents are represented by uncircled numbers.

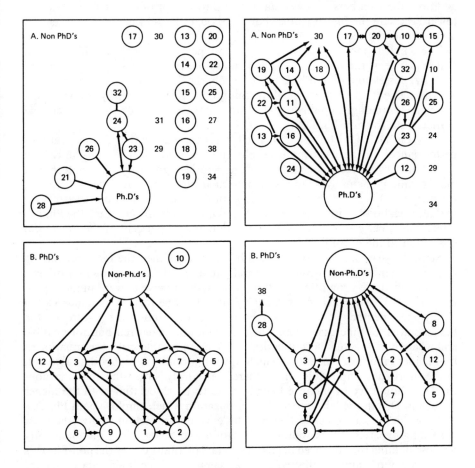

networks shows that, while much of the socialization does occur within work groups, the two networks are somewhat independent and should exert separate influences on information flow. If anything, the formal organization influences communication even more strongly than the informal network. The structure of the work groups influences not only technical discussion but also the upward flow of ideas. In fact, the part of the social network beyond the individual's work group has rather less influence on technical discussions than the complete informal network. Clearly, then, the formal organization is the more important, but by no means the sole determinant of information flow.

## The Impact of Status on Communication

Several experiments by social psychologists have demonstrated that in social systems based on status hierarchies, individuals high on the status ladder will tend to like and communicate frequently with one another while those low in the hierarchy will neither like nor communicate with each other as much. In addition, the members of lower status will direct most of their communication toward those in the higher status clique, although the subjects of their attention do not generally reciprocate it.

The small laboratory provides an almost perfect example of this. Even a casual glance at the figures on page 5 shows the impact of status (exemplified here by possession of a Ph. D. degree) on the laboratory's communication network. The Ph. D.'s form a tightly knit group; they apparently communicate quite freely among themselves but seldom meet socially or discuss technical matters with the non-Ph. D.'s.

This Ph. D. cliquism could in itself drastically disrupt the organization's performance, but an even more serious effect is evident. The non-Ph. D.'s in the laboratory scarcely socialize with one another, and they discuss technical matters among themselves far less than do their Ph. D. colleagues. Furthermore, the non-Ph. D.'s direct the majority of both their social attention (64 per cent) and technical discussions (60 per cent) to the Ph. D.'s. By contrast, the Ph. D's direct only 6 per cent of their social attention and 24 per cent of their technical discussion to the non-Ph. D.'s.

Some 15 years ago, H. H. Kelley, Ph. D.'48, explained the tendency among the lower members of a two-level hierarchy to direct their attention upward as a form of substitute promotion for those who wish to move upward in the organization. A few years later, A. R. Cohen found that one form of communication with upper members of the hierarchy (conjectures about the nature of the higher status job) increases both when "locomotion is desired but not possible and where it is possible but not desirable." We can best describe the situation in the smaller laboratory as one in which upward mobility is highly desirable but, in the short run, impossible. It is, therefore, hardly surprising that the non-Ph. D.'s should try to enhance their own status by associating with the higher status Ph. D.'s in the laboratory. An organization which employs both Ph. D.'s and non-Ph. D.'s together in the same tasks is almost certain to give the most rewarding experiences, as well as publication and recognition, predominantly to those holding the advanced degree. This state of affairs drives the non-Ph. D.'s to a strategy of gaining reflected glory as satellites of the higher status group; they therefore tend to avoid associating with their lower status colleagues in the effort to gain vicariously the kudos denied to them in reality.

## Technological Gatekeepers

Thus far I have restricted myself to the problems of exchanging information between people. Just as important to research management, however, is the stage that immediately precedes this in the chain of communication—the methods and sources that individuals use to gather their information. Looking back at those individuals who were chosen most frequently by their colleagues for technical discussion, or who were cited as sources of critical incident information, we are now able to compare their behavior with that of their colleagues to see whether these "opinion leaders" display any systematic differences in their use of the information system. We compare these "opinion leaders" with their apparently less-informed colleagues in terms of their use of friends outside the laboratory, of technical staff within, and of the technical literature.

Table 1 illustrates the difference between the information gatherers and their colleagues in the small laboratory. The technological gatekeepers clearly read more of the literature and consult more with outside sources than does the average professional in the laboratory; the contrast is especially pronounced in the case of professional journals (those sponsored by scientific and engineering societies).

We also used another criterion of information flow to identify the main sources of information in the laboratory, asking the scientists to indicate the source of any information which influenced the course of their most recently completed research projects. Twelve people in the smaller laboratory cited seven colleagues as the sources of that information, and Table 2 compares these seven with the other professionals in terms of information gathering behavior. The pattern of greater outside contacts and more exposure to the literature reappears.

Thus, there appear to be two distinct classes of individuals within this laboratory. The majority have few information contacts beyond the bounds of the organization. Their internal sources are the other class—the small minority which has extensive contacts outside the laboratory. Information flow in this laboratory is a two-step process, wherein six or seven individuals act as technological gatekeepers for their colleagues. Indeed, the study showed that two of these gatekeepers were responsible for introducing all four of the "most important technical ideas" that had been introduced into the organization during the preceding year.

The individual gatekeepers vary somewhat in the actual sources of information that they use. Some rely more upon literature than discussions, while others operate in reverse manner. If a gatekeeper has a greater number of contacts outside his laboratory, he does not necessarily read the literature more, and vice versa. Therefore, since the gatekeepers do not all tend the same gate, the laboratory as a whole receives a balanced quota of information from the outside world.

The opinion leaders in the laboratory are not of a monolithic sort. Each has his own sources of information and information from each gatekeeper has its own particular function in the laboratory. The situation closely resembles that in the world of mass communication to which I referred earlier in this article. In that context, opinion leaders could be differentiated by topic: those influential in public affairs were not necessarily influential in determining fashion patterns, for example.

We can perhaps extend the analogy between the laboratory and mass communications a little further by examining the source literature of the opinion leaders in the two situations. Studies of mass communication showed that movie leaders read movie magazines more, public affairs leaders read more

**TABLE 1:** Comparison of Communication Behavior and Technical-Discussion Choices

**TABLE 2:** Comparison of Communication Behavior and Identification as the Source of Special Technical Information During One of the Lab's Projects.

Based on Mann-Whitney U-Test performed between the two groups.

| | Number of Times Chosen on Technical-Discussion Matrix | | | Seven individuals cited | Others | Level of statistical significance |
|---|---|---|---|---|---|---|
| | Six or more | Four or fewer | Level of statistical significance | | | |
| Percentage who are above median in using personal friends outside the laboratory as an information source | 64% | 25% | 0.06 | 67% | 30% | 0.10 |
| Percentage who are above median in using technical specialists within the laboratory as an information source | 50 | 40 | 0.47 | 57 | 40 | 0.17 |
| Percentage who are above median in total number of technical periodicals read | 88 | 40 | 0.01 | 100 | 45 | 0.05 |
| Percentage who are above median in number of professional and scientific periodicals read | 75 | 35 | 0.001 | 86 | 35 | 0.03 |

news magazines, fashion leaders read more fashion magazines, and so on. This background strongly suggests that we should look in more detail at the content of the messages processed by the various gatekeepers in R & D laboratories. By analogy, the selection of channels by scientific and technological gatekeepers may be based on the qualitative nature of the information in which the gatekeeper specializes, different channels varying in their ability to provide different types of information. As an example, the literature has been shown to provide information which is important for keeping abreast of the state of a technological field, while oral sources are probably better in providing more specific detailed information about particular techniques. Gatekeepers who specialize in knowledge of the state-of-the-art would thus tend to read the literature more, while those specializing in particular research techniques would interact more with individuals outside the laboratory.

The studies I have described hold two very significant implications for the managers of research and development laboratories. First, they suggest that managers should aim to understand the factors which influence the flow of technical information in the organization; some of these factors are under the management's control and can be used to improve the communication system in action. Second, they emphasize that management should recognize the value of technological gatekeepers; all too frequently rewards by-pass the individuals responsible for information transfer, and managers often fail to make effective use of these individuals.

# Personal Growth
# and Career Development

## THE INDIVIDUAL,
## THE ORGANIZATION,
## AND THE CAREER:
## A CONCEPTUAL SCHEME

Edgar H. Schein

### Introduction

The purpose of this paper is to present a conceptual scheme and a set of variables which make possible the description and analysis of an individual's movement through an organization. We usually think of this set of events in terms of the word "career," but we do not have readily available concepts for describing the multitude of separate experiences and adventures which the individual encounters during the life of his organizational career. We also need concepts which can articulate the relationship between 1) the career seen as a set of attributes and experiences of the *individual* who joins, moves through, and finally leaves an organization, and 2) the career as defined by the *organization*—a set of expectations held by individuals inside the organization which guide their decisions about whom to move, when, how, and at what "speed." It is in the different perspectives which are held toward careers by those who act them out and those who make decisions about them, that one may find some of the richest data for understanding the relationship between individuals and organizations.

The ensuing discussion will focus first on structural variables, those features of the organization, the individual, and the career which are the more or less stable elements. Then we will consider a number of "process" variables which

The ideas in this paper derive from research conducted from 1958–1964 with funds from the Office of Naval Research, Contract NONR 1841 (83) and subsequently with funds from the Sloan Research Fund, M.I.T. Reprinted from Sloan School of Management, M.I.T., Working Paper No. 326–68, with permission of Edgar H. Schein.

will attempt to describe the dynamic interplay between parts of the organization and parts of the individual in the context of his ongoing career. Basically there are two kinds of processes to consider: 1) the influence of the organization on the individual, which can be thought of as a type of *acculturation* or *adult socialization*; and 2) the influence of the individual on the organization, which can be thought of as a process of *innovation* (Schein, 1968).

Both socialization and innovation involve the relationship between the individual and the organization. They differ in that the former is initiated by the organization and reflects the relatively greater power of the social system to induce change in the individual, whereas the latter is initiated by the individual and reflects his power to change the social system. Ordinarily these two processes are discussed as if they were mutually exclusive of each other and as if they reflected *properties* of the organization or the individual. Thus certain organizations are alleged to produce conformity in virtually all of their members, while certain individuals are alleged to have personal strengths which make them innovators wherever they may find themselves. By using the concept of career as a process over time which embodies many different kinds of relationships between an organization and its members, I hope it can be shown that typically the same person is both influenced (socialized) and in turn influences (innovates), and that both processes coexist (though at different points in the life of a career) within any given organization.

## I. The Structure of the Organization

Organizations such as industrial concerns, government agencies, schools, fraternities, hospitals, and military establishments which have a continuity beyond the individual careers of their members can be characterized structurally in many different ways. The particular conceptual model one chooses will depend on the purposes which the model is to fulfill. The structural model which I would like to propose for the analysis of careers is not intended to be a general organizational model; rather, it is designed to elucidate that side of the organization which involves the movement of people through it.

My basic proposition is that the organization should be conceived of as a three-dimensional space like a cone or cylinder in which the external vertical surface is essentially round and in which a core or inner center can be identified. What we traditionally draw as a pyramidal organization on organization charts should really be drawn as a cone in which the various boxes of the traditional chart would represent adjacent sectors of the cone but where movement would be possible within each sector toward or away from the center axis of the cone. Figure 1 shows a redrawing of a typical organization chart according to the present formulation.

*Movement* within the organization can then occur along three conceptually distinguishable dimensions:

    a) *Vertically*—corresponding roughly to the notion of increasing or decreasing one's *rank* or *level* in the organization;

    b) *Radially*—corresponding roughly to the notion of increasing or decreasing one's *centrality* in the organization, one's degree of being more or less "on the inside";

    c) *Circumferentially*—corresponding roughly to the notion of changing one's function or one's division of the organization.

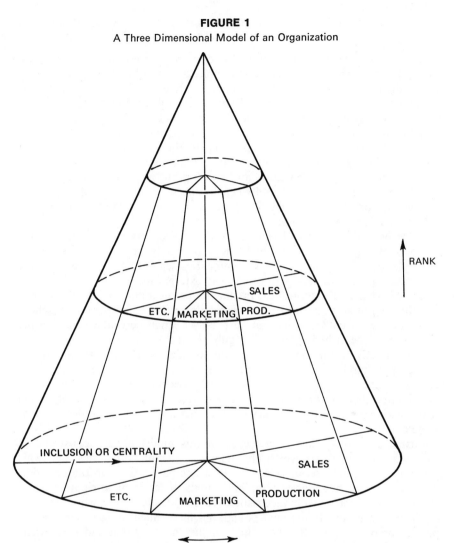

**FIGURE 1**

A Three Dimensional Model of an Organization

Whether movement along one of these dimensions is ever independent of movement along another one is basically an empirical matter. For present purposes it is enough to establish that it would be, in principle, possible for an individual to move along any one of the dimensions without changing his position on either of the other ones.

Corresponding to the three types of movement one can identify three types of *boundaries* which characterize the internal structure of the organization:

a) *Hierarchical boundaries*—which separate the hierarchical levels from each other;

b) *Inclusion boundaries*—which separate individuals or groups who differ in the degree of their centrality;[1]

[1] The organization as a multi-layered system corresponds to Lewin's concept of the personality as a multi-layered system like an onion (Lewin, 1948).

c) *Functional or departmental boundaries*—which separate departments, divisions, or different functional groupings from each other.

Boundaries can vary in 1) *number,* 2) *degree of permeability,* and 3) type of *filtering properties* they possess. For example, in the military there are a great many functional boundaries separating the different line and staff activities, but the overall policy of rotation and keeping all officers highly flexible makes these boundaries highly permeable in the sense that people move a great deal from function to function. On the other hand, a university would also have many functional boundaries corresponding to the different academic departments, but these would be highly impermeable in the sense that no one would seriously consider the movement of an English professor to a Chemistry department, or vice versa. A small family-run business, to take a third example, is an organization with very few functional boundaries in that any manager performs all of the various functions.

Similarly, with respect to hierarchical or inclusion boundaries one can find examples of organizations in which there are many or few levels, many or few degrees of "being in," with the boundaries separating the levels or inner regions being more or less permeable. The external inclusion boundary is, of course, of particular significance, in that its permeability defines the ease or difficulty of initial entry into the organization. Those companies or schools which take in virtually anyone but keep only a small percentage of high performers can be described as having a highly permeable external inclusion boundary, but a relatively impermeable inclusion boundary fairly close to the exterior. On the other hand, the company or school which uses elaborate selection procedures to take in only very few candidates, expects those taken in to succeed, and supports them accordingly, can be described as having a relatively impermeable external inclusion boundary but no other impermeable boundaries close to the exterior.

Further refinement can be achieved in this model if one considers the particular types of filters which characterize different boundaries, i.e., which specify the process or set of rules by which one passes through the boundary. Thus hierarchical boundaries filter individuals in terms of attributes such as seniority, merit, personal characteristics, types of attitudes held, who is sponsoring them, and so on. Functional boundaries filter much more in terms of the specific competencies of the individual, or his "needs" for broader experience in some scheme of training and development (the latter would certainly not be considered in reference to a hierarchical boundary). Inclusion boundaries are probably the most difficult to characterize in terms of their filtering system in that the system may change as one gets closer to the inner core of the organization. Competence may be critical in permeating the external boundary, but factors such as personality, seniority, and willingness to play a certain kind of political game may be critical in becoming a member of the "inner circle."[2] Filter properties may be formally stated requirements for admission or may be highly informal norms shared by the group to be entered.

With reference to individual careers, organizations can be analyzed and described on the basis of 1) number of boundaries of each type, 2) the boundary

---

[2] One of the best descriptions of such filters in an organization can be found in Dalton's (1959) discussion of career advancement in the companies to be studied.

permeability of the different boundaries, and 3) the filtering system which characterizes them. For example, most universities have two hierarchical boundaries (between the ranks of assistant, associate, and full professor), two inclusion boundaries (for initial entry and tenure), and as many functional boundaries as there are departments and schools. Filters for promotion and tenure may or may not be the same depending on the university, but will generally involve some combination of scholarly or research publication, teaching ability, and "service" to the institution. Organizations like industrial ones which do not have a tenure system will be harder to diagnose as far as inclusion filters go, but the inclusion boundaries are just as much a part of their system. The variables identified thus far are basically intended as a set of categories in terms of which to describe and compare different types of organizations in respect to the career paths they generate.

A final variable which needs to be considered is the *shape* of the three-dimensional space which characterizes the organization. The traditional pyramidal organization would presumably become in this scheme a cone. An organization with very many levels could be thought of as a very steep cone, while one with few levels could be thought of as a flat cone. The drawing of the organization as a cone implies, however, that the highest level person is also the most central which is, of course, not necessarily the case. If the top of the organization is a management team, one might think of a truncated cone; if there is a powerful board of directors who represent a higher level but a wider range of centrality one might think of an inverted cone, the point of which touches the apex of the main cone and which sits on top of the main one. In universities where the number of full professors is as large as the number of assistant professors, one might think of the organization more as a cylinder with a small cone on top of it representing the administration.

I am not stating any requirements that the shape of the organization be symmetrical. If a certain department is very large but very peripheral, it might best be thought of as a large bulge on an otherwise round shape. If one considers internal inclusion boundaries one may have some departments which are in their entirety very central and thus reach the vertical axis (core), while other departments do not contain anyone who is very central in the organization and thus do not reach the core at all. The shape of the inner core is also highly variable. It may be an inverted cone which would imply that the number of central people *increases* with rank. Or it might be a cylinder which would imply that there are equal numbers of central people at all ranks. Or it might be some highly asymmetrical shape reflecting the reality that the number of central people varies with length of service, department, political connections with higher ranks, access to critical company informations, etc.[3]

## Some Problems of Measuring Organizational Structure

The problem of measurement varies greatly as a function of the degree to which boundaries and their filtering characteristics are explicitly acknowledged by a given organization and by the wider society. Thus, hierarchical boundaries which separate levels are a widely accepted fact of organizational life and the

[3] Dalton (1959) has identified what he calls "vertical cliques" which cover different ranks as well as departments of an industrial organization.

rules for permeating them tend to be fairly explicit. To the extent that implicit informal factors do operate it becomes more difficult to measure the filtering properties of the hierarchical boundaries in any given organization.

Functional boundaries are generally the easiest to identify because our typical analysis of organizations emphasizes different functions and departments. Similarly, the rules of entry to a function or department tend to be fairly explicit.

The inclusion boundaries are the hardest to identify and measure because to a considerable extent their very existence usually remains implicit. While it may be clear to everyone in a company that there is an inner circle (which may cut across many rank levels), this fact may be denied when an outsider probes for the data. The filtering mechanism may be even more difficult to identify because even the willing informant, including members of the inner circle, may be unclear about the actual mechanisms by which people move toward the center. Even the *concept* of centrality is unclear in that it does not discriminate between a) an individual person's *feeling* of being central or peripheral, and b) some *objective criterion* of his actual position in the organization's social structure.

In the discussion thus far I have meant by the term "centrality" the person's objective position as measured by the degree to which company secrets are entrusted to him, by ratings of others of his position, and by his power. His subjective rating of himself might correlate highly with these other measures and thus might prove to be a simpler measuring device, but it does not basically define centrality because a person may misperceive his own position.

It may be argued that I have over-stated the assumption that the organization is an integrated unified entity. It may after all be only a group of individual people or sub-groups coordinating their activities to some degree but operating from quite different premises. Therefore there are no "organizational" boundaries, only individual approaches to the movement and promotion of their subordinates.

There is ample evidence for the assertion that people who associate with each other around a common task for any length of time *do* develop group boundaries of various sorts and a set of norms which define their probability and filtering properties (e.g. Homans, 1950). But it is quite possible that several such groups co-exist within a larger social system and develop different norms. In applying the concepts which I am outlining in this paper it is therefore necessary to identify as the "organization" a group which has interacted for a sufficient length of time to have developed some common norms. Later, in analyzing the progress of a career, it will of course be necessary to consider the difficulties which are created for the individual as he moves from a group with one set of norms about boundaries to another group with a different set of norms about boundaries, even though both groups are part of the same larger organization.

## II. The Structure of the Individual

Any given individual can be thought of as a more or less integrated set of social selves organized around a basic image or concept of self. His basic temperament, intellectual equipment, learned patterns of feeling expression, and psychological defenses underlie and partially determine this self-image and the kinds of social selves which the individual constructs for himself to deal with his environment. But our focus is on the constructed selves which make it possible for the individual to fulfill various role expectations in his environment, not on the more enduring underlying qualities.

I am using the concept of a constructed social self in the sense of Mead (1934) and more recently Becker (1961) and Goffman (1955, 1957, 1959), as a set of assumptions about, perceptions of, and claims on a given social situation in which role expectations may be more or less well defined. The basic rules of conduct and interaction in terms of which the person orients himself to any social situation are largely culturally determined, but these basic rules still leave each individual a wide latitude in how he will choose to present himself in any given situation (the "line" he will take), and how much social value or status he will claim for himself (his "face").

This conception of the individual places primary emphasis on those aspects of his total being which are the most immediate product of socialization, which most immediately engage other persons in daily life, and which are most dependent on the reinforcement or confirmation of others. For example, at a *basic* level, a person may be temperamentally easily frustrated, may have developed a character structure around the repression of strong aggressive impulses, and may rely heavily on denial and reaction-formation as defense mechanisms. These characteristics describe his basic underlying personality structure but they tell us practically nothing of how he presents himself to others, what his self-image is, how he takes characteristic occupational or social roles, how much value he places on himself, and what kind of interaction patterns he engages in with others.

Focusing on his constructed selves, on the other hand, might show us that this person presents himself to others as very even tempered and mild mannered, that in group situations he takes a role of harmonizing any incipient fights which develop between others, that he tries to appear as the logical voice of reason in discussions and is made uneasy by emotions, that he prefers to analyze problems and advise others rather than getting into action situations (i.e., he prefers some kind of "staff" position), and that he does not get too close to people or depend too heavily upon them. None of the latter characteristics are inconsistent with the basic structure, but they could not have been specifically predicted from the basic structure. Persons with the same kind of underlying character structure might enter similar interactive situations quite differently. In other words, I am asserting that it is not sufficient to describe a person in terms of basic personality structure, if we are to understand his relationship to organizations. Furthermore, it is possible to analyze the person's functioning at the social self level and this level of analysis is most likely to be productive for the understanding of career patterns and the reciprocal influence process between individual and organization.

Each of us learns to construct somewhat different selves for the different kinds of situations in which we are called on to perform, and for the different kinds of roles we are expected to take. Thus, I am a somewhat different person at work than at home; I present myself somewhat differently to my superior than to my subordinate, to my wife than to my children, to my doctor than to a salesman, when I am at a party than when I am at work, and so on. The long and complex process of socialization teaches us the various norms, rules of conduct, values and attitudes, and desirable role behaviors through which one's obligations in situations and roles can be fulfilled. All of these patterns become part of us so that to a large extent we are not conscious of the almost instantaneous choices we make among possible patterns as we "compose ourselves" for entry into a new social situation. Yet these patterns can be immediately brought to consciousness if the presented self chosen is one which does not fit the situation, that is, fails to get confirmation from others.

Failure to get confirmation of a self which involves a certain claimed value is felt by the actor as a threat to his face; he finds himself in a situation in which he is about to lose face if he and the others do not take action to reequilibrate the situation (Goffman, 1955). A simple example of this process can be seen if a person presents himself to others as a humorous fellow who can tell a good joke, tries telling a joke which turns out not to be seen as funny, and "recoups" or avoids the loss of face which is threatened by the silence of others by humorously derogating his own joke telling ability, thereby signalling to the others that he is now claiming a different and somewhat less "valuable" (i.e., more humble) self. The others may signal their acceptance of the latter self by various reassurances, but all parties know very well the unmistakeable meaning of the silence following the first joke.

The various selves which we bring to situations and from which we choose as we present ourselves to others, overlap in varying degrees in that many of the attributes possessed by the person are relevant to several of his selves. Thus, emotional sensitivity may be just as relevant when a person is dealing with a customer in a sales relationship as it is with his wife and children in a family relationship. The person's attributes and underlying character structure thus provide some of the common threads which run through the various social selves he constructs, and provide one basis for seeking order and consistency among them.

Another basis for such order and consistency is to be found in the role demands the person faces. That is, with respect to each role which the person takes or to which he aspires, one can distinguish certain central expectations, certain essential attributes which the person must have or certain behaviors he must be willing to engage in, in order to fulfill the role minimally (pivotal attributes or norms). Other attributes and behaviors are desirable and relevant though not necessary (*relevant* attributes or norms), while still another set can be identified as irrelevant with respect to the role under analysis, though this other set may define various "latent" role capacities the person may have (*peripheral* attributes or norms).[4] The pivotal, relevant, and peripheral attributes of a role will define to some degree the filters which operate at the boundary guarding access to that role.

These changes which occur in a person during the course of his career, as a result of adult socialization or acculturation, are changes in the nature and integration of his social selves. It is highly unlikely that he will change substantially in his basic character structure and his pattern of psychological defenses, but he may change drastically in his social selves in the sense of developing new attitudes and values, new competencies, new images of himself, and new ways of entering and conducting himself in social situations. As he faces new roles which bring new demands, it is from his repertory of attributes and skills that he constructs or reconstructs himself to meet these demands.

A final point concerns the problem of locating what we ordinarily term as

---

[4]This analysis is based on the distinction made by Nadel (1957) and utilized in a study of out-patient nurses by Bennis *et al.* (1959).

the person's beliefs, attitudes, and values at an appropriate level of his total personality. It has been adequately demonstrated (e.g., Adorne *et al.*, 1950; Smith, Bruner, and White, 1956; Katz, 1960) that beliefs, attitudes, and values are intimately related to basic character structure and psychological defenses. But this relationship differs in different people according to the functions which beliefs, attitudes, and values serve for them. Smith *et al.* distinguish three such functions: 1) *reality testing*—where beliefs and attitudes are used by the person to discover and test the basic reality around him; 2) *social adjustment*—where beliefs and attitudes are used by the person to enable him to relate comfortably to others, express his membership in groups, and his social selves; and 3) *externalization*—where beliefs and attitudes are used to express personal conflicts, conscious and unconscious motives, and feelings.

The kind of function which beliefs and attitudes serve for the individual and the kind of flexibility he has in adapting available social selves to varying role demands will define for each individual some of his strengths and weaknesses with respect to organizational demands and the particular pattern of socialization and innovation which one might expect in his career.

For example, a given individual might well have a number of highly labile social selves in which his beliefs and attitudes serve only a social adjustment function. At the same time, he might have one or more other highly stable selves in which he shows great rigidity of belief and attitude. The process of socialization might then involve extensive adaptation and change on the part of the person in his "labile" social selves without touching other more stable parts of him. He might show evidence of having been strongly influenced by the organization, but only in certain areas.[5] Whether this same person would be capable of innovating during his career would depend on whether his job would at any time call on his more stable social selves. The activation of such stable selves might occur only with promotion, the acquisition of increasing responsibility, or acceptance into a more central region of the organization.

When we think of organizations infringing on the private lives of their members we think of a more extensive socialization process which involves changes in more stable beliefs and attitudes which are integrated into more stable social selves. Clearly it is possible for such "deeper" influence to occur, but in assessing depth of influence in any given individual-organizational relationship we must be careful not to overlook adaptational patterns which look like deep influence but are only the activation of and changes in relatively more labile social selves.

### Some Problems of Measuring Individual Structure

I do not know of any well worked out techniques for studying a person's repertory of social selves, their availability, lability, and associated beliefs and attitudes. Something like rating behavior during role-playing or socio-drama would be a possible method but it is difficult to produce in full force the situational and role demands which elicit from us the social selves with which we play for keeps. Assessment techniques which involve observing the person in actual ongoing situations are more promising but more expensive. It is possible that a well motivated person would find it possible to provide accurate data

---

[5]For a relevant analysis of areas which the organization is perceived to be entitled to influence see Schein and Ott (1962) and Schein and Lippitt (1965).

through self-description, i.e. tell accurately how he behaves in situations that he typically faces.

If observation and interview both are impractical, it may be possible to obtain written self-descriptions or adjective check-list data (where the adjectives are specifically descriptive of interactional or social behavior) in response to hypothetical problem situations which are posed for the individual. The major difficulty with this technique would be that it is highly likely that much of the taking of a social self is an unconscious process which even a well motivated subject could not reconstruct accurately. Hence his data would be limited to his conscious self-perceptions. Such conscious self-perceptions could, of course, be supplemented by similar descriptions of the subject made by others.

### III. The Structure of the Career

The career can be looked at from a number of points of view. The individual moving through an organization builds certain perspectives having to do with advancement, personal success, nature of the work, and so on (Becker *et al.,* 1961). Those individuals in the organization who take the "organizational" point of view, build perspectives in terms of the development of human resources, allocation of the right people to the right slots, optimum rates of movement through departments and levels, and so on. A third possible perspective which one can take toward the career is that of the outside observer of the whole process, in which case one is struck by certain basic similarities between organizational careers and other transitional processes which occur in society such as socialization, education, the acculturation of immigrants, initiation into groups, etc. If one takes this observer perspective one can describe the structure and process of the career in terms of a set of basic *stages* which create transitional and terminal *statuses* or *positions*, and involve certain psychological and organizational processes (see Table 1).

In the first column of the Table 1, I have placed the basic stages as well as the key transitional events which characterize movement from one stage to another. The terminology chosen deliberately reflects events in organizations such as schools, religious orders, or fraternities where the stages are well articulated. These same stages and events are assumed to exist and operate in industrial, governmental, and other kinds of organizations even though they are not as clearly defined or labelled. Where a stage does not exist for a given organization, we can ask what the functional equivalent of that stage is. For example, the granting of tenure and the stage of permanent membership is not clearly identified in American business or industrial concerns, yet there are powerful norms operating in most such organizations to retain employees who have reached a certain level and/or have had a certain number of years of service. These norms lead to personnel policies which on the average guarantee the employee a job and thus function as equivalents to a more formal tenure system.

It should be noted that the kind of stages and terminology chosen also reflects the assumption that career movement is basically a process of learning or socialization (during which organizational influence is at a maximum), followed by a process of performance (during which individual influence on the organization is at a maximum), followed by a process of either becoming obsolete or learning new skills which lead to further movement. These are relatively broad categories

## TABLE 1
### Basic Stages, Positions, and Processes Involved in a Career

| Basic Stages and Transitions | Statuses or Positions | Psychological and Organizational Processes: transactions between individual and organization |
|---|---|---|
| 1. Pre-entry | Aspirant, applicant, rushee | Preparation, education, anticipatory socialization |
| Entry (trans.) | Entrant, postulant, recruit | Recruitment, rushing, testing, screening, selection, acceptance ("hiring"); passage through external inclusion boundary; rites of entry; induction and orientation |
| 2. Basic training, novitiate | Trainee, novice, pledge | Training, indoctrination, socialization, testing of the man by the organization, tentative acceptance into group |
| Initiation, first vows (trans.) | Initiate, graduate | Passage through first inner inclusion boundary, acceptance as member and conferring of organizational status, rite of passage and acceptance |
| 3. First regular assignment | New member | First testing by the man of his own capacity to function; granting of real responsibility (playing for keeps); passage through functional boundary with assignment to specific job or department |
| Sub-stages<br>3a. Learning the job<br>3b. Maximum performance<br>3c. Becoming obsolete<br>3d. Learning new skills, etc. | | Indoctrination and testing of man by immediate work group leading to acceptance or rejection; if accepted further education and socialization (learning the ropes); preparation for higher status through coaching, seeking visibility, finding sponsors, etc. |
| Promotion or leveling off (trans.) | | Preparation, testing, passage through hierarchical boundary, rite of passage; may involve passage through functional boundary as well (rotation) |
| 4. Second assignment<br>Sub-stages | Legitimate member (fully accepted) | Processes under no. 3 repeat |
| 5. Granting of tenure | Permanent member | Passage through another inner conclusion boundary |
| Termination and exit (trans.) | Old timer, senior citizen | Preparation for exit, cooling the mark out, rites of exit (testimonial dinners, etc.) |
| 6. Post-exit | Alumnus emeritus, retired | Granting of peripheral status |

which are not fully refined in the table. For example, in the case of becoming obsolete a further set of alternative stages may be provided by the organizational structure—1) retraining for new career; 2) lateral transfer and permanent leveling off with respect to rank, but not necessarily with respect to inclusion; 3) early forced exit (early "retirement"); 4) retention in the given stage in spite of marginal performance (retaining "dead wood" in the organization).

In the second column of the table are found the kinds of terms which we use to characterize the statuses or positions which reflect the different stages of the career. In the third column I have tried to list the kinds of interactional processes which occur between the individual and the organization. These processes can be thought of as reflecting preparation of the incumbent for boundary transition, preparation of the group for his arrival, actual transition processes such as tests, rites of passage, status conferring ceremonies, and post transition processes prior to preparation for new transitions.[6]

Basically the dynamics of the career can be thought of as a *sequence of boundary passages*. The person can move up, around, and in, and every career is some sequence of moves along these three paths. Thus, it is possible to move primarily inward without moving upward or around as in the case of the janitor who has remained a janitor all of his career but, because of association with others who have risen in the hierarchy, enjoys their confidences and a certain amount of power through his opportunities to coach newcomers.

It is also possible to move primarily upward without moving inward or around, as in the case of the scarce highly trained technical specialist who must be elevated in order to be held by the organization but who is given little administrative power or confidential information outside of his immediate area. Such careers are frequently found in universities where certain scholars can become full professors without ever taking the slightest interest in the university as an organization and where they are not seen as being very central to its functioning.

The problem of the professional scientist or engineer in industry hinges precisely on this issue, in that the scientist often feels excluded in spite of "parallel ladders," high salaries, frequent promotions, and fancy titles. Moving in or toward the center of an organization implies increase in power and access to information which enables the person to influence his own destiny. The "parallel ladder" provides rank but often deprives the professional in industry of the kind of power and sense of influence which is associated with centrality.

Finally, movement around without movement in or up is perhaps most clearly exemplified in the perpetual student, or the person who tries some new skill or work area as soon as he has reasonably mastered what he had been doing. Such circumferential or lateral movement is also a way in which organizations handle those whom they are unwilling to promote or get rid of. Thus, they get transferred from one job to another, often with the polite fiction that the transfers constitute promotions of a sort.

In most cases, the career will be some combination of movement in all three dimensions—the person will have been moved up, will have had experience in several departments, and will have moved into a more central position in the organization. Whether any given final position results from smooth or even movement or represents a zig-zagging course is another aspect to consider. Because sub-cultures always tend to exist within a large organization, one may assume that any promotion or transfer results in some *temporary* loss of centrality, in that the person will not immediately be accepted by the new group into which he has been moved. In fact, one of the critical skills of getting ahead may be the person's capacity to regain a central position in any new group into which he is placed.[7] In the military service, whether a person is ultimately accepted as a good leader or not may depend upon his capacity to take a known difficult assignment in which he temporarily loses acceptance and centrality

---

[6]See Strauss (1959) for an excellent description of some of these processes.

[7]In a fascinating experiment with children, Merei, 1941, showed that a strong group could resist the impact of a strong leader child and force the leader child to conform to group norms, but that the skillful leader child first accepted the norms, gained acceptance and centrality, and then began to influence the group toward his own goals.

and to succeed in spite of this in gaining high productivity and allegiance from the men.

The attempt to describe the career in terms of sequential steps or stages introduces some possible distortions. For example, various of the stages may be collapsed in certain situations into a single major event. A young man may report for work and be given as his first assignment a highly responsible job, may be expected to learn as he actually performs, and is indoctrinated by his experiences at the same time that he is using them as a test of his self. The whole assignment may serve the function of an elaborate initiation rite during which the organization tests the man as well. The stages outlined in the chart all occur in one way or another, but they may occur simultaneously and thus be difficult to differentiate.

Another distortion is the implication in the chart that boundaries are crossed in certain set sequences. In reality it may be the case that the person enters a given department on a provisional basis before he has achieved any basic acceptance by the organization so that the functional boundary passage precedes inclusion boundary passage. On the other hand, it may be more appropriate to think of the person as being located in a kind of organizational limbo during his basic training, an image which certainly fits well those training programs which rotate the trainee through all of the departments of the organization without allowing him to do any real work in any of them.

A further complexity arises from the fact that each department, echelon, and power clique is a sub-organization with a sub-culture which superimposes on the major career pattern a set of, in effect, sub-careers within each of the sub-organizations. The socialization which occurs in sub-units creates difficulties or opportunities for the person to the degree that the sub-culture is well integrated with the larger organizational culture. If conflicts exist, the person must make a complex analysis of the major organizational boundaries to attempt to discover whether subsequent passage through a hierarchical boundary (promotion) for example, is more closely tied to acceptance or rejection of sub-cultural norms (i.e., does the filter operate more in terms of the person's capacity to show loyalty even in the face of frustration or in terms of disloyalty for the sake of larger organizational goals even though this entails larger personal risks?).

## IV. Implications and Hypotheses

Thus far I have tried to develop a set of concepts and a kind of model of the organization, the individual, and the career. The kinds of concepts chosen were intended to be useful in identifying the interactions between the individual and the organization as he pursues his career within the organization. We need concepts of this sort to make it possible to compare organizations with respect to the kinds of career paths they generate, and to make it possible to describe the vicissitudes of the career itself. Perhaps the most important function of the concepts, however, is to provide an analytical frame of reference which will make it possible to generate some hypotheses about the crucial process of organizational influences on the individual (socialization) and individual influences on the organization (innovation). Using the concepts defined above, I would now like to try to state some hypotheses as a first step toward building a genuinely socio-psychological theory of career development.

*Hypothesis 1.* Organizational *socialization* will occur primarily in connection with the passage through hierarchical and inclusion boundaries; efforts at *education* and *training* will occur primarily in connection with the passage through functional boundaries. In both instances, the amount of effort at socialization and/or training will be at a maximum just prior to boundary passage, but will continue for some time after boundary passage.

The underlying assumption behind this hypothesis is that 1) the organization is most concerned about correct values and attitudes at the point where it is granting a member more authority and/or centrality, and 2) the individual is most vulnerable to socialization pressures just before and after boundary passage. He is vulnerable before because of the likelihood that he is anxious to move up or in and is therefore motivated to learn organizational norms and values; he is vulnerable after boundary passage because of the new role demands and his needs to reciprocate with correct attitudes and values for having been passed. It is a commonly observed organizational fact that a griping employee often becomes a devoted, loyal follower once he has been promoted and has acquired responsibility for the socialization of other employees.[8]

*Hypothesis 2. Innovation,* or the individual's influence on the organization, will occur *in the middle* of a given stage of the career, at a maximum distance from boundary passage.

The person must be far enough from the earlier boundary passage to have learned the requirements of the new position and to have earned centrality in the new sub-culture, yet must be far enough from his next boundary passage to be fully involved in the present job without being concerned about preparing himself for the future. Also, his power to induce change is lower if he is perceived as about to leave (the lame duck phenomenon). Attempts to innovate closer to boundary passage either will meet resistance or will produce only temporary change.

*Hypothesis 3.* In general, the process of socialization will be more prevalent in the early stages of a career and the process of innovation late in the career, *but both processes occur at all stages.*

Figure 2 attempts to diagram the relationships discussed above. The boundaries that are most relevant to these influence processes are the hierarchical ones in that the power of the organization to socialize is most intimately tied to the status rewards it can offer. One cannot ignore, however, the crucial role which inclusion boundaries and centrality may play in affecting the amount of socialization or innovation. If it is a correct assumption that genuinely creative innovative behavior can occur only when the person is reasonably secure in his position, this is tantamount to saying that he has to have a certain amount of acceptance and centrality to innovate. On the other hand, if the acceptance and centrality involves a sub-culture which is itself hostile to certain organizational goals, it becomes more difficult for the person to innovate (except in reference to sub-cultural norms). This is the case of the men in the production shop with fancy rigs and working routines which permit them to get the job done faster and more comfortably (thus innovating in the service of sub-group norms),

---

[8]See also Lieberman (1956) for an excellent research study demonstrating attitude change after promotion.

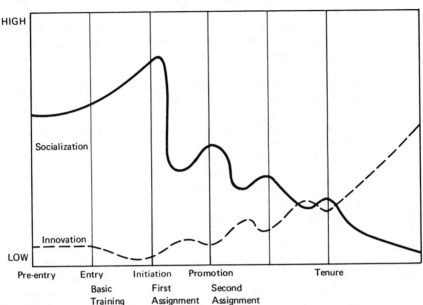

**FIGURE 2**

Socialization and Innovation During The Stages of the Career

HIGH

Socialization

Innovation

LOW

Pre-entry     Entry     Initiation    Promotion         Tenure

              Basic      First      Second

         Training   Assignment  Assignment

yet which are guarded from management eyes and used only to make life easier for the men themselves. One thing which keeps these processes from being shared is the sub-group pressure on the individual and his knowledge that his acceptance by the sub-group hinges on his adherence to its norms. Innovation by individuals will always occur to some degree, but it does not necessarily lead to any new ideas or processes which are functional for the total organization.

Whether or not organizational innovation occurs, then becomes more a function of the degree to which sub-group norms are integrated with the norms and goals of the total organization. In complex organizations there are many forces acting which tend to make groups defensive and competitive, thus increasing the likelihood of their developing conflicting norms (Schein, 1965). Where this happens the process of innovation can still be stimulated through something akin to the "heroic cycle" by which societies revitalize themselves. Campbell shows how the myth of the hero in many cultures is essentially similar (Campbell, 1956). Some respected member of the total organization or society is sent away (freed from the sub-group norms) to find a magic gift which he must bring back to revitalize the organization. By temporarily stepping outside the organization the person can bring back new ideas and methods without directly violating sub-group norms and thus protect his own position as well as the face of the other group members.

*Hypothesis 4.* Socialization or influence will involve primarily the more labile social selves of the individual, while innovation will involve primarily the more stable social selves of the individual, provided the individual is not held captive in the organization.

I am assuming that if socialization forces encounter a stable part of the person which he is unable or unwilling to change, he will leave the organization if he can. On the other hand, if a given way of operating which flows from a stable portion of the individual is incompatible with other organizational procedures or norms, i.e., if innovation is impossible, the individual will also leave. The only condition under which neither of these statements would hold is the condition in which the individual is physically or psychologically unable to leave.

*Hypothesis 5.* A change in the more stable social selves as a result of socialization will occur only under conditions of coercive persuasion, i.e., where the individual cannot or does not psychologically feel free to leave the organization.

Conditions under which coercive persuasion would operate can be produced by a variety of factors: a tight labor market in which movement to other organizations is constrained; an employment contract which involves a legal or moral obligation to remain with the organization; a reward system which subtly but firmly entraps the individual through stock options, pension plans, deferred compensation plans and the like.

If conditions such as those mentioned above do operate to entrap the individual and, if he in turn begins to conform to organizational norms even in terms of the more stable parts of his self, he will indeed become unable to innovate. It is this pattern which has been identified by Merton as operating in bureaucratic frameworks and which writers like W.H. Whyte have decried with the label of "organizational man." It should be noted, however, that this pattern occurs only under certain conditions; it should not be confused with normal processes of socialization, those involving the more labile parts of the person's self and the more pivotal role requirements or norms of the organization.

An important corollary of this hypothesis is that if organizations wish to insure a high rate of innovation, they must also insure highly permeable external boundaries, i.e., must insure that employees feel free to leave the organization. The less permeable the exit boundary, the greater the pressures for total conformity.

### Summary

In this paper I have tried to present a set of concepts about the nature of the organization, the nature of the individual, and the nature of the career—the set of events which tie the individual and the organization together. My purpose has been to provide a frame of reference and a set of concepts which would make it possible to think in more empirical terms about a variable like "career," yet which would relate this variable both to organizational and psychological variables. Using concepts such as "organizational boundaries," labile and stable "social selves," career stages and transitional processes, I have tried to identify some hypotheses about organizational influences on the individual (socialization) and individual influences on the organization (innovation).

**References**

Adorno, T. W. *The authoritarian personality.* New York: Harper, 1950.

Becker, H. S. *et al., Boys in white.* Chicago: University of Chicago Press, 1961.

Bennis, W. G. *et al.,* The role of the nurse in the OPD. Boston University Research Rept. No. 39, 1959.

Campbell, J. *The hero with a thousand faces.* New York: Meridian, 1956.

Dalton, M. *Men who manage*. New York: Wiley, 1959.

Goffman, E. On face work, *Psychiatry*, 1955, 18, 213–231.

Goffman, E. Alienation from interaction. *Human Relations*, 1957, 10, 47–60.

Goffman, E. *The presentation of self in everyday life*. Garden City, New York: Doubleday Anchor, 1959.

Homans, G. C. *The human group*. New York: Harcourt Brace, 1950.

Katz, D. (ed.) Attitude change, *Public Opinion Quarterly*, 1960, 24, 163–365.

Lewin, K. *Resolving social conflicts*. New York: Harper, 1948.

Lieberman, S. The effects of changes in roles on the attitudes of role occupants. *Human Relations*, 1956, 9, 385–402.

Mead, G. H. *Mind, self, and society*. Chicago, Ill.: University of Chicago Press, 1934.

Merei, F. Group leadership and institutionalization. *Human Relations*, 1941, 2, 23–39.

Nadel, F. *The theory of social structure*. Glencoe, Illinois: Free Press, 1957.

Schein, E. H. & Ott, J. S. The legitimacy of organizational influence. *Amer. J. of Sociology*, 1962, 6, 682–689.

Schein, E. H. *Organizational psychology*. Englewood Cliffs, N. J.: Prentice-Hall, 1965.

Schein, E. H. & Lippitt, G. L. Supervisory attitudes toward the legitimacy of influencing subordinates. *J. Appl. Behavioral Science*, 1966, 2, 199–209.

Schein, E. H. Organizational socialization. Industrial Management Review (M.I.T.), 1968.

Smith, M. B., Bruner, J. S., and White, R. W. *Opinions and personality*. New York Wiley, 1956.

Strauss, A. *Mirrors and masks*. Glencoe, Ill.: Free Press, 1959.

# GOAL-SETTING AND
# SELF-DIRECTED BEHAVIOR CHANGE

DAVID A. KOLB
RICHARD E. BOYATZIS

Two recent developments, one theoretical and one practical, have led behavior change researchers to pay more attention to self-directed techniques of behavior change. In practice, there is a growing demand for behavioral science solutions to human problems. More and more individuals are seeing that the various forms of psychotherapy can provide viable solutions to their personal problems. In addition, social welfare agencies are seeking to change their role

This research was supported in part by the Industrial Relations Section, Sloan School of Management, M.I.T. Computation was done at the M.I.T. Computation Center. We wish to express our appreciation to William McKelvey, Sara Winter, James Curtis and Robert Zuckerman for assistance in research design and administration, to George Farris for assistance in data interpretation, and to Robert Euritt, George Farris, Michael Fulenwider, William McKelvey, Irwin Rubin, Suresh Srivastva and Sara Winter who served as T-Group trainers, and to the students who through their efforts made this research possible.

from that of policeman and distributor of government funds to that of an agent for individual and community development. This growing demand for the practical application of behavioral science knowledge has made practitioners painfully aware of the fact that, using the existing techniques of behavior change which are so dependent on the change agent for their success, there can never be enough professionally trained personnel to meet this demand. So in desperation the practitioner is asking, "How crucial am I in the change process? Is it possible to develop change techniques that people can use themselves?"

Until recently the theoretical answer has been no. Therapeutic models of change, both the analytic and learning theory based, have conceived of the patient as passive and reactive. In the tradition of their medical origins it is the doctor who was the active and curative agent in the therapeutic process. In an analysis of psychological journals, Allport (1960) found that psychologists exclusively used a reactive model of a man to interpret their results. In the psychologist's mind man was an animal who reacted to stimuli and who was controlled by his environment. The concept of will—man's ability to control and change his own behavior—was nowhere to be found in respectable psychological theories. The idea of self-directed change appeared only in common sense psychologies like those of Norman Vincent Peale and Dale Carnegie.

Currently, however, there are a great number of theorists who challenge the reactive conception of man. Hartmann, Kris and Loewenstein (1947) and other ego psychologists began to reinterpret psychoanalytic theory laying increasing emphasis on the power of ego processes in the rational direction and control of one's behavior. More recently White (1957) has detailed the research evidence for pro-active, competence motivation in human beings—motives urging men and animals to ignore safety and security, and to take on new, difficult, and challenging tasks. Of this group of men it is perhaps Carl Rogers who has been most influential in applying the new growth-oriented theory of man to the practice of behavior change. He created an entirely new theory and method of psychotherapy—client-centered therapy (1951). As the name implies, in client-centered therapy the client is the active and curative agent in the therapeutic relationship. The therapist's job is to create in a nondirective way the therapeutic conditions which will facilitate self-inquiry and personal growth in the client. By emphasizing man's creative and problem-solving abilities and his growth potential the pro-active theorists imply that self-directed change is not only theoretically possible but that it occurs as a natural life process.

These two conflicting models of man pose something of a dilemma, for we cannot accept one and discard the other without doing an injustice to the data. Research evidence and common sense observations can be marshalled to support both theories—man is passive and controlled by his environment as well as creative and self-directing. The noted ethologist Konrad Lorenz (1963) suggests, however, that this dilemma is an illusion. There is no contradiction, he maintains, between the fact that man's behavior is governed by causal stimulus-response type laws and the fact that man strives toward goals and can modify his behavior by an act of will. "The appreciation of the fact that life processes are directed at aims or goals, and the realization of the other fact that they are, at the same time, determined by causality, not only do not preclude each other but they only make sense in combination. If man did not strive toward goals, his questions as to causes would have not sense; if he has no insight into cause and effect, he is powerless to guide effects toward determined goals, however rightly he may have understood the meaning of these goals . . . (p. 231). Increasing knowledge of the natural causes of his own behavior can certainly increase a man's faculties and enable him to put his free will into action . . . (p. 232)."

Thus in his integration of the two models of man Lorenz suggests a methodology for self-directed change. If we can increase an individual's understanding of the psychological laws which govern his behavior, we can increase his capacity for self-direction. To explore the characteristics of the process of self-directed change we have developed a simple method for self-directed behavior change.

The major emphasis of the method is on self-research. Each subject is encouraged to reflect on his own behavior, and to select a limited and well-defined goal which he would like to achieve. The next step is to undertake a continuing and accurate assessment of his behavior in the area related to his change goal. He keeps an objective record of his behavior in this area, generally in the form of a graph which measures progress toward the goal from day to day. The subject decides for himself how long the project should continue and when his goal is attained.

When business-school students used this method to change themselves as part of their participation in self-analytic groups (Kolb, Winter and Berlew, 1968), two factors were found that predicted the students' success in changing. Change was found to be related to the individual's commitment to his change goal and the amount of feedback he received from other group members during the last half of the group. Improving the change method to increase goal commitment and feedback increased the percentage of students successfully attaining their goals from 5% to 61%.

The research reported in this paper is a more detailed exploration of the dynamics of the goal-setting process in self-directed behavior change. More specifically, we seek answers to the following questions:

1. Does conscious goal-setting facilitate goal achievement?
2. What characteristics of the goal-setting process are related to subsequent success or failure in goal-achievement?

### Goal-Setting and Goal-Achievement

There has been a great deal of attention given to the relationship between goal-setting and goal-achievement in the psychological literature. Most of these studies, however, have been conducted in the level of aspiration experimental paradigm and have been concerned mainly with the question—How does successful or unsuccessful goal-achievement affect goal-setting? (Lewin, et al. 1944; Festinger, 1942; Frank, 1941). The major result of these studies has been that success increases aspirations and failure, to a lesser extent, decreases aspirations. Comparatively little attention has been given to the reverse question which is central to understanding the role of goal-setting in self-directed behavior change—How does goal-setting affect success in goal-achievement?

McClelland's theory of motivation gives a partial answer to this question (McClelland, 1965). Motives in his theory are affectively toned associative networks arranged in a hierarchy of importance within the individual. In other words a motive is an emotionally toned pattern of thinking. The influence which a motive holds over an individual's behavior is determined by the extent to which this pattern of thinking dominates an individual's consciousness. Hundreds of studies have been conducted within this theoretical framework showing the relationship between achievement motivation and behavior as well as other motives such as power, affiliation, aggression and sex (McClelland, 1961; Atkinson, 1958). In addition a number of behavior change programs have reported success in changing achievement motivated behavior by changing (among other things) the position of the achievement motive in a person's motive heirarchy by helping him develop and clearly conceptualize the associative network defining the motive (Kolb, 1965; McClelland, 1965; Litwin and Aronoff, 1971). These studies all lend support to the notion that dominance of a goal (i.e., achievement desires) in consciousness will lead to behavior toward that goal (i.e., achievement related behavior).

Organizational psychology provides another source of evidence for the importance of conscious goal-setting for goal achievement. The field has long recognized the importance of goal-setting and programs of management by objectives have made this process quite explicit in industrial management (Drucker, 1954). Studies of organizations have shown productivity and satisfaction are greater when the worker sets his own goals (Likert, 1967; McGregor, 1960). One excellent field study of performance appraisal interviews by Kay, French and Myer (1962) gives empirical support to the hypothesis that conscious goal-setting leads to goal achievement. The authors found that when managers' improvement needs were translated into specific goals during performance appraisal interviews, 65.2% of these goals were subsequently achieved. When improvement needs were not translated into specific goals only 27.3% were subsequently accomplished. Kay and French conclude that, "Appreciable improvements in performance were realized only when specific goals were established with time deadlines set and results measures agreed upon. Regardless of how much emphasis the manager gave to an improvement need in the appraisal discussion, if this did not get translated into a specific goal, very little performance improvement was achieved" (p. 1).

Two studies in the level of aspiration literature have attempted to show the effect that stating a level of aspiration has a subsequent performance. Kausler (1959) gave a simple arithmetic test to three groups of students, two of which were asked to state levels of aspiration. He found that when mathematical ability was held constant those who were asked to state their level of aspiration performed significantly better than those who were not. Rao (1956) conducted an experiment in which he examined the effects of level of aspiration and feedback on performance. His conclusion was that task performance was decreased when either a level of aspiration was not stated or feedback was withheld.

Finally, our previous research on self-directed behavior change (Kolb, Winter and Berlew, 1968) suggested that when the self-directed change method was modified to emphasize conscious goal-setting the percent of successful goal achievement increased from 44% to 61%.

There is, then, some empirical support for the hypothesis that conscious goal-setting facilitates goal achievement. The purpose of the study reported here is to ascertain whether conscious goal-setting will facilitate the achievement of personal improvement goals by individuals using the self-directed behavior change method.

Hypothesis I. Individuals will change more on those dimensions of their self-concept which they define as relevant to their consciously set change goal than they will on dimensions of their self-concept which they define as not relevant. This difference will be independent of the difficulty of the change goal.

This hypothesis differs from those of previously reported research in that it does not involve an experimental manipulation of the independent variable, goal-setting. This difference overcomes one problem with previous research designs but creates another. The problem with the previous experimental designs is that it is impossible to determine whether the improvements in performance were a result of conscious goal-setting or a result of the influence attempts of the experimenter which are inherent in asking an individual to set goals. By asking a person to say how many arithmetic problems he is going to do or by defining with him what specifically he is going to do to improve his job performance the experimenter or manager is in effect telling the person to achieve the goal. Research on the social psychology of experimental situations suggests that this influence, even if unconscious, can be very great (Milgram, 1968; Orne, 1962; Rosenthal, 1963). In the current experiment, subjects are free to choose whatever goal they wish thus eliminating the effect of experimenter persuasion. The problem with the current design, however, is that it is difficult to conclude that it is conscious goal-setting that causes greater goal achievement. Individuals may simply choose goals that are easier to achieve. In an attempt to overcome this problem we will test whether goal-setting facilitates change in difficult as well as easy goals.

### Characteristics of the Goal-Setting Process

In addition to assessing the effect of conscious goal-setting on goal achievement, this research seeks to determine those characteristics of the goal-setting process which facilitate goal achievement. From a content analysis of individuals' initial goal statements five hypotheses will be tested. These include an exploration of the individual's awareness of his goal, his expectation of success, and his level of psychological safety. The remaining two hypotheses are concerned with the individual's evaluation of his progress—the extent to which he proposes to measure his progress and the degree to which he controls his own reinforcement and evaluates himself.

*Awareness.* Most forms of psychotherapy attempt to increase the patient's awareness of the forces affecting his behavior with the implicit assumption that this insight will change the patient's behavior. Two recent psychotherapy research programs have been able to define the role of awareness in personality change more specifically. Gendlin, *et al.* (1968) has devised a process measure of what he calls the client's focusing ability. He describes the role of focusing ability in therapy as follows:

> The therapist calls the client's attention to an as yet unclear partly cognitive and situational complex which is concretely felt by the client. The client must then be willing and able to focus his attention directly on this felt complex so that he can concretely feel and struggle with it (p. 218).

Gendlin finds that clients who display this kind of focusing ability in therapy interviews improve after therapy while those who do not show focusing ability do not improve. Truax and Carkhuff (1964) have developed a process measure which they call intrapersonal exploration that is similar to focusing ability in that it emphasizes awareness of feelings associated with one's problems. They also find that presence of intrapersonal exploration in psychotherapy interviews is indicative of successful change.

In a study of the personality characteristics of individuals who are successful in self-directed behavior change projects Winter, Griffith and Kolb (1968) found results that suggest that successful change is a function of one's ability to maintain awareness of the dissonance between one's ideal self and one's current self.

> Hypothesis II. Individuals who are successful in achieving their change goal will initially show a greater awareness of forces related to that change goal than will individuals who are unsuccessful in achieving their change goal.

*Expectation of Success.* A number of studies in psychotherapy have shown that an individual's expectations of success or failure can in fact determine his success or failure in therapy (Goldstein, 1962; Frank, 1963). We would predict that this would be even more likely in a self-directed change project since the individual plays a more central role in his own change effort.

> Hypothesis III. Individuals who are successful in achieving their change goals will show in their initial goal choice papers more indications that they expect success than will individuals who are not successful in achieving their goal.

*Psychological Safety.* The concept of psychological safety is one which many students of the behavior change process have felt to be essential for successful change (Maslow, 1954; Rogers, 1951; McClelland, 1965; Schein, 1968). Rogers gives some insights into how lack of psychological safety (threat) or its presence can effect the goal-setting process:

> Any experience which is inconsistent with the organization of the self (or structure) may be perceived as a threat, and the more of these perceptions there are, the more rigidly the self-structure is organized to maintain itself.

> Under certain conditions, involving primarily complete absence of any threat to the self-structure, experiences which are inconsistent with it may be perceived, and examined, and the structure of self revised to assimilate and include such experiences (Rogers, 1951, p. 508).

Thus if a person experiences low psychological safety he is likely to defensively distort his weaknesses and be unable to commit himself to new ideals which are different from his present self.

> Hypothesis IV. Individuals who are successful in achieving their change goals will indicate greater psychological safety during the goal-setting process than will individuals who are not successful.

*Measurability of the Change Goal.* In addition to goal-setting, previous research on self-directed change has shown that information feedback related to one's change goal is essential for achievement of that goal (Kolb, Winter, Berlew, 1968). It seems important, therefore, that a person's change goal be conceived in such a way that feedback from others and the environment could modify it, i.e., the goal should be measurable. We have already mentioned the Kay, French and Myer study which found improvements in performance only "when specific goals were established with time deadlines set and results measures agreed upon." If an individual has defined his goal in such a way that he can measure whether or not he is achieving it, then he should be more capable of identifying and using feedback.

Hypothesis V. Individuals who are successful in achieving their change goals will be more likely to give consideration to measuring progress toward their goal than those who are not successful.

*Self-controlled Evaluation.* The final hypothesis is related to one of the initial assumptions underlying the self-directed change method—that changes in behavior are most likely to be successful if the process of changing is seen by the individual to be under his own control. The previously cited Kay, French and Myer study found that if a subordinate viewed his efforts in the goal-setting process as of equal importance and efficacy as his superior's, his achievement of these goals was significantly higher than those who viewed their influence in the process as minimal or less than they deserved. We have already mentioned organizational studies which show the importance of self control in the goal-setting process.

This need for self control of the change process extends beyond initial goal-setting to a need for self control of the process of evaluating progress toward the goal. The studies by Rotter and his associates of internal versus external control of reinforcement (Lefcourt, 1966) have found distinct differences between people who see positive and negative events as being a consequence of their own actions and, therefore, under their personal control (Internality) and people who see positive and negative events as caused by external forces and beyond personal control (Externality). Rotter finds that:

The individual who has a strong belief that he can control his own destiny is likely to:

a) be more alert to those aspects of the environment which provide useful information for his future behavior

b) takes steps to improve his environmental condition

c) place greater value on skill or achievement reinforcements and be generally more concerned

d) be resistive to subtle attempts to influence him (Rotter, 1966, p. 25).

Thus from Rotter's research we would predict that individuals who see the evaluation of their progress as being self-controlled and self-reinforced will be more successful than those who see evaluation as being controlled by others.

Rogers, in his attempts to identify the characteristics of effective helping relationships, also stresses the importance of self-evaluation:

I have come to feel that the more I can keep a relationship free of judgment and evaluation, the more this will permit the other person to reach the point where he recognizes that the locus of evaluation, the center of responsibility, lies within himself. The meaning and value of his experience is in the last analysis something which is up to him and no amount of external judgment can alter this. (Rogers, 1961, p. 55).

Hypothesis VIA. Individuals who are successful in achieving their change goals will be more likely to feel that the control of reinforcement that they receive during the change process rests with themselves than those who are not successful.

Hypothesis VIB. Individuals who are successful in achieving their change goals will be less likely to feel that control of reinforcement that they receive during the change process rests with others than those who are not successful.

## Experimental Procedure

The experimental procedure used in this study is a modification of earlier applications of the self-directed change method to self-analytic groups (Kolb, Winter and Berlew, 1968; Winter, Griffith and Kolb, 1968). The setting for the experiment was a semester-long course in psychology and human organization, required of master's candidates in management at the M. I. T. Sloan School. Offered as an optional part of the course, 111 students participated in 30 hours of T-Group training usually divided into two 2-hour sessions each week. There were 8 groups of approximately 15 students each. These groups were structured slightly differently from the traditional T-Group method (see Schein and Bennis, 1965, chapter 3) in that they were focused around a task—helping one another achieve personal change goals via the self-directed change method. Students chose, at the beginning of the T-Group, individual change goals which they wanted to achieve. They picked goals like having more empathy, being a more effective leader, and talking more; and customarily they shared these goals with other group members asking them for feedback on their progress. This procedure served to define clearly the groups' task as one of helping others achieve their personal change goals.

The students were about 1/2 undergraduates and 1/2 master's candidates in management. There were two females. About 10% of the students were foreign nationals with varying degrees of fluency in the English language. Subjects varied in age from 19 to 35 with most in their early twenties.

Before the T-Groups began students were asked to write a short paper describing how they saw themselves behaving in a group situation and how they would ideally like to behave in the same situation. They were asked to fill out a 60-pair semantic differential describing their real and ideal selves. It was made clear to the students that these papers would not affect their course grade.

The students then heard a lecture on self-directed change, including a discussion of factors influencing behavior change and several case studies. After the lecture, during the first week of the T-Groups, students chose change goals relevant to their behavior in groups. Each person was asked to write a short paper describing his goal and answer certain questions regarding the goal and his commitment to it. This goal-choice paper was designed to provide data about the characteristics of the person's initial goal. Students were given the following outline to assist them in writing their papers.

The Process of Goal Choice:

    I. Self-evaluation
        1. What are your major strengths and weaknesses in a group as you see them?
        2. Are there any areas in which you really want to change?
        3. Why do you feel these changes would be desirable?
    II. Focusing on one measurable goal
        1. Describe as accurately and concretely as possible the goal you have chosen to work toward.
        2. What considerations influenced your choice of this particular goal?

3. How do you plan to measure your progress toward this goal? How will you know when you have attained it? What change will be observable to others?

III. Anticipating the change process
1. Given your choice of the above goal, what are the factors in yourself, in other people, and in the environment which will help or hinder your progress?

Included with the goal choice paper assignment was a list of the 60 adjective pairs from the real-self, ideal-self semantic differential. Students were asked to circle those adjectives pairs which "best represented the dimensions along which you plan to change." This data was used to determine those aspects of an individual's self-concept which were related to his change goal for testing Hypothesis I.

At the end of each T-Group session each member was asked to fill out a feedback form on which they recorded the feedback they received from others that day. The forms also asked for a daily rating of progress. The purpose of these feedback forms was to stimulate students' awareness of the feedback they were receiving.

The project concluded with a written report by each student on their self-directed change project. In the report they were asked to describe their change process and their success in achieving their goal. They were also asked to indicate their success in changing on a five point scale ranging from (1) "I have made no progress in achieving my goal," to (5) "I have completely achieved my goal."

In conjunction with their final report, students completed again the real-self, ideal-self semantic differential.

*Identification of High Change and Low Change Subjects.* Three measures of change were used in this study. The first is based on the discrepancy between real-self descriptions and ideal-self descriptions on the semantic differential. A before discrepancy score was obtained by subtracting the ideal score from the real score of each pair of adjectives on the forms filled out at the beginning of the experiment. An after discrepancy was obtained the same way using the forms filled out at the conclusion of the experiment. To obtain the change score for each adjective pair the magnitude of the after discrepancy was subtracted from the magnitude of the before discrepancy. Thus a positive score would indicate that a person was closer to his ideal-self after his change project than he was before.

An average *goal-related* change score was then computed for each subject by totaling the change scores for each of the adjective pairs he checked as describing his change goal and dividing by the number of adjective pairs checked. An average non-goal-related change score was computed for each subject by following the same procedure for those adjectives which he did not check. These two scores were used to test Hypothesis I.

The second change measure is based on the subjects' self evaluation of their success in achieving their change goal (the five point rating scale included in their final report). It is used in order to make results gathered here comparable with the results of previous research (Kolb, Winter and Berlew, 1968; Winter, Griffith and Kolb, 1968) which used an experimenter rating of success in goal achievement based on a reading of subjects' final reports. The subjects' rating was used because it was felt that the subject's own rating of his success might more accurately represent aspects of his own experience than the experimenter's rating. A comparison of the former experimenter ratings of the final report with the subjects' ratings show an 85% agreement between the scores.

The third measure of change is based on the group leaders' ratings of change. The group leader of each T-Group was asked to indicate each individual's change toward his goal on a five-point scale. The Kendall Tau correlation between these leader ratings and the subject's own ratings was .35 (p < .01). In addition a significant correlation (.39, p < .01) was found between the subject's rating of his success and his average goal-related change score on the semantic differential.

To form a group of clearly successful and a group of clearly unsuccessful subjects, the 51 individuals (in the self-rated change analysis) and the 35 individuals (in the case of the trainer rated change analysis) who were reported to have made moderate progress in achieving their goals were eliminated from data analysis. This left a group of low change subjects who reported "no progress" or "very slight progress" (N = 32 for self-rated change and N = 34 for trainer rated change) and a group of high change subjects who reported "almost completely achieving my goal" or "completely achieving my goal" (N = 28 for self-rated change and N = 42 for trainer rated change).

The hypotheses concerning the characteristics of the goal-setting process associated with success or failure in goal achievement were tested using both the self rated and trainer rated measures of change.

## Results

Hypothesis I was concerned with the effect of goal-setting on goal achievement. The data describing the test of this hypothesis are shown in Table 1. Individuals showed an average change of .35 on adjective dimensions related to their goal while showing an average change of .16 on non-goal related dimensions. This difference is highly significant (p < .005, 1-tail). An inspection of the adjective pairs that individuals indicated as relevant to their change goal showed that the median number of pairs indicated by an individual was 12 of the 60 adjectives. The number of adjectives indicated ranged from 1 to 46. The median number of times that any single adjective pair was checked was 22 with a range of 4 to 88. From this it can be concluded that individuals tended to use several adjective dimensions to describe their change goal and that all of the 60 adjective dimensions on the semantic differential were used.

To determine whether these differences were simply a result of the fact that subjects tended to choose easy dimensions to change on, a measure of difficulty of change was computed for each adjective dimension. This was accomplished by computing the average change score for each of the 60 adjective dimensions when this dimension was not circled as relevant to the individual's change goal. This change score became an operational definition of difficulty of change without the benefit of goal-setting. The adjectives were rank ordered according to this change score and then divided into three groups of twenty—a group of easy change adjective dimensions, a moderate group and a group of difficult change dimensions. For each group the mean change per dimension when these adjectives were not goal related was then compared to the mean change when the adjectives were described as goal related. (The reader will note that the sample size is depleted in these comparisons since in some cases, for example,

## TABLE 1
Self Concept Change in Goal-related and Non-goal-related Dimensions

| | Average Change Per Adjective Dimension | | |
| --- | --- | --- | --- |
| | Goal-related Dimensions | Non-goal-related Dimensions | Significance of Differences[1] |
| All Adjective Dimensions | .35 n = 111 | .16 n = 111 | < .005 |
| Easy Change Dimensions | .52 n = 110 | .31 n = 110 | < .03 |
| Moderate Dimensions | .19 n = 96 | .17 n = 96 | < .30 |
| Difficult Change Dimensions | .17 n = 105 | .02 n = 105 | < .035 |

[1]Wilcoxon Matched Pairs signed rank test, 1-tail

an individual might not describe any easy adjectives as related to his change goal.) The result of these comparisons show significantly more change on goal related dimensions in the easy and difficult dimensions and a similar but small and unsignificant difference in the moderate dimensions. Although the small facilitating effect of goal-setting on moderately difficult adjective dimensions is difficult to explain, the facilitating effect shown on both easy and difficult dimensions suggests that the results for all adjective dimensions were not simply a result of choosing easy adjectives.

To further test this relationship, goal related change and non-goal related change were correlated with the subject's own estimation of the difficulty of his goal which he indicated on a five-point scale at the time of his goal choice. In both cases there was no significant relationship ($r = -.04$ in both instances). An inspection of scatter plots for both correlations showed no indication of a curvilinear relationship. Thus we conclude that the effect of goal-setting or goal achievement is not due to the adjective difficulty or to self-perceived difficulty of goal achievement.

*Hypothesis II.* Awareness and Goal Achievement. The goal choice papers of high change and low change subjects were scored for the number of forces which they mentioned as affecting their change goal. The coding scheme developed by Thomas, Bennis and Fulenwider (1966) was used to score the papers for (1) the total number of forces mentioned, (2) the number of forces which facilitated progress toward the goal, (3) the number of forces which inhibited progress toward the goal, (4) the number of self-related forces, and (5) the number of other-related and environmental forces. The papers were scored on these and all other categories to be described by a scorer who was unaware of the subjects' change score. A sample of 15 papers scored by two independent coders showed a 98% agreement in scoring.

The following are examples of the different types of forces scored in the goal-choice papers. The word in parenthesis after the statement describes whether the force was self or other related.

I. Inhibiting Forces:
"I'm afraid of letting my feelings be known, I'm afraid of making mistakes in front of the group." (self)
"If the group is prepared to sit back and just listen obviously I am going to receive little stimulus to improve communication as they do not seem able to reach my level." (others)

II. Increasing Forces:
"I can accept criticism from others, so that others will accept criticism from me." (self)
"The factors that might help my progress are my innate appreciation for competition and recognition (self), as well as encouragement from the group to initiate ideas." (others)

The average total number of forces and the average number of the sub-types of forces are shown for High and Low change groups in Table 2. The data confirm the hypothesis that high change subjects show a greater initial awareness of forces relating to their change goal. Although no specific hypotheses were made about the sub-types of forces, the data is interesting but unclear. Successful changers according to the self-rated change scale see significantly more facilitating forces and other related forces while successful changers according to the trainer-rating scale see significantly more inhibiting and self-related forces.

*Hypothesis III.* Expectations of Success and Goal Achievement. All of the goal choice papers were scored for statements which indicated that the writer expected to be successful in achieving his goal. Statements like the following were scored—"I expect to achieve my goal by the end of the course." Only explicit statements of expectations of success were scored. Statements of desire for success ("I want to achieve my goal") or a conditional expectation ("If I can keep active, I expect to arrive at my goal") were not scored. Two independent scorers showed an 82% agreement on scoring expectations of success. In the self-rated change analysis, 43% of the subjects in the high change group stated in their goal choice papers that they expected success; only 9% of the low change subjects stated success expectations. This difference is highly significant (p < .001). In the trainer-rated change analysis, 26% of the subjects in the high change group stated an expectation of success and 9% of the subjects in the low change group stated an expectation of success. This difference is also statistically significant (p < .03).

*Hypothesis IV.* Psychological Safety and Goal Achievement. The goal choice papers of high and low change subjects were scored for psychological safety according to the following category definition:

*Negative Statements of Psychological Safety*
One point is given for each statement by a person of feeling threatened. This is determined by statements of feelings like shy, withdrawn, ineffective, worthless (feeling unworthy), uneasy in front of people, afraid of others, others' reactions, of himself, and feeling self-conscious. General statements of a "lack of self-confidence" were not coded. Evidence of feelings must be present.

Examples of negative statements are:
"I am afraid of not being accepted or included by them."

High and Low Change Subjects' Awareness of Forces Related to Their Change Goal

| | Self-Rated Change | | | Trainer-Rated Change | | |
|---|---|---|---|---|---|---|
| | High Change Subjects N = 28 | Low Change Subjects N = 32 | Level of Significance[1] | High Change Subjects N = 42 | Low Change Subjects N = 34 | Level of Significance[1] |
| Mean Number of Forces Mentioned | 3.69 | 2.44 | <.02 | 3.16 | 2.23 | <.04 |
| Mean Number of Facilitating Forces | 1.76 | .75 | <.001 | 1.42 | 1.29 | NS |
| Mean Number of Inhibiting Forces | 1.93 | 1.69 | NS | 1.88 | .94 | <.006 |
| Mean Number of Self-Related Forces | 2.07 | 2.03 | NS | 2.09 | 1.64 | <.05 |
| Mean Number of Other Related Forces | 1.62 | .41 | <.0001 | 1.02 | .58 | NS |

[1]Mann-Whitney U-Test, 1-tail for total number of forces
2-tail for sub-groupings

"This, coupled with my inner feelings of uneasiness in front of a group
. . ."

*Positive Statements of Psychological Safety*
One point is given for each statement by a person of feeling safe in the
environment. This is coded by statements like: feeling successful, having
good ideas, and being a good leader.

Examples of positive statements are:

"I find I have the ability to stimulate thought by bringing up cogent questions and comments."

"I see myself as perceptive of group members and motives." The total psychological safety score equals total negative statements minus total positive statements.

Two independent coders showed a high reliability (r = .89) on psychological
safety scores.

In the case of self-rated change, subjects who were successful in achieving
their goal had a mean psychological safety score of .28 while unsuccessful subjects had a mean psychological safety score of 1.31 (low scores indicate high
psychological safety). The difference between the two groups is significant at
the .05 level (1-tail) using the Mann-Whitney U-Test. In the case of trainer-
rated change, high changers showed a mean psychological safety score of .29
while low changers showed a mean score of 1.23 (again, a low score indicates
high psychological safety). Although the difference is not significant using a
Mann-Whitney U-Test (p = .10, 1-tail), the trend is in the same direction as
that found using the self-rated measure of change tending to substantiate the
hypothesis. We can thus conclude that subjects who were successful in changing were more psychologically safe during the initial goal-setting process than
subjects who were not successful.

*Hypothesis V.* Measurement and Goal Achievement. Although students
were instructed to give consideration in their goal choice papers to how progress
toward their goal might be measured, some did so and others did not. The
following is an example of a subject who stated a method for measuring his
progress:

> I intend to measure my success by two methods: (1) by an intuitive
> feeling of how much I have contributed to the group activity during
> a session, and (2) by actually measuring the number of times that I
> verbally participate during a group meeting.

The number of high change subjects and low change subjects who mentioned a measurement method were compared. While only 34% of the low
change subjects mentioned a method for measuring progress, 79% of the high
change subjects mentioned a measurement method in the self-rated change
analysis. This difference is highly significant (p < .001). In the case of trainer-
rated change, 61% of the high change subjects mentioned a method of measuring
progress toward their goal, while 41% of the low change subjects mentioned a
method of measurement. This difference is also significant (p < .04).

*Hypothesis VIA and VIB.* Self Evaluation, Other Evaluation and Goal
Achievement. The goal choice papers of high and low change subjects were
coded for indications of self evaluation of progress toward their goal and for

indications of group evaluation of progress. Examples of self evaluation methods are, "I will record the number of times I speak up in the group on a graph and evaluate my progress after each session," "I will observe how uneasy I feel each time I speak and will know I am progressing toward my goal when I start to feel comfortable." Examples of group evaluation methods are, "The group will tell me how at ease I look each time I speak, and whether or not I appear to be improving," "The others in the group will tell me whether or not my statements are coherent and relevant to the subject being discussed."

Two independent scorers showed a 90% agreement on both group and self-evaluation categories. To test hypothesis VIA the percent of subjects in the high and low change groups who showed self-evaluation methods were compared. In the self-rated change analysis, 64% of the high change subjects indicated a self-evaluation method while only 32% of the low change subjects indicated a self-evaluation method ($p < .006$, 1-tail). In the trainer-rated analysis, 57% of the high changers indicated a self-evaluation method while 35% of the low changers indicated a self-evaluation method ($p < .02$, 1-tail). Hypothesis VIB was tested by comparing the percent of subjects in the high and low change groups who indicated group-evaluation methods. In the case of self-rated change, 28% of the low change subjects indicated a group evaluation method while 32% of the high change subjects indicated a group evaluation method. In the case of trainer-rated change, 20% of the low changers indicated a group evaluation while 21% of the high changers indicated a group evaluation. Neither of these differences were in the direction predicted or were statistically significant. Thus it appears that self-controlled evaluation facilitates goal achievement while group-controlled evaluation is unrelated to goal achievement.

## Conclusions and Implications

The experiment presents convincing evidence that conscious goal-setting plays an important role in the process of self-directed behavior change. Individuals tend to change more in those areas of their self-concept which are related to their consciously set change goals. These changes are independent of the difficulty of the change goal and thus do not appear to be a result of an initial choice of easy to achieve goals. The results would suggest a modification of those Freudian and learning theory based approaches to behavior change that treat consciousness as an epiphenomenon by placing heavy emphasis on unconscious forces and behavioral conditioning. While this experiment, since it does not involve an experimental manipulation of goal setting, does not conclusively prove that conscious goal-setting caused the subsequent changes in self-concept, taken with other experimental studies cited in this paper it does strongly suggest that conscious goal-setting facilitates goal achievement.

The analysis of the initial goal descriptions of subjects who were subsequently successful and unsuccessful in achieving their goals provides evidence for those specific characteristics of the goal setting process which are crucial for goal achievement. Awareness of forces related to the change goal, high expectations of success, high psychological safety, a concern for measuring progress, and an emphasis on self-controlled evaluation all appear to be precursors of successful goal achievement.

While the data in this experiment are not sufficiently quantified to allow tests of the interrelationships among the variables identified as important characteristics of the goal-setting process, the results suggest some tentative outlines for a cybernetic model of behavior change. Nearly every student of personality and behavior change has recognized that human personality is a dynamic feedback system with self-sustaining and self-reinforcing qualities. Sullivan, for example, sees this aspect of personality (which he calls the self system) to be the major stumbling block to constructive personality change. Hall and Lindsey (1957) describe his concept of the self system this way:

> The self system as the guardian of one's security tends to become isolated from the rest of the personality; it excludes information that is incongruous with its present organization and fails thereby to profit from experience. Since the self guards the person from anxiety, it is held in high esteem and protected from criticism. As the self system grows in complexity and independence it prevents the person from making objective judgments of his own behavior and it glosses over obvious contradictions between what the person really is and what his self system says he is (p. 139).

Since individuals tend to act in accord with their self system, threats to the self system will cause a person's activities to become more and more inappropriate and rigid leading to further failure and insecurity which in turn leads to further distortions in the self system and so on. The characteristics of the goal-setting process which we have found to be associated with successful self-directed change give some clues about the nature of the intervening variables in this process. Figure 1 shows how the goal-setting characteristics fit into a cybernetic model of the change process. Interrelationships among the variables are simplified to illustrate the dominant feedback loop. For purpose of illustration, let us describe the interaction of these characteristics in an unsuccessful change process beginning with low psychological safety. Low psychological safety can lead to decreased awareness. This decrease in awareness would in turn lead to a decreased sense of self-control which would lead to fewer expectations of success. Low expectations of success would produce few attempts to achieve the goal which would in turn produce fewer opportunities for feedback from the environment. All this would tend to produce failure in achieving the goal. The failure feelings thus aroused would tend to further decrease psychological safety producing an amplification of this positive feedback loop.

### Implications for Helping Interventions

This cybernetic model of the behavior change process suggests several intervention strategies that may serve to create more effective helping relationships with individuals who are seeking change. Since feedback loops are composed of elements which need not have a prior or an hierarchical causal order, helping interventions can be directed to the point or points in the feedback loop where they will be most effective in producing change. As Phillips and Wiener put it:

> Within the cybernetic framework, although not unique to it, variables are selected and regulated in the feedback chain which are most amenable to manipulation and control. In structured therapy, elusive causes are not sought that might operate to produce a disordered system: the therapist goes directly to the element (information) in the feedback loop that has a meaningful coefficient of efficiency in maintaining the loop, and he proceeds immediately to try to insert the change (1966, p. 96).

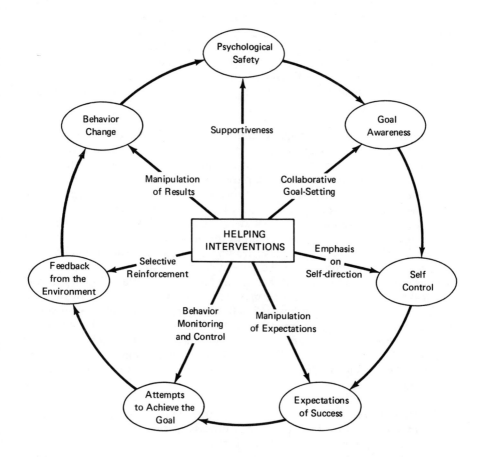

Figure 1
A Simple Cybernetic Model of Behavior Change and Helping Interventions

Thus, cybernetic models of the change process hold forth the promise of an eclectic approach to the choice of helping strategies based on research which identifies those elements in the feedback loop which have the highest "coefficient of efficiency."

The simplified model of change shown in Figure 1 suggests seven types of intervention which may prove effective in breaking into the self-defeating cycle of failure.

*1. Supportiveness.* Rogerian theory has been based primarily on the supportive strategy of increasing the clients' security and self-confidence through the therapists' unconditional positive regard, accurate empathy, and genuineness (Rogers, 1961). Truax and his associates (Truax and Carkhuff, 1964) have shown that these three therapist characteristics are related to constructive personality change in both Rogerian and other forms of therapy. In addition they find that the presence of these variables in the therapist are positively related to intrapersonal exploration on the part of the patient. These results suggest that supportive interventions aimed at increasing psychological safety have a relatively higher coefficient of efficiency in that they produce positive change and gains in another element in the feedback loop—awareness (intrapersonal exploration).

*2. Collaborative goal-setting.* Attempts to increase awareness of personal improvement goals through an explicit process of collaborative goal setting have not often been a part of behavior change programs. However, the use of this strategy in achievement motivation training programs and in organizational settings as well as in research on self-directed behavior change suggests that goal-setting procedures may indeed be a highly effective intervention method. In fact, a careful examination of behavior therapy method of change suggests that in addition to applying, for example, the principles of reciprocal inhibition (Wolpe, 1958) the therapist is also leading the patient through a process of explicit goal setting. By asking the patient to define and rank order the fear evoking situations in his life and then telling him to try to relax while visualizing the weakest fear situation until he masters it and then proceeding to the next weakest and so on, the therapist is in effect helping the patient to set realistic goals and work to achieve them in a way that is quite similar to the self-directed change method. At this point no research evidence exists which can tell us whether it is the process of reciprocal inhibition or collaborative goal-setting which is the change producing intervention. Similar questions can be raised about other behavior therapy methods.

*3. Emphasis on self-direction.* While few therapeutic systems place a heavy emphasis on self control of the change process in their methodology, it is a common assumption that true psychotherapeutic change does not occur until the patient works through his dependence upon the therapist and achieves self-direction. The literature on cognitive dissonance gives experimental evidence for the importance of self-direction in attitude change. These experiments show that attitude change is greatest and most enduring when the person feels that he has freely chosen to alter his point of view (Secord and Backman, 1964). Recognizing the importance of self-direction in personality change, self-help societies like Alcoholics Anonymous and Synanon (for narcotics addicts) have made the principles of personal responsibility and voluntary commitment to change a central part of their ideology. DeCharms (1968) has formulated a concept of self-direction which he calls the origin-pawn variable. In a recent program of research he has been successful in increasing academic performance by training ghetto children to be origins rather than pawns.

*4. Manipulation of expectations.* Research evidence on the impact of an individual's expectations on his own chances for successful change has already been presented. As yet few direct attempts have been made to directly increase individuals' expectations of success. A significant exception is the previously cited work on achievement motivation training. That manipulation of expectations can produce behavior change is shown by a well-executed study by

Rosenthal and Jacobson (1968). They found that intellectual gains could be produced in children by nothing more than giving names of children who had been selected at random to their new teachers at the beginning of the school year and describing them to these teachers as children who could be expected to show unusual gains in intelligence during the year. This research suggests that helping interventions that increase expectations of success may be a very effective method of breaking the cycle of failure.

*5. Behavior monitoring and control.* Behavior therapy attempts to elicit behaviors consistent with constructive personality change goals are of two types—stimulus control and modeling (Schwitzgebel and Kolb, 1973). In stimulus control methods environmental conditions which serve as either discriminating or eliciting stimuli for desired behavioral responses are used to increase the probability of a desired response, or decrease a response to be avoided. A simple example would be the case of the student who moves his study area away from his bed in order to keep from falling asleep. Modeling can be defined as "the systematic provision of opportunities for observing the behavior of others, wherein the cues to behavior came from the behavior of others. In short, this is vicarious learning" (Brayfield, 1968, p. 480). A number of studies, most notably by Bandura and Walters (1963), have shown that the observation of a given behavior in a model increases the occurence of that behavior.

In self-directed behavior change projects another method has been successfully used to elicit goal directed behavior—behavior monitoring. By keeping continuous records of progress toward their goal, subjects are constantly reminded of the goal they are trying to achieve, thus producing more attempts to achieve that goal (Zach, 1965; Goldiamond, 1965; Schwitzgebel, 1964). The fact that high change subjects in the research presented in this paper gave more attention than low change subjects to how their progress could be measured provides additional evidence for the efficiency of behavior-monitoring procedures.

*6. Selective reinforcement.* Perhaps the best documented strategy for producing change is the manipulation of environmental feedback through the use of selective reinforcement. The methods of operant shaping and intermittent positive reinforcement have been used to alter such insignificant behaviors as use of pronouns and such major behavioral patterns as delinquent behavior and schizophrenic symptoms (Schwitzgebel and Kolb, 1973). Research on self-directed change suggests that in certain circumstances the total amount of information feedback may also be related to change (Kolb, Winter and Berlew, 1968).

*7. Manipulation of results.* A final intervention method which deserves consideration is the manipulation of results of change. While this method has not been used systematically as a therapeutic intervention, it is a common device in experimental research. For example, the literature on level of aspiration is replete with examples of artificial manipulation of performance results, which show measurable changes in future goal-setting and performance. While there are obvious problems of credibility for the change agent with such artificial distortions of reality this method might prove to be a promising helping strategy.

It can be seen from the above discussion that the elements of the goal-setting process that are crucial for successful goal achievement as well as feedback from the environment and the final change score itself may all be changed by helping interventions. The task for future research is to determine how effective these interventions, taken singly or in combination, can be in changing the cycle of insecurity and failure to one of psychological safety and success. The most effective intervention strategy may well prove to be the information feedback procedures of behavior therapy approaches in combination with the goal-setting procedures of self-directed change.

## References

Allport, G. W. *Personality and social encounter.* Boston: Beacon Press, 1960.

Aronoff, J., Litwin, G. Achievement motivation training and executive advancement, *Journal of Applied Behavioral Science,* 1971, Vol. 7, 215-229.

Atkinson, J. W. (Ed.) *Motives in fantasy, action and society.* New Jersey: Van Nostrand, 1958.

Bandura, A. and Walters, R. H. *Social learning and personality development.* New York: Holt, Rinehart and Winston, 1963.

Brayfield, A. Human resources development, *American Psychologist,* 1968, Vol. 23, 479-482.

DeCharms, R. *Personal causation.* New York: Academic Press, 1968.

Drucker, P. F. *The practice of management.* New York: Harper Brothers, 1954.

Festinger, L. A theoretical interpretation of shifts in level of aspiration, *Psychological Review,* 1942, Vol. 49, 235-250.

Frank, J. D. Recent studies of the level of aspiration, *Psychological Bulletin,* 1941, Vol. 38, 218-226.

Frank, J. D. *Persuasion and healing.* New York: Schoeken Books, 1963.

Gendlin, E., Beebe, J. III, Cassens, J., Klein, M., and Gaerlander, M. Focusing ability in psychotherapy, personality and creativity, in, *Research in psychotherapy: Vol. III,* American Psychological Association, 1968.

Goldiamond, I. Self-control procedures in personal behavior problems, *Psychological Reports,* 1965, Vol. 17, 851-868.

Goldstein, A. *Therapist-patient expectancies in psychotherapy.* New York: Pergamon Press, 1962.

Hartman, H. E. and Loewenstein, R. M. Comments on the formation of psychic structure, in, *The psychoanalytic study of the child.* New York: International University Press, Vol. 2, 1947.

Hall, C. S., Lindzey, G. *Theories of personality.* New York: Wiley and Sons, 1957.

Kausler, D. H. Aspiration level as a determinant of performance, *Journal of Personality,* 1959, Vol. 27, 346-351.

Kay, E. French and Meyer, H. *A study of the performance appraisal interview,* Management Development and Employee Relations Services, General Electric, New York, 1962.

Kolb, D. A. Achievement motivation training for under-achieving high school boys, *Journal of Personality and Social Psychology,* 1965, Vol. 2, 783-792.

Kolb, D. A., Winter, S., and Berlew, D. Self-directed change: Two studies, *Journal of Applied Behavioral Science,* 1968, Vol. 4, 453-473.

Lefcourt, H. M. Internal versus external control of reinforcement, *Psychological Bulletin,* 1966, Vol. 65, 206-220.

Lewis, K., Dembo, T., Festinger, L., Sears, P. S. Level of aspiration, in, *Personality and behavior disorders*. New York: Ronald Press, 1944.

Likert, R. *The human organization*. New York: McGraw-Hill, 1967.

Lorenz, K. *On aggression*. New York: Harcourt, Brace and World, 1963.

Maslow, A. *Motivation and personality*. New York: Harper Brothers, 1954.

McClelland, D. C. *The achieving society*. New York: Van Nostrand, 1961.

McClelland, D. C. Toward a theory of motive acquisition, *American Psychologist*, 1965, Vol. 20, 321–333.

McGregor, D. *The human side of enterprise*. New York: McGraw-Hill, 1960.

Milgram, S. Behavioral study of obedience, In, *Interpersonal dynamics*. Homewood, Illinois: Dorsey Press, 1968.

Orne, M. On the social psychology of the psychological experiment: With particular reference to demand characteristics and their implications, *American Psychologist*, 1962, Vol. 17, 776–783.

Phillips, E. L. and Wiener, D. *Short-term psychotherapy and structured behavior change*. New York: McGraw-Hill, 1966.

Rao, K. U. The effect of interference with certain aspects of goal-setting on level of aspiration behavior, *Psychological Studies*, 1959, Vol. 1, 1–10.

Rogers, C. R. *Client centered therapy*. Boston: Houghton-Mifflin, 1951.

Rogers, C. R. *On becoming a person*. Boston: Houghton-Mifflin, 1961.

Rosenthal. R. On the social psychology of the psychological experiment: The experimenter's hypothesis as unintended determinant of experimental results, *American Scientist*, 1963, Vol. 51, 268–283.

Rosenthal, R. and Jacobson, L. Teacher expectations for the disadvantaged, *Scientific American*, 1968, Vol 218, 19–23.

Rotter, J. B. Generalized expectancies for internal versus external control of reinforcement, *Psychological Monographs*, 1966, Vol. 80.

Schein, E. H. Personal change through interpersonal relationships, *Interpersonal dynamics*. Homewood, Illinois: Dorsey Press, 1968.

Schein, E. H. and Bennis, W. G. *Personal and organizational change through group methods*. New York: Wiley and Sons, 1965.

Schwitzgebel. R. A simple behavioral system for recording and implementing change in natural settings. Unpublished doctoral dissertation, Harvard School of Education, 1964.

Schwitzgebel, R. and Kolb, D. A. *Changing human behavior: Principles of planned intervention*. New York: McGraw-Hill, 1973.

Secord, P. F. and Backman, C. W. *Social psychology*. New York: McGraw-Hill, 1964.

Thomas, J., Bennis, W., and Fulenwider, M. Problem analysis diagram. Unpublished manuscript, Sloan School of Management, M.I.T., 1966.

Truax, C. and Carkhoff, R. For better or for worse: The process of psychotherapeutic personality change, in, *Recent advances in the study of behavior change*. Montreal: McGill University Press, 1964.

White, R. W. Motivation reconsidered: The concept of competence, *Psychological Review*, 1959, Vol 66, 297–333.

Wolpe, J. *Psychotherapy by reciprocal inhibition*. Stanford: Stanford University Press, 1958.

Zachs, J. Collaborative therapy for smokers. Unpublished manuscript, Harvard University, 1965.

# Helping
# and Consulting


## ON THE DYNAMICS OF
## THE HELPING RELATIONSHIP

DAVID A. KOLB
RICHARD E. BOYATZIS

Most of us as teachers, managers, parents, or friends find ourselves increasingly involved in giving and receiving help. This process of sharing wealth, knowledge, or skill with one who happens to have less of these valuable commodities is far from being a simple exchange, easily accomplished. Rather, we find that the way to an effective helping relationship is fraught with many psychological difficulties that can either sidetrack or destroy the relationship. Carl Rogers, in his classic article, "The Characteristics of a Helping Relationship" defines a helping relationship as one "in which at least one of the parties has the intent of promoting the growth, development, maturity, improved functioning, improved coping with life of the other" (Rogers, 1961, pp. 39–40). This definition would include parent and child, teacher and students, manager and subordinates, therapist and patient, consultant and client, and many other less formally defined relationships.

The purpose of this paper and the program of research of which it is a part is to understand more fully the dynamics of helping relationships in order to discover how these relationships may be made more effective. The first part of the paper describes the model that has guided our investigations and the second part reports an experiment which tests some of the propositions implied by the model.

The model of the helping relationship at this point is unfortunately not a precise set of mathematical interrelationships among operationally defined variables, but rather is a preliminary attempt to translate case observations and

This research was supported in part by the Sloan Research Fund of M. I. T. The work was done in part at the M. I. T. Computation Center. The authors wish to express their gratitude to the students who through their efforts made this research possible and to Robert Euritt, George Farris, Michael Fulenwider, William McKelvey, Irwin Rubin, Suresh Srivastva, and Sara Winter who served as T-Group trainers.

empirical findings from studies of helping relationships in education, welfare, assistance and therapy programs into a single theoretical framework which will eventually allow operational definitions of variables and tests of interrelationship. The model itself, depicted in Figure 1, emphasizes five key elements in the helping relationship: 1) the task or problem around which the helping relationship develops, 2) the helper with his motives (achievement motivation, power motivation, and affiliation motivation) and his self-image, 3) the receiver of help and his motives and self-image, 4) the environment and psychological climate in which the helping activities occur, and 5) the information feedback which occurs during the helping process.

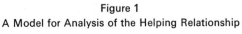

Figure 1
A Model for Analysis of the Helping Relationship

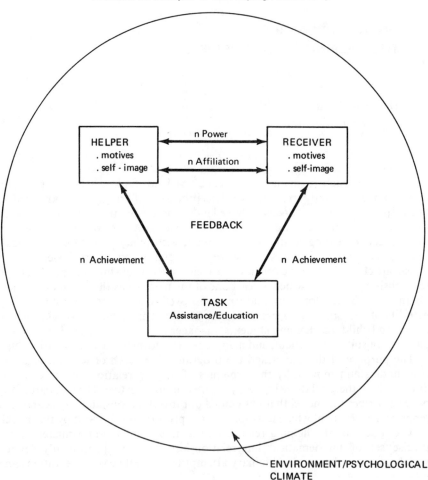

### The Task

The tasks around which helping relationships develop are widely varied—they range from tying a shoe to changing attitudes about birth control to improving the effectiveness of an organization. It is possible to classify all tasks on a single dimension, namely, the extent to which it is required that the receiver of help be capable of accomplishing the task independently when the helper is no longer present. At one end of this dimension are tasks defined as assistance; situations where there is no emphasis on the client's independent task performance. Giving a vagrant a dime for a cup of coffee is a good example of this end of the continuum. Many welfare and foreign aid programs are close to this end of the dimension. The emphasis is on the solution of an immediate problem with no provision for handling recurrences of that problem or similar problems. This type of assistance aimed only at symptom relief is likely to induce a dependency on the helper, making termination of the relationship difficult. When the relationship has been concluded, the client may blame the helper for inadequate help if he cannot replicate a successful result.

The other end of the continuum is education. Here the emphasis is on increasing the client's ecological wisdom, i.e., on developing the client's ability to solve problems like his present problem when they occur by using the resources of his natural environment. The helper avoids using the special knowledge, skills, or other resources he may command to relieve the client's immediate need, but instead works with the client, in the client's frame of reference, to increase his problem solving ability. The "felt needs" approach to community development is perhaps the purest example of an educational helping relationship.

While the educational approach in most cases holds the greatest potential for the client's long-term benefit, it can cause great frustration to a client with strong needs for symptom relief. In addition the educational approach will in some cases be seen by the client as an intrusion on his privacy and an escalation of his problem. India, for example, was quite willing to receive assistance in the form of surplus food, but grew resentful at U. S. insistence that such assistance be coupled with an educational program to solve their basic problems of food production.

### The Helper and Receiver of Help

The personal characteristics of the helper and receiver of help are major factors influencing the process and outcome of the helping relationship. Two types of characteristics are particularly important—the motives and self-image of helper and client. At least three motives seem necessary to understand the dynamics of the helping relationship—power motivation ($n$ Power), affiliation motivation ($n$ Affiliation), and achievement motivation ($n$ Achievement.) These motives are important because they determine how the helper and client will orient themselves to one another and to their task.

The helper and the client's power motivation determines how much they will be concerned about influencing and controlling one another. By asking for and/or receiving help offered, the client places himself in a dependent position, where he often feels weaker than and vulnerable to the source of help. The helper at the same time must deal with tendencies to feel superior thereby letting the satisfactions of power and control overshadow the sometimes elusive goal of acting in the client's best interest. If the helper and client are unable to resolve power struggles and bring about a situation of power equalization, the relationship can degenerate into rebellion or passivity by the client or rejection by the helper ("He doesn't appreciate what I am trying to do for him"). One empirical example of the detrimental effects of a helper's over-concern with power can be seen in Prakash's (1968) study of effective and ineffective organization change agents. He found that ineffective change agents were more concerned with their own personal goals and with their political position within the organization than were the effective change agents who were more concerned about task accomplishment.

The helper's and receiver's affiliation motivation determines how much they will be concerned about intimacy and understanding. To be helpful, the helper must know his client and understand how he perceives his problem. The intimacy required for effective understanding is hard to come by in situations where the helper has impossible demands on his time, and yet a lack of intimacy can leave the helper and client in two different worlds speaking two different languages. Too great a concern about affiliation by the helper and his client, on the other hand, can produce pressure toward conformity and mutual sympathy which may cause the helper to lose his perspective on the client's problem and the client to lose his respect for the helper's expertise.

The achievement motivation of the helper and receiver of help determines how concerned they will be about accomplishing their task or solving their problem. A major question here is—How is the goal of the helping relationship defined? Does the helper decide "what's good for" the client or does the client retain the power to decide what help he wants? In the first case the client is likely to have little motivation to accomplish the helper's task and in the second the helper's motivation is likely to be reduced. Only when the interpersonal issues of influence and intimacy have been resolved does it appear possible that the helper and client can agree on a goal to which they are mutually committed. Even if this is accomplished there is still a problem of what are often strong desires to achieve the goal of the helping relationship. Help is often so late in coming that both helper and client feel strong needs to accomplish *something*. The result is usually assistance programs designed to eliminate the client's immediate desperation rather than programs of education designed to help the client diagnose the causes of the problem and learn to solve the problem himself.

There is an interaction among motives in any helping relationship. It is possible for the helper and client to be so highly power motivated that they become preoccupied with controlling one another at the expense of understanding one another and/or accomplishing their task. Similarly, as we have suggested, high achievement motivation can cause the helper and receiver to orient themselves to accomplishing the task without attending to the interpersonal processes of influence and understanding necessary for having the receiver of help learn to solve the problem on his own. In a case like this, the offer of "Here, let me help you," by the helper is often his cue to push the client aside and do the task himself leaving the client nearly as ignorant about how to solve the problem as before. And finally, high affiliation motivation can lead to concerns about intimacy and understanding that preclude attempts to influence others and to accomplish tasks.

The implication of this analysis for helping relationships is that moderate levels of achievement, affiliation and power motivation in the helper and client are optimal for effective help to take place. The dynamics of the helping relationship are such that influence, intimacy and understanding, and a concern for task accomplishment are all necessary for effective help to take place; yet excess concern in any one area can lead to the deterioration of an effective helping relationship.

The self-image and attitudes of the helper and client are also important defining variables in a helping relationship. The client must see himself as capable of improvement and willing to receive help. If this is not so, a major portion of helping activity must center on building self-confidence and optimism before learning can take place. The helper on the other hand must see himself as capable of helping and yet at the same time must not feel himself to be the "know-it-all" expert who has never experienced his own ignorance. This latter point is related to the issues of influence and intimacy discussed earlier. The helper must be willing to influence and at the same time have empathy with the feelings of the person he is helping.

### The Environment and Psychological Climate

It is a truism in contemporary social psychology that behavior is a function of both the person and the environment. While one could imagine many environmental variables which could influence the process of helping such as comfort of surroundings, freedom from distraction, etc., we have limited ourselves for the present time to a consideration of those environmental factors which are related to influence, intimacy and understanding, and task accomplishment. Atkinson (1964) and Feather (1966) and Litwin (1961) have argued that the tendency (T) to act in these three ways can be predicted by the strength of the individual's motivation (M) power, affiliation, and achievement; times the individual's perceived probability (P) that action in terms of one or more of these motives will be rewarded; times the amount (I) of power, affiliation, and achievement rewards he expects to get. Thus, the individual acts to maximize his satisfaction following the formula $T = M \times P \times I$ for three motives: power, affiliation, and achievement. While M refers to the individual's motivation; P and I refer to the individual's perception of the environment.

This analysis has important implications for predictions about effective helping, for if the environment tends to reward one motive disproportionately it can alter the behavior of an otherwise moderately motivated helper and client. One example of this occurs in the Peace Corps where volunteers who might otherwise establish very effective relationships with host country nationals become bogged down in issues of power and control because the host country people (and sometimes the volunteer himself) perceive the Peace Corps to be a political agent of U. S. foreign policy.

### Feedback

The last element of the model is the information feedback which occurs during the helping process. Two aspects of information feedback are important here. First, there is the source which controls information. Feedback can be controlled by the task as in the case of programmed instruction, or by the receiver of help as in self-research methods (Kolb, Winter, and Berlew, 1968; Schwitzgebel, 1964) or by the helper as in traditional teaching methods.

The second aspect of information feedback is the characteristics of the information itself, whether it is accurate or distorted, intense or mild, positive or negative, and so on. This second aspect of feedback has been the subject of a great deal of theoretical speculation, especially among students of sensitivity training. For example, Schein and Bennis (1965) suggest the following criteria for valid, helpful feedback:

1. The feedback should be based on publicly observed behavior in the T-Group,
2. it should be contiguous in time to the experience it refers to, and
3. it should be modified through all the data sources (i.e., group members) available.

A major question about the characteristics of helpful feedback concerns whether this feedback should be positive (pleasant for the client to hear) or negative (unpleasant). While there are those who feel that negative feedback is sometimes helpful in that it serves to "unfreeze" the client's self-satisfied concept of himself and increase his motivation to change (*cf.* Bennis, Schein, Berlew, and Steele, 1965), most learning theorists have concluded that in the long run reward is more effective than punishment. One example of reward centered feedback is found in the programmed instruction technique of "error free learning." Rogers, too, places heavy emphasis on the importance of positive feedback to the client in his concept of unconditional positive regard. "I find that the more acceptance and liking I feel toward this individual, the more I will be creating a relationship which he can use. By acceptance I mean a warm regard for him as a person of unconditional self-worth—of value no matter what his condition, or his feelings... This acceptance of each fluctuating aspect of this other person makes it for him a relationship of warmth and safety, and the safety of being liked and prized as a person seems a highly important element in a helping relationship (Rogers, 1961, p. 34)." To support his conclusion Rogers cites psychotherapy research by Halkides (1958) which showed that therapists who demonstrated a high degree of unconditional positive regard for their clients were more successful than those who did not.

### An Experimental Study of Effective Helpers, Ineffective Helpers and Non-Helpers

To test some of the hypotheses implied in the model presented above we designed an experiment to study helping as it took place in self-analytic groups (T-Groups, see Schein and Bennis, 1965, for full description). We decided in this study to focus on the characteristics of effective helpers, leaving aside for the time-being questions about the characteristics of effective receivers of help. More specifically we were interested in studying the motives and self-image of helpers and describing the kind of feedback they gave to those they were trying to help.

The first step was to define what constituted help in a T-Group situation. *We defined an effective helper as one who in an environment where giving help is seen as appropriate (the T-Group), attempts to help others while the others see this help as significant and important to them.* This definition implies two comparison groups—ineffective helpers who attempt to give others help but these others do not regard the help as important, and non-helpers who do not attempt to help. While this definition of help has some problems in that it is based on the receiver's subjective judgment of how important the information given by the helper was; it nonetheless seems an important aspect of any helping process. If the client does not regard the information that he receives from his helper to be significant it seems unlikely that he will use this information to modify his behavior. Thus this definition of help can be seen as necessary but possibly not a sufficient aspect of the helping process. What we learn about giving help here can be considered necessary for effective help in situations where the relationship is based on information exchange, but other factors may be important in relationships were the client is required to act on the basis of information he has received from the helper.

### Hypotheses

The following hypotheses were made about differences among effective helpers, ineffective helpers, and non-helpers:

Hypothesis IA: Effective helpers will have moderate scores on power affiliation and achievement motivation.

Hypothesis IB: Ineffective helpers will have high scores on power and achievement motivation and low scores on affiliation motivation.

Hypothesis IC: Non-helpers will have high scores on affiliation motivation and low scores on power and achievement motivation.

Hypothesis IA is an application of the model of the helping relationship to this experimental situation. Hypothesis IB is based on the notion that what ineffective helpers had to say was not regarded as significant because receivers of help felt that the helper was trying to control them (high power motivation) and that he did not understand them (low affiliation motivation). We also predicted that the ineffective helpers would be less effective because they were over-concerned with the group's task accomplishment (high achievement motivation). We predicted in hypothesis IC that non-helpers would not try to influence others (low power motivation) or try to accomplish the group's task of helping others (low achievement motivation), but would be highly concerned about understanding and empathy with other group members (high affiliation motivation).

Hypothesis II: There will be significant differences in self-image among effective helpers, ineffective helpers, and non-helpers.

Since so little is known about the relationship between self-image and the process of giving help, no specific hypotheses were made here.

Hypothesis IIIA: Receivers of help will perceive more positive feedback from effective helpers and more negative feedback from ineffective helpers.

Hypothesis IIIB: Receivers of help will perceive more affection related feedback from effective helpers and more control related feedback from ineffective helpers.

Due to limitations of the experimental design which will be described next in the procedure section, it was only possible to test differences between the types of feedback given by effective and ineffective helpers since non-helpers gave very few feedbacks that were recorded by the receivers of help. In addition, since the type of feedback was described by the receivers of help rather than independent observers, differences between feedback received from effective and ineffective helpers may be due to: 1) the type of feedback the helper gave, 2) the type of feedback the receiver heard, or 3) some combination of 1 and 2. Thus, any results concerning Hypotheses IIIA and IIIB must be cautiously interpreted with this in mind.

Hypothesis IIIA is based on our earlier reasoning that positive feedback is generally more helpful than negative feedback. Hypothesis IIIB is based on the differential motive patterns that we predicted for helpers and ineffective helpers, i.e., ineffective helpers will be higher in need for power and lower in the need for affiliation than effective helpers. Thus they will give more feedback related to control (power) and less feedback related to affection (affiliation). (No data was collected about feedback related to task accomplishment.)

**Procedure**

The setting for the experiment was a semester long course in psychology and human organization, required of master's candidates in management at the M. I. T. Sloan School. As part of the course 111 students participated in 30 hours of T-Group training usually divided into two two-hour sessions each week. There were 8 groups of approximately 15 students each. These groups were structured differently from the traditional T-Group method (see Schein and Bennis, 1965, chapter 3) in that they were focused around a task—helping one another achieve personal change goals. The method used was the self-directed change method developed by Kolb, Winter and Berlew (1968). With this approach students chose, at the beginning of the T-Group, individual change goals which they wanted to achieve. They picked goals like having more empathy, being a more effective leader, and talking more; and customarily they shared these goals with other group members asking them for feedback on their progress. This procedure served to define clearly the group's task as one of helping others achieve their goals.

The students were about 1/2 undergraduates and 1/2 master's candidates in management. There were two females. About 10% of the students were foreign nationals with varying degrees of fluency in the English language. Subjects ranged in age from 19 to 35 with most in their early twenties.

Data Collection

At the beginning of the course students filled out a 60 item semantic differential to describe their self-image and took the standard six-picture Thematic Apperception Test (TAT) described by Atkinson (1958). This test was scored for $n$ Achievement, $n$ Power, and $n$ Affiliation by expert scorers who had demonstrated their scoring reliability according to the procedures specified by Atkinson (1958). The $n$ Power scores were obtained by using Winter's (1967) improved and modified version of Veroff's (Atkinson, 1968) power motivation scoring system. The expert scorer demonstrated scoring reliability using practice stories by Winter.

Data feedback on helping was gathered from group members themselves at the end of each session. Each individual at the end of each session filled out the form shown in Figure 2. This form asked group members to indicate to whom they had given feedback and from whom they had received feedback during the session. In addition it asked them to describe up to three pieces of feedback which had been most significant to them and to indicate from which group member it had come. The definitions of the feedback description categories are described below as they were given to the group members. The descriptive categories were chosen to represent a wide variety of theoretical notions about what constitutes help and non-helpful feedback.

# Description of Feedback Dimensions

| Category of Dimension | Explanation or Description |
|---|---|
| LIKE-DISLIKE NEUTRAL | Do you like the *person* who gave you this feedback? Do you dislike him? Are you neutral towards him? Rate on scale −2 to +2. |
| VERBAL- NON-VERBAL | Was this feedback *spoken* to you (VERBAL), or was it communicated through gestures, facial expressions, nods, etc. (NON-VERBAL)? Check one or the other. |
| STRONG- WEAK | This dimension refers to the intensity of the feedback. Was it emphatic and vigorous, or was it expressed mildly? Check one or the other. |
| HERE-AND-NOW | This dimension refers to the content of the feedback. Did it refer to events or behavior taking place now or recently in the group (HERE-AND-NOW), or did it refer to things in the past not shared by other group members (THERE-AND-THEN)? Check one or the other. |
| POSITIVE- NEGATIVE | Did the feedback agree with you or encourage you? Did you like to hear it (POSITIVE)? Or did it disagree with you, discourage you? Was it "painful" to hear (NEGATIVE)? Check one or the other. |
| SUPPORTED | This dimension refers to the reaction of other group members to the feedback. Did they corroborate, agree with or support it, or did they disagree or remain silent about it (NON-SUPPORTED)? Check one or the other. |
| OWNED- NOT-OWNED | This dimension refers to the person giving you the feedback. Did he attach himself personally to the feedback; did he make it clear that it was his own opinion or feeling (OWNED)? Or was it not clear that the feedback represented the giver's own opinion (NOT-OWNED)? *Examples:* Owned—"I think you talk too much." (or) "Nobody in this group listens to me." Not-owned—"Does the group feel that John talks too much?: (or) "Isn't this group supposed to listen to people?" Check one or the other. Hint—not-owned feedback is often in question form. |
| DIRECTED- NON-DIRECTED | This dimension refers to *you* as the receiver of feedback. Was the feedback directed or applied to you personally; did it have your "name" on it (DIRECTED)? Or did you have to make the application to yourself from a general statement (NON-DIRECTED)? *Examples:* Directed—"John Smith is not sensitive to my feelings " Non-directed—"Some people in this group are not sensitive to my feelings." Check one or the other. |
| EVALUATIVE- NON-EVALUATIVE | This dimension applies to the pressure of an implicit or explicit value judgment *in* the feedback. *Example:* Evaluative—"I think it's wrong that you should try to control the group." Non-evaluative—"I think you are trying to control the group." Check one or the other. Hint— value judgements are often expressed by tone of voice as well as in words. |
| SPONTANEOUS- SOLICITED | Solicited feedback is feedback that you specifically asked for. Spontaneous feedback is feedback that someone gives you without being asked. Check one or the other. |
| INCLUSION-DIRECTED | Was the feedback related to any aspect of your participation or non-participation in the group, acceptance or rejection by the group, interaction with the group, etc.? |
| CONTROL-DIRECTED | Did the feedback pertain to any aspect of your influence, lack of influence, leadership, control in the group, etc.? |
| AFFECTION-DIRECTED | Was the feedback related to your warmth, friendliness, unfriendliness, openness, etc.? |
| RELATED TO YOUR SELF-CHANGE PROJECT | Was the feedback related to the self-change project you have chosen? |

## Figure 2—Feedback Form

Name _____    Date _____

I.   List below in boxes 1, 2, and 3, the three pieces of feedback from today's session that stand out most in your mind. Do this by recording in these boxes the initials of the giver of the feedback. You may also record here the central theme of the feedback if you wish. Try to put the feedback that stands out most in your mind in box 1, etc. A piece of feedback is defined here as a piece of information from one individual. A giver may be listed as many times as appropriate.

II.  Beginning with column 1, go down the column checking those categories which describe the feedback you received. Descriptions of each category appear on the cover sheet. When you have completed column 1, continue in the same fashion in columns 2 and 3.

| | 1 | 2 | 3 |
|---|---|---|---|
| Using a −2 to +2 scale, indicate your feelings about the person who gave you the feedback. −2 = dislike very much; −1 = dislike slightly; 0 = neutral to; +1 = like somewhat; +2 = like very much. | | | |
| VERBAL (spoken feedback) / NON-VERBAL (gestured feedback) | | | |
| STRONG (intense, vigorous feedback) / WEAK (mild feedback) | | | |
| HERE-AND-NOW (feedback about event or behavior in group) / THERE-AND-THEN (about event outside of group experience) | | | |
| POSITIVE (pleasant to hear) / NEGATIVE (unpleasant) | | | |
| SUPPORTED (corroborated by others) / NON-SUPPORTED (not corroborated) | | | |
| OWNED (giver makes it clear that feedback represents his own opinion) / NOT OWNED (not clear that feedback represents the giver's own opinion) | | | |
| DIRECTED (giver applies remark directly to you) / NON-DIRECTED (from general statement, you make application to yourself) | | | |
| EVALUATIVE (giver is making value judgment) / NON-EVALUATIVE (giver is not making value judgment) | | | |
| SOLICITED (you requested feedback) / SPONTANEOUS (you did not request feedback) | | | |
| Feedback refers to your participation, non-participation, interaction, etc. (INCLUSION) | | | |
| Feedback refers to your leadership, influence, lack of influence, etc. (CONTROL) | | | |
| Feedback refers to your friendliness, unfriendliness, etc. (AFFECTION) | | | |
| Related to your self change project | | | |

III. Check below the names of the people you gave feedback to (G) and received feedback from (R) in today's session.

| Name | G | R |   | Name | G | R |
|------|---|---|---|------|---|---|
| | | | | | | |
| | | | | | | |
| | | | | | | |
| | | | | | | |
| | | | | | | |
| | | | | | | |

IV.  How close are you to your goal today? Rate on a scale 1 to 9 with 1 being farthest from your goal and 9 being closest to it. _____

The above procedure yielded approximately 15 forms per group session with each group having about 11 sessions. With the exception of one group, all of the groups submitted complete data. The group with incomplete data had to be eliminated from our analysis.

The procedure for defining effective, ineffective, and non-helping was simple. To begin with each group was analyzed separately, since different groups developed somewhat differently due to different trainer styles and member needs. Thus a member was classified as an effective, ineffective, or non-helper in relation to other group members who shared the same climate as he did, not in relation to the total experimental population. For each member of the group, the investigators totaled the number of times he had been mentioned as a giver of a significant feedback, i.e., his initials had been placed on the top of one of the three columns in Figure 2. The investigators also totaled the number of times the member indicated that he had given feedback to other group members, i.e., the number of checks he placed in the "G" box after members' names in Figure 2. With these two variables—for each member the number of significant feedbacks members had received from him and the number of feedbacks he reported giving—a matrix of the group members was plotted as shown in Figure 3.

Figure 3
Definition of Effective, Ineffective and Non-helpers

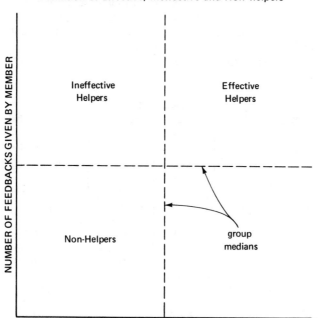

Subjects who were above the group median in number of feedbacks given and below the group median in number of significant feedbacks received were classed as ineffective helpers, i.e., they gave a lot of feedback but few people regarded this feedback as significant. Subjects who were below the group median on both variables were classed as non-helpers. Those who were above both medians were classed as effective helpers, i.e., they gave a lot of feedback and many members reported receiving significant feedbacks from them. As might be expected few subjects (12 out of 98) fell into the fourth quadrant. Those that did were classed as effective helpers since they in all cases came very close to the median of number of feedbacks given. (We assumed that many of those who fell in this quadrant did so because they failed to check the names of all of the people to whom they had given feedback.) The effective, ineffective and non-helpers from each group were then combined to form a total sample of 98 subjects—47 effective helpers, 24 ineffective helpers, and 27 non-helpers.

**Results and Discussion**

Motivation

*N* Achievement, *n* Power and *n* Affiliation scores for the three groups are shown in Table 1, and portrayed graphically in Figure 4. As Figure 4 indicates, the results for all three motives were in the direction predicted, although in several cases difference did not reach the .05 level of significance. The most clear cut differences were shown on *n* Affiliation and *n* Power. Ineffective helpers scored much lower on *n* Affiliation than did effective helpers or non-helpers. The difference in *n* Affiliation scores between non-helpers and effective helpers, however, was not significant. Ineffective helpers scored much higher on *n* Power than did effective helpers or non-helpers. There was no significant difference between the *n* Power scores of effective helpers and non-helpers. *N* Achievement scores were significantly higher for ineffective helpers than for effective helpers, but again the difference between effective helpers and non-helpers was not statistically meaningful.

**TABLE 1**

Motive Scores of Effective Helpers, Ineffective Helpers and Non-helpers

| Gp | A n=35 | B n=14 | C n=10 | P value* | | |
|---|---|---|---|---|---|---|
| Motive | Effective Helpers | Ineffective Helpers | Non-helpers | A v. B | A v. C | B v. C |
| *n* Achievement | 9.20 | 13.50 | 8.64 | .04 | NS | .09 |
| *n* Power | 4.51 | 7.14 | 3.50 | .01 | NS | .001 |
| *n* Affiliation | 5.37 | 3.29 | 6.64 | .03 | NS | .02 |

*Mann-Whitney U-Test 1 tail, NS = P > .10

Viewed overall, these results can generally be seen as supporting the hypothesis that effective helpers are moderately motivated in *n* Achievement, *n* Power, and *n* Affiliation, while ineffective helpers are high in the need for power and achievement and low on *n* Affiliation, and non-helpers are low in needs for power and achievement and high on *n* Affiliation. However, a more cautious conclusion based only on statistically significant differences would suggest that inef-

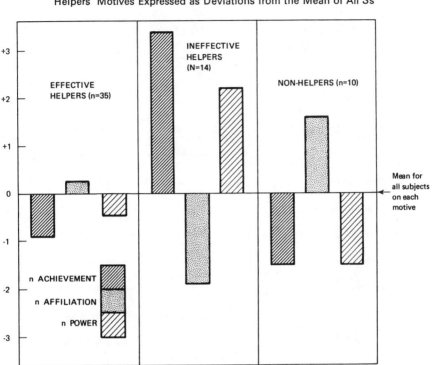

Figure 4
Helpers' Motives Expressed as Deviations from the Mean of All Ss

fective helpers are differentiated from effective helpers and non-helpers by very high $n$ Achievement and $n$ Power scores and very low $n$ Affiliation scores. In this experiment none of the three motives significantly differentiates effective helpers and non-helpers.

### Self-image

The semantic differential data on the self-image of effective, ineffective, and non-helpers is shown in Table 2. Only those adjective pairs which differentiated at least two of the three groups beyond the .05 level (2-tail) are shown in the table. While no specific hypotheses were made about self-image, this data is interesting in that it seems to support the conception of effective helpers, ineffective helpers, and non-helpers suggested by the motivation results. The non-helpers are different from both the effective and ineffective helpers in that they describe themselves as more passive, democratic, not cynical, submissive, followers, guarded, quiet, timid, not influential, inarticulate, self-conscious and preferring to listen. The general picture that emerges from these adjectives is that of an accepting, democratic person who lacks the self-confidence to influence others.

Ineffective helpers, on the other hand, describe themselves differently from non-helpers ($p < .05$ 2-tail) and effective helpers ($p < .10$ 2-tail)—seeing themselves as organized, impatient, open and superior. These adjectives seem to portray an extreme self-confidence with impatience and lack of interest in others.

The most interesting part of Table 2 is that the effective helpers consistently (with three exceptions) place themselves between the ineffective and non-helpers.

# TABLE 2
Self Image of Effective Helpers, Ineffective Helpers and Non-helpers

A = These adjectives differentiate Non-Helpers from both Effective and Ineffective Helpers (Mann-Whitney U-Test p < .05 2 tail)

B = These adjectives differentiate Non-Helpers from Ineffective Helpers (p < .05 2 tail) and Effective Helpers from Ineffective Helpers (p < .10 2 tail)

C = These adjectives differentiate Non-Helpers from Effective Helpers only (p < .05).

No adjectives differentiate Effective from Ineffective Helpers at the .05 level 2-tail.

They are, it appears, self-confident without being overbearing—a moderation which is suggested by their moderate motive scores in achievement, affiliation, and power.

The above results while only suggestive are extremely useful in that they help to sharpen our mental image of two types of help that are doomed to failure—the brash, over-confident, superior approach which places the client on the defensive, and the timid, hesitant, passive approach which may raise questions about the helper's qualifications and lead to a lack of confidence in the helper. The description of the successful helper is somewhat vague from the self-descriptions in Table 2 because no adjectives significantly differentiate effective helpers from the other two groups.

### Feedback

The types of feedback given by effective and ineffective helpers is shown in Table 3. The figures after each category represent the percent of the total number of significant feedbacks received from each group. Totals equal greater than $100\%$ because more than one characteristic was checked on each piece of feedback. The hypothesis that receivers would report more control feedback from ineffective helpers was supported ($33\%$ vs. $26\%$ $p < .03$ 1-tail). The hypothesis that less affection feedback would be received from them was not supported, however.

The hypothesis that effective helpers would give more positive feedback and ineffective helpers more negative feedback was also supported by the data. It is difficult, however, to assess the implication of this result. We cannot say conclusively that effective helpers *gave* more positive than negative feedback—we can only say that more positive feedback was heard from effective helpers. This can either be due to the fact that effective helpers did give more positive feedback or due to the fact that negative feedback given by effective helpers was ignored by receivers of help.

The other unpredicted results are difficult to explain. A greater percentage of non-verbal feedback ($6\%$ vs. $3\%$) and non-owned feedback ($8\%$ vs. $3\%$) was received from effective helpers than from ineffective helpers. The most plausible explanation seems to be that the ineffective helpers were unable to communicate so subtly—using non-verbal expressions or opinions they did not clearly identify as their own—because they lacked the empathy to time such or because their controlling behavior caused receivers defensively to block out such communications.

### Summary

The results of this experiment suggest that the helping relationship is best viewed as one involving a complex interaction of at least three motives—$n$ Achievement, $n$ Affiliation, and $n$ Power. Effective helpers appear to be those individuals who score moderately on these three motives. A similar moderation appears in the self-image of effective helpers. They are not as brash and over-confident as ineffective helpers nor as timid and self-conscious as non-helpers. The feedback that is received from effective helpers tends to be more positive and less related to control issues than feedback from ineffective helpers. Also, receivers of help get more nonverbal and not-owned feedback from effective helpers.

**TABLE 3**

Comparison of Types of Feedback Given by
Effective (n = 47) and Ineffective Helpers (n = 24)

| FEEDBACK CATEGORY | EFFECTIVE HELPERS | INEFFECTIVE HELPERS | P of DIFFERENCE |
|---|---|---|---|
| Verbal | 92 | 96 | .007 |
| Non-Verbal | 6 | 3 | .008 |
| Strong | 63 | 59 | NS |
| Weak | 34 | 40 | NS |
| Here and Now | 87 | 86 | NS |
| There and Then | 10 | 13 | NS |
| Positive | 55 | 45 | .04 1 tail |
| Negative | 42 | 54 | .04 1 tail |
| Supported | 64 | 66 | NS |
| Non-Supported | 33 | 33 | NS |
| Owned | 90 | 96 | .002 |
| Not Owned | 8 | 3 | .002 |
| Directed | 83 | 86 | NS |
| Non-Directed | 14 | 13 | NS |
| Evaluative | 71 | 71 | NS |
| Non-Evaluative | 26 | 27 | NS |
| Solicited | 27 | 33 | NS |
| Spontaneous | 70 | 65 | NS |
| Inclusion | 47 | 44 | NS |
| Control | 26 | 33 | .03 1 tail |
| Affection | 22 | 20 | .12 1 tail |
| Related to Self-Change Project | 52 | 52 | NS |

1. Figures represent % of total Significant Feedback received from each group. These total greater than 100% because more than one characteristic was checked on each piece of feedback.
2. Probabilities marked 1-tail were predicted in advance, all others are 2-tail, (NS = 7.10)

In future research other implications of the model of the helping relationship should be explored. We are currently involved in investigating the characteristics of effective receivers of help following the same research paradigm described here. The generality of the model should at some point be tested by research in a situation where the task is not an interpersonal one. Also, the impact of different psychological climates on the helping process should be investigated.

## References

Atkinson, J. (ed.) *Motives in fantasy, action and society.* Princeton, New Jersey: Van Nostrand, 1958.

Atkinson, J. *An introduction to motivation.* Princeton, New Jersey: Van Nostrand, 1964.

Atkinson, J. and Feather, N. T. *A theory of achievement motivation.* New York: John Wiley and Sons, 1966.

Bennis, W.; Schein, E.; Berlew, D.; and Steele, F. *Interpersonal dynamics.* Homewood, Illinois: Dorsey Press, 1964.

Halkides, G. *An experimental study of four conditions necessary for therapeutic change.* Unpublished doctoral dissertation, University of Chicago, 1958.

Kolb, D, Winter, S.; Berlew, D. Self-directed change: Two studies, *Journal of Applied Behavioral Science,* 1968, Vol. 4, 453–473.

Prakash, S. *Some characteristics of an effective organization development agent.* Unpublished master's thesis, Sloan School of Management, Massachusetts Institute of Technology, 1968.

Rogers, C. *On becoming a person.* Cambridge, Massachusetts: Riverside Press, 1961.

Schein, E. and Bennis, W. *Personal and organizational change through group methods.* New York: John Wiley and Sons, 1965.

Schwitzgebel, R. *A simple behavioral system for recording and implementing change in natural settings.* Unpublished doctoral thesis, Harvard University, 1964.

Winter, David G. *Power motivation in thought and action.* Unpublished doctoral thesis, Harvard University, 1967.

# SOME CRITERIA FOR CHOOSING THE DEPTH OF ORGANIZATIONAL INTERVENTION STRATEGY

ROGER HARRISON

Some Criteria for Choosing the Depth of Organizational
Intervention Strategy

During the years since World War II there has been a great proliferation of behavioral science based methods by which consultants seek to facilitate growth and change in individuals, groups and organizations. The methods

Delivered at the Fourth International Congress of Group Psychotherapy in Vienna, Austria in September 1968.

range from operations analysis and manipulation of the organization chart, through the use of Grid Laboratories, T Groups and non-verbal techniques. As was true in the development of clinical psychology and psychotherapy, the early stages of this developmental process tend to be accompanied by considerable competition, criticism and argument about the relative merits of various approaches. It is my conviction that controversy over the relative goodness or badness, effectiveness or ineffectiveness, of various change strategies really accomplishes very little in the way of increased knowledge or unification of behavioral science. As long as we are arguing about what method is better than another, we tend not to learn very much about how various approaches fit together or complement one another, and we certainly avoid the difficult and ambiguous task of bringing these competing points of view within one overarching system of knowledge about human processes.

As our knowledge increases, it begins to be apparent that these competing change strategies are not really different ways of doing the same thing—some more effective and some less effective—but rather that they are different ways of doing different things. They touch the individual, the group or the organization in different aspects of their functioning. They require differing kinds and amounts of commitment on the part of the client for them to be successful, and they demand different varieties and levels of skills and abilities on the part of the practitioner.

I believe there is a real need for conceptual models which differentiate intervention strategies from one another in a way which permits rational matching of strategies to organizational change problems. The purpose of this paper is to present a modest beginning which I have made towards a conceptualization of strategies, and to derive from this conceptualization some criteria for choosing appropriate methods of intervention in particular applications.

The point of view of this paper is that the depth of individual emotional involvement in the change process can be a central concept in such a taxonomy. In focusing on this dimension, we are concerned with the extent to which core areas of the personality or self are the focus of the change attempt. Strategies which touch the more deep, personal, private and central aspects of the individual or his relationships with others fall toward the deeper end of this continuum. Strategies which deal with more external aspects of the individual, and which focus upon the more formal and public aspects of role behavior, tend to fall toward the surface end of the depth dimension. This dimension has the advantage that it is relatively easy to rank change strategies upon it to get fairly close consensus as to the ranking. It is a widely discussed dimension of difference which has meaning and relevance to practitioners and their clients. I hope in this paper to promote greater flexibility and rationality in choosing appropriate depths of intervention. I shall approach this task by examining the effects of interventions at various depths. I shall also explore the ways in which two important organizational processes tend to make demands and to set limits upon the depth of intervention which can produce effective change in organizational functioning. These two processes are the autonomy of organization members and their own perception of their needs for help.

Before illustrating the concept by ranking five common intervention strategies along the dimension of depth, I should like to define the dimension somewhat more precisely. We are concerned here with how deep, value-laden, emotionally-charged and central to the individual's sense of self are the issues and processes about which the consultant attempts directly to obtain information and which he seeks to influence. If the consultant seeks information about relatively public and observable aspects of behavior and relationship, and if he tries to influence directly only these relatively surface characteristics and processes, we would then categorize his intervention strategy as being more on the surface. If, on the other hand, the consultant seeks information about very deep, private and self-relevant perceptions, attitudes or feelings, and if he intervenes in a way which directly affects these processes then we would classify his intervention strategy as one of considerable depth. To illustrate the surface end of the dimension let us look first at operations research or operations analysis. This strategy is concerned with the roles and functions to be performed within the organization, generally with little regard to the individual characteristics of persons occupying the roles. The change strategy is to manipulate role relationships; in other words, to re-distribute the tasks, the resources and the relative power attached to various roles in the organization. This is essentially a process of rational analysis in which the tasks which need to be performed are determined and specified, and sliced up into role definitions for persons and groups in the organization. The operations analyst does not ordinarily need to know much about particular people. Indeed, his function is to design the organization in such a way that its successful operation does not depend too heavily upon any skills, abilities, values or attitudes of individuals in various roles. He may perform this function adequately without knowing in advance who the individuals are who will fill these slots. Persons are assumed to be moderately interchangeable, and in order to make this approach work it is necessary to design the organization so that the capacities of the individual which are utilized in role performance are relatively public and observable, and are possessed by a fairly large proportion of the population. The approach is certainly one of very modest depth.

Somewhat deeper are those strategies which are based upon evaluating of performance and attempting to manipulate it directly. Included in this approach are much of the industrial psychologist's work in selection, placement and employee appraisal and counseling. The intervenor is concerned with what the individual is able and likely to do and achieve, rather than with processes internal to the individual. Direct attempts to influence performance may be made through the application of rewards and punishments such as promotions, salary increases, transfers within the organizations. An excellent illustration of this focus on end results is the practice of management by objectives. The intervention process is focused on establishing mutually agreed upon goals for performance between the individual and his supervisor. The practice is considered to be particularly advantageous because it permits the supervisor to avoid a focus on personal characteristics of the subordinate, particularly those deeper, more central characteristics which managers generally have difficulty in discussing with those who work for them. The process is designed to limit information exchange to that which is public and observable, the setting of performance goals, and the success or failure of the individual in attaining them.

Because of its focus on end results, rather than on the process by which those results are achieved, management by objectives must be considered less deep than the broad area of concern with work style which I shall term instrumental process analysis. We are concerned here not only with performance but with the processes by which that performance is achieved. However, we are primarily concerned with styles and processes of work rather than with the processes of interpersonal relationships which I would classify as being deeper on the basic dimension.

In instrumental process analysis we are concerned with how a person likes to organize and conduct his work, and with the impact which this style of work has on others in the organization. Principally, we are concerned with how a person perceives his role, what he values and disvalues in it, what he works hard on and what he chooses to ignore. We are also interested in the instrumental acts which the individual directs toward others: delegating authority or reserving decisions to himself, communicating or withholding information, collaborating or competing with others on work related issues. The focus on instrumentality means that we are interested in the person primarily as a doer of work or a performer of functions related to the goals of the organization. We are interested in what facilitates or inhibits his effective task performance.

We are not interested per se in whether his relationships with others are happy or unhappy, whether they perceive him as too warm or too cold, too authoritarian or too laissez-faire, or any other of the many interpersonal relationships which arise as people associate in organizations. However, I do not mean to imply that the line between instrumental relationships and interpersonal ones is an easy one to draw in action and practice, or even that it is desirable that this be done. What I am saying is that an intervention strategy can focus on instrumentality or it can focus on interpersonal relationships, and that there are important consequences of this difference in depth of intervention.

When we intervene at the level of instrumentality, it is to change work behavior and working relationships. Frequently this involves the process of bargaining or negotiation between groups and individuals. Diagnoses are made of the satisfactions or dissatisfactions of organization members with one another's work behavior. Reciprocal adjustments, bargains and trade-offs can then be arranged in which each party gets some modification in the behavior of the other at the cost to him of some reciprocal accommodation. Much of the intervention strategy which has been developed around Blake's concept of the Managerial Grid is at this level and involves bargaining and negotiation of role behavior as an important change process.

At the deeper level of interpersonal relationships the focus is on feelings, attitudes, and perceptions which organization members have about others. At this level we are concerned with the quality of human relationships within the organization, with warmth and coldness of members to one another, and with the experiences of acceptance and rejection, love and hate, trust and suspicion between groups and individuals. At this level the consultant probes for feelings, attitudes and perceptions. He works to create relationships of openness about feelings and to help members to develop mutual understanding of one another as persons. Interventions are directed toward helping organization members to be more comfortable in being authentically themselves with one another, and the degree of mutual caring and concern is expected to increase. Sensitivity training using T Groups is a basic intervention strategy at this level. T-Group educators emphasize increased personalization of relationships, the development of trust and openness, and the exchange of feelings. Interventions at this level deal directly and intensively with interpersonal emotionality. This is the first intervention strategy we have examined which is at a depth where the feelings of organization members about one another are a direct focus of the intervention strategy. At the other levels, feelings certainly exist and may be expressed, but they are not a direct concern of the intervention. The transition from the task orientation of instrumental process analysis to the feeling orientation of interpersonal process analysis seems, as I shall suggest later, to be a critical one for many organization members.

The deepest level of intervention which will be considered in this paper is that of intrapersonal analysis. Here the consultant uses a variety of methods to reveal the individual's deeper attitudes, values and conflicts regarding his own functioning, identity and existence. The focus is generally on increasing the range of experiences which the individual can bring into awareness and cope with. The material may be dealt with at the fantasy or symbolic level, and the intervention strategies include many which are non-interpersonal and non-verbal. Some examples of this kind of approach are in the use of marathon T-Group sessions, the creative risk-taking laboratory approach of Byrd, and some aspects of the task group therapy approach of Clark. These approaches all tend to bring into focus very deep and intense feelings about one's own identity and one's relationships with significant others.

In order to understand the importance of the dimension of depth of interventions let us consider the effect upon the organization members of interventions at different levels. The first of the important concomitants of depth is the degree of dependence of the client on the special competence of the change agent. At the surface end of the depth dimension, the methods of intervention are easily communicated and made public. The client may reasonably expect to learn something of the change agent's skills to improve his own practice.

At the deeper levels, such as interpersonal and intrapersonal process analyses, it is harder for the client to understand the methods of intervention. The change agent is more likely to be seen as a person of special and unusual powers not found in ordinary men. Skills of intervention and change are less frequently learned by organization members, and the change process may tend to become personalized around the change agent as leader. Programs of change which are so dependent upon personal relationships and individual expertise are difficult to institutionalize. When the change agent leaves the system, he may not only take his expertise with him but the entire change process as well.

A second aspect of the change process which varies with depth is the extent to which the benefits of an intervention are transferable to members of the organization not originally participating in the change process. At surface levels of operations analysis and performance evaluation, the effects are institutionalized in the form of procedures, policies and practices of the organization which may have considerable permanence beyond the tenure of individuals. At the level of instrumental behavior, the continuing effects of intervention are more likely to reside in the informal norms of groups within the organization regarding such matters as delegation, communication, decision-making, competition and collaboration, and conflict resolution.

At the deepest levels of intervention, the target of change is the individual's inner life, and if the intervention is successful, the permanence of individual change should be greatest. There are indeed dramatic reports of cases in which persons have changed their careers and life goals as a result of such interventions, and the persistence of such change appears to be relatively high.

One consequence, then, of the level of intervention is that with greater depth of focus the individual increasingly becomes both the target and the carrier of change. In the light of this analysis, it is not surprising to observe that deeper levels of intervention are increasingly being used at higher organizational levels and in scientific and service organizations where the contribution of the individual has greatest impact.

Another concomitant of depth is that as the level of intervention becomes deeper, the information needed to intervene effectively becomes less available. At the less personal level of operations analysis, the information is often a matter of record. At the level of performance evaluation, it is a matter of observation. On the other hand, reactions of others to a person's work style are less likely to be discussed freely, and the more personal responses to his interpersonal style are even less likely to be readily given. At the deepest levels, important information may not be available to the individual himself. Thus, as we go deeper the consultant must use more of his time and skill uncovering information which is ordinarily private and hidden. This is one reason for the greater costs of interventions at deeper levels of focus.

Another aspect of the change process which varies with the depth of intervention is the personal risk and unpredictability of outcome for the individual. At deeper levels we deal with aspects of the individual's view of himself and his relationships with others which are highly charged emotionally. We intervene in processes which bind and channel a great deal of psychological energy. If in the change process the individual's self perceptions are strongly disconfirmed, the imbalance in the equilibrium of forces may produce sudden changes in behavior, attitudes and personality integration.

Because of the private and hidden nature of the processes into which we intervene at deeper levels, it is difficult to predict the individual impact of the change process in advance. The need for clinical sensitivity and skill on the part of the practitioner thus increases, since he must be prepared to diagnose and deal with developing situations involving considerable stress upon individuals.

The foregoing analysis suggests a criterion by which to match intervention strategies to particular organizational problems. It is to *intervene at a level just deep enough to provide enduring solutions of the problems at hand.* This criterion derives directly from the observations above. The cost, skill demands, client dependency and variability of outcome all increase with depth of intervention. Further, as the depth of intervention increases, the effects tend to locate more in the individual and less in the organization. The danger of losing the organization's investment in the change with the departure of the individual becomes a significant consideration.

While this general criterion is simple and straightforward, its application is not. In particular, although the criterion should operate in the direction of less depth of intervention, there is a general trend in modern organizational life which tends to push the intervention level always deeper. This trend is toward increased self-direction of organization members and increased independence of external pressures and incentives. I believe there is a direct relationship between the autonomy of individuals and the depth of intervention needed to effect organizational change.

Before going on to discuss this relationship, I shall acknowledge freely that I cannot prove the existence of a trend toward a general increase in freedom of individuals within organizations. I only intend to assert the great importance of the degree of individual autonomy in determining the level of intervention which will be effective.

In order to understand the relationship between autonomy and depth of intervention, it is necessary to conceptualize a dimension which parallels and is implied by the depth dimension we have been discussing. This is the dimension of predictability and variability among persons in their responses to the different kinds of incentives which may be used to influence behavior in the organization. The key assumption in this analysis is that the more unpredictable and unique is the individual's response to the particular kinds of controls and incentives one can bring to bear upon him, the more one must know about that person in order to influence his behavior.

Most predictable and least individual is the response of the person to economic and bureaucratic controls when his needs for economic income and security are high. It is not necessary to delve very deeply into a person's inner processes in order to influence his behavior, if we know that he badly needs his income and his position and if we are in a position to control his access to these rewards. Responses to economic and bureaucratic controls tend to be relatively simple, impersonal and on the surface.

If for any reason organization members become relatively uninfluenceable through the manipulation of their income and economic security, the management of performance becomes strikingly more complex, and the need for more personal information about the individual increases. Except very generally, we do not know automatically or in advance what styles of instrumental or interpersonal interaction will be responded to as negative or positive incentives by the individual. One person may appreciate close supervision and direction; another may value independence of direction. One may prefer to work alone; another may function best when he is in close communication with others. One may thrive in close, intimate personal interaction; while others are made uncomfortable by any but cool and distant relationships with colleagues.

What I am saying is that when bureaucratic and economic incentives lose their force for whatever reason, the improvement of performance *must* involve linking organizational goals to the individual's attempts to meet his own needs for satisfying instrumental activities and interpersonal relationships. It is for this reason that I make the assertion that increases in personal autonomy dictate change interventions at deeper and more personal levels. In order to obtain the information necessary to link organizational needs to individual goals, one must probe fairly deeply into the attitudes, values and emotions of the organization members.

If the need for deeper personal information becomes great when we intervene at the instrumental and interpersonal levels, it becomes even greater when one is dealing with organization members who are motivated less through their transactions with the environment and more in response to internal values and standards. An example is the researcher, engineer or technical specialist whose work behavior may be influenced more by his own values and standards of creativity or professional excellence than by his relationships with others. The deepest organizational interventions at the intrapersonal level may be required in order to effect change when working with persons who are highly self-directed.

Let me summarize my position about the relationship between autonomy, influence and level of intervention. As the individual becomes less subject to economic and bureaucratic pressures, he tends to seek more intangible rewards in the organization which come from both the instrumental and interpersonal aspects of the system. I view this as a shift from greater external to more internal control and as an increase in autonomy. Further shifts in this direction may involve increased independence of rewards and punishments mediated by others, in favor of operation in accordance with internal values and standards.

I view organizations as systems of reciprocal influence. Achievement of organization goals is facilitated when individuals can seek their own satisfactions through activity which promotes the goals of the organization. As the satis-factions which are of most value to the individual change, so must the reciprocal influence systems, if the organization goals are to continue to be met.

If the individual changes are in the direction of increased independence of external incentives, then the influence systems must change to provide oppor-tunities for individuals to achieve more intangible, self-determined satisfactions in their work. However, people are more differentiated, complex and unique in their intangible goals and values than in their economic needs. In order to create systems which offer a wide variety of intangible satisfactions, much more private, emotion- and value-laden information about individuals is needed to create and maintain systems based chiefly on economic and bureaucratic controls. For this reason, deeper interventions are called for when the system it is desired to change contains a high proportion of relatively autonomous individuals.

There are a number of factors promoting autonomy which I have observed in my work organizations. Wherever a number of these factors obtain, it is prob-ably an indication that deeper levels of intervention are required to effect lasting improvements in organizational functioning. These factors all tend to free the individual from dependence upon economic and bureaucratic controls. I shall simply list these indicators briefly in categories to show what kinds of things might signify to the practitioner that deeper levels of intervention may be ap-propriate.

The first category includes anything which makes the evaluation of individual performance difficult:

> —a long time span between the individual's actions and the results by which effectiveness of performance is to be judged;
>
> —non-repetitive, unique tasks which cannot be evaluated by reference to the performance of others on similar tasks;
>
> —specialized skills and abilities possessed by an individual which cannot be evaluated by a supervisor who does not possess the skills or knowledge himself.

The second category concerns economic conditions:

> —arrangements which secure the job tenure and/or income of the indi-vidual;
>
> —a market permitting easy transfer from one organization to another (e.g. engineers in the U.S. aerospace industry);
>
> —unique skills and knowledge of the individual which make him difficult to replace.

The third category includes characteristics of the system or its environment which lead to independence of the parts of the organization and decentraliza-tion of authority.

> —an organization which works on a project basis instead of producing a standard line of products;
>
> —an organization in which subparts must be given latitude to deal rapidly and flexibly with frequent environmental change.

I should like to conclude the discussion of this criterion for depth of intervention with a brief reference to the ethics of intervention, a problem which merits considerably more thorough treatment than I can give it here.

There is considerable concern in the U.S. about invasion of privacy by behavioral scientists. I would agree that such invasion of privacy is an actual as well as a fantasied concomitant of the use of organizational change strategies of greater depth. The recourse by organizations to such strategies has been widely viewed as an indication of greater organizational control over the most personal and private aspects of the lives of the members. The present analysis suggests, however, that recourse to these deeper interventions actually reflects the greater *freedom* of organization members from traditionally crude and impersonal means of organizational control. There is no reason to be concerned about man's attitudes or values or interpersonal relationships when his job performance can be controlled by brute force, by economic coercion or by bureaucratic rules and regulations. The "invasion of privacy" only becomes worth the cost, bother and uncertainty of outcome when the individual has achieved relative independence from control by other means. Put another way, it only makes organizational sense to try to get a man to *want* to do something if you cannot *make* him do it. And regardless of what intervention strategy is used, the individual still retains considerably greater control over his own behavior than he had when he could be manipulated more crudely. As long as we can maintain a high degree of voluntarism regarding the nature and extent of an individual's participation in the deeper organizational change strategies, these strategies can work toward adapting the organization to the individual quite as much as they work the other way around. Only when an individual's participation in one of the deeper change strategies is coerced by economic or bureaucratic pressures, do I feel that the ethics of the intervention clearly run counter to the values of a democratic society.

So far our attention to the choice of level of intervention has focused upon locating the depth at which the information exists which must be exchanged to facilitate system improvement. Unfortunately, the choice of an intervention strategy cannot practically be made with reference to this criterion alone. Even if a correct diagnosis is made of the level at which the relevant information lies, we may not be able to work effectively at the desired depth because of client norms, values, resistances and fears.

In an attempt to develop a second criterion for depth of intervention which takes such dispositions on the part of the client into account, I have considered two approaches which represent somewhat polarized orientations to the problem. One approach is based upon analyzing and overcoming client resistance; the other is based upon discovering and joining forces with the self-articulated wants or "felt needs" of the client.

There are several ways of characterizing these approaches; to me, the simplest is to point out that when the change agent is resistance-oriented he tends to lead or influence the client to work at a depth greater than that at which the latter feels comfortable. When resistance-oriented, the change agent tends to mistrust the client's statement of his problems and of the areas where he wants help. He suspects the client's presentation of being a smokescreen or defense against admission of his "real" problems and needs. The consultant works to expose the underlying processes and concerns and to influence the client to work at a deeper level.

The resistance-oriented approach grows out of the work of clinicians and psychotherapists, and it characterizes much of the work of organizational consultants who specialize in sensitivity training and deeper intervention strategies.

On the other hand, change agents may be oriented to the self-articulated wants of clients or, as they are sometimes called, their "felt needs." When so oriented, the consultant tends more to follow and facilitate the client in working at whatever level the latter sets for himself. He may assist the client in defining problems and needs and in working on solutions, but he tends to try to anchor his work in the norms, values and accepted standards of behavior of the organization.

I believe that there is a tendency for change agents working at the interpersonal and deeper levels to adopt a rather consistent resistance-oriented approach. Some consultants seem to take a certain quixotic pride in dramatically and self-consciously violating organizational norms. Various techniques have been developed for pressuring or seducing organization members into departing from organizational norms in the service of the change. The "marathon T Group" is a case in point, where the increased irritability and fatigue of prolonged contact and lack of sleep move participants to deal with one another more emotionally, personally and spontaneously than they would normally be willing to do.

in changing organizational norms, their effects are relatively short-lived, because the social structures and interpersonal linkages have not been created which can utilize for day-to-day problem solving the deeper information produced by the intervention. It is true that the consultant may succeed in producing information, but he is less likely to succeed in creating social structures which can continue that work in his absence. The problem is directly analogous to that of the community developer who succeeds by virtue of his personal influence in getting villagers to build a school or a community center which falls into disuse as soon as he leaves, due to the lack of any integration of these achievements into the social structure and day-to-day life of the community. Community developers have had to learn through bitter failure and frustration that ignoring or subverting the standards and norms of a social system often results in temporary success followed by a reactionary increase in resistance to the influence of the change agent. On the other hand, felt needs embody those problems, issues and difficulties which have a high conscious priority on the part of community or organization members. We can expect individuals and groups to be ready to invest time, energy and resources in dealing with their felt needs, while they will be relatively passive or even resistant toward those who attempt to "help" them with externally defined needs. Community developers have found that attempts to help with felt needs are met by greater receptivity, support and integration within the structure and life of the community than are intervention attempts which rely primarily upon the developer's value system for setting need priorities.

The emphasis of many organizational change agents on confronting and working through resistances was developed originally in the practice of individual psychoanalysis and psychotherapy, and it is also a central concept in the conduct of therapy groups and sensitivity training laboratories. In all of these situations, the change agent has a high degree of environmental control and is at least temporarily in a high status position with respect to the client. To a degree that is frequently underestimated by practitioners, we manage to create a situation in which it is more unpleasant for the client to leave than it is to stay and submit to the pressure to confront and work through resistances. I believe that the tendency is for behavioral scientists to tend to overplay their hands when they move from the clinical and training situations where they have environmental control to the organizational consulting situation, where their control is sharply attenuated.

This attenuation derives only partially from the relative ease with which the client can terminate the relationship. Even if this most drastic step is not taken, the consultant can be tolerated, misled and deceived in ways which are relatively difficult in the therapeutic or human relations training situations. He can also be openly defied and blocked if he runs afoul of strongly shared group norms, whereas when the consultant is dealing with a group of strangers, he can often utilize differences among the members to overcome this kind of resistance. I suspect that in general, behavioral scientists underestimate their power in working with individuals and groups of strangers, and overestimate it when working with individuals and groups in organizations. I emphasize this point because I believe that a good many potentially fruitful and mutually satisfying consulting relationships are terminated early because of the consultant's taking the role of overcomer of resistance to change, rather than that of collaborator in the client's attempts at solving his problems. It is these considerations which lead me to suggest my second criterion for the choice of organization intervention strategy: *Intervene at a level no deeper than that at which energy and resources of organization members can be committed to problem solving and to change.* These energies and resources can be mobilized through obtaining legitimation for the intervention in the norms of the organization and through devising intervention strategies which have clear relevance to consciously felt needs on the part of the organization members.

Unfortunately, it is doubtless true that the forces which influence the conditions we desire to change often exist at deeper levels than can be dealt with by adhering to the criterion of working within organization norms and meeting felt needs. The level at which an individual or group is willing and ready to invest energy and resources is probably always determined partly by a realistic assessment of the problems and partly by a defensive need and to avoid confrontation and significant change. It is thus not likely that our two criteria for selection of intervention depth will result in the same decisions when practically applied. It is not the same to intervene at the level where behavior-determining forces are most potent as it is to work on felt needs as they are articulated by the client. This, it seems to me, is the consultant's dilemma. It always has been. We are continually faced with the choice between leading the client into areas which are threatening, unfamiliar and dependency-provoking for him (and, where our own expertise shows to best advantage) or, on the other hand, being guided by the client's own understanding of his problems and his willingness to invest resources in particular kinds of relatively familiar and non-threatening strategies.

When time permits, this dilemma is ideally dealt with by intervening first at a level where there is good support from the norms, power structure and felt needs of organizational members. The consultant can then, over a period of time, develop trust, sophistication and support within the organization to explore deeper levels at which particularly important forces may be operating. This would probably be agreed to, at least in principle, by most organizational consultants. The point at which I feel I differ from a significant number of workers in this field is that I would advocate that interventions should *always* be limited to the depth of the client's felt needs and readiness to legitimize intervention. I believe we should always avoid moving deeper at a pace which outstrips a client system's willingness to subject itself to exposure, dependency and threat. What I am saying is that if the dominant response of organization members indicates that an intervention violates system norms regarding exposure, privacy and confrontation, then one has intervened too deeply and should pull back to a level at which organization members are more ready to invest their own energy in the change process. This point of view is thus in opposition to that which sees negative reactions primarily as indications of resistances which are to be brought out into the open, confronted and worked through as a central part of the intervention process. I believe that behavioral scientists acting as organizational consultants have tended to place overmuch emphasis on the overcoming of resistance to change and have underemphasized the importance of enlisting in the service of change the energies and resources which the client can consciously direct and willingly devote to problem solving.

What is advocated here is that we in general accept the client's felt needs or presented problems as real and that we work on them at a level at which he can serve as a competent and willing collaborator. This position is in opposition to that which sees the presenting problem as more or less a smokescreen or barrier. I am not advocating this point of view because I value the right or privacy of organization members more highly than I value their growth and development, or the solving of organizational problems. (This is an issue which concerns me, but it is enormously more complex than the ones which I am dealing with in this paper.) Rather, I place first priority on collaboration with the client, because I do not think we are frequently successful consultants without it.

In my own practice I have observed that the change in client response is frequently quite striking when I move from a resistance-oriented approach to an acceptance of the client's norms and definitions of his own needs. With quite a few organizational clients in the U.S., the line of legitimacy seems to lie somewhere between interventions at the instrumental level and those focused on interpersonal relationships. Members who exhibit hostility, passivity, and dependence when I initiate intervention at the interpersonal level may become dramatically more active, collaborative and involved when I shift the focus to the instrumental level.

If I intervene directly at the level of interpersonal relationships, I can be sure that at least some members, and often the whole group, will react with anxiety, passive resistance and low or negative commitment to the change process. Furthermore, they express their resistance in terms of norms and values regarding the appropriateness or legitimacy of dealing at this level. They say things like, "It isn't right to force people's feelings about one another out into the open"; "I don't see what this has to do with improving organizational effectiveness"; "People are being encouraged to say things which are better left unsaid."

If I then switch to a strategy which focuses on decision-making, delegation of authority, information exchange and other instrumental questions, these complaints about illegitimacy and the inappropriateness of the intervention are usually sharply reduced. This does not mean that the clients are necessarily comfortable or free from anxiety in the discussions, nor does it mean that strong negative feelings may not be expressed about one another's behavior. What is different is that the clients are more likely to work with instead of against me, to feel and express some sense of ownership in the change process, and to see many more possibilities for carrying it on among themselves in the absence of the consultant.

What I have found is that when I am resistance-oriented in my approach to the client, I am apt to feel rather uncomfortable in "letting sleeping dogs lie." When, on the other hand, I orient myself to the client I am uncomfortable when I feel I am leading or pushing the client to operate very far outside the shared norms of the organization. I have tried to indicate why I believe the latter orientation is more appropriate. I realize of course that many highly sophisticated and talented practitioners will not agree with me.

In summary, I have tried to show in this paper that the dimension of depth should be central to the taxonomy of intervention strategies. I have presented what I believe are the major consequences of intervening at greater or lesser depth, and from these consequences I have suggested two criteria for choosing the appropriate depth of intervention:

—first, to intervene at a depth just deep enough to effect enduring solutions to the problems at hand;

—second, to intervene at a level no deeper than that at which the energy and resources can be committed to problem solving and to change.

I have analyzed the tendency for increases in individual autonomy in organizations to push the appropriate level of intervention deeper when the first criterion is followed. Opposed to this is the countervailing tendency of the second criterion to dictate working at more of a surface level in order to enlist the energy and support of the organization members in the change process. Arguments have been presented for resolving this dilemma in favor of the second, more conservative criterion. The dilemma remains, of course; the continuing tension under which the change agent works is between the desire to lead and push, or to collaborate and follow. The middle ground is never very stable, and I suspect we show our values and preferences by which criterion we choose to maximize when we are under the stress of difficult and ambiguous client-consultant relationships.

# Planned Change
# and Organizational Development

## INFLUENCE AND ORGANIZATIONAL CHANGE[1]

GENE W. DALTON[2]

During the last few years a new term, "organizational development," has been rapidly finding its way into the organization charts of American corporations. Because of the recency of this phenomenon it is sometimes difficult to ascertain the extent to which the activities carried out under this title are old activities being carried out under a new name or a new set of activities aimed at an old but increasingly urgent problem. But one fact does emerge: there is an increasing number of men in these organizations whose primary function is to foster change. This has always been part of the job of a manager, and often a significant part; but now there is an increasing number of men in the organizations who are essentially specialists in the process of organizational change.

Almost inevitably, a part of the requirement of this new role will be an ability to be explicit about the change process itself, for the O.D. specialist will be an adviser and helper more often than an initiator. In this role of counselor, he will need a framework or model for both thinking and talking about the means by which individuals and groups are influenced to change their behavior in organizations. A model has a number of uses. It can help order the available data and clarify discussion. It can provide some much-needed categories so that similarities between similar acts can be highlighted. It can point out the multiple functions which some act performs without forcing us to talk about everything at once.

For several years my colleagues and I have been studying an organization in which a new director of a research and development center set out to change the behavior of a substantial number of managers and engineers. We observed

[1]First presented and published as a paper at a Conference on Organizational Behavioral Models, Kent State University, May 1969, and reprinted here by permission. The central ideas of the paper were developed in G. W. Dalton, L. B. Barnes, and A. Zaleznik, *The Distribution of Authority in Formal Organizations* (Boston: Division of Research, Harvard Business School, 1968). The research was generously supported by the B. F. Goodrich Endowment and the Ford Foundation Research in Organizational Behavior and Administration.

[2]Professor of Management, Brigham Young University.

his efforts over time and attempted to measure their effects. Over a period of a year and a half it became increasingly evident that he had been successful in influencing one group of the men but had had little effect on the others. This result both baffled and challenged us. In our attempt to understand the difference, we examined the studies we could find which described instances where someone had successfully influenced others to change their behavior. From the analysis of these studies and of our own data we constructed an elementary model of the influence process in organizational change. I am proposing that it may serve as a useful point of departure for those engaged in organization development, as well as for those of us who study organizational life.

### Organizational and Individual Change

First I should clarify what I mean by organizational change. As used here, the term refers to any significant alteration of the behavior patterns of a large number of the individuals who constitute that organization. I make a point of this because students of organizations, in their efforts to characterize an organization as a system or organism, too often lose sight of the fact that the "behavior" of an organization is made up of the actions and interactions of the individuals in it. We read so frequently about an organization "adapting" to market shifts, economic conditions, and scientific discoveries that we slide over the internal processes by which an organization does that adapting. The biological analogy of an organism adapting to its environment can be dramatic and conceptually helpful, but students of organizations typically make only partial use of the analogy. They stop at this generalized level of explanation and fail to follow their biologist colleagues, whose concepts they have borrowed, to the next step of examining the internal processes by which the system adapts.

Our focus will be on the response within the organization to factors in its environment. Typically, one or more individuals in the organization see something in the environment which calls for different behavior on the part of the members of the organization. He (or they) then tries to move others in the organization to make this change in their behavior. This is fundamentally an influence process, and it is the process I shall be representing here. The primary data chosen for illustration come from our own study plus studies of change in organizational settings by Guest,[3] Seashore and Bowers,[4] Jaques,[5] and Blake, Mouton, Barnes, and Greiner.[6] These all focused on the internal change process.

Some of the best reported studies of the influence process, however, were made in nonorganizational settings: experimental studies of attitude change, individual and group psychotherapy, religious conversion, and so-called thought reform. In deciding whether to draw from these, I was faced with the question

[3]Robert H. Guest, *Organizational Change: The Effect of Successful Leadership* (Homewood, Ill.: Richard D. Irwin, Inc. and The Dorsey Press, 1962).

[4]S. E. Seashore and D. G. Bowers, *Changing the Structure and Functioning of an Organization* (Ann Arbor: University of Michigan, Survey Research Center, Monograph No. 33, 1963).

[5]Elliot Jaques, *The Changing Culture of a Factory* (London: Tavistock Publications, Ltd., 1951).

[6]Robert R. Blake, Jane S. Mouton, Louis B. Barnes, and Larry E. Greiner, "Breakthrough in Organization Development," *Harvard Business Review*, November-December 1964.

as to whether studies of individual change can materially aid our understanding of organizational change, and my answer was affirmative. Certainly, membership in a formal organization places the individual within a potent influence network, and any explanation of changes in his behavior and attitudes must take this network into account. But we must not allow ourselves to presume that behavior in formal organizations is discontinuous from human behavior elsewhere. The object of change in planned change programs is the behavior and attitudes of individuals. Within an organization, those attitudes and actions form an inextricable part of larger formal and informal systems, but the workings of social processes ultimately take place as intrapersonal and interpersonal processes.

### Sequencing

In our study of the events at the Nampa Development Center, one of the first things we noted was the importance of time. Often the most significant fact about a given event was that it followed other events or that it created a condition which influenced subsequent events. This is also the one point on which other students of change agree—that behavioral and attitudinal change takes place in sequential steps or phases.

Probably the most fruitful conception of the change process, judging from the frequency of its use by others and by the research it has stimulated, is the three-step model advanced by Kurt Lewin:[7] unfreezing the system which is operating in a given pattern, moving to a new pattern, and refreezing into this new pattern. Lewin postulated that systems tend to operate in a given pattern or at a given level as long as there is a relative balance of forces acting on the system.

A sequential model achieves a number of functions. It provides a dimension along which to order events and draws attention to events and conditions at the boundaries of the phenomena under examination. Too often, I think, those of us managing or studying organizations tend to be ahistorical in our approach.[8] For example, in our own study, when we conceived of "unfreezing" broadly, we were led to examine not only the unsettling effects of the director's changes in the organizational structure, but also the conditions in the organization at the time he became director and the events leading up to them. Using this one dimension, time, we could characterize the change process at the center, where successful, as follows:

**FIGURE 1**

| Unfreezing | | Change | Refreezing |
|---|---|---|---|
| Tension and the need for change was experienced within the organization. | Change was advocated by the new director. | Individuals within the organization tested out the proposed changes. | New behavior and attitudes were either reinforced and internalized, or rejected and abandoned. |

[7]Kurt Lewin, "Group Decision and Social Change," in T. M. Newcomb and E. L. Hartley (eds.), *Readings in Social Psychology* (New York: Holt, Rinehart & Winston, Inc., 1958).

[8]For a notable exception, see L. E. Greiner, "Antecedents of Planned Organizational Change," *Journal of Applied Behavioral Science*, Vol. 3, No. 1 (1967).

### Subprocesses

So far, so good. Time is important, and a sequential model such as Lewin's is useful in pointing to the tendency toward orderly movement related to prior events. But, as we compared the successful and unsuccessful attempts to exert influence, it also became obvious that there was not one process at work but several, all moving simultaneously. Where influence was successful, changes occurred not only in the way an individual related to the influencing agent, but also to his co-worker and to himself. As interaction patterns were dissolving and reforming, changes were taking place within the individuals involved, changes in their feelings about themselves and in the objectives they sought.

We identified four major subprocesses that tended to characterize successful change in our own study and in the other empirical studies of change we examined.

The four subprocesses are characterized by movement:

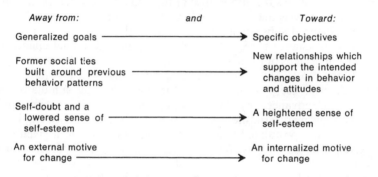

A Model for Induced Change

If we combine these four subprocesses with our notion of sequencing, we arrive at the diagram in Figure 2. Following this diagram, we shall look at the two antecedent conditions which were present in each case of successful planned change examined. Then we shall look separately at each of the four subprocesses pictured.

### Internal Tension as an Antecedent Condition

At the risk of stating a truism, let me point out that one of the most important conditions necessary for the successful initiation of change is a sense of tension or a felt need for change among those who are the targets of influence. In nearly every instance, in the studies reviewed, where one person or group successfully influenced the behavior of others, those influenced were experiencing a more-than-usual amount of tension or stress.

In our own study, a major project on which many of the men had worked for years had just been discontinued and the technology sold to a competitor. The decision by top management not to manufacture or market the product, which had been announced just prior to the new director's appointment, had generated a sense of disappointment and frustration at the center, since many had come to identify their own future with the success of the project. The men were also concerned about the falling prices of their division's major product and at the center's apparent lack of success in recent years at translating their technical capabilities into dramatic new products.

## FIGURE 2

### A Model of Induced Change

| Tension Experienced within the System | Intervention of a Prestigious Influencing Agent | Individuals Attempt to Implement the Proposed Changes | New Behavior and Attitudes Reinforced by Achievement, Social Ties, and Internalized Values—Accompanied by Decreasing Dependence on Influencing Agent |
|---|---|---|---|
| ⟶ | Generalized objectives established | Growing specificity of objectives ⟶ —establishment of subgoals | Achievement and resetting of specific objectives ⟶ |
| Tension within existing social ties ⟶ | Prior social ties interrupted or attenuated ⟶ | Formation of new alliances and relationships centering around new ⟶ activities | New social ties reinforce altered behavior and attitudes ⟶ |
| Lowered sense of self-esteem ⟶ | Esteem-building begun on basis of agent's attention and ⟶ assurance | Esteem-building based on task accomplishment ⟶ | Heightened sense of self-esteem ⟶ |
| ⟶ | External motive for change ⟶(New schema provided) | Improvisation and reality-testing ⟶ | Internalized motive for change ⟶ |

Guest, in his three-year study of leadership and organizational change in an automobile assembly plant, reported that before the arrival of the new production manager, who succeeded in "turning the plant around" from the least to the most efficient plant in the division, there was great tension. Labor grievances were high, turnover was twice that in other plants and the plant was under constant pressure from division headquarters.[9]

Seashore and Bowers, in their study of an ultimately successful change effort by a consulting-research team from the University of Michigan, reported that in the year prior to the interventions of the team, "Banner [the company] dropped to a very marginal profit position. . . . Waste, service, and quality problems arose. . . . There was a sense of things getting out of control, a feeling shared and expressed by many non-managerial people."[10]

Elliot Jaques, in his pioneering study of social and technical change in the Glacier Metal Company, reported the impact of a crisis which resulted in a large number of layoffs and "great anxiety about job security." The procedure adopted [to handle the layoffs] had lessened some of the morale problems—but

[9]Guest, op. cit.
[10]Seashore and Bowers, op. cit.

it did not and could not remove everyone's anxiety about job security."[11] Jaques, in fact, concluded that a necessary factor in allowing for a working through of group problems was a "problem severe and painful enough for its members to wish to do something about it."

Blake, Mouton, Barnes, and Greiner, describing a major organizational change effort featuring a training program, noted the presence of great tension in the Sigma plant prior to the training consultant's arrival at the plant. A merger had taken place, bringing the plant under a new headquarters staff, and a serious problem arose over the "use of Sigma manpower on construction work of new projects." When the headquarters staff began to "prod Sigma," the plant management "became defensive" and according to one of the managers at headquarters, "some of our later sessions became emotional. Strained relations between different departments and levels within the plant began to develop."[12] Greiner reported that "plant morale slipped badly, insecurity arose and performance slumped," while a manager within the plant reported that "everything seemed to get out of control."[13]

This uniformity was also evident in other settings where there was a successful attempt to influence attitudes and behavior. The religious convert usually is experiencing self-doubt and guilt before he gives careful heed to the missionary or revivalist. A need for change is already felt by the person who walks into the Christian Science reading room or the revivalist tent. Certain organizations, such as Alcoholics Anonymous, whose central aim is to induce specific behavioral change, refuse to admit anyone unless he is consciously experiencing distress. An applicant to A.A. must openly admit the failure of previous individual efforts and his need for help.[14] Jerome Frank suggests that in psychotherapy the presence of prior emotional distress is closely related to the results of the treatment. He argues as follows:

> The importance of emotional distress in the establishment of a fruitful psychotherapeutic relationship is suggested by the facts that the greater the over-all degree of expressed distress, as measured by a symptom check list, the more likely the patient is to remain in treatment, while conversely two of the most difficult categories of patients to treat have nothing in common except lack of distress.[15]

Even in Chinese "thought-reform" prisons, where the interrogator had the power to induce new stress, the presence of internal tension prior to imprisonment appears to have been a crucial factor in the prisoner's susceptibility to influence and attitude change. Schein and his associates, who studied the Chinese thought-reform program as it was reported by American civilian prisoners in Chinese prisons, assigned a crucial role to the sense of guilt experienced by the individual. They reported that "if the prisoner-to-be was susceptible to social guilt, he was particularly vulnerable to the pressure of the cellmates in a group cell."[16]

[11] Jaques, *op. cit.*
[12] Blake *et al., op. cit.*
[13] *Ibid.*
[14] O. H. Mowrer, *The New Group Therapy* (Princeton, N.J.: D. Van Nostrand Co., 1964).
[15] Jerome Frank, *Persuasion and Healing* (New York: Schocken Books, 1963).
[16] Edgar H. Schein *et al., Coercive Persuasion* (New York: W. W. Norton & Co., 1961).

It is important to note that these are qualitatively different situations, in many ways, from industrial settings; alcoholics, Communist prisoners, and psychiatric patients share an emotional distress and lack of control over their own actions which differentiate them from men working in industrial organizations. But as in the industrial studies, attempts to influence behavior have a high probability of success only when the individuals have been experiencing internal stress.

In an organization, of course, the need for change isn't experienced uniformly throughout the organization and its locus helps determine the methods used to effect change. If the tension is felt primarily by those at the top of the authority structure but not by those below, change efforts will be exerted through the existing authority structure. Resistance usually takes the form of circumvention and token compliance. If, on the other hand, the tension exists at the bottom of the legitimate power structure, but not at the top, attempts to change the organization take the form of a revolt and an attack on the existing authority structure, as in campus riots and wildcat strikes. The extent and locus of tension also help determine outcomes. In our own study, two groups, the senior scientists and junior managers, were relatively more frustrated than others at the center and it was among the men in these groups that the new director found the greatest acceptance of the changes he proposed.

### Authority and Prestige of the Influencer

The forces for change represented by tension and the desire for change must be mobilized, however, and given direction, while forces acting to resist change in a given direction must be overcome, neutralized, or enlisted. In an organization, unless there is to be protracted resistance, someone must gain the acceptance and possible support of individuals not seeking change and even those who feel threatened by it.

A second prerequisite for successfully induced change, therefore, appears to be that the initiation comes from a respected and, ideally, a trusted source. The persons being influenced need confidence that the change can, in fact, be effected and a large part of this confidence comes initially from their confidence in the power and judgment of the influencing agent. When men are unsure of their capacity to cope effectively with the situation, they identify with someone whom they perceive as having the knowledge or power to successfully cope with it and who states *where* they need to change. As such, he is then placed in a position where his expectations can become "self-fulfilling prophecies."[17]

In the organizational studies reviewed, successful attempts of change were either initiated by the formal head of the organizational unit involved or were given his strong support. In Guest's study, the initiator was the new plant manager, who brought with him a strong reputation for success in his previous position. Furthermore, it quickly became obvious to the other employees that he had the support of the district management.[18] (Pelz reported that upward influence with one's own superior was a necessary condition for influence with sub-

[17]R. Rosenthall and L. F. Jacobsen, "Teacher Expectations for the Disadvantaged," *Scientific American,* April 1968.

[18]Guest, *op. cit.*

[19]D. C. Pelz, "Influence: A Key to Effective Leadership in the First-Line Supervisor," *Personnel,* Vol. 29 (1952).

ordinates.[19]) Jaques also had the active support of the managing director of Glacier Metals.[20]

The changes at the "Banner Corporation"[21] were initiated by the highest official at the plant. He gained support from Rensis Likert and brought in an agent from the Survey Research Center who carried with him the prestige of the university as well as the authority of an experienced manager. The change effort at the Sigma plant had a similar dual sponsorship, receiving active support from the plant manager and a consultant, Robert Blake, who "had an impressive reputation with the management in other parts of [the headquarters company]."[22] (As a contrast to these successful change efforts, consider for a moment the many ineffectual training programs for first- and second-line supervisors in which the top management group did not participate and therefore never fully understood or supported.)

Nonorganizational studies show the same link between prestige and influence: individuals tend to believe and do those things suggested by authoritative, prestigeful sources.[23] Goal-setting studies reported by Mace indicated that setting goals for individuals and associating these goals with prestigeful authorities like "scientific progress" or "the advancement of research" tended to have a favorable effect on performance.[24]

Studies of operant conditioning of verbal behavior, where one person reinforces certain verbal signals emitted by another person, indicate that when the conditioner has some prestige or power in the subject's eyes, the influence tends to be stronger and more consistent. Students were more consistently influenced by their instructors, for example, than by fellow students. (Of course, this was several years ago. Perhaps today instructors over 30 may not enjoy the same influence.)

Another area of study focusing on the persuasive influence of a prestigeful figure is faith-healing and the so-called "placebo effect" in medicine. Jerome Frank reports that even healers regarded by the community as charlatans or quacks, were able, in some instances, to bring about change and symptom relief among persons who regarded them as sources of authority and power. Their success appeared to rest on their ability to evoke the patient's expectancy of help. In medical treatment, the fact that relief and healing can be brought about solely by the patient's expectation of help from the physician, is demonstrated by experiments verifying the so-called "placebo effect." In these studies, the doctor administers a pharmacologically inert substance to the patient rather than an active medication. Since the placebo is inert, its beneficial effects derive from the patient's confidence in the doctor's prescription and in the institutions of science and medicine which he represents. There is evidence that placebos can have marked physiological effects. Studies have shown that their use has been accompanied by healing of tissue damage ranging from warts to peptic ulcers. A similar effect is the "hello-goodbye" effect in psychotherapy. Patients who merely had contact with a prestigeful (in their eyes) psychiatrist improved

[20]Jaques, op. cit.
[21]Seashore and Bowers, op. cit.
[22]Blake, Mouton, Barnes, and Greiner, op. cit.
[23]C. J. Hovland, I. L. Janis, and H. Kelley, Communication and Persuasion: Psychological Studies of Opinion Change (New Haven, Conn.: Yale University Press, 1953).
[24]C. A. Mace, "Satisfaction in Work," Occupational Psychology, Vol. 22 (1948), pp. 5–12.

significantly over the individuals in a control group who were placed on a waiting list and did not see a psychiatrist. In fact, these minimal contact patients showed almost as much improvement of certain kinds as a third group who underwent prolonged treatment.[25]

Even in thought-reform prisons, there is some suggestion that interrogators or cellmates with higher education and intelligence, as this was perceived by the prisoner, were more likely to be able to influence the prisoner than were those whom he "looked down on."[26] Statistical evidence on American prisoners of war in Korea show the small proportion (about 15 percent) of the prisoners who were classified as collaborators came primarily from low-status positions in American society,[27] and were therefore among the group most likely to see their interrogators and discussion leaders as prestigeful persons. In one of the most graphic accounts by a prisoner who successfully resisted influence by his interrogators, Gonzales reports that he never came to think of his interrogators as authorities in any real sense nor in any way superior to himself except that they were more numerous than he.[28] There is, of course, abundant evidence in our own study and elsewhere to refute a claim that any change initiated by a high status person will be successful. The process of change is more complex than that. But prestige and power on the part of the initiator seem to be a necessary, if not sufficient, condition for introducing large-scale change in any system. Where the person planning to initiate change does not already possess prestige and power in the organization, as Loomis has pointed out, it is his first task to develop "social capital" for himself, i.e., to build his reputation and power in the social system he intends to change.[29]

**The Subprocesses**

Now let us turn from the conditions which precede and facilitate change to an examination of the change process itself. The subtleties and interdependencies of the process, of course, are difficult and, in many ways, impossible to represent or describe because the phenomena occur simultaneously and are "of a piece." But as is shown in the diagram, we were able to distinguish four major subprocesses, all of which seemed to proceed simultaneously in those instances where individuals and groups were influenced to change their behavior and where these new behavior patterns persisted. Movement along each of these four streams characterized the junior managers and senior scientists at Nampa, but were either absent or restricted among the other men at the center whose behavior and attitude changed least.

Movement along each of these streams, where present, appeared to follow a consistent pattern or direction, and while each seemed distinct and separable, movement along all four appeared to occur simultaneously. The first two deal with changes in shared objectives and relationships, while the last two concern changes within the individual.

[25]Frank, *op. cit.*

[26]Schein *et al., op. cit.*

[27]J. Segal, "Correlates of Collaboration and Resistance Behavior among U.S. Army's POW's in Korea," *Journal of Social Issues*, Vol. 13, pp. 31–40.

[28]V. Gonzales and J. Gorkin, *El Campesino: Life and Death in Soviet Russia* (New York: G. P. Putnam's Sons, 1952).

[29]C. P. Loomis, "Tentative Types of Directed Social Change Involving Systematic Linkage," *Rural Sociology*, Vol. 24, No. 4 (December 1959).

The first pattern which consistently seems to characterize successful attempts to bring about behavioral and attitudinal change is a movement from generalized goals toward specific and concrete objectives. As the change progresses, the targets take on greater immediacy and concreteness; one of the clearest signals that a new pattern of behavior will not be established and maintained is the objectives remaining general and nonspecific. In the Nampa Center the changes outlined for all the groups began at a very general level. The junior managers, for example, were told that they were to take on more responsibility for the administration of their groups and to "plan the technical work" for their groups. The senior managers were told to spend at least half their time doing long-range planning. Soon afterward, the junior managers were asked to prepare budget requests for their groups. Later they were given responsibility for performing a specific technical objective and a target date was set for completion, and soon they were working out a week-by-week projected schedule. The assignment given the senior managers to do long-range planning, however, remained essentially at that level of generality, with neither the director nor the senior managers working out intermediate or subobjectives. Fifteen months later, of course, it was the junior and not the senior managers whose attitudes and behavior had changed in the intended direction.

In each of the other studies, whenever someone successfully influenced another person or group of persons to change their behavior or attitudes, movement toward greater specificity of goals was a prominent feature. Sometimes the person initiating the change set the subgoals, sometimes those being influenced set them; most often it was a joint or alternating arrangement. But the consistent element was that someone set concrete subgoals and the behavior change moved along step by step. Guest reported that the new manager at Plant Y began by outlining a "few general goals," such as better planning. He set up meetings for discussing general problems, but attention was steadily brought to focus on improving specific areas, such as accounting methods and inspection procedures.[30] Jaques' report of a three-year period of change in the Glacier Metal Company described how the project team worked successfully with councils and management groups at various levels and departments throughout the organizations. The process followed in their work, with each group showing remarkable consistency, began with the general goals of "understanding their difficulties," moved to a goal of understanding their own "here-and-now" relationships, and finally headed toward the resolution of specific problems or the writing of a new constitution.[31]

The plant manager's initially announced objective at "Banner Corporation" was to introduce "participation management" into the organization. After several months, four subgoals were explicitly stated as a way of implementing the overall goal:

a) Increased emphasis on the work group as a functioning unit.

b) More supportive behavior from supervisors.

c) Greater employee participation in decision making.

d) Increased interaction and influence among work group members.

[30]Guest, *op. cit.*
[31]Jaques, *op. cit.*

A series of meetings with all the supervisors in the experimental department followed, in which the objective became more and more operational in the minds of the supervisors. Finally, these intermediate goals were translated into more specific goals, such as bringing the employees into the decisions about a new shift rotation scheme.[32] The changes reported by Blake *et al.* at the Sigma refinery followed an identical pattern,[33] beginning with a training program in which the objectives for the participants were the general goals of understanding the concepts and assessing their own present management style. Other meetings followed in which the objectives were to explore ways to transfer the new concepts and personal learning of the seminars to the operation of their own group. The objective became even more concrete as the men consciously tried to use some of their new problem-solving methods in working out a program for reducing utility costs and in negotiating a difficult union-management contract.

Outside organizational settings, the most carefully conceptualized example of this aspect of the change process is found in the descriptions of the therapeutic process.[34] At the beginning of the relationship between the patient and the therapist, the mutually understood objective is usually relatively general in character: to help the patient to operate more effectively in his environment, to find relief from serious distress, or to achieve an understanding of the patient's problems and their causes. Explorations may begin by looking at the patient's past behavior, his relationships outside therapy, and his feelings about these. But nearly all schools of therapy agree that as the relationship continues, the patient comes to show feelings and behavior toward the therapist similar to those making trouble for him outside therapy. The examination of these concrete specific events acted out in their own relationship is undertaken as a means of achieving the more general objective. Religious conversion begins with the goals of total repentance and "casting off the old man for the new," but where the conversion has lasting effects, this general goal moves toward the specific objectives of giving up certain practices, making contributions or proselyting others. Then as an individual makes small behavioral commitments in a certain direction, he justifies and rationalizes these acts by accepting values and explanations which reduce dissonance between these acts and his self-image. He becomes his own socializing agent. Even in the thought-reform prisons, the early demand of the interrogator for confession of guilt narrows and focuses to the objective of producing a written document confessing specific "criminal acts" which the interrogator will accept.

### Altering Old Relationships and Establishing New Social Ties

The second pattern which seemed to characterize successful change was the loosening of old relationships and the establishment of new social ties which support the intended changes in attitude and behavior. Old behavior and attitudes are often deeply imbedded in the relationships which have been built up over the years, and as long as the individuals involved maintain these relationships unaltered, changes are unlikely to occur. By the same token, new behavior patterns are most readily and firmly established when they are conditions of

---

[32]Seashore and Bowers, *op. cit.*
[33]*Op. cit.*
[34]M. I. Stein, *Contemporary Psychotherapies* (Glencoe, Ill.: Free Press, 1961).

regular membership in a new group, for group members exercise the most powerful tool for shaping behavior: selective reinforcement of responses with immediate rewards.

In other studies this is the dimension of the change process that has been most explicitly recognized: the beliefs, attitudes, and activities of a person are closely related to those of his reference groups. New attitudes and new activity patterns are most likely to be established when an individual becomes associated with a new reference group.[35] Certainly, not all of an individual's former associations will counteract an intended change, nor will new groups formed in a change situation always work in the direction that the influencing agent intends; but, in general, any significant changes in activities or attitudes include some movement from old object relationships toward new ones.

Behavioral scientists did not originate the idea that an alteration of old relationships facilitates change in individuals or groups. Most influencing institutions in our society separate the individual whom they wish to influence from his regular social contacts and routines. Convents, monasteries, and prisons tend to make this a total separation, and educational institutions make the same separation to a lesser degree by their physical distance from home and a demanding work load. Perhaps the best reported study of this is the work done by Newcomb at Bennington College. During their four years at the college, the girls tended to take on the attitudes of the faculty and student leaders, and to relinquish those of their parents.[36] The individual's greater susceptibility to influence when he is separated from social contacts which support his current beliefs was ingeniously demonstrated by the famous Asch experiments: when subjects were placed in a situation where no other person agreed with the subject's own judgments, a third of the subjects came to doubt their own perceptions to the extent that they reported seeing what the others reported in over half the trials. Yet, if only one person in the group confirmed a subject's own perception, his resistance to social pressure was significantly increased.[37] Rice, in his study of change in a textile weaving mill in India, found some confirmation for his argument that this need for removal from previous contacts applied also to groups where the group was the focus of change. Otherwise the prior social relationships continued to support the behavior patterns and attitudes which the change program was trying to alter.[38]

Breaking up or loosening former social ties may act to unfreeze an individual or group, but this alone provides no assurance that any resulting changes will be in a given direction or that they will have any permanency. Establishing new relationships which reward the desired behaviors and confirm the modified attitudes also seems to be essential. Otherwise, there will be an active seeking to return to former activities and attitudes and to the relationships which supported and reinforced them.

[35]B. Berelson and G. A. Steiner, *Human Behavior: An Inventory of Scientific Findings* (New York: Harcourt, Brace & Co., 1964).

[36]T. M. Newcomb, "Attitude Development as a Function of Reference Groups: The Bennington Study," in E. E. Maccoby, T. T. Newcomb, and E. L. Hartley (eds.), *Readings in Social Psychology* (New York: Holt, Rinehart & Winston, Inc., 1958).

[37]S. E. Asch, "Effects of Group Pressure upon the Modification and Distortion of Judgments," in H. Guetzkow (ed.), *Groups, Leadership, and Men* (Pittsburgh: Carnegie Press, 1951).

[38]A. K. Rice, *Productivity and Social Organization: The Ahmedabad Experiment* (London: Tavistock Publications, Ltd., 1958).

In our study of the Nampa Center, all the men in the experimental sections reported some disruption of their former relationships. Changes in job requirements and work schedules broke up former important interaction patterns in all the groups, but there was a sharp difference among the groups in the extent to which new relations were established. The men in the groups which eventually changed most were assigned to new decision-making committees with their peers from other parts of the company. When decisions were made in the groups there were strong pressures from the other members of the group to defend these decisions, even in dealings with the senior managers. The men who eventually changed least, on the other hand, established no new relationships. Their previous ties were attenuated, but they formed no new relationships which might have pulled them more closely into new patterns of activities and beliefs.

One of the most interesting studies illustrating this phenomenon was the follow-up study of an International Harvester Company training program emphasizing human relations skills which the investigators categorized as "consideration." Tested before and after the two-week training program, the foremen's attitude test scores showed an immediate increase on "consideration," but, over time, the scores shifted until these foremen actually scored lower in consideration than did a control group who had not been trained. Only those foremen whose immediate superiors scored high on consideration continued to score high themselves. The other foremen, whose superiors did not place a high value on consideration, returned to a pattern very close to that of their chiefs. Daily interaction completely negated the effect of the training program. The foremen's ties had been interrupted only during the two weeks' training period. Then they returned to a situation where the most significant relationship was with their own supervisors. No continuing new relationships had been established which would act to confirm and reinforce any attitude changes begun in the training program.[39]

A study which differs in important ways from the International Harvester study, yet confirms its findings, is the Barnes and Greiner investigation of the effects of Blake's organization development program at the Sigma oil refinery. At Sigma the management and staff members at all levels of the plant went through an initial training program during which men were taken out of their regular work groups and placed among relative strangers. They then returned to their old work groups, as in the International Harvester program, but with the difference that their superiors and colleagues had also been through the same training experience. In addition, a second series of meetings was held in which the teams who worked together jointly examined their own operations and made mutual commitments to change. A follow-up study revealed that the program had had an impact on the plant's operations and on the behavior and attitudes of some of the men but, again, not all. In this case, 92 percent of the supervisors who were rated as most changed by their subordinates worked in groups where a majority of their colleagues were also rated as "most improved" by their subordinates, while only 26 percent of the supervisors rated as "least improved" worked in such groups. In fact, it appeared to the investigators that even the presence of only one "least improved" cynic was enough to have a strong dampening effect, since 60 percent of the "most improved" supervisors

[39]E. A. Fleishman, E. F. Harris, and H. E. Burtt, *Leadership and Supervision in Industry* (Columbus, Ohio: Personnel Research Board, Ohio State University, 1945).

worked in settings where there were no "least improved" colleagues whatsoever.[40] As in the Nampa and International Harvester studies, there was no behavioral change unless relationships changed to support the new behavior. The Sigma study, however, differs in one significant way: the major reinforcing relationships in the refinery study were with the *same* people with whom they had worked before. The parties to the relationship had not changed, but the relationships had. This, of course, has important implications for an administrator who wishes to maintain his work teams intact, but hopes to alter behavior and attitudes in these groups. Still, the major point to be made here is that unless the relationships change, behavioral change is more difficult.

Some of the other studies involved an actual breakup of former associations, while in others the parties did not change but the relationships between those parties did. Guest, in his study of a successful change, reported a high incidence of personnel shifts' breaking up old social ties and establishing new relationships which supported the new behavior patterns. There were few discharges, but a program of planned and deliberate lateral transfers and promotions was instituted. Only 25 percent of the plant's supervisors held the same job throughout the period studied. Moreover, the plant manager set up a new pattern of interactions through an increased use of meetings.

> The scope and function of the meetings established by the new manager stood in marked contrast to those of the earlier period: there were more of them, they were regularly scheduled, they covered a wider range of activities, more people took part in them....[41]

Relationships in these meetings were established around new attitudes and behaviors, and support and reinforcement for the new behavior patterns came from these ties.

The studies reported by Jaques and by Seashore and Bowers, however, focused on changes in the nature of the existing relationships. Jaques found that at Glacier Metals a number of new relationships had been established around the new activities (new worker-management committees, etc.), but the primary thrust of the research team's efforts was to alter the expectations and the reinforcement patterns in the existing relationships. This came primarily through what they termed "role clarification" and "working through." Role clarification consisted of a joint examination of the several roles members were expected to play in the group and in the organization as well as the achievement of a common set of expectations about the new ways in which those roles were to be filled. Jaques described "working through" as a serious attempt to voice the unrecognized difficulties, often socially taboo, which had been preventing the group from going ahead with whatever task it may have had. The research team's focus on "working through" was not to aid in the solution of any one problem but to alter the relationship and the manner of working together. Jaques' underlying thesis was that, "Once a group has developed insight and skill in recognizing forces related to status, prestige, security, [etc.] . . . these forces no longer colour subsequent discussion nor impede progress to the same extent as before."[42]

---

[40]Blake *et al., op. cit.*
[41]Guest, *op. cit.*
[42]Jaques, *op. cit.*

The most vivid example of new social interactions acting to bring about the intended change itself is in the "struggle sessions" in thought-reform prisons. In some reform prisons on the Chinese mainland, Western prisoners were placed in cells with a group of "advanced" prisoners, who had already made confessions or were in the process. These prisoners, who themselves were taking on the reformed attitudes, and who were given to know that the progress of the entire cell was dependent on the performance of the least-reformed member, exerted strong pressures (accusations, browbeating) on their new member. The potency of this pressure from fellow prisoners was so pronounced that Schein concluded it was the single most effective device used to influence the prisoners to confess and change attitudes.[43] The Communist prison struggle groups are an extreme form of a group influencing a new member to assume new behaviors and attitudes, but the same process goes on in all groups with lowered intensity. The entering member is required to demonstrate adherence to the norms and values of the group to a greater extent, even, than established members.[44]

The establishment of new social ties for confirmation and reinforcement of changes already begun has also traditionally been a part of evangelistic programs. John Wesley organized his converts into small units of 12 or less. This small group, with a chosen leader, met together weekly to tell of their experiences. The leader visited a member each week to collect dues and to verify the sincerity of his conversion. Quarterly, each member was reissued a ticket of membership admitting him to sacrament meetings. Backsliding was watched carefully, and even three or four absences could bring the loss of one's ticket and expulsion from the Society.[45] The importance of the establishment of new social relationships which confirm and support change begun is probably best illustrated by examining change attempts where new ties are not established. Following a Billy Graham crusade in New York City, an informal survey of individuals who came forward and converted during the crusade found that only those who were subsequently integrated into local churches maintained their faith. For others, the conversion became merely a temporary and lapsed response.[46]

There are those who lay complete stress on group membership and social pressure in explaining the change process. Such explanations seem incomplete, and that is obviously not our position here, but movement along this dimension appears to be a necessary if not sufficient condition for inducing significant and lasting behavioral change.

### Heightening Self-Esteem

Changes in self-esteem on the part of the person being influenced also appear to be an integral part of the process. Interestingly, a movement toward greater self-esteem seems to be a facilitating factor, not only in the establishment of new patterns of thought and action, but also in the unfreezing of old patterns. The abandonment of previous patterns of behavior and thought is easier when an individual is moving toward an increased sense of his own

---

[43]Schein et al., op. cit.
[44]George C. Homans, The Human Group (New York: Harcourt, Brace & Co., 1950).
[45]W. Sargent, Battle for the Mind (Garden City, N.Y.: Doubleday & Co., 1957).
[46]Schein et al., op. cit.

worth. The movement along this continuum is away from a sense of self-doubt toward a feeling of positive worth—from a feeling of partial inadequacy toward a confirmed sense of personal capacity. The increased sense of one's own potential is evident throughout this continuum, not merely at the end. This may seem a paradox, but the contradiction is more apparent than real.

As noted earlier, one of the preconditions for successful change is the experience of stress within the system. Though stress is usually present even before the intervention of the change agent, the agent himself can play an extremely important role in challenging the individual's sense of adequacy. His means of doing this may be explicit or implicit. The negative diagnosis may be openly stated, as when the religious revivalist points to the prospective proselyte's indulgent life and calls him to repentance. The older members at an A.A. meeting may confront the alcoholic with the fact that he is destroying himself and his family. The Communist prison interrogator may insist on the prisoner's "criminal acts against the people." On the other hand, the negative diagnosis may be communicated implicitly by the agent's acting to introduce change in the object system, such as a psychotherapist embarking on a program of treatment after he has had exploratory talks with the patient.

In organizational change, we also find both patterns. A new executive may confront the members of the organization with the inconsistencies and inefficiencies in their operations, as he did in the Nampa case. An outside consultant, however, will more often seek a confrontation among the members of the organization. For example, Robert Blake, in working with the management of the Sigma plant, suggested an initial meeting between plant managers and the headquarters staff, at which the problems uncovered "shocked" the plant management. From this meeting came the impetus to design a development program in which each of the members of the supervisory group were likewise confronted by others' perceptions of his behavior.[47] Jaques and the research team at Glacier Metals worked with the staff in their meetings and helped them to "express feelings which they had been suppressing sometimes for years." Many, for the first time, were able to assess the consequences of some of their behavior.[48]

On the other hand, the manager of the plant studied by Guest entered into a situation where the men had already had abundant evidence of the unsatisfactory consequences of their behavior. He felt it necessary only to acknowledge this evidence.

> In the first meeting with all supervision he put forward what he called "a few basic goals" for the organization in terms of expected efficiency and quality. He stated candidly to the group that Plant Y had a bad reputation. He said he had heard that many members of the group were not capable of doing their jobs. He said he was "willing to prove that this was not so, and until shown otherwise, I personally have confidence in the group."[49]

In each of these instances, the manager or consultant signaled that the men needed to change; that their former performance was not adequate or appropriate. How, then, does this kind of action foster a heightened sense of worth? The

[47]Blake *et al., op. cit.*
[48]Jaques, *op. cit.*
[49]Guest, *op. cit.*

men cannot help feeling they are of some worth, receiving this much attention from someone whom they respect. He is making an investment in them. Even though he is communicating a negative evaluation of their present behavior or attitudes, he is also indicating that he has higher expectations. He is saying, in effect, that he respects their potential. Finally, when he communicates his negative diagnosis he also offers hope, implying that there is a better way and that he knows that better way. The effect on self-esteem is negative at this point in that the attention received derives from their past inadequacy—their need to change. But it is positive in that it lays a foundation for a new beginning, and promise of better results in the future.

In instances of successful change, there is a movement toward increased self-regard as the person finds himself capable of making the changes in behavior. He experiences a sense of accomplishment, a relief from tension, and a reintegration around a new pattern of activity and thought. The junior managers at Nampa, for example, had the opportunity to assume new roles and take on new tasks. As they accomplished these tasks, which had been previously performed by their superiors, they gained a new confidence rooted in their own achievements.

This gain in self-esteem was evident in each of the studies. Early in each of the organizational studies, managers began listening to their subordinates and responding to them. In each case subordinates began taking on responsibilities and participating in decisions that had been withheld from them in the past. The confidence gained from success in these early attempts led to further steps. In Guest's study, men expressed an increasing feeling of competence ("Just gradually we learned how to do the job") and confidence in their future ("The foreman knows that he's got the stuff, he's going to be recognized and promoted"). Toward the end of the period studied, the "promotion" theme was mentioned often in the interviews, while only three years earlier none had expressed the hope of advancing.[50] At the Sigma Refinery, studied by Barnes and Greiner, a new set of programs for increasing productivity and improving costs were confidently and successfully carried out.[51] At Glacier, Jaques reported that increased confidence and self-esteem was demonstrated in a capacity to tackle formerly taboo problems with considerably less anxiety.

The study of the "Banner Corporation," conducted by Seashore and Bowers, is perhaps the most interesting of the four concerning this factor, in that managers and consultants were explicit about the need for increased self-esteem. The consultants set a goal to build "supportive supervisory behavior," which they defined as increasing "the extent to which subordinates (at all levels) experienced positive, ego-sustaining relations with superiors and peers whenever they undertook to act in ways which would promote their common goals."[52] Paradoxically, it was at "Banner" that increased confidence was most difficult to attain; the early attempts at supervisory support became the focus of misunderstanding and ill-will. The supervisors attempted in good faith to be "supportive" but often found no way to link this up to accomplishment. Indiscriminate support not only failed to build self-esteem but actually undermined it. This factor, plus a deteriorating economic situation and some formal organi-

[50]Ibid.
[51]Blake et al., op. cit.
[52]Seashore and Bowers, op. cit.

zational blocks controlled by higher management, retarded progress to the point where the representative from the Survey Research Center proposed a suspension of the field work. It was only after a reorganization, allowing the plant greater freedom, that the latent gains from the early change efforts began to produce the spiraling achievement and confidence that increased plant productivity.

The best known study demonstrating that a heightening of self-worth is an integral part of the influence process comes from the Relay Assembly Test Room Experiments begun in 1924 by the Western Electric Company at their Hawthorne works. The tests, of course, were initially designed to examine the "relation of quality and quantity of illumination to efficiency in industry," but the baffled experimenters found that productivity increased in their "test groups" and "control groups" in almost equal magnitude. They were obtaining greater efficiency, but it apparently was not "illumination that was making the difference!" Further study, this time experimentally varying rest pauses and working hours, again revealed no simple correlation between the experimentally imposed changes and rate of output. Production rose steadily even when the experimental conditions were returned to their original condition. This time, however, the experimenters took careful note of other factors, one of which was the experimenters' influence on the girls to increase productivity. Ostensibly, the experiment had not been an attempt to change behavior, and the experimenters disclaimed any conscious desire to influence the girls toward increased production. The superintendent's notes concerning the first meeting held with the girls indicated that great care was taken to convince them that the purpose of the test was not to boost production:

> The group were assured that the test was not being set up to determine the maximum output, and they were asked to work along at a comfortable pace and particularly not to attempt to see how much they could possibly do.[53]

But in fact the girls received signals which conveyed an exactly opposite message.[54] The superintendent's next words were:

> If increased output resulted from better or more satisfactory working conditions, both parties would be the gainers.[55]

Increased productivity *was* what interested the experimenters! The girls could see that it was the production output which was being recorded so meticulously and subjected to such careful scrutiny.[56]

In retrospect, the treatment the girls were given seems almost perfectly de-

[53]F. J. Roethlisberger and W. J. Dickson, *Management and the Worker* (Cambridge, Mass.: Harvard University Press, 1939).

[54]Committee on Work in Industry, National Research Council, *Fatigue of Workers: Its Relation to Industrial Production* (New York: Reinhold Publishing Corp., 1941), pp. 56–66.

[55]Roethlisberger and Dickson, *op. cit.*

[56]There seems little doubt that the girls received this message whether the experimenters were consciously trying to convey it or not. Studies have shown that even when one person in a close interpersonal relationship is trying to be "nondirective," the other person's behavior can still be strongly influenced by the subtle signals of approval and disapproval which the first person unintentionally gives. E. J. Murray. "A Content Analysis Method for Studying Psychotherapy," *Psychological Monographs*, Vol. 70 (1956).

signed to increase their sense of self-esteem. A new supervisor who was promoted to department chief became the test observer and he treated them very differently from their previous superior. The observer and the experimenters made every effort to obtain the girls' whole-hearted cooperation for each change, consulting them about each change and even canceling some changes which did not meet with their approval. The girls' health, well-being, and opinions were the subject of genuine concern. Investigators spent full time recording and analyzing their output and the superintendent of the inspection branch visited the room frequently, accompanied by an intermittent stream of industrial psychologists and university professors. Each of the girls became a valued member of a cohesive and cooperative group, and as their efficiency increased, so did their sense of confidence.

The experimenters had sought to hold all factors constant except those which were explicitly manipulated in each period. In their attempts to provide an optimal climate for objective research, however, the things which were changed most were the very factors most likely to facilitate change. Each of the conditions and processes so far described was present: (1) the girls, in a new and unfamiliar situation, were initially tense and unsure; (2) persons holding great prestige in the girls' eyes introduced the change; (3) initially the objective which the researchers sought was vague and unclear to the girls, but, judging from the reports, it became increasingly clear to the girls that the research had a specific objective—to find ways to increase productivity; (4) the girls were separated from their former associates and formed a new group built around new activities and attitudes; and finally, (5) the experimenters created conditions which gave the girls a greater sense of importance and worth. The Relay Assembly Test Room Experiment Series has been cited by many writers to illustrate many things, but whatever else it demonstrates, it provides us with a carefully reported instance of influence and induced change—with increasing self-esteem an integral part of that process.

### Internalization

Internalization of the motive for change was the fourth part of the influence process. The motivating force toward a particular change originates outside the individuals to be influenced. They may be actively searching for more adequate behavior, but the actual kind or direction of the change originates outside. Someone else introduces the plan, the scheme, the interpretation, the suggestion, or the idea. Where the new behavior patterns are to become lasting, however, the individuals involved must internalize or come to "own" the rationale for the change.

Internalization occurs as an individual finds the ideas and the prescribed behavior intrinsically rewarding in helping him to cope with external and internal stresses. He adopts the new behavior because he sees it as useful for the solution of a problem or because it is congenial to his own orientation.[57] In the

[57]We are very close here to Kelman's formulation of identification. (See "Processes of Opinion Change," *Public Opinion Quarterly*, Spring, 1961; and "Compliance, Identification and Internalization, Through Processes of Attitude Change," *Journal of Conflict Resolution*, Vol. 2, No. 1 (March 1958). Kelman, however, argues that internalization is not a necessary part of the influence process. An individual, he reasons, may adopt a new behavior pattern through *compliance*, not because he believes in the

Nampa Center as well as in the historical and experimental settings mentioned earlier, internalization seemed to consist of three elements:

1. Provision of a new cognitive structure.
2. Application and improvisation.
3. Verification through experience.

*Provision of a new cognitive structure.* To judge from the studies examined, the first step in the internalization process is the influencing agent's introduction of a new conceptual framework. The new framework may be restricted to a way of conceiving of a limited set of phenomena or it may be far-reaching in its attempt to explain the totality of a person's experience. In either case, the individual is given a new means for reordering the information he has about himself and his environment. Implicit in the framework are relationships of acts to outcomes so that certain ends call for certain behavior. The framework also provides a language which not only communicates the cognitive structure, but creates an "associative net"[58] by which the individual can relate the events in his own life to the new scheme. Once an idea has been acquired, it serves as a discriminative stimulus and increases the probability that a wide range of relevant behaviors will occur.[59]

This provision of a new cognitive structure by the person seeking to exert influence was a part of all the organizational change studies examined. The new director in our study spent a considerable amount of time differentiating his views of authority from that which underlay the manner in which the Nampa Center had been administered before. At the "Banner Corporation," the plant manager and the consultants agreed that the first step was to "provide the plant management group of 14 people with a thorough grounding in the concepts and research basis for participation management." A series of seminars were agreed upon partly "to explore the concepts" and to "outline a conceptual scheme."[60] At the Piedmont Oil Refinery, a training program which emphasized a conceptual scheme developed by Robert Blake, called the Management Grid, initiated the change, providing the managers at the plant with new ways of conceiving of their experiences and actions.[61] In other instances, such as the automobile assembly plant studied by Guest, the new scheme was not presented as formally. The new manager met with the plant in various meetings and told them "what he believed in." He outlined in writing a long-range program and he set up a

---

content, but in order to gain a specific reward or avoid some anticipated punishment. Or he may, through identification, accept influence in order to establish or maintain a relationship with another person or group. This distinction between compliance, identification, and internalization may be made conceptually, but in complex interpersonal relations, in which social influence is being exerted over an extended period of time, neither compliance to external demands nor identification with new reference groups appear to operate successfully without internalization of content on the part of the persons being influenced. Certainly in the Nampa situation, it would be difficult to explain the changes we have noted in terms of compliance or identification alone.

[58]David C. McClelland, "Toward a Theory of Motive Acquisition," *American Psychologist*, May 1965.

[59]A. H. Brayfield, "Human Resources Development," *American Psychologist*, Vol. 23, No. 7 (July 1968).

[60]Seashore and Bowers, *op. cit.*

[61]Blake *et al., op. cit.*

series of regular meetings to examine their operations. Gradually, the men were brought to "a greater awareness of how the total organization fitted together."[62]

The introduction of a new conception of experience as a part of the internalization process is even more apparent in nonorganizational settings. The religious evangelist presents a world view which explains events in terms of spiritual force and points to the relationships of man's actions to this force. The Communistic prison interrogator advances a world view which interprets events as part of a struggle between "progress" and "reaction." From this world view proceeds a prescription of "progressive" and "reactionary" behavior. Different forms of psychotherapy provide a conception of health and sickness that enables the patient to reconceive of his life and supplies him with a consistent way of interpreting his experiences.

*Application and improvisation.* Introduction of a new cognitive structure is not sufficient for internalizing to take place, however. The individual must in some way "make it his own." Our data suggest that he must actively participate in trying to understand the scheme and apply it to his own problems. Where internalization occurs, typically the guidelines are general enough that the person being influenced is forced to improvise. Thus the new cognitive structure has to be amplified and integrated into the individual's existing thought patterns. King and Janis demonstrated the effectiveness of improvisation for inducing opinion change in an experiment with college students.[63] Three groups of male students were presented with a written document concerning the induction of graduating college students into the military service, a topic of personal importance to them. Men in one group were asked only to study the statement. Men in a second group were asked to read it aloud with as much effect as possible so that the statement could be tape-recorded and played to judges. Those in the third group were asked to read the statement, then to role-play the part of an advocate of the views stated in the paper. Results of questionnaires filled out several months before and immediately after the experiment showed that only the group who had had to improvise showed a significant opinion change. Moreover, the experimenters' analysis showed that the difference between the groups could not be attributed to closer attention to the written statement nor higher satisfaction with their performance.

In the studies at "Banner," Piedmont, and Guest's auto assembly plant, the supervisors had to improvise to make the suggested ideas operational in their own department. At "Banner," the managers and supervisors had to build on their own ideas in order to implement "participation management" in their own part of the plant. At Piedmont, the men had an idea at the end of the training session about the aims of "9,9" management, but they had to improvise to apply the ideas to their own unique situation. At the auto assembly plant studied by Guest the supervisors were impressed by the way the new manager treated them and by his use of meetings to gather the relevant information and to plan the work. But they had to take his pattern, modify it, and improvise to make the new approach work for them.

Schein and his associates reported that in the Chinese thought-reform pris-

[62]Guest, *op. cit.*

[63]B. King and I. Janis, "Comparison of the Effectiveness of Improvised vs. Non-Improvised Role Playing in Producing Opinion Change," *Human Relations*, Vol. 9, pp. 177–86.

ons, the prisoners were kept under extreme pressure to make a confession of their guilt.[64] But they were not told what the content of the confession was to be. The prisoner had to supply the material for the confession himself. He was only told repeatedly to stop holding back and to make a complete confession. Only then would there be any promise that the pressure would cease. His task was to produce a confession which would demonstrate to the satisfaction of his captors his complete and unqualified acceptance of the Communist scheme of things. To do this he had to improvise with material from his own experience. Usually, completely fabricated confessions were condemned and rejected. For an acceptable selection and interpretation of this material he had to look for cues from his interrogator, his fellow prisoners who had successfully confessed, and from the controlled mass media. The prisoner had to try repeatedly to demonstrate that he had come to interpret the events in his life in terms of the constructs of his captors. Having had to use these constructs to analyze his own life experiences, the prisoner found the Communistic world view less implausible and foreign.

*Verification through experience.* Testing a new scheme through one's own experience is probably the most important of the three elements of internalization, and it is too often overlooked in the rush to examine the irrational aspects of the influence process. The individual adopts the attitude or behavior and gives it meaning independent of the original source only as he finds it valid in working with his own problems. He must test it against the world as he perceives that world.

At Nampa the junior managers were told that they would be the contact men for their projects with research and sales, and before long they were assigned to committees with important and urgent tasks with these men. In approximately the same manner, the senior scientists were given an openended assignment: to make themselves more useful to the line projects. Soon afterward they were assigned to committees where the task was to plan and execute line projects. Specific organizational mechanisms were provided by the director to help both groups achieve their objectives, and thus they consistently found their experience coinciding with their expectations.

For the other two groups the situation was very different. The senior managers' assignment to do long-range technical planning was no more openended than the assignments given the two groups just discussed, but no mechanisms were established to implement this difficult assignment. Moreover, the senior managers could see that the director was not in the same power position to support them in their role as long-range planners as he was for the junior managers and senior scientists in their new roles.

Though the situation for the junior scientists was different, the net result was the same. The director did have the power to support his assertion that the changes would give the junior scientists more responsibility and autonomy, but he provided no specific organizational mechanisms to help bring this about.

At "Banner," experimenters first introduced participative management in an industrial engineering project; efficiency rose and morale remained high. So later they set up an experimental department, and again the early results were close enough to those anticipated that the superintendents in the plant chose to extend the new management methods to other departments. At Plant Y the

[64]Schein *et al., op. cit.*

supervisors tried new methods of running their departments and produced better results. Following the new manager's lead in holding regular meetings, they found it possible to coordinate their efforts better. They took chances, made mistakes, and were not fired. In recommending technical changes they found each change gave them "that much more chance to think ahead so we won't get in the hole next time." At Sigma the management at the plant drew heavily on the approaches developed in the Grid Laboratory sessions in deciding how to handle a manpower reduction, and the results were so encouraging that they sought to use the approach on more of their operating problems.

In each of the above instances, the new scheme found confirmation in the individual's experience, but there is also the other side of the coin. One of the striking outcomes of the Chinese thought-reform program among Western prisoners is that among most returned prisoners, it did *not* produce long-range ideological changes independent of the external support provided in the prison setting. Only a very few former prisoners maintained an espousal of the ideological position "taught" in the prison after they had had time to reevaluate the prison experience and had new sources of information which they could check. What would have happened to these prisoners had they returned to a Communist society is impossible to say, but where the viewpoint of his captors failed to find validation in the prisoner's experience after the prison experience, it was not internalized. Of course, in those areas where the Chinese captors' schema *did* continue to be congruent with their experience, the change in the ex-prisoners' attitudes and behavior continued to be effected.[65]

In one sense, this part of the internalization process may be termed reality-testing, but this is not to say that uniform views of reality prevail. Indeed, an individual's perception of reality may be distorted, but for an individual to integrate the new construct into his system of beliefs he must validate it through his perception of reality.

### Implications

So much for the model itself, what are its implications? For those who have a major interest in organizational change, a model such as this raises three kinds of issues:

1. Technical.
2. Moral.
3. Social.

By the term "technical," I refer simply to the issues concerning how someone can do his task more effectively. In this vein, even an elementary paradigm like this shows the utility of such a device to a practitioner. If nothing else, it serves as a check list, forcing him to ask himself what he has neglected. For example, the importance of tension and the recognition by those involved that some change is required would seem to be nothing beyond common sense. But how often is it ignored by the managers, or by the organizational development staff man who is eager to demonstrate the utility of his methods? It is my hope that better models will keep the organizational development specialist from becom-

[65]*Ibid.*

ing a victim of the "law of the instrument" (i.e., if you give a boy a hammer, he'll find things to hit) and push him toward an improvement of his diagnostic skills.

The near-necessity that the change be introduced or supported by those with power and respect has been learned many times, the hard way, by those in management training. Although a chief executive's actual participation may not be necessary or in some cases even desirable, his understanding and support can be vital. A full recognition of this feature of organizational change processes may lead the O.D. staff man to spend more time as a counselor to the line executive and less time in training sessions. The line manager may accomplish more using means available to him than the staff specialist can with many times the effort. But this will require those engaged in organizational development work to educate themselves, not only in training methods, but also in the creative design of formal structures and in the behavioral effects of information and measurement systems.

Movement toward increasingly specific goals, while seeming the most obvious, is, from my observation, probably the dimension on which most change efforts flounder. General goals, often widely and genuinely shared, too frequently die for the lack of the crucial idea as to how the first few concrete steps can be taken. Laboratory training often provides a first useful step, but the steps which can help an individual or a group translate the goal from there into daily job performance arise only from planning and creative collaboration of the parties involved.

The use of laboratory training methods has made a major contribution to organizational change in providing a means, however imperfect, of changing relationships without requiring that work teams be broken up or that change wait upon shifts in personnel. But more needs to be learned about the use of groups to support and reinforce change and experimentation. Work by Schein[66] and others suggests that there is much to be learned about helping individuals enter and exit from organizational units with greater understanding in order to maximize their own effectiveness and freedom.

At an intuitive level, we all understand the part self-esteem plays in change, but the message from the learning theorists about the superior effectiveness of positive reinforcements as a teaching strategy has yet to be fully utilized. Concerning internalization, it is my opinion that as we improve our models of behavioral change, we will become even more impressed with the importance of the cognitive constructs. The constructs used more widely now by those in industry (such as McGregor's X and Y) benefit from the impact which a dichotomy provides, but they also suffer from the polarization it induces. In my opinion, we need new constructs and have been living on the conceptual capital of a prior decade for some time.

The moral issues raised by the use of some explicit representation of the influence process are probably heightened by citing examples drawn from clearly coercive instances of influence as I have done here. In one sense, this is a semantic issue. "Influence" as a descriptive term may cause concern, while "leadership" would have an opposite effect. But there is more here than semantics. Manipulation does occur. Anyone who deals with others in a responsible

[66]Edgar H. Schein, "Organizational Socialization and the Profession of Management," *Industrial Management Review*, Winter, 1968.

position is in danger of becoming manipulative. His only effective means of coping with this danger is an intelligent awareness of his own actions and motives and an openness in his dealings with others. A refusal to examine his aims and the processes in which his actions play a part can do no more than serve as a psychological defense against some guilt he may feel. We are all in the business of influencing others. It is not our understanding or consciousness which presents the real moral issues, but our motives and methods. These can be better scrutinized when made explicit.

The social implications are primarily potential rather than actual. Given the swiftness of technological change, it seems imperative that we understand and learn to manage the social change which must accompany it. From scientific invention until the manufacture of the product, the time lag for photography was 112 years. The telephone took half that time—56 years. That period for the transistor was only five years, and the integrated circuit went into production in three years. This technological pace is becoming increasingly unforgiving of those who fail to anticipate and remain abreast. Organizations, groups, and individuals that do not change rapidly enough must be shunted aside, and, at best, placed under some disguised form of caretaking. Even if, in our abundance, we can afford this economically, there is an increasing intolerance in our society, particularly among the young, of our failure to change our organizations to keep pace with shifts in the environment and our failure to keep all segments of our population in the swift mainstream. They impatiently demand that we plan for and cope with change more effectively and humanely—now. These demands cannot completely be dismissed as naïve, for within almost all our organizations are individuals who are aware of the environmental shifts and who have some vision of the required behavioral changes. Management's challenge is to translate that awareness to effective action. The implication for students of organizations, it seems to me, is that mine should be only one of an increasing number of attempts to become explicit about the process by which planned change takes place.

# HOW TO DEAL
# WITH RESISTANCE
# TO CHANGE

PAUL R. LAWRENCE

One of the most baffling and recalcitrant of the problems which business executives face is employee resistance to change. Such resistance may take a number of forms—persistent reduction in output, increase in the number of "quits" and requests for transfer, chronic quarrels, sullen hostility, wildcat or slowdown strikes, and, of course, the expression of a lot of pseudological reasons why the change will not work. Even the more petty forms of this resistance can be troublesome.

All too often when executives encounter resistance to change, they "explain" it by quoting the cliché that "people resist change" and never look further. Yet changes must continually occur in industry. This applies with particular force to the all-important "little" changes that constantly take place—changes in work methods, in routine office procedures, in the location of a machine or a desk, in personnel assignments and job titles. No one of these changes makes the headlines, but in total they account for much of our increase in productivity. They are not the spectacular once-in-a-lifetime technological revolutions that involve mass layoffs or the obsolescence of traditional skills, but they are vital to business progress.

Does it follow, therefore, that business management is forever saddled with the onerous job of "forcing" change down the throats of resistant people? My answer is *no*. It is the thesis of this article that people do *not* resist technical change as such and that most of the resistance which does occur is unnecessary. I shall discuss these points, among others:

1. A solution which has become increasingly popular for dealing with resistance to change is to get the people involved to "participate" in making the change. But as a practical matter "participation" as a device is not a good way for management to think about the problem. In fact, it may lead to trouble.

2. The key to the problem is to understand the true nature of resistance. Actually, what employees resist is usually not technical change but social change—the change in their human relationships that generally accompanies technical change.

3. Resistance is usually created because of certain blind spots and attitudes which staff specialists have as a result of their preoccupation with the technical aspects of new ideas.

4. Management can take concrete steps to deal constructively with these staff attitudes. The steps include emphasizing new standards of performance for staff specialists and encouraging them to think in different ways, as well as making use of the fact that signs of resistance can serve as a practical warning signal in directing and timing technological changes.

5. Top executives can also make their own efforts more effective at meetings of staff and operating groups where change is being discussed. They can do this by shifting their attention from the facts of schedules, technical details, work assignments, and so forth, to what the discussion of these items indicates about developing resistances and receptiveness to change.

Let us begin by taking a look at some recent research into the nature of resistance to change. There are two studies in particular that I should like to discuss. They highlight contrasting ways of interpreting resistance to change and of coping with it in day-to-day administration.

### Is Participation Enough?

The first study was conducted by Lester Coch and John R. P. French, Jr., in a clothing factory.[1] It deserves special comment because, it seems to me, it is

[1] See Lester Coch and John R. P. French, Jr., "Overcoming Resistance to Change," *Human Relations*, Vol. 1, No. 4, 1948, p. 512.

the most systematic study of the phenomenon of resistance to change that has been made in a factory setting. To describe it briefly:

> The two researchers worked with four different groups of factory operators who were being paid on a modified piece-rate basis. For each of these four groups a minor change in the work procedure was installed by a different method, and the results were carefully recorded to see what, if any, problems of resistance occurred. The four experimental groups were roughly matched with respect to efficiency ratings and degree of cohesiveness; in each group the proposed change modified the established work procedure about the same degree.
>
> The work change was introduced to the first group by what the researchers called a "no-participation" method. This small group of operators was called into a room where some staff people told the members that there was a need for a minor methods change in their work procedures. The staff people then explained the change to the operators in detail, and gave them the reasons for the change. The operators were then sent back to the job with instructions to work in accordance with the new method.
>
> The second group of operators was introduced to the work change by a "participation-through-representation" method—a variation of the approach used with the third and fourth groups, which turned out to be of little significance.
>
> The third and fourth groups of operators were both introduced to the work change on a "total participation" basis. All the operators in these groups met with the staff men concerned. The staff men dramatically demonstrated the need for cost reduction. A general agreement was reached that some savings could be effected. The groups then discussed how existing work methods could be improved and unnecessary operations eliminated. When the new work methods were agreed on, all the operators were trained in the new methods, and all were observed by the time-study men for purposes of establishing a new piece rate on the job.

### Research Findings

The researchers reported a marked contrast between the results achieved by the different methods of introducing this change.

*No-Participation Group.* The most striking difference was between Group #1, the no-participation group, and Groups #3 and #4, the total-participation groups. The output of Group #1 dropped immediately to about two-thirds of its previous output rate. The output rate stayed at about this level throughout the period of 30 days after the change was introduced. The researchers further reported:

> "Resistance developed almost immediately after the change occurred. Marked expressions of aggression against management occurred, such as conflict with the methods engineer, . . . hostility toward the supervisor, deliberate restriction of production, and lack of cooperation with the supervisor. There were 17% quits in the first 40 days. Grievances were filed about piece rates; but when the rate was checked, it was found to be a little 'loose'."

*Total-Participation Groups.* In contrast with this record, Groups #3 and #4 showed a smaller initial drop in output and a very rapid recovery not only to the previous production rate but to a rate that exceeded the previous rate. In these groups there were no signs of hostility toward the staff people or toward the supervisors, and there were no quits during the experimental period.

Without going into all the researchers' decisions based on these experiments, it can be fairly stated that they concluded that resistance to methods changes could be overcome by *getting the people involved in the change to participate in making it.*

This was a very useful study, but the results are likely to leave the manager of a factory still bothered by the question, "Where do we go from here?" The trouble centers around that word "participation." It is not a new word. It is seen often in management journals, heard often in management discussions. In fact, the idea that it is a good thing to get employee participation in making changes has become almost axiomatic in management circles.

But participation is not something that can be conjured up or created artificially. You obviously cannot buy it as you would buy a typewriter. You cannot hire industrial engineers and accountants and other staff people who have the ability "to get participation" built into them. It is doubtful how helpful it would be to call in a group of supervisors and staff men and exhort them, "Get in there and start participation."

Participation is a feeling on the part of people, not just the mechanical act of being called in to take part in discussions. Common sense would suggest that people are more likely to respond to the way they are customarily treated—say, as people whose opinions are respected because they themselves are respected for their own worth—rather than by the stratagem of being called to a meeting or asked some carefully calculated questions. In fact, many supervisors and staff men have had some unhappy experiences with executives who have read about participation and have picked it up as a new psychological gimmick for getting other people to think they "want" to do as they are told—as a sure way to put the sugar coating on a bitter pill.

So there is still the problem of how to get this thing called participation. And, as a matter of fact, the question remains whether participation was the determining factor in the Coch and French experiment or whether there was something of deeper significance underlying it.

## Resistance to What?

Now let us take a look at a second series of research findings about resistance to change. Recently, while making some research observations in a factory manufacturing electronic products, a colleague and I had an opportunity to observe a number of incidents that for us threw new light on this matter of resistance to change.[2] One incident was particularly illuminating:

We were observing the work of one of the industrial engineers and a production operator who had been assigned to work with the engineer on assembling and testing an experimental product that the engineer was developing. The engineer and the operator were in almost constant daily contact in their work. It was a common occurrence for the engineer to suggest an idea for some modification in a part of the new product; he would then discuss his idea with the operator and ask her to try out the change to see how it worked. It was also a

---

[2]For a complete report of the study, see Harriet O. Ronken and Paul R. Lawrence, *Administering Changes: A Case Study of Human Relations in a Factory* (Boston, Division of Research, Harvard Business School, 1952).

common occurrence for the operator to get an idea as she assembled parts and to pass this idea on to the engineer, who would then consider it and, on occasion, ask the operator to try out the idea and see if it proved useful.

A typical exchange between these two people might run somewhat as follows:

> *Engineer:* "I got to thinking last night about that difficulty we've been having on assembling the x part in the last few days. It occurred to me that we might get around that trouble if we washed the part in a cleaning solution just prior to assembling it."
>
> *Operator:* "Well, that sounds to me like it's worth trying."
>
> *Engineer:* "I'll get you some of the right kind of cleaning solution, and why don't you try doing that with about 50 parts and keep track of what happens."
>
> *Operator:* "Sure, I'll keep track of it and let you know how it works."

With this episode in mind, let us take a look at a second episode involving the same production operator. One day we noticed another engineer approaching the production operator. We knew that this particular engineer had had no previous contact with the production operator. He had been asked to take a look at one specific problem on the new product because of his special technical qualifications. He had decided to make a change in one of the parts of the product to eliminate the problem, and he had prepared some of these parts using his new method. Here is what happened:

> He walked up to the production operator with the new parts in his hand and indicated to her by a gesture that he wanted her to try assembling some units using his new part. The operator picked up one of the parts and proceeded to assemble it. We noticed that she did not handle the part with her usual care. After she had assembled the product, she tested it and it failed to pass inspection. She turned to the new engineer and, with a triumphant air, said, "It doesn't work."
>
> The new engineer indicated that she should try another part. She did so, and again it did not work. She then proceeded to assemble units using all of the new parts that were available. She handled each of them in an unusually rough manner. None of them worked. Again she turned to the engineer and said that the new parts did not work.
>
> The engineer left, and later the operator, with evident satisfaction, commented to the original industrial engineer that the new engineer's idea was just no good.

### Social Change

What can we learn from these episodes? To begin, it will be useful for our purposes to think of change as having both a technical and a social aspect. The *technical* aspect of the change is the making of a measurable modification in the physical routines of the job. The *social* aspect of the change refers to the way those affected by it think it will alter their established relationships in the organization.

We can clarify this distinction by referring to the two foregoing episodes. In both of them, the technical aspects of the changes introduced were virtually identical: the operator was asked to use a slightly changed part in assembling the finished product. By contrast, the social aspects of the changes were quite different.

In the first episode, the interaction between the industrial engineer and the operator tended to sustain the give-and-take kind of relationship that these two people were accustomed to. The operator was used to being treated as a person with some valuable skills and knowledge and some sense of responsibility about her work; when the engineer approached her with his idea, she felt she was being dealt with in the usual way. But, in the second episode, the new engineer was introducing not only a technical change but also a change in the operator's customary way of relating herself to others in the organization. By his brusque manner and by his lack of any explanation, he led the operator to fear that her usual work relationships were being changed. And she just did not like the new way she was being treated.

The results of these two episodes were quite different also. In the first episode there were no symptoms of resistance to change, a very good chance that the experimental change would determine fairly whether a cleaning solution would improve product quality, and a willingness on the part of the operator to accept future changes when the industrial engineer suggested them. In the second episode, however, there were signs of resistance to change (the operator's careless handling of parts and her satisfaction in their failure to work), failure to prove whether the modified part was an improvement or not, and indications that the operator would resist any further changes by the engineer. We might summarize the two contrasting patterns of human behavior in the two episodes in graphic form; see Exhibit 1.

**EXHIBIT 1**
Two Contrasting Patterns of Human Behavior

| | *Change* | | |
| | *Technical aspect* | *Social aspect* | *Results* |
| --- | --- | --- | --- |
| Episode 1 | Clean part prior to assembly | Sustaining the customary work relationship of operator | 1. No resistance<br>2. Useful technical result<br>3. Readiness for more change |
| Episode 2 | Use new part in assembly | Threatening the customary work relationship of operator | 1. Signs of resistance<br>2. No useful technical result<br>3. Lack of readiness for more change |

It is apparent from these two patterns that the variable that determines the result is the *social* aspect of the change. In other words, the operator did not resist the technical change as such but rather the accompanying change in her human relationships.

Confirmation

This conclusion is based on more than one case. Many other cases in our research project substantiate it. Furthermore, we can find confirmation in the research experience of Coch and French, even though they came out with a different interpretation.

Coch and French tell us in their report that the procedure used with Group #1, the no-participation group, was the usual one in the factory for introducing work changes. And yet they also tell us something about the customary treatment of the operators in their work life. For example, the company's labor relations policies are progressive, the company and the supervisors place a high value on fair and open dealings with the employees, and the employees are encouraged to take up their problems and grievances with management. Also, the operators are accustomed to measuring the success and failure of themselves as operators against the company's standard output figures.

Now compare these *customary* work relationships with the way the Group #1 operators were treated when they were introduced to this particular work change. There is quite a difference. When the management called them into the room for indoctrination, they were treated as if they had no useful knowledge of their own jobs. In effect, they were told that they were not the skilled and efficient operators they had thought they were, that they were doing the job inefficiently, and that some "outsider" (the staff expert) would now tell them how to do it right. How could they construe this experience *except* as a threatening change in their usual working relationship? It is the story of the second episode in our research case all over again. The results were also the same, with signs of resistance, persistently low output, and so on.

Now consider experimental Groups #3 and #4, the total-participation groups. Coch and French referred to management's approach in their case as a "new" method of introducing change, but from the point of view of the *operators* it must not have seemed new at all. It was simply a continuation of the way they were ordinarily dealt with in the course of their regular work. And what happened? The results—reception to change, technical improvement, better performance—were much like those reported in the first episode between the operator and the industrial engineer.

So the research data of Coch and French tend to confirm the conclusion that the nature and size of the technical aspect of the change does not determine the presence or absence of resistance nearly so much as does the social aspect of the change.

**Roots of Trouble**

The significance of these research findings, from management's point of view, is that executives and staff experts need, not expertness in using the devices of participation, but a real understanding, in depth and detail, of the specific social arrangements that will be sustained or threatened by the change or by the way in which it is introduced.

These observations check with everyday management experience in industry. When we stop to think about it, we know that many changes occur in our factories without a bit of resistance. We know that people who are working closely with one another continually swap ideas about short cuts and minor changes in procedure that are adopted so easily and naturally that we seldom notice them or even think of them as change. The point is that because these people work so closely with one another, they intuitively understand and take account of the existing social arrangements for work and so feel no threat to themselves in such everyday changes.

By contrast, management actions leading to what we commonly label "change" are usually initiated outside the small work group by staff people. These are the changes that we notice and the ones that most frequently bring on symptoms of resistance. By the very nature of their work, most of our staff specialists in industry do not have the intimate contact with operating groups that allows them to acquire an intuitive understanding of the complex social arrangements which their ideas may affect. Neither do our staff specialists always have the day-to-day dealings with operating people that lead them to develop a natural respect for the knowledge and skill of these people. As a result, all too often the staff men behave in a way that threatens and disrupts the established social relationships. And the tragedy is that so many of these upsets are inadvertent and unnecessary.

Yet industry must have its specialists—not only many kinds of engineering specialists (product, process, maintenance, quality, and safety engineers) but also cost accountants, production schedulers, purchasing agents, and personnel men. Must top management therefore reconcile itself to continual resistance to change, or can it take constructive action to meet the problem? 

I believe that our research in various factory situations indicates why resistance to change occurs and what management can do about it. Let us take the "why" factors first.

### Self-Preoccupation

All too frequently we see staff specialists who bring to their work certain blind spots that get them into trouble when they initiate change with operating people. One such blind spot is "self-preoccupation." The staff man gets so engrossed in the technology of the change he is interested in promoting that he becomes wholly oblivious to different kinds of things that may be bothering people. Here are two examples:

> In one situation the staff people introduced, with the best of intentions, a technological change which inadvertently deprived a number of skilled operators of much of the satisfaction that they were finding in their work. Among other things, the change meant that, whereas formerly the output of each operator had been placed beside his work position where it could be viewed and appreciated by him and by others, it was now being carried away immediately from the work position. The workmen did not like this.

> The sad part of it was that there was no compelling cost or technical reason why the output could not be placed beside the work position as it had been formerly. But the staff people who had introduced the change were so literal-minded about their ideas that when they heard complaints on the changes from the operators, they could not comprehend what the trouble was. Instead, they began repeating all the logical arguments why the change made sense from a cost standpoint. The final result here was a chronic restriction of output and persistent hostility on the part of the operators.

> An industrial engineer undertook to introduce some methods changes in one department with the notion firmly in mind that this assignment presented him with an opportunity to "prove" to higher management the value of his function. He became so preoccupied with his personal desire to make a name for his particular techniques that he failed to pay any attention to some fairly obvious and practical considerations which the operating people were calling to his attention but which did not show up in his time-study techniques. As could be expected, resistance quickly developed to all his ideas, and the only "name" that he finally won for his techniques was a black one.

Obviously, in both of these situations the staff specialists involved did not take into account the social aspects of the change they were introducing. For different reasons they got so preoccupied with the technical aspects of the change that they literally could not see or understand what all the fuss was about.

We may sometimes wish that the validity of the technical aspect of the change were the sole determinant of its acceptability. But the fact remains that the social aspect is what determines the presence or absence of resistance. Just as ignoring this fact is the sure way to trouble, so taking advantage of it can lead to positive results. We must not forget that these same social arrangements that at times seem so bothersome are essential for the performance of work. Without a network of established social relationships a factory would be populated with a collection of people who had no idea of how to work with one another in an organized fashion. By working *with* this network instead of *against* it, management's staff representatives can give new technological ideas a better chance of acceptance.

### Operators' Know-How Overlooked

Another blind spot of many staff specialists is to the strengths as well as to the weaknesses of firsthand production experience. They do not recognize that the production foreman and the production operator are in their own way specialists themselves—specialists in actual experience with production problems. This point should be obvious, but it is amazing how many staff specialists fail to appreciate the fact that even though they themselves may have a superior knowledge of the technology of the production process involved, the foreman or the operators may have a more practical understanding of how to get daily production out of a group of men and machines.

The experience of the operating people frequently equips them to be of real help to staff specialists on at least two counts: (1) The operating people are often able to spot practical production difficulties in the ideas of the specialists—and iron out those difficulties before it is too late. (2) The operating people are often able to take advantage of their intimate acquaintance with the existing social arrangements for getting work done. If given a chance, they can use this kind of knowledge to help detect those parts of the change that will have undesirable social consequences. The staff experts can then go to work on ways to avoid the trouble area without materially affecting the technical worth of the change.

Further, some staff specialists have yet to learn the truth that, even after the plans for a change have been carefully made, it takes *time* to put the change successfully into production use. Time is necessary even though there may be no resistance to the change itself. The operators must develop the skill needed to use new methods and new equipment efficiently; there are always bugs to be taken out of a new method or piece of equipment even with the best of engineering. When a staff man begins to lose his patience with the amount of time that these steps take, the people he is working with will begin to feel that he is pushing them; *this* amounts to a change in their customary work relationships, and resistance will start building up where there was none before.

The situation is aggravated if the staff man mistakenly accuses the operators of resisting the idea of the change, for there are few things that irritate people more than to be blamed for resisting change when actually they are doing their best to learn a difficult new procedure.

Many of the problems of resistance to change arise around certain kinds of *attitudes* that staff men are liable to develop about their jobs and their own ideas for introducing change. Fortunately, management can influence these attitudes and thus deal with the problems at their source.

### Broadening Staff Interests

It is fairly common for a staff man to work so hard on one of his ideas for change that he comes to identify himself with it. This is fine for the organization when he is working on the idea by himself or with his immediate colleagues; the idea becomes "his baby," and the company benefits from his complete devotion to his work.

But when he goes to some group of operating people to introduce a change, his very identification with his ideas tends to make him unreceptive to any suggestions for modification. He just does not feel like letting anyone else tamper with his pet ideas. It is easy to see, of course, how this attitude is interpreted by the operating people as a lack of respect for their suggestions.

This problem of the staff man's extreme identification with his work is one which, to some extent, can only be cured by time. But here are four suggestions for speeding up the process:

1. The manager can often, with wise timing, encourage the staff man's interest in a different project that is just starting.

2. The manager can also, by his "coaching" as well as by example, prod the staff man to develop a healthier respect for the contributions he can receive from operating people; success in this area would, of course, virtually solve the problem.

3. It also helps if the staff man can be guided to recognize that the satisfaction he derives from being productive and creative is the same satisfaction he denies the operating people by his behavior toward them. Experience shows that staff people can sometimes be stimulated by the thought of finding satisfaction in sharing with others in the organization the pleasures of being creative.

4. Sometimes, too, the staff man can be led to see that winning acceptance of his ideas through better understanding and handling of human beings is just as challenging and rewarding as giving birth to an idea.

### Using Understandable Terms

One of the problems that must be overcome arises from the fact that the typical staff man is likely to have the attitude that the reasons why he is recommending any given change may be so complicated and specialized that it is impossible to explain them to operating people. It may be true that the operating people would find it next to impossible to understand some of the staff man's analytical techniques, but this does not keep them from coming to the conclusion that the staff specialist is trying to razzledazzle them with tricky figures and formulas—insulting their intelligence—if he does not strive to his utmost to translate his ideas into terms understandable to them. The following case illustrates the importance of this point:

> A staff specialist was temporarily successful in "selling" a change based on a complicated mathematical formula to a foreman who really did not

understand it. The whole thing backfired, however, when the foreman tried to sell it to his operating people. They asked him a couple of sharp questions that he could not answer. His embarrassment about this led him to resent and resist the change so much that eventually the whole proposition fell through. This was unfortunate in terms not only of human relations but also of technological progress in the plant.

There are some very good reasons, both technical and social, why the staff man should be interested in working with the operating people until his recommendations make "sense." (This does not mean that the operating people need to understand the recommendations in quite the same way or in the same detail that the staff man does, but that they should be able to visualize the recommendations in terms of their job experiences.) Failure of the staff man to provide an adequate explanation is likely to mean that a job the operators had formerly performed with understanding and satisfaction will now be performed without understanding and with less satisfaction.

This loss of satisfaction not only concerns the individual involved but also is significant from the standpoint of the company which is trying to get maximum productivity from the operating people. A person who does not have a feeling of comprehension of what he is doing is denied the opportunity to exercise that uniquely human ability—the ability to use informed and intelligent judgment on what he does. If the staff man leaves the operating people with a sense of confusion, they will also be left unhappy and less productive.

Top line and staff executives responsible for the operation should make it a point, therefore, to know how the staff man goes about installing a change. They can do this by asking discerning questions when he reports to them, listening closely to reports of employee reaction, and, if they have the opportunity, actually watching the staff man at work. At times they may have to take such drastic action as insisting that the time of installation of a proposed change be postponed until the operators are ready for it. But, for the most part, straightforward discussions with the staff man in terms of what they think of his approach should help him, over a period of time, to learn what is expected of him in his relationships with operating personnel.

### New Look at Resistance

Another attitude that gets staff men into trouble is the *expectation* that all the people involved will resist the change. It is curious but true that the staff man who goes into his job with the conviction that people are going to resist any idea he presents with blind stubbornness is likely to find them responding just the way he thinks they will. The process is clear: whenever he treats the people who are supposed to buy his ideas as if they were bullheaded, he changes the way they are used to being treated; and they *will* be bullheaded in resisting *that* change!

I think that the staff man—and management in general—will do better to look at it this way: When resistance *does* appear, it should not be thought of as something to be *overcome*. Instead, it can best be thought of as a useful red flag—a signal that something is going wrong. To use a rough analogy, signs of resistance in a social organization are useful in the same way that pain is useful to the body as a signal that some bodily functions are getting out of adjustment.

The resistance, like the pain, does not tell what is wrong but only that something is wrong. And it makes no more sense to try to overcome such resistance than it does to take a pain killer without diagnosing the bodily ailment. Therefore, when resistance appears, it is time to listen carefully to find out what the trouble is. What is needed is not a long harangue on the logics of the new recommendations but a careful exploration of the difficulty.

It may happen that the problem is some technical imperfection in the change that can be readily corrected. More than likely, it will turn out that the change is threatening and upsetting some of the established social arrangments for doing work. Whether the trouble is easy or difficult to correct, management will at least know what it is dealing with.

### New Job Definition

Finally, some staff specialists get themselves in trouble because they assume they have the answer in the thought that people will accept a change when they have participated in making it. For example:

> In one plant we visited, an engineer confided to us (obviously because we, as researchers on human relations, were interested in psychological gimmicks!) that he was going to put across a proposed production layout change of his by inserting in it a rather obvious error, which others could then suggest should be corrected. We attended the meeting where this stunt was performed, and superficially it worked. Somebody caught the error, proposed that it be corrected, and our engineer immediately "bought" the suggestion as a very worth-while one and made the change. The group then seemed to "buy" his entire layout proposal.

> It looked like an effective technique—oh, so easy—until later, when we became better acquainted with the people in the plant. Then we found out that many of the engineer's colleagues considered him a phony and did not trust him. The resistance they put up to his ideas was very subtle, yet even more real and difficult for management to deal with.

Participation will never work so long as it is treated as a device to get somebody else to do what you want him to. Real participation is based on respect. And respect is not acquired by just trying; it is acquired when the staff man faces the reality that he needs the contributions of the operating people.

If the staff man defines his job as not just generating ideas but also getting those ideas into practical operation, he will recognize his real dependence on the contributions of the operating people. He will ask them for ideas and suggestions, not in a backhanded way to get compliance, but in a straightforward way to get some good ideas and avoid some unnecessary mistakes. By this process he will be treating the operating people in such a way that his own behavior will not be perceived as a threat to their customary work relationships. It will be possible to discuss, and accept or reject, the ideas on their own merit.

The staff specialist who looks at the process of introducing change and at resistance to change in the manner outlined in the preceding pages may not be hailed as a genius, but he can be counted on in installing a steady flow of technical changes that will cut costs and improve quality without upsetting the organization.

Now what about the way the top executive goes about his *own* job as it involves the introduction of change and problems of resistance?

One of the most important things he can do, of course, is to deal with staff people in much the same way that he wants them to deal with the operators. He must realize that staff people resist social change, too. (This means, among other things, that he should not prescribe particular rules to them on the basis of this article!)

But most important, I think, is the way the administrator conceives of his job in coordinating the work of the different staff and line groups involved in a change. Does he think of his duties *primarily* as checking up, delegating and following through, applying pressure when performance fails to measure up? Or does he think of them *primarily* as facilitating communication and understanding between people with different points of view—for example, between a staff engineering group and a production group who do not see eye to eye on a change they are both involved in? An analysis of management's actual experience—or, at least, that part of it which has been covered by our research— points to the latter as the more effective concept of administration.

I do not mean that the executive should spend his time with the different people concerned discussing the human problems of change as such. He *should* discuss schedules, technical details, work assignments, and so forth. But he should also be watching closely for the messages that are passing back and forth as people discuss these topics. He will find that people—himself as well as others— are always implicitly asking and making answers to questions like: "How will he accept criticism?" "How much can I afford to tell him?" "Does he really get my point?" "Is he playing games?" The answers to such questions determine the degree of candor and the amount of understanding between the people involved.

When the administrator concerns himself with these problems and acts to facilitate understanding, there will be less logrolling and more sense of common purpose, fewer words and better understanding, less anxiety and more acceptance of criticism, less griping and more attention to specific problems—in short, better performance in putting new ideas for technological change into effect.